TCP/IP and Linux Protocol Implementation: Systems Code for the Linux Internet

Jon Crowcroft
Iain Phillips

Wiley Computer Publishing

John Wiley & Sons, Inc.
NEW YORK • CHICHESTER • WEINHEIM • BRISBANE • SINGAPORE • TORONTO

Publisher: Robert Ipsen
Editor: Carol A. Long
Assistant Editor: Adaobi Obi
Managing Editor: Micheline Frederick
Text Design & Composition: Interactive Composition Corporation

This book is printed on acid-free paper. ♾

Published by John Wiley & Sons, Inc., New York

Published simultaneously in Canada.

Library of Congress Cataloging-in-Publication Data:

TCP/IP and Linux protocol implementation : systems code for the Linux Internet/
Jon Crowcroft, Iain Phillips [editors].
p. cm. – (Wiley Networking Council series)
Includes bibliographical references and index.
ISBN 0-471-40882-4 (cloth : alk. paper)
1. TCP/IP (Computer network protocol) 2. Linux. 3. Internet. I. Crowcroft, Jon. II. Phillips, Iain, 1967- III. Series.

TK5105.585 .T34 2001
004.6′2—dc21 2001045453

Printed in the United States of America.

10 9 8 7 6 5 4 3 2 1

Wiley Networking Council Series

NETWORKING council

Series Editors:

Scott Bradner
Senior Technical Consultant, Harvard University

Vinton Cerf
Senior Vice President, MCI WorldCom

Lyman Chapin
Chief Scientist, BBN/GTE

Books in series:

- High Speed Networking: A Systematic Approach to High-Bandwidth Low-Latency Communication
  James P. G. Sterbenz, Joseph D. Touch ISBN: 0-471-33036-1
- Planning for PKI: Best Practices Guide for Deploying Public Key Infrastructure
  Russ Housley, Tim Polk ISBN: 0-471-39702-4
- Understanding Policy-Based Networking
  Dave Kosiur ISBN: 0-471-38804-1
- Delivering Internet Connections over Cable: Breaking the Access Barrier
  Mark E. Laubach, David J. Farber, Stephen D. Dukes ISBN: 0-471-38950-1
- The NAT Handbook: Implementing and Managing Network Address Translation
  Bill Dutcher ISBN: 0-471-39089-5
- WAN Survival Guide: Strategies for VPNs and Multiservice Networks
  Howard C. Berkowitz ISBN: 0471-38428-3
- ISP Survival Guide: Strategies for Running a Competitive ISP
  Geoff Huston ISBN: 0-471-31499-4
- Implementing IPsec: Making Security Work on VPNs, Intranets, and Extranets
  Elizabeth Kaufman, Andrew Newman ISBN: 0-471-34467-2
- Internet Performance Survival Guide: QoS Strategies for Multiservice Networks
  Geoff Huston ISBN: 0-471-37808-9
- ISP Liability Survival Guide: Strategies for Managing Copyright, Spam, Cache, and Privacy Regulations
  Tim Casey ISBN: 0-471-37748-1
- VPN Applications Guide: Real Solutions for Enterprise Networks
  Dave McDysan ISBN: 0-471-37175-0
- Converged Networks and Services: Internetworking IP and the PSTN
  Igor Faynberg, Hui-Lan Lu, and Lawrence Gabuzda ISBN: 0-471-35644-1

For more information, please visit the Networking Council Web site at: www.wiley.com/networkingcouncil

Contents

List of Figures

List of Tables

Preface

This book is about the implementation of the Internet Protocol suite in the Linux operating system.

Linux provides all the components necessary to build clients, servers, and full-featured routers, and so it is possible to conceive of a world where we build almost all of the Internet out of Linux systems.

Of course, there is strength in diversity, and so luckily for the Internet software gene pool, we have alternatives that keep each other honest. Thus there are many operating systems and hardware platforms on which the Internet is built in practice. What makes Linux particularly interesting, and what is relevant for readers of this book, is that the source code of the operating systems and many of the applications is freely available, and that the software runs on many hardware platforms, ranging from the embedded microprocessor to the multiprocessor and huge cluster systems that can function as core network routers or major site servers.

Importance

There are a number of Fortune 100 companies now using Linux for servers, not just in the technology sector, but also in banking, health care, and just about any other business you can think of. Some of these have started to use Linux as a router platform too. Given the open nature of the system and its level of sophistication, both in terms of functionality and performance, this is entirely reasonable. We believe that this trend will increase over the next few years as the commoditization of the Internet rolls on.

Intended Audience

The material in this book is systems code. This means that it is tethered to hardware and other environmental specifics. While the Linux kernel is portable, it is not *generic:* It has a specific goal and purpose. The assumption we have made in writing this book is that a reader will be familiar with the general ideas of operating systems and communications protocols.

This is not a book for someone wishing to write an Internet application. There are several excellent books for that purpose. Indeed, most of the major operating systems share an API (sockets) for that purpose. The emphasis here is on the system specifics rather than the communications applications. In fact we deliberately avoid most aspects of so-called user-land or user-space programming, and concentrate on the kernel internals.

As network researchers and educators, we have increasingly found it useful to explain (or create) ideas in communications by examples. Thus the goal of this book is to use the Linux kernel implementation of the Internet Protocol suite as an example. If you are learning or researching Internet Protocol protocols and services, transport protocols and services, or adapting either of these areas to novel communications media, then this is a book for you.

The level of the material assumes an engineering-level knowledge of communication, operating systems, and hardware system concepts. We assume you're acquainted with these already. If not, then there are some excellent books, such as the classic work on hardware by Patterson and Hennessy [24]. There are many on communications (e.g., Kurose and Ross [25]) and operating systems (e.g., Silberschatz and Peterson [23]).

Unintended Audience

This book is not about system administration. For an excellent book on system administration for Linux routers, see the book by Mancill [27]. We have also made a (somewhat arbitrary) decision to exclude non-Internet mainstream protocols from the book (e.g., IPX, AppleTalk, DECnet, ax25, X.25, ECONET, IRDA, ATM, are all not covered here).

Another criterion used to decide what went in and what didn't was whether the protocol required kernel support. Protocols that are entirely user-land-based are really portable across a range of platforms, and so are not part of the Linux world exclusively. In general, this means that we exclude Internet applications altogether, except where they are close to the low level (e.g., where the application's raison d'être is solely to manage a low-level function).

Finally, we worked largely to the 2.4.0 kernel release from early 2001. Things that were in earlier releases but are not here, or are in later releases but aren't present here, are obviously not covered (maybe in volume 2). We found our way around the code with help (of course) from the Linux Documentation Project, and from a variety of tools (ctags and vi, etags and emacs, the Red Hat source code navigator, grep, ls-R, find, and so on—all those things that make UNIX-like systems the tools of choice for systems developers).

Roadmap, Outline, and Organization

The book is in 10 chapters. Chapter 1 is a very brief reminder of the way that the Internet Protocol suite works. Chapter 2 is an introduction to the Linux operating system kernel. Chapter 3 is a walk-through of the life cycle of a single packet, from creation to transmission, and from reception to consumption. Chapter 4 is a recapitulation of Interprocess communication; in other words, an overview of socket programming. Chapter 5 is about the kernel infrastructure support for communications in general. Chapter 6 is a walk-through of the implementation of the network layer code and support. Chapter 7 is about transport protocol implementations. Chapter 8 covers routing, while Chapter 9 is about the rich Linux support for different packet forwarding treatments. We wrap up with Chapter 10, which is about network security, covering various network filtering techniques and applications.

The approach taken is largely code-centric, but with explanations and illustrations of the way the code fits together and is used by other layers.

Each chapter covers the concepts and implementation from one or more of five perspectives:

Data structures. We show by example the way that protocol state and packet data is stored.

Wire format of packets. We show the format of packets as transmitted/forwarded/received.

Algorithm/code. The rules for processing user, network, and timer events are detailed.

Process. The progression of the set of tasks involved in communication are illustrated.

Operational. We cover the set of actions carried out by the system manager, network manager, and an ordinary user.

The structure of most chapters covers these five perspectives, and then connects them together through a story—the life of some component activity of the Internet Protocol architecture as exemplified by the Linux implementation.

Acknowledgments

This book is dedicated to the followers of *li*.

Thanks also to Orion Hodson, Tristan Henderson, Panos Gevros, and other denizens of (virtual) G11, and to Adam Greenhalgh, Julia Schnabul, John Andrews, and Tony Mancill for feedback. Thanks especially to Carsten Heinz for his excellent listings style and assistance fixing my overly naive use of the word said. Thanks to Jamal Hadi Salim for information about SMP forwarding, and to T'so for helpful comments on security.

Of course, we would have nothing if not for the valiant efforts of the authors of the code in implementing, bug fixing, and performance tweaking. A list of implementors who signed code that we look at is appended at the end of the bibliography.

Jon Crowcroft

Iain Phillips

CHAPTER 1

Overview of the Internet Protocols

"To some of us, preserving the Net for free speech is more important than anything in the free world."

—Ron Newman, netizen

Figure 1.1 Comments, what comments: `linux/net/khttpd/waitheaders.c`.

```
/* WONDERFUL. NO COMMENTS. --ANK */
```

1.1 Roadmap

This chapter is a self-contained overview of the Internet protocols. We start with an overview of the history of TCP/IP and then cover the basic concepts of IPv4, including routing, addressing, reliability, and performance management. A brief introduction to IPv6, IPSec, mobile IP, and multicast.

1.2 Introduction

The history of the Internet is the history of the world's most successful software system. Unlike previous networks (postal, telephone, broadcast) that were largely built out of custom hardware, the Internet is mostly made from software components, running on relatively simple, general-purpose computing hardware.

Of course there is a little bit of hardware involved, as well as people using the system. The important point is that most of the hardware components are general-purpose programmable computers, and as such, have all the flexibility that such devices enjoy. Of particular relevance to this book is the fact that the performance of the hardware in the form of personal computers running off-the-shelf operating systems such as Linux, is now sufficient to fulfill most of the important roles in the Internet.

What are the main components of the Internet? We can look at them from many viewpoints, but from 20,000 feet they might be the following:

Users. Users are either people, or their agents, that access content over the Internet using networked applications to download Web pages or move email or even run VoIP.

Content. In the end, users want content—whether it is to access a Web page, acquire a real-world good or service, or hear the voice of their friend.

Service providers. Service providers are organizations to which users subscribe (have some contract-like relationship with) that manage connectivity by acquiring lower-level services and coordinating them. Service providers may provide *content*, *applications*, or *Internet connectivity*. This space is constantly expanding as more and more layers of business are refined out of the global information market. Traditionally, Internet service providers (ISPs) bought bit-transport capacity, and added value by managing a collection of links and routers. More recently at least two more layers have been added, with content and application service providers offering *overlay* services, with collections of coordinated, managed end systems connected to one or more ISPs offering optimized performance for this set of users or that.

Hosts, or end systems. End systems are hosts (general-purpose computers) that run client, server, or peer-to-peer application software. The term has become somewhat muddied in recent years due to the emergence of the other business layers, and also due to some hacks required to make security and addressing deploy pragmatically (see Chapter 10 for some details on this). Thus we have seen the evolution of *middle boxes*, which provide a variety of services ranging from proxying, caching, firewalls, address translation, and so on. Pure end systems have users (i.e., clients, servers, or peers).

Middle boxes. Middle boxes are end systems that don't have explicit users (clients or servers) attached, but intermediate at the application, transport, or network level in the protocol stream to provide some kind of value-added service or optimization.

Intermediate systems, or routers. Intermediate systems that provide a router (or as it used to be commonly known, *IP gateway*) service are, from the point of view of end systems, almost completely transparent. They connect links together and construct a set of paths for packets, across a set of links. A router may be an end system for the purposes of management.

Links. A link is some piece of transmission medium that interconnects hosts and routers, or just routers. Links are increasingly diverse in their technologies and architectures. In fact, recently it has become clear that the Internet uses some technologies that provide more than traditional serial line or local area network links as if they are merely point-to-point, or broadcast medium technologies. There are moves afoot to generalize the model of the Internet so that it can be used recursively below the IP layer (so called generalized multi-protocol label switching, for example), but there is neither time nor space to discuss this interesting topic here.

To glue this all together we have a vast infrastructure of software:

Applications. Applications allow the user to copy or access files across the network, FTP or NFS, send and receive email and news such as SMTP and NNTP, and browse or download content such as the family of WWW protocols. Applications are usually instantiated via some type of client that nowadays has a graphical user interface (GUI), or even a voice or touch-screen-activated interface on palm devices.

Protocols. Communicating applications cause flows of information. They do this by using protocols, which are programming rules for distributed applications. Most applications are only *distributed* in a limited sense of being client-to-server, or peer-to-peer, so that there is usually only a pair of systems to be coordinated from the user's point of view. Of course, the Internet has many simultaneous users, so that some types of applications on the Internet need to coordinate with many others. In fact, this is what distinguishes a pure end system from a middle box, and also more specifically, from a router; a pure end system need only concern itself explicitly with one other system, whereas all kinds of intermediaries necessarily concern themselves with other multiple systems simultaneously even in a given communications context. There is one exception to this rule: multicast, which we'll look at briefly in Chapter 8.

Protocols include two main important types of rules in their definitions: packet formats and rules of operation. In programming terms, packet formats are implemented as data structures with a specific machine-independent encoding. Protocol rules of operation cannot be expressed in narrative form. There are far too many possible ways that a network can be used. Instead, they are typically expressed in terms of a set of states and actions. In Chapter 7, we will look at the clearest example of this, which is the way that the Transmission Control Protocol (TCP) is defined and implemented.

Layers: Physical, network and application. Inevitably, the complexity of such a system of components is best understood by introducing some systematic way of categorizing its modularization. The natural way that designers tend to do this is by *layering*. In a network, it is clear that the physical transmission link and its framing rules for packets that the standard and network interface card dictate is a given. The Internet Protocol *has* to be fitted *on top of* this. By this we mean that the Internet is an overlay on a service made out of lots of links of differing kinds, and in general, users of the Internet Protocol layer don't really care what the details of the link layers are. This is an example of *information hiding*.

The idea of layering occurs in programming as well as in design. When a design is layered, however, this does not imply that the implementation must slavishly follow the same boundaries. For example, the application may actually care what the size of the physically largest packet a link can transmit is.

Names, addresses, routes. These are confusing concepts—in a way we often define examples of these in the context of one layer, only to redefine them differently at different layers:

A *name* tells you what it is: e.g.,"Clore Lecture Theatre," or "Jon Crowcroft," or http://www.cs.ucl.ac.uk/index.html.

An *address* tells you where something is: e.g., "151 Gower Street", or "Room 101", or `128.16.5.31`.

A *route* tells you how to get there: e.g., "go in the second door, up the stairs, turn left, and stop at the door marked stop."

Security. Security is generally concerned with defending against attacks such as theft or denial of service. It is hard for software to defend against physical attacks. However, we can provide means to reduce the chances of logical attacks. Logical attacks such as theft of content, theft of identity, or theft of privacy cannot be completely ruled out, but there are a variety of techniques for making it expensive (i.e., computationally hard) to misbehave. The ones implemented in the Linux kernel and supporting software relevant to the actual lower protocol levels are discussed in Chapter 10. However, security is part of a much larger picture, and we would advise concerned users to read a good book on network security (for example on firewalls) before embarking on any use of the Internet.

Metering, accounting. If you are providing a service, you may want to account for usage. There are quite a few tools for doing this at the microscopic level of detail—one advantage of Linux is that it is relatively easy to build on these and add layers of software to accumulate statistics and summarize them.

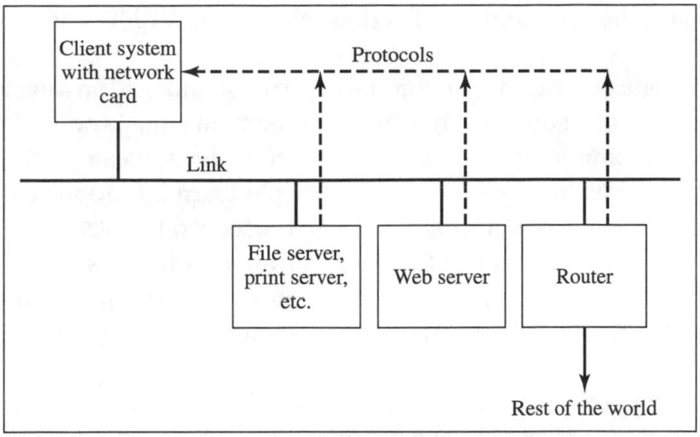

Figure 1.2 LAN.

1.3 Protocols

Packets contain data and control.

To get information from memory to processor, the CPU uses a bus protocol, sends commands and addresses on some (parallel) wires, and gets data over other wires.

To get data across a network that is usually only one wire wide (serial), a computer uses a protocol, but everything must be in the messages—datagrams, like a telegram, carry addresses, data, and other instructions to the postman.

1.3.1 A Note on Programming Languages and Methodologies

Most of the Internet is programmed in the *C* language. This is especially true of lower-level protocols and systems. Most operating systems running today are written in C, although many applications are programmed in higher-level languages. There are several reasons for using C. Partly it is historic: previous systems had been written in assembler, but this is completely non-portable and extremely hard to maintain. C reveals just enough of the underlying hardware to allow the programmer access to specific memory locations and structures, as well as interfacing to assembler, while offering enough high-level programming tools (functions, modules, and so on) to retain some degree of maintainability.

It is possible to write highly portable C, but it is also possible to write non-portable code. It is also possible to write very obscure code (there are competitions in *obfuscated C*!), but luckily, the influence of several decades of experience has led to programming styles and conventions that make C code quite easy to comprehend.

These styles and conventions vary from community to community, however in the Linux system there are some fairly strong agreements on how code should be written, laid out, and integrated. One of the key advantages of open source approaches to systems development is that people learn by (good) examples. The Linux kernel benefits additionally from strong central control over what is allowed into a release. A different model pertains with the systems that are packaged together by the large number of Linux *distribution* companies now in the world, where it is up to those organizations to maintain consistency.

More importantly, in general over the last few years, the practice of *object oriented (OO) design and programming* has become widespread. There was a trend towards using *C++* or even *Objective C* for a while, but these proved more complex than necessary. For application (and high-level network) programming, *Java* is now in the ascendancy. However, the techniques can be applied *semi-manually* in C, and we will see that this is widespread throughout the Linux kernel code. In fact, there is a school of thought that it has always been the case amongst good programmers that they use patterns in common with OO programming.

For example, for a modular kernel, it is required to package code with a standard set of methods (or functions and arguments and their types), and little means of modifying the internals of that module—this applies to device drivers, protocols within a layer, and even larger units of operating system functionality such as filesystems and schedulers. At design time, this leads to safer code. At implementation time, it leads to extensibility. At build (*link*) time, this allows the system to be statically configured. Finally, at run time it allows a system to be configured dynamically as needed. This means that the system can be as small as needed.

It has a side effect on the design, which is that, usually, systems such as this are highly *regular*. That means that once a programmer has learned how to do something, it represents a general lesson.

C Style

There are quite a few different styles possible in C. Since there are a large number of examples in this book, we don't think it is necessary to spell out the style here, but rather discuss the reasons for some rules (of thumb).

Readability. Having a standard layout makes it easier for people to read your code (and find, and hopefully fix, bugs). It also allows people to share syntax-directed editor functions (emacs, usually). Not all programmers have three 21-inch displays at their disposal—it's friendly to make the code fit on a standard screen/window width. In kernel code, change logging is absolutely essential. A single line at the start of the module is only enough if there are indications throughout of the changes referencing the author too.

Automatic processing. There are a number of programs that are used to process code (e.g., for generating call graphs or code statistics). Some of these may rely on conventions for placing open braces at the start of a line, for example.

Maintenance. Code should contain enough comments that you can figure out its basic operation quickly, but not so many that you cannot find the actual statements. It is conventional to comment code in English. The bulk of Linux code is written by people who chose names for variables from the English vocabulary—it's a fait accompli. Function and variable names should communicate use and function (and to some extent, scope).

Portability. Be pedantic about types. Be extra pedantic about commenting the mapping between data structures and protocol wire formats. Be clear about byte order and alignment of fields.

Risk. There are no reasons for deliberate obfuscation of statements—for example, if you have a complex logical expression, bracket it to make it clear rather than relying on (possibly incorrect) memory of operator precedence.

In an ideal world, all code is accompanied by separate documentation as well, written *at the same time* as the code (e.g., as dictated by the extreme programming style). Such documentation should include examples of use and examples of test output. The world is unfortunately less than 100% ideal.

C Structures, Memory, and Wire Format

It is doubly useful that the fields in a compound data structure such as the C record structure, when compiled on a specific machine architecture with a specific compiler, have a known layout in memory. This allows the systems and communications programmer to be able to map external data into memory and vice versa (typically via buffers handed to input/output interfaces through some control register addressed in a device driver).

When reading a protocol definition, there are typically three places that the programmer needs to look, and in general the order that works best is:

1. *Packet format definitions.* Internet protocols are handily (and not accidentally) designed *and* defined using fields that are typically convenient, basic data types of a modern computer: byte (*octet*), and

16-, 32-, and 64-bit words. Most packet headers are aggregates of these (we'll see IP, TCP, and many others throughout the book). Making sure that we can access and manipulate the fields conveniently, correctly, and efficiently is the first thing that we try to get right—normally, a packet header is defined as a C structure in a C header file.

The only glitches in this approach are to do with variations between C compilers and machine architectures for the fine details—e.g., *endian*-ness of a byte, a short and long word. This is normally hidden in a single place through the use of functions or macros that can be used immediately pre-transmission, or post-reception, allowing the programmer to treat C fields as native data objects (e.g., for arithmetic) throughout the bulk of the code.

2. *Rules of operation (e.g., a state machine, or language/grammar of the protocol*). This can often directly be mapped into the core of an implementation (most TCP code for input packet handling is written directly, line by line, from the RFC).

3. *Interfaces to lower and higher layers, and to system functions*. Here we can see the set of functions and parameters for the service interface for the protocol (called by a higher layer), the calls to send and receive (or be called with a packet that has been received), together with infrastructure calls (timers, memory allocation/freeing, critical region protection, and so on).

High-level data structures (object-oriented) are useful for large systems and for re-use. Examples of this abound in UNIX—e.g., APIs to filesystems, device drivers, networks, and in some cases quite complex emulations of C++ in C (e.g., Kuznetzov's elegant structures of operations in the queuing discipline code, which we will see in Chapter 9).

The C language makes a nodding allowance for some higher-level approaches to programming. Typically, we can keep code in a directory hierarchy (see Section 2.4 for the Linux kernel source code layout). Within a given directory, we keep the code for a given level of abstraction. A collection of functions in a given source code file (a *module* in C terms; *not* to be confused with a module in Linux dynamic load terms), performs closely related functions—almost literally, an object. To make an object more generic, C provides a simple but extremely efficient and powerful mechanism of function pointers. A reference to a function can be passed as yet another parameter—this allows us to write code that can be quite generic, and only fill in the details at call time. It is common in Linux to wrap up these types of interfaces in a data structure with a standard set of pointers to the set of detailed functions—since C has a function prototype, this can be made reasonably type safe (though the programmer is free to mess this up, with disastrous consequences when kernel programming—it's a good way to learn some discipline).

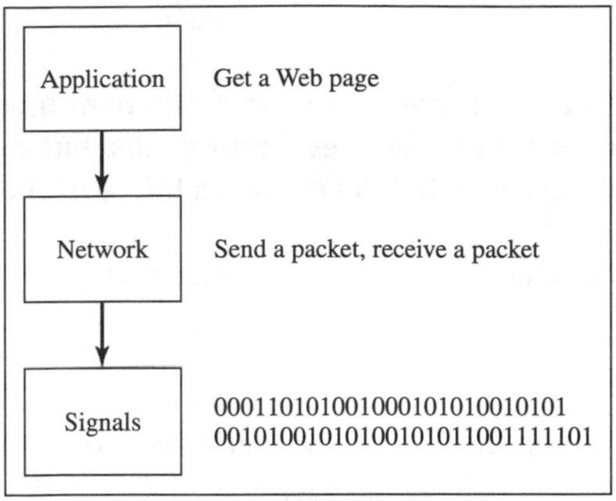

Figure 1.3 Layers of abstraction.

1.4 Protocol Stacks

Since the dawn of time, at least with regard to communications, systems have been composed out of protocols that are *layered* on each other to add more and more functionality.

Each layer implements a service (something relatively simple such as "send or receive a packet"), but is internally quite complex (e.g., involves fragmentation, address resolution, and so on). A higher layer enhances a lower layer. Common elements are kept in as low a layer as possible, but only so far as they are needed by the vast majority of higher-level users. Otherwise, they are implemented as another higher-layer protocol. This is a version of the famous *end-to-end* design principle.

Thus it is very natural to use an object-oriented style of programming with a strong separation of interface, defined by its methods and their parameters, from the internal implementation of the actual protocol. This layering leads to the idea of a protocol *stack*. The isolation of layers is enforced to some extent using information hiding (local variables, C `statics` and so on) as well as operating system techniques (separation of address space via memory management).

To counteract this, the real world imposes certain responsibilities on us, such as management and performance, which sometimes require us to design protocols that make use directly of internal functions in a lower layer, or report or even modify the state of a lower layer. There are many examples of this including TCP header compression (see Chapter 7), as well as most firewall applications (see Chapter 10). This is particularly true in the lower levels such as in driving link devices, and in the Internet Protocol layer and transport. Nevertheless, the OO approach works well, and use of controlled *holes* through the interface (global variables or other techniques) is usually kept to a minimum.

Next, let's look at the specifics of some layers, in terms of the service, and the protocol.

1.4.1 The Basics

To date, the Internet community has studiously avoided defining its own link protocols, and has endeavored merrily to operate one level above this, but to port the Internet Protocol software to every new link layer within hours of the technology being available.

The IP protocol is therefore the global glue that keeps the Internet alive.

1.4.2 IP

The conventional way of looking at an Internet Protocol header is as shown in Figure 1.4.

Figure 1.4 The RFC-style IP header definition.

```
0                   1                   2                   3
  0 1 2 3 4 5 6 7 8 9 0 1 2 3 4 5 6 7 8 9 0 1 2 3 4 5 6 7 8 9 0 1
 +-+-+-+-+-+-+-+-+-+-+-+-+-+-+-+-+-+-+-+-+-+-+-+-+-+-+-+-+-+-+-+-+
 |Version|  IHL  |Type of Service|          Total Length         |
 +-+-+-+-+-+-+-+-+-+-+-+-+-+-+-+-+-+-+-+-+-+-+-+-+-+-+-+-+-+-+-+-+
 |         Identification        |Flags|      Fragment Offset    |
 +-+-+-+-+-+-+-+-+-+-+-+-+-+-+-+-+-+-+-+-+-+-+-+-+-+-+-+-+-+-+-+-+
 |  Time to Live |    Protocol   |         Header Checksum       |
 +-+-+-+-+-+-+-+-+-+-+-+-+-+-+-+-+-+-+-+-+-+-+-+-+-+-+-+-+-+-+-+-+
 |                       Source Address                          |
 +-+-+-+-+-+-+-+-+-+-+-+-+-+-+-+-+-+-+-+-+-+-+-+-+-+-+-+-+-+-+-+-+
 |                    Destination Address                        |
 +-+-+-+-+-+-+-+-+-+-+-+-+-+-+-+-+-+-+-+-+-+-+-+-+-+-+-+-+-+-+-+-+
 |                    Options                    |    Padding    |
 +-+-+-+-+-+-+-+-+-+-+-+-+-+-+-+-+-+-+-+-+-+-+-+-+-+-+-+-+-+-+-+-+
```

In Linux, and in C, this is rendered this way:

Figure 1.5 The C-style IP header definition.

```
struct iphdr {
#if defined(__LITTLE_ENDIAN_BITFIELD)
        __u8    ihl:4,
                version:4;
#elif defined (__BIG_ENDIAN_BITFIELD)
        __u8    version:4,
                ihl:4;
#else
#error "Please_fix_<asm/byteorder.h>"
#endif
        __u8    tos;
        __u16   tot_len;
        __u16   id;
        __u16   frag_off;
```

```
        __u8    ttl;
        __u8    protocol;
        __u16   check;
        __u32   saddr;
        __u32   daddr;
        /*The options start here. */
};
```

You may be asking why there is so much in an IP header. We have a version number (4 or 6), the Internet header length (in 32-bit words, so the value is 5 for IPv4), the type of service, which we cover in some depth in Chapter 9, the total length (includes user data and upper layer protocol headers), the fragmentation information (see Chapter 6), the time to live (see Chapter 6), the protocol (identifies the next layer protocol up), the header checksum, and finally the source and destination addresses (described in Chapters 3, 6, and 8). This seems like a lot of data for every packet, but remember that this is a datagram network, so all packets have to carry enough of a survival kit.

1.4.3 Routes

IP is a simple protocol. However, getting IP packets around in a global network is a complex business. The smart part of the job of a router is to compute routes. The easy bit is to send packets on their way. Recently the easy part got harder, because people wanted to control the relative performance that packets are forwarded with for different users or different applications. We look at the two different pieces of routing and forwarding in Chapters 8 and 9, respectively.

For now, let's just introduce the basic idea of how routers work. The task of routing is the task of building a map, and then finding a fast way to index it when presented with a packet's destination and the question, "OK, so you're holding the map, and here's where we are trying to get to; now do we go left, right, or straight ahead?"

Basically, you need to know how to get to any address—so have all the routers tell each other about all the addresses on the map; then have them build a forwarding table, by searching the map for all addresses and building an index. When a packet arrives, the destination address in the packet is an index to the map—it says: where to go next (i.e., which turn to take at this intersection).

IP is carefully designed so that destinations make quite efficient indexes. To subvert this, the Internet has evolved so that the map is extremely complex and hard to compute routes over.

IP addresses therefore currently identify points of connection in the Internet. The usual term used is an *interface*. Any interface can have one (and even more than one) IP address. IP routing is the function of getting a packet from one interface across a sequence of other interfaces to a destination interface. This model is somewhat generalized in IPv6, which we discuss in Chapter 6.

1.4.4 TCP

Similarly, the transport protocol header for TCP is defined in the RFC, and illustrated as shown in Figure 1.6.

Figure 1.6 The RFC-style IP header definition.

```
 0                   1                   2                   3
 0 1 2 3 4 5 6 7 8 9 0 1 2 3 4 5 6 7 8 9 0 1 2 3 4 5 6 7 8 9 0 1
+-+-+-+-+-+-+-+-+-+-+-+-+-+-+-+-+-+-+-+-+-+-+-+-+-+-+-+-+-+-+-+-+
|          Source Port          |       Destination Port        |
+-+-+-+-+-+-+-+-+-+-+-+-+-+-+-+-+-+-+-+-+-+-+-+-+-+-+-+-+-+-+-+-+
|                        Sequence Number                        |
+-+-+-+-+-+-+-+-+-+-+-+-+-+-+-+-+-+-+-+-+-+-+-+-+-+-+-+-+-+-+-+-+
|                    Acknowledgment Number                      |
+-+-+-+-+-+-+-+-+-+-+-+-+-+-+-+-+-+-+-+-+-+-+-+-+-+-+-+-+-+-+-+-+
|  Data |           |U|A|P|R|S|F|                               |
| Offset| Reserved  |R|C|S|S|Y|I|            Window             |
|       |           |G|K|H|T|N|N|                               |
+-+-+-+-+-+-+-+-+-+-+-+-+-+-+-+-+-+-+-+-+-+-+-+-+-+-+-+-+-+-+-+-+
|           Checksum            |         Urgent Pointer        |
+-+-+-+-+-+-+-+-+-+-+-+-+-+-+-+-+-+-+-+-+-+-+-+-+-+-+-+-+-+-+-+-+
|                    Options                    |    Padding    |
+-+-+-+-+-+-+-+-+-+-+-+-+-+-+-+-+-+-+-+-+-+-+-+-+-+-+-+-+-+-+-+-+
|                             data                              |
+-+-+-+-+-+-+-+-+-+-+-+-+-+-+-+-+-+-+-+-+-+-+-+-+-+-+-+-+-+-+-+-+
```

This, in C, is defined as follows:

Figure 1.7 The TCP header definition: `linux/include/linux/tcp.h`.

```
struct tcphdr {
        __u16   source;
        __u16   dest;
        __u32   seq;
        __u32   ack_seq;
#if defined(__LITTLE_ENDIAN_BITFIELD)
        __u16   res1:4,
                doff:4,
                fin:1,
                syn:1,
```

```
                rst:1,
                psh:1,
                ack:1,
                urg:1,
                ece:1,
                cwr:1;
#elif defined(__BIG_ENDIAN_BITFIELD)
        __u16   doff:4,
                res1:4,
                cwr:1,
                ece:1,
                urg:1,
                ack:1,
                psh:1,
                rst:1,
                syn:1,
                fin:1;
#else
#error "Adjust_your_<asm/byteorder.h> defines"
#endif
        __u16   window;
        __u16   check;
        __u16   urg_ptr;
};
```

The fields in TCP convey end-to-end functionally, and again, we have to emphasize that each packet must be as standalone as possible in an IP network environment, since the routing system may cause packets to arrive misordered, and the transmission system may cause packets to vanish or be corrupted in flight.

TCP is the Transmission Control Protocol, which provides the most common end-to-end protocol for most applications' reliability requirements.

TCP packets are encapsulated in IP packets, and as far as the IP routing substrate is aware, that is really almost completely transparent (with the exception of fancy forwarding treatment, or filtering, as discussed in Chapters 9 and 10).

So long as IP can get a TCP payload from one host to another, and can get TCP payloads back too, then that's the minimum requirement TCP has from the IP layer.

What's in the TCP header? Well, the first thing that's needed is some way to identify the use or application that is running a TCP connection, so we need some way of distinguishing IP packets carrying TCP payloads. To this end, TCP headers contain 16-bit identifiers called *ports* which are used for both source and destination. These enable the IP layer and TCP layer software to do multiplexing, i.e., to support a large number of distinguishable sessions between any host and any other host. Well-known ports in the destination field identify the application, while dynamically allocated ports in the source field allow multiple instances of use of the same application between any pair of hosts.

To get the delivery semantics correct, packets contain sequence numbers so that the TCP code in an end system can construct an ordered delivery of bytes between the sender and the receiving application. Given that the network is potentially unreliable, packets also contain acknowledgment numbers that are used to report back to a sender what has been received correctly in order so far by a recipient TCP. This is a full-duplex operation, as is flow and congestion control, which is achieved by several complex Window schemes, which are discussed in some detail in Chapter 6. After the TCP header payload, the rest of the contents of an IP packet will be some amount (for example, on an Ethernet, up to 1,500 bytes) of stuff that is data as far as TCP is concerned, but which is some application protocol as far as the upper-layer protocol using TCP is concerned.

1.4.5 Packet Exchange Patterns

In Chapter 6 and elsewhere we look at several packet exchange scenarios. It's worth talking here a bit about this way of understanding a protocol by way of introduction.

TCP has a very complex set of rules by which it operates—RFC 793 is 85 pages long, and there are now several other RFCs that define additional functionality for TCP such as congestion control, window scaling, ECN behavior, protection against wrapped sequence numbers, and so on. Given that a pair of communicating systems are autonomous, it is entirely possible for one end of a TCP session to generate any packet or sequence of packets you can imagine within the header format illustrated in Figure 1.6, at just about any time. Many of these will even be legal packets (with sensible sequence and acknowledgment numbers, window sizes, and so on). To exhaustively list all the combinations of legal send and receive behaviors is not a sensible approach to thinking about a protocol such as TCP. Instead, we typically use illustrations of *typical* or commonly implemented behavior, rather than trying to consider the many pathological possibilities.

One part of the way TCP works that makes life a little more complex to consider is that in practice, TCP contains several subprotocols that operate nearly independently within the same flow of packets being exchanged within a single session. The reason for this is that the data exchange is only a part of what is being sent to and fro. There are also a number of *control messages*. Every TCP packet has all the same fields and has the capability of *piggybacking* a control function or exchange, along with any data in the rest of the payload. Of course, sometimes (quite often) TCP packets are pure control, for example at the start and end of connections, or in one-way data flows where the packets coming the other way are all pure acknowledgments. Even then, the header information is *sub-multiplexing* several functions, such as ordering, reliability, flow control and congestion control, through updating window fields and so on.

We can look at a simple example of how a protocol operates to achieve some degree of reliability:

```
Wait for data
Tx Data(1)
Rx data (1)
Ack data(1)
Wait for ack
Wait for ack
Wait for data (2)
Get ack, Tx More data(2)
Say the data is lost in transit -
What to do? TIMEOUT!!!
Retransmit data (2)
...
...
Rx data (2).
```

Note there are so many permutations of the scenario above that there are better ways to express behavior in a more general manner—one common way is to capture the set of desired actions for the set of feasible events in a single structure called a finite state machine, or FSM. This is a two-dimensional matrix with two indices: the current state and the current event. The contents of each entry is a function that carries out the desired action and sets the state variable to the next state. The total number of different paths through such a matrix for a sequence of events can be huge, but it is a compact and robust representation for the entire system, and it can be directly implemented and tested.

Here is an example of simple flow control in action:

```
Tx(1);wait for ack(1)
Rx(1);Ack(1)
Tx(2) Tx(3);wait for ack(3)
Rx(2);Ack(2);Rx(3);Ack(3)
TxTxTxTx;wait for ack(7)


etc, etc etc
but if a packet is lost, but if we are ''out of steam''
we lost a packet,
it doesn't get acked.
we TIMEOUT,
and rtx - maybe we ought to
slow down
```

In the history of communications, and the Internet specifically, there has been a long-running argument about the fact that the datagram network is connectionless and usually *stateless*. This argument is based on a naive view of layering (some would say a religious view) that holds that "you cannot look outside the packet header of the protocol at *this* layer when processing this layer." In fact, this is nonsense, and as we will see in later chapters, in practice it is very common to do this for lots of good reasons (TCP and RTP header compression, header prediction, differentiated services, masquerading, and many others). For now, suffice it to say that the common notion that has become accepted is that of a *flow*.

A flow roughly corresponds to a user session. The simplest form this can take is a single Web page download, or an ssh session. There are more complex examples of flows that include aggregations of traffic between two machines, or between two sites, or between one machine and a number of sites. All of these are identifiable by some combination of packet header information gleaned from the IP and transport headers—the simplest example is the IPv4 integrated services (or differentiated services) 5-tuple, consisting of the IP protocol number, source and destination IP addresses (host interfaces), and transport source and destination port numbers. More complex examples can be built by either wildcarding some fields and pattern matching, or by looking at even higher-level information.

Flows are a very useful concept, and we will revisit them in later chapters (especially in Chapter 8). For now, we can think of them as the unit of resource control (whether for allocating resources, or blocking for security reasons). Linux has powerful mechanisms for identifying flows efficiently.

There is some debate in the Internet measurement community about how easy it is in practice to use flow information (statistics about the pattern of end points, and distribution of duration for flows). The debate is important for large network operators in provisioning their networks, and is a topic for several other books.

1.4.6 Performance Trends

Networks get faster and bigger, as well as smaller and slower, year by year.

The host count on the Internet increases by around 100% every eight months, and any number we write down (e.g., as I type this, there are now around 50 million public, and probably 200 million private, networked computers) will be out of date before you finish reading this sentence.

A typical link speed was 56 Kbps in 1976, but now 622 Mbps is not uncommon wide area, and people are working on designing terabit/second routers.

Specific examples of national institutional network access in the U.K. National University network, SuperJANET, were 64 Kbps in 1980, 2 Mbps in 1990, 155 Mbps in 1995, 1 Gbps in 2001, and currently deploying 2 to 10 Gbps, to be rolled out by 2002. However, note that Moore's Law has computer speeds tracking this performance quite nicely. Not only that, but commodity PCs are also falling in price, so that there is a win-win scenario with using them as a networking end system, router, or middle box.

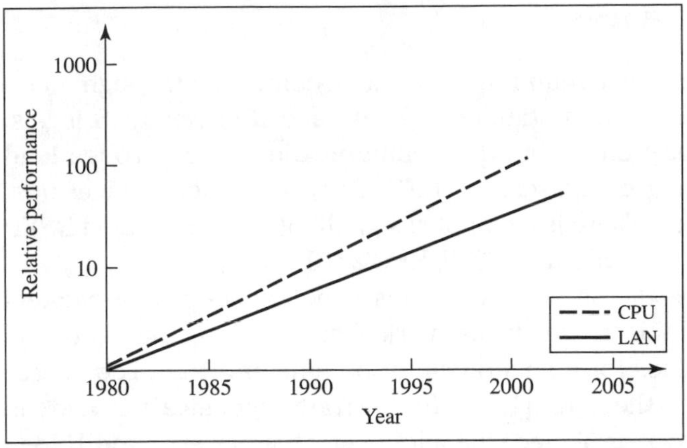

Figure 1.8 Trends.

1.5 Security

Security concerns discussed above briefly can be expanded on a little, although, as we said, it really is important to be well educated about cyber-crime-prevention.

Typical questions to ask yourself before hooking up a machine to the Net include:

- Who can use your computer?
- Who can use your network?
- Whose computer can you use?
- Whose network can you use?
- Access control, privacy, depend on protocols.
- Authentication protocols plus encryption techniques.

This of course still leaves denial-of-service and traffic pattern analysis. The best defense against these may be to invoke a different model of costs, such as performance management through pricing. We'll look at this next.

1.6 Performance

As the network becomes a more important component in your enterprise, you may have concerns about controlling the absolute or relative performance that different users and applications can obtain. There is now a plethora of techniques for doing this, and Linux implements most of them very well in its most recent versions, and is a favorite amongst engineers looking at this area.

1.6.1 Integrated Services

The most stringent performance requirements can be controlled through meeting the IETF's Integrated Services standards. These specify three QoS levels. Currently, the service is best-effort, but this definition adds the controlled-load service (RFC 2211), the guaranteed service (RFC 2212), and other services possible (RFC 2215, RFC 2216). There is a complex signalling protocol called RSVP (Resource Reservation Protocol) (RFC 2205, RFC 2210).

The standards describe the service semantics which specify how packets with a given service should be treated by network elements along the path. This is achieved by setting values for a general set of parameters ⟨`service name`⟩ ⟨`parameter name`⟩, both in the range [1, 254] for the traffic specification, and the service specification, known as TSpec (the allowed traffic pattern) and RSpec (the service request specification).

Performance is in terms of a token bucket (rate, bucket size) and is controlled through a token bucket filter that measures the total data sent. To make sure we do not add traffic to a network that is already full, the routers (and/or sources and receivers) running this scheme carry out a calculation called *Admission Control.*

While running this scheme, traffic is also subject to policing. This means that conforming routers check that the TSpec is adhered to, and packet handling may change if the TSpec is violated (e.g., degrade service level, drop, mark, and so on).

The idea of the controlled-load service is to provide a virtual network that looks very much like a path for best-effort, but under unloaded conditions.

The idea of the guaranteed service is to offer a specified assured data rate with bounded delay. This is a deterministic guarantee, but offers no guarantees on jitter.

1.6.2 Differentiated Services

Integrated service is expensive to offer in router state (processing and memory) terms, so a less complex model is defined, called *differentiated services.*

Again, an architecture demands a service model (RFC 2475), and this entails tiered service levels, indicated now through simple packet markings (RFC 2474) rather than via out-of-band (RSVP) signalling. Packets are intended to be marked by the network, not by the application, so differentiated services would support legacy applications. It is intended to be simpler to implement than INTSERV, and can be introduced onto current networks.

It should scale better since state is no longer kept (necessarily) per flow, and the aggregate treatment of packets from a source is defined.

Service classes that have been defined so far include:

- Premium (low delay)—EF (RFC 2598)
- Assured (high data rate, low loss)—AF (RFC 2597)

Ongoing research is defining mechanisms to specify the service level agreement (SLA) via a service level specification (SLS). This will include a statement of the policy between a user and a provider, with policing at ingress, and a service provided by network (end system unaware).

Packet marking is achieved through use of the IPv4 ToS byte or IPv6 traffic-class byte, now known as the DS byte. Traffic classifiers that work to mark packets according to the SLA, act on either a multifield (MF) (as in integrated services) DS byte + other header fields, or a behavior aggregate (BA), recursively reusing the DS field only. DS codepoints define values for the DS byte, and SLAs are implemented by understanding the aggregate per-hop behavior (PHB) together with the aggregate treatment within the network.

So typically we would specify the rate and delay in the SLS. Expedited forwarding (EF) (RFC 2598) defines a virtual leased line (VLL) service, with data rate specified in SLS and more loosely defined performance for the other parameters, such as low delay, low jitter, and low loss.

Assured forwarding (AF) (RFC 2597) defines four classes (1–4) with three levels of drop precedence per class (1–3), where AF11 is best and AF43 is worst.

Traffic conditioners act at the ingress to the network to meter traffic and apply a marker, and if appropriate, a shaper/dropper. Metering of traffic is the function of deciding whether a flow (aggregate) is in-profile or out-of-profile. Remarking can be used as the flow(s) traverse multiple providers with different implementations of the PHBs, to a new DS codepoint, and to reshape or drop packets.

When is allocation made to SLA? This can be at subscription, per user/user-group/site/customer, and could be multifield, policy-based, or within an organization, per application/user/user-group.

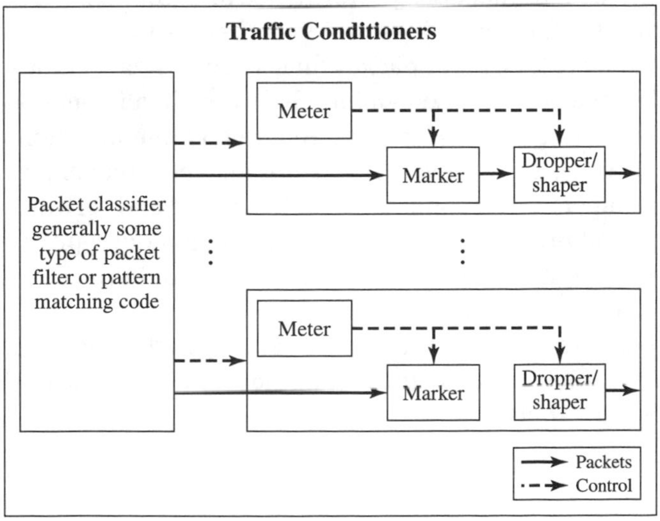

Figure 1.9 Differentiated services metering and marking.

Table 1.1 Integrated versus Differentiated Services

FUNCTION	INTSERV	DIFFSERV
signalling	from application	network management, application
granularity	flow	flow, source, site, aggregate
mechanism	destination address, protocol, port	packet class
scope	end-to-end	edge-to-edge

We could graph behavior aggregates using ad hoc tools of network management statically, or, possibly dynamically using RSVP.

Since the same DS codepoints could be used for different services by different providers, and different providers using the same PHBs may have different behavior, we have to define edge-to-edge semantics. There is also the problem currently of the lack of symmetry: protocols such as TCP (ideally) require symmetric QoS. Finally, differentiated services for multicast, to support for multiparty, symmetric communication, are as yet undefined.

1.7 Summary

In this chapter, we have sketched an overview of the Internet protocol suite. The interesting thing about the design philosophy embodied in the split of functions between the unreliable IP layer and the reliable TCP layer[1] is that it fits the evolution of technology so well. Link and physical layer systems have continued to evolve that are affordable with tremendous performance and low cost (both for local area networks and for long-haul links and switches), so long as we don't expect them to mask faults at the bit or packet time scale. Instead, end-to-end protocols such as TCP have been devised and implemented in all common operating systems for the end user to be offered the required communications semantics. The split has also led to twenty years of optimization techniques familiar to software programmers being applied to the IP routing and forwarding layer, and to the end-to-end protocols, so that now on a commodity-priced computer, we can have near gigabit-per-second performance without even using significant amounts of CPU or memory resources.

In the next chapter, we take a tour around the Linux operating system, looking at its general features, before coming back in the rest of the book to look at TCP and IP and all their friends and family.

[1] If we can characterize what may also have been an astronomical quantity of blind luck, as design!

CHAPTER 2

Introduction to the Linux Operating System

```
echo '16i[q]sa[ln0=aln100%Pln100/snlbx]sbA0D4D465452snlbxq'|dc
```

—Submitted by Simon Chapman to the Irish Linux community Web site

2.1 Roadmap

In this chapter, we review the purpose and functions of an operating system and put the networking mechanisms in this context. We look at the overall features of Linux. Then we study a day in the life of a process, a file, the operating system as a whole (from boot to shutdown), a device driver, a kernel module, and a system call.

We explain the difference between user space programming and the kernel view of the world, and take a detailed look at support for concurrency, and the consequence for control for access to shared resources, with the idea of critical regions, and mechanisms for preventing inconsistency such as interrupt disabling, semaphores, and spinlocks.

We then follow the story of a day in the life of a file, covering the variety of file types and file access that make up the rich world of Linux input and output, and the unification of process, device, and module management.

Following that, we take a look at a day in the life of an operating system, from boot until shutdown.

Similarly, we follow a day in the life of a device driver, looking at interfaces (the view from above—unifying all devices), and down to hardware, interrupts, and DMA.

Because of its special status in network code, we dissect a day in the life of a kernel module, and show how this gives Linux the properties of a microkernel, but without the overhead of server or helper processes with their associated context and IPC overheads.

Getting down to more detail, we examine a day in the life of a system call, and getting from one space to another.

After that, we take a look at the operating system's idea of time and events.

We wrap up the chapter with a look at multiprocessor support, and in particular, the effect of symmetric multiprocessing (SMP) design on other parts of the operating system and networking implementation.

2.2 What Is an Operating System?

An operating system (OS) provides *services*. Typical services that a user wants include management of storage through a filesystem and backup system; the ability to run application programs; easy access to the network; and management of a Graphical User Interface.

There are several different approaches to designing and building such software. At its simplest, much of an operating system is a collection of libraries of commonly used functions. An OS usually also incorporates a number of useful utility programs (operations and management applications). However, what makes an operating system different from other collections of code is that much of the OS code interfaces between the hardware and applications.

Services are provided through a set of layers of software which unify common elements and hide the idiosyncratic details of the underlying hardware. Access to hardware requires use of specific instructions and memory addresses that the system may wish to protect the normal user from accidentally disturbing. Hardware may autonomously wake up and attempt to access memory or interrupt the processor at any moment—this is especially true of user interface hardware (mice, keyboards) and networking interfaces. While user programs (applications) are increasingly being implemented by programmers who are familiar with an event-driven programming paradigm, it is still hard to design systems that manage large numbers of competing streams of events—gone are the says when cooperative multitasking was a viable way for the everyday program to manage resources on a system. Now this role is largely taken by the *kernel* of the operating system. Applications are largely insulated from this level of complexity.

Different operating systems have been designed with different types of users in mind. This means that the three general purpose operating systems in most common use today in the world, UNIX, Windows, and MAC OS, have undergone very different pressures during their development. This has led to quite a different emphasis in how services are provided.

The principle differences lie in whether the system was originally designed to support a single or multiple users; whether the user is a technical expert or someone with no interest in developing computing systems further; and whether the user has intense multimedia requirements, or mainly text and graphics. MAC OS and Windows historically both targeted single-user systems, while the Apple offering emphasized multimedia. UNIX systems have always targeted the technical systems developer, engineer, or scientist. As such, UNIX has traditionally run on large computing systems as well as small desktop ones. Because there were many different vendors providing different processors and systems for scientific- and engineering-based computing, UNIX systems have always been designed with the ability to run on a variety of hardware platforms.

An analogy for the different services is to think about a car; in a car, you have an operating system that the normal user thinks about—navigation tools, the accelerator, the brake, the steering wheel, and so on; you have the operating system that the maintenance engineer thinks about: the tire pressure, the engine management system, the fuel supply, and so on; there is the operating system that the mechanic is concerned with: the steering, the suspension, the braking system, and so on. Each has their place. In some system designs, there is more effort on the user side, while in others (off-road vehicles) there is more on the engineering. To some extent, recent work with Linux is trying to cross this divide and cover both territories, by extensive work on application and GUI support. Fundamentally, the kernel of an operating system is rooted in the efficient exploitation of the hardware to meet one of these goals.

To make efficient use of an expensive resource such as an old mainframe, minicomputer, or supercomputer, the UNIX designers adopted a number of the techniques from the large commercial operating systems of the 1970s. Over the last decade, there has been a clear trend to adopt these same ideas in desktop systems, but at the same time, UNIX-like systems such as Linux have been designed to work in just the same type of constrained environments. In particular, UNIX-like systems are the industry standard for network servers, systems that run application-level services accessible over the network, which is one of the reasons for this book.

Networks are another example of a potentially expensive, or at least shared, resource. As described in the introduction, they are typically shared among many users. This means that operating system support for network access, and access from the network to operating system resources, must follow the rules for sharing the network.

Linux provides a general set of means for computing resources to be shared between multiple users at the same, and at different, times. Linux unifies different hardware under a resource management umbrella, to allow safe and efficient use of the processor, memory, and input and output devices.

2.2.1 MultiUser

Since the 1970s, there has been a saying that "Everything in UNIX is a file." What is meant by this is that the standard abstraction for any object on the system is provided by the overloading of the concept of a file.

Of course, normally, files are objects stored on disk. Files are organized in filesystems. Any filesystem (and Linux supports quite a few different ones) consists of a way of organizing storage devices (*file-stores*), a way of organizing files within a naming hierarchy (directories, files within directories, and so on), and a way of formatting data within files (UNIX has traditionally kept this as simple as can be). UNIX *unifies* the view of a number of objects in the system by using the filename space to name, and therefore provide access to, devices and (in modern UNIX systems) processes, as well as to simple stored data. This unification makes the system programmers' tasks easier—there are fewer system interfaces than in other families of operating systems. We will see throughout the book how this makes access to the communications facilities quite straightforward. We will also see that in some cases, this unification comes at a cost—sometimes the analogy between a file and some other type of object stretches the use of the system call interface in some rather odd ways, and this shows in the use of some of the parameters.

An important aspect of the filesystems is the identification of ownership of files. In the data structures associated with any file, whether it is a normal plain file, a directory, a handle on a device, or even a process, there are fields that show the ownership of the file and the permissions associated with different users (user, group, others). This data is stored with the files on disk, and is kept in memory when a file is opened by a program—the data structure that stores all this is called an `inode`. At the root of all things, all files have an *inode number*.

Traditional interaction between the user and the system was via command line interfaces (the *shell*). Of course, on modern systems, we expect to use a graphical user interface (GUI). The underlying system for this on UNIX is X-Windows, which for 20 years now has provided networked graphical interfaces to programs running on remote systems. GUIs come into their own when coupled with multitasking systems—it is common for many classes of user to combine and overlap a number of loosely related tasks (e.g., editing and previewing a letter, or programming, debugging, and viewing documentation, or browsing the net and taking notes). A windowing system combined with a tasking system is essential to the modern user. Let's look a bit further at tasks.

2.2.2 MultiTasking

Main Street shops now sell computers that execute nearly 1,000 million instructions per second. Yet much of the time, the user is sitting in front of his computer (or holding his palmtop) thinking deep thoughts about what to type next. In the meantime, the computer might as well get on with something useful. In the early days of computing, people would hardwire in to the operating system some useful task in the *idle loop* such as computing the next few million decimal places in π. Nowadays, we do the same thing more flexibly—for example, screen savers may download some data from the radio telescopes around the world and try to find some meaningful signal in the noise (Search for Extraterrestrial Intelligence, or SETI). Multitasking is the ability of the operating system to provide the illusion of serving many masters at once. The illusion is easiest to see as a user when you fire up some background task such as printing. The two tasks, a foreground one (e.g., an editor) and a background one (e.g., printing) are carried out by the system by alternating between the programs, running part of one, then part of the other, and so on. Programs that have started and not finished are known as *processes*. All processes have a process ID.

A system that has enough cycles per second to fool a user in this way, and enough memory to hold the code and data for multiple programs, is relatively simple. The key idea is that a process can be described by taking a snapshot of the state of the processor and the code and data at any instant (between one instruction and the next)—this snapshot is known as the *context*. The operating system can save the context of a running program into some special location in memory associated with the process, and *switch* to another process by restoring its context—really, this is just a case of loading all the registers with the last values that this other process had, and setting the CPU's program counter to the next address to start getting code from. The part of the operating system that carries out this *context switching* is called the scheduler. When there are several processes to choose from, the scheduler may make use of all sorts of bookkeeping data to base the decision on. Linux supports several different schedulers nowadays. This can be very useful for specialist applications such as real-time systems (e.g., in physical process control systems in factories, where time is of the essence).

Multitasking is really essential for providing a clean programming abstraction for an open platform where users can safely run different applications in a windowing environment. Multitasking is also non-optional when building network servers. Nowadays, a server (e.g., a Web server) may receive many requests nearly simultaneously, and will need to schedule dealing with servers in many different ways. There are several different ways that this can be done, but a multitasking system is really one of the simplest. We will see later on in this book that there are reasons why general multitasking is sometimes a little too slow for really high-throughput Web serving.

General purpose servers are very common in the networking business—these may provide a number of networked services such as network time (via Network Time Protocol) to synchronize the clocks on a set of remote computers, network printing, email, logging, file serving, and so on. The general term used for programs that provide useful services on a UNIX system is *daemon*.

Processes are associated with users, just as files are. In UNIX, processes are created in an ancestor-descendant way from a primordial process (init, a process that UNIX starts when it finishes booting—see later). Child processes inherit their parent's user identity. To change identity, a process may set its user ID, although only to reduce the access rights that a child may obtain. This sounds draconian, but is in fact, quite general.

Linux also keeps track of time. This is fairly essential for a number of networking protocols, as well as being important for bookkeeping (e.g., file creation, access and modification times, process startup, and system usage statistics).

There is a lot more context associated with a task that Linux manages in order to keep life simpler for the application programmer.

For example, the filesystem provides a hierarchical organization of directories. This is useful for users and applications as a navigation aid. To help keep things brief, the *current working directory* is part of the state associated with a process. In keeping with the simple (but effective) approach to security, UNIX allows a process to change its view of where the root of the filesystem is. This allows parents to restrict childrens' views of things.

Processes start life with three standard channels to the outside world: input, output, and errors. These are associated with the *controlling terminal* or *tty*. Parents pass these through to their children (of course a process is at liberty to *detach* from a controlling terminal so that it can run *in background*). A group of processes controlled by the same terminal are managed together. The idea of groups of processes is very useful in networking, since one can manage the state of the group together, particularly through the use of *signals*.

Signals provide a way for the operating system to notify a process of an event. This idea originates from the requirement for raising exceptions (software interrupts) in a task: for an extreme example, many UNIX systems can send a signal to all processes when the power is about to die. Nowadays, signals are used for many asynchronous communications, alongside more normal file, pipe, and socket communication tools, of which we will see more next.

The kernel and user processes may use signals to communicate (albeit abruptly) with another process. If a process wishes to communicate in a more civilized manner, with another process on the same machine, there are several choices. If the programmer wants a record of the communication, the simplest technique is just to use files. UNIX doesn't restrict the reading and writing of files by default to a specific process, but there are tools to control access to files and provide synchronization. A more common technique is the use of a pair of file-like channels, called a *pipe*. Finally, the programmer might use full-fledged communications channels such as a *socket*, which can be used for purely local, or inter-machine, inter-process communication.

To summarize, we can take the view from below as the operating system context, or the view from above, the application/user context. The viewpoints are like a dual personality, or the subconscious and conscious.[1]

[1] A more fanciful model of system calls might be the visual metaphor used in Jean Cocteau's film of the Orpheus and Eurydice legend when the poet follows his true love into hell, by going through mirrors.

2.2.3 MultiDevice

Modern computers support a massive range of devices. As well as traditional keyboards, screens, and storage devices, we have a range of network interface types, including fixed and wireless, and a number of multimedia devices (audio, video capture, 3D, and so on).

At the lowest level, the operating system needs to manage input and output from and to these devices. There is a surprising amount of commonality in the functions required to match the OS to the different hardware.

A large percentage of the code associated with any operating system is so-called device driver code. Device drivers hide the specifics of a piece of hardware to control an I/O device, and provide the standard systems and application programming interfaces to the device, translating between the generic model and any idiosyncrasies that a specific device may possess. Of course, a particular hardware configuration only needs drivers for the devices it possesses. Linux supports the concept of *modules*, which allows on-demand dynamic loading of code for operating system subcomponents such as device drivers, which makes it even more economical on memory.

All UNIX systems identify the kind of device driver by a unique number called the *major number* and the specific device by its *minor number*. Major numbers are allocated by an authority, although free ones can be used by configuration or as needed, while minor numbers are allocated as needed by the system or by configuration (e.g., through *mknod*).

Linux divides devices into three basic classes:

Character. These devices are typically serial lines (traditionally for keyboard-type input), but also parallel interfaces, mice, sound cards, frame buffers, and so on. The main emphasis here is on interaction with humans and external machines.

Block. These are for storage-type devices (floppy, hard, and optical disks). Most importantly, these support filesystems.

Network. This a special case where Linux differs from other UNIX-like systems in its treatment of these as a distinct device type, and as networking is the main topic of this book, this is discussed in detail later. The critical difference between character and block devices, and network devices, is that the network device usually has another intelligent computer at the far end, rather than a human user, or just dumb storage.

What makes devices similar? The ability to read and write data to a device is the main common strand. What makes devices different? A number of things, ranging from performance (data rate, latency, and so on), through to intelligence (dumb keyboards, smart audio, and network cards, and so on), and most importantly management and control complexity.

As discussed before, operating system services are layered. Applications typically access files, and Linux supports various filesystems that reside within kernel space, but make use of block devices to access storage devices. Applications may carry out interprocess communication via networking protocols that (largely) reside in the operating system, but make use of network device drivers to access local and wide area networks. The exception to this three-layered pattern is that applications wishing to carry out interaction with users via keyboard and screen generally do so directly. The case of the graphical application using a frame buffer for output and mouse for input is slightly exceptional here, as this is generally done via the X-Windows system, which resides in user space, but requires a special process to manage the frame buffer display and pointer devices, rather than using a kernel resident task.

We've already mentioned that the filesystem naming is also used to name devices. The naming convention for network devices is somewhat different and is discussed later. Now we introduce the idea of *binding* of names. Binding is a word full of resonance: from the binding power of certain kinds of magic in *The Lord of the Rings* through to the ancient art of book binding. The use of the word binding in computer science is no less important.

In the context of I/O, binding is concerned with associating one or both ends of a channel, which is identified by some short descriptor, with some *named* entity. In the filesystem namespace, we need to make a storage device that contains a filesystem visible in the name hierarchy. This is done through *mounting* the device, which attaches the root of the filesystem of the device into the overall hierarchy. In the driver namespace, a driver is associated with a specific device through the major plus minor device numbers. In the process namespace, processes are associated with a process identifier through the `/proc` mechanism (more later). In the communications world, we associate a channel with a pair of endpoints through some Internet naming and addressing system, of which more later. In the windowing system, an external server associates regions of the screen with window identifiers.

At the lower level, device drivers may make use of a number of different programming techniques for access between the device to move data to and from the processor or memory. The simplest technique is called *polling*, and depends on continual access to a device to see if it has data ready (or it is ready for data). Few devices work like this in real systems. More commonly, the device has a modicum of intelligence and can make use of *interrupts* to notify the processor that data is ready. Different processor families have different hardware techniques for providing interrupt-handling facilities. Typically, most systems provide some number of channels; on the PC these are known as interrupt requests, or IRQs. There may be more devices than IRQs, in which case the devices have to share interrupts, and a processor has to be programmed to distinguish which device interrupted. Each IRQ is associated with an interrupt service routine (ISR). Typically, the operating system installs code at a set of addresses that is where the interrupts are *vectored* to. Think of an interrupt as an *unsolicited* procedure call, with a few side effects. These side effects are important (they involve changing processor mode from user to kernel, for example). We will see later how they work, and how we synchronize between processes, kernel tasks, and interrupt handlers. Many devices also have enough intelligence to move data to and fro from memory to device controller buffers and vice versa—this is direct memory access (DMA) and is typically set up by device drivers to take more work away from the CPU, and to get some measure of parallelism between normal work and I/O work. Most faster (block mode and network) devices work this way.

Linux has one more trick up its sleeve with regard to interrupt handling. Interrupt service routines often have a critical time within which they must respond to a device, at least initially. However, there may be a lot of housekeeping work which can then be done with more slack. Linux ISRs schedule the later work to be dealt with by what is known as a *bottom half*. The bottom half routines often involve moving data up to application space, and rescheduling processes and so on. A list of bottom half routines is scanned, and any ready routines are called explicitly during the last stages of system calls. In symmetric multiprocessor Linux, bottom halves have been re-engineered using a more general mechanism, which we'll look at briefly later on.

The fact that an interrupt changes processor mode (typically from user to kernel), and therefore allows code in an ISR to access privileged resources, makes it the ideal way to implement system calls. System calls have also been known as traps for this reason: they are like a trapdoor down from the user space into the cellar that is the kernel. Most UNIX implementations vector all the system calls through one IRQ, and then use a jump table to access the actual system call code. System calls rigorously check the validity of parameters (e.g., data buffer addresses, and lengths thereof, for read and write must reside within the user's process' address space). System calls may de-schedule a user process if necessary.

2.2.4 From Input/Output to Interprocess Communication

"Everything is a file" is a UNIX mantra. In fact, there are several activities supported by operating systems that can be made to look like files, but hide a multitude of sins of commission and omission behind this simple face.

For example, there are at least four radically different things that can be accessed by the same system calls, but are not all files:

File. A file is an array of bytes on a storage device. In the UNIX view of the world, we can open, close, read, and write it. There's a huge amount of code in Linux dedicated to supporting files on a range of different storage devices with a variety of different goals, including foreign operating system support and performance goals.

Pipe. A pipe is a means of communicating between two related processes. It looks like a file, but we can't do some things to a pipe that we could do to a file (e.g., seek).

Socket. One view of the concept of a socket is the extension of a pipe between two processes to include two more steps: firstly, communication between unrelated processes; secondly, communication between processes on different CPUs or different computer systems. Sockets are supported by a large amount of communications protocol code, in the analogous way to the support for files on many different filesystems.

Device. A device is a piece of hardware. Some things a device can do are support input and output, but it doesn't actually perform it directly—for example, a device might tell you its temperature. Devices may be for storage, for communication, or for something completely different (robots, car engine management systems, and so on).

The things in common between these are simple. The aspects that differ are complex. In common is that all UNIX communication is via filesystem interface code, and starts with getting a handle on a channel via a system call such as `open()`, using a name for the end point (file, device, computer/process). Subsequent communication might use `read()` and `write()`, or other calls, but there are then other things that the programmer might wish to do, including polling, or controlling some facet of the communications channel. We'll see later on that in one case (communications routing protocols) this is so complex that Linux ends up supporting a control channel as another file I/O channel (the routing `rtnetlink` interface) rather than *overloading* yet further one of the overburdened system calls such as `setsockopt()` or `ioctl()`.

2.2.5 Processor Independence

The core components of most modern operating systems are reasonably independent of processor architecture. This is due simply to the modern software engineering practice of using high-level languages and of separation of concerns for services and hardware.

However, Linux appears to enjoy a degree of portability across processor architectures beyond many other systems (apart from its UNIX cousins), due perhaps partly to the efforts of its implementors in retaining a clear goal of including any other processor architecture work in the operating system. Another factor in this has historically been the relatively small size of the Linux kernel source, which means that identifying architecture dependence is a smaller task than with some commercial systems. This is becoming less true as more variations (e.g., multiprocessor support) mean that there is more complexity in the kernel, which may depend on hardware architectural differences.

However, the vast bulk of the hardware-specific code is in the device support, which is where things are necessarily processor-, bus-, and I/O architecture-dependent in any case, so this is not of any concern.

There are some parts of the low-level memory management, time management, and scheduler that have some assembler and a few C code routines that need attention when moving to another hardware platform.

Types

Linux defines a set of C types for use in the kernel (and elsewhere, if you like) to aid in remembering what is and what is not portable. These are built on top of the POSIX standard definitions, and architecture specific types.

Figure 2.1 POSIX C-type definitions: `linux/include/linux/posix_types.h`.

```
/*
 * This allows for 1024 file descriptors: if NR_OPEN is ever grown
 * beyond that you'll have to change this too. But 1024 fd's seem to be
 * enough even for such "real" unices like OSF/1, so hopefully this is
 * one limit that doesn't have to be changed [again].
 *
 * Note that POSIX wants the FD_CLEAR(fd,fdsetp) defines to be in
 * <sys/time.h> (and thus <linux/time.h>) - but this is a more logical
 * place for them. Solved by having dummy defines in <sys/time.h>.
 */

/*
 * Those macros may have been defined in <gnu/types.h>. But we always
 * use the ones here.
 */
#undef __NFDBITS
#define __NFDBITS     (8 * sizeof(unsigned long))

#undef __FD_SETSIZE
#define __FD_SETSIZE  1024

#undef __FDSET_LONGS
#define __FDSET_LONGS (__FD_SETSIZE/__NFDBITS)

#undef __FDELT
#define __FDELT(d)    ((d) / __NFDBITS)

#undef __FDMASK
#define __FDMASK(d)   (1UL << ((d) % __NFDBITS))

typedef struct {
       unsigned long fds_bits [__FDSET_LONGS];
} __kernel_fd_set;

```

```
/* Type of a signal handler. */
typedef void (*__kernel_sighandler_t)(int);

/* Type of a SYSV IPC key. */
typedef int __kernel_key_t;
```

Figure 2.2 i386 ASM header interface C-type definitions: `linux/include/asm-i386/types.h`.

```
typedef unsigned short umode_t;

/*
 * __xx is ok: it doesn't pollute the POSIX namespace. Use these in the
 * header files exported to user space
 */

typedef __signed__ char __s8;
typedef unsigned char __u8;

typedef __signed__ short __s16;
typedef unsigned short __u16;

typedef __signed__ int __s32;
typedef unsigned int __u32;

#if defined(__GNUC__) && !defined(__STRICT_ANSI__)
typedef __signed__ long long __s64;
typedef unsigned long long __u64;
#endif

/*
 * These aren't exported outside the kernel to avoid name space clashes
 */
#ifdef __KERNEL__

typedef signed char s8;
typedef unsigned char u8;

typedef signed short s16;
typedef unsigned short u16;

typedef signed int s32;
typedef unsigned int u32;

typedef signed long long s64;
typedef unsigned long long u64;

#define BITS_PER_LONG 32

/* Dma addresses are 32-bits wide. */

typedef u32 dma_addr_t;
```

Figure 2.3 Kernel C-type definitions: `linux/include/linux/types.h`.

```
typedef __kernel_fd_set      fd_set;
typedef __kernel_dev_t       dev_t;
typedef __kernel_ino_t       ino_t;
typedef __kernel_mode_t      mode_t;
typedef __kernel_nlink_t     nlink_t;
typedef __kernel_off_t       off_t;
typedef __kernel_pid_t       pid_t;
typedef __kernel_daddr_t     daddr_t;
typedef __kernel_key_t       key_t;
typedef __kernel_suseconds_t suseconds_t;

#ifdef __KERNEL__
typedef __kernel_uid32_t     uid_t;
typedef __kernel_gid32_t     gid_t;
typedef __kernel_uid16_t     uid16_t;
typedef __kernel_gid16_t     gid16_t;

#ifdef CONFIG_UID16
/* This is defined by include/asm-{arch}/posix_types.h */
typedef __kernel_old_uid_t   old_uid_t;
typedef __kernel_old_gid_t   old_gid_t;
#endif /* CONFIG_UID16 */

/* libc5 includes this file to define uid_t, thus uid_t can never change
 * when it is included by non-kernel code
 */
#else
typedef __kernel_uid_t       uid_t;
typedef __kernel_gid_t       gid_t;
#endif /* __KERNEL__ */

#if defined(__GNUC__) && !defined(__STRICT_ANSI__)
typedef __kernel_loff_t      loff_t;
#endif

/*
 * The following typedefs are also protected by individual ifdefs for
 * historical reasons:
 */
#ifndef _SIZE_T
#define _SIZE_T
typedef __kernel_size_t      size_t;
#endif

#ifndef _SSIZE_T
#define _SSIZE_T
typedef __kernel_ssize_t     ssize_t;
#endif
```

Figure 2.4 Kernel C-type definitions: `linux/include/linux/types.h`.

```
62   #ifndef _PTRDIFF_T
63   #define _PTRDIFF_T
64   typedef __kernel_ptrdiff_t   ptrdiff_t;
65   #endif
66
67   #ifndef _TIME_T
68   #define _TIME_T
69   typedef __kernel_time_t       time_t;
70   #endif
71
72   #ifndef _CLOCK_T
73   #define _CLOCK_T
74   typedef __kernel_clock_t      clock_t;
75   #endif
76
77   #ifndef _CADDR_T
78   #define _CADDR_T
79   typedef __kernel_caddr_t      caddr_t;
80   #endif
81
82   /* bsd */
83   typedef unsigned char     u_char;
84   typedef unsigned short    u_short;
85   typedef unsigned int      u_int;
86   typedef unsigned long     u_long;
87
88   /* sysv */
89   typedef unsigned char     unchar;
90   typedef unsigned short    ushort;
91   typedef unsigned int      uint;
92   typedef unsigned long     ulong;
```

Figure 2.5 Kernel C-type definitions: `linux/include/linux/types.h`.

```
94    #ifndef __BIT_TYPES_DEFINED__
95    #define __BIT_TYPES_DEFINED__
96
97    typedef        __u8        u_int8_t;
98    typedef        __s8        int8_t;
99    typedef        __u16       u_int16_t;
100   typedef        __s16       int16_t;
101   typedef        __u32       u_int32_t;
102   typedef        __s32       int32_t;
103
104   #endif /* !(__BIT_TYPES_DEFINED__) */
105
106   typedef        __u8        uint8_t;
107   typedef        __u16       uint16_t;
108   typedef        __u32       uint32_t;
109
110   #if defined(__GNUC__) && !defined(__STRICT_ANSI__)
111   typedef        __u64       uint64_t;
```

```
typedef         __u64           u_int64_t;
typedef         __s64           int64_t;
#endif
```

2.2.6 Concurrency Control

A very important part of an operating system is that it has to manage a set of co-operating tasks. In a modern system these include I/O processors (at the very least, DMA-capable devices, but often complex disk controllers with internal schedulers), but possibly even multiple processors running different parts of the operating system concurrently. In any case, it is conventional to provide the illusion of concurrency to the application programmer, so that different application processes can run apparently sequentially, using kernel services in a way that appears to be independent, but is in fact interleaved. This makes many types of application programming much simpler, while making efficient use of computing resources at the same time. For example, a word processor is simply a program that appears to control all the input and output from the user typing at a keyboard and using a mouse, and to the screen, and all the input and output from and to files, in a sequential way. In fact, the computer may be carrying out a whole host of other tasks simultaneously, both on behalf of this specific user (e.g., printing, backing up, and so on) and for other users. Indeed, breaking down the details of device and filesystem access into smaller steps reveals that not all of these are sequential either. What happens on a single processor is that the illusion of a single *virtual machine* is provided by a scheduler that can switch context between different user processes (and within the kernel, a dispatcher that can switch between different interrupt contexts). This is known as *interleaving.* When a computer has multiple processors (even a single processor, but with smart independent I/O such as DMA, which we look at more later), then the concurrency is actual rather than illusory. Without modifying all the applications or large pieces of kernel code, this leads to potential (at best, near linear in CPU count) improvements in performance for the overall set of tasks (though not necessarily for a single process) as you add more processors to a system.

When execution is interleaved in an arbitrary way for strands of code that access the same data, there is a need to control access to the data (to *serialize*) the code at certain points to maintain data consistency. It is common to hear kernel hackers refer to *race conditions*, which are situations when concurrent pieces of code leave data in an inconsistent state in some situations (but not in all). It is hard to debug such errors since they occur in only some combinations of interleaved execution (some, out of very many possible ones) and heavily depend on timing. Even the introduction of simple tracing or debugging code may make them vanish. Sections of potentially concurrent code that access the same data are known as *critical regions* and require separation. As well as this, we also need low-level communication between processes via global variables to be specifically synchronized.

To this end, Linux provides a wide range of primitives. These depend on whether one is controlling concurrency for a user process or for the kernel.

At the highest level of the operating system (synchronizing with user processes), the user process scheduling level needs a `sleep_on` (interruptible) and a `wakeup` function.

User processes (when a CPU is in user mode) can be interrupted at any time (this is expected), and one device interrupting can interrupt itself or another device's interrupt service routine. In kernel mode, interrupts do not occur inside a routine at the same priority or lower. At the lowest level, the basic requirement to support this is for atomic operations (e.g., a single *test and set* instruction that is uninterruptable, at least in a single-processor architecture). Different hardware architectures provide slightly different atomic instructions, so Linux provides a set of macros to hide this.

For kernel-critical regions, we can divide the functions into two approaches—the first simply disable interrupts, rendering code serial; the second provides synchronization.

Kernel-level locks work on the interrupt level, and can be separate for reading and writing functions. The *spin* versions work across multiple processors in an SMP environment, and employ simple busy waiting. To maximize concurrency, separate read and write locks are provided. `cli` and `sti` are *clear* and *set* interrupts respectively.

Table 2.1 Kernel-Critical Region Serialization

single processor requirement	non-SMP implementation
spinlock irq	cli()
spin unlock irq	sti()
spinlock irqsave	save flags, cli()
spin unlock irqrestore	restore flags, sti()
read lock irq	cli()
read unlock irq	sti()
read lock irqsave	save flags, cli()
read unlock irqrestore	restore flags, sti()
write lock irq	cli()
write unlock irq	sti()
write lock irqsave	(save flags cli)
write lock irqrestore	(sti)

In addition to this, the kernel has wait queues, which we can then put a thread on (add wait queue/remove wait queue) and kernel-level semaphores to provide ordered access to a region: The classic `down (down interruptible)` and `up` functions operate on a semaphore.

Linux has a mechanism for deferred interrupts. These allow hardware interrupt service routines to be as short as possible (which can maximize the rate at which they can be handled) and put off handling the bulk of the work (usually to do with higher-level functionality) until later, using what it calls a *bottom half* level:

- `start_bh_atomic() = atomic_inc (&gobval bh_lock)`
- `end_bh_atomic() = atomic_dec (&global bh_lock)`
- `bh_mask` is set and cleared by `enable_bh(n)`, `disable_bh(n)` for nth bh
- `do_bottom_half()` checks that there is no lock (no global `bh_lock`) and no interrupt handlers (global irq count null), and that interrupts are enabled (`irq-lock` is free)

In SMP (in Linux 2.4) we have *software interrupts* that are interrupts that are SMP able (i.e., non-serialized). On top of these, we have a serialized task mechanism called a *tasklet*—these are how bottom halves are implemented, as serialized software interrupts. The old deferred interrupt code, such as bottom halves, is run by one of the new tasklets. Spinlocks actually do busy waiting between CPUs, but then this is no longer a problem (it doesn't lead to priority inversion, for example). A nice way to think of a spinlock is to say, "What I want to access is locked now, but to wait will require a context switch, which is slow and expensive. So I'll spin around for a while in the hope that the lock unlocks soon, rather than context switch immediately." This might add, say, 25% effect in the event of the unlock not occurring, but this might only happen 1 in 10 times, so the benefit is obvious.

Note Bene—cause for confusion (term also used for *signal* and for *system call trap*.

Table 2.2 Spinlock Outline

spinlock requirement SMP implementation
use atomic test on one cpu
only if clear, proceed
otherwise loop, reading bit until clear and then
loop back to atomic test and set.

Table 2.3 Kernel Spin Read/Write Locks

lock requirement	SMP implementation
read lock irq (rwlp)	cli(), read lock(rwlp)
read unlock irq (rwlp)	read unlock(rwlp), sti()
etc.	etc.

So we have a whole plethora of techniques at our disposal that have different levels of applicability.

2.2.7 Memory Management

The Linux kernel model of memory is (typically) as simple as can be: Linux uses *linear* addresses, which are flat 32-bit address spaces of 4 Gbytes, rather than making segmentation visible. However, this is the model. In practice we cannot allocate a real 4 Gbytes to the kernel and to each process, so we need to use paging to manage mapping from linear addresses to real address space. Also, some hardware architectures (e.g., Intel) oblige one to use at least a limited form of segmented addresses.

Segmented addresses are *logical* addresses made out of two distinct components: the *base* and *offset*. When the CPU (or some devices) access memory, addresses are translated from those used in the code into physical addresses by one or two stages. If we just use paging, then we just need to use the linear address to access the page table. If we are also using segmentation, then the segment descriptor needs to be accessed. This is done on the Intel platform by implicit access via a non-programmable register that contains the segment descriptor. Typically on such hardware, segments are used merely to separate three segments: the kernel, user code, and data. The rest of memory management (and all of it on other platforms) is done via page table hardware. Depending on the exact nature of the page table, some number of the high (i.e., most significant) bits of a linear address (the one the code references) are used to index a page table. Typically, since most page tables are not fully occupied, we use a combination of caches and translation look-aside buffers to get space/performance tradeoffs. A complete discussion of segmentation and paging can be found in most good operating system books (see [7] for an excellent discussion).

Linux processes (as with most operating systems) are built out of statically allocated memory at load time for the text (code), data, and stack. However, they can allocate memory dynamically as well.

The kernel is also built out of a statically allocated set of memory (at boot/startup time) for the kernel code and data, and dynamic memory. However, the kernel has to manage memory more dynamically for two reasons. Firstly, we have processes being loaded, started, and stopped all the time. Secondly, the requirement for process memory may exceed the actual physical memory in a machine.

To this end, Linux implements a virtual memory system (like many operating systems) that extends the limits of physical memory by using disk space. To organize the memory systems into a coherent framework, the unit of allocation and mapping is the page. At the lowest level, this is typically managed by memory management, mapping, and paging hardware, which predetermines a limited set of page sizes (for efficiency reasons). The most common size is 4 Kbytes. The full set of descriptors of possible pages are in memory themselves and are represented by the page table, which is an array of descriptors with an associated set of flags indicating how the page is being used. Efficiency considerations have to do with the tradeoff between the page table size, and the cost of *paging* from disk to memory and back, and the accuracy of matching the unit of allocation to the unit of request for memory. Of course, actual usage doesn't map simply onto convenient 4 Kbytes page chunks of memory.

Some page use puts constraints on the memory addresses (e.g., devices that cannot go via the MMU and/or can only access low parts of the address space) and this is specified in the flags on request.

At the next level of abstraction, many kernel functions require variable length pieces of memory allocated and freed dynamically that are often much shorter than a whole page. Linux implements a system called a *slab* allocation algorithm that is based on the idea that there is a common set of objects of a common set of sizes that is frequently allocated and freed (e.g., process descriptors, file table entries, and so on). The slab allocator groups requests into caches of similar sizes. Another important feature of memory allocated from slabs is that it can be aligned to a multiple of bytes or words, or even an entire page size, so that accesses can be faster and even avoid the address mapping process.

Memory management is quite a complex process in general, and has to be tuned often to the mix of jobs a system typically runs. In practice, it is the pattern of memory freeing that can dominate the performance.

In the communications code, most memory allocation is done by a special purpose function, and uses its own set of data structures to overlay the memory with some patterns that are highly optimized to network packet header processing. This is the *socket buffer* structure, the `alloc_skb()`, and related functions. These in turn call `kmalloc()` (and `kfree()`) to allocate general purpose dynamic memory for general purpose use. Typically, these call `kmem_cache_alloc()` to allocate memory from the appropriate cache block size. The use of these functions for networking is discussed in more detail in Chapter 5.

The exception to this is the use of lower-level access to memory allocation, typically for I/O buffers in device drivers when we need to restrict the possible locations to which memory is allocated. This is often because devices do not access memory via the page table or the segment register, or have restricted numbers of bits in the device's register that is used to specific buffers' locations.

2.3 What More Could You Ask For?

As well as normal multiuser, multitasking UNIX (as you would expect), Linux 2 supports:

Platform independence. Several processor architectures (e.g., Intel, ARM, Alpha, Motorola, and lots of exotics).

Multiprocessor. Symmetric multiprocessor operation.

Sophisticated scheduling. Multiple user process schedulers (two classes of real-time scheduler and some smarter than standard time slicing, and also run-to-completion as well as normal UNIX semantics).

Efficient execution startup. Copy on write demand load executables (i.e., fork uses no memory, exec uses no memory, mmaps the file, but doesn't demand page until a new data page is needed).

Efficient application memory utilization. Shared libraries (so processes are smaller as well as faster).

Efficient system memory utilization. Modules (runtime loadable kernel code—e.g., most drivers, most alternate schedulers, and filesystem code are not present until needed).

Sophisticated filesystems. Several alternate filesystems (e.g., UNIX, NFS, EFT, DOS, NTFS, and Samba).

Binary compatibility. Multiple execution formats.

Industry desktop compatibility. WINE (Windows emulator).

Internationalization. National language support and other normal stuff.

Applications include some fairly convincing Microsoft clones, plus several desktops that make X less clunky (and more Mac/Windowslike—including shortcuts such as URL/Web ones).

2.3.1 Reliability, Efficiency, Safety, Security

Another factor in Linux success is the robustness of the system. In general, networks and operating systems are robust because of two main factors: simplicity and feedback. The end-to-end model [9] describes a system design principle for networks (and OSs) that prescribes inclusion of functions at the lower layers only if they are *generally* required in the layers above. In a network protocol architecture, this is as clear as it is in an operating system. Devices do not concern themselves with applications, just as link layer protocols do not contain features that serve merely one application, transport, or network layer protocol.

An emergent feature of the end-to-end model that is common across operating systems and network systems is that considerations of statefulness (maintaining history across a sequence of invocations of a service) is not a useful feature in a low-level function. This is true in Linux of device drivers and filesystems, and network protocol stacks at the lower layers as well.

This leads to remarkable lifetime and safety, as well as reasonable transparency when there are failures.[2]

It means that application writers (and this applies beautifully to network server implementation patterns) are free to choose the performance/reliability tradeoffs they desire.

Because of the *generic* design of its layers, Linux will also run in 4 Mbytes of memory (but won't run very far or fast). This is done simply by leaving out what you don't want. With modules, this happens automatically and for free, although you can do this statically at kernel configure time if you prefer. On a 486 with 16 Mbytes, it will run X (KDE, Gnome, and so on) and be usable. On a Pentium 2 with 56 Mbytes of memory it is really quite impressive. This means that it is evidentially a scalable system, which is very interesting if you want to run a range of systems such as desktop, small server, router, and large cluster.

Linux is extremely good at resource sharing. In networking, we tend to refer to this as multiplexing. Multiplexing is a simple idea—it requires the system to keep track of resource shares. This is a large part of what network and transport protocol state machines are for. It is also a large part of an operating system's functionality. User, process, and I/O management are all about keeping track of ownership and utilization of resources. Schedulers and security subsystems carry out this work.

Of course, there are some differences between intrasystem resource management and intersystem problems. For example, systems separated by a network are autonomous. This means that there are potentially multiple administrative domains: Each operating system has a set of users, superusers, and so on. Each system owns a set of resources and can separately and unilaterally allocate them. In network terms, this translates into policies that can be local or global, link-wide, network-wide, or worldwide. To make these work in a scalable fashion is a large problem, so typically we only very loosely couple the local and global management, if at all.

2.4 The Source Code Organization

The reference site for the Linux kernel is `http://www.kernel.org/`. For the purpose of stability for this book (which is absolutely *not* for building up-to-date kernels), we have a mirror of the 2.4.0 code at ftp://cs.ucl.ac.uk/darpa/linux/.

The Linux source code is the subject of the GNU General Public License copyright statement. This is part of a philosophy of open source. Now is not the time or place to discuss the details of this. The GPL is in the file `COPYING`.

[2]When I first built and installed a Linux 2.4.0 kernel under a Red Hat 7.1 distribution, it ran 24/7 until I wanted to do an upgrade—for two months.

The directory structure of the source code tree is important to understand. It is quite simple. Assuming we are at the top of the source code tree (wherever you put it in your filesystems), it then looks like this:

Table 2.4 Source Code Directory Tree Organization

arch/	processor hardware model platform-dependent code
drivers/	device-specific code
fs/	file systems code
include/	header files
init/	kernel startup code
kernel/	core code for processes, modules, scheduling
lib/	general purpose kernel support functions
mm/	memory management code
net/	the networking code

Of these, this book is mostly about the code in the one main net/ subdirectory, and the network-specific subdirectories in the include/ and driver/ subdirectories.

Table 2.5 Source Code Network Subdirectory Tree Organization

core/	common code for device access, filtering, netlink, socket glue, etc.
ipv4/	IP version 4 code, TCP code, UDP code, ICMP, IGMP, and forwarding table code.
ipv6/	same as IPv4 but for IPv6
sched/	packet scheduling for output link resource management, IP or non-IP
packet/	raw packet access protocol family, below or non-IP
khttpd/	misguided attempt to put the HTTP application in kernel
sunrpc/	implementation of Sun's remote procedure call (for NFS)
wanrouter/	support for multiprotocol router
netlink/	protocol management protocol socket code
ethernet/	generic Ethernet code (specific Ethernet cards in ../dev/
802/	generic IEEE 802 link layer protocol code
atm/	generic asynchronous transfer mode network/link code, including MPOA and IP specifics

Table 2.5 *Continued*

`ax25/`	amateur packet radio X.25 link protocol code, below IP
`x25/`	wide area x.25 protocol network code, below or non-IP
`rose/`	remote operations service code—layer on x.25, non-IP
`lapb/`	link access procedure, balanced link layer protocol code, below IP
`netrom/`	netrom IP device code
`bridge/`	EEE 802.1d spec bridge implementation below IP level
`ipx/`	Novell's IPX protocol (not IP)
`unix/`	UNIX domain socket code—see Chapter 4, non-IP
`irda/`	Infrared digital access—that IR non-IP device
`decnet/`	DECNET (old Digital Equipment Corporation non-IP protocol suite)
`econet/`	ECONET—cheap and cheerful (non-IP) network
`appletalk/`	for talking to Macs using native (non-IP) protocols

Going one stage further down the tree, let's look at the IPv4 directory, shown in Table 2.6.

Table 2.6 IPv4 Subdirectory Tree Organization

`linux/net/ipv4/netfilter/`	contains the IPv4-specific filter code—see Chapter 10

2.5 A Day in the Life of a Process

A process starts life as a compiled program sitting on a disk, and a user somewhere with a desire to run the program. By interacting with the system (via some other program, e.g., a shell, or perhaps via cron), the user informs the system that they want this program to run.

A process lives in a memory address space of its own, made out of its own set of pages, and runs with the CPU in *user mode*. A process can extend its memory (using the sbrk system call via `malloc()`) and can share memory (see Chapter 4 on IPC). It can also memory map files.

Processes live in a family tree, and new processes are spawned through `fork()` and various forms of the `exec()` system calls copying the process table entry, creating a new process ID, and then overlaying or allocating new memory for a new executable, and loading it from disk. In some cases, we clone many copies of a process (e.g., for Web serving in very old CERN HTTP daemons). Nowadays, this is more commonly done through a threads system.

Processes make use of kernel services to share resources (as discussed previously) such as CPU, memory, disk, files, networks, and so on.

In their extremely useful book, Beck et al. [5], describe the two different ways that we can look at the relationship between a process and the kernel. To paraphrase what they say:

Process viewpoint. From above, the kernel provides services to processes. Processes access these services by making *system calls*, which appear to be calls to library functions that carry out some work and return. Processes feel like they are on their own—they appear to have a system dedicated to them. When a user program enters a system call, the kernel takes over and has more privileges to access more of the system—because of this, parameters to system calls are extremely constrained, well defined, and carefully checked.

Kernel viewpoint. From below, the kernel runs the system. The kernel can access all memory, all devices, and all additional hardware (kernel registers, MMU, and so on). The kernel is structured as a set of cooperating tasks, but there are no protection domains between these tasks, and the switching between them is entirely cooperative. Programming mistakes are disastrous (hence, why systems programmers are paid more than application programmers). When the kernel runs a user's code, it runs it in a less privileged mode to make sure that user programming errors do not infect it. We can see this seperation of concerns illustrated in Figure 2.6.

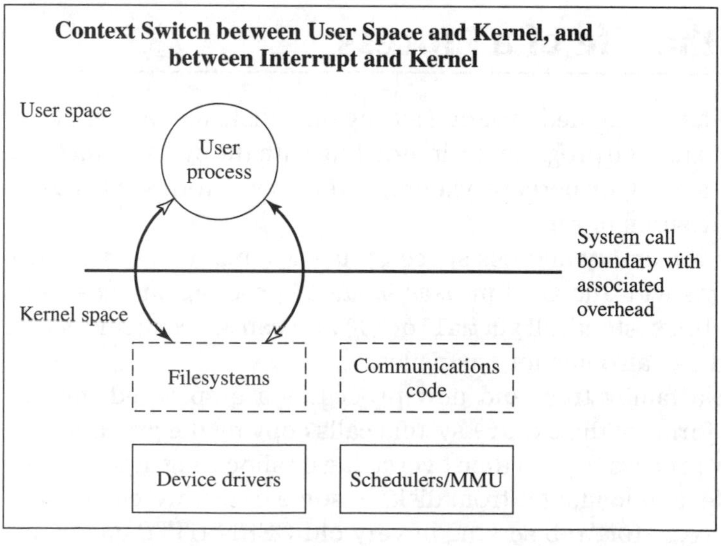

Figure 2.6 System calls.

Figure 2.7 The scheduler i: `linux/kernel/sched.c`.

```
#endif /* CONFIG_SMP */
}

void schedule_tail(struct task_struct *prev)
{
        __schedule_tail(prev);
}

/*
 *  'schedule()' is the scheduler function. It's a very simple and nice
 * scheduler: it's not perfect, but certainly works for most things.
 *
 * The goto is "interesting".
 *
 *   NOTE!! Task 0 is the 'idle' task, which gets called when no other
 * tasks can run. It can not be killed, and it cannot sleep. The 'state'
 * information in task[0] is never used.
 */
asmlinkage void schedule(void)
{
        struct schedule_data * sched_data;
        struct task_struct *prev, *next, *p;
        struct list_head *tmp;
        int this_cpu, c;


        if (!current->active_mm) BUG();
need_resched_back:
        prev = current;
        this_cpu = prev->processor;

        if (in_interrupt())
                goto scheduling_in_interrupt;
```

Figure 2.8 The scheduler ii: `linux/kernel/sched.c`.

```
        release_kernel_lock(prev, this_cpu);

        /* Do "administrative" work here while we don't hold any locks */
        if (softirq_active(this_cpu) & softirq_mask(this_cpu))
                goto handle_softirq;
handle_softirq_back:

        /*
         * 'sched_data' is protected by the fact that we can run
         * only one process per CPU.
         */
        sched_data = & aligned_data[this_cpu].schedule_data;

        spin_lock_irq(&runqueue_lock);
```

Figure 2.9 The scheduler iii: `linux/kernel/sched.c`.

```
        /* move an exhausted RR process to be last.. */
        if (prev->policy == SCHED_RR)
                goto move_rr_last;
move_rr_back:

        switch (prev->state) {
                case TASK_INTERRUPTIBLE:
                        if (signal_pending(prev)) {
                                prev->state = TASK_RUNNING;
                                break;
                        }
                default:
                        del_from_runqueue(prev);
                case TASK_RUNNING:
        }
        prev->need_resched = 0;

        /*
         * this is the scheduler proper:
         */

repeat_schedule:
        /*
         * Default process to select..
         */
        next = idle_task(this_cpu);
        c = -1000;
        if (prev->state == TASK_RUNNING)
                goto still_running;

still_running_back:
        list_for_each(tmp, &runqueue_head) {
                p = list_entry(tmp, struct task_struct, run_list);
                if (can_schedule(p, this_cpu)) {
```

Figure 2.10 The scheduler iv: `linux/kernel/sched.c`.

```
                        int weight = goodness(p, this_cpu, prev->active_mm);
                        if (weight > c)
                                c = weight, next = p;
                }
        }

        /* Do we need to re-calculate counters? */
        if (!c)
                goto recalculate;
        /*
         * from this point on nothing can prevent us from
         * switching to the next task, save this fact in
         * sched_data.
         */
        sched_data->curr = next;
```

```
#ifdef CONFIG_SMP
        next->has_cpu = 1;
        next->processor = this_cpu;
#endif
        spin_unlock_irq(&runqueue_lock);

        if (prev == next)
                goto same_process;

#ifdef CONFIG_SMP
        /*
         * maintain the per-process 'last schedule' value.
         * (this has to be recalculated even if we reschedule to
         * the same process) Currently this is only used on SMP,
         * and it's approximate, so we do not have to maintain
         * it while holding the runqueue spinlock.
         */
        sched_data->last_schedule = get_cycles();

        /*
         * We drop the scheduler lock early (it's a global spinlock),
         * thus we have to lock the previous process from getting
         * rescheduled during switch_to().
         */

#endif /* CONFIG_SMP */
```

Figure 2.11 The scheduler iv: `linux/kernel/sched.c`.

```
        kstat.context_swtch++;
        /*
         * there are 3 processes which are affected by a context switch:
         *
         * prev == .... ==> (last => next)
         *
         * It's the 'much more previous' 'prev' that is on next's stack,
         * but prev is set to (the just run) 'last' process by switch_to().
         * This might sound slightly confusing but makes tons of sense.
         */
        prepare_to_switch();
        {
                struct mm_struct *mm = next->mm;
                struct mm_struct *oldmm = prev->active_mm;
                if (!mm) {
                        if (next->active_mm) BUG();
                        next->active_mm = oldmm;
                        atomic_inc(&oldmm->mm_count);
                        enter_lazy_tlb(oldmm, next, this_cpu);
                } else {
                        if (next->active_mm != mm) BUG();
                        switch_mm(oldmm, mm, next, this_cpu);
                }

                if (!prev->mm) {
```

```
639                        prev->active_mm = NULL;
640                        mmdrop(oldmm);
641                }
642        }
643
644        /*
645         * This just switches the register state and the
646         * stack.
647         */
648        switch_to(prev, next, prev);
649        __schedule_tail(prev);
650
651  same_process:
```

Figure 2.12 The scheduler v: linux/kernel/sched.c.

```
652        reacquire_kernel_lock(current);
653        if (current->need_resched)
654                goto need_resched_back;
655
656        return;
657
658  recalculate:
659        {
660                struct task_struct *p;
661                spin_unlock_irq(&runqueue_lock);
662                read_lock(&tasklist_lock);
663                for_each_task(p)
664                        p->counter = (p->counter >> 1) + NICE_TO_TICKS(p->nice);
665                read_unlock(&tasklist_lock);
666                spin_lock_irq(&runqueue_lock);
667        }
668        goto repeat_schedule;
669
670  still_running:
671        c = goodness(prev, this_cpu, prev->active_mm);
672        next = prev;
673        goto still_running_back;
674
675  handle_softirq:
676        do_softirq();
677        goto handle_softirq_back;
678
679  move_rr_last:
680        if (!prev->counter) {
681                prev->counter = NICE_TO_TICKS(prev->nice);
682                move_last_runqueue(prev);
683        }
684        goto move_rr_back;
685
686  scheduling_in_interrupt:
687        printk("Scheduling in interrupt\n");
688        BUG();
689        return;
```

```
690    }
691
692    static inline void __wake_up_common (wait_queue_head_t *q, unsigned int mode,
693                                    unsigned int wq_mode, const int sync)
694    {
695          struct list_head *tmp, *head;
696          struct task_struct *p, *best_exclusive;
697          unsigned long flags;
698          int best_cpu, irq;
699
700          if (!q)
```

Figure 2.13 The scheduler tail: `linux/kernel/sched.c`.

```
446              * fast path falls through. We have to clear has_cpu before
447              * checking prev->state to avoid a wakeup race - thus we
448              * also have to protect against the task exiting early.
449              */
450             task_lock(prev);
451             prev->has_cpu = 0;
452             mb();
453             if (prev->state == TASK_RUNNING)
454                     goto needs_resched;
455
456    out_unlock:
457             task_unlock(prev);    /* Synchronise here with release_task() if prev is TASK_ZOMBIE */
458             return;
459
460             /*
461              * Slow path - we 'push' the previous process and
462              * reschedule_idle() will attempt to find a new
463              * processor for it. (but it might preempt the
464              * current process as well.) We must take the runqueue
465              * lock and re-check prev->state to be correct. It might
466              * still happen that this process has a preemption
467              * 'in progress' already - but this is not a problem and
468              * might happen in other circumstances as well.
469              */
470    needs_resched:
471             {
472                     unsigned long flags;
473
474                     /*
475                      * Avoid taking the runqueue lock in cases where
476                      * no preemption-check is necessery:
477                      */
478                     if ((prev == idle_task(smp_processor_id())) ||
479                                             (policy & SCHED_YIELD))
480                             goto out_unlock;
481
482                     spin_lock_irqsave(&runqueue_lock, flags);
483                     if (prev->state == TASK_RUNNING)
```

Figure 2.14 The wake-up common code : `linux/kernel/sched.c`.

```
346   static inline void wake_up_process_synchronous(struct task_struct * p)
347   {
348         unsigned long flags;
349
350         /*
351          * We want the common case fall through straight, thus the goto.
352          */
353         spin_lock_irqsave(&runqueue_lock, flags);
354         p->state = TASK_RUNNING;
355         if (task_on_runqueue(p))
356               goto out;
357         add_to_runqueue(p);
358   out:
359         spin_unlock_irqrestore(&runqueue_lock, flags);
360   }
361
362   static void process_timeout(unsigned long __data)
363   {
364         struct task_struct * p = (struct task_struct *) __data;
365
366         wake_up_process(p);
367   }
368
369   signed long schedule_timeout(signed long timeout)
```

Figure 2.15 The sleepon code : `linux/kernel/sched.c`.

```
803   {
804         SLEEP_ON_VAR
805
806         current->state = TASK_INTERRUPTIBLE;
807
808         SLEEP_ON_HEAD
809         timeout = schedule_timeout(timeout);
810         SLEEP_ON_TAIL
811
812         return timeout;
```

Figure 2.16 The Linux kernel system call entry code—save and restore overhead: `linux/arch/i386/kernel/entry.S`.

```
86    #define SAVE_ALL \
87          cld; \
88          pushl %es; \
89          pushl %ds; \
90          pushl %eax; \
91          pushl %ebp; \
92          pushl %edi; \
93          pushl %esi; \
```

```
        pushl %edx; \
        pushl %ecx; \
        pushl %ebx; \
        movl $(__KERNEL_DS),%edx; \
        movl %edx,%ds; \
        movl %edx,%es;

#define RESTORE_ALL     \
        popl %ebx;      \
        popl %ecx;      \
        popl %edx;      \
        popl %esi;      \
        popl %edi;      \
        popl %ebp;      \
        popl %eax;      \
1:      popl %ds;       \
2:      popl %es;       \
        addl $4,%esp;   \
3:      iret;           \
.section .fixup,"ax"; \
4:      movl $0,(%esp); \
        jmp 1b;         \
5:      movl $0,(%esp); \
        jmp 2b;         \
6:      pushl %ss;      \
        popl %ds;       \
        pushl %ss;      \
        popl %es;       \
        pushl $11;      \
        call do_exit;   \
.previous;              \
.section __ex_table,"a";\
        .align 4;       \
        .long 1b,4b;    \
        .long 2b,5b;    \
        .long 3b,6b;    \
.previous
```

Figure 2.17 The Linux kernel system call entry code—example of entry: `linux/arch/i386/kernel/entry.S`.

```
ENTRY(lcall7)
        pushfl                  # We get a different stack layout with call gates,
        pushl %eax              # which has to be cleaned up later..
        SAVE_ALL
        movl EIP(%esp),%eax     # due to call gates, this is eflags, not eip..
        movl CS(%esp),%edx      # this is eip..
        movl EFLAGS(%esp),%ecx  # and this is cs..
        movl %eax,EFLAGS(%esp)  #
        movl %edx,EIP(%esp)     # Now we move them to their "normal" places
        movl %ecx,CS(%esp)      #
        movl %esp,%ebx
        pushl %ebx
```

```
        andl $-8192,%ebx       # GET_CURRENT
        movl exec_domain(%ebx),%edx  # Get the execution domain
        movl 4(%edx),%edx      # Get the lcall7 handler for the domain
        pushl $0x7
        call *%edx
        addl $4, %esp
        popl %eax
        jmp ret_from_sys_call
```

At the end of the day, when a process is done, it exits. Typically, there may be various pieces of tidying up to do, so the well-behaved parent process will wait for the kernel to finish closing all files and so on before continuing. An example of a network task that needs finishing up is a TCP connection, which needs shutting down properly even if a process rudely exits (e.g., due to crashing because of a bug). This is a good example of why transport protocols such as TCP (see Chapter 6) are in the kernel.

2.6 A Day in the Life of a File

Files in Linux come in a variety of types. A discussion of the virtual filesystem is beyond the scope of this book (see [5] again, or [7], for an excellent overview). Suffice it to say that we have already discussed the use of the namespace to manage a set of different operating system resources including devices as well as disk storage. On disk storage, so-called regular files are accessed via the standard system calls, and basically consist of a 1-D array of bytes. Other structures can be built above this as applications need them. Standard techniques are used to improve read and write access via caching and read-ahead (and write-behind on some systems).

There is also the possibility of memory mapping a file, which means that subsequent random access will be far more efficient (unless thrashing in the paging system is incurred).

Files reside in a filesystem, which is created when a disk is formatted and partitioned. Each partition is laid out with a doubly linked list of *superblocks* and ordinary blocks that can be used for file information or file contents. The superblock contains information about the filesystem type (which indicates the allowed operations on a filesystem). Typically, operations read, update, or delete blocks or *inodes*. The `inode` structure is the core data structure that holds all the file attributes such as ownership, access times, and block location information. An in-core copy is held whenever a file is open, as well as several blocks of the actual file, and also contains information about any memory mapping of the file.

Files are created by allocating an inode and some blocks.

In addition to regular filesystems, there are also networked filesystems (e.g., accessed via NFS or Samba) and virtual filesystems. Of the latter, the most important is the `/proc` filesystem. The kernel maintains a bunch of information about active processes and uses the access procedures in the `/proc` filesystem to allow applications to manage this data. This is generally useful for access to quite arbitrary kernel data without having to allow direct access across the user/kernel memory address spaces.

2.7 A Day in the Life of an Operating System

It has become commonplace for users to leave their computers running all the time. However, one does have to start them up when you bring them home from the shop, and from time to time, one has to shut them down (even if only to throw away), though usually for upgrading.

2.7.1 The Start of Time

When you power up your machine, the hardware generates a special signal which *should* propagate to all devices, memory, and the processor to cause a *power up reset*. This sets everything into a *known state*, so that when software starts, it can make certain assumptions about how things are.

From this point on, the details depend on the processor architecture, but in practice, all systems arrange for the processor (or at least one of them) to start its instruction fetch-and-execute cycle at some *well-known* address.

Normally, we organize the memory hardware so that this address (a physical address, since the memory management unit is not active yet) actually is a piece of ROM (read-only memory) that holds a standard well-known program, which allows some very basic operations to be done, including some rudimentary input and output. On a PC this is the BIOS (basic I/O system). Normally, this will run some self-tests on the hardware, then initiate a real bootstrap process.

This consists of looking on some storage device (such as a floppy disk or hard drive) for a bootable operating system—usually stored in a well-known place (the *boot sector* of the disk).

In fact, as systems have become larger over the years, what is normally stored in the boot sector is a second-stage bootstrap, or *boot loader* program. If you want to boot multiple systems and manage this via Linux, then this program is the Linux loader program, *LILO*.

The loader needs to be able to load arbitrary code onto arbitrary addresses, so normally it copies itself to high memory and then sets up the addressing modes so that it can load code all over memory. It then starts to read in the configured (or selected) operating system from the (selected or configured) boot device.

Finally, the boot loader changes some of the systems settings and jumps into the newly loaded code, which goes through the operating systems specific initialization.

Here we go.

Figure 2.18 The Linux kernel startup code i: `linux/init/main.c`.

```
498  }
499  #else
500  #define smp_init()    do { } while (0)
501  #endif
502
503  #else
504
505  /* Called by boot processor to activate the rest. */
506  static void __init smp_init(void)
507  {
508       /* Get other processors into their bootup holding patterns. */
509       smp_boot_cpus();
510       smp_threads_ready=1;
511       smp_commence();
512  }
513
514  #endif
515
516  /*
517   *    Activate the first processor.
518   */
519
520  asmlinkage void __init start_kernel(void)
521  {
522       char * command_line;
```

Figure 2.19 The Linux kernel startup code ii: `linux/init/main.c`.

```
523       unsigned long mempages;
524       extern char saved_command_line[];
525  /*
526   * Interrupts are still disabled. Do necessary setups, then
527   * enable them
528   */
529       lock_kernel();
530       printk(linux_banner);
531       setup_arch(&command_line);
532       printk("Kernel command line: %s\n", saved_command_line);
533       parse_options(command_line);
534       trap_init();
535       init_IRQ();
536       sched_init();
```

```
        time_init();
        softirq_init();

        /*
         * HACK ALERT! This is early. We're enabling the console before
         * we've done PCI setups etc, and console_init() must be aware of
         * this. But we do want output early, in case something goes wrong.
         */
        console_init();
#ifdef CONFIG_MODULES
        init_modules();
#endif
        if (prof_shift) {
                unsigned int size;
                /* only text is profiled */
                prof_len = (unsigned long) &_etext - (unsigned long) &_stext;
                prof_len >>= prof_shift;

                size = prof_len * sizeof(unsigned int) + PAGE_SIZE-1;
                prof_buffer = (unsigned int *) alloc_bootmem(size);
        }

        kmem_cache_init();
        sti();
        calibrate_delay();
#ifdef CONFIG_BLK_DEV_INITRD
```

Figure 2.20 The Linux kernel startup code iii: `linux/init/main.c`.

```
        if (initrd_start && !initrd_below_start_ok &&
                        initrd_start < min_low_pfn << PAGE_SHIFT) {
                printk(KERN_CRIT "initrd overwritten (0x%08lx < 0x%08lx) - "
                    "disabling it.\n",initrd_start,min_low_pfn << PAGE_SHIFT);
                initrd_start = 0;
        }
#endif
        mem_init();
        kmem_cache_sizes_init();
#ifdef CONFIG_3215_CONSOLE
        con3215_activate();
#endif
#ifdef CONFIG_PROC_FS
        proc_root_init();
#endif
        mempages = num_physpages;

        fork_init(mempages);
        proc_caches_init();
        vfs_caches_init(mempages);
        buffer_init(mempages);
        page_cache_init(mempages);
        kiobuf_setup();
        signals_init();
```

```
        bdev_init();
        inode_init(mempages);
#if defined(CONFIG_SYSVIPC)
        ipc_init();
#endif
#if defined(CONFIG_QUOTA)
```

2.7.2 As Time Goes By

Once the system is up, it runs the `idle()` process and awaits some work to do.

2.7.3 The End of Time

At the end of the day, when you want to shut down the system, the appropriate signal is sent to all the running processes, and the system synchronizes the filesystems and halts.

2.8 A Day in the Life of a Device Driver

A device is a generic object with a set of standard routines. It is initialized, then there are a set of standard functions for input and output, as well as interrupt handlers.

Here we look at the three main types of devices, and how they make themselves known to the operating system when the drivers come onstream.

Figure 2.21 Linux character device registration: `linux/fs/devices.c`.

```
        if (major == 0) {
                write_lock(&chrdevs_lock);
                for (major = MAX_CHRDEV-1; major > 0; major--) {
                        if (chrdevs[major].fops == NULL) {
                                chrdevs[major].name = name;
                                chrdevs[major].fops = fops;
                                write_unlock(&chrdevs_lock);
                                return major;
                        }
                }
                write_unlock(&chrdevs_lock);
                return -EBUSY;
        }
        if (major >= MAX_CHRDEV)
                return -EINVAL;
        write_lock(&chrdevs_lock);
        if (chrdevs[major].fops && chrdevs[major].fops != fops) {
                write_unlock(&chrdevs_lock);
```

```
                return -EBUSY;
        }
        chrdevs[major].name = name;
        chrdevs[major].fops = fops;
        write_unlock(&chrdevs_lock);
        return 0;
}

int unregister_chrdev(unsigned int major, const char * name)
{
        if (major >= MAX_CHRDEV)
                return -EINVAL;
        write_lock(&chrdevs_lock);
        if (!chrdevs[major].fops || strcmp(chrdevs[major].name, name)) {
                write_unlock(&chrdevs_lock);
                return -EINVAL;
        }
        chrdevs[major].name = NULL;
        chrdevs[major].fops = NULL;
        write_unlock(&chrdevs_lock);
        return 0;
}

/*
```

Figure 2.22 Linux block device registration: `linux/fs/block_dev.c`.

```
        len = sprintf(p, "\nBlock devices:\n");
        for (i = 0; i < MAX_BLKDEV ; i++) {
                if (blkdevs[i].bdops) {
                        len += sprintf(p+len, "%3d %s\n", i, blkdevs[i].name);
                }
        }
        return len;
}

/*
        Return the function table of a device.
        Load the driver if needed.
*/
const struct block_device_operations * get_blkfops(unsigned int major)
{
        const struct block_device_operations *ret = NULL;

        /* major 0 is used for non-device mounts */
        if (major && major < MAX_BLKDEV) {
#ifdef CONFIG_KMOD
                if (!blkdevs[major].bdops) {
                        char name[20];
                        sprintf(name, "block-major-%d", major);
                        request_module(name);
                }
#endif
```

```
504                    ret = blkdevs[major].bdops;
505            }
506        return ret;
507    }
508
509    int register_blkdev(unsigned int major, const char * name, struct block_device_operations
                *bdops)
510    {
```

Figure 2.23 Linux network device registration i: `linux/net/core/dev.c`.

```
2151
2152        /*
2153         *      See which interface the caller is talking about.
2154         */
2155
2156        switch(cmd)
2157        {
2158                /*
2159                 *      These ioctl calls:
2160                 *      - can be done by all.
2161                 *      - atomic and do not require locking.
2162                 *      - return a value
2163                 */
2164
2165            case SIOCGIFFLAGS:
2166            case SIOCGIFMETRIC:
2167            case SIOCGIFMTU:
2168            case SIOCGIFHWADDR:
2169            case SIOCGIFSLAVE:
2170            case SIOCGIFMAP:
2171            case SIOCGIFINDEX:
2172            case SIOCGIFTXQLEN:
2173                    dev_load(ifr.ifr_name);
2174                    read_lock(&dev_base_lock);
2175                    ret = dev_ifsioc(&ifr, cmd);
2176                    read_unlock(&dev_base_lock);
2177                    if (!ret) {
2178                            if (colon)
2179                                    *colon = ':';
2180                            if (copy_to_user(arg, &ifr, sizeof(struct ifreq)))
2181                                    return -EFAULT;
2182                    }
2183                    return ret;
2184
2185                /*
2186                 *      These ioctl calls:
2187                 *      - require superuser power.
2188                 *      - require strict serialization.
2189                 *      - do not return a value
2190                 */
```

Figure 2.24 Linux network device registration ii: `linux/net/core/dev.c`.

```
2192                case SIOCSIFFLAGS:
2193                case SIOCSIFMETRIC:
2194                case SIOCSIFMTU:
2195                case SIOCSIFMAP:
2196                case SIOCSIFHWADDR:
2197                case SIOCSIFSLAVE:
2198                case SIOCADDMULTI:
2199                case SIOCDELMULTI:
2200                case SIOCSIFHWBROADCAST:
2201                case SIOCSIFTXQLEN:
2202                case SIOCSIFNAME:
2203                case SIOCETHTOOL:
2204                        if (!capable(CAP_NET_ADMIN))
2205                                return -EPERM;
2206                        dev_load(ifr.ifr_name);
2207                        dev_probe_lock();
2208                        rtnl_lock();
2209                        ret = dev_ifsioc(&ifr, cmd);
2210                        rtnl_unlock();
2211                        dev_probe_unlock();
2212                        return ret;
```

Figure 2.25 Linux network device registration iii: `linux/net/core/dev.c`.

```
2214                case SIOCGIFMEM:
2215                        /* Get the per device memory space. We can add this but currently
2216                           do not support it */
2217                case SIOCSIFMEM:
2218                        /* Set the per device memory buffer space. Not applicable in our case */
2219                case SIOCSIFLINK:
2220                        return -EINVAL;
2221
2222                /*
2223                 *      Unknown or private ioctl.
2224                 */
2225
2226                default:
2227                        if (cmd >= SIOCDEVPRIVATE &&
2228                            cmd <= SIOCDEVPRIVATE + 15) {
2229                                dev_load(ifr.ifr_name);
2230                                dev_probe_lock();
2231                                rtnl_lock();
2232                                ret = dev_ifsioc(&ifr, cmd);
2233                                rtnl_unlock();
2234                                dev_probe_unlock();
2235                                if (!ret && copy_to_user(arg, &ifr, sizeof(struct ifreq)))
2236                                        return -EFAULT;
2237                                return ret;
2238                        }
2239    #ifdef WIRELESS_EXT
2240                        /* Take care of Wireless Extensions */
2241                        if (cmd >= SIOCIWFIRST && cmd <= SIOCIWLAST) {
```

```
2242                              /* If command is 'set a parameter', or
2243                               * 'get the encoding parameters', check if
2244                               * the user has the right to do it */
2245                              if (IW_IS_SET(cmd) || (cmd == SIOCGIWENCODE)) {
2246                                      if(!capable(CAP_NET_ADMIN))
2247                                              return -EPERM;
2248                              }
2249                              dev_load(ifr.ifr_name);
2250                              rtnl_lock();
2251                              ret = dev_ifsioc(&ifr, cmd);
2252                              rtnl_unlock();
2253                              if (!ret && IW_IS_GET(cmd) &&
2254                                  copy_to_user(arg, &ifr, sizeof(struct ifreq)))
2255                                      return -EFAULT;
2256                              return ret;
2257                      }
2258 #endif /* WIRELESS_EXT */
2259                      return -EINVAL;
2260      }
2261 }
```

Figure 2.26 Linux network device registration iv: `linux/net/core/dev.c`.

```
2264 /**
2265  *      dev_new_index -       allocate an ifindex
2266  *
2267  *      Returns a suitable unique value for a new device interface
2268  *      number. The caller must hold the rtnl semaphore or the
2269  *      dev_base_lock to be sure it remains unique.
2270  */
2271
2272 int dev_new_index(void)
2273 {
2274      static int ifindex;
2275      for (;;) {
2276              if (++ifindex <= 0)
2277                      ifindex=1;
2278              if (__dev_get_by_index(ifindex) == NULL)
2279                      return ifindex;
2280      }
2281 }
2282
2283 static int dev_boot_phase = 1;
```

Figure 2.27 Linux network device registration v: `linux/net/core/dev.c`.

```
2285 /**
2286  *      register_netdevice   - register a network device
2287  *      @dev: device to register
2288  *
2289  *      Take a completed network device structure and add it to the kernel
2290  *      interfaces. A %NETDEV_REGISTER message is sent to the netdev notifier
```

```
 *      chain. 0 is returned on success. A negative errno code is returned
 *      on a failure to set up the device, or if the name is a duplicate.
 *
 *      Callers must hold the rtnl semaphore. See the comment at the
 *      end of Space.c for details about the locking. You may want
 *      register_netdev() instead of this.
 *
 *      BUGS:
 *      The locking appears insufficient to guarantee two parallel registers
 *      will not get the same name.
 */

int register_netdevice(struct net_device *dev)
{
        struct net_device *d, **dp;
#ifdef CONFIG_NET_DIVERT
        int ret;
#endif

        spin_lock_init(&dev->queue_lock);
        spin_lock_init(&dev->xmit_lock);
        dev->xmit_lock_owner = -1;
#ifdef CONFIG_NET_FASTROUTE
        dev->fastpath_lock=RW_LOCK_UNLOCKED;
#endif
```

Figure 2.28 Linux network device registration 2: `linux/net/core/dev.c`.

```
        if (dev_boot_phase) {
#ifdef CONFIG_NET_DIVERT
                ret = alloc_divert_blk(dev);
                if (ret)
                        return ret;
#endif /* CONFIG_NET_DIVERT */

                /* This is NOT bug, but I am not sure, that all the
                   devices, initialized before netdev module is started
                   are sane.

                   Now they are chained to device boot list
                   and probed later. If a module is initialized
                   before netdev, but assumes that dev->init
                   is really called by register_netdev(), it will fail.

                   So that this message should be printed for a while.
                 */
                printk(KERN_INFO "early initialization of device %s is deferred\n", dev->name);

                /* Check for existence, and append to tail of chain */
                for (dp=&dev_base; (d=*dp) != NULL; dp=&d->next) {
                        if (d == dev || strcmp(d->name, dev->name) == 0) {
                                return -EEXIST;
```

```
2341                          }
2342                  }
2343                  dev->next = NULL;
2344                  write_lock_bh(&dev_base_lock);
2345                  *dp = dev;
2346                  dev_hold(dev);
2347                  write_unlock_bh(&dev_base_lock);
2348
2349                  /*
2350                   *       Default initial state at registry is that the
2351                   *       device is present.
2352                   */
2353
2354                  set_bit(__LINK_STATE_PRESENT, &dev->state);
2355
2356                  return 0;
2357          }
```

Figure 2.29 Linux network device registration 2: `linux/net/core/dev.c`.

```
2358
2359    #ifdef CONFIG_NET_DIVERT
2360            ret = alloc_divert_blk(dev);
2361            if (ret)
2362                    return ret;
2363    #endif /* CONFIG_NET_DIVERT */
2364
2365            dev->iflink = -1;
2366
2367            /* Init, if this function is available */
2368            if (dev->init && dev->init(dev) != 0)
2369                    return -EIO;
2370
2371            dev->ifindex = dev_new_index();
2372            if (dev->iflink == -1)
2373                    dev->iflink = dev->ifindex;
2374
2375            /* Check for existence, and append to tail of chain */
2376            for (dp=&dev_base; (d=*dp) != NULL; dp=&d->next) {
2377                    if (d == dev || strcmp(d->name, dev->name) == 0) {
2378                            return -EEXIST;
2379                    }
2380            }
2381            /*
2382             *      nil rebuild_header routine,
2383             *      that should be never called and used as just bug trap.
2384             */
2385
2386            if (dev->rebuild_header == NULL)
2387                    dev->rebuild_header = default_rebuild_header;
```

Figure 2.30 Linux network device registration 2: `linux/net/core/dev.c`.

```
        /*
         *      Default initial state at registry is that the
         *      device is present.
         */

        set_bit(__LINK_STATE_PRESENT, &dev->state);

        dev->next = NULL;
        dev_init_scheduler(dev);
        write_lock_bh(&dev_base_lock);
        *dp = dev;
        dev_hold(dev);
        dev->deadbeaf = 0;
        write_unlock_bh(&dev_base_lock);

        /* Notify protocols, that a new device appeared. */
        notifier_call_chain(&netdev_chain, NETDEV_REGISTER, dev);

        net_run_sbin_hotplug(dev, "register");

        return 0;
}
```

2.9 A Day in the Life of a Kernel Module

One of the critically acclaimed features of Linux today is that it achieves the flexibility of a microkernel without the need for server processes with the inevitable overhead of domain-crossing interprocess communication. This is done through modules. This is illustrated in Figure 2.31.

Modules are simply runtime loadable code that is linked into the kernel. This is achieved through a relatively simple interface that works by defining a very generic set of routines to initialize and clean up a module, and to export an interface with a set of symbols (variables, functions, and so on) and module cross-dependencies. Dealing with cross dependencies is not rocket science—it is what link loaders do every day when you compile and link an application that uses several functions from several different libraries. What happens is that kernel code is annotated via explicit listing of the symbols that are exported, then some utilities are used to build an index of the symbols (see `/proc/ksyms`), and the module management tools use these to resolve what is and isn't needed.

There are some applications for managing modules that live in `/sbin`, such as `insmod`, `rmmod`, and `modprobe`. The first two can be used manually (or via scripts) to add or delete a module. The latter is actually invoked by the kernel (so the kernel that uses modules requires a filesystem with at least `/sbin` so

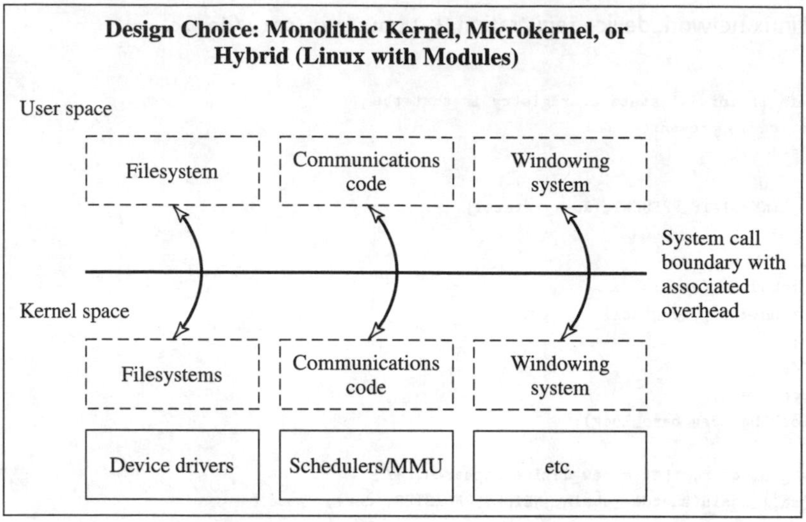

Figure 2.31 Monolithic kernel, microkernel, or hybrid kernel?

that it can run this external program) to manage the module dependencies on demand.

An example of the most adventurous use of modules is the MIT Click Project [26], which implements a component-based router completely as a collection of modules, configured through a programming language, and then installed via the kernel module mechanism.

2.10 SMP

Linux supports symmetric multiprocessing (SMP). What this means is that if you have a multiprocessor system, the Linux kernel will be executed on behalf of processes on more than one processor. This is not rocket science either, but it does make the interlocks between critical regions potentially a little more complex. It also makes performance analysis of a system (particularly a large file, web, or router server-type system) much more complex. This is a topic for an entire other book.

A large number of Linux 2.4 changes to the networking code from previous releases are associated with what is known as *softnet*. This is the change to remove the bottleneck associated with a lot of networking code being run from bottom halves in the deferred interrupt model, and instead to run it from software interrupts. There are two soft interrupts allocated to networking, the `NET_RX_SOFTIRQ` and `NET_TX_SOFTIRQ`. These trigger the appropriate handler. Since these are different interrupts from the actual hardware interrupts, they can be concurrent with hardware interrupts (and with other kernel and user processing) on a multiprocessor platform. The second part of reducing the bottleneck due to serialization was to change the various kernel locks to use spins. Finally, instead of scheduling a network bottom-half handler, we schedule a network thread by calling `netif_wake_queue()`.

This is defined in `include/linux/netdevice.h`. Essentially, `netif_start_queue()`, and `netif_stop_queue()` manage a given interface by tagging it as active or not, and waking up the queue schedules an interrupt, as shown in the code extract labelled Figure 2.32.

Figure 2.32 SMP netdevice scheduling: `linux/include/linux/netdevice.h`.

```
extern struct softnet_data softnet_data[NR_CPUS];

#define HAVE_NETIF_QUEUE

static inline void __netif_schedule(struct net_device *dev)
{
        if (!test_and_set_bit(__LINK_STATE_SCHED, &dev->state)) {
                unsigned long flags;
                int cpu = smp_processor_id();

                local_irq_save(flags);
                dev->next_sched = softnet_data[cpu].output_queue;
                softnet_data[cpu].output_queue = dev;
                __cpu_raise_softirq(cpu, NET_TX_SOFTIRQ);
                local_irq_restore(flags);
        }
}

static inline void netif_schedule(struct net_device *dev)
{
        if (!test_bit(__LINK_STATE_XOFF, &dev->state))
                __netif_schedule(dev);
}

static inline void netif_start_queue(struct net_device *dev)
{
        clear_bit(__LINK_STATE_XOFF, &dev->state);
}

static inline void netif_wake_queue(struct net_device *dev)
{
        if (test_and_clear_bit(__LINK_STATE_XOFF, &dev->state))
                __netif_schedule(dev);
}

static inline void netif_stop_queue(struct net_device *dev)
{
        set_bit(__LINK_STATE_XOFF, &dev->state);
}

static inline int netif_queue_stopped(struct net_device *dev)
{
```

```
        return test_bit(__LINK_STATE_XOFF, &dev->state);
}

static inline int netif_running(struct net_device *dev)
{
        return test_bit(__LINK_STATE_START, &dev->state);
}
```

2.10.1 Application Support

This book is not about applications per se. Suffice it to say that support for applications extends beyond the actual operating system into application-level libraries, as well as threads, interprocess communication, and a number of toolkits and GUIs.

2.11 A Day in the Life of Time

A notion of time, in the sense of ordering events, but also in terms of an absolute clock and the concepts of *duration* and *interval*, are very important in operating systems, and especially with regard to communications and distributed systems. Most operating systems in use today on the desktop, and for network server-based computers, do not provide the user with a direct *real-time* support. However, within the lower levels of the kernel, and right down to the hardware level, there is usually some support at least for measuring intervals, if not for actually *scheduling* events on exact boundaries. There is also usually some support for scheduling events at some approximate later time (after *at least* some duration).

The way this works in detail at the lowest level depends rather on the exact hardware support in a given processor and system architecture.

However, at the next level up, Linux has consistent support for managing dynamic timers in the kernel, and offers a standard UNIX *interval timer* mechanism to the application programmer.

RTC (real-time clock). Starting at the lowest level, let's assume that the hardware provides a real-time clock, which ticks at some relatively low frequency (compared to the processor clock for fetching and executing instructions, at least), for example a few tens or hundreds of Hz (cycles per second). More importantly, this is backed up by battery, so that it moves forward even when the system is deprived of power, which means that it is a stable store of state and is useful for long-term protocols (see later in "TCP Initial Sequence Number" for example) across reboots.

TSC (time stamp counter). Secondly, there is some type of clock input to the processor that is used to cycle through the fetch and execute cycle—this is on the order of hundreds of MHz, or even several GHz nowadays. This typically increments a particular register or location (e.g., the time stamp counter register in the 386 family), which can be read from software in the system.

PIT (programmable interval timer). Thirdly, there is usually some provision for a programmable device that can interrupt after some interval has elapsed, on the order of milliseconds accuracy, up to seconds away—usually, this is programmed to provide a periodic *clock interrupt* every `HZ` where this is defined in the kernel (e.g., 100 times per second). The term *jiffies* refers to the number of ticks since the system booted, and counts the number of clock interrupts.

The clock interrupt handler deals with a hardware exception, and thus must not take too much time to do its work (or else there's not enough time to use the CPU for any real computing—worse still, if we take too long, we might even miss a clock interrupt, although we could tell later on by reading the TSC, but by then it might be too late to take any actual actions that had been intended). Instead, clock interrupt actions are divided, as are other interrupts, into two types: *urgent*, and *deferred*.

The main urgent task is simply to record the system uptime. A number of other tasks can be handled by one of two bottom-half handlers: `TIMER_BH` and `TQUEUE_BH` (or, in Linux 2.4 by a tasklet associated with these). These include: making a record of how long the current process(es) have been running and other resource utilization levels, checking if any interval timers for any tasks have expired, and calling the appropriate call-back functions if so.

The main relevant kernel service then to other kernel functions is that one can install, delete, and alter timer functions, which are essentially lists of a simple data structure, defined in `include/linux/timer.h`. These define after how many jiffies a given function is to be called. kernel/timer.c defines some simple functions to create a list entry, initialize it, and load and set the function pointer and expiry time for the timer.

Figure 2.33 Linux timer structure: `linux/include/linux/timer.h`.

```
struct timer_list {
        struct list_head list;
        unsigned long expires;
        unsigned long data;
        void (*function)(unsigned long);
};
```

Figure 2.34 Updating the Linux timer structure: `linux/include/linux/timer.h`.

```
/*
 * mod_timer is a more efficient way to update the expire field of an
 * active timer (if the timer is inactive it will be activated)
 * mod_timer(a,b) is equivalent to del_timer(a); a->expires = b; add_timer(a).
 * If the timer is known to be not pending (ie, in the handler), mod_timer
 * is less efficient than a->expires = b; add_timer(a).
 */
int mod_timer(struct timer_list *timer, unsigned long expires);

extern void it_real_fn(unsigned long);

static inline void init_timer(struct timer_list * timer)
{
        timer->list.next = timer->list.prev = NULL;
}

static inline int timer_pending (const struct timer_list * timer)
{
        return timer->list.next != NULL;
}
```

Figure 2.35 Linux timer calls—add_timer: `linux/kernel/timer.c`.

```
void add_timer(struct timer_list *timer)
{
        unsigned long flags;

        spin_lock_irqsave(&timerlist_lock, flags);
        if (timer_pending(timer))
                goto bug;
        internal_add_timer(timer);
        spin_unlock_irqrestore(&timerlist_lock, flags);
        return;
bug:
        spin_unlock_irqrestore(&timerlist_lock, flags);
        printk("bug: kernel timer added twice at %p.\n",
                        __builtin_return_address(0));
}
```

Figure 2.36 Linux timer calls—internal_add_timer: `linux/kernel/timer.c`.

```
static unsigned long timer_jiffies;

static inline void internal_add_timer(struct timer_list *timer)
{
        /*
         * must be cli-ed when calling this
         */
        unsigned long expires = timer->expires;
```

```
        unsigned long idx = expires - timer_jiffies;
        struct list_head * vec;

        if (idx < TVR_SIZE) {
                int i = expires & TVR_MASK;
                vec = tv1.vec + i;
        } else if (idx < 1 << (TVR_BITS + TVN_BITS)) {
                int i = (expires >> TVR_BITS) & TVN_MASK;
                vec = tv2.vec + i;
        } else if (idx < 1 << (TVR_BITS + 2 * TVN_BITS)) {
                int i = (expires >> (TVR_BITS + TVN_BITS)) & TVN_MASK;
                vec = tv3.vec + i;
        } else if (idx < 1 << (TVR_BITS + 3 * TVN_BITS)) {
                int i = (expires >> (TVR_BITS + 2 * TVN_BITS)) & TVN_MASK;
                vec = tv4.vec + i;
        } else if ((signed long) idx < 0) {
                /* can happen if you add a timer with expires == jiffies,
                 * or you set a timer to go off in the past
                 */
                vec = tv1.vec + tv1.index;
        } else if (idx <= 0xffffffffUL) {
                int i = (expires >> (TVR_BITS + 3 * TVN_BITS)) & TVN_MASK;
                vec = tv5.vec + i;
        } else {
                /* Can only get here on architectures with 64-bit jiffies */
                INIT_LIST_HEAD(&timer->list);
                return;
        }
        /*
         * Timers are FIFO!
         */
        list_add(&timer->list, vec->prev);
}
```

From user space, interval timers are set up with `setitimer()` and `alarm()` system calls, and result in a `SIGIO` event.

2.12 Summary

In this chapter, we have presented an overview of the Linux operating system, pointing out various salient features of process, user, and I/O management, but not paying a lot of regard to network services yet.

In the next chapter, we take a vertical cut through the whole protocol stack to see how it all fits together, and a rapid tour through the topics of the rest of the book.

CHAPTER

3

The Brief Life of a Packet

"It is better to give than to receive."
—traditional saying

"Be conservative in what you send, and liberal in what you receive."
—Jon Postel

3.1 Roadmap

In this chapter we take a lightweight structured walk-through of the process of constructing and sending a packet in Linux, and then receiving and decoding the packet at the far side. We do this by way of three different examples, each seen from three different viewpoints: firstly, we look at the transfer of some data over a TCP connection (e.g., part of an HTTP download); then we look at a UDP packet exchange (e.g., part of a DNS lookup); finally, we look at a one-way RTP flow. The viewpoints are taken from the source code, from the execution, and from the *wire*. In the last case, we also consider a router as part of the wire, and go into a bit more detail about its operation: looking at an extended case that entails capturing some audio, putting it into an RTP packet, calling the socket API to send a packet, going through the socket kernel code (`skbuffs`, and so on), adding the UDP header, firewall filter checking, and multicasting. Then the packet traverses a link (SLIP or PPP) to a router that is also Linux, running diffserv—so we get a look at a packet being scheduled in packet queuing code, by a WRR or another scheduler, then forwarded over an Ethernet, then finally received by a driver, IP layer, demultiplexed and passed up through UDP to the process that is scheduled, where it reads the socket and outputs the audio.

This is a way to explain Internet communications ideas combined from many RFCs and related Internet documents,[1] where the view of a single protocol is expanded through an operational example *and* a top-down view of the entire protocol stack in one go.

Thus we also provide a rapid introduction to the rest of the book at a fast-track technical level.

3.1.1 User, Application, and Protocol Viewpoints

There are at least three very different views of communication that one can take:

User. From a user perspective, in modern systems, communication is made as transparent as possible; when clicking on an anchor in a Web page, there is no indication whether the download is local or very remote. Many FTP implementations include GUIs that make copying files the same whether remote or local. Usually the only visible differences are in the areas of naming (specifying a remote system name as part of a URL or FTP site name, although this can often be hidden in a global extension to a normal object or file naming system) and security—access to a remote system usually (though not within an organization) entails presenting more credentials than when accessing local resources.

Application. An application is programmed to talk to an application programming interface to a lower-level system. Normally, such an API hides detail, and, especially in the area of data communication, this detail may be of a very complex and rich structure. If the API is to a lower-level protocol, then it will hide the concurrency and state machine present in the lower level and attempt to present a more sequential, simpler style of programming for everyday implementors to understand and use.

Protocol. The protocol perspective is the most complex. Here we need to understand the way that information is exchanged. We need to consider the fact that each end point in a communication session is autonomous, and has its own quirks, failures, and successes. The channels between end points are imperfect, introducing errors, independent failures, and performance degradation.

Each of these perspectives can be illustrated in different ways. From the user perspective, one is interested in resource naming and visible performance parameters. From the application perspective, one is interested in the APIs

[1]See for example, *TCP/IP Illustrated Volume 1.*

and interface programming. From the protocol perspective, one really wants to understand the range of sequences of possible events and the way that state is changed by events.

From a user perspective, we can show information models and organization of how resources are mapped into cyberspace. From an API perspective, we can document the interfaces—the function prototypes, prerequisites, and results of functions, and how they relate in families to each other, are usually part of good systems documentation in any case. However, as we move through the layers of abstraction to lower levels, often these APIs become more complex and the interactions more subtle. From a protocol perspective, we need to understand the behavior of senders and receivers and the structure of information exchanged.

This latter view is often best illustrated through looking at the operational examples of a protocol, showing the actual data exchanged on the wire for correct and common error cases. In this sense, understanding a protocol stack implementation is often best done by effectively *debugging* it.

In the Linux community, the use of high-level tools for debugging the kernel is somewhat frowned upon. To some extent, this is justifiable since most high-level debugging tools (e.g., GDB) introduce changes to the function call mechanisms and therefore actually alter timing that in low-level code (especially interrupt handling, but also anything that involves any fancy concurrency and scheduling) will alter the behavior of the system under examination, often critically to the point where the problem being chased is no longer evident.

However, one can conduct the same type of activity by hand. Thus, in this chapter we start doing what the rest of this book does in detail, which is to take a structured walk through the Linux kernel communications stack. In doing so we occasionally take a look at a trace of packets on the wire, and occasionally take a look at a trace of function calls, but largely, especially given space and time considerations, we concentrate on the code itself. This is because there is really one main example piece of code, while there are an infinite variety of examples of execution traces of the code.

Many tracing, debugging, and profiling tools do abound, and I would encourage you to use them to help find problems (especially nonintrusive tracing for performance problems). For now, lets look at some of the code.

Sending

In the following figure, we try to illustrate the overall structure of the code, showing the way the control flows from the application down to the driver, and thence out onto the transmission medium.

Here we can see the flow of information from the application, which uses system calls from the filesystem API and socket API such as `send`, `sendto`, `sendmsg`, `writev`, and `write`, to interface to the lower-level protocols in the kernel. The parameters to these system calls are passed through what is normally

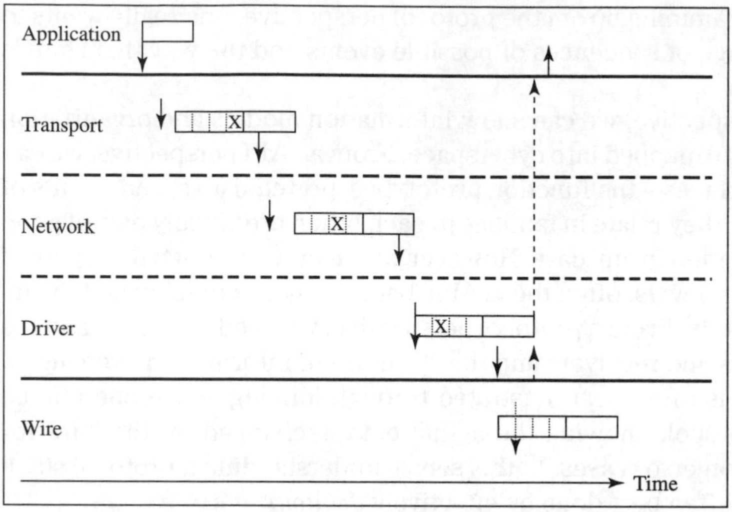

Figure 3.1 The overall transmission process: from application to wire.

a synchronous, blocking procedure call to the lower level, and actually makes things like reading and writing to a remote application look extremely similar to reading and writing from a local file or application (in Chapter 4, we look in detail at interprocess-communication APIs). The parameters are typically data and addressing information, and these are passed through to the transport protocol in the correct family, for example UDP, TCP, and so on.

The kernel then triggers the appropriate state machine for the protocol and then passes information through to the IP level, which then does the necessary route work, and then adds any appropriate IP header information, finally queuing the data for driver output. The device is then usually woken and actual transmission occurs. In fact, several of these stages may be deferred to allow more efficient use of CPU, memory, and network resources, so that a network scheduler is then part of the picture. In fact there are several complex levels of scheduling that are not always explicit. Sometimes, it is simply a matter of using a flow control and on-off scheduler mechanism; for instance, when looking at device output for busy links (or device input for full queues), we may rely simply on semaphores or other mechanisms to handshake between the layers and wake up a device driver, which does link and physical layer work to send or receive a packet.

Receiving

In the following figure we try to show the converse process—from unsolicited arrival of a frame from the wire, up to delivery to an application that had, in fact, been earlier primed with the idea that it might want to receive some data sometime soon.

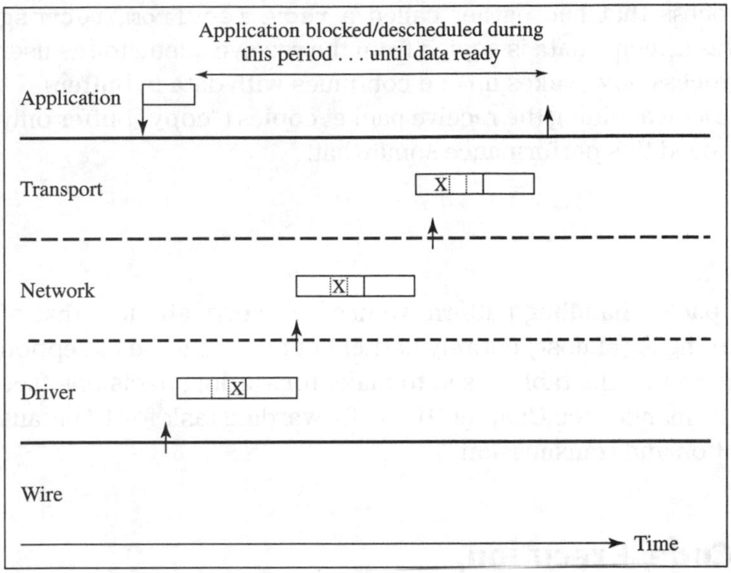

Figure 3.2 The overall reception process: from wire to application.

Physical reception causes hardware to wake up, and typically interrupt. Most modern network devices include both interrupt and DMA hardware. The interrupt service routine pulls a packet off a device and puts it in memory, and flags the network bottom half that the packet(s) are ready. Bottom halves and other Linux mechanisms (software interrupts, tasklets, and other SMP capabilities) are discussed in Chapter 2 and later on in the book.

The general system scheduler (after a system call) runs the network bottom half (and can dispatch tasklets or software interrupts) on completion of any kernel work on behalf of any user process that called a system call. The bottom halves basically complete work that the hardware interrupts started—for example, they can dequeue any packets in the interface queue for IP input and send any more packets waiting to send.

IP input checks packets, carries out any reassembly work needed, and gets a route if the packet is to be forwarded rather than destined for a local application process. If it is for local delivery, IP then demultiplexes the packets according to the IP protocol number to the appropriate transport handler receive function (UDP, TCP, and so on).

TCP (and UDP) input then do further packet header checking, update state machinery, and then demultiplex the packet further to the correct socket (i.e., to the queue of data pending for any user process that has an outstanding read on that socket, which is connected to the appropriate port numbers).

Once the transport protocol demultiplexing routine has put data on the appropriate socket receive queue, it calls `wakeup` on any process waiting for data, thus making any such process ready for general running by the system scheduler.

Sometimes a process that had earlier called a `recv`, `recvfrom`, `recvmsg` `read/readv` and was asleep—data is copied from the receive queue to the user space buffer; the process now wakes up and continues with data in buffers.

Recent Linux work on avoiding the receive packet copies ("copy" buffer only on `write`) has improved this performance somewhat.

Forwarding

The final case of a packet handling pattern we need to worry about is that of forwarding. Forwarding is (almost) entirely kernel bound—with the exception of the process of managing the tables used to make forwarding decisions (see Chapter 8) and performance (see Chapter 9), the forwarding task for IP entails back-to-back reception and transmission.

3.1.2 Source Code, Execution, and Wire Viewpoints

In the rest of this chapter we look at the source code and trace through some simple vertical cuts across the stack for some examples, with a very slimmed-down view of what occurs on the wire during these executions.

3.1.3 State, Memory, and So On

Throughout the code, protocols need to keep track of where they are. Rather than just using a set of randomly allocated, messy global memory, most protocols gather together all the appropriate information on a given flow (at their level—e.g., an IP route, a TCP connection, a UDP session) in one data structure—in BSD UNIX this is generally referred to as the Protocol Control Block. In Linux, the general, all-purpose data structure of `skbuffs` is also used to hold this data. It contains information to fit a packet into a sequence, to multiplex packets downwards (locally route them), to demultiplex them when receiving and passing them upwards (e.g., link to the user socket structure to queue data, and so on), as well as very complex state machinery for parts of the TCP machine.

3.2 TCP Example

First we look at the example of the Transmission Control Protocol (TCP) and follow through the code applied to a single data packet as it is transmitted, then subsequently as one is received.

3.2.1 Socket Level

In this simple example, we assume that an application process (Netscape, Apache, and so on) has called `write()` on the socket maps into a system call (see Chapter 2), which subsequently calls `tcp_sendmsg()` and deschedules the process (see also Chapter 2).

3.2.2 TCP Output

Here we are at the socket glue, then the TCP work—in the source distribution, this (as does most of the rest of the code discussed in this chapter) resides in the `linux/net/ipv4/` directory in the (version 2.4) kernel distribution tree.

An extract from the code referenced below is displayed in Figure 3.3.

```
inet_sendmsg()
sk->prot->sendmsg() ...
tcp_ipv4.c:
struct proto tcp_prot { }
tcp.c:
tcp_sendmsg()
tcp_output.c:
tcp_send\_skb()
tcp_transmit_skb()
err = tp->af_specific->queue_xmit(skb);
which maps to ip_queue_xmit()
```

Then in `tcp_transmit_skb()`, the state/header changes are managed. This is discussed in detail in Chapter 7.

Figure 3.3 Filling in some key TCP fields: `linux/net/ipv4/tcp_output.c`.

```
        th = (struct tcphdr *) skb_push(skb, tcp_header_size);
        skb->h.th = th;
        skb_set_owner_w(skb, sk);

        /* Build TCP header and checksum it. */
        th->source              = sk->sport;
        th->dest                = sk->dport;
        th->seq                 = htonl(tcb->seq);
        th->ack_seq             = htonl(tp->rcv_nxt);
        *(((__u16 *)th) + 6)    = htons(((tcp_header_size >> 2) << 12) | tcb->flags);
        if (tcb->flags & TCPCB_FLAG_SYN) {
                /* RFC1323: The window in SYN & SYN/ACK segments
                 * is never scaled.
                 */
                th->window      = htons(tp->rcv_wnd);
        } else {
                th->window      = htons(tcp_select_window(sk));
        }
        th->check               = 0;
        th->urg_ptr             = 0;
```

3.2.3 IP Output Work

TCP calls IP functions to carry out output. Some of this work is structured as follows, and a relevant extract from the code is illustrated in Figure 3.4 following.

```
ip_output.c:
ip_queue_xmit()
ip_route_output()
NF_HOOK()
```

`ip_route_output()` is an inline function defined in `linux/include/net/route.h` and interfaces to `ip_route_output_key()`, which is explained in Chapter 8. `NF_HOOK` is part of the network filter support in Linux that is machinery to do the low-level work for firewalls and other functions, and is discussed in more detail in Chapter 10.

```
netfilter.h:

NF_HOOK(pf, hook, skb, indev, outdev, okfn)
NF_hook\_slow((pf), (hook), (skb), (indev), (outdev), (okfn))
ip_queue_xmit2
skb->dst->output(skb)
```

This queues, or calls `okfn()`, which maps to `op_queue_xmit2()`. The `skb->dst` structure was filled in by a local route lookup and is a link-level output routine.

In `ip_queue_xmit`, header changes are as follows:

Figure 3.4 Filling in some key IP bits: `linux/net/ipv4/ip_output.c`.

```
/* OK, we know where to send it, allocate and build IP header. */
iph = (struct iphdr *) skb_push(skb, sizeof(struct iphdr) + (opt ? opt->optlen : 0));
*((__u16 *)iph) = htons((4 << 12) | (5 << 8) | (sk->protinfo.af_inet.tos & 0xff));
iph->tot_len = htons(skb->len);
iph->frag_off = 0;
iph->ttl     = sk->protinfo.af_inet.ttl;
iph->protocol = sk->protocol;
iph->saddr   = rt->rt_src;
iph->daddr   = rt->rt_dst;
skb->nh.iph  = iph;
/* Transport layer set skb->h.foo itself. */
```

This is covered in detail in Chapter 6.

3.2.4 Link-Level Output

Output at the link level can be complex (see Chapter 8). It includes specific technical details of driving devices, but also the important part is that this is where Linux provides different treatment for different traffic types by providing fancy queueing and scheduling management.

In general, we call the device-specific function to start output on the device. This does the book work, then informs the device that there is work to do, which then typically is done by DMA—this is covered in some detail in Chapter 5.

3.2.5 Link-Level Input

Link-level input requires dealing with hardware and software interrupts and DMA devices—this is also covered in Chapter 5 in detail. Some relevant extracts from the code are displayed in Figures 3.5, 3.6, 3.7, and 3.8.

Figure 3.5 Network device driver Rx i: `linux/net/core/dev.c`.

```
1028    static void netdev_wakeup(void)
1029    {
1030            unsigned long xoff;
1031
1032            spin_lock(&netdev_fc_lock);
1033            xoff = netdev_fc_xoff;
1034            netdev_fc_xoff = 0;
1035            while (xoff) {
1036                    int i = ffz(~xoff);
1037                    xoff &= ~(1<<i);
1038                    netdev_fc_slots[i].stimul(netdev_fc_slots[i].dev);
1039            }
1040            spin_unlock(&netdev_fc_lock);
1041    }
```

Figure 3.6 Network device driver Rx ii: `linux/net/core/dev.c`.

```
1044    static void get_sample_stats(int cpu)
1045    {
1046    #ifdef RAND_LIE
1047            unsigned long rd;
1048            int rq;
1049    #endif
1050            int blog = softnet_data[cpu].input_pkt_queue.qlen;
1051            int avg_blog = softnet_data[cpu].avg_blog;
1052
1053            avg_blog = (avg_blog >> 1)+ (blog >> 1);
1054
1055            if (avg_blog > mod_cong) {
1056                    /* Above moderate congestion levels. */
1057                    softnet_data[cpu].cng_level = NET_RX_CN_HIGH;
1058    #ifdef RAND_LIE
1059                    rd = net_random();
1060                    rq = rd % netdev_max_backlog;
1061                    if (rq < avg_blog) /* unlucky bastard */
```

```
1062                              softnet_data[cpu].cng_level = NET_RX_DROP;
1063    #endif
1064            } else if (avg_blog > lo_cong) {
1065                    softnet_data[cpu].cng_level = NET_RX_CN_MOD;
1066    #ifdef RAND_LIE
1067                    rd = net_random();
1068                    rq = rd % netdev_max_backlog;
1069                            if (rq < avg_blog) /* unlucky bastard */
1070                                    softnet_data[cpu].cng_level = NET_RX_CN_HIGH;
1071    #endif
1072            } else if (avg_blog > no_cong)
1073                    softnet_data[cpu].cng_level = NET_RX_CN_LOW;
1074            else /* no congestion */
1075                    softnet_data[cpu].cng_level = NET_RX_SUCCESS;
1076
1077            softnet_data[cpu].avg_blog = avg_blog;
1078    }
```

Network device interrupts end up calling the function `netif_rx()` via the `net_devices` structure in `linux/net/core/dev.c`.

Figure 3.7 Network device driver Rx iii: `linux/net/core/dev.c`.

```
1135    enqueue:
1136                            dev_hold(skb->dev);
1137                            __skb_queue_tail(&queue->input_pkt_queue,skb);
1138                            __cpu_raise_softirq(this_cpu, NET_RX_SOFTIRQ);
1139                            local_irq_restore(flags);
1140    #ifndef OFFLINE_SAMPLE
1141                            get_sample_stats(this_cpu);
1142    #endif
1143                            return softnet_data[this_cpu].cng_level;
1144                    }
1145
1146            if (queue->throttle) {
1147                    queue->throttle = 0;
1148    #ifdef CONFIG_NET_HW_FLOWCONTROL
1149                    if (atomic_dec_and_test(&netdev_dropping))
1150                            netdev_wakeup();
1151    #endif
1152            }
1153            goto enqueue;
1154        }
1155
1156        if (queue->throttle == 0) {
1157            queue->throttle = 1;
1158            netdev_rx_stat[this_cpu].throttled++;
1159    #ifdef CONFIG_NET_HW_FLOWCONTROL
1160            atomic_inc(&netdev_dropping);
1161    #endif
1162        }
```

```
drop:
        netdev_rx_stat[this_cpu].dropped++;
        local_irq_restore(flags);

        kfree_skb(skb);
        return NET_RX_DROP;
}
```

Figure 3.8 Network device driver Rx iv: `linux/net/core/dev.c`.

```
/* Deliver skb to an old protocol, which is not threaded well
   or which do not understand shared skbs.
 */
static int deliver_to_old_ones(struct packet_type *pt, struct sk_buff *skb, int last)
{
        static spinlock_t net_bh_lock = SPIN_LOCK_UNLOCKED;
        int ret = NET_RX_DROP;


        if (!last) {
                skb = skb_clone(skb, GFP_ATOMIC);
                if (skb == NULL)
                        return ret;
        }

        /* The assumption (correct one) is that old protocols
           did not depened on BHs different of NET_BH and TIMER_BH.
         */

        /* Emulate NET_BH with special spinlock */
        spin_lock(&net_bh_lock);

        /* Disable timers and wait for all timers completion */
        tasklet_disable(bh_task_vec+TIMER_BH);

        ret = pt->func(skb, skb->dev, pt);

        tasklet_enable(bh_task_vec+TIMER_BH);
```

Then the software interrupt schedules the rest, which eventually results in a call to `net_rx_action`.

Next, `net_rx_action()`, which dequeues the packet, calls a packet handler based on the packet type (via a table)—if it is IP, this calls `ip_rcv()` in `ip_input.c`, which checks various things.

3.2.6 IP Input Work

IP input has to decipher the packet, so the first thing to do is figure out if it is really for me, e.g., is it IP version 4.

In ip_input, ip_rcv() checks, then calls, NH_HOOK (to run filters), which may call, or queue directly, ip_rcv_finish(), which calls ip_route_input() in route.c, which fills in the internal route.

This includes a function (forward or local delivery), and calls ip_local_deliver() in ip_input again, and this then calls ipprot->handler.

This pointer was previously filled in (via the inet_protocol structure) in protocol.c, which matches the protocol to the protocol handler function—in this case, TCP—tcp_v4_rcv().

This is investigated in more detail in Chapter 6.

3.2.7 TCP Input Work

In the IPv4 case, the relevant TCP input code is kicked off from tcp_ipv4.c, which looks up if we have a connection __tcp_v4_lookup, then tries to queue in process context, or else calls tcp_v4_do_rcv(), then tcp_rcv_established(), which actually processes the TCP header (header prediction, and so on) and calls tcp_event_data_recv(), does any acknowledgment needed, and calls sk->data_ready. The last function queues data to the socket.

3.2.8 Socket Input Work

In core/sock.c, we see that the main effect is triggered because sk->data_ready = sock_def_readable;.

Figure 3.9 Socket receive wake-up process: linux/net/core/sock.c.

```
void sock_def_readable(struct sock *sk, int len)
{
        read_lock(&sk->callback_lock);
        if (sk->sleep && waitqueue_active(sk->sleep))
                wake_up_interruptible(sk->sleep);
        sk_wake_async(sk,1,POLL_IN);
        read_unlock(&sk->callback_lock);
}
```

3.2.9 On the Wire

```
16:09:07.462590 brahms.cs.ucl.ac.uk.ssh > ovavu.cs.ucl.ac.uk.1023: P
2466:2574(108) ack 971 win 17376 <nop,nop,timestamp 7115105 382435932>
(DF)
```

3.3 DNS/UDP Example

Here we look at the difference if the packet were a UDP packet; for example, part of a DNS exchange. To a large extent, these are restricted to the actual UDP protocol function itself.

3.3.1 UDP Output

In udp.c, the main function of interest is udp_sendmsg() for output.

Figure 3.10 UDP output i: linux/net/ipv4/udp.c.

```
488          if (msg->msg_name) {
489                  struct sockaddr_in * usin = (struct sockaddr_in*)msg->msg_name;
490                  if (msg->msg_namelen < sizeof(*usin))
491                          return -EINVAL;
492                  if (usin->sin_family != AF_INET) {
493                          if (usin->sin_family != AF_UNSPEC)
494                                  return -EINVAL;
495                  }
496
497                  ufh.daddr = usin->sin_addr.s_addr;
498                  ufh.uh.dest = usin->sin_port;
499                  if (ufh.uh.dest == 0)
500                          return -EINVAL;
501          } else {
502                  if (sk->state != TCP_ESTABLISHED)
503                          return -ENOTCONN;
504                  ufh.daddr = sk->daddr;
505                  ufh.uh.dest = sk->dport;
506                  /* Open fast path for connected socket.
507                     Route will not be used, if at least one option is set.
508                   */
509                  connected = 1;
510          }
511          ipc.addr = sk->saddr;
512          ufh.uh.source = sk->sport;
513
514          ipc.opt = NULL;
515          ipc.oif = sk->bound_dev_if;
516          if (msg->msg_controllen) {
517                  err = ip_cmsg_send(msg, &ipc);
518                  if (err)
519                          return err;
520                  if (ipc.opt)
521                          free = 1;
522                  connected = 0;
523          }
524          if (!ipc.opt)
525                  ipc.opt = sk->protinfo.af_inet.opt;
526
527          ufh.saddr = ipc.addr;
528          ipc.addr = daddr = ufh.daddr;
```

Figure 3.11 UDP output ii: `linux/net/ipv4/udp.c`.

```
530            if (ipc.opt && ipc.opt->srr) {
531                    if (!daddr)
532                            return -EINVAL;
533                    daddr = ipc.opt->faddr;
534                    connected = 0;
535            }
536            tos = RT_TOS(sk->protinfo.af_inet.tos);
537            if (sk->localroute || (msg->msg_flags&MSG_DONTROUTE) ||
538                (ipc.opt && ipc.opt->is_strictroute)) {
539                    tos |= RTO_ONLINK;
540                    connected = 0;
541            }
542
543            if (MULTICAST(daddr)) {
544                    if (!ipc.oif)
545                            ipc.oif = sk->protinfo.af_inet.mc_index;
546                    if (!ufh.saddr)
547                            ufh.saddr = sk->protinfo.af_inet.mc_addr;
548                    connected = 0;
549            }
550
551            if (connected)
552                    rt = (struct rtable*)sk_dst_check(sk, 0);
553
554            if (rt == NULL) {
555                    err = ip_route_output(&rt, daddr, ufh.saddr, tos, ipc.oif);
556                    if (err)
557                            goto out;
558
559                    err = -EACCES;
560                    if (rt->rt_flags&RTCF_BROADCAST && !sk->broadcast)
561                            goto out;
562                    if (connected)
563                            sk_dst_set(sk, dst_clone(&rt->u.dst));
564            }
```

Figure 3.12 UDP output iii: `linux/net/ipv4/udp.c`.

```
566            if (msg->msg_flags&MSG_CONFIRM)
567                    goto do_confirm;
568    back_from_confirm:
569
570            ufh.saddr = rt->rt_src;
571            if (!ipc.addr)
572                    ufh.daddr = ipc.addr = rt->rt_dst;
573            ufh.uh.len = htons(ulen);
574            ufh.uh.check = 0;
575            ufh.iov = msg->msg_iov;
576            ufh.wcheck = 0;
577
578            /* RFC1122: OK. Provides the checksumming facility (MUST) as per */
```

```
        /* 4.1.3.4. It's configurable by the application via setsockopt() */
        /* (MAY) and it defaults to on (MUST). */

        err = ip_build_xmit(sk,
                            (sk->no_check == UDP_CSUM_NOXMIT ?
                             udp_getfrag_nosum :
                             udp_getfrag),
                            &ufh, ulen, &ipc, rt, msg->msg_flags);
```

3.3.2 UDP Input

UDP is small enough that it is all in one C file, udp.c. For receive, the function of interest is udp_recvmsg().

Figure 3.13 UDP input i: linux/net/ipv4/udp.c.

```
        skb = skb_recv_datagram(sk, flags, noblock, &err);
        if (!skb)
                goto out;

        copied = skb->len - sizeof(struct udphdr);
        if (copied > len) {
                copied = len;
                msg->msg_flags |= MSG_TRUNC;
        }

        if (skb->ip_summed==CHECKSUM_UNNECESSARY) {
                err = skb_copy_datagram_iovec(skb, sizeof(struct udphdr), msg->msg_iov,
                                              copied);
        } else if (msg->msg_flags&MSG_TRUNC) {
                if (__udp_checksum_complete(skb))
                        goto csum_copy_err;
                err = skb_copy_datagram_iovec(skb, sizeof(struct udphdr), msg->msg_iov,
                                              copied);
        } else {
                err = copy_and_csum_toiovec(msg->msg_iov, skb, sizeof(struct udphdr));

                if (err)
                        goto csum_copy_err;
        }

        if (err)
                goto out_free;

        sock_recv_timestamp(msg, sk, skb);

        /* Copy the address. */
        if (sin)
        {
                sin->sin_family = AF_INET;
                sin->sin_port = skb->h.uh->source;
```

```
                sin->sin_addr.s_addr = skb->nh.iph->saddr;
                memset(sin->sin_zero, 0, sizeof(sin->sin_zero));
        }
        if (sk->protinfo.af_inet.cmsg_flags)
                ip_cmsg_recv(msg, skb);
        err = copied;
```

Figure 3.14 UDP input ii: `linux/net/ipv4/udp.c`.

```
out_free:
        skb_free_datagram(sk, skb);
out:
        return err;

csum_copy_err:
        UDP_INC_STATS_BH(UdpInErrors);

        /* Clear queue. */
        if (flags&MSG_PEEK) {
                int clear = 0;
                spin_lock_irq(&sk->receive_queue.lock);
                if (skb == skb_peek(&sk->receive_queue)) {
                        __skb_unlink(skb, &sk->receive_queue);
                        clear = 1;
                }
                spin_unlock_irq(&sk->receive_queue.lock);
                if (clear)
                        kfree_skb(skb);
        }

        skb_free_datagram(sk, skb);

        return -EAGAIN;
}
```

3.3.3 On the Wire

```
16:11:35.321380 brahms.cs.ucl.ac.uk.1904 > bells.cs.ucl.ac.uk.domain:
60803+ (43)
16:11:35.323169 bells.cs.ucl.ac.uk.domain > brahms.cs.ucl.ac.uk.1904:
60803* 1/2/2 (172)
```

```
14:19:51.488399 0:20:af:ab:e1:6e 8:0:20:7d:a5:36 ip 85:
brahms.cs.ucl.ac.uk.2167 > bells.cs.ucl.ac.uk.domain: 6517+ (43)
14:19:51.490923 8:0:20:7d:a5:36 0:20:af:ab:e1:6e ip 214:
bells.cs.ucl.ac.uk.domain > brahms.cs.ucl.ac.uk.2167: 6517* 1/2/2
(172)
14:22:05.123790 0:20:af:ab:e1:6e Broadcast arp 42: arp who-has
merci.cs.ucl.ac.uk tell brahms.cs.ucl.ac.uk
```

3.4 RTP/UDP (Multicast) Example

For multicast, most higher-level protocols are built on top of UDP, so again we need to look in udp.c.

Sending is the same as for unicast, but the receive case has to handle the chance that there is more than one process waiting for copies of a multicast packet, so receiving is a tad different, as we can see in udp_v4_mcast_deliver().

Figure 3.15 UDP receive multicast: linux/net/ipv4/udp.c.

```
read_lock(&udp_hash_lock);
sk = udp_hash[ntohs(uh->dest) & (UDP_HTABLE_SIZE - 1)];
dif = skb->dev->ifindex;
sk = udp_v4_mcast_next(sk, uh->dest, daddr, uh->source, saddr, dif);
if (sk) {
        struct sock *sknext = NULL;

        do {
                struct sk_buff *skb1 = skb;

                sknext = udp_v4_mcast_next(sk->next, uh->dest, daddr,
                                        uh->source, saddr, dif);
                if(sknext)
                        skb1 = skb_clone(skb, GFP_ATOMIC);

                if(skb1)
                        udp_queue_rcv_skb(sk, skb1);
                sk = sknext;
        } while(sknext);
} else
        kfree_skb(skb);
read_unlock(&udp_hash_lock);
```

3.4.1 On the Wire

```
16:25:49.747290 d230-17.uoregon.edu.1025 > 224.2.163.188.23824: udp 332
16:25:49.790001 hocus.cs.ucl.ac.uk > 224.1.127.255: igmp nreport 224.1.127.255
    [ttl 1]
16:25:49.829479 d230-17.uoregon.edu.1025 > 224.2.163.188.23824: udp 332
16:25:49.853864 d230-17.uoregon.edu.1025 > 224.2.163.188.23824: udp 332
16:25:49.898744 d230-17.uoregon.edu.1025 > 224.2.163.188.23824: udp 332
16:25:49.992876 d230-17.uoregon.edu.1025 > 224.2.163.188.23824: udp 332
16:25:50.104227 d230-17.uoregon.edu.1025 > 224.2.163.188.23824: udp 332
16:25:50.135776 d230-17.uoregon.edu.1025 > 224.2.163.188.23824: udp 332
16:25:50.212101 d230-17.uoregon.edu.1025 > 224.2.163.188.23824: udp 332
16:25:50.272045 d230-17.uoregon.edu.1025 > 224.2.163.188.23824: udp 332
16:25:50.276215 Ez.Stanford.EDU.33235 > 224.2.163.188.23825: udp 88
```

3.4.2 But with a Router in the Path...

We know where we are going, but not how to get there—some kind strangers along the way will help. These are routers. See Chapters 8 and 9 for more details on Linux as a router.

Linux works well as a router. Basically, you need to consider input, then output—the decision above, where a packet was discovered to be destined for me in the call in `route.c`, validates the source address for the input device, then decides if it's for me, multicast, loopback, or someone else, and adds it to a hash-based cache table of most recent routes.

Then if we are forwarding, we do `fib_lookup()`. This fills in the routing structure, including a reference to the input handler—if it's a non-local delivery, this will be set to `ip_forward()` in `ip_forward.c`.

`ip_forward` does various checks (router alerts, route options, and so on), `ttl` processing, `mtu` work, fragmenting, and generating `ICMP` errors if necessary, NAT, if needed, then calls `NF_HOOK` (for net filter work, again see Chapter 10), and then will schedule a call to `ip_forward_finish`, which checks the route cache for a fast route decision, and then does `ip_send(skb)`.

Then `ip_send()` does fragmentation or not, and calls `ip_finish_output()`, does yet more NF work, then calls `dst->neighbour->output(skb)` and/or `hh->hh_output(skb)`.

3.5 Three Views of the Traces of Ping

As an illustration of the actual total API, including another protocol case, that of a *raw* socket used to do ICMP access, let's look at the strace of the ping program usage: ping bells, as shown in Figure 3.16.

Figure 3.16 Use of ping.

```
PING bells.cs.ucl.ac.uk (128.16.5.31) from 128.16.6.226 : 56(84) bytes of data.

64 bytes from bells.cs.ucl.ac.uk (128.16.5.31): icmp_seq=0 ttl=255 time=819 usec
```

On the wire, a ping is an exchange of ICMP echo messages, and might look as shown in Figure 3.17.

Figure 3.17 Wire view of ping.

```
10:38:11.705142 0:c0:4f:d3:db:c3 0:20:af:ab:e1:6e ip 98: ovavu.cs.ucl.ac.uk > brahms.cs.ucl.ac.
     uk: icmp: echo request

10:38:11.705270 0:20:af:ab:e1:6e 0:c0:4f:d3:db:c3 ip 98: brahms.cs.ucl.ac.uk > ovavu.cs.ucl.ac.
     uk: icmp: echo reply
```

Finally, from a systems viewpoint, we can see the set of calls made by the application by running *strace* on the ping command, and getting a listing of all the system calls it makes, as shown in the excerpt in Figure 3.18. In this *strace*, you can also see the stage of looking up the IP address of the destination, since the ping command (as above) had been given a DNS name—on the system under consideration, it is possible to configure this as a local NIS lookup, a lookup in `/etc/hosts`, or a DNS lookup, with a sequence of stages of what to do next if one type of lookup fails.

Figure 3.18 Strace of ping.

```
execve("/bin/ping", ["ping", "-c", "1", "bells"], [/* 24 vars */]) = 0
open("/lib/libresolv.so.2", O_RDONLY) = 3
getpid()                            = 4510
getuid()                            = 0
socket(PF_INET, SOCK_RAW, IPPROTO_ICMP) = 3
setuid(0)                           = 0
gettimeofday({960371553, 351449}, NULL) = 0
open("/etc/resolv.conf", O_RDONLY)  = 4
read(4, "search cs.ucl.ac.uk\nnameserver 1"..., 4096) = 43
socket(PF_UNIX, SOCK_STREAM, 0)     = 4
connect(4, {sin_family=AF_UNIX, path="
                                                                        /var/run/.
    nscd_socket"}, 110) = -1 ECONNREFUSED (Connection refused)
open("/etc/nsswitch.conf", O_RDONLY) = 4
open("/etc/host.conf", O_RDONLY)    = 4
open("/etc/hosts", O_RDONLY)        = 4
open("/lib/libnss_nisplus.so.2", O_RDONLY) = 4
uname({sys="Linux", node="ovavu.cs.ucl.ac.uk", ...}) = 0
open("/var/nis/NIS_COLD_START", O_RDONLY) = -1 ENOENT (No such file or directory)
socket(PF_INET, SOCK_DGRAM, IPPROTO_IP) = 4
connect(4, {sin_family=AF_INET, sin_port=htons(53), sin_addr=inet_addr("128.16.5.31")}}, 16) = 0
send(4, "V\'\1\0\0\1\0\0\0\0\0\0\5bells\2cs\3ucl\2ac\2uk\0"..., 36, 0) = 36
time(NULL)                          = 960371553
poll([{fd=4, events=POLLIN, revents=POLLIN}], 1, 5000) = 1
recvfrom(4, "V\'\205\200\0\1\0\1\0\4\0\6\5bells\2cs\3ucl\2ac\2uk\0"..., 1024, 0, {sin_family=
    AF_INET, sin_port=htons(53), sin_addr=inet_addr("128.16.5.31")}}, [16]) = 262
close(4)                            = 0
socket(PF_INET, SOCK_DGRAM, IPPROTO_IP) = 4
connect(4, {sin_family=AF_INET, sin_port=htons(1025), sin_addr=inet_addr("128.16.5.31")}}, 16)
    = 0
getsockname(4, {sin_family=AF_INET, sin_port=htons(1031), sin_addr=inet_addr("128.16.6.226")
    }}, [16]) = 0
close(4)                            = 0
bind(3, {sin_family=AF_INET, sin_port=htons(0), sin_addr=inet_addr("128.16.6.226")}}, 16) = 0
setsockopt(3, IPPROTO_RAW1, [-6202], 4) = 0
rt_sigaction(SIGINT, {0x804a670, [], SA_INTERRUPT|0x4000000}, NULL, 8) = 0
rt_sigaction(SIGALRM, {0x8049e74, [], SA_INTERRUPT|0x4000000}, NULL, 8) = 0
gettimeofday({960371553, 403056}, NULL) = 0
gettimeofday({960371553, 403316}, NULL) = 0
sendmsg(3, {msg_name(16)={sin_family=AF_INET, sin_port=htons(0), sin_addr=inet_addr
    ("128.16.5.31")}}, msg_iov(1)=[{"\10\0Uo\236\21\0\0a\33>9t\'\6\0\10\t\n\v\f\r
    \16\17\20\21"..., 64}], msg_controllen=0, msg_flags=0}, 0) = 64
rt_sigaction(SIGALRM, {0x804a670, [], SA_INTERRUPT|0x4000000}, NULL, 8) = 0
```

```
setitimer(ITIMER_REAL, {it_interval={0, 0}, it_value={10, 0}}, NULL) = 0
time(NULL)                              = 960371553
recvfrom(3, "E\0\0TR\250\0\0\377\1\\\337\200\20\5\37\200\20\6\342\0"..., 192, 0, {sin_family=
     AF_INET, sin_port=htons(4288), sin_addr=inet_addr("128.16.5.31")}}, [16]) = 84
gettimeofday({960371553, 407464}, NULL) = 0
uname({sys="Linux", node="ovavu.cs.ucl.ac.uk", ...}) = 0
socket(PF_INET, SOCK_DGRAM, IPPROTO_IP) = 4
connect(4, {sin_family=AF_INET, sin_port=htons(53), sin_addr=inet_addr("128.16.5.31")}}, 16) = 0
send(4, "V(\1\0\0\1\0\0\0\0\0\0\00231\0015\00216\003128\7in-add"..., 42, 0) = 42
time(NULL)                              = 960371553
poll([{fd=4, events=POLLIN, revents=POLLIN}], 1, 5000) = 1
recvfrom(4, "V(\205\200\0\1\0\1\0\3\0\3\00231\0015\00216\003128\7in"..., 1024, 0, {sin_family=
     AF_INET, sin_port=htons(53), sin_addr=inet_addr("128.16.5.31")}}, [16]) = 215
close(4)                                = 0
write(1, "PING bells.cs.ucl.ac.uk (128.16."..., 159PING bells.cs.ucl.ac.uk (128.16.5.31) from
      128.16.6.226 : 56(84) bytes of data.
64 bytes from bells.cs.ucl.ac.uk (128.16.5.31): icmp_seq=0 ttl=255 time=4.1 ms
rt_sigaction(SIGALRM, {SIG_IGN}, NULL, 8) = 0
write(1, "\n", 1
)              = 1
write(1, "--- bells.cs.ucl.ac.uk ping stat"..., 141--- bells.cs.ucl.ac.uk ping statistics ---
1 packets transmitted, 1 packets received, 0% packet loss round-trip min/avg/max = 4.1/4.1/4.1
     ms
) = 141
_exit(0)                                = ?
```

CHAPTER

4

Interprocess Communication

"Socket Scientist"

—Job description seen at an IETF meeting.

4.1 Roadmap

In this chapter we look at the programming interfaces provided for interprocess communication (IPC). As luck would have it, the de facto standard for application programmers is a truly cross-platform capability, generically referred to as *sockets*, and even extends to Microsoft's Windows systems, although it originates with the BBN and Berkeley UNIX family, dating from the early 1980s.

There are other IPC mechanisms that operate within a single system, which we do not cover in depth as they do not rely on the TCP/IP protocols. These are generally simpler to use, and also may (in some cases) be more efficient, provided that the programmer only wants to achieve *local* communication between processes that are known to only reside on the same computer (for all time).

These other mechanisms include:

Pipes. Pipes are the oldest mechanim in the UNIX family of operating systems, but are restricted to processes that are directly related in the creation tree. Pipes are analagous to a temporary file, which has no actual representation in the mounted filestore (neither disk space nor in the file namespace). Linux pipes are *pairs* of file descriptors, one of which is used for reading, the other for writing, in each direction. As with any Linux files, a pipe is a 1-D array of bytes. However, note that you can't *seek* on a pipe. This would be tantamount to time travel (like reading a file before it is written). A pipe is implemented in the kernel as an inode that has a virtual filesystem type (see Chapter 2) that allows `read()` and `write()` calls and internally keeps a simple buffer, with appropriate locks, to implement the channel between the two (or possibly more) processes.

Named pipes or FIFOs. FIFOs get around the limitation of pipes that a pipe has no *explicit* name, and therefore cannot be accessed except by processes related in the ancestor/descendant tree of the process that created the pipe, and therefore have a copy of the file descriptor(s) for the pipe. Instead, FIFOs have a representation in the filesystem *namespace*, although they do not occupy any actual filestore disk blocks. Thus the VFS functions for opening and creating a FIFO are different than for a standard pipe, and have to include a reference to the filename. In fact, a named pipe or FIFO is created the same way that a device file is created, via a `mknod()` call.

Shared memory. Linux includes the so-called System V IPC mechanisms, which derive from the AT&T UNIX System development tree. Shared memory segments are one of three different IPC resources that can be allocated by a process and then used to communicate with other arbitrary processes. The resources also include the semaphore and message types as below. Shared memory is very efficient in terms of preventing the data copying that is sometimes associated with crossing process-process memory protection domain boundaries, although Linux's copy-on-write semantics probably mean that sockets are nearly as efficient. One benefit of the System V mechanisms is that they cleanly separate synchronization (achieved via semaphores, messages, and bulk memory usage. The shared memory mechanisms also include access-right mechanisms modeled directly on the filesystem access right and process ownership structure of {owner, group, other} and {read, write} permissions.

Semaphores. Semaphores are used to place a set of processes in an ordered execution sequence so that consistency of shared memory segments can be maintained. They provide user processes using shared memory with the same functionality as kernel semaphores do for kernel threads. Obviously, executing a semaphore operation typically suspends the calling process until the relevant semaphore is clear.

Messages. The System V messaging facility allows for sending, and receiving, FIFO-queued messages.

In the rest of this chapter, we concentrate on an overview of the socket API and its implementation, and cover management and control and the life of a socket.

4.2 Socket API

We discussed in Chapter 2 in general why the interface for application programmers to kernel services is not implemented simply as a subroutine library. This is especially true of the API to the transport level that isolates the networked application programmer from network layer errors, and from the complexity of dealing with error recovery and timing matters, as well as enforcing the correct handling of independent failure modes at each end of an end-to-end session.

The kernel needs to control access to shared (also known as *multiplexed*) resources such as network devices. The transport, network, and link-level protocols need access to all of memory (mmu/dma, and so on). The kernel decides on scheduling for a share of resources. Thus, we restrict the less-sophisticated programmer from access to these complex responsibilities via system calls. System calls are traps, exceptions, or software interrupts, and use a special instruction to change processor mode. Once in kernel space, we can decide what to do and can deschedule a process (or not, e.g., a simple syscall like `getpid()`). There is not necessarily a one-to-one mapping between the set of function calls that implement the socket API library and system calls. In different UNIX versions, it has depended on history whether this is the case, or whether the calls map through a single call or a smaller set of actual system calls. This is also affected by the ability of different hardware architectures to support vectored software interrupts or similar mechanisms (221 calls on an i386 family in the 2.4 kernel).

4.3 The Actual Socket API

The actual socket API looks something like Figure 4.1.

Figure 4.1 `socket()`.

```

\#include <sys/types.h>
\#include <sys/socket.h>

int socket(int domain, int type, int protocol);
```

The `socket()` system call created an end point for interprocess communication. It returns the socket descriptor, which is used in later calls to set up the state for protocols that require that, and to send and receive data to a far end. The API is supposed to be quite general-purpose, and not tied specifically to the TCP/IP protocol suite, and to prove this, there are in fact quite a few *protocol families* implemented below this API. Which family is intended is indicated by the *domain* parameter. Linux currently supports the families listed in Table 4.1.

Table 4.1 Linux Socket Protocol Families Implemented

PROTOCOL FAMILY	USE
PF_UNIX,PF_LOCAL	local communication
PF_INET	IPv4 Internet (discussed in Chapter 6)
PF_INET6	IPv6 Internet (discussed in Chapter 6)
PF_IPX	IPX—Novell
PF_NETLINK	kernel user interface device (discussed in Chapters 7 and 8)
PF_X25	ITU-T X.25/ISO-8208 protocol
PF_AX25	amateur radio AX.25 protocol
PF_ATMPVC	access to raw ATM PVCs
PF_APPLETALK	AppleTalk
PF_PACKET	low-level packet interface (deprecated)

UNIX domain sockets are analagous to the named pipes discussed earlier. The `netlink` socket is used to provide a control channel between user space and kernel protocol control functions, and is discussed later. The other socket protocol families supported come from a variety of protocol worlds, but the ones we are most concerned with in this book are the `PF_INET` and `PF_INET6` ones.

For a given protocol family, one then also defines a socket *type*, which essentally selects a protocol *semantic*, although the semantics can be refined later with calls to `setsockopt()`. Semantics currently defined include those given in Table 4.2.

Table 4.2 Linux Socket Protocol Semantics

TYPE	SEMANTIC
SOCK_STREAM	reliable (connection-oriented), ordered, duplex byte stream delivery
SOCK_DGRAM	single shot (connectionless, unreliable) packet
SOCK_SEQPACKET	packetized delivery, otherwise similar to stream
SOCK_RAW	low-level protocol access
SOCK_RDM	as with sequence packet, but not ordered
SOCK_PACKET	deprecated (like raw but different)

The final parameter in the `socket()` call indicates the specific protocol required. In general, for a given family, for a given semantic, there is usually only one protocol supplied in a protocol suite. However, if there is more than one, this allows one to select the appropriate one wished for.

Once a socket descriptor is returned, there are a set of further calls to carry out protocol state setup and data exchange. It is also possible to change the behavior of these calls in terms of whether they are *blocking* and whether they are *synchronous*.

The `fcntl()` call allows one to set up a socket so that calls to input routines that would normally block (i.e., not return from the kernel) until the operation is complete, return immediately and indicate whether they worked or need to be recalled. Subsequently, the use of `poll()`, or `select()` calls allows one to check if there is input (for up to some specified amount of time). `fcntl()` can also be used to set up a process group to receive *signals* for input and output events, instead of having to explicitly call input read routines. We show examples of both of these mechanisms later in this chapter.

The other routines in the socket API include those listed in Table 4.3.

Table 4.3 Other Socket API Calls

FUNCTION	USE
bind	associate a socket descriptor with a local name or address
connect	associate a socket descriptor with the *far end* of the protocol (has side effect of setting up connections for connection-oriented protocols)
listen	wait for a connection to be set up from a (any) *far end*
accept	agree to a connection set up requested from a now specific far end
shutdown	tear down the protocol state on this socket
getsockname	map from socket descriptor to the local name (address) bound to it
setsockopt	request some non-default socket parameter settings
getsockopt	find out the current status of some socket parameters
ioctl	general purpose workaround system call on descriptors
send	send a buffer full of data on a socket
recv	receive up to a buffer full of data on a socket
read/readv	read some data into buffer(s)
write/writev	send some data from buffer(s)
select	check I/O status on a socket descriptor
socketpair	see pipes (equivalent)
getprotoent	see `/etc/protocols`

The following table illustrates the socket options that can be set or retrieved by `setsockopt()` or `getsockopt()` and what they are intended for.

Table 4.4 Other Socket API Calls

SOCKET OPTION	PURPOSE
SO_KEEPALIVE	sets the protocol pinging the far end
SO_OOBINLINE	moves *out-of-band* data passing into the in-band data stream
SO_RCVLOWAT and SO_SNDLOWAT	sets a receive (or send) low watermark on the before the socket layer fetches data from (passes data to) the protocol—always 1
SO_RCVTIMEO and SO_SNDTIMEO	alter the timeout before reporting an error—fixed per protocol in linix
SO_BSDCOMPAT	for bug emulation
SO_PASSCRED	PF_UNIX domain-specific
SO_PEERCRED	PF_UNIX domain-specific
SO_BINDTODEVICE	on a multihomed machine, allows one to limit the interface packets are sent and received via
SO_DEBUG	for processes with adequate (root) rights, can debug
SO_REUSEADDR	in PF_INET, allows more than one process to `bind()` to given port—useful for multicast
SO_TYPE	report (cannot set) the protocol type (as above) of the socket
SO_DONTROUTE	only allow local communication
SO_BROADCAST	set the broadcast address
SO_SNDBUF	configures the maximum socket transmit side buffer size
SO_RCVBUF	configures the maximum socket receive side buffer space
SO_LINGER	says how long `close()` blocks for waiting to process queued messages
SO_PRIORITY	sets up priority associated with socket—see Chapter 9 for details
SO_ERROR	return details of error
SO_ATTACH_FILTER	these are CONFIG_FILTER socket options—see Chapter 10 (libpcap)
SO_DETACH_FILTER	same as SO_ATTACH_FILTER

When a socket is set up and the protocol is specified, there are further *protocol-specific* parameters that may be configured. Generally, these are set up via the sysctl() interface. Examples of these are mainly TCP-specific parameters—some of these are listed in the following table. The internal implementation of these is discussed in Chapter 7. These work using the /proc interface (see /proc/sys/net/ipv4/ for details).

Table 4.5 TCP Sysctls

TCP SYSCTL	PURPOSE
tcp_window_scaling	enable RFC 1323 TCP window scaling
tcp_sack	enable RFC 2018 TCP SACK
tcp_timestamps	enable RFC 1323 TCP timestamps
tcp_fin_timeout	dally before FIN, before forcing socket closed
tcp_keepalive_probes	maximum TCP keep-alive probes
tcp_keepalive_time	seconds before sending probe on idle connection
tcp_max_ka_probes	how many keep-alive probes are sent
tcp_stdurg	enable the strict RFC 793 interpretation of the TCP urgent-pointer field
tcp_syncookies	enable TCP syncookies—the kernel must be compiled with CONFIG_SYN_COOKIES—see Chapter 10
tcp_max_syn_backlog	length of the per-socket backlog queue
tcp_retries1	max count of SYN ACK retransmit
tcp_retries2	max count for retransmit data packet in established connection
tcp_syn_retries	max count for SYN (re)tries
tcp_retrans_collapse	try to send full-sized packets during retransmit

Also, there are socket-level parameters. See Table 4.6.

Table 4.6 TCP setsockopt Options

TCP-SPECIFIC SETSOCKOPT	PURPOSE
TCP_NODELAY	disable the Nagle algorithm packets are always sent as soon as possible
TCP_MAXSEG	confiure the MSS for a connection
TCP_CORK	toggle sending of partial frames—almost oppostite of Nagle

There are even a couple of TCP-specific `ioctl()`'s, too, given in Table 4.7.

Table 4.7 TCP ioctl Options

TCP-SPECIFIC SETSOCKOPT	PURPOSE
FIONREAD	returns the amount of queued, unread data in the receive buffer
SIOCATMARK	returns true when the all-urgent data has been already received
TIOCOUTQ	returns the amount of unsent data in the socket send queue

4.4 Using the Socket API

Communication between separate processes involves moving data between one address space and another—in former times, this was known as crossing protection *domain* boundaries. Because of this, the various communications facilities are named under this confusing use of the word domain (it has *nothing* to do with the domain name system at all).

The example C code in Figure 4.2 illustrates the use of an *INET* domain socket, with stream semantics. This basically makes use of TCP code in the kernel—in the example here, communication is between a parent and child process, so the socket is simply being used to replace a pipe.

Figure 4.2 Socket programming i–main: `pix/sock.c.`

```
#include <stdio.h>
#include <sys/types.h>
#include <sys/socket.h>
#include <netinet/in.h>
#include <netdb.h>


#include <errno.h>
extern int errno;

int child_pid;     /* Handy child handle */

main(argc, argv)
char *argv[];
{
  long host = 0;
  short port;

  if (argc < 3) {
    printf("What host(i.j.k.l)/port?\n");
    exit(-1);
```

```
  }

  host = inet_addr(argv[1]);
  port = (short)atoi(argv[2]);

  if ((child_pid = fork()) == 0)
    client(host, port); /* Child Code */
  else
    server(port); /* Parent */

}
```

The fork() call sets up the second process (child) so that now we have two processes, one of which is a client, the other a server. They then set up a connection-oriented socket to communicate with each other.

Figure 4.3 Socket programming ii—client: pix/sock.c.

```

client(host, port)
long host;
short port;
{

  char buff[80];
  int len;
  int asock;
  struct sockaddr_in where, there;
  int ret;

  /* Wait for child to set up listen */
  sleep(1);

  asock = socket(AF_INET, SOCK_STREAM, 0);
  check(asock, "socket");

  where.sin_family = AF_INET;
  where.sin_addr.s_addr = 0;
  where.sin_port = 0;
  ret = bind(asock, &where, sizeof(struct sockaddr_in));
  check(ret, "bind");

  there.sin_family = AF_INET;
  there.sin_addr.s_addr = host;
  there.sin_port = htons(port);
  ret = connect(asock, &there, sizeof(struct sockaddr_in));
  check(ret, "connect");

  while((len = read(0, buff, 1)) > 0)
    write(asock, buff, 1); /* Write to pipe */

```

```
  fprintf(stderr, "\nChild gone\n");
  shutdown(asock, 1);
  close(asock);
  exit(0);
}
```

The client side here is the proactive end that takes the initiative and opens the connection. The server side is (hopefully) already sitting there waiting (listening) for an inbound connection, which it then accepts.

Figure 4.4 Socket programming iii—server: `pix/sock.c`.

```
server(port)
short port;
{
  char buff[80];
  int len;
  int status;
  int asock, ns;  /* Socket descriptor thingy */
  struct sockaddr_in where, there;
  int thing = sizeof(struct sockaddr_in);


  asock = socket(AF_INET, SOCK_STREAM, 0);
  check(asock, "socket");

  where.sin_family = AF_INET;
  where.sin_addr.s_addr = INADDR_ANY; /* System Knows */
  where.sin_port = htons(port);

  status = bind(asock, &where, sizeof(struct sockaddr_in));
  check (status, "bind");
  status = listen(asock, 1);
  check(status, "listen");

  ns = accept(asock, &there, &thing);
  check(ns, "accept");

  while ((len = read(ns, buff, 1)) > 0)
    write(2, buff, len); /* Write to terminal */

  shutdown(asock, 0);
  close(asock);

  fprintf(stderr, "\nParent gone\n");
  wait(status);    /* Wait for child to finish */
  exit(0);
}
```

```
110   check(status, sysname)
111   int status;
112   char *sysname;
113   {
114     if (status < 0) {
115       perror(sysname);
116       exit(-1);
117     }
118   }
```

Normally, of course, the client and server would be unrelated processes on unrelated computers.

4.4.1 Polling a Socket

It is often useful to be able to check if data is available on an interface without actually waiting until it is. This is known as polling. The way it is done from the UNIX filesystem and socket API is via the `select()` system call. This takes a mask parameter that allows one to poll several file descriptors simultaneously. This is very useful for programs that wish to provide the appearance of concurrent user interface interaction and network I/O, for example, network management programs, or networked graphics programs.

Figure 4.5 Select: `pix/poll.c`.

```
1    #include <stdio.h>
2    #include <sys/types.h>
3    #include <sys/time.h>
4    #include <stdlib.h>
5
6
7    struct timeval timeout,then,now;
8
9    main(argc, argv)
10   int     argc;
11   char    *argv[];
12   {
13           int selret;
14
15           if (argc != 3) {
16                   printf("usage: timer <#seconds> <#microseconds>");
17                   exit(-1);
18           }
19
20           timeout.tv_sec = atol(argv[1]);
21           timeout.tv_usec = atol(argv[2]);
22
```

```
        gettimeofday(&then,(struct timezone *)0);
        if ((selret=select(0, NULL, NULL, NULL, &timeout)) < 0) {
                check(selret, "select");
        gettimeofday(&now,(struct timezone *)0);
        printf("Delay = %d microseconds\n",(now.tv_sec - then.tv_sec)*1000000 +
                now.tv_usec - then.tv_usec);
        exit(0);
}
```

As well as `select()`, many systems implement the `poll()` call.

Figure 4.6 `poll()`.

```

#include <sys/poll.h>

    int poll(struct pollfd *ufds, unsigned int nfds, int timeout);
```

`poll()` is a variation on the theme of `select`. It specifies an array of nfds structures of the type shown below.

Figure 4.7 `pollfd`.

```

        struct pollfd {
                int fd;           /* file descriptor */
                short events;     /* requested events */
                short revents;    /* returned events */
        };
```

The timeout is in milliseconds, rather than the more complex structure in `select()`.

4.4.2 Nonblocking I/O

In some cases, we are not interested in waiting to see if output has finished yet or not, but we do wish to start it. In other cases, the programmer would like to read as much data as there is available immediately if it is ready, but not to wait if there is no data yet. For this purpose, *nonblocking* I/O is provided, and is triggered by setting a flag in the process data associated with the file descriptor.

Figure 4.8 NBIO: `pix/nbio.c`.

```
setnb()
{
        int     on = 1;
        int     iret;

        if ((iret=ioctl(0, FIONBIO, (char *) &on)) < 0)
                check(iret, "ioctl FIONBIO error");
}
```

Finally, we may wish to carry out some set of tasks, but be interrupted with the arrival of new data—this can be done in user space with the use of `signals`. For I/O, this is set up as follows.

4.4.3 Asynchronous I/O

Figure 4.9 illustrates asynchronous input. Here the application continues with its current work after registering an interest in callbacks for given events.

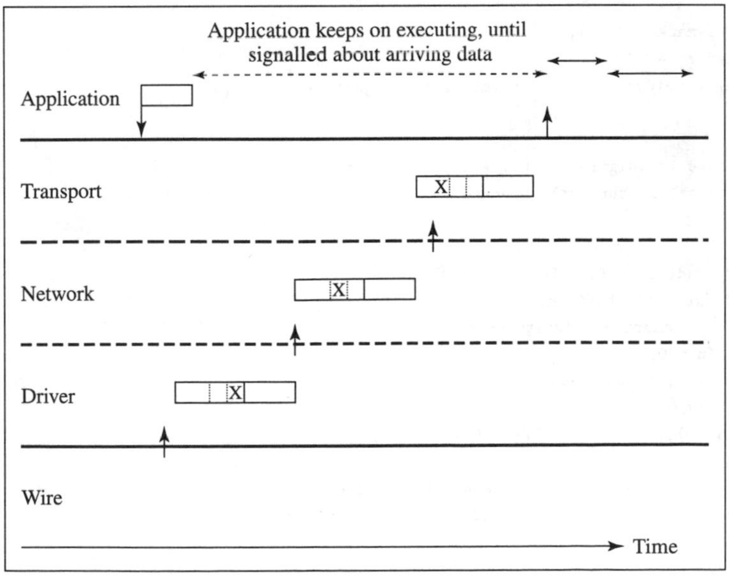

Figure 4.9 Asynchronous reception.

An example of an application using this is shown in Figure 4.10.

Figure 4.10 SIGIO: `pix/asynch.c`.

```
#include        <signal.h>
#include        <fcntl.h>

#define BUFFSIZE 4096

int     sigflag; /* gotta be global! */

int sigio_handler()
{
        sigflag = 1;            /* just set flag and return */
}

main()
{
        int     n, fret;
        char    buff[BUFFSIZE];

        signal(SIGIO, sigio_handler);
        fret=fcntl(0, F_SETOWN, getpid());
        check(fret, "F_SETOWN error");

        fret=fcntl(0, F_SETFL, FASYNC);
        check(fret, "F_SETFL FASYNC error");

/* This turns asynch into a loop which blocks in sigpause... */

        for (;;) {
                sigblock(sigmask(SIGIO));
                while (sigflag == 0)
                        sigpause(0);            /* wait for a signal */

                /*
                 * We're here if (sigflag != 0). Also, we know that the
                 * SIGIO signal is currently blocked.
                 */

                if ( (n = read(0, buff, BUFFSIZE)) > 0) {
                        if (write(1, buff, n) != n)
                                check(-1, "write error");
                } else if (n < 0)
                        check(n, "read error");
                else if (n == 0)
                        exit(0);                /* EOF */

                sigflag = 0;                    /* turn off our flag */
                sigsetmask(0);                  /* and reenable signals */
        }
}
```

Alternative Programming Models

Other languages such as Java have built in mechanisms for concurrency such as *threads*. It can be very elegant for event handling programs to program using these.

4.4.4 System Include Files

There are several include files in the preceding examples that are quite generic to all socket programming, and provide the definitions of types to use the socket system layer. These are installed in `/usr/include/netinet` from the source tree.

Figure 4.11 IP user view of address structure: `linux/include/linux/in.h`.

```
/* Structure describing an Internet (IP) socket address. */
#define __SOCK_SIZE__ 16               /* sizeof(struct sockaddr)   */
struct sockaddr_in {
  sa_family_t          sin_family;     /* Address family            */
  unsigned short int   sin_port;       /* Port number               */
  struct in_addr       sin_addr;       /* Internet address          */

  /* Pad to size of 'struct sockaddr'. */
  unsigned char        __pad[__SOCK_SIZE__ - sizeof(short int) -
                       sizeof(unsigned short int) - sizeof(struct in_addr)];
};
#define sin_zero       __pad           /* for BSD UNIX comp. -FvK   */
```

The IPv6 version of this is as follows (and is, not surprisingly, more complex).

Figure 4.12 IP user view of the IPv6 address structure: `linux/include/linux/in6.h`.

```
struct in6_addr
{
        union
        {
                __u8            u6_addr8[16];
                __u16           u6_addr16[8];
                __u32           u6_addr32[4];
        } in6_u;
#define s6_addr                 in6_u.u6_addr8
#define s6_addr16               in6_u.u6_addr16
#define s6_addr32               in6_u.u6_addr32
};

struct sockaddr_in6 {
```

```
        unsigned short int   sin6_family;   /* AF_INET6 */
        __u16                sin6_port;     /* Transport layer port # */
        __u32                sin6_flowinfo; /* IPv6 flow information */
        struct in6_addr      sin6_addr;     /* IPv6 address */
        __u32                sin6_scope_id; /* scope id (new in RFC2553) */
};
```

Here also, and in related include files, there are definitions of the structures used to communicate through the socket layer calls such as `setsockopt()`.

4.5 Summary

In this chapter, we have taken a brief look at the application programmers interface to kernel communications services, with a survey of some of the different models for programming.

In the next chapter, we will look at the infrastructure *within* the kernel for implementing link, network, and transport layer protocols.

CHAPTER

5

Protocol Implementation Framework

"The penguins had the most powerful army in the world. So had the porpoises."

—Anatole France

5.1 Roadmap

This chapter covers the overall background to kernel protocol implementation. It is bottom up in that we start with hardware and interrupts, go through drivers, then look at buffering and multiplexing, and finally examine the socket glue.

To some extent, we have given an overview of this in the preceding chapters, but here we go into more detail about the protocol implementation framework and the architecture within which the functions for multiplexing and layering fit. We look at the split between kernel versus user space again, and pay particular attention to the Linux structures defined for network protocol buffers that encourage efficient memory management as data and control are passed up and down the stack.

We look at interrupt handling and DMA for different I/O devices, and how to deal with expected versus unexpected events.

We look at the support for network devices and show the way that this encourages (at least to some extent) modularity, abstraction, and hiding.

We look at a day in the life of a network interrupt. Then we look at handling users' calls to the socket layer. We then take a walk through a day in the life of a buffer. Following that, we wrap up with a look at the day in the life of a protocol control block.

5.2 A Day in the Life of a Software Interrupt

5.2.1 Concurrency in the Linux Communications Stack

As discussed in Chapter 2, the design of kernel functionality, including communications services, is concerned with both reliability and performance. The reliability is largely a feature of correctness of the protocol specifications and implementations, but performance is much more of an art. It is measured by several metrics, including code size, execution time, and memory use. Code size in Linux is typically on the low side. Execution time must also include the degree to which concurrency (both interleaving and true multiprocessor concurrency) are exploited. Memory use is constrained by good discipline in the allocation of buffers and other dynamic structures (e.g., protocol management structures), and timeliness in freeing up resources when no longer needed, or needed elsewhere. Another consideration is fairness, which is a topic for a whole book on its own.

Within OS, a protocol stack is arranged as a pair of loosely coupled producer/consumer chains for output and input. This avoids well-known deadlock problems and gives a natural model for buffer use disciplines, *and* for critical region protection. State management (through the Protocol Control Block for each session) provides a connection between one system call and the next, and between threads that handle interrupts and threads handling system calls. Queues and counters provide data for flow control. Sleep/wake-up semaphores/queues are used to synchronize the sequence of processes/threads.

Critical regions are then kept to a minimum. User processes can only get to the kernel through system calls, and once there, the kernel has control, except for timer and device driver interrupts. Thus we can have three levels of code accessing *global* data in the protocol stack state (PCB and socket structures):

- Upper-layer call
- Timer-event
- Lower-layer call

Using interrupt level setting or spinlocks as explained in Chapter 2 makes sure that code accessing or modifying the global state in the protocol stack from one of these three "directions" is not preempted inappropriately.

5.2.2 Producer/Consumer Chain

Ideally, a protocol stack consists of two chains of tasks, one for output, one for input. These are loosely coupled (e.g., via resource management, or via the protocol itself, for example when a data packet requires acknowledgment, and acknowledgments are piggybacked on data). This is illustrated in Figure 5.1.

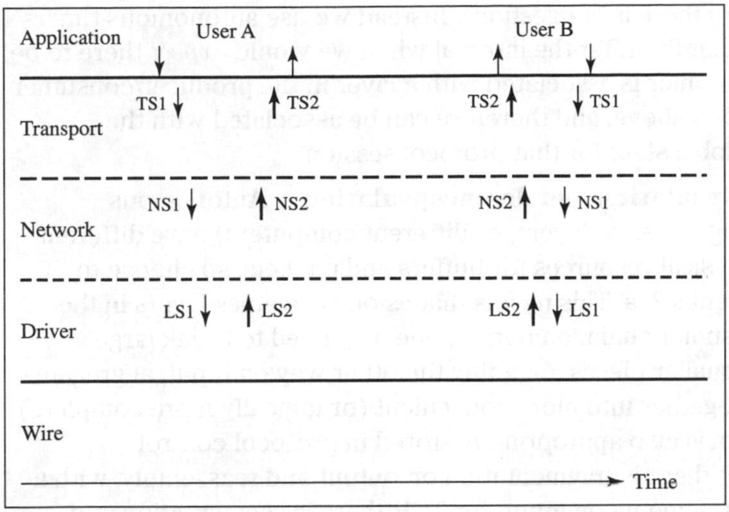

Figure 5.1 Producer/consumer chain.

In principle, there is a variety of ways to implement these chains of tasks. In practice, the TCP/IP protocols make life relatively regular for the modern operating systems programmer, since the IP level is so straightforward (at least superficially—see Chapter 6 for the glaring reality). This means that the interference between input and output chains is relatively simple, and restricted to a few places where we need to have communication via the protocol state machine, typically in TCP, or through resource management in the buffer allocation in the output flow or input flow.

Then protocols in the chains or flows have to look after a number of communication specific tasks, including:

Multiplexing and demultiplexing. State is held at the socket, transport protocol, network, and driver level to indicate how to handle incoming packets and pass them on to the appropriate handler at the next level up. Socket state gives session-to-process mapping. Transport protocol state to some extent repeats this data. Network protocol state is longer lived—essentially, in the IP world, it represents the binding of the IP protocol identifier to a transport protocol. Then at the driver level, there are indications in the frame level which network layer to demultiplex a packet to, and when sending a packet, there is a binding between an IP address and the link layer addressing, maintained by address resolution tables (or neighbor tables).

Reliability and resource control. Reliability and resource management both require timers. The problem that they have in common is that when things *stop* working, that is exactly the time that the system doesn't have resources to tell you. For example, packet loss may happen because of congestion, which is when there is not enough bandwidth to send packets (e.g., to tell you there is congestion). Instead we use autonomous timers (watchdogs) that fire after the interval when we would *expect* there to be an event. Each timer is associated with a layer in the producer/consumer chains described above, and therefore can be associated with the appropriate global state for that protocol session.

Buffering, encapsulation and de-encapsulation. Autonomous communicating systems (layers, or different computers) have different logical and physical resources for buffers and packets, so choose to allocate different sizes. This means that as one traverses layers in the producer/consumer chain, on output, one may need to break large packets into smaller pieces, or, going the other way on input, aggregate small pieces together into more convenient (or logically more complete) units. This data is also appropriately stored in protocol control blocks—for IP, there is fragmentation on output and reassembly, with a timer for lost fragments on input; for TCP, there is segmentation and reassembly, which operates directly to the socket layer.

As discussed in Chapter 3, the way that network input and output work is driven from software interrupts. For output, the producer is the application process. For input, it is the network interrupt.

Concurrency Problems—What if We Had No Discipline

There are a variety of problems with interleaving code from different places. Three well-known problems are:

Deadlock. a has x and needs y, b has y and needs x to proceed, as shown in Figure 5.2.

Livelock. A sequence of trades of x and y without either party ending up with the necessary full set of resources, as illustrated in Figure 5.3.

Fairness. This is discussed further in Chapter 9.

If one process, thread, task, or driver gets more turns at the CPU (or memory, bus, or whatever resource is congested) we have what is called *unfairness*.

Fairness is complex, but typically, a round-robin scheduler can control fairness. In general, protocol fairness is even more complex as it includes fairness of more than one system (far end, links in between, and so forth).

5.2.3 What about Real Multiprocessor Systems?

Of course, the model above of a simple producer-consumer chain potentially breaks down (or is at least a lot more complex) on a true multiprocessor system.

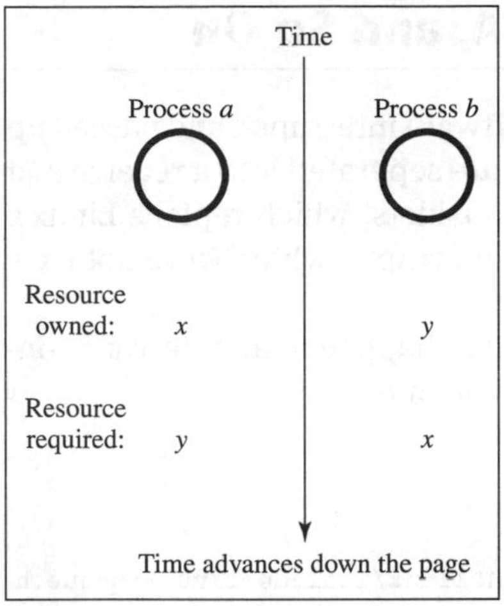

Figure 5.2 Deadlock.

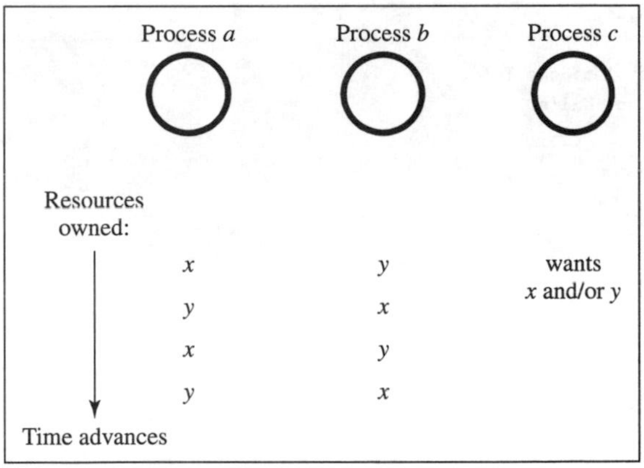

Figure 5.3 Livelock.

Linux is now pretty much fully symmetric multiprocessor-capable. Atomic access to shared data must be protected across processors, since any layer (e.g., driver interrupt, software interrupt, system call handler) may run on any processor.

In Chapter 2, we discussed the mutual exclusion support that this requires, the technique called a spinlock. For input and output, this is a relatively simple (localized) change to all the communications code that has happened in the last few years of evolution of the Linux kernel, so that now we have greatly enhanced performance in multiprocessor hardware systems. The remaining area for performance enhancement is in SMP forwarding, but this is a topic for future research at the moment, as mentioned before.

5.3 Bottom Up: Interrupts, DMA, and So On

Now network interrupts are dealt with under software interrupts, and passed up the food chain by such. The software interrupts are seperated into a receive and transmit side, and essentially schedule a set of tasklets, which replace Linux's older mechanism of *bottom halves* or deferred interrupts, which were not easy to make work under SMP.

Instead, Linux now has a structure for tasks that happen in an interrupt context, and thus can be per processor in an SMP machine.

Figure 5.4 Task queue structure—copyright statement: `linux/include/linux/tqueue.h`.

```
/*
 * tqueue.h --- task queue handling for Linux.
 *
 * Mostly based on a proposed bottom-half replacement code written by
 * Kai Petzke, wpp@marie.physik.tu-berlin.de.
 *
 * Modified for use in the Linux kernel by Theodore Ts'o,
 * tytso@mit.edu. Any bugs are my fault, not Kai's.
 *
 * The original comment follows below.
 */

#ifndef _LINUX_TQUEUE_H
#define _LINUX_TQUEUE_H

#include <linux/spinlock.h>
#include <linux/list.h>
#include <asm/bitops.h>
#include <asm/system.h>

/*
 * New proposed "bottom half" handlers:
 * (C) 1994 Kai Petzke, wpp@marie.physik.tu-berlin.de
 *
 * Advantages:
 * - Bottom halfs are implemented as a linked list. You can have as many
 *   of them, as you want.
 * - No more scanning of a bit field is required upon call of a bottom half.
 * - Support for chained bottom half lists. The run_task_queue() function can be
 *   used as a bottom half handler. This is for example useful for bottom
 *   halfs, which want to be delayed until the next clock tick.
 *
 * Notes:
 * - Bottom halfs are called in the reverse order that they were linked into
 *   the list.
 */
```

In Figure 5.5 we see the definition of the core data structure to describe the tasklet queue structure:

Figure 5.5 Task queue (TQ) structures: `linux/include/linux/tqueue.h`.

```
struct tq_struct {
        struct list_head list;        /* linked list of active bh's */
        unsigned long sync;           /* must be initialized to zero */
        void (*routine)(void *);      /* function to call */
        void *data;                   /* argument to function */
};

typedef struct list_head task_queue;

#define DECLARE_TASK_QUEUE(q) LIST_HEAD(q)
#define TQ_ACTIVE(q)         (!list_empty(&q))

extern task_queue tq_timer, tq_immediate, tq_disk;
```

Now we have to support legacy-deferred interrupts, since a great deal of code is still written in terms of this older Linux construct.

Figure 5.6 TQ mapping to deferred processing/bh_: `linux/include/linux/tqueue.h`.

```
/*
 * To implement your own list of active bottom halfs, use the following
 * two definitions:
 *
 * DECLARE_TASK_QUEUE(my_tqueue);
 * struct tq_struct my_task = {
 *      routine: (void (*)(void *)) my_routine,
 *      data: &my_data
 * };
 *
 * To activate a bottom half on a list, use:
 *
 *      queue_task(&my_task, &my_tqueue);
 *
 * To later run the queued tasks use
 *
 *      run_task_queue(&my_tqueue);
 *
 * This allows you to do deferred processing. For example, you could
 * have a task queue called tq_timer, which is executed within the timer
 * interrupt.
 */
```

It is common to define some inline functions in the header (the same place as relevant structures are defined).

Figure 5.7 TQ inline functions, queue, and run: `linux/include/linux/tqueue.h`.

```
extern spinlock_t tqueue_lock;

/*
 * Queue a task on a tq. Return non-zero if it was successfully
 * added.
 */
static inline int queue_task(struct tq_struct *bh_pointer, task_queue *bh_list)
{
	int ret = 0;
	if (!test_and_set_bit(0,&bh_pointer->sync)) {
		unsigned long flags;
		spin_lock_irqsave(&tqueue_lock, flags);
		list_add_tail(&bh_pointer->list, bh_list);
		spin_unlock_irqrestore(&tqueue_lock, flags);
		ret = 1;
	}
	return ret;
}

/*
 * Call all "bottom halfs" on a given list.
 */

extern void __run_task_queue(task_queue *list);

static inline void run_task_queue(task_queue *list)
{
	if (TQ_ACTIVE(*list))
		__run_task_queue(list);
}
```

Now, let's look at the soft IRQ mechanisms that use this.

Figure 5.8 Soft IRQs—main copyright, and so on: `linux/kernel/softirq.c`.

```
/*
 *	linux/kernel/softirq.c
 *
 *	Copyright (C) 1992 Linus Torvalds
 *
 * Fixed a disable_bh()/enable_bh() race (was causing a console lockup)
 * due bh_mask_count not atomic handling. Copyright (C) 1998 Andrea Arcangeli
 *
 * Rewritten. Old one was good in 2.2, but in 2.3 it was immoral. --ANK (990903)
 */

```

```
#include <linux/config.h>
#include <linux/mm.h>
#include <linux/kernel_stat.h>
#include <linux/interrupt.h>
#include <linux/smp_lock.h>
#include <linux/init.h>
#include <linux/tqueue.h>
```

In the next extract, the comment makes it clear that SMP interaction with soft IRQs is not yet a well-understood performance area.

Figure 5.9 Soft IRQs—main comment: `linux/kernel/softirq.c.`

```
/*
   - No shared variables, all the data are CPU local.
   - If a softirq needs serialization, let it serialize itself
     by its own spinlocks.
   - Even if softirq is serialized, only local cpu is marked for
     execution. Hence, we get something sort of weak cpu binding.
     Though it is still not clear, will it result in better locality
     or will not.
   - These softirqs are not masked by global cli() and start_bh_atomic()
     (by clear reasons). Hence, old parts of code still using global locks
     MUST NOT use softirqs, but insert interfacing routines acquiring
     global locks. F.e. look at BHs implementation.

   Examples:
   - NET RX softirq. It is multithreaded and does not require
     any global serialization.
   - NET TX softirq. It kicks software netdevice queues, hence
     it is logically serialized per device, but this serialization
     is invisible to common code.
   - Tasklets: serialized wrt itself.
   - Bottom halves: globally serialized, grr...
 */
```

Here is the code that actually acts on the soft IRQ, and fields it to the appropriate handler.

Figure 5.10 Soft IRQs—handler i: `linux/kernel/softirq.c.`

```
static struct softirq_action softirq_vec[32] __cacheline_aligned;

asmlinkage void do_softirq()
{
        int cpu = smp_processor_id();
        __u32 active, mask;

```

```
55          if (in_interrupt())
56                  return;
57
58          local_bh_disable();
59
60          local_irq_disable();
61          mask = softirq_mask(cpu);
62          active = softirq_active(cpu) & mask;
63
64          if (active) {
65                  struct softirq_action *h;
66
67  restart:
68                  /* Reset active bitmask before enabling irqs */
69                  softirq_active(cpu) &= ~active;
70
71                  local_irq_enable();
72
73                  h = softirq_vec;
74                  mask &= ~active;
75
76                  do {
77                      if (active & 1)
78                              h->action(h);
79                      h++;
80                      active >>= 1;
81                  } while (active);
```

This part then makes sure that we don't nest hard and soft IRQs arbitrarily, which would lead to bad things happening.

Figure 5.11 Soft IRQs—handler ii: `linux/kernel/softirq.c`.

```
83                  local_irq_disable();
84
85                  active = softirq_active(cpu);
86                  if ((active &= mask) != 0)
87                          goto retry;
88          }
89
90          local_bh_enable();
91
92          /* Leave with locally disabled hard irqs. It is critical to close
93           * window for infinite recursion, while we help local bh count,
94           * it protected us. Now we are defenceless.
95           */
96          return;
97
98  retry:
99          goto restart;
100 }
```

This section kicks off the soft IRQ vectors.

Figure 5.12 Soft IRQs—setup: `linux/kernel/softirq.c`.

```
static spinlock_t softirq_mask_lock = SPIN_LOCK_UNLOCKED;

void open_softirq(int nr, void (*action)(struct softirq_action*), void *data)
{
        unsigned long flags;
        int i;

        spin_lock_irqsave(&softirq_mask_lock, flags);
        softirq_vec[nr].data = data;
        softirq_vec[nr].action = action;

        for (i=0; i<NR_CPUS; i++)
                softirq_mask(i) |= (1<<nr);
        spin_unlock_irqrestore(&softirq_mask_lock, flags);
}
```

Tasklets

As we mentioned before in Chapter 2, Linux recently replaced the whole bottom-half mechanism for deferred interrupts with two levels—the lowest level was soft interrupts, shown in the preceding code, and is used especially for networking. The next level is the general tasklet framework that enables processors in an SMP system to pick a deferred interrupt task from a queue.

Figure 5.13 Soft IRQs—tasklet handler: `linux/kernel/softirq.c`.

```
/* Tasklets */

struct tasklet_head tasklet_vec[NR_CPUS] __cacheline_aligned;

static void tasklet_action(struct softirq_action *a)
{
        int cpu = smp_processor_id();
        struct tasklet_struct *list;

        local_irq_disable();
        list = tasklet_vec[cpu].list;
        tasklet_vec[cpu].list = NULL;
        local_irq_enable();

        while (list != NULL) {
                struct tasklet_struct *t = list;

                list = list->next;

                if (tasklet_trylock(t)) {
```

```
                        if (atomic_read(&t->count) == 0) {
                                clear_bit(TASKLET_STATE_SCHED, &t->state);

                                t->func(t->data);
                                /*
                                 * talklet_trylock() uses test_and_set_bit that imply
                                 * an mb when it returns zero, thus we need the explicit
                                 * mb only here: while closing the critical section.
                                 */
#ifdef CONFIG_SMP
                                smp_mb__before_clear_bit();
#endif
                                tasklet_unlock(t);
                                continue;
                        }
                        tasklet_unlock(t);
                }
                local_irq_disable();
                t->next = tasklet_vec[cpu].list;
                tasklet_vec[cpu].list = t;
                __cpu_raise_softirq(cpu, TASKLET_SOFTIRQ);
                local_irq_enable();
        }
}
```

In the preceding code, we see the way that tasklets are dequeued when the general handler is called and then the `t->func()` is applied to the `t->data`.

Next, the exact same struture is seen (just the function declaration) to handle the high-priority version of the tasklet queue—maybe eventually in some later Linux release, tasklets will be in a multilevel queue, although it's not clear that many levels of deferred interrupt priority make a lot of sense when it gives you finer-grain concurrency, but coarse-grain multiprocessing is cheap.

Figure 5.14 Soft IRQs—tasklet high-priority handler: `linux/kernel/softirq.c`.

```
struct tasklet_head tasklet_hi_vec[NR_CPUS] __cacheline_aligned;

static void tasklet_hi_action(struct softirq_action *a)
```

The whole tasklet framework has to be kicked into action, and that's what we see here.

Figure 5.15 Soft IRQs—tasklet initialization and destruction: `linux/kernel/softirq.c`.

```
void tasklet_init(struct tasklet_struct *t,
                  void (*func)(unsigned long), unsigned long data)
{
        t->func = func;
```

```
        t->data = data;
        t->state = 0;
        atomic_set(&t->count, 0);
}

void tasklet_kill(struct tasklet_struct *t)
{
        if (in_interrupt())
                printk("Attempt to kill tasklet from interrupt\n");

        while (test_and_set_bit(TASKLET_STATE_SCHED, &t->state)) {
                current->state = TASK_RUNNING;
                do {
                        current->policy |= SCHED_YIELD;
                        schedule();
                } while (test_bit(TASKLET_STATE_SCHED, &t->state));
        }
        tasklet_unlock_wait(t);
        clear_bit(TASKLET_STATE_SCHED, &t->state);
}
```

Bottom Halves

In the past, we had bottom halves. We still have a lot of legacy code written in terms of these, so the code must be called from the tasklet framework. It just follows the rules about serialization outlined in Chapter 2.

Figure 5.16 Soft IRQs—handler for legacy bottom-half code: `linux/kernel/softirq.c`.

```
/* Old style BHs */

static void (*bh_base[32])(void);
struct tasklet_struct bh_task_vec[32];

/* BHs are serialized by spinlock global_bh_lock.

   It is still possible to make synchronize_bh() as
   spin_unlock_wait(&global_bh_lock). This operation is not used
   by kernel now, so that this lock is not made private only
   due to wait_on_irq().

   It can be removed only after auditing all the BHs.
 */
spinlock_t global_bh_lock = SPIN_LOCK_UNLOCKED;

static void bh_action(unsigned long nr)
{
        int cpu = smp_processor_id();

        if (!spin_trylock(&global_bh_lock))
                goto resched;
```

```
252
253              if (!hardirq_trylock(cpu))
254                      goto resched_unlock;
255
256              if (bh_base[nr])
257                      bh_base[nr]();
258
259              hardirq_endlock(cpu);
260              spin_unlock(&global_bh_lock);
261              return;
262
263      resched_unlock:
264              spin_unlock(&global_bh_lock);
265      resched:
266              mark_bh(nr);
267      }
```

This installs the bh_ in the tasklet queue.

Figure 5.17 Soft IRQs—handler for legacy bottom-half code: `linux/kernel/softirq.c`.

```
269      void init_bh(int nr, void (*routine)(void))
270      {
271              bh_base[nr] = routine;
272              mb();
273      }
274
275      void remove_bh(int nr)
276      {
277              tasklet_kill(bh_task_vec+nr);
278              bh_base[nr] = NULL;
279      }
```

This sets up the whole soft IRQ and tasklet system and starts it going.

Figure 5.18 Soft IRQs—initialize `softirq` and run tasklets: `linux/kernel/softirq.c`.

```
281      void __init softirq_init()
282      {
283              int i;
284
285              for (i=0; i<32; i++)
286                      tasklet_init(bh_task_vec+i, bh_action, i);
287
288              open_softirq(TASKLET_SOFTIRQ, tasklet_action, NULL);
289              open_softirq(HI_SOFTIRQ, tasklet_hi_action, NULL);
```

```
290    }
291
292    void __run_task_queue(task_queue *list)
293    {
294            struct list_head head, *next;
295            unsigned long flags;
296
297            spin_lock_irqsave(&tqueue_lock, flags);
298            list_add(&head, list);
299            list_del_init(list);
300            spin_unlock_irqrestore(&tqueue_lock, flags);
301
302            next = head.next;
303            while (next != &head) {
304                    void (*f) (void *);
305                    struct tq_struct *p;
306                    void *data;
307
308                    p = list_entry(next, struct tq_struct, list);
309                    next = next->next;
310                    f = p->routine;
311                    data = p->data;
312                    wmb();
313                    p->sync = 0;
314                    if (f)
315                            f(data);
316            }
317    }
```

5.4 Device Level, Bottom Up, One Level Up

Moving up one level from generic interrupts, we take a look at network device
support.

For many years, operating systems have provided a standard abstraction/
interface for classes of device, so that higher-level operating system (and application) software can be common across all such devices. UNIX traditionally
divides devices into two classes, character (low rate, interactive, and serial line,
typically) and block (disk, display, and so on). It's possible to squeeze network
devices into the block mode paradigm, but its messy. Linux adds a third type of
device—a network. This is discussed in some detail in Chapter 2.

Typically, a device has a name to place it in the file namespace, but also has
an identifier: UNIX has major/minor numbers. A driver is a structure (class)
with a set of entry points (functions/methods). At boot (or module load) time,
the device is initialized by calling its init() function—this resets the device,
installs any relevant interrupt handlers, and so on. It then registers with the OS.
The rest of the time, we manage I/O with a device with open, close, queue_xmit,
and interrupts/notifications.

Device driver details manage specifics like:

- Bus interface/memory/I/O address of device registers
- DMA and timer chip use
- IRQS, and so on

Notice the asymmetry of input and output—output is requested, whereas input arrives unexpectedly (i.e., at this level we could never sensibly implement a device driver by polling) Input results in packets being queued, and `netif_rx()` called to find out which higher-level protocol function to dispatch.

The traditional catchall interface is via the `ioctl()` call. This allows one to set and get a number of network-specific device control parameters—for example:

- Link up/down
- Broadcast address
- ARP (see Chapter 6)
- MTU
- Statistics, and so on

We can see these by saying `ifconfig <dev>`. The command `netstat -i` will tell you what network devices you have. We look at this further in Chapter 6.

Address resolution is done either algorithmically, or through a table, or through a helper task that runs the Address Resolution Protocol (ARP). ARP is invoked from output when the IP address is known but the destination link layer (or strictly, Media Access Control) address is unknown. ARP is demultiplexed in `netif_rx()` for input frames with ARP type—it makes sure that it enters table updates and maintains these with a lifetime so that they expire when not used in a timely fashion. It can be overridden by configuration management.

In general, output is multiplexed by indicating frametype (IP, ARP, or other). Input demultiplexes, by looking at frametype, and using to *upcall* the right higher level (from inside `netif_rx()`, from the input interrupt).

As discussed before, buffer disciplines are asymmetric: for output, the higher level allocates buffer and calls a stack of send routines, and the lowest level frees, while for input, the low level has a pool, hands up to the upper the level, which, when done with a buffer, frees.

What if the packet is *not for us*? Basically, it will either bridge, route, or discard. Bridging is intensive (it requires the Ethernet interface to be in promiscuous mode, which is most expensive in packet discard). We don't discuss that further.

Routing is a built-in part of Linux and requires a forwarding table, and is discussed in much more detail in Chapters 8 and 9. Discard is often the most common case and requires efficient handling. There has been lots of good work on efficient filtering, mainly from the implementation of network monitoring and firewall mechanisms, which are discussed in Chapter 10.

Most hardware (at the driver level) batches packet handling to reduce the interrupt count to much less than one per packet. This is good for performance, although it results potentially in bursts of IP packets arriving at the higher levels (or for forwarding). This doesn't cause problems too often in the common cases, and can be controlled using network schedulers and shapers, as discussed in Chapter 9.

Now we take a detailed look at a specific network device by walking though the driver code.

5.4.1 Network Device Driver API

We covered the overall view of drivers in Chapter 2. In this section, we take a look at the specifics of a network device in more detail, and then use a classic example of an Ethernet driver for a very well-known device to provide some specifics.

The Linux network device driver interface information is basically all held in one general data structure—it is fairly horrible, as it combines various protocol layers in one place.

Here is the main network device data structure.

Figure 5.19 Network/OS device-level abstraction 0: `linux/include/linux/netdevice.h`.

```
/*
 *      The DEVICE structure.
 *      Actually, this whole structure is a big mistake. It mixes I/O
 *      data with strictly "high-level" data, and it has to know about
 *      almost every data structure used in the INET module.
 *
 *      FIXME: cleanup struct net_device such that network protocol info
 *      moves out.
 */

struct net_device
{

        /*
         * This is the first field of the "visible" part of this structure
         * (i.e. as seen by users in the "Space.c" file). It is the name
         * the interface.
         */
        char                    name[IFNAMSIZ];

        /*
         *      I/O specific fields
         *      FIXME: Merge these and struct ifmap into one
         */
```

```
	unsigned long		rmem_end;	/* shmem "recv" end	*/
	unsigned long		rmem_start;	/* shmem "recv" start */
	unsigned long		mem_end;	/* shared mem end	*/
	unsigned long		mem_start;	/* shared mem start	*/
	unsigned long		base_addr;	/* device I/O address */
	unsigned int		irq;		/* device IRQ number */
```

Common across all network devices is initialization.

Figure 5.20 Network/OS device-level abstraction i: `linux/include/linux/netdevice.h`.

```
	/*
	 *	Some hardware also needs these fields, but they are not
	 *	part of the usual set specified in Space.c.
	 */

	unsigned char		if_port;	/* Selectable AUI, TP,..*/
	unsigned char		dma;		/* DMA channel		*/

	unsigned long		state;

	struct net_device	*next;

	/* The device initialization function. Called only once. */
	int			(*init)(struct net_device *dev);

	/* ------- Fields preinitialized in Space.c finish here ------- */

	struct net_device	*next_sched;

	/* Interface index. Unique device identifier */
	int			ifindex;
	int			iflink;
```

Then we have the generic network device data and statistics, including MAC addresses—for a LAN card we have to support broadcast address(es), as well as unicast, and various modes such as *promiscuous*, where the card accepts frames to all addresses, not just those in its address filter table.

Figure 5.21 Network/OS device-level abstraction ii: `linux/include/linux/netdevice.h`.

```
	struct net_device_stats* (*get_stats)(struct net_device *dev);
	struct iw_statistics* (*get_wireless_stats)(struct net_device *dev);

	/*
	 * This marks the end of the "visible" part of the structure. All
	 * fields hereafter are internal to the system, and may change at
```

```
         * will (read: may be cleaned up at will).
         */

        /* These may be needed for future network-power-down code. */
        unsigned long           trans_start;  /* Time (in jiffies) of last Tx */
        unsigned long           last_rx;      /* Time of last Rx     */

        unsigned short          flags; /* interface flags (a la BSD) */
        unsigned short          gflags;
        unsigned                mtu;   /* interface MTU value       */
        unsigned short          type;  /* interface hardware type   */
        unsigned short          hard_header_len;     /* hardware hdr length */
        void                    *priv; /* pointer to private data   */

        struct net_device       *master; /* Pointer to master device of a group,
                                          * which this device is member of.
                                          */

        /* Interface address info. */
        unsigned char           broadcast[MAX_ADDR_LEN];      /* hw bcast add */
        unsigned char           pad;          /* make dev_addr aligned to 8 bytes */
        unsigned char           dev_addr[MAX_ADDR_LEN]; /* hw address */
        unsigned char           addr_len;     /* hardware address length    */

        struct dev_mc_list      *mc_list;     /* Multicast mac addresses    */
        int                     mc_count;     /* Number of installed mcasts */
        int                     promiscuity;
        int                     allmulti;

        int                     watchdog_timeo;
        struct timer_list       watchdog_timer;

        /* Protocol specific pointers */

        void                    *atalk_ptr;   /* AppleTalk link     */
```

In Chapter 9, we'll see how output queuing disciplines are attached to a device—here we see that the generic network driver level is where the hooks for this are.

Figure 5.22 Network/OS device-level abstraction iii: `linux/include/linux/netdevice.h`.

```
        void                    *ip_ptr;      /* IPv4 specific data */
        void                    *dn_ptr;      /* DECnet specific data */
        void                    *ip6_ptr;     /* IPv6 specific data */
        void                    *ec_ptr;      /* Econet specific data */

        struct Qdisc            *qdisc;
        struct Qdisc            *qdisc_sleeping;
        struct Qdisc            *qdisc_list;
```

```
        struct Qdisc            *qdisc_ingress;
        unsigned long           tx_queue_len; /* Max frames per queue allowed */

        /* hard_start_xmit synchronizer */
        spinlock_t              xmit_lock;
        /* cpu id of processor entered to hard_start_xmit or -1,
           if nobody entered there.
         */
        int                     xmit_lock_owner;
        /* device queue lock */
        spinlock_t              queue_lock;
        /* Number of references to this device */
        atomic_t                refcnt;
        /* The flag marking that device is unregistered, but held by an user */
        int                     deadbeaf;

        /* Net device features */
        int                     features;
#define NETIF_F_SG              1       /* Scatter/gather IO. */
#define NETIF_F_IP_CSUM         2       /* Can checksum only TCP/UDP over IPv4. */
#define NETIF_F_NO_CSUM         4       /* Does not require checksum. F.e. loopack. */
#define NETIF_F_HW_CSUM         8       /* Can checksum all the packets. */
#define NETIF_F_DYNALLOC        16      /* Self-dectructable device. */
#define NETIF_F_HIGHDMA         32      /* Can DMA to high memory. */
#define NETIF_F_FRAGLIST        1       /* Scatter/gather IO. */

        /* Called after device is detached from network. */
```

Figure 5.23 Network/OS device-level abstraction iv: `linux/include/linux/netdevice.h`.

```
        void                    (*uninit)(struct net_device *dev);
        /* Called after last user reference disappears. */
        void                    (*destructor)(struct net_device *dev);

        /* Pointers to interface service routines. */
        int                     (*open)(struct net_device *dev);
        int                     (*stop)(struct net_device *dev);
        int                     (*hard_start_xmit) (struct sk_buff *skb,
                                                    struct net_device *dev);
        int                     (*hard_header) (struct sk_buff *skb,
                                                struct net_device *dev,
                                                unsigned short type,
                                                void *daddr,
                                                void *saddr,
                                                unsigned len);
        int                     (*rebuild_header)(struct sk_buff *skb);
#define HAVE_MULTICAST
        void                    (*set_multicast_list)(struct net_device *dev);
#define HAVE_SET_MAC_ADDR
        int                     (*set_mac_address)(struct net_device *dev,
                                                   void *addr);
#define HAVE_PRIVATE_IOCTL
```

```
        int                 (*do_ioctl)(struct net_device *dev,
                                        struct ifreq *ifr, int cmd);
#define HAVE_SET_CONFIG
        int                 (*set_config)(struct net_device *dev,
                                          struct ifmap *map);
#define HAVE_HEADER_CACHE
        int                 (*hard_header_cache)(struct neighbour *neigh,
                                                 struct hh_cache *hh);
        void                (*header_cache_update)(struct hh_cache *hh,
                                                   struct net_device *dev,
                                                   unsigned char * haddr);
#define HAVE_CHANGE_MTU
        int                 (*change_mtu)(struct net_device *dev, int new_mtu);

#define HAVE_TX_TIMEOUT
        void                (*tx_timeout) (struct net_device *dev);

        int                 (*hard_header_parse)(struct sk_buff *skb,
                                                 unsigned char *haddr);
        int                 (*neigh_setup)(struct net_device *dev, struct neigh_parms *);
        int                 (*accept_fastpath)(struct net_device *, struct dst_entry*);

        /* open/release and usage marking */
        struct module *owner;

        /* bridge stuff */
        struct net_bridge_port *br_port;
```

5.4.2 Network Reception

This is a generic receive handle/demultiplex function called from receive interrupts from all network device drivers.

Figure 5.24 Network device driver Rx: `linux/net/core/dev.c`.

```
static void netdev_wakeup(void)
{
        unsigned long xoff;

        spin_lock(&netdev_fc_lock);
        xoff = netdev_fc_xoff;
        netdev_fc_xoff = 0;
        while (xoff) {
                int i = ffz(~xoff);
                xoff &= ~(1<<i);
                netdev_fc_slots[i].stimul(netdev_fc_slots[i].dev);
        }
        spin_unlock(&netdev_fc_lock);
}
```

5.4.3 A Specific Device Driver—3c501

This is a 3Com Ethernet card driver from Linux 2.4. This is a pretty old device, but it has enough intelligence to show some of the features of Linux. In fact, some of its limitations also mean that a driver for it must also exhibit some classic workarounds for well-known device problems—some device problems never go away even in state-of-the-art hardware.

The `net_device` structure illustrates what data is associated with the hardware specifics of a network device, including bus interface and memory and interrupt priority, as well as external card specifics.

Basically, we are usually given an I/O address that a card is memory-mapped to, and then a given card has a number of registers for control and status—in this case there are also addresses we can read internal configuration back from the card (e.g., a manufacturer-assigned Ethernet address, for example).

Figure 5.25 Ethernet driver 0—data: `linux/drivers/net/3c501.c`.

```
#define RX_STATUS (ioaddr + 0x06)
#define RX_CMD  RX_STATUS
#define TX_STATUS (ioaddr + 0x07)
#define TX_CMD  TX_STATUS
#define GP_LOW  (ioaddr + 0x08)
#define GP_HIGH (ioaddr + 0x09)
#define RX_BUF_CLR (ioaddr + 0x0A)
#define RX_LOW  (ioaddr + 0x0A)
#define RX_HIGH (ioaddr + 0x0B)
#define SAPROM  (ioaddr + 0x0C)
#define AX_STATUS (ioaddr + 0x0E)
#define AX_CMD  AX_STATUS
#define DATAPORT (ioaddr + 0x0F)
#define TX_RDY 0x08          /* In TX_STATUS */

#define EL1_DATAPTR   0x08
#define EL1_RXPTR     0x0A
#define EL1_SAPROM    0x0C
#define EL1_DATAPORT  0x0f

/*
 *      Writes to the ax command register.
 */

#define AX_OFF 0x00                 /* Irq off, buffer access on */
#define AX_SYS 0x40                 /* Load the buffer */
#define AX_XMIT 0x44                /* Transmit a packet */
#define AX_RX  0x48                 /* Receive a packet */
#define AX_LOOP 0x0C                /* Loopback mode */
#define AX_RESET 0x80
```

The transmission and reception are (typically) separated out, and there are status bits that indicate specific conditions associated with the type of link. Ethernets have lots of ways that frames or the media can present problems, and device manufacturers like to enable the device driver writer to be able to get at all of these—in most cases, the actions in the driver are simple (do nothing except count statistics) and it's up to network managers to look at the statistics and notice problems.

Figure 5.26 Ethernet driver 1—data: `linux/drivers/net/3c501.c`.

```
/*
 *      Normal receive mode written to RX_STATUS. We must intr on short packets
 *      to avoid bogus rx lockups.
 */

#define RX_NORM 0xA8           /* 0x68 == all addrs, 0xA8 only to me. */
#define RX_PROM 0x68           /* Senior Prom, uhmm promiscuous mode. */
#define RX_MULT 0xE8           /* Accept multicast packets. */
#define TX_NORM 0x0A           /* Interrupt on everything that might hang the chip */

/*
 *      TX_STATUS register.
 */

#define TX_COLLISION 0x02
#define TX_16COLLISIONS 0x04
#define TX_READY 0x08

#define RX_RUNT 0x08
#define RX_MISSED 0x01         /* Missed a packet due to 3c501 braindamage. */
#define RX_GOOD 0x30           /* Good packet 0x20, or simple overflow 0x10. */
```

3c501 Initialization

Here we see initialization of the device. There are some specifics to do with interfacing to the operating system so that the data is available and the driver for the card can be started. We see the retrieval of the *station* or MAC address from the card here.

Figure 5.27 Ethernet driver 2—init a: `linux/drivers/net/3c501.c`.

```
        /*
         *      Reserve I/O resource for exclusive use by this driver
         */

        if (!request_region(ioaddr, EL1_IO_EXTENT, dev->name))
                return -ENODEV;
```

```
280
281             /*
282              *      Read the station address PROM data from the special port.
283              */
284
285             for (i = 0; i < 6; i++)
286             {
287                     outw(i, ioaddr + EL1_DATAPTR);
288                     station_addr[i] = inb(ioaddr + EL1_SAPROM);
289             }
290             /*
291              *      Check the first three octets of the S.A. for 3Com's prefix, or
292              *      for the Sager NP943 prefix.
293              */
294
295             if (station_addr[0] == 0x02 && station_addr[1] == 0x60
296                     && station_addr[2] == 0x8c)
297             {
298                     mname = "3c501";
299             } else if (station_addr[0] == 0x00 && station_addr[1] == 0x80
300             && station_addr[2] == 0xC8)
301             {
302                     mname = "NP943";
303             }
304             else {
305                     release_region(ioaddr, EL1_IO_EXTENT);
306                     return -ENODEV;
307             }
```

Here we probe to find the IRQ that the device is on.

Figure 5.28 Ethernet driver 2—init b: `linux/drivers/net/3c501.c`.

```
309             /*
310              *      We auto-IRQ by shutting off the interrupt line and letting it float
311              *      high.
312              */
313
314             if (dev->irq < 2)
315             {
316                     autoirq_setup(2);
317                     inb(RX_STATUS);        /* Clear pending interrupts. */
318                     inb(TX_STATUS);
319                     outb(AX_LOOP + 1, AX_CMD);
320
321                     outb(0x00, AX_CMD);
322
323                     autoirq = autoirq_report(1);
324
325                     if (autoirq == 0)
326                     {
```

```
327                    printk("%s probe at %#x failed to detect IRQ line.\n",
328                         mname, ioaddr);
329                    release_region(ioaddr, EL1_IO_EXTENT);
330                    return -EAGAIN;
331               }
332          }
333
334     outb(AX_RESET+AX_LOOP, AX_CMD);          /* Loopback mode. */
335     dev->base_addr = ioaddr;
336     memcpy(dev->dev_addr, station_addr, ETH_ALEN);
337
338     if (dev->mem_start & 0xf)
339          el_debug = dev->mem_start & 0x7;
340     if (autoirq)
341          dev->irq = autoirq;
342
343     printk(KERN_INFO "%s: %s EtherLink at %#lx, using %sIRQ %d.\n", dev->name, mname, dev->
             base_addr,
344                    autoirq ? "auto":"assigned ", dev->irq);
```

If all is well so far, we try to allocate space for the net device structure.

Figure 5.29 Ethernet driver 2—init C: `linux/drivers/net/3c501.c`.

```
346  #ifdef CONFIG_IP_MULTICAST
347       printk(KERN_WARNING "WARNING: Use of the 3c501 in a multicast kernel is NOT recommended.\
             n");
348  #endif
349
350       if (el_debug)
351            printk("%s", version);
352
353       /*
354        *    Initialize the device structure.
355        */
356
357       dev->priv = kmalloc(sizeof(struct net_local), GFP_KERNEL);
358       if (dev->priv == NULL) {
359            release_region(ioaddr, EL1_IO_EXTENT);
360            return -ENOMEM;
361       }
362       memset(dev->priv, 0, sizeof(struct net_local));
```

This section of the startup fills in the device structure with the function pointers for this specific driver. If all is well, it then does the generic Ethernet initialization (since there is a lot in common across all Ethernet devices).

Figure 5.30 Ethernet driver 2—init d: `linux/drivers/net/3c501.c`.

```
        lp=dev->priv;
        spin_lock_init(&lp->lock);

        /*
         *      The EL1-specific entries in the device structure.
         */

        dev->open = &el_open;
        dev->hard_start_xmit = &el_start_xmit;
        dev->tx_timeout = &el_timeout;
        dev->watchdog_timeo = HZ;
        dev->stop = &el1_close;
        dev->get_stats = &el1_get_stats;
        dev->set_multicast_list = &set_multicast_list;

        /*
         *      Setup the generic properties
         */

        ether_setup(dev);

        return 0;
}

/**
 *      el1_open:
 *      @dev: device that is being opened
 *
 *      When an ifconfig is issued which changes the device flags to include
 *      IFF_UP this function is called. It is only called when the change
 *      occurs, not when the interface remains up. #el1_close will be called
```

3C501 Start Transmission

DMA network devices have quite a lot of autonomy (i.e., they can get on with quite a lot of work in parallel with the processor(s)). Sometimes, though, they can be quite slow about some phases, so it is common practice to separate out the work, and make as few (and as short) critical regions as possible.

Figure 5.31 Ethernet driver 2—txstart a: `linux/drivers/net/3c501.c`.

```
/**
 * el_start_xmit:
 * @skb: The packet that is queued to be sent
 * @dev: The 3c501 card we want to throw it down
 *
 * Attempt to send a packet to a 3c501 card. There are some interesting
 * catches here because the 3c501 is an extremely old and therefore
```

```
 * stupid piece of technology.
 *
 * If we are handling an interrupt on the other CPU we cannot load a packet
 * as we may still be attempting to retrieve the last RX packet buffer.
 *
 * When a transmit times out we dump the card into control mode and just
 * start again. It happens enough that it isnt worth logging.
 *
 * We avoid holding the spin locks when doing the packet load to the board.
 * The device is very slow, and its DMA mode is even slower. If we held the
 * lock while loading 1500 bytes onto the controller we would drop a lot of
 * serial port characters. This requires we do extra locking, but we have
 * no real choice.
 */
```

The next few code extracts show the continuation of the transmission *startup* code. Essentially (as the comments indicate), we are telling the card that there is data ready to send, and where it is, then we tell it to go away and send it, and interrupt us when done.

Figure 5.32 Ethernet driver 2—txstart a: `linux/drivers/net/3c501.c`.

```
static int el_start_xmit(struct sk_buff *skb, struct net_device *dev)
{
        struct net_local *lp = (struct net_local *)dev->priv;
        int ioaddr = dev->base_addr;
        unsigned long flags;

        /*
         *      Avoid incoming interrupts between us flipping txing and flipping
         *      mode as the driver assumes txing is a faithful indicator of card
         *      state
         */

        spin_lock_irqsave(&lp->lock, flags);

        /*
         *      Avoid timer-based retransmission conflicts.
         */

        netif_stop_queue(dev);
```

Figure 5.33 Ethernet driver 2—txstart b: `linux/drivers/net/3c501.c`.

```
        do
        {
                int gp_start = 0x800 - (ETH_ZLEN < skb->len ? skb->len : ETH_ZLEN);
                unsigned char *buf = skb->data;

```

```
            lp->tx_pkt_start = gp_start;
            lp->collisions = 0;

            lp->stats.tx_bytes += skb->len;

            /*
             *     Command mode with status cleared should [in theory]
             *     mean no more interrupts can be pending on the card.
             */

            outb_p(AX_SYS, AX_CMD);
            inb_p(RX_STATUS);
            inb_p(TX_STATUS);

            lp->loading = 1;
            lp->txing = 1;

            /*
             *     Turn interrupts back on while we spend a pleasant afternoon
             *     loading bytes into the board
             */

            spin_unlock_irqrestore(&lp->lock, flags);

            outw(0x00, RX_BUF_CLR);       /* Set rx packet area to 0. */
            outw(gp_start, GP_LOW);       /* aim - packet will be loaded into buffer start */
            outsb(DATAPORT,buf,skb->len); /* load buffer (usual thing each byte increments the
                                             pointer) */
            outw(gp_start, GP_LOW);       /* the board reuses the same register */
```

Figure 5.34 Ethernet driver 2—txstart b: `linux/drivers/net/3c501.c`.

```
            if(lp->loading != 2)
            {
                  outb(AX_XMIT, AX_CMD);        /* fire ... Trigger xmit. */
                  lp->loading=0;
                  dev->trans_start = jiffies;
                  if (el_debug > 2)
                        printk(" queued xmit.\n");
                  dev_kfree_skb (skb);
                  return 0;
            }
            /* A receive upset our load, despite our best efforts */
            if(el_debug>2)
                  printk("%s: burped during tx load.\n", dev->name);
            spin_lock_irqsave(&lp->lock, flags);
      }
      while(1);

}
```

3c501 Interrupt Handling

At the top level, we have to handle a generic device interrupt from this device and figure out then what actually happened that it is trying to tell us about (i.e., another example of demultiplexing).

Figure 5.35 Ethernet driver 3—interrupt a1: `linux/drivers/net/3c501.c`.

```
581
582          /*
583           *      What happened ?
584           */
585
586          axsr = inb(AX_STATUS);
587
588          /*
589           *      Log it
590           */
591
592          if (el_debug > 3)
593                  printk(KERN_DEBUG "%s: el_interrupt() aux=%#02x", dev->name, axsr);
594
595          if(lp->loading==1 && !lp->txing)
596                  printk(KERN_WARNING "%s: Inconsistent state loading while not in tx\n",
597                          dev->name);
```

So we read the status from the card to figure out which event triggered this.

Figure 5.36 Ethernet driver 3—interrupt a2: `linux/drivers/net/3c501.c`.

```
599          if (lp->txing)
600          {
601
602                  /*
603                   *      Board in transmit mode. May be loading. If we are
604                   *      loading we shouldn't have got this.
605                   */
606
607                  int txsr = inb(TX_STATUS);
608
609                  if(lp->loading==1)
610                  {
611                          if(el_debug > 2)
612                          {
613                                  printk(KERN_DEBUG "%s: Interrupt while loading [", dev->name);
614                                  printk(" txsr=%02x gp=%04x rp=%04x]\n", txsr, inw(GP_LOW),
615                                          inw(RX_LOW));
616                          }
617                          lp->loading=2;          /* Force a reload */
618                          spin_unlock(&lp->lock);
                             return;
```

```
        }

        if (el_debug > 6)
                printk(KERN_DEBUG " txsr=%02x gp=%04x rp=%04x", txsr, inw(GP_LOW),inw(
                      RX_LOW));
```

In many cases it may have been an error condition (such is life on a CSMA/CD network). In a few cases, we are done with something, and we want to get on with the next piece of work, so we call `netif_wake_queue` to find what more there might be to send.

Figure 5.37 Ethernet driver 3—interrupt b1: `linux/drivers/net/3c501.c`.

```
        if ((axsr & 0x80) && (txsr & TX_READY) == 0)
        {
                /*
                 *      FIXME: is there a logic to whether to keep on trying or
                 *      reset immediately ?
                 */
                if(el_debug>1)
                        printk("%s: Unusual interrupt during Tx, txsr=%02x axsr=%02x"
                                " gp=%03x rp=%03x.\n", dev->name, txsr, axsr,
                inw(ioaddr + EL1_DATAPTR), inw(ioaddr + EL1_RXPTR));
                lp->txing = 0;
                netif_wake_queue(dev);
        }
        else if (txsr & TX_16COLLISIONS)
        {
                /*
                 *      Timed out
                 */
                if (el_debug)
                        printk("%s: Transmit failed 16 times, Ethernet jammed?\n",dev->name)
                              ;
                outb(AX_SYS, AX_CMD);
                lp->txing = 0;
                lp->stats.tx_aborted_errors++;
                netif_wake_queue(dev);
        }
```

Figure 5.38 Ethernet driver 3—interrupt b2: `linux/drivers/net/3c501.c`.

```
        else if (txsr & TX_COLLISION)
        {
                /*
                 *      Retrigger xmit.
                 */
```

```

                if (el_debug > 6)
                    printk(" retransmitting after a collision.\n");
                /*
                 *     Poor little chip can't reset its own start pointer
                 */

                outb(AX_SYS, AX_CMD);
                outw(lp->tx_pkt_start, GP_LOW);
                outb(AX_XMIT, AX_CMD);
                lp->stats.collisions++;
                spin_unlock(&lp->lock);
                return;
            }
            else
            {
                /*
                 *     It worked.. we will now fall through and receive
                 */
                lp->stats.tx_packets++;
                if (el_debug > 6)
                    printk(" Tx succeeded %s\n",
                        (txsr & TX_RDY) ? "." : "but tx is busy!");
                /*
                 *     This is safe the interrupt is atomic WRT itself.
                 */

                lp->txing = 0;
                netif_wake_queue(dev); /* In case more to transmit */
            }
        }
```

Of course, there is also the case that we have received a packet. Then we want to deal with that, too.

Figure 5.39 Ethernet driver 3—interrupt c: `linux/drivers/net/3c501.c`.

```
        else
        {
            /*
             *     In receive mode.
             */

            int rxsr = inb(RX_STATUS);
            if (el_debug > 5)
                printk(" rxsr=%02x txsr=%02x rp=%04x", rxsr, inb(TX_STATUS),inw(RX_LOW));
            /*
             *     Just reading rx_status fixes most errors.
             */
            if (rxsr & RX_MISSED)
                lp->stats.rx_missed_errors++;
            else if (rxsr & RX_RUNT)
```

```
700                    {       /* Handled to avoid board lock-up. */
701                            lp->stats.rx_length_errors++;
702                            if (el_debug > 5)
703                                    printk(" runt.\n");
704                    }
705                    else if (rxsr & RX_GOOD)
706                    {
707                            /*
708                             *      Receive worked.
709                             */
710                            el_receive(dev);
711                    }
712                    else
713                    {
714                            /*
715                             *      Nothing? Something is broken!
716                             */
717                            if (el_debug > 2)
718                                    printk("%s: No packet seen, rxsr=%02x **resetting 3c501***\n",
719                                            dev->name, rxsr);
720                            el_reset(dev);
721                    }
722                    if (el_debug > 3)
723                            printk(".\n");
724            }
```

Many problems can still be present even though the hardware has delivered a packet and an interrupt to say so. We have to check for these (remember the Postel quote at the start of Chapter 3?).

Figure 5.40 Ethernet driver 3—interrupt d: `linux/drivers/net/3c501.c`.

```
726        /*
727         *      Move into receive mode
728         */
729
730        outb(AX_RX, AX_CMD);
731        outw(0x00, RX_BUF_CLR);
732        inb(RX_STATUS);         /* Be certain that interrupts are cleared. */
733        inb(TX_STATUS);
734        spin_unlock(&lp >lock);
735        return;
736  }
737
738
739  /**
740   * el_receive:
741   * @dev: Device to pull the packets from
742   *
743   * We have a good packet. Well, not really "good", just mostly not broken.
744   * We must check everything to see if it is good. In paticular we occasionally
```

```
 * get wild packet sizes from the card. If the packet seems sane we PIO it
 * off the card and queue it for the protocol layers.
 */
```

Here we start the work of receiving a packet in earnest. We check for simply illegal packet lengths, for example.

Figure 5.41 Ethernet driver 4—receive: `linux/drivers/net/3c501.c`.

```
/**
 * el_receive:
 * @dev: Device to pull the packets from
 *
 * We have a good packet. Well, not really "good", just mostly not broken.
 * We must check everything to see if it is good. In paticular we occasionally
 * get wild packet sizes from the card. If the packet seems sane we PIO it
 * off the card and queue it for the protocol layers.
 */

static void el_receive(struct net_device *dev)
{
	struct net_local *lp = (struct net_local *)dev->priv;
	int ioaddr = dev->base_addr;
	int pkt_len;
	struct sk_buff *skb;

	pkt_len = inw(RX_LOW);

	if (el_debug > 4)
		printk(" el_receive %d.\n", pkt_len);

	if ((pkt_len < 60) || (pkt_len > 1536))
	{
		if (el_debug)
			printk("%s: bogus packet, length=%d\n", dev->name, pkt_len);
		lp->stats.rx_over_errors++;
		return;
	}
```

Finally, if all is well, we call `netif_rx` on the socket buffer that has the packet data.

Figure 5.42 Ethernet driver 4—receive: `linux/drivers/net/3c501.c`.

```
	/*
	 *	Command mode so we can empty the buffer
	 */

	outb(AX_SYS, AX_CMD);
```

```
774                skb = dev_alloc_skb(pkt_len+2);
775
776                /*
777                 *      Start of frame
778                 */
779
780                outw(0x00, GP_LOW);
781                if (skb == NULL)
782                {
783                        printk("%s: Memory squeeze, dropping packet.\n", dev->name);
784                        lp->stats.rx_dropped++;
785                        return;
786                }
787                else
788                {
789                        skb_reserve(skb,2);   /* Force 16 byte alignment */
790                        skb->dev = dev;
791                        /*
792                         *      The read increments through the bytes. The interrupt
793                         *      handler will fix the pointer when it returns to
794                         *      receive mode.
795                         */
796                        insb(DATAPORT, skb_put(skb,pkt_len), pkt_len);
797                        skb->protocol=eth_type_trans(skb,dev);
798                        netif_rx(skb);
799                        lp->stats.rx_packets++;
800                        lp->stats.rx_bytes+=pkt_len;
801                }
802                return;
803        }
```

3c501 Device-Specific Statistics

Figure 5.43 Ethernet driver 4—stats: `linux/drivers/net/3c501.c`.

```
879     {
880             struct net_local *lp = (struct net_local *)dev->priv;
881             return &lp->stats;
882     }
883
884     /**
885      * set_multicast_list:
886      * @dev: The device to adjust
887      *
888      * Set or clear the multicast filter for this adaptor to use the best-effort
889      * filtering supported. The 3c501 supports only three modes of filtering.
890      * It always receives broadcasts and packets for itself. You can choose to
891      * optionally receive all packets, or all multicast packets on top of this.
892      */
893
894     static void set_multicast_list(struct net_device *dev)
```

5.4.4 Link Driver-Level Configuration

The widely used `netstat -i` command shows data such as shown in Figure 5.44.

Figure 5.44 Netstat -i.

```

Kernel Interface table
Iface   MTU Met    RX-OK RX-ERR RX-DRP RX-OVR TX-OK TX-ERR TX-DRP
TX-OVR Flg
eth0  1476   0  7545013      3      0      3  2303995      0      0 0 BRU
lo    3924   0       18      0      0      0       18      0      0 0 LRU
```

Meanwhile, the `ifconfig` command reveals

Figure 5.45 `ifconfig.`

```

[ucachgd@ovavu ucachgd]$ /sbin/ifconfig eth0
eth0      Link encap:10Mbps Ethernet HWaddr 00:C0:4F:D3:DB:C3
          inet addr:128.16.6.226 Bcast:128.16.15.255
Mask:255.255.240.0
          UP BROADCAST RUNNING MULTICAST MTU:1476 Metric:1
          RX packets:2147483647 errors:7545063 dropped:3 overruns:0
          TX packets:3 errors:0 dropped:0 overruns:207165461
          Interrupt:10 Base address:0x300
```

3c501 Multicast Support

Here is how the driver supports multicast:

Figure 5.46 Ethernet driver 4—multicast: `linux/drivers/net/3c501.c.`

```
 * optionally receive all packets, or all multicast packets on top of this.
 */

static void set_multicast_list(struct net_device *dev)
{
        int ioaddr = dev->base_addr;

        if(dev->flags&IFF_PROMISC)
        {
                outb(RX_PROM, RX_CMD);
                inb(RX_STATUS);
        }
        else if (dev->mc_list || dev->flags&IFF_ALLMULTI)
```

```
904              {
905                      outb(RX_MULT, RX_CMD); /* Multicast or all multicast is the same */
906                      inb(RX_STATUS);        /* Clear status. */
907              }
908              else
909              {
910                      outb(RX_NORM, RX_CMD);
911                      inb(RX_STATUS);
912              }
913      }
914
915      #ifdef MODULE
916
917      static struct net_device dev_3c501 = {
918              init:           el1_probe,
919              base_addr:      0x280,
920              irq:            5,
921      };
922
923      static int io=0x280;
924      static int irq=5;
925      MODULE_PARM(io, "i");
926      MODULE_PARM(irq, "i");
927
928      /**
929       * init_module:
930       *
931       * When the driver is loaded as a module this function is called. We fake up
932       * a device structure with the base I/O and interrupt set as if it was being
933       * called from Space.c. This minimises the extra code that would otherwise
934       * be required.
935       *
```

3c501 Module Support

Finally, Figure 5.47 has the interface to the kernel so that the device driver can
be installed as a module.

Figure 5.47 Ethernet driver 4—modules: `linux/drivers/net/3c501.c`.

```
954      */
955
956      void cleanup_module(void)
957      {
958              /*
959               *      No need to check MOD_IN_USE, as sys_delete_module() checks.
960               */
961
962              unregister_netdev(&dev_3c501);
963
```

```
        /*
         *      Free up the private structure, or leak memory :-)
         */

        kfree(dev_3c501.priv);
        dev_3c501.priv = NULL; /* gets re-allocated by el1_probe1 */

        /*
         *      If we don't do this, we can't re-insmod it later.
         */
        release_region(dev_3c501.base_addr, EL1_IO_EXTENT);
}

#endif /* MODULE */

/*
 * Local variables:
 *  compile-command: "gcc -D__KERNEL__ -Wall -Wstrict-prototypes -O6 -fomit-frame-pointer
        -m486 -c -o 3c501.o 3c501.c"
 *  kept-new-versions: 5
 * End:
 */
```

5.5 Top Down: Socket Glue Level

Earlier in this chapter, we looked bottom up from the generic to the specifics of driver (link)-level support for networking.

In the previous chapter, we looked at the API used to program networked applications. Now, working further down from the top level, we can look at how the user/system interface level maps onto kernel code; the kernel code looks as follows.

First, as this level was complex, there are a lot of programmers to give due credit to.

Figure 5.48 Socket interface code—authors, and so on: `linux/net/socket.c`.

```
/*
 * NET          An implementation of the SOCKET network access protocol.
 *
 * Version:     @(#)socket.c   1.1.93 18/02/95
 *
 * Authors:     Orest Zborowski, <obz@Kodak.COM>
 *              Ross Biro, <bir7@leland.Stanford.Edu>
 *              Fred N. van Kempen, <waltje@uWalt.NL.Mugnet.ORG>
 *
 * Fixes:
 *              Anonymous       :       NOTSOCK/BADF cleanup. Error fix in
 *                                      shutdown()
```

```
 *              Alan Cox        :       verify_area() fixes
 *              Alan Cox        :       Removed DDI
 *              Jonathan Kamens :       SOCK_DGRAM reconnect bug
 *              Alan Cox        :       Moved a load of checks to the very
 *                                      top level.
 *              Alan Cox        :       Move address structures to/from user
 *                                      mode above the protocol layers.
 *              Rob Janssen     :       Allow 0 length sends.
 *              Alan Cox        :       Asynchronous I/O support (cribbed from the
 *                                      tty drivers).
 *              Niibe Yutaka    :       Asynchronous I/O for writes (4.4BSD style)
 *              Jeff Uphoff     :       Made max number of sockets command-line
 *                                      configurable.
 *              Matti Aarnio    :       Made the number of sockets dynamic,
 *                                      to be allocated when needed, and mr.
 *                                      Uphoff's max is used as max to be
 *                                      allowed to allocate.
 *              Linus           :       Argh. removed all the socket allocation
 *                                      altogether: it's in the inode now.
 *              Alan Cox        :       Made sock_alloc()/sock_release() public
 *                                      for NetROM and future kernel nfsd type
 *                                      stuff.
 *              Alan Cox        :       sendmsg/recvmsg basics.
 *              Tom Dyas        :       Export net symbols.
 *              Marcin Dalecki  :       Fixed problems with CONFIG_NET="n".
 *              Alan Cox        :       Added thread locking to sys_* calls
 *                                      for sockets. May have errors at the
 *                                      moment.
 *              Kevin Buhr      :       Fixed the dumb errors in the above.
 *              Andi Kleen      :       Some small cleanups, optimizations,
 *                                      and fixed a copy_from_user() bug.
 *              Tigran Aivazian :       sys_send(args) calls sys_sendto(args, NULL, 0)
 *              Tigran Aivazian :       Made listen(2) backlog sanity checks
 *                                      protocol-independent
```

There is a copy of the GNU General Public License here, too.

Figure 5.49 Socket interface code—main copyright, and so on: `linux/net/socket.c`.

```
 *
 *              This program is free software; you can redistribute it and/or
 *              modify it under the terms of the GNU General Public License
 *              as published by the Free Software Foundation; either version
 *              2 of the License, or (at your option) any later version.
 *
 *
 *      This module is effectively the top level interface to the BSD socket
 *      paradigm.
 *
 */
```

Moving on, we can see the set of C prototypes for the set of exported functions from this API.

Figure 5.50 Socket interface code—prototypes: `linux/net/socket.c`.

```
static int sock_no_open(struct inode *irrelevant, struct file *dontcare);
static loff_t sock_lseek(struct file *file, loff_t offset, int whence);
static ssize_t sock_read(struct file *file, char *buf,
                         size_t size, loff_t *ppos);
static ssize_t sock_write(struct file *file, const char *buf,
                          size_t size, loff_t *ppos);
static int sock_mmap(struct file *file, struct vm_area_struct * vma);

static int sock_close(struct inode *inode, struct file *file);
static unsigned int sock_poll(struct file *file,
                              struct poll_table_struct *wait);
static int sock_ioctl(struct inode *inode, struct file *file,
                      unsigned int cmd, unsigned long arg);
static int sock_fasync(int fd, struct file *filp, int on);
static ssize_t sock_readv(struct file *file, const struct iovec *vector,
                          unsigned long count, loff_t *ppos);
static ssize_t sock_writev(struct file *file, const struct iovec *vector,
                          unsigned long count, loff_t *ppos);
```

As explained in Chapter 2, the socket code is yet another variant of the virtual filesystem API, so it must provide the mappings for the generic functions therein. These are wrapped up in the `file_operations` structure.

Figure 5.51 Socket interface code—file operation mappings, and so on: `linux/net/socket.c`.

```
/*
 *    Socket files have a set of 'special' operations as well as the generic file ones. These don't appear
 *    in the operation structures but are done directly via the socketcall() multiplexor.
 */

static struct file_operations socket_file_ops = {
        llseek:         sock_lseek,
        read:           sock_read,
        write:          sock_write,
        poll:           sock_poll,
        ioctl:          sock_ioctl,
        mmap:           sock_mmap,
        open:           sock_no_open,  /* special open code to disallow open via /proc */
        release:        sock_close,
        fasync:         sock_fasync,
        readv:          sock_readv,
        writev:         sock_writev
};
```

Slightly more bottom up again, we also have to have linkage to the set of protocols that the socket layer supports. This is done through an array of `net_proto_family` structures, each one holding pointers to the relevant input and output functions (and others) for that protocol family. These are discussed briefly in Chapter 3, and also in Chapter 7 on transport protocols.

Figure 5.52 Socket interface code—protocol families supported: `linux/net/socket.c`.

```
/*
 *      The protocol list. Each protocol is registered in here.
 */

static struct net_proto_family *net_families[NPROTO];

#ifdef CONFIG_SMP
static atomic_t net_family_lockct = ATOMIC_INIT(0);
static spinlock_t net_family_lock = SPIN_LOCK_UNLOCKED;
```

Locking Sockets

As discussed in Chapters 3 and 4, this is the layer in which a lot of concurrency can occur (between user processes and kernel transport protocols), thus there needs to be support for mutual exclusion and synchronization. Here is some of it.

Figure 5.53 Socket interface code—lock code: `linux/net/socket.c`.

```
/* The strategy is: modifications net_family vector are short, do not
   sleep and veeery rare, but read access should be free of any exclusive
   locks.
 */

static void net_family_write_lock(void)
{
        spin_lock(&net_family_lock);
        while (atomic_read(&net_family_lockct) != 0) {
                spin_unlock(&net_family_lock);

                current->policy |= SCHED_YIELD;
                schedule();

                spin_lock(&net_family_lock);
        }
}

static __inline__ void net_family_write_unlock(void)
{
        spin_unlock(&net_family_lock);
}
```

```
static __inline__ void net_family_read_lock(void)
{
        atomic_inc(&net_family_lockct);
        spin_unlock_wait(&net_family_lock);
}

static __inline__ void net_family_read_unlock(void)
{
        atomic_dec(&net_family_lockct);
}

#else
#define net_family_write_lock() do { } while(0)
#define net_family_write_unlock() do { } while(0)
#define net_family_read_lock() do { } while(0)
#define net_family_read_unlock() do { } while(0)
#endif
```

Each CPU needs to keep copies of this data.

Figure 5.54 Socket interface code—global counters and statistics: `linux/net/socket.c`.

```
/*
 *      Statistics counters of the socket lists
 */

static union {
        int     counter;
        char    __pad[SMP_CACHE_BYTES];
} sockets_in_use[NR_CPUS] __cacheline_aligned = {{0}};

/*
 *      Support routines. Move socket addresses back and forth across the kernel/user
 *      divide and look after the messy bits.
 */

#define MAX_SOCK_ADDR 128           /* 108 for Unix domain -
                                       16 for IP, 16 for IPX,
                                       24 for IPv6,
                                       about 80 for AX.25
                                       must be at least one bigger than
                                       the AF_UNIX size (see net/unix/af_unix.c
                                       :unix_mkname()).
                                     */
```

When moving buffers between a user process and the socket layer (actually, any virtual filesystem instance), we need to check that the buffer *is actually* owned by the user, so that we don't make any terrible privilege violations. Checks need to happen from user to kernel.

Figure 5.55 Check buffer addresses passed between the user and kernel: `linux/net/socket.c`.

```
/**
 *      move_addr_to_kernel   -      copy a socket address into kernel space
 *      @uaddr: Address in user space
 *      @kaddr: Address in kernel space
 *      @ulen: Length in user space
 *
 *      The address is copied into kernel space. If the provided address is
 *      too long an error code of -EINVAL is returned. If the copy gives
 *      invalid addresses -EFAULT is returned. On a success 0 is returned.
 */

int move_addr_to_kernel(void *uaddr, int ulen, void *kaddr)
{
        if(ulen<0||ulen>MAX_SOCK_ADDR)
                return -EINVAL;
        if(ulen==0)
                return 0;
        if(copy_from_user(kaddr,uaddr,ulen))
                return -EFAULT;
        return 0;
}
```

We also check buffers when copying data from the kernel to the user.

Figure 5.56 More legality checks: `linux/net/socket.c`.

```
/**
 *      move_addr_to_user     -      copy an address to user space
 *      @kaddr: kernel space address
 *      @klen: length of address in kernel
 *      @uaddr: user space address
 *      @ulen: pointer to user length field
 *
 *      The value pointed to by ulen on entry is the buffer length available.
 *      This is overwritten with the buffer space used. -EINVAL is returned
 *      if an overlong buffer is specified or a negative buffer size. -EFAULT
 *      is returned if either the buffer or the length field are not
 *      accessible.
 *      After copying the data up to the limit the user specifies, the true
 *      length of the data is written over the length limit the user
 *      specified. Zero is returned for a success.
 */

```

```
242    int move_addr_to_user(void *kaddr, int klen, void *uaddr, int *ulen)
243    {
244          int err;
245          int len;
246
247          if((err=get_user(len, ulen)))
248                  return err;
249          if(len>klen)
250                  len=klen;
251          if(len<0 || len> MAX_SOCK_ADDR)
252                  return -EINVAL;
253          if(len)
254          {
255                  if(copy_to_user(uaddr,kaddr,len))
256                          return -EFAULT;
257          }
258          /*
259           *      "fromlen shall refer to the value before truncation.."
260           *                      1003.1g
261           */
262          return __put_user(klen, ulen);
263    }
```

5.5.1 Virtual Filesystem Socket Instance Functions

Now we can look at the actual instances of the virtual *filesystem* functions that implement the socket (i.e., protocol interface) functions.

This function returns filesystem status—for a socket, that's not really terribly meaningful, but we try:

Figure 5.57 Socket glue—socket `statfs: linux/net/socket.c`.

```
265    #define SOCKFS_MAGIC 0x534F434B
266    static int sockfs_statfs(struct super_block *sb, struct statfs *buf)
267    {
268          buf->f_type = SOCKFS_MAGIC;
269          buf->f_bsize = 1024;
270          buf->f_namelen = 255;
271          return 0;
272    }
273
274    static struct super_operations sockfs_ops = {
275          statfs:         sockfs_statfs,
276    };
```

Read a block from a file:

Figure 5.58 Socket glue—socket `fs` `read`: `linux/net/socket.c`.

```
static struct super_block * sockfs_read_super(struct super_block *sb, void *data, int silent)
{
        struct inode *root = new_inode(sb);
        if (!root)
                return NULL;
        root->i_mode = S_IFDIR | S_IRUSR | S_IWUSR;
        root->i_uid = root->i_gid = 0;
        root->i_atime = root->i_mtime = root->i_ctime = CURRENT_TIME;
        sb->s_blocksize = 1024;
        sb->s_blocksize_bits = 10;
        sb->s_magic = SOCKFS_MAGIC;
        sb->s_op        = &sockfs_ops;
        sb->s_root = d_alloc(NULL, &(const struct qstr) { "socket:", 7, 0 });
        if (!sb->s_root) {
                iput(root);
                return NULL;
        }
        sb->s_root->d_sb = sb;
        sb->s_root->d_parent = sb->s_root;
        d_instantiate(sb->s_root, root);
        return sb;
}
```

The following operations really make very little sense at all on sockets (of any address family).

Figure 5.59 Socket glue—socket `fs` `mnt`, `delete`, `dentry`: `linux/net/socket.c`.

```
static struct vfsmount *sock_mnt;
static DECLARE_FSTYPE(sock_fs_type, "sockfs", sockfs_read_super,
        FS_NOMOUNT|FS_SINGLE);
static int sockfs_delete_dentry(struct dentry *dentry)
{
        return 1;
}
static struct dentry_operations sockfs_dentry_operations = {
        d_delete:       sockfs_delete_dentry,
};
```

Seeking is another thing that we do on storage device type filesystems, but which doesn't make a whole lot of sense on a socket.

Figure 5.60 Socket glue—`seek` (and ye shall not find): `linux/net/socket.c`.

```
/*
 *	Sockets are not seekable.
 */

static loff_t sock_lseek(struct file *file, loff_t offset, int whence)
{
	return -ESPIPE;
}
```

Memory mapping a socket doesn't really make sense.

Figure 5.61 Socket glue—`mmap`: `linux/net/socket.c`.

```
static int sock_mmap(struct file * file, struct vm_area_struct * vma)
{
	struct socket *sock = socki_lookup(file->f_dentry->d_inode);

	return sock->ops->mmap(file, sock, vma);
}
```

Mapping Socket and File Descriptors

Now we need to map descriptors so that we can use filesystem management code on socket descriptors as if they are file descriptors.

The first function finds a spare file descriptor.

Figure 5.62 Socket glue—find a spare file descriptor: `linux/net/socket.c`.

```
/*
 *	Obtains the first available file descriptor and sets it up for use.
 *
 *	This functions creates file structure and maps it to fd space
 *	of current process. On success it returns file descriptor
 *	and file struct implicitly stored in sock->file.
 *	Note that another thread may close file descriptor before we return
 *	from this function. We use the fact that now we do not refer
 *	to socket after mapping. If one day we will need it, this
 *	function will inincrement ref. count on file by 1.
 *
 *	In any case returned fd MAY BE not valid!
 *	This race condition is inavoidable
 *	with shared fd spaces, we cannot solve is inside kernel,
 *	but we take care of internal coherence yet.
 */
```

We then need to map inodes to socket descriptors, and vice versa.

Figure 5.63 Socket glue—get a file descriptor for a `sock` fd: `linux/net/socket.c`.

```
329   static int sock_map_fd(struct socket *sock)
330   {
331         int fd;
332         struct qstr this;
333         char name[32];
334
335         /*
336          *      Find a file descriptor suitable for return to the user.
337          */
338
339         fd = get_unused_fd();
340         if (fd >= 0) {
341               struct file *file = get_empty_filp();
342
343               if (!file) {
344                     put_unused_fd(fd);
345                     fd = -ENFILE;
346                     goto out;
347               }
348
349               sprintf(name, "[%lu]", sock->inode->i_ino);
350               this.name = name;
351               this.len = strlen(name);
352               this.hash = sock->inode->i_ino;
353
354               file->f_dentry = d_alloc(sock_mnt->mnt_sb->s_root, &this);
355               if (!file->f_dentry) {
356                     put_filp(file);
357                     put_unused_fd(fd);
358                     fd = -ENOMEM;
359                     goto out;
360               }
```

The next part fills in the file function points and other administrative parts of the structure.

Figure 5.64 Socket glue—get a file descriptor for a `sock` fd: `linux/net/socket.c`.

```
361               file->f_dentry->d_op = &sockfs_dentry_operations;
362               d_add(file->f_dentry, sock->inode);
363               file->f_vfsmnt = mntget(sock_mnt);
364
365               sock->file = file;
366               file->f_op = sock->inode->i_fop = &socket_file_ops;
367               file->f_mode = 3;
368               file->f_flags = O_RDWR;
```

```
369                     file->f_pos = 0;
370                     fd_install(fd, file);
371             }
372
373     out:
374             return fd;
375     }
```

We need to map the other way, too.

Figure 5.65 Socket glue—look up a file descriptor to a `sock` fd: `linux/net/socket.c`.

```
377     extern __inline__ struct socket *socki_lookup(struct inode *inode)
378     {
379             return &inode->u.socket_i;
380     }
```

Figure 5.66 Socket glue—look up a file descriptor to a `sock` fd: `linux/net/socket.c`.

```
382     /**
383      *      sockfd_lookup -        Go from a file number to its socket slot
384      *      @fd: file handle
385      *      @err: pointer to an error code return
386      *
387      *      The file handle passed in is locked and the socket it is bound
388      *      too is returned. If an error occurs the err pointer is overwritten
389      *      with a negative errno code and NULL is returned. The function checks
390      *      for both invalid handles and passing a handle which is not a socket.
391      *
392      *      On a success the socket object pointer is returned.
393      */
394
395     struct socket *sockfd_lookup(int fd, int *err)
396     {
397             struct file *file;
398             struct inode *inode;
399             struct socket *sock;
400
401             if (!(file = fget(fd)))
402             {
403                     *err = -EBADF;
404                     return NULL;
405             }
406
407             inode = file->f_dentry->d_inode;
408             if (!inode->i_sock || !(sock = socki_lookup(inode)))
409             {
410                     *err = -ENOTSOCK;
411                     fput(file);
```

```
412                     return NULL;
413             }
414
415             if (sock->file != file) {
416                     printk(KERN_ERR "socki_lookup: socket file changed!\n");
417                     sock->file = file;
418             }
419             return sock;
420     }
```

We need to allow free passage between the inode and socket descriptor space. Here is where we allocate and associate the relevant numbers.

Figure 5.67 Socket glue—allocate a socket inode: `linux/net/socket.c`.

```
422     extern __inline__ void sockfd_put(struct socket *sock)
423     {
424             fput(sock->file);
425     }
426
427     /**
428      *      sock_alloc      -       allocate a socket
429      *
430      *      Allocate a new inode and socket object. The two are bound together
431      *      and initialised. The socket is then returned. If we are out of inodes
432      *      NULL is returned.
433      */
434
435     struct socket *sock_alloc(void)
436     {
437             struct inode * inode;
438             struct socket * sock;
439
440             inode = get_empty_inode();
441             if (!inode)
442                     return NULL;
443
444             inode->i_sb = sock_mnt->mnt_sb;
445             sock = socki_lookup(inode);
446
447             inode->i_mode = S_IFSOCK|S_IRWXUGO;
448             inode->i_sock = 1;
449             inode->i_uid = current->fsuid;
450             inode->i_gid = current->fsgid;
451
452             sock->inode = inode;
453             init_waitqueue_head(&sock->wait);
454             sock->fasync_list = NULL;
455             sock->state = SS_UNCONNECTED;
456             sock->flags = 0;
457             sock->ops = NULL;
```

```
        sock->sk = NULL;
        sock->file = NULL;

        sockets_in_use[smp_processor_id()].counter++;
        return sock;
}
```

Of course, we also need to be able to return these identifiers to the pool of free ones.

Figure 5.68 Socket glue—free a socket inode: `linux/net/socket.c`.

```
/**
 *      sock_release    -       close a socket
 *      @sock: socket to close
 *
 *      The socket is released from the protocol stack if it has a release
 *      callback, and the inode is then released if the socket is bound to
 *      an inode not a file.
 */

void sock_release(struct socket *sock)
{
        if (sock->ops)
                sock->ops->release(sock);

        if (sock->fasync_list)
                printk(KERN_ERR "sock_release: fasync list not empty!\n");

        sockets_in_use[smp_processor_id()].counter--;
        if (!sock->file) {
                iput(sock->inode);
                return;
        }
        sock->file=NULL;
}
```

This was all for the convenience of the operating system so that we have a single unified interface between the system call code and various lower-level services, both filesystem and interprocess communication, including a unified set of identifiers.

Back to the VFS Socket Code Instances

Now we return to looking at more instances of socket functions that implement virtual filesystem functions—here is the code for accessing the `open()` call.

Figure 5.69 Socket glue—block opening a socket inode: `linux/net/socket.c`.

```
/*
 *      In theory you can't get an open on this inode, but /proc provides
 *      a back door. Remember to keep it shut otherwise you'll let the
 *      creepy crawlies in.
 */

static int sock_no_open(struct inode *irrelevant, struct file *dontcare)
{
        return -ENXIO;
}
```

Then we need the inverse of this to deal with tearing things down (either explicitly or after process exits).

Figure 5.70 Socket glue—shutdown: `linux/net/socket.c`.

```

/*
 *      Shutdown a socket.
 */

asmlinkage long sys_shutdown(int fd, int how)
{
        int err;
        struct socket *sock;

        if ((sock = sockfd_lookup(fd, &err))!=NULL)
        {
                err=sock->ops->shutdown(sock, how);
                sockfd_put(sock);
        }
        return err;
}
```

Finally, some real work is involved when we want to actually send or receive messages on a socket.

Figure 5.71 Socket glue—send and receive messages on a socket: `linux/net/socket.c`.

```
int sock_sendmsg(struct socket *sock, struct msghdr *msg, int size)
{
        int err;
        struct scm_cookie scm;

        err = scm_send(sock, msg, &scm);
```

```
        if (err >= 0) {
                err = sock->ops->sendmsg(sock, msg, size, &scm);
                scm_destroy(&scm);
        }
        return err;
}

int sock_recvmsg(struct socket *sock, struct msghdr *msg, int size, int flags)
{
        struct scm_cookie scm;

        memset(&scm, 0, sizeof(scm));

        size = sock->ops->recvmsg(sock, msg, size, flags, &scm);
        if (size >= 0)
                scm_recv(sock, msg, &scm, flags);

        return size;
}
```

We also need to support the `read()` call.

Figure 5.72 Socket glue—read: `linux/net/socket.c`.

```
/*
 *      Read data from a socket. ubuf is a user mode pointer. We make sure the user
 *      area ubuf...ubuf+size-1 is writable before asking the protocol.
 */

static ssize_t sock_read(struct file *file, char *ubuf,
                        size_t size, loff_t *ppos)
{
        struct socket *sock;
        struct iovec iov;
        struct msghdr msg;
        int flags;

        if (ppos != &file->f_pos)
                return -ESPIPE;
        if (size==0)            /* Match SYS5 behaviour */
                return 0;

        sock = socki_lookup(file->f_dentry->d_inode);

        msg.msg_name=NULL;
        msg.msg_namelen=0;
        msg.msg_iov=&iov;
        msg.msg_iovlen=1;
        msg.msg_control=NULL;
        msg.msg_controllen=0;
        iov.iov_base=ubuf;
```

```
        iov.iov_len=size;
        flags = !(file->f_flags & O_NONBLOCK) ? 0 : MSG_DONTWAIT;

        return sock_recvmsg(sock, &msg, size, flags);
}
```

Similarly, there's also the `write()` system call.

Figure 5.73 Socket glue—write: `linux/net/socket.c.`

```
/*
 *      Write data to a socket. We verify that the user area ubuf..ubuf+size-1
 *      is readable by the user process.
 */

static ssize_t sock_write(struct file *file, const char *ubuf,
                          size_t size, loff_t *ppos)
{
        struct socket *sock;
        struct msghdr msg;
        struct iovec iov;

        if (ppos != &file->f_pos)
                return -ESPIPE;
        if(size==0)             /* Match SYS5 behaviour */
                return 0;

        sock = socki_lookup(file->f_dentry->d_inode);

        msg.msg_name=NULL;
        msg.msg_namelen=0;
        msg.msg_iov=&iov;
        msg.msg_iovlen=1;
        msg.msg_control=NULL;
        msg.msg_controllen=0;
        msg.msg_flags=!(file->f_flags & O_NONBLOCK) ? 0 : MSG_DONTWAIT;
        if (sock->type == SOCK_SEQPACKET)
                msg.msg_flags |= MSG_EOR;
        iov.iov_base=(void *)ubuf;
        iov.iov_len=size;

        return sock_sendmsg(sock, &msg, size);
}
```

Noncontiguous I/O Buffer Parameters

The following routines manage the calls that users make with noncontiguous buffers (`iovec[]` structures).

Figure 5.74 Socket glue—`readv/writev` service routine: `linux/net/socket.c`.

```
int sock_readv_writev(int type, struct inode * inode, struct file * file,
                      const struct iovec * iov, long count, long size)
{
        struct msghdr msg;
        struct socket *sock;

        sock = socki_lookup(inode);

        msg.msg_name = NULL;
        msg.msg_namelen = 0;
        msg.msg_control = NULL;
        msg.msg_controllen = 0;
        msg.msg_iov = (struct iovec *) iov;
        msg.msg_iovlen = count;
        msg.msg_flags = (file->f_flags & O_NONBLOCK) ? MSG_DONTWAIT : 0;

        /* read() does a VERIFY_WRITE */
        if (type == VERIFY_WRITE)
                return sock_recvmsg(sock, &msg, size, msg.msg_flags);

        if (sock->type == SOCK_SEQPACKET)
                msg.msg_flags |= MSG_EOR;

        return sock_sendmsg(sock, &msg, size);
}
```

The preceding function is a service function for the separate handlers here.

Figure 5.75 Socket glue—`readv` and `writev`: `linux/net/socket.c`.

```
static ssize_t sock_readv(struct file *file, const struct iovec *vector,
                          unsigned long count, loff_t *ppos)
{
        size_t tot_len = 0;
        int i;
        for (i = 0 ; i < count ; i++)
                tot_len += vector[i].iov_len;
        return sock_readv_writev(VERIFY_WRITE, file->f_dentry->d_inode,
                                 file, vector, count, tot_len);
}

static ssize_t sock_writev(struct file *file, const struct iovec *vector,
                           unsigned long count, loff_t *ppos)
{
        size_t tot_len = 0;
        int i;
        for (i = 0 ; i < count ; i++)
                tot_len += vector[i].iov_len;
        return sock_readv_writev(VERIFY_READ, file->f_dentry->d_inode,
                                 file, vector, count, tot_len);
}
```

When a user process calls the `sendto()` socket API call, it maps into this.

Figure 5.76 Socket glue—`sendto` i: `linux/net/socket.c`.

```
1159    /*
1160     *      Send a datagram to a given address. We move the address into kernel
1161     *      space and check the user space data area is readable before invoking
1162     *      the protocol.
1163     */
1164
1165    asmlinkage long sys_sendto(int fd, void * buff, size_t len, unsigned flags,
1166                               struct sockaddr *addr, int addr_len)
1167    {
1168            struct socket *sock;
1169            char address[MAX_SOCK_ADDR];
1170            int err;
1171            struct msghdr msg;
1172            struct iovec iov;
1173
1174            sock = sockfd_lookup(fd, &err);
1175            if (!sock)
1176                    goto out;
1177            iov.iov_base=buff;
1178            iov.iov_len=len;
1179            msg.msg_name=NULL;
1180            msg.msg_iov=&iov;
1181            msg.msg_iovlen=1;
1182            msg.msg_control=NULL;
1183            msg.msg_controllen=0;
1184            msg.msg_namelen=addr_len;
```

More of this `sendto()` (probably a datagram) follows.

Figure 5.77 Socket glue—`sendto` ii: `linux/net/socket.c`.

```
1185            if(addr)
1186            {
1187                    err = move_addr_to_kernel(addr, addr_len, address);
1188                    if (err < 0)
1189                            goto out_put;
1190                    msg.msg_name=address;
1191            }
1192            if (sock->file->f_flags & O_NONBLOCK)
1193                    flags |= MSG_DONTWAIT;
1194            msg.msg_flags = flags;
1195            err = sock_sendmsg(sock, &msg, len);
1196
1197    out_put:
1198            sockfd_put(sock);
1199    out:
```

```
        return err;
}

/*
 *      Send a datagram down a socket.
 */

asmlinkage long sys_send(int fd, void * buff, size_t len, unsigned flags)
{
        return sys_sendto(fd, buff, len, flags, NULL, 0);
}
```

When a user process calls `recvfrom()`, it maps to this code. This means we have a user who wants to receive a packet (typically a datagram).

Figure 5.78 Socket glue—recvfrom: `linux/net/socket.c`.

```
/*
 *      Receive a frame from the socket and optionally record the address of the
 *      sender. We verify the buffers are writable and if needed move the
 *      sender address from kernel to user space.
 */

asmlinkage long sys_recvfrom(int fd, void * ubuf, size_t size, unsigned flags,
                             struct sockaddr *addr, int *addr_len)
{
        struct socket *sock;
        struct iovec iov;
        struct msghdr msg;
        char address[MAX_SOCK_ADDR];
        int err,err2;

        sock = sockfd_lookup(fd, &err);
        if (!sock)
                goto out;
```

Figure 5.79 Socket glue—recvfrom: `linux/net/socket.c`.

```
        msg.msg_control=NULL;
        msg.msg_controllen=0;
        msg.msg_iovlen=1;
        msg.msg_iov=&iov;
        iov.iov_len=size;
        iov.iov_base=ubuf;
        msg.msg_name=address;
        msg.msg_namelen=MAX_SOCK_ADDR;
        if (sock->file->f_flags & O_NONBLOCK)
                flags |= MSG_DONTWAIT;
```

```
        err=sock_recvmsg(sock, &msg, size, flags);

        if(err >= 0 && addr != NULL && msg.msg_namelen)
        {
                err2=move_addr_to_user(address, msg.msg_namelen, addr, addr_len);
                if(err2<0)
                        err=err2;
        }
        sockfd_put(sock);
out:
        return err;
}
```

Figure 5.80 Socket glue—`recvfrom: linux/net/socket.c.`

```
/*
 *      Receive a datagram from a socket.
 */

asmlinkage long sys_recv(int fd, void * ubuf, size_t size, unsigned flags)
{
        return sys_recvfrom(fd, ubuf, size, flags, NULL, NULL);
}
```

Socket-Layer VFS Function for ioctl

The `ioctl()` call really is an all-purpose, Swiss army knife of a system call:

Figure 5.81 Socket glue—`ioctl: linux/net/socket.c.`

```
/*
 *      With an ioctl arg may well be a user mode pointer, but we don't know what to do
 *      with it - that's up to the protocol still.
 */

int sock_ioctl(struct inode *inode, struct file *file, unsigned int cmd,
           unsigned long arg)
{
        struct socket *sock;
        int err;

        unlock_kernel();
        sock = socki_lookup(inode);
        err = sock->ops->ioctl(sock, cmd, arg);
        lock_kernel();

        return err;
}
```

Polling, as discussed in Chapter 4, is like `select()`, only simpler.

Figure 5.82 Socket glue—`poll`: `linux/net/socket.c`.

```
/* No kernel lock held - perfect */
static unsigned int sock_poll(struct file *file, poll_table * wait)
{
	struct socket *sock;

	/*
	 *	We can't return errors to poll, so it's either yes or no.
	 */
	sock = socki_lookup(file->f_dentry->d_inode);
	return sock->ops->poll(file, sock, wait);
}
```

Closing a socket frees up the appropriate resources, of course.

Figure 5.83 Socket glue—`close`: `linux/net/socket.c`.

```
int sock_close(struct inode *inode, struct file *filp)
{
	/*
	 *	It was possible the inode is NULL we were
	 *	closing an unfinished socket.
	 */

	if (!inode)
	{
		printk(KERN_DEBUG "sock_close: NULL inode\n");
		return 0;
	}
	sock_fasync(-1, filp, 0);
	sock_release(socki_lookup(inode));
	return 0;
}
```

Asynchronous Events on Sockets

The use of asynchronous input was discussed in Chapter 4. Here we see how it is mapped through the virtual filesystem again onto the socket code. Asynchronous input events are of course more likely on a network interface than a disk.

The socket layer associates a list of functions to call with the socket via a *callback* field, which are then invoked by the lower layers as necessary. Notice careful locking of the socket to avoid inconsistency in callbacks during changes to the list.

Figure 5.84 Socket glue—asynch events on sockets i: `linux/net/socket.c`.

```
/*
 *      Update the socket async list
 *
 *      Fasync_list locking strategy.
 *
 *      1. fasync_list is modified only under process context socket lock
 *         i.e. under semaphore.
 *      2. fasync_list is used under read_lock(&sk->callback_lock)
 *         or under socket lock.
 *      3. fasync_list can be used from softirq context, so that
 *         modification under socket lock have to be enhanced with
 *         write_lock_bh(&sk->callback_lock).
 *                                                      --ANK (990710)
 */
```

Figure 5.85 has more of the function.

Figure 5.85 Socket glue—asynch events on sockets ii: `linux/net/socket.c`.

```
static int sock_fasync(int fd, struct file *filp, int on)
{
        struct fasync_struct *fa, *fna=NULL, **prev;
        struct socket *sock;
        struct sock *sk;

        if (on)
        {
                fna=(struct fasync_struct *)kmalloc(sizeof(struct fasync_struct), GFP_KERNEL);
                if(fna==NULL)
                        return -ENOMEM;
        }


        sock = socki_lookup(filp->f_dentry->d_inode);

        if ((sk=sock->sk) == NULL)
                return -EINVAL;

        lock_sock(sk);

        prev=&(sock->fasync_list);

        for (fa=*prev; fa!=NULL; prev=&fa->fa_next,fa=*prev)
                if (fa->fa_file==filp)
                        break;
```

Figure 5.86 has the next part.

Figure 5.86 Socket glue—asynch events on sockets iii: `linux/net/socket.c`.

```
751        if(on)
752        {
753                if(fa!=NULL)
754                {
755                        write_lock_bh(&sk->callback_lock);
756                        fa->fa_fd=fd;
757                        write_unlock_bh(&sk->callback_lock);
758
759                        kfree(fna);
760                        goto out;
761                }
762                fna->fa_file=filp;
763                fna->fa_fd=fd;
764                fna->magic=FASYNC_MAGIC;
765                fna->fa_next=sock->fasync_list;
766                write_lock_bh(&sk->callback_lock);
767                sock->fasync_list=fna;
768                write_unlock_bh(&sk->callback_lock);
769        }
```

Here's where we handle removing a callback from the list.

Figure 5.87 Socket glue—asynch events on sockets else off ii: `linux/net/socket.c`.

```
770        else
771        {
772                if (fa!=NULL)
773                {
774                        write_lock_bh(&sk->callback_lock);
775                        *prev=fa->fa_next;
776                        write_unlock_bh(&sk->callback_lock);
777                        kfree(fa);
778                }
779        }
780
781 out:
782        release_sock(sock->sk);
783        return 0;
784 }
```

The next piece of code actually fields the asynchronous calls.

Figure 5.88 Socket glue–finish asynch events on sockets: `linux/net/socket.c`.

```
/* This function may be called only under socket lock or callback_lock */

int sock_wake_async(struct socket *sock, int how, int band)
{
        if (!sock || !sock->fasync_list)
                return -1;
        switch (how)
        {
        case 1:

                if (test_bit(SOCK_ASYNC_WAITDATA, &sock->flags))
                        break;
                goto call_kill;
        case 2:
                if (!test_and_clear_bit(SOCK_ASYNC_NOSPACE, &sock->flags))
                        break;
                /* fall through */
        case 0:
        call_kill:
                __kill_fasync(sock->fasync_list, SIGIO, band);
                break;
        case 3:
                __kill_fasync(sock->fasync_list, SIGURG, band);
        }
        return 0;
}
```

Creating a Socket

Figure 5.89 Socket glue–create a socket i: `linux/net/socket.c`.

```
int sock_create(int family, int type, int protocol, struct socket **res)
{
        int i;
        struct socket *sock;

        /*
         *      Check protocol is in range
         */
        if(family<0 || family>=NPROTO)
                return -EAFNOSUPPORT;

        /* Compatibility.

           This uglymoron is moved from INET layer to here to avoid
           deadlock in module load.
         */
```

```
        if (family == PF_INET && type == SOCK_PACKET) {
                static int warned;
                if (!warned) {
                        warned = 1;
                        printk(KERN_INFO "%s uses obsolete (PF_INET,SOCK_PACKET)\n", current->comm)
                                ;
                }
                family = PF_PACKET;
        }
```

Start up the module if it isn't already going.

Figure 5.90 Socket glue—create a socket ii: `linux/net/socket.c`.

```
        /* Attempt to load a protocol module if the find failed.
         *
         * 12/09/1996 Marcin: But! this makes REALLY only sense, if the user
         * requested real, full-featured networking support upon configuration.
         * Otherwise module support will break!
         */
        if (net_families[family]==NULL)
        {
                char module_name[30];
                sprintf(module_name,"net-pf-%d",family);
                request_module(module_name);
        }
```

Associate the module with the right protocol.

Figure 5.91 Socket glue—create a socket: `linux/net/socket.c`.

```
/*
 *      Allocate the socket and allow the family to set things up. if
 *      the protocol is 0, the family is instructed to select an appropriate
 *      default.
 */

        if (!(sock = sock_alloc()))
        {
                printk(KERN_WARNING "socket: no more sockets\n");
                i = -ENFILE;            /* Not exactly a match, but its the
                                           closest posix thing */
                goto out;
        }

        sock->type = type;

        if ((i = net_families[family]->create(sock, protocol)) < 0)
        {
```

```
                sock_release(sock);
                goto out;
        }

        *res = sock;

out:
        net_family_read_unlock();
        return i;
}
```

Creating a Socket Pair

Socket pairs are a useful way to emulate a pipe.

Figure 5.92 Socket glue—asm glue to create a socket: `linux/net/socket.c`.

```
asmlinkage long sys_socket(int family, int type, int protocol)
{
        int retval;
        struct socket *sock;

        retval = sock_create(family, type, protocol, &sock);
        if (retval < 0)
                goto out;

        retval = sock_map_fd(sock);
        if (retval < 0)
                goto out_release;

out:
        /* It may be already another descriptor 8) Not kernel problem. */
        return retval;

out_release:
        sock_release(sock);
        return retval;
}
```

Figure 5.93 Socket glue—asm glue to create a socket pair: `linux/net/socket.c`.

```
/*
 *      Create a pair of connected sockets.
 */

asmlinkage long sys_socketpair(int family, int type, int protocol, int usockvec[2])
{
        struct socket *sock1, *sock2;
```

```
918          int fd1, fd2, err;
919
920          /*
921           * Obtain the first socket and check if the underlying protocol
922           * supports the socketpair call.
923           */
924
925          err = sock_create(family, type, protocol, &sock1);
926          if (err < 0)
927                  goto out;
928
929          err = sock_create(family, type, protocol, &sock2);
930          if (err < 0)
931                  goto out_release_1;
932
933          err = sock1->ops->socketpair(sock1, sock2);
934          if (err < 0)
935                  goto out_release_both;
936
937          fd1 = fd2 = -1;
```

Figure 5.94 Socket glue—create a socket pair: `linux/net/socket.c`.

```
939          err = sock_map_fd(sock1);
940          if (err < 0)
941                  goto out_release_both;
942          fd1 = err;
943
944          err = sock_map_fd(sock2);
945          if (err < 0)
946                  goto out_close_1;
947          fd2 = err;
948
949          /* fd1 and fd2 may be already another descriptors.
950           * Not kernel problem.
951           */
952
953          err = put_user(fd1, &usockvec[0]);
954          if (!err)
955                  err = put_user(fd2, &usockvec[1]);
956          if (!err)
957                  return 0;
958
959          sys_close(fd2);
960          sys_close(fd1);
961          return err;
962
963  out_close_1:
964          sock_release(sock2);
965          sys_close(fd1);
966          return err;
967
968  out_release_both:
```

```
        sock_release(sock2);
out_release_1:
        sock_release(sock1);
out:
        return err;
}
```

Bind, Listen, Accept

All three of these functions are associated with the process of binding one or the other end of a connection to an identifier (effectively an IP address) or an active protocol association (i.e., transport-level connection).

`bind()` takes the socket and associates the local end of it with an address (typically, an IPv4 or IPv6 address).

Figure 5.95 Socket glue–bind a socket: `linux/net/socket.c`.

```
/*
 *      Bind a name to a socket. Nothing much to do here since it's
 *      the protocol's responsibility to handle the local address.
 *
 *      We move the socket address to kernel space before we call
 *      the protocol layer (having also checked the address is ok).
 */

asmlinkage long sys_bind(int fd, struct sockaddr *umyaddr, int addrlen)
{
        struct socket *sock;
        char address[MAX_SOCK_ADDR];
        int err;

        if((sock = sockfd_lookup(fd,&err))!=NULL)
        {
                if((err=move_addr_to_kernel(umyaddr,addrlen,address))>=0)
                        err = sock->ops->bind(sock, (struct sockaddr *)address, addrlen);
                sockfd_put(sock);
        }
        return err;
}
```

tt `listen()` deals with awaiting an inbound connection request.

Figure 5.96 Socket glue–listen on a socket: `linux/net/socket.c`.

```
/*
 *      Perform a listen. Basically, we allow the protocol to do anything
 *      necessary for a listen, and if that works, we mark the socket as
 *      ready for listening.
```

```
 */

asmlinkage long sys_listen(int fd, int backlog)
{
        struct socket *sock;
        int err;

        if ((sock = sockfd_lookup(fd, &err)) != NULL) {
                if ((unsigned) backlog > SOMAXCONN)
                        backlog = SOMAXCONN;
                err=sock->ops->listen(sock, backlog);
                sockfd_put(sock);
        }
        return err;
}
```

`accept()` is called when an inbound connection request informs the application by a return value from `listen()`.

Figure 5.97 Socket glue—accept on a socket: `linux/net/socket.c`.

```
/*
 *      For accept, we attempt to create a new socket, set up the link
 *      with the client, wake up the client, then return the new
 *      connected fd. We collect the address of the connector in kernel
 *      space and move it to user at the very end. This is unclean because
 *      we open the socket then return an error.
 *
 *      1003.1g adds the ability to recvmsg() to query connection pending
 *      status to recvmsg. We need to add that support in a way thats
 *      clean when we restucture accept also.
 */
```

And there's some more work here on accepting a connection.

Figure 5.98 Socket glue—accept on a socket i: `linux/net/socket.c`.

```
asmlinkage long sys_accept(int fd, struct sockaddr *upeer_sockaddr, int *upeer_addrlen)
{
        struct socket *sock, *newsock;
        int err, len;
        char address[MAX_SOCK_ADDR];

        sock = sockfd_lookup(fd, &err);
        if (!sock)
                goto out;

        err = -EMFILE;
        if (!(newsock = sock_alloc()))
```

```
                goto out_put;

        newsock->type = sock->type;
        newsock->ops = sock->ops;

        err = sock->ops->accept(sock, newsock, sock->file->f_flags);
        if (err < 0)
                goto out_release;
```

If all is well, we go ahead.

Figure 5.99 Socket glue—accept on a socket ii: `linux/net/socket.c`.

```
        if (upeer_sockaddr) {
                if(newsock->ops->getname(newsock, (struct sockaddr *)address, &len, 2)<0) {
                        err = -ECONNABORTED;
                        goto out_release;
                }
                err = move_addr_to_user(address, len, upeer_sockaddr, upeer_addrlen);
                if (err < 0)
                        goto out_release;
        }

        /* File flags are not inherited via accept() unlike another OSes. */

        if ((err = sock_map_fd(newsock)) < 0)
                goto out_release;

out_put:
        sockfd_put(sock);
out:
        return err;

out_release:
        sock_release(newsock);
        goto out_put;
}
```

At the other end of things, the active (client) end of a protocol calls this to cause the protocol to try to set up a connection to a given remote address.

Figure 5.100 Socket glue—connect on a socket: `linux/net/socket.c`.

```
/*
 *      Attempt to connect to a socket with the server address. The address
 *      is in user space so we verify it is OK and move it to kernel space.
 *
```

```
1085   *      For 1003.1g we need to add clean support for a bind to AF_UNSPEC to
1086   *      break bindings
1087   *
1088   *      NOTE: 1003.1g draft 6.3 is broken with respect to AX.25/NetROM and
1089   *      other SEQPACKET protocols that take time to connect() as it doesn't
1090   *      include the -EINPROGRESS status for such sockets.
1091   */
1092
1093   asmlinkage long sys_connect(int fd, struct sockaddr *uservaddr, int addrlen)
1094   {
1095         struct socket *sock;
1096         char address[MAX_SOCK_ADDR];
1097         int err;
1098
1099         sock = sockfd_lookup(fd, &err);
1100         if (!sock)
1101               goto out;
1102         err = move_addr_to_kernel(uservaddr, addrlen, address);
1103         if (err < 0)
1104               goto out_put;
1105         err = sock->ops->connect(sock, (struct sockaddr *) address, addrlen,
1106                           sock->file->f_flags);
1107   out_put:
1108         sockfd_put(sock);
1109   out:
1110         return err;
1111   }
```

Bookkeeping of Connection Identifiers

We can ask the socket layer for the addresses that the local, or far end, of a connection are bound to.

Figure 5.101 Socket glue—get the local name (address) of a socket: `linux/net/socket.c`.

```
1113   /*
1114    *      Get the local address ('name') of a socket object. Move the obtained
1115    *      name to user space.
1116    */
1117
1118   asmlinkage long sys_getsockname(int fd, struct sockaddr *usockaddr, int *usockaddr_len)
1119   {
1120         struct socket *sock;
1121         char address[MAX_SOCK_ADDR];
1122         int len, err;
1123
1124         sock = sockfd_lookup(fd, &err);
1125         if (!sock)
1126               goto out;
1127         err = sock->ops->getname(sock, (struct sockaddr *)address, &len, 0);
1128         if (err)
```

```
                goto out_put;
        err = move_addr_to_user(address, len, usockaddr, usockaddr_len);

out_put:
        sockfd_put(sock);
out:
        return err;
}
```

In this case, it is like asking "Where did a connection come from?"

Figure 5.102 Socket glue—get the far end's name (address) for a socket: `linux/net/socket.c`.

```
/*
 *      Get the remote address ('name') of a socket object. Move the obtained
 *      name to user space.
 */

asmlinkage long sys_getpeername(int fd, struct sockaddr *usockaddr, int *usockaddr_len)
{
        struct socket *sock;
        char address[MAX_SOCK_ADDR];
        int len, err;

        if ((sock = sockfd_lookup(fd, &err))!=NULL)
        {
                err = sock->ops->getname(sock, (struct sockaddr *)address, &len, 1);
                if (!err)
                        err=move_addr_to_user(address,len, usockaddr, usockaddr_len);
                sockfd_put(sock);
        }
        return err;
}
```

Here we set various socket layer parameters (see the previous chapter for the use and meaning of these).

Figure 5.103 Socket glue—`setsockopt`: `linux/net/socket.c`.

```
/*
 *      Set a socket option. Because we don't know the option lengths we have
 *      to pass the user mode parameter for the protocols to sort out.
 */

asmlinkage long sys_setsockopt(int fd, int level, int optname, char *optval, int optlen)
```

```
{
        int err;
        struct socket *sock;

        if ((sock = sockfd_lookup(fd, &err))!=NULL)
        {
                if (level == SOL_SOCKET)
                        err=sock_setsockopt(sock,level,optname,optval,optlen);
                else
                        err=sock->ops->setsockopt(sock, level, optname, optval, optlen);
                sockfd_put(sock);
        }
        return err;
}
```

Here we get various socket parameters (see the previous chapter).

Figure 5.104 Socket glue—`getsockopt`: `linux/net/socket.c`.

```
/*
 *      Get a socket option. Because we don't know the option lengths we have
 *      to pass a user mode parameter for the protocols to sort out.
 */

asmlinkage long sys_getsockopt(int fd, int level, int optname, char *optval, int *optlen)
{
        int err;
        struct socket *sock;

        if ((sock = sockfd_lookup(fd, &err))!=NULL)
        {
                if (level == SOL_SOCKET)
                        err=sock_getsockopt(sock,level,optname,optval,optlen);
                else
                        err=sock->ops->getsockopt(sock, level, optname, optval, optlen);
                sockfd_put(sock);
        }
        return err;
}
```

BSDisms—These Calls Are Derived Specifically from BSD UNIX

As well as reading, writing, `sendto`, `recvfrom`, and the `iovec` versions, we also have the interface for message-like structures that derives from the

BSD UNIX family.

Figure 5.105 Socket glue—sendmsg i: `linux/net/socket.c`.

```
1323  /*
1324   *      BSD sendmsg interface
1325   */
1326
1327  asmlinkage long sys_sendmsg(int fd, struct msghdr *msg, unsigned flags)
1328  {
1329          struct socket *sock;
1330          char address[MAX_SOCK_ADDR];
1331          struct iovec iovstack[UIO_FASTIOV], *iov = iovstack;
1332          unsigned char ctl[sizeof(struct cmsghdr) + 20]; /* 20 is size of ipv6_pktinfo */
1333          unsigned char *ctl_buf = ctl;
1334          struct msghdr msg_sys;
1335          int err, ctl_len, iov_size, total_len;
1336
1337          err = -EFAULT;
1338          if (copy_from_user(&msg_sys,msg,sizeof(struct msghdr)))
1339                  goto out;
1340
1341          sock = sockfd_lookup(fd, &err);
1342          if (!sock)
1343                  goto out;
1344
1345          /* do not move before msg_sys is valid */
1346          err = -EINVAL;
1347          if (msg_sys.msg_iovlen > UIO_MAXIOV)
1348                  goto out_put;
1349
1350          /* Check whether to allocate the iovec area*/
1351          err = -ENOMEM;
1352          iov_size = msg_sys.msg_iovlen * sizeof(struct iovec);
1353          if (msg_sys.msg_iovlen > UIO_FASTIOV) {
1354                  iov = sock_kmalloc(sock->sk, iov_size, GFP_KERNEL);
1355                  if (!iov)
1356                          goto out_put;
1357          }
```

Figure 5.106 Socket glue—sendmsg ii: `linux/net/socket.c`.

```
1359          /* This will also move the address data into kernel space */
1360          err = verify_iovec(&msg_sys, iov, address, VERIFY_READ);
1361          if (err < 0)
1362                  goto out_freeiov;
1363          total_len = err;
1364
1365          err = -ENOBUFS;
1366
1367          if (msg_sys.msg_controllen > INT_MAX)
1368                  goto out_freeiov;
1369          ctl_len = msg_sys.msg_controllen;
```

```
1370            if (ctl_len)
1371            {
1372                    if (ctl_len > sizeof(ctl))
1373                    {
1374                            ctl_buf = sock_kmalloc(sock->sk, ctl_len, GFP_KERNEL);
1375                            if (ctl_buf == NULL)
1376                                    goto out_freeiov;
1377                    }
1378                    err = -EFAULT;
1379                    if (copy_from_user(ctl_buf, msg_sys.msg_control, ctl_len))
1380                            goto out_freectl;
1381                    msg_sys.msg_control = ctl_buf;
1382            }
1383            msg_sys.msg_flags = flags;
1384
1385            if (sock->file->f_flags & O_NONBLOCK)
1386                    msg_sys.msg_flags |= MSG_DONTWAIT;
1387            err = sock_sendmsg(sock, &msg_sys, total_len);
1388
1389    out_freectl:
1390            if (ctl_buf != ctl)
1391                    sock_kfree_s(sock->sk, ctl_buf, ctl_len);
1392    out_freeiov:
1393            if (iov != iovstack)
1394                    sock_kfree_s(sock->sk, iov, iov_size);
1395    out_put:
1396            sockfd_put(sock);
1397    out:
1398            return err;
1399    }
```

Figure 5.107 Socket glue—`recvmsg` i: `linux/net/socket.c`.

```
1401    /*
1402     *      BSD recvmsg interface
1403     */
1404
1405    asmlinkage long sys_recvmsg(int fd, struct msghdr *msg, unsigned int flags)
1406    {
1407            struct socket *sock;
1408            struct iovec iovstack[UIO_FASTIOV];
1409            struct iovec *iov=iovstack;
1410            struct msghdr msg_sys;
1411            unsigned long cmsg_ptr;
1412            int err, iov_size, total_len, len;
1413
1414            /* kernel mode address */
1415            char addr[MAX_SOCK_ADDR];
1416
1417            /* user mode address pointers */
1418            struct sockaddr *uaddr;
1419            int *uaddr_len;
1420
1421            err=-EFAULT;
```

```
1422                if (copy_from_user(&msg_sys,msg,sizeof(struct msghdr)))
1423                        goto out;
1424
1425            sock = sockfd_lookup(fd, &err);
1426            if (!sock)
1427                    goto out;
1428
1429            err = -EINVAL;
1430            if (msg_sys.msg_iovlen > UIO_MAXIOV)
1431                    goto out_put;
1432
1433            /* Check whether to allocate the iovec area*/
1434            err = -ENOMEM;
1435            iov_size = msg_sys.msg_iovlen * sizeof(struct iovec);
1436            if (msg_sys.msg_iovlen > UIO_FASTIOV) {
1437                    iov = sock_kmalloc(sock->sk, iov_size, GFP_KERNEL);
1438                    if (!iov)
1439                            goto out_put;
1440            }
```

Figure 5.108 Socket glue—recvmsg ii: `linux/net/socket.c`.

```
1442            /*
1443             *      Save the user-mode address (verify_iovec will change the
1444             *      kernel msghdr to use the kernel address space)
1445             */
1446
1447            uaddr = msg_sys.msg_name;
1448            uaddr_len = &msg->msg_namelen;
1449            err = verify_iovec(&msg_sys, iov, addr, VERIFY_WRITE);
1450            if (err < 0)
1451                    goto out_freeiov;
1452            total_len=err;
1453
1454            cmsg_ptr = (unsigned long)msg_sys.msg_control;
1455            msg_sys.msg_flags = 0;
1456
1457            if (sock->file->f_flags & O_NONBLOCK)
1458                    flags |= MSG_DONTWAIT;
1459            err = sock_recvmsg(sock, &msg_sys, total_len, flags);
1460            if (err < 0)
1461                    goto out_freeiov;
1462            len = err;
1463
1464            if (uaddr != NULL && msg_sys.msg_namelen) {
1465                    err = move_addr_to_user(addr, msg_sys.msg_namelen, uaddr, uaddr_len);
1466                    if (err < 0)
1467                            goto out_freeiov;
1468            }
1469            err = __put_user(msg_sys.msg_flags, &msg->msg_flags);
1470            if (err)
1471                    goto out_freeiov;
1472            err = __put_user((unsigned long)msg_sys.msg_control-cmsg_ptr,
1473                                                    &msg->msg_controllen);
```

```
1474          if (err)
1475                  goto out_freeiov;
1476          err = len;
1477
1478   out_freeiov:
1479          if (iov != iovstack)
1480                  sock_kfree_s(sock->sk, iov, iov_size);
1481   out_put:
1482          sockfd_put(sock);
1483   out:
1484          return err;
1485   }
```

Other VFS Calls

Figure 5.109 Socket glue—file control (fcntl): linux/net/socket.c.

```
1488   /*
1489    *      Perform a file control on a socket file descriptor.
1490    *
1491    *      Doesn't acquire a fd lock, because no network fcntl
1492    *      function sleeps currently.
1493    */
1494
1495   int sock_fcntl(struct file *filp, unsigned int cmd, unsigned long arg)
1496   {
1497          struct socket *sock;
1498
1499          sock = socki_lookup (filp->f_dentry->d_inode);
1500          if (sock && sock->ops)
1501                  return sock_no_fcntl(sock, cmd, arg);
1502          return(-EINVAL);
1503   }
1504
1505   /* Argument list sizes for sys_socketcall */
1506   #define AL(x) ((x) * sizeof(unsigned long))
1507   static unsigned char nargs[18]={AL(0),AL(3),AL(3),AL(3),AL(2),AL(3),
1508                          AL(3),AL(3),AL(4),AL(4),AL(4),AL(6),
1509                          AL(6),AL(2),AL(5),AL(5),AL(3),AL(3)};
1510   #undef AL
```

Figure 5.110 Socket glue—system call vector: linux/net/socket.c.

```
1512   /*
1513    *      System call vectors.
1514    *
1515    *      Argument checking cleaned up. Saved 20% in size.
1516    * This function doesn't need to set the kernel lock because
1517    * it is set by the callees.
1518    */
1519
```

```
asmlinkage long sys_socketcall(int call, unsigned long *args)
{
        unsigned long a[6];
        unsigned long a0,a1;
        int err;

        if(call<1||call>SYS_RECVMSG)
                return -EINVAL;

        /* copy_from_user should be SMP safe. */
        if (copy_from_user(a, args, nargs[call]))
                return -EFAULT;

        a0=a[0];
```

Figure 5.111 Socket glue—system call vector: `linux/net/socket.c`.

```
        switch(call)
        {
                case SYS_SOCKET:
                        err = sys_socket(a0,a1,a[2]);
                        break;
                case SYS_BIND:
                        err = sys_bind(a0,(struct sockaddr *)a1, a[2]);
                        break;
                case SYS_CONNECT:
                        err = sys_connect(a0, (struct sockaddr *)a1, a[2]);
                        break;
                case SYS_LISTEN:
                        err = sys_listen(a0,a1);
                        break;
                case SYS_ACCEPT:
                        err = sys_accept(a0,(struct sockaddr *)a1, (int *)a[2]);
                        break;
                case SYS_GETSOCKNAME:
                        err = sys_getsockname(a0,(struct sockaddr *)a1, (int *)a[2]);
                        break;
                case SYS_GETPEERNAME:
                        err = sys_getpeername(a0, (struct sockaddr *)a1, (int *)a[2]);
                        break;
                case SYS_SOCKETPAIR:
                        err = sys_socketpair(a0,a1, a[2], (int *)a[3]);
                        break;
                case SYS_SEND:
                        err = sys_send(a0, (void *)a1, a[2], a[3]);
                        break;
                case SYS_SENDTO:
                        err = sys_sendto(a0,(void *)a1, a[2], a[3],
                                         (struct sockaddr *)a[4], a[5]);
                        break;
                case SYS_RECV:
                        err = sys_recv(a0, (void *)a1, a[2], a[3]);
                        break;
```

```
            case SYS_RECVFROM:
                    err = sys_recvfrom(a0, (void *)a1, a[2], a[3],
                                    (struct sockaddr *)a[4], (int *)a[5]);
                    break;
```

Figure 5.112 Socket glue—system call vector: `linux/net/socket.c`.

```
            case SYS_SHUTDOWN:
                    err = sys_shutdown(a0,a1);
                    break;
            case SYS_SETSOCKOPT:
                    err = sys_setsockopt(a0, a1, a[2], (char *)a[3], a[4]);
                    break;
            case SYS_GETSOCKOPT:
                    err = sys_getsockopt(a0, a1, a[2], (char *)a[3], (int *)a[4]);
                    break;
            case SYS_SENDMSG:
                    err = sys_sendmsg(a0, (struct msghdr *) a1, a[2]);
                    break;
            case SYS_RECVMSG:
                    err = sys_recvmsg(a0, (struct msghdr *) a1, a[2]);
                    break;
            default:
                    err = -EINVAL;
                    break;
        }
        return err;
}
```

Associating a Protocol with the Socket Layer

We can dynamically install protocol families at run time.

Figure 5.113 Socket glue—registering a protocol family with the socket module: `linux/net/socket.c`.

```
/*
 *      This function is called by a protocol handler that wants to
 *      advertise its address family, and have it linked into the
 *      SOCKET module.
 */

int sock_register(struct net_proto_family *ops)
{
        int err;

        if (ops->family >= NPROTO) {
                printk(KERN_CRIT "protocol %d >= NPROTO(%d)\n", ops->family, NPROTO);
```

```
                return -ENOBUFS;
        }
        net_family_write_lock();
        err = -EEXIST;
        if (net_families[ops->family] == NULL) {
                net_families[ops->family]=ops;
                err = 0;
        }
        net_family_write_unlock();
        return err;
}
```

We may also want to remove socket protocols, so they need to be deregistered.

Figure 5.114 Socket glue—unregistering a protocol family with the socket module: `linux/net/socket.c`.

```
/*
 *      This function is called by a protocol handler that wants to
 *      remove its address family, and have it unlinked from the
 *      SOCKET module.
 */

int sock_unregister(int family)
{
        if (family < 0 || family >= NPROTO)
                return -1;

        net_family_write_lock();
        net_families[family]=NULL;
        net_family_write_unlock();
        return 0;
}
```

Figure 5.115 Socket glue—initializing the socket VFS module: `linux/net/socket.c`.

```
void __init sock_init(void)
{
        int i;

        printk(KERN_INFO "Linux NET4.0 for Linux 2.4\n");
        printk(KERN_INFO "Based upon Swansea University Computer Society NET3.039\n");

        /*
         *      Initialize all address (protocol) families.
         */

        for (i = 0; i < NPROTO; i++)
                net_families[i] = NULL;

```

```
1660          /*
1661           *      Initialize sock SLAB cache.
1662           */
1663
1664          sk_init();
1665
1666  #ifdef SLAB_SKB
1667          /*
1668           *      Initialize skbuff SLAB cache
1669           */
1670          skb_init();
1671  #endif
1672
1673          /*
1674           *      Wan router layer.
1675           */
1676
1677  #ifdef CONFIG_WAN_ROUTER
1678          wanrouter_init();
1679  #endif
```

Then the socket VFS module itself may be installed or removed at run time, too, as needed.

Figure 5.116 Socket glue–initializing the socket VFS module: `linux/net/socket.c`.

```
1681          /*
1682           *      Initialize the protocols module.
1683           */
1684
1685          register_filesystem(&sock_fs_type);
1686          sock_mnt = kern_mount(&sock_fs_type);
1687          /* The real protocol initialization is performed when
1688           * do_initcalls is run.
1689           */
1690
1691
1692          /*
1693           * The netlink device handler may be needed early.
1694           */
1695
1696  #ifdef CONFIG_RTNETLINK
1697          rtnetlink_init();
1698  #endif
1699  #ifdef CONFIG_NETLINK_DEV
1700          init_netlink();
1701  #endif
1702  #ifdef CONFIG_NETFILTER
1703          netfilter_init();
1704  #endif
1705  }
```

And we also need to keep statistics (per CPU) on the socket module layer.

Figure 5.117 Socket glue—socket stats per CPU: `linux/net/socket.c`.

```
1707  int socket_get_info(char *buffer, char **start, off_t offset, int length)
1708  {
1709          int len, cpu;
1710          int counter = 0;
1711
1712          for (cpu=0; cpu<smp_num_cpus; cpu++)
1713                  counter += sockets_in_use[cpu_logical_map(cpu)].counter;
1714
1715          /* It can be negative, by the way. 8) */
1716          if (counter < 0)
1717                  counter = 0;
1718
1719          len = sprintf(buffer, "sockets: used %d\n", counter);
1720          if (offset >= len)
1721          {
1722                  *start = buffer;
1723                  return 0;
1724          }
1725          *start = buffer + offset;
1726          len -= offset;
1727          if (len > length)
1728                  len = length;
1729          if (len < 0)
1730                  len = 0;
1731          return len;
1732  }
```

5.6 Sideways: A Day in the Life of a Socket Buffer

Linux has a fairly complex sophisticated network buffer type, which is somewhat different than other open source operating systems that have been documented.

Figure 5.118 statically tries to show the regions of the sk_buff structure— these change dynamically as a reference to a buffer is moved up and down the stack. Essentially, buffers are allocated at the producer end of a producer/ consumer chain, passed through the protocol layers, and freed back to the pool at the consumer end. Thus for input, drivers allocate buffers and pass them up through the demultiplexing layers to the socket layer, where data is copied into user space and the buffer freed. For output, the data is copied from user space into buffers allocated by the transport protocol and passed down through the layers until it is transmitted.

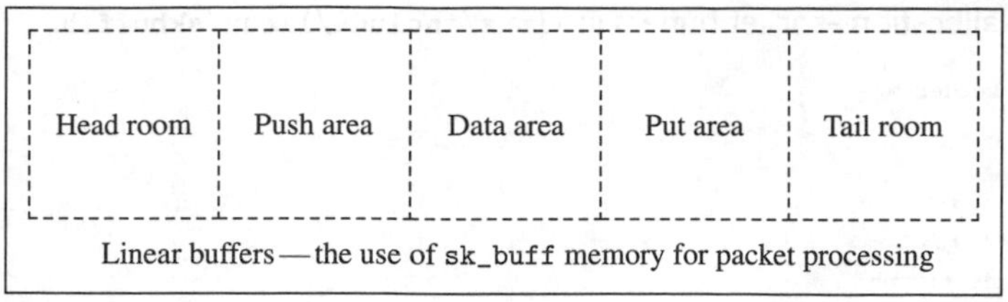

Figure 5.118 `sk_buff` structure layout.

Notice that if this discipline is followed systematically, there is at most one copy (ignoring the DMA from a device into memory), and that even this can be eliminated (and has been in some research Linux systems) by carrying out the kernel/user space mapping via memory management and marking the buffer as copy-on-write.

The `sk_buff` structure is critical to understanding the networking code. It is used to hold a plethora of different types of network data, although principally this is packet buffers (including their nested headers and so forth).

In the next two listings in Figures 5.119 and 5.120, you can see the way that these structures are part of a linked list, and can in fact be on several lists. They can be owned by a socket that is sending or about to receive them (high-level interface), and have a link to a device that they either arrived on or will be sent on (low-level interface). There is a timestamp associated with when they were last timestamped (it depends on the use or last protocol that touched the field and how it wishes to communicate with the next one—this can be particularly useful in scheduling packet output, as discussed in Chapter 9).

Figure 5.119 Memory allocation–socket buffers i: `linux/include/linux/skbuff.h`.

```
struct sk_buff {
        /* These two members must be first. */
        struct sk_buff * next;          /* Next buffer in list                 */
        struct sk_buff * prev;          /* Previous buffer in list             */

        struct sk_buff_head * list;     /* List we are on                      */
        struct sock    *sk;             /* Socket we are owned by              */
        struct timeval stamp;           /* Time we arrived                     */
        struct net_device     *dev;     /* Device we arrived on/are leaving by */
```

The socket buffer structure *overlays* a number of possible interpretations of the actual contents of the memory it points to—the headers have to include transport, network, and link layer information for fast access and multiplexing/demultiplexing, but for each protocol layer, the `union` of all types of different packet header for the different available protocols at that layer is used for programming convenience.

Figure 5.120 Memory allocation–socket buffers ii: `linux/include/linux/skbuff.h`.

```
        /* Transport layer header */
        union
        {
                struct tcphdr *th;
                struct udphdr *uh;
                struct icmphdr *icmph;
                struct igmphdr *igmph;
                struct iphdr   *ipiph;
                struct spxhdr *spxh;
                unsigned char *raw;
        } h;

        /* Network layer header */
        union
        {
                struct iphdr   *iph;
                struct ipv6hdr *ipv6h;
                struct arphdr *arph;
                struct ipxhdr *ipxh;
                unsigned char *raw;
        } nh;

        /* Link layer header */
        union
        {
                struct ethhdr *ethernet;
                unsigned char  *raw;
        } mac;

        struct dst_entry *dst;
```

Manipulating `sk_buffs`

There are a number of functions for manipulating socket buffers. Figure 5.121 has the definitions of the publicly available ones.

Figure 5.121 Memory allocation–socket buffers routines: `linux/include/linux/skbuff.h`.

```
extern void                 __kfree_skb(struct sk_buff *skb);
extern struct sk_buff *     skb_peek_copy(struct sk_buff_head *list);
extern struct sk_buff *     alloc_skb(unsigned int size, int priority);
extern void                 kfree_skbmem(struct sk_buff *skb);
extern struct sk_buff *     skb_clone(struct sk_buff *skb, int priority);
extern struct sk_buff *     skb_copy(const struct sk_buff *skb, int priority);
extern struct sk_buff *     skb_copy_expand(const struct sk_buff *skb,
                                      int newheadroom,
                                      int newtailroom,
                                      int priority);
#define dev_kfree_skb(a)     kfree_skb(a)
```

```
extern void    skb_over_panic(struct sk_buff *skb, int len, void *here);
extern void    skb_under_panic(struct sk_buff *skb, int len, void *here);

/* Backwards compatibility */
#define skb_realloc_headroom(skb, nhr) skb_copy_expand(skb, nhr, skb_tailroom(skb), GFP_ATOMIC)
```

5.6.1 Allocating a Socket Buffer

Figure 5.122 Memory allocation–socket buffers code.

```
struct sk_buff *alloc_skb(unsigned int size,int gfp_mask)
{
        struct sk_buff *skb;
        u8 *data;

        if (in_interrupt() && (gfp_mask & __GFP_WAIT)) {
                static int count = 0;
                if (++count < 5) {
                        printk(KERN_ERR "alloc_skb called nonatomically "
                                "from interrupt %p\n", NET_CALLER(size));
                        BUG();
                }
                gfp_mask &= ~__GFP_WAIT;
        }

        /* Get the HEAD */
        skb = skb_head_from_pool();
        if (skb == NULL) {
                skb = kmem_cache_alloc(skbuff_head_cache, gfp_mask);
                if (skb == NULL)
                        goto nohead;
        }

        /* Get the DATA. Size must match skb_add_mtu(). */
        size = ((size + 15) & ~15);
        data = kmalloc(size + sizeof(atomic_t), gfp_mask);
        if (data == NULL)
                goto nodata;
```

Figure 5.123 Memory allocation–socket buffers code.

```
        /* XXX: does not include slab overhead */
        skb->truesize = size + sizeof(struct sk_buff);

        /* Load the data pointers. */
        skb->head = data;
        skb->data = data;
        skb->tail = data;
        skb->end = data + size;

```

```
203              /* Set up other state */
204              skb->len = 0;
205              skb->cloned = 0;
206
207              atomic_set(&skb->users, 1);
208              atomic_set(skb_datarefp(skb), 1);
209              return skb;
210
211 nodata:
212              skb_head_to_pool(skb);
213 nohead:
214              return NULL;
215 }
```

In TCP, there is a wrapper function for this, called `tcp_alloc_skb()`.

Figure 5.124 TCP memory allocation—socket buffers code.

```
1680 static inline struct sk_buff *tcp_alloc_skb(struct sock *sk, int size, int gfp)
1681 {
1682         struct sk_buff *skb = alloc_skb(size, gfp);
1683
1684         if (skb) {
1685                 if (sk->forward_alloc >= (int)skb->truesize ||
1686                     tcp_mem_schedule(sk, skb->truesize, 0))
1687                         return skb;
1688                 __kfree_skb(skb);
1689         } else {
1690                 tcp_enter_memory_pressure();
1691                 tcp_moderate_sndbuf(sk);
1692         }
1693         return NULL;
1694 }
```

Here we see the definition of the standard functions for accessing the `skbuff` structure.

Figure 5.125 Socket buffer kernel globals: `linux/net/core/skbuff.c`.

```
65 int sysctl_hot_list_len = 128;
66
67 static kmem_cache_t *skbuff_head_cache;
68
69 static union {
70         struct sk_buff_head  list;
71         char                 pad[SMP_CACHE_BYTES];
72 } skb_head_pool[NR_CPUS];
```

5.6.2 Allocating and Freeing a Socket Buffer from the Global Pool

Figure 5.126 Socket buffer head from/to pool: `linux/net/core/skbuff.c`.

```
static __inline__ struct sk_buff *skb_head_from_pool(void)
{
        struct sk_buff_head *list = &skb_head_pool[smp_processor_id()].list;

        if (skb_queue_len(list)) {
                struct sk_buff *skb;
                unsigned long flags;

                local_irq_save(flags);
                skb = __skb_dequeue(list);
                local_irq_restore(flags);
                return skb;
        }
        return NULL;
}

static __inline__ void skb_head_to_pool(struct sk_buff *skb)
{
        struct sk_buff_head *list = &skb_head_pool[smp_processor_id()].list;

        if (skb_queue_len(list) < sysctl_hot_list_len) {
                unsigned long flags;

                local_irq_save(flags);
                __skb_queue_head(list, skb);
                local_irq_restore(flags);

                return;
        }
        kmem_cache_free(skbuff_head_cache, skb);
}
```

The following extract from the `skbuff` code describes the allocation of a socket buffer in some detail.

Figure 5.127 Allocate socket buffer—comment: `linux/net/core/skbuff.c`.

```
/**
 *      alloc_skb       -       allocate a network buffer
 *      @size: size to allocate
 *      @gfp_mask: allocation mask
 *
 *      Allocate a new &sk_buff. The returned buffer has no headroom and a
 *      tail room of size bytes. The object has a reference count of one.
 *      The return is the buffer. On a failure the return is %NULL.
```

```
160    *
161    *       Buffers may only be allocated from interrupts using a @gfp_mask of
162    *       %GFP_ATOMIC.
163    */
```

The code to allocate a socket buffer calls lower-level kernel functions to actually allocate the right type of memory.

Figure 5.128 Allocate socket buffer: `linux/net/core/skbuff.c`.

```
165    struct sk_buff *alloc_skb(unsigned int size,int gfp_mask)
166    {
167            struct sk_buff *skb;
168            u8 *data;
169
170            if (in_interrupt() && (gfp_mask & __GFP_WAIT)) {
171                    static int count = 0;
172                    if (++count < 5) {
173                            printk(KERN_ERR "alloc_skb called nonatomically "
174                                    "from interrupt %p\n", NET_CALLER(size));
175                            BUG();
176                    }
177                    gfp_mask &= ~__GFP_WAIT;
178            }
179
180            /* Get the HEAD */
181            skb = skb_head_from_pool();
182            if (skb == NULL) {
183                    skb = kmem_cache_alloc(skbuff_head_cache, gfp_mask);
184                    if (skb == NULL)
185                            goto nohead;
186            }
187
188            /* Get the DATA. Size must match skb_add_mtu(). */
189            size = ((size + 15) & ~15);
190            data = kmalloc(size + sizeof(atomic_t), gfp_mask);
191            if (data == NULL)
192                    goto nodata;
193
194            /* XXX: does not include slab overhead */
195            skb->truesize = size + sizeof(struct sk_buff);
196
197            /* Load the data pointers. */
198            skb->head = data;
199            skb->data = data;
200            skb->tail = data;
201            skb->end = data + size;
202
203            /* Set up other state */
```

```
204          skb->len = 0;
205          skb->cloned = 0;
206
207          atomic_set(&skb->users, 1);
208          atomic_set(skb_datarefp(skb), 1);
209          return skb;
210
211   nodata:
212          skb_head_to_pool(skb);
213   nohead:
214          return NULL;
215   }
```

Figure 5.129 Initialize socket buffer: `linux/net/core/skbuff.c`.

```
218   /*
219    *      Slab constructor for a skb head.
220    */
221   static inline void skb_headerinit(void *p, kmem_cache_t *cache,
222                              unsigned long flags)
223   {
224          struct sk_buff *skb = p;
225
226          skb->next = NULL;
227          skb->prev = NULL;
228          skb->list = NULL;
229          skb->sk = NULL;
230          skb->stamp.tv_sec=0;  /* No idea about time */
231          skb->dev = NULL;
232          skb->dst = NULL;
233          memset(skb->cb, 0, sizeof(skb->cb));
234          skb->pkt_type = PACKET_HOST; /* Default type */
235          skb->ip_summed = 0;
236          skb->priority = 0;
237          skb->security = 0;    /* By default packets are insecure */
238          skb->destructor = NULL;
239
240   #ifdef CONFIG_NETFILTER
241          skb->nfmark = skb->nfcache = 0;
242          skb->nfct = NULL;
243   #ifdef CONFIG_NETFILTER_DEBUG
244          skb->nf_debug = 0;
245   #endif
246   #endif
247   #ifdef CONFIG_NET_SCHED
248          skb->tc_index = 0;
249   #endif
250   }
```

Figure 5.130 Free socket buffer: `linux/net/core/skbuff.c`.

```
252   /*
253    *      Free an skbuff by memory without cleaning the state.
254    */
255   void kfree_skbmem(struct sk_buff *skb)
256   {
257          if (!skb->cloned || atomic_dec_and_test(skb_datarefp(skb)))
258                  kfree(skb->head);
259
260          skb_head_to_pool(skb);
261   }
```

5.6.3 Manipulating Socket Buffers

Figure 5.131 Clone socket buffer: `linux/net/core/skbuff.c`.

```
295   /**
296    *      skb_clone        -        duplicate an sk_buff
297    *      @skb: buffer to clone
298    *      @gfp_mask: allocation priority
299    *
300    *      Duplicate an &sk_buff. The new one is not owned by a socket. Both
301    *      copies share the same packet data but not structure. The new
302    *      buffer has a reference count of 1. If the allocation fails the
303    *      function returns %NULL otherwise the new buffer is returned.
304    *
305    *      If this function is called from an interrupt gfp_mask() must be
306    *      %GFP_ATOMIC.
307    */
308
309   struct sk_buff *skb_clone(struct sk_buff *skb, int gfp_mask)
310   {
311          struct sk_buff *n;
312
313          n = skb_head_from_pool();
314          if (!n) {
315                  n = kmem_cache_alloc(skbuff_head_cache, gfp_mask);
316                  if (!n)
317                          return NULL;
318          }
319
320          memcpy(n, skb, sizeof(*n));
321          atomic_inc(skb_datarefp(skb));
322          skb->cloned = 1;
323
324          dst_clone(n->dst);
325          n->cloned = 1;
326          n->next = n->prev = NULL;
327          n->list = NULL;
328          n->sk = NULL;
329          atomic_set(&n->users, 1);
```

```
        n->destructor = NULL;
#ifdef CONFIG_NETFILTER
        nf_conntrack_get(skb->nfct);
#endif
        return n;
}
```

The following function copies form, but not content, and bumps reference count.

Figure 5.132 Copy socket buffer structure header: `linux/net/core/skbuff.c`.

```
static void copy_skb_header(struct sk_buff *new, const struct sk_buff *old)
{
        /*
         *      Shift between the two data areas in bytes
         */
        unsigned long offset = new->data - old->data;

        new->list=NULL;
        new->sk=NULL;
        new->dev=old->dev;
        new->priority=old->priority;
        new->protocol=old->protocol;
        new->dst=dst_clone(old->dst);
        new->h.raw=old->h.raw+offset;
        new->nh.raw=old->nh.raw+offset;
        new->mac.raw=old->mac.raw+offset;
        memcpy(new->cb, old->cb, sizeof(old->cb));
        new->used=old->used;
        atomic_set(&new->users, 1);
        new->pkt_type=old->pkt_type;
        new->stamp=old->stamp;
        new->destructor = NULL;
        new->security=old->security;
#ifdef CONFIG_NETFILTER
        new->nfmark=old->nfmark;
        new->nfcache=old->nfcache;
        new->nfct=old->nfct;
        nf_conntrack_get(new->nfct);
#ifdef CONFIG_NETFILTER_DEBUG
        new->nf_debug=old->nf_debug;
#endif
#endif
#ifdef CONFIG_NET_SCHED
        new->tc_index = old->tc_index;
#endif
}
```

Here's the global data part of the code to manipulate socket buffers.

Figure 5.133 Copy socket buffer structure and data: `linux/net/core/skbuff.c`.

```
/**
 *      skb_copy        -       copy an sk_buff
 *      @skb: buffer to copy
 *      @gfp_mask: allocation priority
 *
 *      Make a copy of both an &sk_buff and its data. This is used when the
 *      caller wishes to modify the data and needs a private copy of the
 *      data to alter. Returns %NULL on failure or the pointer to the buffer
 *      on success. The returned buffer has a reference count of 1.
 *
 *      You must pass %GFP_ATOMIC as the allocation priority if this function
 *      is called from an interrupt.
 */

struct sk_buff *skb_copy(const struct sk_buff *skb, int gfp_mask)
{
        struct sk_buff *n;

        /*
         *      Allocate the copy buffer
         */

        n=alloc_skb(skb->end - skb->head, gfp_mask);
        if(n==NULL)
                return NULL;

        /* Set the data pointer */
        skb_reserve(n,skb->data-skb->head);
        /* Set the tail pointer and length */
        skb_put(n,skb->len);
        /* Copy the bytes */
        memcpy(n->head,skb->head,skb->end-skb->head);
        n->csum = skb->csum;
        copy_skb_header(n, skb);

        return n;
}
```

Figure 5.134 Copy and expand socket buffer structure and data: `linux/net/core/skbuff.c`.

```
/**
 *      skb_copy_expand -       copy and expand sk_buff
 *      @skb: buffer to copy
 *      @newheadroom: new free bytes at head
 *      @newtailroom: new free bytes at tail
 *      @gfp_mask: allocation priority
 *
 *      Make a copy of both an &sk_buff and its data and while doing so
```

```
 *      allocate additional space.
 *
 *      This is used when the caller wishes to modify the data and needs a
 *      private copy of the data to alter as well as more space for new fields.
 *      Returns %NULL on failure or the pointer to the buffer
 *      on success. The returned buffer has a reference count of 1.
 *
 *      You must pass %GFP_ATOMIC as the allocation priority if this function
 *      is called from an interrupt.
 */


struct sk_buff *skb_copy_expand(const struct sk_buff *skb,
                                int newheadroom,
                                int newtailroom,
                                int gfp_mask)
{
        struct sk_buff *n;

        /*
         *      Allocate the copy buffer
         */

        n=alloc_skb(newheadroom + (skb->tail - skb->data) + newtailroom,
                    gfp_mask);
        if(n==NULL)
                return NULL;

        skb_reserve(n,newheadroom);

        /* Set the tail pointer and length */
        skb_put(n,skb->len);

        /* Copy the data only. */
        memcpy(n->data, skb->data, skb->len);

        copy_skb_header(n, skb);
        return n;
}
```

Finally, we get to the code that sets up the actual pool of buffers.

Figure 5.135 Initialize socket buffer global data: `linux/net/core/skbuff.c`.

```
void __init skb_init(void)
{
        int i;

        skbuff_head_cache = kmem_cache_create("skbuff_head_cache",
                                              sizeof(struct sk_buff),
                                              0,
                                              SLAB_HWCACHE_ALIGN,
```

```
                                              skb_headerinit, NULL);
        if (!skbuff_head_cache)
                panic("cannot create skbuff cache");

        for (i=0; i<NR_CPUS; i++)
                skb_queue_head_init(&skb_head_pool[i].list);
}
```

5.7 A Day in the Life of a Protocol Control Block

Here is the relevant data for the protocol vis-à-vis the state of a stream-type socket in the INET protocol family.

Figure 5.136 TCP states: `linux/include/net/tcp.h`.

```
 *        Failing this, the port cannot be shared.
 *
 * The interesting point, is test #2. This is what an FTP server does
 * all day. To optimize this case we use a specific flag bit defined
 * below. As we add sockets to a bind bucket list, we perform a
 * check of: (newsk->reuse && (newsk->state != TCP_LISTEN))
 * As long as all sockets added to a bind bucket pass this test,
 * the flag bit will be set.
 * The resulting situation is that tcp_v[46]_verify_bind() can just check
 * for this flag bit, if it is set and the socket trying to bind has
 * sk->reuse set, we don't even have to walk the owners list at all,
 * we return that it is ok to bind this socket to the requested local port.
 *
 * Sounds like a lot of work, but it is worth it. In a more naive
 * implementation (ie. current FreeBSD etc.) the entire list of ports
 * must be walked for each data port opened by an ftp server. Needless
 * to say, this does not scale at all. With a couple thousand FTP
 * users logged onto your box, isn't it nice to know that new data
 * ports are created in O(1) time? I thought so. ;-) -DaveM
 */
struct tcp_bind_bucket {
        unsigned short          port;
        unsigned short          fastreuse;
        struct tcp_bind_bucket *next;
        struct sock             *owners;
        struct tcp_bind_bucket **pprev;
};

struct tcp_bind_hashbucket {
        spinlock_t              lock;
        struct tcp_bind_bucket *chain;
};
```

Figure 5.137 TCP state flags: `linux/include/net/tcp.h`.

```
extern struct tcp_hashinfo {
        /* This is for sockets with full identity only. Sockets here will
         * always be without wildcards and will have the following invariant:
         *
         *          TCP_ESTABLISHED <= sk->state < TCP_CLOSE
         *
         * First half of the table is for sockets not in TIME_WAIT, second half
         * is for TIME_WAIT sockets only.
         */
        struct tcp_ehash_bucket *__tcp_ehash;

        /* Ok, let's try this, I give up, we do need a local binding
         * TCP hash as well as the others for fast bind/connect.
         */
        struct tcp_bind_hashbucket *__tcp_bhash;

        int __tcp_bhash_size;
        int __tcp_ehash_size;

        /* All sockets in TCP_LISTEN state will be in here. This is the only
         * table where wildcard'd TCP sockets can exist. Hash function here
         * is just local port number.
         */
        struct sock *__tcp_listening_hash[TCP_LHTABLE_SIZE];
```

Figure 5.138 TCP connection state: `linux/include/net/tcp.h`.

```
        /* All the above members are written once at bootup and
         * never written again _or_ are predominantly read-access.
         *
         * Now align to a new cache line as all the following members
         * are often dirty.
         */
        rwlock_t __tcp_lhash_lock
                __attribute__((__aligned__(SMP_CACHE_BYTES)));
        atomic_t __tcp_lhash_users;
        wait_queue_head_t __tcp_lhash_wait;
        spinlock_t __tcp_portalloc_lock;
} tcp_hashinfo;

#define tcp_ehash           (tcp_hashinfo.__tcp_ehash)
#define tcp_bhash           (tcp_hashinfo.__tcp_bhash)
#define tcp_ehash_size      (tcp_hashinfo.__tcp_ehash_size)
#define tcp_bhash_size      (tcp_hashinfo.__tcp_bhash_size)
#define tcp_listening_hash (tcp_hashinfo.__tcp_listening_hash)
#define tcp_lhash_lock      (tcp_hashinfo.__tcp_lhash_lock)
#define tcp_lhash_users     (tcp_hashinfo.__tcp_lhash_users)
#define tcp_lhash_wait      (tcp_hashinfo.__tcp_lhash_wait)
#define tcp_portalloc_lock (tcp_hashinfo.__tcp_portalloc_lock)

extern kmem_cache_t *tcp_bucket_cachep;
```

```
141    extern struct tcp_bind_bucket *tcp_bucket_create(struct tcp_bind_hashbucket *head,
142                                                     unsigned short snum);
143    extern void tcp_bucket_unlock(struct sock *sk);
144    extern int tcp_port_rover;
145    extern struct sock *tcp_v4_lookup_listener(u32 addr, unsigned short hnum, int dif);
146
147    /* These are AF independent. */
```

Figure 5.139 TCP state variables: `linux/include/net/tcp.h`.

```
149    {
150            return (lport & (tcp_bhash_size - 1));
151    }
152
153    /* This is a TIME_WAIT bucket. It works around the memory consumption
154     * problems of sockets in such a state on heavily loaded servers, but
155     * without violating the protocol specification.
156     */
157    struct tcp_tw_bucket {
158            /* These _must_ match the beginning of struct sock precisely.
159             * XXX Yes I know this is gross, but I'd have to edit every single
160             * XXX networking file if I created a "struct sock_header". -DaveM
161             */
162            __u32           daddr;
163            __u32           rcv_saddr;
164            __u16           dport;
165            unsigned short  num;
166            int             bound_dev_if;
167            struct sock     *next;
168            struct sock     **pprev;
169            struct sock     *bind_next;
170            struct sock     **bind_pprev;
171            unsigned char   state,
172                            substate; /* "zapped" is replaced with "substate" */
173            __u16           sport;
174            unsigned short  family;
175            unsigned char   reuse,
176                            rcv_wscale; /* It is also TW bucket specific */
177            atomic_t        refcnt;
178
179            /* And these are ours. */
180            int             hashent;
181            int             timeout;
182            __u32           rcv_nxt;
183            __u32           snd_nxt;
184            __u32           rcv_wnd;
185            __u32           syn_seq;
```

There is a lot more to the TCP state machine than this, but we'll look at that in Chapter 7.

5.7.1 Socket and Route-Related Transport State

For historical reasons, some state associated with the transport protocol is kept in the socket structure (it is, in any case, per connection per process for connection-oriented unicast protocols, so this is not a terrible error, although in the future for reliable multicast transport protocols with multiple senders and receiving processes potentially on the same machine, this could be a problem).

The route-related state is discussed in Chapter 8. In any case, one of the most formidable data structures in the Linux communications protocol stack implementation is contained in the innocently named file `sock.h`.

Along with this is the `tcp_opt` structure, which is discussed in detail in Chapter 7.

Figure 5.140 Socket TCP state i, start: `linux/include/net/sock.h`.

```
struct tcp_opt {
        int     tcp_header_len; /* Bytes of tcp header to send      */

/*
 *      Header prediction flags
 *      0x5?10 << 16 + snd_wnd in net byte order
 */
        __u32   pred_flags;

/*
 *      RFC793 variables by their proper names. This means you can
 *      read the code and the spec side by side (and laugh ...)
 *      See RFC793 and RFC1122. The RFC writes these in capitals.
 */
```

There is also IP, level information (e.g., `struct ipv6_pinfo` and `struct inet_opt`), and then socket level data itself.

Figure 5.141 Socket relevant IP option state: `linux/include/net/sock.h`.

```
struct inet_opt
{
        int                     ttl;                    /* TTL setting */
        int                     tos;                    /* TOS */
        unsigned                cmsg_flags;
        struct ip_options       *opt;
        unsigned char           hdrincl;                /* Include headers ? */
        __u8                    mc_ttl;                 /* Multicasting TTL */
        __u8                    mc_loop;                /* Loopback */
        unsigned                recverr : 1,
```

```
                                freebind : 1;
        __u8                    pmtudisc;
        int                     mc_index;               /* Multicast device index */
        __u32                   mc_addr;
        struct ip_mc_socklist *mc_list;                 /* Group array */
};
```

Figure 5.142 Socket IPv6 state: `linux/include/net/sock.h`.

```
struct ipv6_pinfo {
        struct in6_addr         saddr;
        struct in6_addr         rcv_saddr;
        struct in6_addr         daddr;
        struct in6_addr         *daddr_cache;

        __u32                   flow_label;
        __u32                   frag_size;
        int                     hop_limit;
        int                     mcast_hops;
        int                     mcast_oif;

        /* pktoption flags */
        union {
                struct {
                        __u8    srcrt:2,
                                rxinfo:1,
                                rxhlim:1,
                                hopopts:1,
                                dstopts:1,
                                authhdr:1,
                                rxflow:1;
                } bits;
                __u8            all;
        } rxopt;

        /* sockopt flags */
        __u8                    mc_loop:1,
                                recverr:1,
                                sndflow:1,
                                pmtudisc:2;

        struct ipv6_mc_socklist *ipv6_mc_list;
        struct ipv6_fl_socklist *ipv6_fl_list;
        __u32                    dst_cookie;

        struct ipv6_txoptions   *opt;
        struct sk_buff          *pktoptions;
};
```

Figure 5.143 Socket state i, demultiplex data: `linux/include/net/sock.h`.

```
struct sock {
        /* Socket demultiplex comparisons on incoming packets. */
        __u32                   daddr;          /* Foreign IPv4 addr            */
        __u32                   rcv_saddr;      /* Bound local IPv4 addr        */
        __u16                   dport;          /* Destination port             */
        unsigned short          num;            /* Local port                   */
        int                     bound_dev_if;   /* Bound device index if != 0   */

        /* Main hash linkage for various protocol lookup tables. */
        struct sock             *next;
        struct sock             **pprev;
        struct sock             *bind_next;
        struct sock             **bind_pprev;
```

Figure 5.144 Socket state ii, resource data: `linux/include/net/sock.h`.

```
        volatile unsigned char state,           /* Connection state             */
                                zapped;         /* In ax25 & ipx means not linked */
        __u16                   sport;          /* Source port                  */

        unsigned short          family;         /* Address family               */
        unsigned char           reuse;          /* SO_REUSEADDR setting         */
        unsigned char           shutdown;
        atomic_t                refcnt;         /* Reference count              */

        socket_lock_t           lock;           /* Synchronizer...              */
        int                     rcvbuf;         /* Size of receive buffer in bytes */

        wait_queue_head_t       *sleep;         /* Sock wait queue              */
        struct dst_entry        *dst_cache;     /* Destination cache            */
        rwlock_t                dst_lock;
        atomic_t                rmem_alloc;     /* Receive queue bytes committed */
        struct sk_buff_head     receive_queue;  /* Incoming packets             */
        atomic_t                wmem_alloc;     /* Transmit queue bytes committed */
        struct sk_buff_head     write_queue;    /* Packet sending queue         */
        atomic_t                omem_alloc;     /* "o" is "option" or "other" */
        int                     wmem_queued;    /* Persistent queue size */
        int                     forward_alloc;  /* Space allocated forward. */
        __u32                   saddr;          /* Sending source               */
        unsigned int            allocation;     /* Allocation mode              */
        int                     sndbuf;         /* Size of send buffer in bytes */
        struct sock             *prev;
```

Figure 5.145 Socket state iii, socket state itself: `linux/include/net/sock.h`.

```
        /* Not all are volatile, but some are, so we might as well say they all are.
         * XXX Make this a flag word -DaveM
         */
        volatile char           dead,
```

```
                              done,
                              urginline,
                              keepopen,
                              linger,
                              destroy,
                              no_check,
                              broadcast,
                              bsdism;
        unsigned char         debug;
        unsigned char         rcvtstamp;
        unsigned char         userlocks;
        int                   proc;
        unsigned long         lingertime;

        int                   hashent;
        struct sock           *pair;

        /* The backlog queue is special, it is always used with
         * the per-socket spinlock held and requires low latency
         * access. Therefore we special case it's implementation.
         */
        struct {
                struct sk_buff *head;
                struct sk_buff *tail;
        } backlog;

        rwlock_t              callback_lock;

        /* Error queue, rarely used. */
        struct sk_buff_head   error_queue;
```

Figure 5.146 Socket state iv, routing, erroring, and filtering: `linux/include/net/sock.h`.

```
        struct proto          *prot;

#if defined(CONFIG_IPV6) || defined (CONFIG_IPV6_MODULE)
        union {
                struct ipv6_pinfo     af_inet6;
        } net_pinfo;
#endif

        union {
                struct tcp_opt        af_tcp;
#if defined(CONFIG_INET) || defined (CONFIG_INET_MODULE)
                struct raw_opt        tp_raw4;
#endif
#if defined(CONFIG_IPV6) || defined (CONFIG_IPV6_MODULE)
                struct raw6_opt       tp_raw;
#endif /* CONFIG_IPV6 */
#if defined(CONFIG_SPX) || defined (CONFIG_SPX_MODULE)
                struct spx_opt        af_spx;
#endif /* CONFIG_SPX */
```

```
578            } tp_pinfo;
579
580        int              err, err_soft; /* Soft holds errors that don't
581                                          cause failure but are the cause
582                                          of a persistent failure not just
583                                          'timed out' */
584        unsigned short   ack_backlog;
585        unsigned short   max_ack_backlog;
586        __u32            priority;
587        unsigned short   type;
588        unsigned char    localroute;   /* Route locally only */
589        unsigned char    protocol;
590        struct ucred     peercred;
591        int              rcvlowat;
592        long             rcvtimeo;
593        long             sndtimeo;
594
595    #ifdef CONFIG_FILTER
596        /* Socket Filtering Instructions */
597        struct sk_filter    *filter;
598    #endif /* CONFIG_FILTER */
```

Figure 5.147 Socket state v, private protocol info: `linux/include/net/sock.h`.

```
599
600        /* This is where all the private (optional) areas that don't
601         * overlap will eventually live.
602         */
603        union {
604                void *destruct_hook;
605                struct unix_opt af_unix;
606    #if defined(CONFIG_INET) || defined (CONFIG_INET_MODULE)
607                struct inet_opt af_inet;
608    #endif
609    #if defined(CONFIG_ATALK) || defined(CONFIG_ATALK_MODULE)
610                struct atalk_sock    af_at;
611    #endif
612    #if defined(CONFIG_IPX) || defined(CONFIG_IPX_MODULE)
613                struct ipx_opt       af_ipx;
614    #endif
615    #if defined (CONFIG_DECNET) || defined(CONFIG_DECNET_MODULE)
616                struct dn_scp        dn;
617    #endif
618    #if defined (CONFIG_PACKET) || defined(CONFIG_PACKET_MODULE)
619                struct packet_opt    *af_packet;
620    #endif
621    #if defined(CONFIG_X25) || defined(CONFIG_X25_MODULE)
622                x25_cb               *x25;
623    #endif
624    #if defined(CONFIG_AX25) || defined(CONFIG_AX25_MODULE)
625                ax25_cb              *ax25;
626    #endif
627    #if defined(CONFIG_NETROM) || defined(CONFIG_NETROM_MODULE)
```

```
628                 nr_cb                *nr;
629  #endif
630  #if defined(CONFIG_ROSE) || defined(CONFIG_ROSE_MODULE)
631                 rose_cb              *rose;
632  #endif
633  #if defined(CONFIG_PPPOE) || defined(CONFIG_PPPOE_MODULE)
634                 struct pppox_opt     *pppox;
635  #endif
636  #ifdef CONFIG_NETLINK
637                 struct netlink_opt   *af_netlink;
638  #endif
639  #if defined(CONFIG_ECONET) || defined(CONFIG_ECONET_MODULE)
640                 struct econet_opt    *af_econet;
641  #endif
642  #if defined(CONFIG_ATM) || defined(CONFIG_ATM_MODULE)
643                 struct atm_vcc       *af_atm;
644  #endif
645  #if defined(CONFIG_IRDA) || defined(CONFIG_IRDA_MODULE)
646                 struct irda_sock     *irda;
647  #endif
648        } protinfo;
```

Figure 5.148 Socket state vi, timers and callbacks: `linux/include/net/sock.h`.

```
610                 struct atalk_sock    af_at;
611  #endif
612  #if defined(CONFIG_IPX) || defined(CONFIG_IPX_MODULE)
613                 struct ipx_opt       af_ipx;
614  #endif
615  #if defined (CONFIG_DECNET) || defined(CONFIG_DECNET_MODULE)
616                 struct dn_scp        dn;
617  #endif
618  #if defined (CONFIG_PACKET) || defined(CONFIG_PACKET_MODULE)
619                 struct packet_opt    *af_packet;
620  #endif
621  #if defined(CONFIG_X25) || defined(CONFIG_X25_MODULE)
622                 x25_cb               *x25;
623  #endif
624  #if defined(CONFIG_AX25) || defined(CONFIG_AX25_MODULE)
625                 ax25_cb              *ax25;
626  #endif
627  #if defined(CONFIG_NETROM) || defined(CONFIG_NETROM_MODULE)
628                 nr_cb                *nr;
629  #endif
630  #if defined(CONFIG_ROSE) || defined(CONFIG_ROSE_MODULE)
631                 rose_cb              *rose;
632  #endif
633  #if defined(CONFIG_PPPOE) || defined(CONFIG_PPPOE_MODULE)
634                 struct pppox_opt     *pppox;
635  #endif
636  #ifdef CONFIG_NETLINK
637                 struct netlink_opt   *af_netlink;
638  #endif
```

```
#if defined(CONFIG_ECONET) || defined(CONFIG_ECONET_MODULE)
                struct econet_opt       *af_econet;
#endif
#if defined(CONFIG_ATM) || defined(CONFIG_ATM_MODULE)
                struct atm_vcc          *af_atm;
#endif
#if defined(CONFIG_IRDA) || defined(CONFIG_IRDA_MODULE)
                struct irda_sock        *irda;
#endif
        } protinfo;
```

Figure 5.149 Socket state vii, timers and callbacks: `linux/include/net/sock.h`.

```


        /* This part is used for the timeout functions. */
        struct timer_list       timer;          /* This is the sock cleanup timer. */
        struct timeval          stamp;

        /* Identd and reporting IO signals */
        struct socket           *socket;

        /* RPC layer private data */
        void                    *user_data;

        /* Callbacks */
        void                    (*state_change)(struct sock *sk);
        void                    (*data_ready)(struct sock *sk,int bytes);
        void                    (*write_space)(struct sock *sk);
        void                    (*error_report)(struct sock *sk);

        int                     (*backlog_rcv) (struct sock *sk,
                                                struct sk_buff *skb);
        void                    (*destruct)(struct sock *sk);
};
```

5.7.2 Future of the Socket Structure

There is a comment to the effect that it's desired by the code authors to tidy this all up, which describes a much more elegant solution.

Figure 5.150 Proposal to tidy up socket state: `linux/include/net/sock.h`.

```
 * This structure really needs to be cleaned up.
 * Most of it is for TCP, and not used by any of
 * the other protocols.
 */

/*
```

```
 * The idea is to start moving to a newer struct gradualy
 *
 * IMHO the newer struct should have the following format:
 *
 *     struct sock {
 *             sockmem [mem, proto, callbacks]
 *
 *             union or struct {
 *                     ax25;
 *             } ll_pinfo;
 *
 *             union {
 *                     ipv4;
 *                     ipv6;
 *                     ipx;
 *                     netrom;
 *                     rose;
 *                     x25;
 *             } net_pinfo;
 *
 *             union {
 *                     tcp;
 *                     udp;
 *                     spx;
 *                     netrom;
 *             } tp_pinfo;
 *
 *     }
 *
 * The idea failed because IPv6 transition asssumes dual IP/IPv6 sockets.
 * So, net_pinfo is IPv6 are really, and protinfo unifies all another
 * private areas.
```

5.7.3 Reference Counting

Further on, there are two more important facets of the socket state maintenance code. First, we see the reference counting.

Figure 5.151 Socket reference counting comment: `linux/include/net/sock.h`.

```
/*
 * Socket reference counting postulates.
 *
 * * Each user of socket SHOULD hold a reference count.
 * * Each access point to socket (an hash table bucket, reference from a list,
 *   running timer, skb in flight MUST hold a reference count.
 * * When reference count hits 0, it means it will never increase back.
 * * When reference count hits 0, it means that no references from
 *   outside exist to this socket and current process on current CPU
 *   is last user and may/should destroy this socket.
 * * sk_free is called from any context: process, BH, IRQ. When
 *   it is called, socket has no references from outside -> sk_free
```

```
 *   may release descendant resources allocated by the socket, but
 *   to the time when it is called, socket is NOT referenced by any
 *   hash tables, lists etc.
 * * Packets, delivered from outside (from network or from another process)
 *   and enqueued on receive/error queues SHOULD NOT grab reference count,
 *   when they sit in queue. Otherwise, packets will leak to hole, when
 *   socket is looked up by one cpu and unhasing is made by another CPU.
 *   It is true for udp/raw, netlink (leak to receive and error queues), tcp
 *   (leak to backlog). Packet socket does all the processing inside
 *   BR_NETPROTO_LOCK, so that it has not this race condition. UNIX sockets
 *   use separate SMP lock, so that they are prone too.
 */

/* Grab socket reference count. This operation is valid only
   when sk is ALREADY grabbed f.e. it is found in hash table
   or a list and the lookup is made under lock preventing hash table
   modifications.
 */
```

Figure 5.152 Inline functions for socket reference management: `linux/include/net/sock.h`.

```
static inline void sock_hold(struct sock *sk)
{
        atomic_inc(&sk->refcnt);
}

/* Ungrab socket in the context, which assumes that socket refcnt
   cannot hit zero, f.e. it is true in context of any socketcall.
 */
static inline void __sock_put(struct sock *sk)
{
        atomic_dec(&sk->refcnt);
}

/* Ungrab socket and destroy it, if it was the last reference. */
static inline void sock_put(struct sock *sk)
{
        if (atomic_dec_and_test(&sk->refcnt))
                sk_free(sk);
}
```

Figure 5.153 Inline functions for socket reference management: `linux/include/net/sock.h`.

```
/* Detach socket from process context.
 * Announce socket dead, detach it from wait queue and inode.
 * Note that parent inode held reference count on this struct sock,
 * we do not release it in this function, because protocol
 * probably wants some additional cleanups or even continuing
 * to work with this socket (TCP).
 */
```

```
static inline void sock_orphan(struct sock *sk)
{
        write_lock_bh(&sk->callback_lock);
        sk->dead = 1;
        sk->socket = NULL;
        sk->sleep = NULL;
        write_unlock_bh(&sk->callback_lock);
}
```

Figure 5.154 Inline functions for socket reference management: `linux/include/net/sock.h`.

```
static inline void sock_graft(struct sock *sk, struct socket *parent)
{
        write_lock_bh(&sk->callback_lock);
        sk->sleep = &parent->wait;
        parent->sk = sk;
        sk->socket = parent;
        write_unlock_bh(&sk->callback_lock);
}

static inline int sock_i_uid(struct sock *sk)
{
        int uid;

        read_lock(&sk->callback_lock);
        uid = sk->socket ? sk->socket->inode->i_uid : 0;
        read_unlock(&sk->callback_lock);
        return uid;
}

static inline unsigned long sock_i_ino(struct sock *sk)
{
        unsigned long ino;

        read_lock(&sk->callback_lock);
        ino = sk->socket ? sk->socket->inode->i_ino : 0;
        read_unlock(&sk->callback_lock);
        return ino;
}
```

5.7.4 Sockets and Routes

Next, we see the code to associate a socket with a route.

Figure 5.155 Socket route state management: `linux/include/net/sock.h`.

```
static inline struct dst_entry *
__sk_dst_get(struct sock *sk)
{
        return sk->dst_cache;
```

```
1047  }
1048
1049  static inline struct dst_entry *
1050  sk_dst_get(struct sock *sk)
1051  {
1052          struct dst_entry *dst;
1053
1054          read_lock(&sk->dst_lock);
1055          dst = sk->dst_cache;
1056          if (dst)
1057                  dst_hold(dst);
1058          read_unlock(&sk->dst_lock);
1059          return dst;
1060  }
1061
1062  static inline void
1063  __sk_dst_set(struct sock *sk, struct dst_entry *dst)
1064  {
1065          struct dst_entry *old_dst;
1066
1067          old_dst = sk->dst_cache;
1068          sk->dst_cache = dst;
1069          dst_release(old_dst);
1070  }
1071
1072  static inline void
1073  sk_dst_set(struct sock *sk, struct dst_entry *dst)
1074  {
1075          write_lock(&sk->dst_lock);
1076          __sk_dst_set(sk, dst);
1077          write_unlock(&sk->dst_lock);
1078  }
```

Figure 5.156 Socket route state management: `linux/include/net/sock.h`.

```
1080  static inline void
1081  __sk_dst_reset(struct sock *sk)
1082  {
1083          struct dst_entry *old_dst;
1084
1085          old_dst = sk->dst_cache;
1086          sk->dst_cache = NULL;
1087          dst_release(old_dst);
1088  }
1089
1090  static inline void
1091  sk_dst_reset(struct sock *sk)
1092  {
1093          write_lock(&sk->dst_lock);
1094          __sk_dst_reset(sk);
1095          write_unlock(&sk->dst_lock);
1096  }
```

Figure 5.157 Socket route state management: `linux/include/net/sock.h`.

```
1098    static inline struct dst_entry *
1099    __sk_dst_check(struct sock *sk, u32 cookie)
1100    {
1101            struct dst_entry *dst = sk->dst_cache;
1102
1103            if (dst && dst->obsolete && dst->ops->check(dst, cookie) == NULL) {
1104                    sk->dst_cache = NULL;
1105                    return NULL;
1106            }
1107
1108            return dst;
1109    }
1110
1111    static inline struct dst_entry *
1112    sk_dst_check(struct sock *sk, u32 cookie)
1113    {
1114            struct dst_entry *dst = sk_dst_get(sk);
1115
1116            if (dst && dst->obsolete && dst->ops->check(dst, cookie) == NULL) {
1117                    sk_dst_reset(sk);
1118                    return NULL;
1119            }
1120
1121            return dst;
1122    }
```

There is a set of functions to queue data safely to and from a socket (remembering that a socket is shared between user process and kernel threads).

Figure 5.158 Socket queue management interface: `linux/include/net/sock.h`.

```
1125    /*
1126     *      Queue a received datagram if it will fit. Stream and sequenced
1127     *      protocols can't normally use this as they need to fit buffers in
1128     *      and play with them.
1129     *
1130     *      Inlined as it's very short and called for pretty much every
1131     *      packet ever received.
1132     */
1133
1134    static inline void skb_set_owner_w(struct sk_buff *skb, struct sock *sk)
1135    {
1136            sock_hold(sk);
1137            skb->sk = sk;
1138            skb->destructor = sock_wfree;
1139            atomic_add(skb->truesize, &sk->wmem_alloc);
1140    }
```

Figure 5.159 Socket queue management interface: `linux/include/net/sock.h`.

```
1141
1142  static inline void skb_set_owner_r(struct sk_buff *skb, struct sock *sk)
1143  {
1144        skb->sk = sk;
1145        skb->destructor = sock_rfree;
1146        atomic_add(skb->truesize, &sk->rmem_alloc);
1147  }
1148
1149  static inline int sock_queue_rcv_skb(struct sock *sk, struct sk_buff *skb)
1150  {
1151        /* Cast skb->rcvbuf to unsigned... It's pointless, but reduces
1152           number of warnings when compiling with -W --ANK
1153         */
1154        if (atomic_read(&sk->rmem_alloc) + skb->truesize >= (unsigned)sk->rcvbuf)
1155              return -ENOMEM;
1156
1157  #ifdef CONFIG_FILTER
1158        if (sk->filter) {
1159              int err = 0;
1160              struct sk_filter *filter;
1161
1162              /* It would be deadlock, if sock_queue_rcv_skb is used
1163                 with socket lock! We assume that users of this
1164                 function are lock free.
1165               */
1166              bh_lock_sock(sk);
1167              if ((filter = sk->filter) != NULL && sk_filter(skb, filter))
1168                    err = -EPERM;
1169              bh_unlock_sock(sk);
1170              if (err)
1171                    return err;   /* Toss packet */
1172        }
1173  #endif /* CONFIG_FILTER */
1174
1175        skb->dev = NULL;
1176        skb_set_owner_r(skb, sk);
1177        skb_queue_tail(&sk->receive_queue, skb);
1178        if (!sk->dead)
1179              sk->data_ready(sk,skb->len);
1180        return 0;
1181  }
```

Finally, we have some macros to control synchronization between user and kernel via socket wait queues.

Figure 5.160 Socket queue management interface: `linux/include/net/sock.h`.

```
1286  /*
1287   * Macros for sleeping on a socket. Use them like this:
1288   *
1289   * SOCK_SLEEP_PRE(sk)
1290   * if (condition)
1291   *     schedule();
```

```
 * SOCK_SLEEP_POST(sk)
 *
 */

#define SOCK_SLEEP_PRE(sk)    { struct task_struct *tsk = current; \
                              DECLARE_WAITQUEUE(wait, tsk); \
                              tsk->state = TASK_INTERRUPTIBLE; \
                              add_wait_queue((sk)->sleep, &wait); \
                              release_sock(sk);

#define SOCK_SLEEP_POST(sk)   tsk->state = TASK_RUNNING; \
                              remove_wait_queue((sk)->sleep, &wait); \
                              lock_sock(sk); \
                              }

extern __u32 sysctl_wmem_max;
extern __u32 sysctl_rmem_max;
```

5.7.5 Socket Credentials Manager Interface

It's necessary to control use of resources in the socket interface—this is done through keeping a list of credentials for access to socket buffers (basically, typical UNIX user and group identifier information).

An example function is illustrated in Figure 5.161, which maps between given credentials and actual process rights.

Figure 5.161 Socket credential function: `linux/net/core/scm.c`.

```
static __inline__ int scm_check_creds(struct ucred *creds)
{
        if ((creds->pid == current->pid || capable(CAP_SYS_ADMIN)) &&
            ((creds->uid == current->uid || creds->uid == current->euid ||
              creds->uid == current->suid) || capable(CAP_SETUID)) &&
            ((creds->gid == current->gid || creds->gid == current->egid ||
              creds->gid == current->sgid) || capable(CAP_SETGID))) {
               return 0;
        }
        return -EPERM;
}
```

The interface to this code is as shown in the next figure.

Figure 5.162 Socket credential interface: `linux/include/net/scm.h`.

```
struct scm_fp_list
{
        int             count;
        struct file     *fp[SCM_MAX_FD];
```

```
};

struct scm_cookie
{
        struct ucred            creds;          /* Skb credentials    */
        struct scm_fp_list      *fp;            /* Passed files       */
        unsigned long           seq;            /* Connection seqno   */
};
```

5.7.6 A Brief Comparison with BSD Style Stack Infrastructure

By way of contrast, let's look at the way that the BSD UNIX kernel might achieve the synchronization.

Figure 5.163 BSD producer/consumer chain—transport out.

```


-- 1/2 of Transport Protocol
--        Consumer of User events, Producer of Network requests...
        for(ever)
        {
                sleep(tsdu-q-event);

                prev = spl-ts()
                tsdu-pkt = deq(tsdu-q);
                spl-restore(prev)

                -- make up some tpdu (transport pkts)
                -- do all the rtx q stuff and set timers
                -- if this is that service/kind of transport protocol
                -- (and network service isn't enough to give us the
                -- service we are asked for)

                prev = spl-ns()
                enqueue(nsdu-q, tpdu-pkt)
                spl-restore(prev)

                wakeup(nsdu-q-event);

        }
```

Figure 5.164 BSD producer/consumer chain—network out.

```

-- 1/2 of Network Protocol - NS1
--       Consumer of Transport events, Producer of Link requests
        for(ever)
        {
```

```
            sleep(nsdu-q-event);

            prev = spl-ns()
            tsdu-pkt = deq(nsdu-q);
            spl-previous(prev)

            -- make up some npdu (network pkts)
            -- do all the rtx q stuff and set timers
            -- if this is that kind of Network protocol

            prev = spl-ls()
            enqueue(lsdu-q, npdu-pkt)
            spl-restore(prev)

    }
```

Here is a brief outline of what the preceding pseudofunctions do.

Figure 5.165 BSD producer/consumer chain–legend.

```

sleep - waits (suspends this task/process/thread) till some other task
wakes us up with appropriate event).

wakeup - wakeup any task sleeping for this event.

spl-? - set priority level to exclude any tasks from waking up who
need this level of access.

spl-x - restore all previous priority levels.

que - add a buffer/packet to a queue for another process to...

dequeue - remove from a queue some buffer.
```

5.8 Summary

In this chapter, we have looked at the general support for protocols in the kernel, from network device driver and software interrupts, through to the socket glue, taking in the socket buffer data structures, protocol multiplexing, and demultiplexing layers along the way.

In the next chapter, we look at the network layer protocol IP itself, and its associated management protocols.

CHAPTER 6

Infrastructure Protocols

"Three things are inevitable in life: death, taxes, and middleware."
—anonymous

6.1 Roadmap

In this chapter, we cover the protocols that provide an internetworking infrastructure, that is to say IP (versions 4 and 6), and the associated management protocols such as ARP, DHCP, ICMP, and IGMP.

We introduce the basic concepts of the MAC address, IPv4 address, and look at proposed IPv6 addressing and multicast addressing. We then look at autoconfiguration, including ARP and IPv6 stateless autoconfiguration.

Then we look at IP host packet processing for sending and receiving, and briefly forwarding.

6.2 IP

6.2.1 Internet Protocol Output

Figure 6.1 IP output—add header and send: `linux/net/ipv4/ip_output.c`.

```
/*
 *          Add an ip header to a skbuff and send it out.
 */
int ip_build_and_send_pkt(struct sk_buff *skb, struct sock *sk,
                          u32 saddr, u32 daddr, struct ip_options *opt)
```

```
{
        struct rtable *rt = (struct rtable *)skb->dst;
        struct iphdr *iph;

        /* Build the IP header. */
        if (opt)
                iph=(struct iphdr *)skb_push(skb,sizeof(struct iphdr) + opt->optlen);
        else
                iph=(struct iphdr *)skb_push(skb,sizeof(struct iphdr));

        iph->version = 4;
        iph->ihl     = 5;
        iph->tos     = sk->protinfo.af_inet.tos;
        iph->frag_off = 0;
        if (ip_dont_fragment(sk, &rt->u.dst))
                iph->frag_off |= htons(IP_DF);
        iph->ttl     = sk->protinfo.af_inet.ttl;
        iph->daddr   = rt->rt_dst;
        iph->saddr   = rt->rt_src;
        iph->protocol = sk->protocol;
        iph->tot_len = htons(skb->len);
        ip_select_ident(iph, &rt->u.dst);
        skb->nh.iph  = iph;

        if (opt && opt->optlen) {
                iph->ihl += opt->optlen>>2;
                ip_options_build(skb, opt, daddr, rt, 0);
        }
        ip_send_check(iph);

        /* Send it out. */
        return NF_HOOK(PF_INET, NF_IP_LOCAL_OUT, skb, NULL, rt->u.dst.dev,
                         output_maybe_reroute);
}
```

Figure 6.2 IP output—finish sending (note two-stage process): `linux/net/ipv4/ip_output.c`.

```
static inline int ip_finish_output2(struct sk_buff *skb)
{
        struct dst_entry *dst = skb->dst;
        struct hh_cache *hh = dst->hh;

#ifdef CONFIG_NETFILTER_DEBUG
        nf_debug_ip_finish_output2(skb);
#endif /*CONFIG_NETFILTER_DEBUG*/

        if (hh) {
                read_lock_bh(&hh->hh_lock);
                memcpy(skb->data - 16, hh->hh_data, 16);
                read_unlock_bh(&hh->hh_lock);
                skb_push(skb, hh->hh_len);
```

```
                return hh->hh_output(skb);
        } else if (dst->neighbour)
                return dst->neighbour->output(skb);

        printk(KERN_DEBUG "khm\n");
        kfree_skb(skb);
        return -EINVAL;
}

__inline__ int ip_finish_output(struct sk_buff *skb)
{
        struct net_device *dev = skb->dst->dev;

        skb->dev = dev;
        skb->protocol = __constant_htons(ETH_P_IP);

        return NF_HOOK(PF_INET, NF_IP_POST_ROUTING, skb, NULL, dev,
                       ip_finish_output2);
}
```

Figure 6.3 Internet Protocol—output—checksum: `linux/net/ipv4/ip_output.c`.

```
/* Generate a checksum for an outgoing IP datagram. */
__inline__ void ip_send_check(struct iphdr *iph)
{
        iph->check = 0;
        iph->check = ip_fast_csum((unsigned char *)iph, iph->ihl);
}
```

Figure 6.4 IP output—loopback: `linux/net/ipv4/ip_output.c`.

```
/* dev_loopback_xmit for use with netfilter. */
static int ip_dev_loopback_xmit(struct sk_buff *newskb)
{
        newskb->mac.raw = newskb->data;
        skb_pull(newskb, newskb->nh.raw - newskb->data);
        newskb->pkt_type = PACKET_LOOPBACK;
        newskb->ip_summed = CHECKSUM_UNNECESSARY;
        BUG_TRAP(newskb->dst);

#ifdef CONFIG_NETFILTER_DEBUG
        nf_debug_ip_loopback_xmit(newskb);
#endif
        netif_rx(newskb);
        return 0;
}
```

Figure 6.5 IP output—reroute?: `linux/net/ipv4/ip_output.c`.

```
/* Don't just hand NF_HOOK skb->dst->output, in case netfilter hook
   changes route */
static inline int
output_maybe_reroute(struct sk_buff *skb)
{
        return skb->dst->output(skb);
}
```

Figure 6.6 IP output—multicast replication: `linux/net/ipv4/ip_output.c`.

```
int ip_mc_output(struct sk_buff *skb)
{
        struct sock *sk = skb->sk;
        struct rtable *rt = (struct rtable*)skb->dst;
        struct net_device *dev = rt->u.dst.dev;

        /*
         *      If the indicated interface is up and running, send the packet.
         */
        IP_INC_STATS(IpOutRequests);
#ifdef CONFIG_IP_ROUTE_NAT
        if (rt->rt_flags & RTCF_NAT)
                ip_do_nat(skb);
#endif

        skb->dev = dev;
        skb->protocol = __constant_htons(ETH_P_IP);

        /*
         *      Multicasts are looped back for other local users
         */

        if (rt->rt_flags&RTCF_MULTICAST && (!sk || sk->protinfo.af_inet.mc_loop)) {
#ifdef CONFIG_IP_MROUTE
                /* Small optimization: do not loopback not local frames,
                   which returned after forwarding; they will be dropped
                   by ip_mr_input in any case.
                   Note, that local frames are looped back to be delivered
                   to local recipients.

                   This check is duplicated in ip_mr_input at the moment.
                 */
                if ((rt->rt_flags&RTCF_LOCAL) || !(IPCB(skb)->flags&IPSKB_FORWARDED))
#endif
                {
                        struct sk_buff *newskb = skb_clone(skb, GFP_ATOMIC);
                        if (newskb)
                                NF_HOOK(PF_INET, NF_IP_POST_ROUTING, newskb, NULL,
                                        newskb->dev,
                                        ip_dev_loopback_xmit);
                }
```

Figure 6.7 IP output—multicast replication: `linux/net/ipv4/ip_output.c`.

```
                /* Multicasts with ttl 0 must not go beyond the host */

                if (skb->nh.iph->ttl == 0) {
                        kfree_skb(skb);
                        return 0;
                }
        }

        if (rt->rt_flags&RTCF_BROADCAST) {
                struct sk_buff *newskb = skb_clone(skb, GFP_ATOMIC);
                if (newskb)
                        NF_HOOK(PF_INET, NF_IP_POST_ROUTING, newskb, NULL,
                                newskb->dev, ip_dev_loopback_xmit);
        }

        return ip_finish_output(skb);
}
```

Figure 6.8 IP output—drive output: `linux/net/ipv4/ip_output.c`.

```
int ip_output(struct sk_buff *skb)
{
#ifdef CONFIG_IP_ROUTE_NAT
        struct rtable *rt = (struct rtable*)skb->dst;
#endif

        IP_INC_STATS(IpOutRequests);

#ifdef CONFIG_IP_ROUTE_NAT
        if (rt->rt_flags&RTCF_NAT)
                ip_do_nat(skb);
#endif

        return ip_finish_output(skb);
}
```

Figure 6.9 IP output—queue for sending—part 2i: `linux/net/ipv4/ip_output.c`.

```
/* Queues a packet to be sent, and starts the transmitter if necessary.
 * This routine also needs to put in the total length and compute the
 * checksum. We use to do this in two stages, ip_build_header() then
 * this, but that scheme created a mess when routes disappeared etc.
 * So we do it all here, and the TCP send engine has been changed to
 * match. (No more unroutable FIN disasters, etc. wheee...) This will
 * most likely make other reliable transport layers above IP easier
 * to implement under Linux.
 */
```

```
277   static inline int ip_queue_xmit2(struct sk_buff *skb)
278   {
279           struct sock *sk = skb->sk;
280           struct rtable *rt = (struct rtable *)skb->dst;
281           struct net_device *dev;
282           struct iphdr *iph = skb->nh.iph;
283
284           dev = rt->u.dst.dev;
285
286           /* This can happen when the transport layer has segments queued
287            * with a cached route, and by the time we get here things are
288            * re-routed to a device with a different MTU than the original
289            * device. Sick, but we must cover it.
290            */
291           if (skb_headroom(skb) < dev->hard_header_len && dev->hard_header) {
292                   struct sk_buff *skb2;
293
294                   skb2 = skb_realloc_headroom(skb, (dev->hard_header_len + 15) & ~15);
295                   kfree_skb(skb);
296                   if (skb2 == NULL)
297                           return -ENOMEM;
298                   if (sk)
299                           skb_set_owner_w(skb2, sk);
300                   skb = skb2;
301                   iph = skb->nh.iph;
302           }
303
304           if (skb->len > rt->u.dst.pmtu)
305                   goto fragment;
```

Figure 6.10 IP output—queue for sending—part 2ii: `linux/net/ipv4/ip_output.c`.

```
307           if (ip_dont_fragment(sk, &rt->u.dst))
308                   iph->frag_off |= __constant_htons(IP_DF);
309
310           ip_select_ident(iph, &rt->u.dst);
311
312           /* Add an IP checksum. */
313           ip_send_check(iph);
314
315           skb->priority = sk->priority;
316           return skb->dst->output(skb);
317
318   fragment:
319           if (ip_dont_fragment(sk, &rt->u.dst)) {
320                   /* Reject packet ONLY if TCP might fragment
321                    * it itself, if were careful enough.
322                    */
323                   iph->frag_off |= __constant_htons(IP_DF);
324                   NETDEBUG(printk(KERN_DEBUG "sending pkt_too_big to self\n"));
325
326                   icmp_send(skb, ICMP_DEST_UNREACH, ICMP_FRAG_NEEDED,
```

```
327                          htonl(rt->u.dst.pmtu));
328                  kfree_skb(skb);
329                  return -EMSGSIZE;
330          }
331          ip_select_ident(iph, &rt->u.dst);
332          return ip_fragment(skb, skb->dst->output);
333  }
```

Figure 6.11 IP output–queue packet for sending–part 1: `linux/net/ipv4/ip_output.c`.

```
335  int ip_queue_xmit(struct sk_buff *skb)
336  {
337          struct sock *sk = skb->sk;
338          struct ip_options *opt = sk->protinfo.af_inet.opt;
339          struct rtable *rt;
340          struct iphdr *iph;
341
342          /* Make sure we can route this packet. */
343          rt = (struct rtable *)__sk_dst_check(sk, 0);
344          if (rt == NULL) {
345                  u32 daddr;
346
347                  /* Use correct destination address if we have options. */
348                  daddr = sk->daddr;
349                  if(opt && opt->srr)
350                          daddr = opt->faddr;
351
352                  /* If this fails, retransmit mechanism of transport layer will
353                   * keep trying until route appears or the connection times itself
354                   * out.
355                   */
356                  if (ip_route_output(&rt, daddr, sk->saddr,
357                                        RT_TOS(sk->protinfo.af_inet.tos) | RTO_CONN | sk->localroute,
358                                        sk->bound_dev_if))
359                          goto no_route;
360                  __sk_dst_set(sk, &rt->u.dst);
361          }
362          skb->dst = dst_clone(&rt->u.dst);
363
364          if (opt && opt->is_strictroute && rt->rt_dst != rt->rt_gateway)
365                  goto no_route;
```

Figure 6.12 IP output–queue packet for sending–part 1: `linux/net/ipv4/ip_output.c`.

```
367          /* OK, we know where to send it, allocate and build IP header. */
368          iph = (struct iphdr *) skb_push(skb, sizeof(struct iphdr) + (opt ? opt->optlen : 0));
369          *((__u16 *)iph) = htons((4 << 12) | (5 << 8) | (sk->protinfo.af_inet.tos & 0xff));
370          iph->tot_len = htons(skb->len);
371          iph->frag_off = 0;
372          iph->ttl     = sk->protinfo.af_inet.ttl;
373          iph->protocol = sk->protocol;
```

```
        iph->saddr   = rt->rt_src;
        iph->daddr   = rt->rt_dst;
        skb->nh.iph  = iph;
        /* Transport layer set skb->h.foo itself. */

        if(opt && opt->optlen) {
                iph->ihl += opt->optlen >> 2;
                ip_options_build(skb, opt, sk->daddr, rt, 0);
        }

        return NF_HOOK(PF_INET, NF_IP_LOCAL_OUT, skb, NULL, rt->u.dst.dev,
                       ip_queue_xmit2);

no_route:
        IP_INC_STATS(IpOutNoRoutes);
        kfree_skb(skb);
        return -EHOSTUNREACH;
}
```

Figure 6.13 IP output—classic building of IP packet: `linux/net/ipv4/ip_output.c`.

```
/*
 *      Build and send a packet, with as little as one copy
 *
 *      Doesn't care much about ip options... option length can be
 *      different for fragment at 0 and other fragments.
 *
 *      Note that the fragment at the highest offset is sent first,
 *      so the getfrag routine can fill in the TCP/UDP checksum header
 *      field in the last fragment it sends... actually it also helps
 *      the reassemblers, they can put most packets in at the head of
 *      the fragment queue, and they know the total size in advance. This
 *      last feature will measurably improve the Linux fragment handler one
 *      day.
 *
 *      The callback has five args, an arbitrary pointer (copy of frag),
 *      the source IP address (may depend on the routing table), the
 *      destination address (char *), the offset to copy from, and the
 *      length to be copied.
 */

static int ip_build_xmit_slow(struct sock *sk,
                  int getfrag (const void *,
                               char *,
                               unsigned int,
                               unsigned int),
                  const void *frag,
                  unsigned length,
                  struct ipcm_cookie *ipc,
                  struct rtable *rt,
                  int flags)
{
```

Figure 6.14 IP output—classic building of IP packet: `linux/net/ipv4/ip_output.c`.

```
	unsigned int fraglen, maxfraglen, fragheaderlen;
	int err;
	int offset, mf;
	int mtu;
	u16 id = 0;

	int hh_len = (rt->u.dst.dev->hard_header_len + 15)&~15;
	int nfrags=0;
	struct ip_options *opt = ipc->opt;
	int df = 0;

	mtu = rt->u.dst.pmtu;
	if (ip_dont_fragment(sk, &rt->u.dst))
		df = htons(IP_DF);

	length -= sizeof(struct iphdr);

	if (opt) {
		fragheaderlen = sizeof(struct iphdr) + opt->optlen;
		maxfraglen = ((mtu-sizeof(struct iphdr)-opt->optlen) & ~7) + fragheaderlen;
	} else {
		fragheaderlen = sizeof(struct iphdr);

		/*
		 *	Fragheaderlen is the size of 'overhead' on each buffer. Now work
		 *	out the size of the frames to send.
		 */

		maxfraglen = ((mtu-sizeof(struct iphdr)) & ~7) + fragheaderlen;
	}
```

Figure 6.15 IP output—classic building of IP packet: `linux/net/ipv4/ip_output.c`.

```
	if (length + fragheaderlen > 0xFFFF) {
		ip_local_error(sk, EMSGSIZE, rt->rt_dst, sk->dport, mtu);
		return -EMSGSIZE;
	}


	/*
	 *	Start at the end of the frame by handling the remainder.
	 */

	offset = length - (length % (maxfraglen - fragheaderlen));

	/*
	 *	Amount of memory to allocate for final fragment.
	 */

	fraglen = length - offset + fragheaderlen;

	if (length-offset==0) {
```

```
                fraglen = maxfraglen;
                offset -= maxfraglen-fragheaderlen;
        }

        /*
         *      The last fragment will not have MF (more fragments) set.
         */

        mf = 0;
```

Figure 6.16 IP output—classic building of IP packet: `linux/net/ipv4/ip_output.c`.

```
        /*
         *      Don't fragment packets for path mtu discovery.
         */

        if (offset > 0 && sk->protinfo.af_inet.pmtudisc==IP_PMTUDISC_DO) {
                ip_local_error(sk, EMSGSIZE, rt->rt_dst, sk->dport, mtu);
                return -EMSGSIZE;
        }
        if (flags&MSG_PROBE)
                goto out;
```

6.2.2 Fragmentation

Here is where IP output loops over a buffer that is bigger than the MTU size, and generates fragments to send.

Figure 6.17 IP output—classic building of IP packet: `linux/net/ipv4/ip_output.c`.

```
        /*
         *      Begin outputting the bytes.
         */

        do {
                char *data;
                struct sk_buff * skb;

                /*
                 *      Get the memory we require with some space left for alignment.
                 */

                skb = sock_alloc_send_skb(sk, fraglen+hh_len+15, 0, flags&MSG_DONTWAIT, &err);
                if (skb == NULL)
                        goto error;

                /*
```

```
         *      Fill in the control structures
         */

        skb->priority = sk->priority;
        skb->dst = dst_clone(&rt->u.dst);
        skb_reserve(skb, hh_len);

        /*
         *      Find where to start putting bytes.
         */

        data = skb_put(skb, fraglen);
        skb->nh.iph = (struct iphdr *)data;
```

Figure 6.18 IP output—classic building of IP packet: `linux/net/ipv4/ip_output.c`.

```
        /*
         *      Only write IP header onto non-raw packets
         */

        {
                struct iphdr *iph = (struct iphdr *)data;

                iph->version = 4;
                iph->ihl = 5;
                if (opt) {
                        iph->ihl += opt->optlen>>2;
                        ip_options_build(skb, opt,
                                         ipc->addr, rt, offset);
                }
                iph->tos = sk->protinfo.af_inet.tos;
                iph->tot_len = htons(fraglen - fragheaderlen + iph->ihl*4);
                iph->frag_off = htons(offset>>3)|mf|df;
                iph->id = id;
```

Figure 6.19 IP output—classic building of IP packet: `linux/net/ipv4/ip_output.c`.

```
                if (!mf) {
                        if (offset || !df) {
                                /* Select an unpredictable ident only
                                 * for packets without DF or having
                                 * been fragmented.
                                 */
                                __ip_select_ident(iph, &rt->u.dst);
                                id = iph->id;
                        }

                        /*
                         *      Any further fragments will have MF set.
                         */
                        mf = htons(IP_MF);
```

```
557                           }
558                           if (rt->rt_type == RTN_MULTICAST)
559                                   iph->ttl = sk->protinfo.af_inet.mc_ttl;
560                           else
561                                   iph->ttl = sk->protinfo.af_inet.ttl;
562                           iph->protocol = sk->protocol;
563                           iph->check = 0;
564                           iph->saddr = rt->rt_src;
565                           iph->daddr = rt->rt_dst;
566                           iph->check = ip_fast_csum((unsigned char *)iph, iph->ihl);
567                           data += iph->ihl*4;
568                   }
```

Figure 6.20 IP output—classic building of IP packet: `linux/net/ipv4/ip_output.c`.

```
569
570                   /*
571                    *      User data callback
572                    */
573
574                   if (getfrag(frag, data, offset, fraglen-fragheaderlen)) {
575                           err = -EFAULT;
576                           kfree_skb(skb);
577                           goto error;
578                   }
579
580                   offset -= (maxfraglen-fragheaderlen);
581                   fraglen = maxfraglen;
582
583                   nfrags++;
```

Figure 6.21 IP output—classic building of IP packet: `linux/net/ipv4/ip_output.c`.

```
584
585                   err = NF_HOOK(PF_INET, NF_IP_LOCAL_OUT, skb, NULL,
586                               skb->dst->dev, output_maybe_reroute);
587                   if (err) {
588                           if (err > 0)
589                                   err = sk->protinfo.af_inet.recverr ? net_xmit_errno(err) : 0;
590                           if (err)
591                                   goto error;
592                   }
593           } while (offset >= 0);
594
595       if (nfrags>1)
596               ip_statistics[smp_processor_id()*2 + !in_softirq()].IpFragCreates += nfrags;
597   out:
598       return 0;
599
600   error:
601       IP_INC_STATS(IpOutDiscards);
```

```
        if (nfrags>1)
                ip_statistics[smp_processor_id()*2 + !in_softirq()].IpFragCreates += nfrags;
        return err;
}
```

Nonfragmented Transmission

It is common that the transport layer has used MTU discovery to find the maximum packet size tolerable on a path so that fragmentation subsequently is not necessary. In this case, we want superfast code to handle the situation.

Figure 6.22 IP output—fast path for nonfragmented packets: `linux/net/ipv4/ip_output.c`.

```
/*
 *      Fast path for unfragmented packets.
 */
int ip_build_xmit(struct sock *sk,
                  int getfrag (const void *,
                               char *,
                               unsigned int,
                               unsigned int),
                  const void *frag,
                  unsigned length,
                  struct ipcm_cookie *ipc,
                  struct rtable *rt,
                  int flags)
{
        int err;
        struct sk_buff *skb;
        int df;
        struct iphdr *iph;

        /*
         *      Try the simple case first. This leaves fragmented frames, and by
         *      choice RAW frames within 20 bytes of maximum size(rare) to the long path
         */

        if (!sk->protinfo.af_inet.hdrincl) {
                length += sizeof(struct iphdr);

                /*
                 *      Check for slow path.
                 */
                if (length > rt->u.dst.pmtu || ipc->opt != NULL)
                        return ip_build_xmit_slow(sk,getfrag,frag,length,ipc,rt,flags);
        } else {
                if (length > rt->u.dst.dev->mtu) {
                        ip_local_error(sk, EMSGSIZE, rt->rt_dst, sk->dport, rt->u.dst.dev->mtu);
                        return -EMSGSIZE;
```

```
                }
        }
        if (flags&MSG_PROBE)
                goto out;
```

Figure 6.23 IP output—fast path for nonfragmented packets: `linux/net/ipv4/ip_output.c`.

```
        /*
         *      Do path mtu discovery if needed.
         */
        df = 0;
        if (ip_dont_fragment(sk, &rt->u.dst))
                df = htons(IP_DF);

        /*
         *      Fast path for unfragmented frames without options.
         */
        {
        int hh_len = (rt->u.dst.dev->hard_header_len + 15)&~15;

        skb = sock_alloc_send_skb(sk, length+hh_len+15,
                                  0, flags&MSG_DONTWAIT, &err);
        if(skb==NULL)
                goto error;
        skb_reserve(skb, hh_len);
        }

        skb->priority = sk->priority;
        skb->dst = dst_clone(&rt->u.dst);

        skb->nh.iph = iph = (struct iphdr *)skb_put(skb, length);

        if(!sk->protinfo.af_inet.hdrincl) {
                iph->version=4;
                iph->ihl=5;
                iph->tos=sk->protinfo.af_inet.tos;
                iph->tot_len = htons(length);
                iph->frag_off = df;
                iph->ttl=sk->protinfo.af_inet.mc_ttl;
                ip_select_ident(iph, &rt->u.dst);
                if (rt->rt_type != RTN_MULTICAST)
                        iph->ttl=sk->protinfo.af_inet.ttl;
                iph->protocol=sk->protocol;
                iph->saddr=rt->rt_src;
                iph->daddr=rt->rt_dst;
                iph->check=0;
                iph->check = ip_fast_csum((unsigned char *)iph, iph->ihl);
                err = getfrag(frag, ((char *)iph)+iph->ihl*4,0, length-iph->ihl*4);
        }
        else
                err = getfrag(frag, (void *)iph, 0, length);
```

Figure 6.24 IP output—fast path for nonfragmented packets: `linux/net/ipv4/ip_output.c`.

```
        if (err)
                goto error_fault;

        err = NF_HOOK(PF_INET, NF_IP_LOCAL_OUT, skb, NULL, rt->u.dst.dev,
                      output_maybe_reroute);
        if (err > 0)
                err = sk->protinfo.af_inet.recverr ? net_xmit_errno(err) : 0;
        if (err)
                goto error;
out:
        return 0;

error_fault:
        err = -EFAULT;
        kfree_skb(skb);
error:
        IP_INC_STATS(IpOutDiscards);
        return err;
}
```

Here is the actual tight loop over the transport packet buffer, outputting fragments:

Figure 6.25 IP output—fragment: `linux/net/ipv4/ip_output.c`.

```
/*
 *      This IP datagram is too large to be sent in one piece. Break it up into
 *      smaller pieces (each of size equal to IP header plus
 *      a block of the data of the original IP data part) that will yet fit in a
 *      single device frame, and queue such a frame for sending.
 *
 *      Yes this is inefficient, feel free to submit a quicker one.
 */

int ip_fragment(struct sk_buff *skb, int (*output)(struct sk_buff*))
{
        struct iphdr *iph;
        unsigned char *raw;
        unsigned char *ptr;
        struct net_device *dev;
        struct sk_buff *skb2;
        unsigned int mtu, hlen, left, len;
        int offset;
        int not_last_frag;
        struct rtable *rt = (struct rtable*)skb->dst;
        int err = 0;

        dev = rt->u.dst.dev;

```

```
737          /*
738           *      Point into the IP datagram header.
739           */
740
741          raw = skb->nh.raw;
742          iph = (struct iphdr*)raw;
```

Figure 6.26 IP output—fragment: `linux/net/ipv4/ip_output.c`.

```
744          /*
745           *      Setup starting values.
746           */
747
748          hlen = iph->ihl * 4;
749          left = ntohs(iph->tot_len) - hlen;  /* Space per frame */
750          mtu = rt->u.dst.pmtu - hlen; /* Size of data space */
751          ptr = raw + hlen;                    /* Where to start from */
752
753          /*
754           *      Fragment the datagram.
755           */
756
757          offset = (ntohs(iph->frag_off) & IP_OFFSET) << 3;
758          not_last_frag = iph->frag_off & htons(IP_MF);
759
760          /*
761           *      Keep copying data until we run out.
762           */
763
764          while(left > 0) {
765                  len = left;
766                  /* IF: it doesn't fit, use 'mtu' - the data space left */
767                  if (len > mtu)
768                          len = mtu;
769                  /* IF: we are not sending upto and including the packet end
770                     then align the next start on an eight byte boundary */
771                  if (len < left) {
772                          len &= ~7;
773                  }
774                  /*
775                   *      Allocate buffer.
776                   */
```

Figure 6.27 IP output—fragment: `linux/net/ipv4/ip_output.c`.

```
778                  if ((skb2 = alloc_skb(len+hlen+dev->hard_header_len+15,GFP_ATOMIC)) == NULL) {
779                          NETDEBUG(printk(KERN_INFO "IP: frag: no memory for new fragment!\n"));
780                          err = -ENOMEM;
781                          goto fail;
```

```
        }

        /*
         *      Set up data on packet
         */

        skb2->pkt_type = skb->pkt_type;
        skb2->priority = skb->priority;
        skb_reserve(skb2, (dev->hard_header_len+15)&~15);
        skb_put(skb2, len + hlen);
        skb2->nh.raw = skb2->data;
        skb2->h.raw = skb2->data + hlen;

        /*
         *      Charge the memory for the fragment to any owner
         *      it might possess
         */

        if (skb->sk)
                skb_set_owner_w(skb2, skb->sk);
        skb2->dst = dst_clone(skb->dst);
        skb2->dev = skb->dev;

        /*
         *      Copy the packet header into the new buffer.
         */

        memcpy(skb2->nh.raw, raw, hlen);

        /*
         *      Copy a block of the IP datagram.
         */
        memcpy(skb2->h.raw, ptr, len);
        left -= len;
```

Figure 6.28 IP output—fragment: `linux/net/ipv4/ip_output.c`.

```
        /*
         *      Fill in the new header fields.
         */
        iph = skb2->nh.iph;
        iph->frag_off = htons((offset >> 3));

        /* ANK: dirty, but effective trick. Upgrade options only if
         * the segment to be fragmented was THE FIRST (otherwise,
         * options are already fixed) and make it ONCE
         * on the initial skb, so that all the following fragments
         * will inherit fixed options.
         */
        if (offset == 0)
                ip_options_fragment(skb);

```

```
832                     /*
833                      *        Added AC : If we are fragmenting a fragment that's not the
834                      *                  last fragment then keep MF on each bit
835                      */
836                     if (left > 0 || not_last_frag)
837                             iph->frag_off |= htons(IP_MF);
838                     ptr += len;
839                     offset += len;
840
841     #ifdef CONFIG_NETFILTER
842                     /* Connection association is same as pre-frag packet */
843                     skb2->nfct = skb->nfct;
844                     nf_conntrack_get(skb2->nfct);
845     #ifdef CONFIG_NETFILTER_DEBUG
846                     skb2->nf_debug = skb->nf_debug;
847     #endif
848     #endif
```

Figure 6.29 IP output—fragment: `linux/net/ipv4/ip_output.c`.

```
850                     /*
851                      *        Put this fragment into the sending queue.
852                      */
853
854                     IP_INC_STATS(IpFragCreates);
855
856                     iph->tot_len = htons(len + hlen);
857
858                     ip_send_check(iph);
859
860                     err = output(skb2);
861                     if (err)
862                             goto fail;
863             }
864     kfree_skb(skb);
865     IP_INC_STATS(IpFragOKs);
866     return err;
867
868     fail:
869     kfree_skb(skb);
870     IP_INC_STATS(IpFragFails);
871     return err;
872     }
```

Noncontiguous Buffers

As in Chapter 5, we need to handle noncontiguous buffers. It would be excellent
if this could be done across the entire stack without generating packet copies
or new sk_buff allocations.

Figure 6.30 IP output—deal with `iovec` and `checksum` for next function: `linux/net/ipv4/ip_output.c`.

```
874   /*
875    *      Fetch data from kernel space and fill in checksum if needed.
876    */
877   static int ip_reply_glue_bits(const void *dptr, char *to, unsigned int offset,
878                                 unsigned int fraglen)
879   {
880           struct ip_reply_arg *dp = (struct ip_reply_arg*)dptr;
881           u16 *pktp = (u16 *)to;
882           struct iovec *iov;
883           int len;
884           int hdrflag = 1;
885
886           iov = &dp->iov[0];
887           if (offset >= iov->iov_len) {
888                   offset -= iov->iov_len;
889                   iov++;
890                   hdrflag = 0;
891           }
892           len = iov->iov_len - offset;
893           if (fraglen > len) { /* overlapping. */
894                   dp->csum = csum_partial_copy_nocheck(iov->iov_base+offset, to, len,
895                                           dp->csum);
896                   offset = 0;
897                   fraglen -= len;
898                   to += len;
899                   iov++;
900           }
901
902           dp->csum = csum_partial_copy_nocheck(iov->iov_base+offset, to, fraglen,
903                                           dp->csum);
904
905           if (hdrflag && dp->csumoffset)
906                   *(pktp + dp->csumoffset) = csum_fold(dp->csum); /* fill in checksum */
907           return 0;
908   }
```

The next case deals with a common case, where we have a prototype packet received from somewhere (e.g., an ICMP request) and we need to generate the packet going the other way.

Figure 6.31 IP output—build a packet that is a response to something: `linux/net/ipv4/ip_output.c`.

```
910   /*
911    *      Generic function to send a packet as reply to another packet.
912    *      Used to send TCP resets so far. ICMP should use this function too.
913    *
914    *      Should run single threaded per socket because it uses the sock
915    *      structure to pass arguments.
916    */
```

```
void ip_send_reply(struct sock *sk, struct sk_buff *skb, struct ip_reply_arg *arg,
                   unsigned int len)
{
        struct {
                struct ip_options       opt;
                char                    data[40];
        } replyopts;
        struct ipcm_cookie ipc;
        u32 daddr;
        struct rtable *rt = (struct rtable*)skb->dst;

        if (ip_options_echo(&replyopts.opt, skb))
                return;

        daddr = ipc.addr = rt->rt_src;
        ipc.opt = NULL;

        if (replyopts.opt.optlen) {
                ipc.opt = &replyopts.opt;

                if (ipc.opt->srr)
                        daddr = replyopts.opt.faddr;
        }

        if (ip_route_output(&rt, daddr, rt->rt_spec_dst, RT_TOS(skb->nh.iph->tos), 0))
                return;

        /* And let IP do all the hard work.

           This chunk is not reenterable, hence spinlock.
           Note that it uses the fact, that this function is called
           with locally disabled BH and that sk cannot be already spinlocked.
         */
        bh_lock_sock(sk);
        sk->protinfo.af_inet.tos = skb->nh.iph->tos;
        sk->priority = skb->priority;
        sk->protocol = skb->nh.iph->protocol;
        ip_build_xmit(sk, ip_reply_glue_bits, arg, len, &ipc, rt, MSG_DONTWAIT);
        bh_unlock_sock(sk);

        ip_rt_put(rt);
}
```

Initialization

Figure 6.32 IP output—initialize IP layer: `linux/net/ipv4/ip_output.c`.

```
/*
 *      IP protocol layer initialiser
 */

static struct packet_type ip_packet_type =
```

```
{
        __constant_htons(ETH_P_IP),
        NULL,  /* All devices */
        ip_rcv,
        (void*)1,
        NULL,
};

/*
 *      IP registers the packet type and then calls the subprotocol initialisers
 */

void __init ip_init(void)
{
        dev_add_pack(&ip_packet_type);

        ip_rt_init();
        inet_initpeers();

#ifdef CONFIG_IP_MULTICAST
        proc_net_create("igmp", 0, ip_mc_procinfo);
#endif
}
```

6.2.3 Internet Protocol Input

Receiving IP packets—first of all, there is a brief discussion of IP reassembly hacking:

Figure 6.33 Internet Protocol–input–preamble: `linux/net/ipv4/ip_input.c`.

```
 * To Fix:
 *              IP fragmentation wants rewriting cleanly. The RFC 815 algorithm is much more
       efficient
 *              and could be made very efficient with the addition of some virtual memory hacks to
        permit
 *              the allocation of a buffer that can then be 'grown' by twiddling page tables.
 *              Output fragmentation wants updating along with the buffer management to use a
       single
 *              interleaved copy algorithm so that fragmenting has a one copy overhead. Actual
       packet
 *              output should probably do its own fragmentation at the UDP/RAW layer. TCP shouldn'
       t cause
 *              fragmentation anyway.
```

Figure 6.34 IP input–stats for network managers: `linux/net/ipv4/ip_input.c`.

```
struct ip_mib ip_statistics[NR_CPUS*2];
```

Figure 6.35 IP input—router alter handler: `linux/net/ipv4/ip_input.c`.

```
/*
 *      Process Router Attention IP option
 */
int ip_call_ra_chain(struct sk_buff *skb)
{
        struct ip_ra_chain *ra;
        u8 protocol = skb->nh.iph->protocol;
        struct sock *last = NULL;

        read_lock(&ip_ra_lock);
        for (ra = ip_ra_chain; ra; ra = ra->next) {
                struct sock *sk = ra->sk;

                /* If socket is bound to an interface, only report
                 * the packet if it came from that interface.
                 */
                if (sk && sk->num == protocol
                    && ((sk->bound_dev_if == 0)
                        || (sk->bound_dev_if == skb->dev->ifindex))) {
                        if (skb->nh.iph->frag_off & htons(IP_MF|IP_OFFSET)) {
                                skb = ip_defrag(skb);
                                if (skb == NULL) {
                                        read_unlock(&ip_ra_lock);
                                        return 1;
                                }
                        }
                        if (last) {
                                struct sk_buff *skb2 = skb_clone(skb, GFP_ATOMIC);
                                if (skb2)
                                        raw_rcv(last, skb2);
                        }
                        last = sk;
                }
        }

        if (last) {
                raw_rcv(last, skb);
                read_unlock(&ip_ra_lock);
                return 1;
        }
        read_unlock(&ip_ra_lock);
        return 0;
}
```

Figure 6.36 IP input—find IP protocol—not inline: `linux/net/ipv4/ip_input.c`.

```
/* Handle this out of line, it is rare. */
static int ip_run_ipprot(struct sk_buff *skb, struct iphdr *iph,
                         struct inet_protocol *ipprot, int force_copy)
{
        int ret = 0;
```

```

	do {
		if (ipprot->protocol == iph->protocol) {
			struct sk_buff *skb2 = skb;
			if (ipprot->copy || force_copy)
				skb2 = skb_clone(skb, GFP_ATOMIC);
			if(skb2 != NULL) {
				ret = 1;
				ipprot->handler(skb2,
					ntohs(iph->tot_len) - (iph->ihl * 4));
			}
		}
		ipprot = (struct inet_protocol *) ipprot->next;
	} while(ipprot != NULL);

	return ret;
}
```

Figure 6.37 IP input—deliver IP packets 2nd stage: `linux/net/ipv4/ip_input.c`.

```
static inline int ip_local_deliver_finish(struct sk_buff *skb)
{
	struct iphdr *iph = skb->nh.iph;

#ifdef CONFIG_NETFILTER_DEBUG
	nf_debug_ip_local_deliver(skb);
#endif /*CONFIG_NETFILTER_DEBUG*/

	/* Point into the IP datagram, just past the header. */
	skb->h.raw = skb->nh.raw + iph->ihl*4;

	{
		/* Note: See raw.c and net/raw.h, RAWV4_HTABLE_SIZE==MAX_INET_PROTOS */
		int hash = iph->protocol & (MAX_INET_PROTOS - 1);
		struct sock *raw_sk = raw_v4_htable[hash];
		struct inet_protocol *ipprot;
		int flag;

		/* If there maybe a raw socket we must check - if not we
		 * don't care less
		 */
		if(raw_sk != NULL)
			raw_sk = raw_v4_input(skb, iph, hash);

		ipprot = (struct inet_protocol *) inet_protos[hash];
		flag = 0;
		if(ipprot != NULL) {
			if(raw_sk == NULL &&
			   ipprot->next == NULL &&
			   ipprot->protocol == iph->protocol) {
				int ret;

```

```
                        /* Fast path... */
                        ret = ipprot->handler(skb, (ntohs(iph->tot_len) -
                                                (iph->ihl * 4)));

                        return ret;
                } else {
                        flag = ip_run_ipprot(skb, iph, ipprot, (raw_sk != NULL));
                }
        }

        /* All protocols checked.
         * If this packet was a broadcast, we may *not* reply to it, since that
         * causes (proven, grin) ARP storms and a leakage of memory (i.e. all
         * ICMP reply messages get queued up for transmission...)
         */
```

Figure 6.38 IP input—deliver IP packets 1st stage: `linux/net/ipv4/ip_input.c`.

```
/*
 *      Deliver IP Packets to the higher protocol layers.
 */
int ip_local_deliver(struct sk_buff *skb)
{
        struct iphdr *iph = skb->nh.iph;

        /*
         *      Reassemble IP fragments.
         */

        if (iph->frag_off & htons(IP_MF|IP_OFFSET)) {
                skb = ip_defrag(skb);
                if (!skb)
                        return 0;
        }

        return NF_HOOK(PF_INET, NF_IP_LOCAL_IN, skb, skb->dev, NULL,
                       ip_local_deliver_finish);
}
```

Figure 6.39 IP input—finish IP reception: `linux/net/ipv4/ip_input.c`.

```
static inline int ip_rcv_finish(struct sk_buff *skb)
{
        struct net_device *dev = skb->dev;
        struct iphdr *iph = skb->nh.iph;

        /*
```

```
306         *       Initialise the virtual path cache for the packet. It describes
307         *       how the packet travels inside Linux networking.
308         */
309        if (skb->dst == NULL) {
310                if (ip_route_input(skb, iph->daddr, iph->saddr, iph->tos, dev))
311                        goto drop;
312        }
313
314 #ifdef CONFIG_NET_CLS_ROUTE
315        if (skb->dst->tclassid) {
316                struct ip_rt_acct *st = ip_rt_acct + 256*smp_processor_id();
317                u32 idx = skb->dst->tclassid;
318                st[idx&0xFF].o_packets++;
319                st[idx&0xFF].o_bytes+=skb->len;
320                st[(idx>>16)&0xFF].i_packets++;
321                st[(idx>>16)&0xFF].i_bytes+=skb->len;
322        }
323 #endif
```

Figure 6.40 IP input—finish IP reception: `linux/net/ipv4/ip_input.c`.

```
325        if (iph->ihl > 5) {
326                struct ip_options *opt;
327
328                /* It looks as overkill, because not all
329                   IP options require packet mangling.
330                   But it is the easiest for now, especially taking
331                   into account that combination of IP options
332                   and running sniffer is extremely rare condition.
333                                              --ANK (980813)
334                */
335
336                skb = skb_cow(skb, skb_headroom(skb));
337                if (skb == NULL)
338                        return NET_RX_DROP;
339                iph = skb->nh.iph;
340
341                skb->ip_summed = 0;
342                if (ip_options_compile(NULL, skb))
343                        goto inhdr_error;
344
345                opt = &(IPCB(skb)->opt);
346                if (opt->srr) {
347                        struct in_device *in_dev = in_dev_get(dev);
348                        if (in_dev) {
349                                if (!IN_DEV_SOURCE_ROUTE(in_dev)) {
350                                        if (IN_DEV_LOG_MARTIANS(in_dev) && net_ratelimit())
351                                                printk(KERN_INFO "source route option %u.%u.%u.%u
                                                         -> %u.%u.%u.%u\n",
352                                                        NIPQUAD(iph->saddr), NIPQUAD(iph->daddr));
353                                        in_dev_put(in_dev);
```

```
                                        goto drop;
                                }
                                in_dev_put(in_dev);
                        }
                        if (ip_options_rcv_srr(skb))
                                goto drop;
                }
        }

        return skb->dst->input(skb);

inhdr_error:
        IP_INC_STATS_BH(IpInHdrErrors);
drop:
        kfree_skb(skb);
        return NET_RX_DROP;
}
```

Figure 6.41 IP input—main IP reception routine: `linux/net/ipv4/ip_input.c`.

```
/*
 *      Main IP Receive routine.
 */
int ip_rcv(struct sk_buff *skb, struct net_device *dev, struct packet_type *pt)
{
        struct iphdr *iph = skb->nh.iph;

        /* When the interface is in promisc. mode, drop all the crap
         * that it receives, do not try to analyse it.
         */
        if (skb->pkt_type == PACKET_OTHERHOST)
                goto drop;

        IP_INC_STATS_BH(IpInReceives);

        if ((skb = skb_share_check(skb, GFP_ATOMIC)) == NULL)
                goto out;

        /*
         *      RFC 1122: 3.1.2.2 MUST silently discard any IP frame that fails the checksum.
         *
         *      Is the datagram acceptable?
         *
         *      1.      Length at least the size of an ip header
         *      2.      Version of 4
         *      3.      Checksums correctly. [Speed optimisation for later, skip loopback
        checksums]
         *      4.      Doesn't have a bogus length
         */
```

Figure 6.42 IP input—main IP reception routine: `linux/net/ipv4/ip_input.c`.

```
        if (skb->len < sizeof(struct iphdr) || skb->len < (iph->ihl<<2))
                goto inhdr_error;
        if (iph->ihl < 5 || iph->version != 4 || ip_fast_csum((u8 *)iph, iph->ihl) != 0)
                goto inhdr_error;

        {
                __u32 len = ntohs(iph->tot_len);
                if (skb->len < len || len < (iph->ihl<<2))
                        goto inhdr_error;

                /* Our transport medium may have padded the buffer out. Now we know it
                 * is IP we can trim to the true length of the frame.
                 * Note this now means skb->len holds ntohs(iph->tot_len).
                 */
                __skb_trim(skb, len);
        }

        return NF_HOOK(PF_INET, NF_IP_PRE_ROUTING, skb, dev, NULL,
                       ip_rcv_finish);

inhdr_error:
        IP_INC_STATS_BH(IpInHdrErrors);
drop:
        kfree_skb(skb);
out:
        return NET_RX_DROP;
}
```

6.2.4 Internet Protocol Forwarding

Figure 6.43 Internet Protocol—forward last part: `linux/net/ipv4/ip_forward.c`.

```
static inline int ip_forward_finish(struct sk_buff *skb)
{
        struct ip_options * opt = &(IPCB(skb)->opt);

        IP_INC_STATS_BH(IpForwDatagrams);

        if (opt->optlen == 0) {
#ifdef CONFIG_NET_FASTROUTE
                struct rtable *rt = (struct rtable*)skb->dst;

                if (rt->rt_flags&RTCF_FAST && !netdev_fastroute_obstacles) {
                        struct dst_entry *old_dst;
                        unsigned h = ((*(u8*)&rt->key.dst)^(*(u8*)&rt->key.src))&
                              NETDEV_FASTROUTE_HMASK;

                        write_lock_irq(&skb->dev->fastpath_lock);
                        old_dst = skb->dev->fastpath[h];
```

```
                        skb->dev->fastpath[h] = dst_clone(&rt->u.dst);
                        write_unlock_irq(&skb->dev->fastpath_lock);

                        dst_release(old_dst);
                }
#endif
                return (ip_send(skb));
        }

        ip_forward_options(skb);
        return (ip_send(skb));
}
```

Figure 6.44 Internet Protocol—forward first bit: `linux/net/ipv4/ip_forward.c`.

```
int ip_forward(struct sk_buff *skb)
{
        struct net_device *dev2;        /* Output device */
        struct iphdr *iph;      /* Our header */
        struct rtable *rt;      /* Route we use */
        struct ip_options * opt = &(IPCB(skb)->opt);
        unsigned short mtu;

        if (IPCB(skb)->opt.router_alert && ip_call_ra_chain(skb))
                return NET_RX_SUCCESS;

        if (skb->pkt_type != PACKET_HOST)
                goto drop;

        /*
         *      According to the RFC, we must first decrease the TTL field. If
         *      that reaches zero, we must reply an ICMP control message telling
         *      that the packet's lifetime expired.
         */

        iph = skb->nh.iph;
        rt = (struct rtable*)skb->dst;

        if (iph->ttl <= 1)
                goto too_many_hops;

        if (opt->is_strictroute && rt->rt_dst != rt->rt_gateway)
                goto sr_failed;

        /*
         *      Having picked a route we can now send the frame out
         *      after asking the firewall permission to do so.
         */

        skb->priority = rt_tos2priority(iph->tos);
        dev2 = rt->u.dst.dev;
        mtu = rt->u.dst.pmtu;
```

```
110
111          /*
112          *        We now generate an ICMP HOST REDIRECT giving the route
113          *        we calculated.
114          */
115          if (rt->rt_flags&RTCF_DOREDIRECT && !opt->srr)
116                  ip_rt_send_redirect(skb);
```

Figure 6.45 Internet Protocol—forward first bit: `linux/net/ipv4/ip_forward.c`.

```
118          /* We are about to mangle packet. Copy it! */
119          if ((skb = skb_cow(skb, dev2->hard_header_len)) == NULL)
120                  return NET_RX_DROP;
121          iph = skb->nh.iph;
122          opt = &(IPCB(skb)->opt);
123
124          /* Decrease ttl after skb cow done */
125          ip_decrease_ttl(iph);
126
127          /*
128           * We now may allocate a new buffer, and copy the datagram into it.
129           * If the indicated interface is up and running, kick it.
130           */
131
132          if (skb->len > mtu && (ntohs(iph->frag_off) & IP_DF))
133                  goto frag_needed;
134
135  #ifdef CONFIG_IP_ROUTE_NAT
136          if (rt->rt_flags & RTCF_NAT) {
137                  if (ip_do_nat(skb)) {
138                          kfree_skb(skb);
139                          return NET_RX_BAD;
140                  }
141          }
142  #endif
143
144          return NF_HOOK(PF_INET, NF_IP_FORWARD, skb, skb->dev, dev2,
145                          ip_forward_finish);
146
147  frag_needed:
148          IP_INC_STATS_BH(IpFragFails);
149          icmp_send(skb, ICMP_DEST_UNREACH, ICMP_FRAG_NEEDED, htonl(mtu));
150          goto drop;
151
152  sr_failed:
153          /*
154           *        Strict routing permits no gatewaying
155           */
156          icmp_send(skb, ICMP_DEST_UNREACH, ICMP_SR_FAILED, 0);
157          goto drop;
158
159  too_many_hops:
```

```
        /* Tell the sender its packet died... */
        icmp_send(skb, ICMP_TIME_EXCEEDED, ICMP_EXC_TTL, 0);
drop:
        kfree_skb(skb);
        return NET_RX_DROP;
}
```

6.2.5 Internet Protocol Fragmentation Support Functions

Figure 6.46 Internet Protocol—fragmentation—data: `linux/net/ipv4/ip_fragment.c`.

```
/* NOTE. Logic of IP defragmentation is parallel to corresponding IPv6
 * code now. If you change something here, _PLEASE_ update ipv6/reassembly.c
 * as well. Or notify me, at least. --ANK
 */

/* Fragment cache limits. We will commit 256K at one time. Should we
 * cross that limit we will prune down to 192K. This should cope with
 * even the most extreme cases without allowing an attacker to measurably
 * harm machine performance.
 */
int sysctl_ipfrag_high_thresh = 256*1024;
int sysctl_ipfrag_low_thresh = 192*1024;

/* Important NOTE! Fragment queue must be destroyed before MSL expires.
 * RFC 791 is wrong proposing to prolongate timer each fragment arrival by TTL.
 */
int sysctl_ipfrag_time = IP_FRAG_TIME;

struct ipfrag_skb_cb
{
        struct inet_skb_parm  h;
        int                   offset;
};

#define FRAG_CB(skb)  ((struct ipfrag_skb_cb*)((skb)->cb))

/* Describe an entry in the "incomplete datagrams" queue. */
struct ipq {
        struct ipq     *next;         /* linked list pointers              */
        u32            saddr;
        u32            daddr;
        u16            id;
        u8             protocol;
        u8             last_in;
#define COMPLETE               4
#define FIRST_IN               2
#define LAST_IN                1

```

```
        struct sk_buff *fragments;   /* linked list of received fragments */
        int            len;          /* total length of original datagram */
        int            meat;
        spinlock_t     lock;
        atomic_t       refcnt;
        struct timer_list timer;     /* when will this queue expire?     */
        struct ipq     **pprev;
        int            iif;          /* Device index - for icmp replies  */
};
```

Figure 6.47 Fragmentation—hash data: `linux/net/ipv4/ip_fragment.c`.

```
/* Hash table. */

#define IPQ_HASHSZ   64

/* Per-bucket lock is easy to add now. */
static struct ipq *ipq_hash[IPQ_HASHSZ];
static rwlock_t ipfrag_lock = RW_LOCK_UNLOCKED;
int ip_frag_nqueues = 0;

static __inline__ void __ipq_unlink(struct ipq *qp)
{
        if(qp->next)
                qp->next->pprev = qp->pprev;
        *qp->pprev = qp->next;
        ip_frag_nqueues--;
}

static __inline__ void ipq_unlink(struct ipq *ipq)
{
        write_lock(&ipfrag_lock);
        __ipq_unlink(ipq);
        write_unlock(&ipfrag_lock);
}

/*
 * Was: ((((id) >> 1) ^ (saddr) ^ (daddr) ^ (prot)) & (IPQ_HASHSZ - 1))
 *
 * I see, I see evil hand of bigendian mafia. On Intel all the packets hit
 * one hash bucket with this hash function. 8)
 */
static __inline__ unsigned int ipqhashfn(u16 id, u32 saddr, u32 daddr, u8 prot)
{
        unsigned int h = saddr ^ daddr;

        h ^= (h>>16)^id;
        h ^= (h>>8)^prot;
        return h & (IPQ_HASHSZ - 1);
}
```

Memory Allocation and Freeing for Fragments

Figure 6.48 Fragmentation—memory tracking: `linux/net/ipv4/ip_fragment.c`.

```
atomic_t ip_frag_mem = ATOMIC_INIT(0); /* Memory used for fragments */

/* Memory Tracking Functions. */
extern __inline__ void frag_kfree_skb(struct sk_buff *skb)
{
        atomic_sub(skb->truesize, &ip_frag_mem);
        kfree_skb(skb);
}

extern __inline__ void frag_free_queue(struct ipq *qp)
{
        atomic_sub(sizeof(struct ipq), &ip_frag_mem);
        kfree(qp);
}

extern __inline__ struct ipq *frag_alloc_queue(void)
{
        struct ipq *qp = kmalloc(sizeof(struct ipq), GFP_ATOMIC);

        if(!qp)
                return NULL;
        atomic_add(sizeof(struct ipq), &ip_frag_mem);
        return qp;
}
```

Figure 6.49 Fragmentation—free up `ipq`: `linux/net/ipv4/ip_fragment.c`.

```

/* Destruction primitives. */

/* Complete destruction of ipq. */
static void ip_frag_destroy(struct ipq *qp)
{
        struct sk_buff *fp;

        BUG_TRAP(qp->last_in&COMPLETE);
        BUG_TRAP(del_timer(&qp->timer) == 0);

        /* Release all fragment data. */
        fp = qp->fragments;
        while (fp) {
                struct sk_buff *xp = fp->next;

                frag_kfree_skb(fp);
                fp = xp;
        }

```

```
        /* Finally, release the queue descriptor itself. */
        frag_free_queue(qp);
}

static __inline__ void ipq_put(struct ipq *ipq)
{
        if (atomic_dec_and_test(&ipq->refcnt))
                ip_frag_destroy(ipq);
}

/* Kill ipq entry. It is not destroyed immediately,
 * because caller (and someone more) holds reference count.
 */
static __inline__ void ipq_kill(struct ipq *ipq)
{
        if (del_timer(&ipq->timer))
                atomic_dec(&ipq->refcnt);

        if (!(ipq->last_in & COMPLETE)) {
                ipq_unlink(ipq);
                atomic_dec(&ipq->refcnt);
                ipq->last_in |= COMPLETE;
        }
}
```

Figure 6.50 Fragmentation—free up space starting with oldest frags: `linux/net/ipv4/ip_fragment.c`.

```
/* Memory limiting on fragments. Evictor trashes the oldest
 * fragment queue until we are back under the low threshold.
 */
static void ip_evictor(void)
{
        int i, progress;

        do {
                if (atomic_read(&ip_frag_mem) <= sysctl_ipfrag_low_thresh)
                        return;
                progress = 0;
                /* FIXME: Make LRU queue of frag heads. -DaveM */
                for (i = 0; i < IPQ_HASHSZ; i++) {
                        struct ipq *qp;
                        if (ipq_hash[i] == NULL)
                                continue;

                        write_lock(&ipfrag_lock);
                        if ((qp = ipq_hash[i]) != NULL) {
                                /* find the oldest queue for this hash bucket */
                                while (qp->next)
                                        qp = qp->next;
                                __ipq_unlink(qp);
                                write_unlock(&ipfrag_lock);
```

```
223
224                             spin_lock(&qp->lock);
225                             if (del_timer(&qp->timer))
226                                     atomic_dec(&qp->refcnt);
227                             qp->last_in |= COMPLETE;
228                             spin_unlock(&qp->lock);
229
230                             ipq_put(qp);
231                             IP_INC_STATS_BH(IpReasmFails);
232                             progress = 1;
233                             continue;
234                     }
235                     write_unlock(&ipfrag_lock);
236             }
237     } while (progress);
238 }
```

Figure 6.51 Fragmentation—reassembly timeout, expire a packet: `linux/net/ipv4/ip_fragment.c`.

```
240 /*
241  * Oops, a fragment queue timed out. Kill it and send an ICMP reply.
242  */
243 static void ip_expire(unsigned long arg)
244 {
245     struct ipq *qp = (struct ipq *) arg;
246
247     spin_lock(&qp->lock);
248
249     if (qp->last_in & COMPLETE)
250             goto out;
251
252     ipq_kill(qp);
253
254     IP_INC_STATS_BH(IpReasmTimeout);
255     IP_INC_STATS_BH(IpReasmFails);
256
257     if ((qp->last_in&FIRST_IN) && qp->fragments != NULL) {
258             struct sk_buff *head = qp->fragments;
259
260             /* Send an ICMP "Fragment Reassembly Timeout" message. */
261             if ((head->dev = dev_get_by_index(qp->iif)) != NULL) {
262                     icmp_send(head, ICMP_TIME_EXCEEDED, ICMP_EXC_FRAGTIME, 0);
263                     dev_put(head->dev);
264             }
265     }
266 out:
267     spin_unlock(&qp->lock);
268     ipq_put(qp);
269 }
```

Figure 6.52 Fragmentation—create fragment: `linux/net/ipv4/ip_fragment.c`.

```
273   static struct ipq *ip_frag_intern(unsigned int hash, struct ipq *qp_in)
274   {
275         struct ipq *qp;
276
277         write_lock(&ipfrag_lock);
278   #ifdef CONFIG_SMP
279         /* With SMP race we have to recheck hash table, because
280          * such entry could be created on other cpu, while we
281          * promoted read lock to write lock.
282          */
283         for(qp = ipq_hash[hash]; qp; qp = qp->next) {
284               if(qp->id == qp_in->id        &&
285                  qp->saddr == qp_in->saddr &&
286                  qp->daddr == qp_in->daddr &&
287                  qp->protocol == qp_in->protocol) {
288                     atomic_inc(&qp->refcnt);
289                     write_unlock(&ipfrag_lock);
290                     qp_in->last_in |= COMPLETE;
291                     ipq_put(qp_in);
292                     return qp;
293               }
294         }
295   #endif
296         qp = qp_in;
297
298         if (!mod_timer(&qp->timer, jiffies + sysctl_ipfrag_time))
299               atomic_inc(&qp->refcnt);
300
301         atomic_inc(&qp->refcnt);
302         if((qp->next = ipq_hash[hash]) != NULL)
303               qp->next->pprev = &qp->next;
304         ipq_hash[hash] = qp;
305         qp->pprev = &ipq_hash[hash];
306         ip_frag_nqueues++;
307         write_unlock(&ipfrag_lock);
308         return qp;
309   }
```

Figure 6.53 Fragmentation—queue whole packet: `linux/net/ipv4/ip_fragment.c`.

```
311   /* Add an entry to the 'ipq' queue for a newly received IP datagram. */
312   static struct ipq *ip_frag_create(unsigned hash, struct iphdr *iph)
313   {
314         struct ipq *qp;
315
316         if ((qp = frag_alloc_queue()) == NULL)
317               goto out_nomem;
318
319         qp->protocol = iph->protocol;
320         qp->last_in = 0;
321         qp->id = iph->id;
```

```
        qp->saddr = iph->saddr;
        qp->daddr = iph->daddr;
        qp->len = 0;
        qp->meat = 0;
        qp->fragments = NULL;
        qp->iif = 0;

        /* Initialize a timer for this entry. */
        init_timer(&qp->timer);
        qp->timer.data = (unsigned long) qp; /* pointer to queue */
        qp->timer.function = ip_expire;     /* expire function    */
        qp->lock = SPIN_LOCK_UNLOCKED;
        atomic_set(&qp->refcnt, 1);

        return ip_frag_intern(hash, qp);

out_nomem:
        NETDEBUG(printk(KERN_ERR "ip_frag_create: no memory left !\n"));
        return NULL;
}
```

Figure 6.54 Fragmentation—match a fragment to rest of datagram in partial queue: `linux/net/ipv4/ip_fragment.c`.

```
/* Find the correct entry in the "incomplete datagrams" queue for
 * this IP datagram, and create new one, if nothing is found.
 */
static inline struct ipq *ip_find(struct iphdr *iph)
{
        __u16 id = iph->id;
        __u32 saddr = iph->saddr;
        __u32 daddr = iph->daddr;
        __u8 protocol = iph->protocol;
        unsigned int hash = ipqhashfn(id, saddr, daddr, protocol);
        struct ipq *qp;

        read_lock(&ipfrag_lock);
        for(qp = ipq_hash[hash]; qp; qp = qp->next) {
                if(qp->id == id       &&
                   qp->saddr == saddr &&
                   qp->daddr == daddr &&
                   qp->protocol == protocol) {
                        atomic_inc(&qp->refcnt);
                        read_unlock(&ipfrag_lock);
                        return qp;
                }
        }
        read_unlock(&ipfrag_lock);

        return ip_frag_create(hash, iph);
}
```

Figure 6.55 Fragmentation—add segment to queue: `linux/net/ipv4/ip_fragment.c`.

```
/* Add new segment to existing queue. */
static void ip_frag_queue(struct ipq *qp, struct sk_buff *skb)
{
        struct iphdr *iph = skb->nh.iph;
        struct sk_buff *prev, *next;
        int flags, offset;
        int ihl, end;

        if (qp->last_in & COMPLETE)
                goto err;

        offset = ntohs(iph->frag_off);
        flags = offset & ~IP_OFFSET;
        offset &= IP_OFFSET;
        offset <<= 3;          /* offset is in 8-byte chunks */
        ihl = iph->ihl * 4;

        /* Determine the position of this fragment. */
        end = offset + (ntohs(iph->tot_len) - ihl);
```

Figure 6.56 Fragmentation—add segment to queue: `linux/net/ipv4/ip_fragment.c`.

```
        /* Is this the final fragment? */
        if ((flags & IP_MF) == 0) {
                /* If we already have some bits beyond end
                 * or have different end, the segment is corrrupted.
                 */
                if (end < qp->len ||
                    ((qp->last_in & LAST_IN) && end != qp->len))
                        goto err;
                qp->last_in |= LAST_IN;
                qp->len = end;
        } else {
                if (end&7) {
                        end &= ~7;
                        if (skb->ip_summed != CHECKSUM_UNNECESSARY)
                                skb->ip_summed = CHECKSUM_NONE;
                }
                if (end > qp->len) {
                        /* Some bits beyond end -> corruption. */
                        if (qp->last_in & LAST_IN)
                                goto err;
                        qp->len = end;
                }
        }
```

Figure 6.57 Fragmentation—add segment to queue: `linux/net/ipv4/ip_fragment.c`.

```
414            if (end == offset)
415                    goto err;
416
417            /* Point into the IP datagram 'data' part. */
418            skb_pull(skb, (skb->nh.raw+ihl) - skb->data);
419            skb_trim(skb, end - offset);
420
421            /* Find out which fragments are in front and at the back of us
422             * in the chain of fragments so far. We must know where to put
423             * this fragment, right?
424             */
425            prev = NULL;
426            for(next = qp->fragments; next != NULL; next = next->next) {
427                    if (FRAG_CB(next)->offset >= offset)
428                            break; /* bingo! */
429                    prev = next;
430            }
431
432            /* We found where to put this one. Check for overlap with
433             * preceding fragment, and, if needed, align things so that
434             * any overlaps are eliminated.
435             */
436            if (prev) {
437                    int i = (FRAG_CB(prev)->offset + prev->len) - offset;
438
439                    if (i > 0) {
440                            offset += i;
441                            if (end <= offset)
442                                    goto err;
443                            skb_pull(skb, i);
444                            if (skb->ip_summed != CHECKSUM_UNNECESSARY)
445                                    skb->ip_summed = CHECKSUM_NONE;
446                    }
447            }
```

Figure 6.58 Fragmentation—add segment to queue: `linux/net/ipv4/ip_fragment.c`.

```
449            while (next && FRAG_CB(next)->offset < end) {
450                    int i = end - FRAG_CB(next)->offset; /* overlap is 'i' bytes */
451
452                    if (i < next->len) {
453                            /* Eat head of the next overlapped fragment
454                             * and leave the loop. The next ones cannot overlap.
455                             */
456                            FRAG_CB(next)->offset += i;
457                            skb_pull(next, i);
458                            qp->meat -= i;
459                            if (next->ip_summed != CHECKSUM_UNNECESSARY)
460                                    next->ip_summed = CHECKSUM_NONE;
461                            break;
462                    } else {
```

```
463                struct sk_buff *free_it = next;
464
465                        /* Old fragmnet is completely overridden with
466                         * new one drop it.
467                         */
468                        next = next->next;
469
470                        if (prev)
471                                prev->next = next;
472                        else
473                                qp->fragments = next;
474
475                        qp->meat -= free_it->len;
476                        frag_kfree_skb(free_it);
477                }
478        }
```

Figure 6.59 Fragmentation—add segment to queue: `linux/net/ipv4/ip_fragment.c`.

```
480        FRAG_CB(skb)->offset = offset;
481
482        /* Insert this fragment in the chain of fragments. */
483        skb->next = next;
484        if (prev)
485                prev->next = skb;
486        else
487                qp->fragments = skb;
488
489        if (skb->dev)
490                qp->iif = skb->dev->ifindex;
491        skb->dev = NULL;
492        qp->meat += skb->len;
493        atomic_add(skb->truesize, &ip_frag_mem);
494        if (offset == 0)
495                qp->last_in |= FIRST_IN;
496
497        return;
498
499 err:
500        kfree_skb(skb);
501 }
```

Reassembly

The inverse of fragmentation is reassembly. This is not strictly an inverse, since fragmentation can occur at any, and many, hops along a route, wherever the MTU on an output link is smaller than the MTU on the input link. However, reassembly is only done at the receiving end system. The other part of reassembly that is complex is that it requires a timer (the only timer in the IP layer) since one needs to deal with lost or out-of-order delivery of fragments (and to be able to discard fragments for packets that will never be complete).

Figure 6.60 Fragmentation—put fragments together: `linux/net/ipv4/ip_fragment.c`.

```
/* Build a new IP datagram from all its fragments.
 *
 * FIXME: We copy here because we lack an effective way of handling lists
 * of bits on input. Until the new skb data handling is in I'm not going
 * to touch this with a bargepole.
 */
static struct sk_buff *ip_frag_reasm(struct ipq *qp, struct net_device *dev)
{
        struct sk_buff *skb;
        struct iphdr *iph;
        struct sk_buff *fp, *head = qp->fragments;
        int len;
        int ihlen;

        ipq_kill(qp);

        BUG_TRAP(head != NULL);
        BUG_TRAP(FRAG_CB(head)->offset == 0);

        /* Allocate a new buffer for the datagram. */
        ihlen = head->nh.iph->ihl*4;
        len = ihlen + qp->len;

        if(len > 65535)
                goto out_oversize;

        skb = dev_alloc_skb(len);
        if (!skb)
                goto out_nomem;
```

Figure 6.61 Fragmentation—put fragments together: `linux/net/ipv4/ip_fragment.c`.

```
        /* Fill in the basic details. */
        skb->mac.raw = skb->data;
        skb->nh.raw = skb->data;
        FRAG_CB(skb)->h = FRAG_CB(head)->h;
        skb->ip_summed = head->ip_summed;
        skb->csum = 0;

        /* Copy the original IP headers into the new buffer. */
        memcpy(skb_put(skb, ihlen), head->nh.iph, ihlen);

        /* Copy the data portions of all fragments into the new buffer. */
        for (fp=head; fp; fp = fp->next) {
                memcpy(skb_put(skb, fp->len), fp->data, fp->len);

                if (skb->ip_summed != fp->ip_summed)
                        skb->ip_summed = CHECKSUM_NONE;
```

```
550                   else if (skb->ip_summed == CHECKSUM_HW)
551                        skb->csum = csum_add(skb->csum, fp->csum);
552          }
553
554          skb->dst = dst_clone(head->dst);
555          skb->pkt_type = head->pkt_type;
556          skb->protocol = head->protocol;
557          skb->dev = dev;
```

Figure 6.62 Fragmentation—put fragments together: `linux/net/ipv4/ip_fragment.c`.

```
559          /*
560           * Clearly bogus, because security markings of the individual
561           * fragments should have been checked for consistency before
562           * gluing, and intermediate coalescing of fragments may have
563           * taken place in ip_defrag() before ip_glue() ever got called.
564           * If we're not going to do the consistency checking, we might
565           * as well take the value associated with the first fragment.
566           *      --rct
567           */
568          skb->security = head->security;
569
570  #ifdef CONFIG_NETFILTER
571          /* Connection association is same as fragment (if any). */
572          skb->nfct = head->nfct;
573          nf_conntrack_get(skb->nfct);
574  #ifdef CONFIG_NETFILTER_DEBUG
575          skb->nf_debug = head->nf_debug;
576  #endif
577  #endif
578
579          /* Done with all fragments. Fixup the new IP header. */
580          iph = skb->nh.iph;
581          iph->frag_off = 0;
582          iph->tot_len = htons(len);
583          IP_INC_STATS_BH(IpReasmOKs);
584          return skb;
585
586  out_nomem:
587          NETDEBUG(printk(KERN_ERR
588                          "IP: queue_glue: no memory for gluing queue %p\n",
589                          qp));
590          goto out_fail;
591  out_oversize:
592          if (net_ratelimit())
593                  printk(KERN_INFO
594                          "Oversized IP packet from %d.%d.%d.%d.\n",
595                          NIPQUAD(qp->saddr));
596  out_fail:
597          IP_INC_STATS_BH(IpReasmFails);
598          return NULL;
599  }
```

Figure 6.63 Fragmentation—deal with arrival of a fragment: `linux/net/ipv4/ip_fragment.c`.

```
/* Process an incoming IP datagram fragment. */
struct sk_buff *ip_defrag(struct sk_buff *skb)
{
        struct iphdr *iph = skb->nh.iph;
        struct ipq *qp;
        struct net_device *dev;

        IP_INC_STATS_BH(IpReasmReqds);

        /* Start by cleaning up the memory. */
        if (atomic_read(&ip_frag_mem) > sysctl_ipfrag_high_thresh)
                ip_evictor();

        dev = skb->dev;

        /* Lookup (or create) queue header */
        if ((qp = ip_find(iph)) != NULL) {
                struct sk_buff *ret = NULL;

                spin_lock(&qp->lock);

                ip_frag_queue(qp, skb);

                if (qp->last_in == (FIRST_IN|LAST_IN) &&
                    qp->meat == qp->len)
                        ret = ip_frag_reasm(qp, dev);

                spin_unlock(&qp->lock);
                ipq_put(qp);
                return ret;
        }

        IP_INC_STATS_BH(IpReasmFails);
        kfree_skb(skb);
        return NULL;
}
```

6.2.6 Internet Protocol Options

IP options in IPv4 are curious things. They have a high potential value, but since (for over two decades) they have remained relatively unused, most routers process them in the *slow path*. The slow path is the uncommon case code, and contains many more checks than so-called *fast-path processing*. In fact, when router vendors throw hardware solutions at a problem, they are committing designs to silicon that are costly, so typically they reduce the number of options to zero.

Nevertheless, we need to handle them because of host requirements. The loose and strict source route and record options would be very useful if they were widely implemented, although they do represent a nasty security hole in the capability for an ISP to do *traceback*.

The *router alert* is becoming an interesting exception to this, since it is typically used only occasionally in the stream of packets that rely on its effect.

IPv6 makes a different design decision to separate out hop-by-hop options from end-to-end options and give a handle to routers to find the next-header easily. We'll look at this later in this chapter.

Figure 6.64 Internet Protocol—options—build IP option header: `linux/net/ipv4/ip_options.c`.

```
/*
 * Write options to IP header, record destination address to
 * source route option, address of outgoing interface
 * (we should already know it, so that this function is allowed be
 * called only after routing decision) and timestamp,
 * if we originate this datagram.
 *
 * daddr is real destination address, next hop is recorded in IP header.
 * saddr is address of outgoing interface.
 */

void ip_options_build(struct sk_buff * skb, struct ip_options * opt,
                      u32 daddr, struct rtable *rt, int is_frag)
{
        unsigned char * iph = skb->nh.raw;

        memcpy(&(IPCB(skb)->opt), opt, sizeof(struct ip_options));
        memcpy(iph+sizeof(struct iphdr), opt->__data, opt->optlen);
        opt = &(IPCB(skb)->opt);
        opt->is_data = 0;

        if (opt->srr)
                memcpy(iph+opt->srr+iph[opt->srr+1]-4, &daddr, 4);

        if (!is_frag) {
                if (opt->rr_needaddr)
                        ip_rt_get_source(iph+opt->rr+iph[opt->rr+2]-5, rt);
                if (opt->ts_needaddr)
                        ip_rt_get_source(iph+opt->ts+iph[opt->ts+2]-9, rt);
                if (opt->ts_needtime) {
                        struct timeval tv;
                        __u32 midtime;
                        do_gettimeofday(&tv);
                        midtime = htonl((tv.tv_sec % 86400) * 1000 + tv.tv_usec / 1000);
                        memcpy(iph+opt->ts+iph[opt->ts+2]-5, &midtime, 4);
                }
                return;
        }
        if (opt->rr) {
                memset(iph+opt->rr, IPOPT_NOP, iph[opt->rr+1]);
                opt->rr = 0;
                opt->rr_needaddr = 0;
```

```
	}
	if (opt->ts) {
		memset(iph+opt->ts, IPOPT_NOP, iph[opt->ts+1]);
		opt->ts = 0;
		opt->ts_needaddr = opt->ts_needtime = 0;
	}
}
```

Figure 6.65 IP options—echo: `linux/net/ipv4/ip_options.c`.

```
/*
 * Provided (sopt, skb) points to received options,
 * build in dopt compiled option set appropriate for answering.
 * i.e. invert SRR option, copy anothers,
 * and grab room in RR/TS options.
 *
 * NOTE: dopt cannot point to skb.
 */

int ip_options_echo(struct ip_options * dopt, struct sk_buff * skb)
{
	struct ip_options *sopt;
	unsigned char *sptr, *dptr;
	int soffset, doffset;
	int	optlen;
	u32	daddr;

	memset(dopt, 0, sizeof(struct ip_options));

	dopt->is_data = 1;

	sopt = &(IPCB(skb)->opt);

	if (sopt->optlen == 0) {
		dopt->optlen = 0;
		return 0;
	}

	sptr = skb->nh.raw;
	dptr = dopt->__data;

	if (skb->dst)
		daddr = ((struct rtable*)skb->dst)->rt_spec_dst;
	else
		daddr = skb->nh.iph->daddr;
```

Figure 6.66 IP options—echo: `linux/net/ipv4/ip_options.c`.

```
	if (sopt->rr) {
		optlen = sptr[sopt->rr+1];
		soffset = sptr[sopt->rr+2];
```

```
114              dopt->rr = dopt->optlen + sizeof(struct iphdr);
115              memcpy(dptr, sptr+sopt->rr, optlen);
116              if (sopt->rr_needaddr && soffset <= optlen) {
117                      if (soffset + 3 > optlen)
118                              return -EINVAL;
119                      dptr[2] = soffset + 4;
120                      dopt->rr_needaddr = 1;
121              }
122              dptr += optlen;
123              dopt->optlen += optlen;
124      }
125      if (sopt->ts) {
126              optlen = sptr[sopt->ts+1];
127              soffset = sptr[sopt->ts+2];
128              dopt->ts = dopt->optlen + sizeof(struct iphdr);
129              memcpy(dptr, sptr+sopt->ts, optlen);
```

Figure 6.67 IP options—echo: `linux/net/ipv4/ip_options.c`.

```
130              if (soffset <= optlen) {
131                      if (sopt->ts_needaddr) {
132                              if (soffset + 3 > optlen)
133                                      return -EINVAL;
134                              dopt->ts_needaddr = 1;
135                              soffset += 4;
136                      }
137                      if (sopt->ts_needtime) {
138                              if (soffset + 3 > optlen)
139                                      return -EINVAL;
140                              if ((dptr[3]&0xF) != IPOPT_TS_PRESPEC) {
141                                      dopt->ts_needtime = 1;
142                                      soffset += 4;
143                              } else {
144                                      dopt->ts_needtime = 0;
145
146                                      if (soffset + 8 <= optlen) {
147                                              __u32 addr;
148
149                                              memcpy(&addr, sptr+soffset-1, 4);
150                                              if (inet_addr_type(addr) != RTN_LOCAL) {
151                                                      dopt->ts_needtime = 1;
152                                                      soffset += 8;
153                                              }
154                                      }
155                              }
156                      }
157                      dptr[2] = soffset;
158              }
159              dptr += optlen;
160              dopt->optlen += optlen;
161      }
```

Figure 6.68 IP options—echo: `linux/net/ipv4/ip_options.c`.

```
162        if (sopt->srr) {
163                unsigned char * start = sptr+sopt->srr;
164                u32 faddr;
165
166                optlen = start[1];
167                soffset = start[2];
168                doffset = 0;
169                if (soffset > optlen)
170                        soffset = optlen + 1;
171                soffset -= 4;
172                if (soffset > 3) {
173                        memcpy(&faddr, &start[soffset-1], 4);
174                        for (soffset-=4, doffset=4; soffset > 3; soffset-=4, doffset+=4)
175                                memcpy(&dptr[doffset-1], &start[soffset-1], 4);
176                        /*
177                         * RFC 1812 requires to fix illegal source routes.
178                         */
179                        if (memcmp(&skb->nh.iph->saddr, &start[soffset+3], 4) == 0)
180                                doffset -= 4;
181                }
182                if (doffset > 3) {
183                        memcpy(&start[doffset-1], &daddr, 4);
184                        dopt->faddr = faddr;
185                        dptr[0] = start[0];
186                        dptr[1] = doffset+3;
187                        dptr[2] = 4;
188                        dptr += doffset+3;
189                        dopt->srr = dopt->optlen + sizeof(struct iphdr);
190                        dopt->optlen += doffset+3;
191                        dopt->is_strictroute = sopt->is_strictroute;
192                }
193        }
194        while (dopt->optlen & 3) {
195                *dptr++ = IPOPT_END;
196                dopt->optlen++;
197        }
198        return 0;
199 }
```

Figure 6.69 IP options—zero-out disallowed options in frags: `linux/net/ipv4/ip_options.c`.

```
201 /*
202  *      Options "fragmenting", just fill options not
203  *      allowed in fragments with NOOPs.
204  *      Simple and stupid 8), but the most efficient way.
205  */
206
207 void ip_options_fragment(struct sk_buff * skb)
208 {
209        unsigned char * optptr = skb->nh.raw;
210        struct ip_options * opt = &(IPCB(skb)->opt);
211        int l = opt->optlen;
```

```
212            int optlen;
213
214        while (l > 0) {
215                switch (*optptr) {
216                case IPOPT_END:
217                        return;
218                case IPOPT_NOOP:
219                        l--;
220                        optptr++;
221                        continue;
222                }
223                optlen = optptr[1];
224                if (optlen<2 || optlen>l)
225                  return;
226                if (!IPOPT_COPIED(*optptr))
227                        memset(optptr, IPOPT_NOOP, optlen);
228                l -= optlen;
229                optptr += optlen;
230        }
231        opt->ts = 0;
232        opt->rr = 0;
233        opt->rr_needaddr = 0;
234        opt->ts_needaddr = 0;
235        opt->ts_needtime = 0;
236        return;
237 }
```

Option Clearing

This is the preamble to processing options:

Figure 6.70 IP options—validate inbound packet header options: linux/net/ipv4/
ip_options.c.

```
239 /*
240  * Verify options and fill pointers in struct options.
241  * Caller should clear *opt, and set opt->data.
242  * If opt == NULL, then skb->data should point to IP header.
243  */
244
245 int ip_options_compile(struct ip_options * opt, struct sk_buff * skb)
246 {
247        int l;
248        unsigned char * iph;
249        unsigned char * optptr;
250        int optlen;
251        unsigned char * pp_ptr = NULL;
252        struct rtable *rt = skb ? (struct rtable*)skb->dst : NULL;
253
254        if (!opt) {
255                opt = &(IPCB(skb)->opt);
256                memset(opt, 0, sizeof(struct ip_options));
257                iph = skb->nh.raw;
```

```
            opt->optlen = ((struct iphdr *)iph)->ihl*4 - sizeof(struct iphdr);
            optptr = iph + sizeof(struct iphdr);
            opt->is_data = 0;
    } else {
            optptr = opt->is_data ? opt->__data : (unsigned char*)&(skb->nh.iph[1]);
            iph = optptr - sizeof(struct iphdr);
    }
```

Next, we deal with NO-OP and option end case:

Figure 6.71 IP options–validate inbound packet header options: `linux/net/ipv4/ip_options.c`.

```
    for (l = opt->optlen; l > 0; ){
            switch (*optptr) {
                  case IPOPT_END:
                    for (optptr++, l--; l>0; l--) {
                            if (*optptr != IPOPT_END) {
                                    *optptr = IPOPT_END;
                                    opt->is_changed = 1;
                            }
                    }
                    goto eol;
                  case IPOPT_NOOP:
                    l--;
                    optptr++;
                    continue;
            }
            optlen = optptr[1];
            if (optlen<2 || optlen>l) {
                    pp_ptr = optptr;
                    goto error;
            }
```

Process loose and strict source route options:

Figure 6.72 IP options–validate inbound packet header options: `linux/net/ipv4/ip_options.c`.

```
            switch (*optptr) {
                  case IPOPT_SSRR:
                  case IPOPT_LSRR:
                    if (optlen < 3) {
                            pp_ptr = optptr + 1;
                            goto error;
                    }
                    if (optptr[2] < 4) {
                            pp_ptr = optptr + 2;
                            goto error;
```

```
296                         }
297                         /* NB: cf RFC-1812 5.2.4.1 */
298                         if (opt->srr) {
299                                 pp_ptr = optptr;
300                                 goto error;
301                         }
302                         if (!skb) {
303                                 if (optptr[2] != 4 || optlen < 7 || ((optlen-3) & 3)) {
304                                         pp_ptr = optptr + 1;
305                                         goto error;
306                                 }
307                                 memcpy(&opt->faddr, &optptr[3], 4);
308                                 if (optlen > 7)
309                                         memmove(&optptr[3], &optptr[7], optlen-7);
310                         }
311                         opt->is_strictroute = (optptr[0] == IPOPT_SSRR);
312                         opt->srr = optptr - iph;
313                         break;
```

Route record:

Figure 6.73 IP options—validate inbound packet header options: linux/net/ipv4/ ip_options.c.

```
314                   case IPOPT_RR:
315                         if (opt->rr) {
316                                 pp_ptr = optptr;
317                                 goto error;
318                         }
319                         if (optlen < 3) {
320                                 pp_ptr = optptr + 1;
321                                 goto error;
322                         }
323                         if (optptr[2] < 4) {
324                                 pp_ptr = optptr + 2;
325                                 goto error;
326                         }
327                         if (optptr[2] <= optlen) {
328                                 if (optptr[2]+3 > optlen) {
329                                         pp_ptr = optptr + 2;
330                                         goto error;
331                                 }
332                                 if (skb) {
333                                         memcpy(&optptr[optptr[2]-1], &rt->rt_spec_dst, 4);
334                                         opt->is_changed = 1;
335                                 }
336                                 optptr[2] += 4;
337                                 opt->rr_needaddr = 1;
338                         }
339                         opt->rr = optptr - iph;
340                         break;
```

Timestamp option processing:

Figure 6.74 IP options—validate inbound packet header options: linux/net/ipv4/ ip_options.c.

```
341                    case IPOPT_TIMESTAMP:
342                 if (opt->ts) {
343                         pp_ptr = optptr;
344                         goto error;
345                 }
346                 if (optlen < 4) {
347                         pp_ptr = optptr + 1;
348                         goto error;
349                 }
350                 if (optptr[2] < 5) {
351                         pp_ptr = optptr + 2;
352                         goto error;
353                 }
354                 if (optptr[2] <= optlen) {
355                         __u32 * timeptr = NULL;
356                         if (optptr[2]+3 > optptr[1]) {
357                                 pp_ptr = optptr + 2;
358                                 goto error;
359                         }
360                         switch (optptr[3]&0xF) {
361                             case IPOPT_TS_TSONLY:
362                                 opt->ts = optptr - iph;
363                                 if (skb)
364                                         timeptr = (__u32*)&optptr[optptr[2]-1];
365                                 opt->ts_needtime = 1;
366                                 optptr[2] += 4;
367                                 break;
368                             case IPOPT_TS_TSANDADDR:
369                                 if (optptr[2]+7 > optptr[1]) {
370                                         pp_ptr = optptr + 2;
371                                         goto error;
372                                 }
373                                 opt->ts = optptr - iph;
374                                 if (skb) {
375                                         memcpy(&optptr[optptr[2]-1], &rt->rt_spec_dst, 4);
376                                         timeptr = (__u32*)&optptr[optptr[2]+3];
377                                 }
378                                 opt->ts_needaddr = 1;
379                                 opt->ts_needtime = 1;
380                                 optptr[2] += 8;
381                                 break;
```

Figure 6.75 IP options—validate inbound packet header options: `linux/net/ipv4/` `ip_options.c`.

```
382                              case IPOPT_TS_PRESPEC:
383                                 if (optptr[2]+7 > optptr[1]) {
384                                        pp_ptr = optptr + 2;
385                                        goto error;
386                                 }
387                                 opt->ts = optptr - iph;
388                                 {
389                                        u32 addr;
390                                        memcpy(&addr, &optptr[optptr[2]-1], 4);
391                                        if (inet_addr_type(addr) == RTN_UNICAST)
392                                               break;
393                                        if (skb)
394                                               timeptr = (__u32*)&optptr[optptr[2]+3];
395                                 }
396                                 opt->ts_needtime = 1;
397                                 optptr[2] += 8;
398                                 break;
399                              default:
400                                 if (!skb && !capable(CAP_NET_RAW)) {
401                                        pp_ptr = optptr + 3;
402                                        goto error;
403                                 }
404                                 break;
405                           }
406                        if (timeptr) {
407                                 struct timeval tv;
408                                 __u32 midtime;
409                                 do_gettimeofday(&tv);
410                                 midtime = htonl((tv.tv_sec % 86400) * 1000 + tv.tv_usec
                                             / 1000);
411                                 memcpy(timeptr, &midtime, sizeof(__u32));
412                                 opt->is_changed = 1;
413                        }
414                  } else {
415                        unsigned overflow = optptr[3]>>4;
416                        if (overflow == 15) {
417                                 pp_ptr = optptr + 3;
418                                 goto error;
419                        }
420                        opt->ts = optptr - iph;
421                        if (skb) {
422                                 optptr[3] = (optptr[3]&0xF)|((overflow+1)<<4);
423                                 opt->is_changed = 1;
424                        }
425                  }
426               break;
```

Router alert option handling:

Figure 6.76 IP options—end of options processing: `linux/net/ipv4/ip_options.c`.

```
427                    case IPOPT_RA:
428                      if (optlen < 4) {
429                              pp_ptr = optptr + 1;
430                              goto error;
431                      }
432                      if (optptr[2] == 0 && optptr[3] == 0)
433                              opt->router_alert = optptr - iph;
434                      break;
435                    case IPOPT_SEC:
436                    case IPOPT_SID:
437                    default:
438                      if (!skb && !capable(CAP_NET_RAW)) {
439                              pp_ptr = optptr;
440                              goto error;
441                      }
442                      break;
443              }
444              l -= optlen;
445              optptr += optlen;
446        }
447
448  eol:
449        if (!pp_ptr)
450                return 0;
451
452  error:
453        if (skb) {
454                icmp_send(skb, ICMP_PARAMETERPROB, 0, htonl((pp_ptr-iph)<<24));
455        }
456        return -EINVAL;
457  }
```

Figure 6.77 IP options—unmangle what previous function did: `linux/net/ipv4/ip_options.c`.

```
460  /*
461   *      Undo all the changes done by ip_options_compile().
462   */
463
464  void ip_options_undo(struct ip_options * opt)
465  {
466        if (opt->srr) {
467                unsigned char * optptr = opt->__data+opt->srr-sizeof(struct iphdr);
468                memmove(optptr+7, optptr+3, optptr[1]-7);
469                memcpy(optptr+3, &opt->faddr, 4);
470        }
471        if (opt->rr_needaddr) {
472                unsigned char * optptr = opt->__data+opt->rr-sizeof(struct iphdr);
```

```
473                     optptr[2] -= 4;
474                     memset(&optptr[optptr[2]-1], 0, 4);
475             }
476             if (opt->ts) {
477                     unsigned char * optptr = opt->__data+opt->ts-sizeof(struct iphdr);
478                     if (opt->ts_needtime) {
479                             optptr[2] -= 4;
480                             memset(&optptr[optptr[2]-1], 0, 4);
481                             if ((optptr[3]&0xF) == IPOPT_TS_PRESPEC)
482                                     optptr[2] -= 4;
483                     }
484                     if (opt->ts_needaddr) {
485                             optptr[2] -= 4;
486                             memset(&optptr[optptr[2]-1], 0, 4);
487                     }
488             }
489     }
```

Figure 6.78 IP options—make space for options: linux/net/ipv4/ip_options.c.

```
491     int ip_options_get(struct ip_options **optp, unsigned char *data, int optlen, int user)
492     {
493             struct ip_options *opt;
494
495             opt = kmalloc(sizeof(struct ip_options)+((optlen+3)&~3), GFP_KERNEL);
496             if (!opt)
497                     return -ENOMEM;
498             memset(opt, 0, sizeof(struct ip_options));
499             if (optlen) {
500                     if (user) {
501                             if (copy_from_user(opt->__data, data, optlen)) {
502                                     kfree(opt);
503                                     return -EFAULT;
504                             }
505                     } else
506                             memcpy(opt->__data, data, optlen);
507             }
508             while (optlen & 3)
509                     opt->__data[optlen++] = IPOPT_END;
510             opt->optlen = optlen;
511             opt->is_data = 1;
512             opt->is_setbyuser = 1;
513             if (optlen && ip_options_compile(opt, NULL)) {
514                     kfree(opt);
515                     return -EINVAL;
516             }
517             *optp = opt;
518             return 0;
519     }
```

Figure 6.79 IP options—forwarding options—for example, route record: `linux/net/ipv4/ip_options.c`.

```
void ip_forward_options(struct sk_buff *skb)
{
        struct  ip_options * opt     = &(IPCB(skb)->opt);
        unsigned char * optptr;
        struct rtable *rt = (struct rtable*)skb->dst;
        unsigned char *raw = skb->nh.raw;

        if (opt->rr_needaddr) {
                optptr = (unsigned char *)raw + opt->rr;
                ip_rt_get_source(&optptr[optptr[2]-5], rt);
                opt->is_changed = 1;
        }
        if (opt->srr_is_hit) {
                int srrptr, srrspace;

                optptr = raw + opt->srr;

                for ( srrptr=optptr[2], srrspace = optptr[1];
                     srrptr <= srrspace;
                     srrptr += 4
                     ) {
                        if (srrptr + 3 > srrspace)
                                break;
                        if (memcmp(&rt->rt_dst, &optptr[srrptr-1], 4) == 0)
                                break;
                }
                if (srrptr + 3 <= srrspace) {
                        opt->is_changed = 1;
                        ip_rt_get_source(&optptr[srrptr-1], rt);
                        skb->nh.iph->daddr = rt->rt_dst;
                        optptr[2] = srrptr+4;
                } else
                        printk(KERN_CRIT "ip_forward(): Argh! Destination lost!\n");
                if (opt->ts_needaddr) {
                        optptr = raw + opt->ts;
                        ip_rt_get_source(&optptr[optptr[2]-9], rt);
                        opt->is_changed = 1;
                }
        }
        if (opt->is_changed) {
                opt->is_changed = 0;
                ip_send_check(skb->nh.iph);
        }
}
```

Figure 6.80 IP options—receive SSR and process: `linux/net/ipv4/ip_options.c`.

```
568        struct ip_options *opt = &(IPCB(skb)->opt);
569        int srrspace, srrptr;
570        u32 nexthop;
571        struct iphdr *iph = skb->nh.iph;
572        unsigned char * optptr = skb->nh.raw + opt->srr;
573        struct rtable *rt = (struct rtable*)skb->dst;
574        struct rtable *rt2;
575        int err;
576
577        if (!opt->srr)
578                return 0;
579
580        if (skb->pkt_type != PACKET_HOST)
581                return -EINVAL;
582        if (rt->rt_type == RTN_UNICAST) {
583                if (!opt->is_strictroute)
584                        return 0;
585                icmp_send(skb, ICMP_PARAMETERPROB, 0, htonl(16<<24));
586                return -EINVAL;
587        }
588        if (rt->rt_type != RTN_LOCAL)
589                return -EINVAL;
```

Figure 6.81 IP options—receive SSR and process: `linux/net/ipv4/ip_options.c`.

```
591        for (srrptr=optptr[2], srrspace = optptr[1]; srrptr <= srrspace; srrptr += 4) {
592                if (srrptr + 3 > srrspace) {
593                        icmp_send(skb, ICMP_PARAMETERPROB, 0, htonl((opt->srr+2)<<24));
594                        return -EINVAL;
595                }
596                memcpy(&nexthop, &optptr[srrptr-1], 4);
597
598                rt = (struct rtable*)skb->dst;
599                skb->dst = NULL;
600                err = ip_route_input(skb, nexthop, iph->saddr, iph->tos, skb->dev);
601                rt2 = (struct rtable*)skb->dst;
602                if (err || (rt2->rt_type != RTN_UNICAST && rt2->rt_type != RTN_LOCAL)) {
603                        ip_rt_put(rt2);
604                        skb->dst = &rt->u.dst;
605                        return -EINVAL;
606                }
607                ip_rt_put(rt);
608                if (rt2->rt_type != RTN_LOCAL)
609                        break;
610                /* Superfast 8) loopback forward */
611                memcpy(&iph->daddr, &optptr[srrptr-1], 4);
612                opt->is_changed = 1;
613        }
614        if (srrptr <= srrspace) {
```

```
                opt->srr_is_hit = 1;
                opt->is_changed = 1;
        }
        return 0;
}
```

6.2.7 Internet Protocol Socket Glue

Figure 6.82 Internet Protocol–socket glue–some spare constants: `linux/net/ipv4/ip_sockglue.c`.

```
#define IP_CMSG_PKTINFO         1
#define IP_CMSG_TTL             2
#define IP_CMSG_TOS             4
#define IP_CMSG_RECVOPTS        8
#define IP_CMSG_RETOPTS         16
```

Figure 6.83 IP socket glue–various CMSGs: `linux/net/ipv4/ip_sockglue.c`.

```
/*
 *      SOL_IP control messages.
 */

static void ip_cmsg_recv_pktinfo(struct msghdr *msg, struct sk_buff *skb)
{
        struct in_pktinfo info;
        struct rtable *rt = (struct rtable *)skb->dst;

        info.ipi_addr.s_addr = skb->nh.iph->daddr;
        if (rt) {
                info.ipi_ifindex = rt->rt_iif;
                info.ipi_spec_dst.s_addr = rt->rt_spec_dst;
        } else {
                info.ipi_ifindex = 0;
                info.ipi_spec_dst.s_addr = 0;
        }

        put_cmsg(msg, SOL_IP, IP_PKTINFO, sizeof(info), &info);
}
```

Figure 6.84 IP socket glue–various CMSGs: `linux/net/ipv4/ip_sockglue.c`.

```
static void ip_cmsg_recv_ttl(struct msghdr *msg, struct sk_buff *skb)
{
        int ttl = skb->nh.iph->ttl;
        put_cmsg(msg, SOL_IP, IP_TTL, sizeof(int), &ttl);
}

```

```
static void ip_cmsg_recv_tos(struct msghdr *msg, struct sk_buff *skb)
{
        put_cmsg(msg, SOL_IP, IP_TOS, 1, &skb->nh.iph->tos);
}

static void ip_cmsg_recv_opts(struct msghdr *msg, struct sk_buff *skb)
{
        if (IPCB(skb)->opt.optlen == 0)
                return;

        put_cmsg(msg, SOL_IP, IP_RECVOPTS, IPCB(skb)->opt.optlen, skb->nh.iph+1);
}


void ip_cmsg_recv_retopts(struct msghdr *msg, struct sk_buff *skb)
{
        unsigned char optbuf[sizeof(struct ip_options) + 40];
        struct ip_options * opt = (struct ip_options*)optbuf;

        if (IPCB(skb)->opt.optlen == 0)
                return;

        if (ip_options_echo(opt, skb)) {
                msg->msg_flags |= MSG_CTRUNC;
                return;
        }
        ip_options_undo(opt);

        put_cmsg(msg, SOL_IP, IP_RETOPTS, opt->optlen, opt->__data);
}
```

Figure 6.85 IP socket glue—field CMSGs to right place: `linux/net/ipv4/ip_sockglue.c`.

```
void ip_cmsg_recv(struct msghdr *msg, struct sk_buff *skb)
{
        unsigned flags = skb->sk->protinfo.af_inet.cmsg_flags;

        /* Ordered by supposed usage frequency */
        if (flags & 1)
                ip_cmsg_recv_pktinfo(msg, skb);
        if ((flags>>=1) == 0)
                return;

        if (flags & 1)
                ip_cmsg_recv_ttl(msg, skb);
        if ((flags>>=1) == 0)
                return;

        if (flags & 1)
                ip_cmsg_recv_tos(msg, skb);
        if ((flags>>=1) == 0)
                return;
```

```
132
133              if (flags & 1)
134                      ip_cmsg_recv_opts(msg, skb);
135              if ((flags>>=1) == 0)
136                      return;
137
138              if (flags & 1)
139                      ip_cmsg_recv_retopts(msg, skb);
140      }
```

Figure 6.86 IP socket glue—send CMSGs: `linux/net/ipv4/ip_sockglue.c`.

```
142     int ip_cmsg_send(struct msghdr *msg, struct ipcm_cookie *ipc)
143     {
144          int err;
145          struct cmsghdr *cmsg;
146
147          for (cmsg = CMSG_FIRSTHDR(msg); cmsg; cmsg = CMSG_NXTHDR(msg, cmsg)) {
148                  if (cmsg->cmsg_len < sizeof(struct cmsghdr) ||
149                      (unsigned long)(((char*)cmsg - (char*)msg->msg_control)
150                              + cmsg->cmsg_len) > msg->msg_controllen) {
151                          return -EINVAL;
152                  }
153                  if (cmsg->cmsg_level != SOL_IP)
154                          continue;
155                  switch (cmsg->cmsg_type) {
156                  case IP_RETOPTS:
157                          err = cmsg->cmsg_len - CMSG_ALIGN(sizeof(struct cmsghdr));
158                          err = ip_options_get(&ipc->opt, CMSG_DATA(cmsg), err < 40 ? err : 40, 0);
159                          if (err)
160                                  return err;
161                          break;
162                  case IP_PKTINFO:
163                  {
164                          struct in_pktinfo *info;
165                          if (cmsg->cmsg_len != CMSG_LEN(sizeof(struct in_pktinfo)))
166                                  return -EINVAL;
167                          info = (struct in_pktinfo *)CMSG_DATA(cmsg);
168                          ipc->oif = info->ipi_ifindex;
169                          ipc->addr = info->ipi_spec_dst.s_addr;
170                          break;
171                  }
172                  default:
173                          return -EINVAL;
174                  }
175          }
176          return 0;
177     }
```

Figure 6.87 IP socket glue–router alert handler for user level: `linux/net/ipv4/ip_sockglue.c`.

```
180   /* Special input handler for packets catched by router alert option.
181      They are selected only by protocol field, and then processed likely
182      local ones; but only if someone wants them! Otherwise, router
183      not running rsvpd will kill RSVP.
184
185      It is user level problem, what it will make with them.
186      I have no idea, how it will masquearde or NAT them (it is joke, joke :-)),
187      but receiver should be enough clever f.e. to forward mtrace requests,
188      sent to multicast group to reach destination designated router.
189    */
190   struct ip_ra_chain *ip_ra_chain;
191   rwlock_t ip_ra_lock = RW_LOCK_UNLOCKED;
192
193   int ip_ra_control(struct sock *sk, unsigned char on, void (*destructor)(struct sock *))
194   {
195          struct ip_ra_chain *ra, *new_ra, **rap;
196
197          if (sk->type != SOCK_RAW || sk->num == IPPROTO_RAW)
198                  return -EINVAL;
199
200          new_ra = on ? kmalloc(sizeof(*new_ra), GFP_KERNEL) : NULL;
```

Figure 6.88 IP socket glue–router alert handler for user level: `linux/net/ipv4/ip_sockglue.c`.

```
202          write_lock_bh(&ip_ra_lock);
203          for (rap = &ip_ra_chain; (ra=*rap) != NULL; rap = &ra->next) {
204                  if (ra->sk == sk) {
205                          if (on) {
206                                  write_unlock_bh(&ip_ra_lock);
207                                  if (new_ra)
208                                          kfree(new_ra);
209                                  return -EADDRINUSE;
210                          }
211                          *rap = ra->next;
212                          write_unlock_bh(&ip_ra_lock);
213
214                          if (ra->destructor)
215                                  ra->destructor(sk);
216                          sock_put(sk);
217                          kfree(ra);
218                          return 0;
219                  }
220          }
221          if (new_ra == NULL) {
222                  write_unlock_bh(&ip_ra_lock);
223                  return -ENOBUFS;
224          }
225          new_ra->sk = sk;
226          new_ra->destructor = destructor;
```

```
        new_ra->next = ra;
        *rap = new_ra;
        sock_hold(sk);
        write_unlock_bh(&ip_ra_lock);

        return 0;
}
```

Figure 6.89 IP socket glue—ICMP error to socket error mapping: `linux/net/ipv4/ip_sockglue.c`.

```
void ip_icmp_error(struct sock *sk, struct sk_buff *skb, int err,
                   u16 port, u32 info, u8 *payload)
{
        struct sock_exterr_skb *serr;

        if (!sk->protinfo.af_inet.recverr)
                return;

        skb = skb_clone(skb, GFP_ATOMIC);
        if (!skb)
                return;

        serr = SKB_EXT_ERR(skb);
        serr->ee.ee_errno = err;
        serr->ee.ee_origin = SO_EE_ORIGIN_ICMP;
        serr->ee.ee_type = skb->h.icmph->type;
        serr->ee.ee_code = skb->h.icmph->code;
        serr->ee.ee_pad = 0;
        serr->ee.ee_info = info;
        serr->ee.ee_data = 0;
        serr->addr_offset = (u8*)&(((struct iphdr*)(skb->h.icmph+1))->daddr) - skb->nh.raw;
        serr->port = port;

        skb->h.raw = payload;
        skb_pull(skb, payload - skb->data);

        if (sock_queue_err_skb(sk, skb))
                kfree_skb(skb);
}
```

Figure 6.90 IP socket glue—local error problem: `linux/net/ipv4/ip_sockglue.c`.

```
void ip_local_error(struct sock *sk, int err, u32 daddr, u16 port, u32 info)
{
        struct sock_exterr_skb *serr;
        struct iphdr *iph;
        struct sk_buff *skb;
```

```
271
272              if (!sk->protinfo.af_inet.recverr)
273                      return;
274
275              skb = alloc_skb(sizeof(struct iphdr), GFP_ATOMIC);
276              if (!skb)
277                      return;
278
279              iph = (struct iphdr*)skb_put(skb, sizeof(struct iphdr));
280              skb->nh.iph = iph;
281              iph->daddr = daddr;
282
283              serr = SKB_EXT_ERR(skb);
284              serr->ee.ee_errno = err;
285              serr->ee.ee_origin = SO_EE_ORIGIN_LOCAL;
286              serr->ee.ee_type = 0;
287              serr->ee.ee_code = 0;
288              serr->ee.ee_pad = 0;
289              serr->ee.ee_info = info;
290              serr->ee.ee_data = 0;
291              serr->addr_offset = (u8*)&iph->daddr - skb->nh.raw;
292              serr->port = port;
293
294              skb->h.raw = skb->tail;
295              skb_pull(skb, skb->tail - skb->data);
296
297              if (sock_queue_err_skb(sk, skb))
298                      kfree_skb(skb);
299      }
```

Figure 6.91 IP socket glue—map IP reception errors to socket: `linux/net/ipv4/ip_sockglue.c`.

```
301      /*
302       *      Handle MSG_ERRQUEUE
303       */
304      int ip_recv_error(struct sock *sk, struct msghdr *msg, int len)
305      {
306           struct sock_exterr_skb *serr;
307           struct sk_buff *skb, *skb2;
308           struct sockaddr_in *sin;
309           struct {
310                   struct sock_extended_err ee;
311                   struct sockaddr_in      offender;
312           } errhdr;
313           int err;
314           int copied;
315
316           err = -EAGAIN;
317           skb = skb_dequeue(&sk->error_queue);
318           if (skb == NULL)
319                   goto out;
```

```

        copied = skb->len;
        if (copied > len) {
                msg->msg_flags |= MSG_TRUNC;
                copied = len;
        }
        err = memcpy_toiovec(msg->msg_iov, skb->data, copied);
        if (err)
                goto out_free_skb;

        sock_recv_timestamp(msg, sk, skb);

        serr = SKB_EXT_ERR(skb);

        sin = (struct sockaddr_in *)msg->msg_name;
        if (sin) {
                sin->sin_family = AF_INET;
                sin->sin_addr.s_addr = *(u32*)(skb->nh.raw + serr->addr_offset);
                sin->sin_port = serr->port;
        }
```

Figure 6.92 IP socket glue—map IP reception errors to socket: `linux/net/ipv4/ip_sockglue.c`.

```
        memcpy(&errhdr.ee, &serr->ee, sizeof(struct sock_extended_err));
        sin = &errhdr.offender;
        sin->sin_family = AF_UNSPEC;
        if (serr->ee.ee_origin == SO_EE_ORIGIN_ICMP) {
                sin->sin_family = AF_INET;
                sin->sin_addr.s_addr = skb->nh.iph->saddr;
                if (sk->protinfo.af_inet.cmsg_flags)
                        ip_cmsg_recv(msg, skb);
        }

        put_cmsg(msg, SOL_IP, IP_RECVERR, sizeof(errhdr), &errhdr);

        /* Now we could try to dump offended packet options */

        msg->msg_flags |= MSG_ERRQUEUE;
        err = copied;

        /* Reset and regenerate socket error */
        spin_lock_irq(&sk->error_queue.lock);
        sk->err = 0;
        if ((skb2 = skb_peek(&sk->error_queue)) != NULL) {
                sk->err = SKB_EXT_ERR(skb2)->ee.ee_errno;
                spin_unlock_irq(&sk->error_queue.lock);
                sk->error_report(sk);
        } else {
                spin_unlock_irq(&sk->error_queue.lock);
        }

```

```
369   out_free_skb:
370          kfree_skb(skb);
371   out:
372          return err;
373   }
```

Setting Socket Options

In the previous chapter we saw the generic socket layer for dealing with socket options. Here we have the IP protocol-specific part of that function. Other protocol families would have different instances of this code:

Figure 6.93 IP socket glue—`setsockopt` entry for IP: `linux/net/ipv4/ip_sockglue.c`.

```
376   /*
377    *      Socket option code for IP. This is the end of the line after any TCP,UDP etc options on
378    *      an IP socket.
379    */
380
381   int ip_setsockopt(struct sock *sk, int level, int optname, char *optval, int optlen)
382   {
383          int val=0,err;
384
385          if (level != SOL_IP)
386                  return -ENOPROTOOPT;
387
388          if ((((1<<optname) & ((1<<IP_PKTINFO) | (1<<IP_RECVTTL) |
389                            (1<<IP_RECVOPTS) | (1<<IP_RECVTOS) |
390                            (1<<IP_RETOPTS) | (1<<IP_TOS) |
391                            (1<<IP_TTL) | (1<<IP_HDRINCL) |
392                            (1<<IP_MTU_DISCOVER) | (1<<IP_RECVERR) |
393                            (1<<IP_ROUTER_ALERT) | (1<<IP_FREEBIND))) ||
394                              optname == IP_MULTICAST_TTL ||
395                              optname == IP_MULTICAST_LOOP) {
396               if (optlen >= sizeof(int)) {
397                       if (get_user(val, (int *) optval))
398                               return -EFAULT;
399               } else if (optlen >= sizeof(char)) {
400                       unsigned char ucval;
401
402                       if (get_user(ucval, (unsigned char *) optval))
403                               return -EFAULT;
404                       val = (int) ucval;
405               }
406          }
```

Figure 6.94 IP socket glue—`setsockopt` entry for IP: `linux/net/ipv4/ip_sockglue.c`.

```
408             /* If optlen==0, it is equivalent to val == 0 */
409
410     #ifdef CONFIG_IP_MROUTE
411             if (optname >= MRT_BASE && optname <= (MRT_BASE + 10))
412                     return ip_mroute_setsockopt(sk,optname,optval,optlen);
413     #endif
414
415             err = 0;
416             lock_sock(sk);
417
418             switch (optname) {
419                     case IP_OPTIONS:
420                     {
421                             struct ip_options * opt = NULL;
422                             if (optlen > 40 || optlen < 0)
423                                     goto e_inval;
424                             err = ip_options_get(&opt, optval, optlen, 1);
425                             if (err)
426                                     break;
427                             if (sk->type == SOCK_STREAM) {
428                                     struct tcp_opt *tp = &sk->tp_pinfo.af_tcp;
429     #if defined(CONFIG_IPV6) || defined(CONFIG_IPV6_MODULE)
430                                     if (sk->family == PF_INET ||
431                                         (!((1<<sk->state)&(TCPF_LISTEN|TCPF_CLOSE))
432                                          && sk->daddr != LOOPBACK4_IPV6)) {
433     #endif
434                                             if (opt)
435                                                     tp->ext_header_len = opt->optlen;
436                                             tcp_sync_mss(sk, tp->pmtu_cookie);
437     #if defined(CONFIG_IPV6) || defined(CONFIG_IPV6_MODULE)
438                                     }
439     #endif
440                             }
441                             opt = xchg(&sk->protinfo.af_inet.opt, opt);
442                             if (opt)
443                                     kfree(opt);
444                             break;
445                     }
```

Figure 6.95 IP socket glue—`setsockopt` entry for IP: `linux/net/ipv4/ip_sockglue.c`.

```
446                     case IP_PKTINFO:
447                             if (val)
448                                     sk->protinfo.af_inet.cmsg_flags |= IP_CMSG_PKTINFO;
449                             else
450                                     sk->protinfo.af_inet.cmsg_flags &= ~IP_CMSG_PKTINFO;
451                             break;
452                     case IP_RECVTTL:
453                             if (val)
```

```
454                            sk->protinfo.af_inet.cmsg_flags |= IP_CMSG_TTL;
455                    else
456                            sk->protinfo.af_inet.cmsg_flags &= ~IP_CMSG_TTL;
457                    break;
458            case IP_RECVTOS:
459                    if (val)
460                            sk->protinfo.af_inet.cmsg_flags |= IP_CMSG_TOS;
461                    else
462                            sk->protinfo.af_inet.cmsg_flags &= ~IP_CMSG_TOS;
463                    break;
464            case IP_RECVOPTS:
465                    if (val)
466                            sk->protinfo.af_inet.cmsg_flags |= IP_CMSG_RECVOPTS;
467                    else
468                            sk->protinfo.af_inet.cmsg_flags &= ~IP_CMSG_RECVOPTS;
469                    break;
470            case IP_RETOPTS:
471                    if (val)
472                            sk->protinfo.af_inet.cmsg_flags |= IP_CMSG_RETOPTS;
473                    else
474                            sk->protinfo.af_inet.cmsg_flags &= ~IP_CMSG_RETOPTS;
475                    break;
```

Figure 6.96 IP socket glue—setsockopt entry for IP: linux/net/ipv4/ip_sockglue.c.

```
476            case IP_TOS:   /* This sets both TOS and Precedence */
477                        /* Reject setting of unused bits */
478  #ifndef CONFIG_INET_ECN
479                    if (val & ~(IPTOS_TOS_MASK|IPTOS_PREC_MASK))
480                            goto e_inval;
481  #else
482                    if (sk->type == SOCK_STREAM) {
483                            val &= ~3;
484                            val |= sk->protinfo.af_inet.tos & 3;
485                    }
486  #endif
487                    if (IPTOS_PREC(val) >= IPTOS_PREC_CRITIC_ECP &&
488                        !capable(CAP_NET_ADMIN)) {
489                            err = -EPERM;
490                            break;
491                    }
492                    if (sk->protinfo.af_inet.tos != val) {
493                            sk->protinfo.af_inet.tos=val;
494                            sk->priority = rt_tos2priority(val);
495                            sk_dst_reset(sk);
496                    }
497                    break;
498            case IP_TTL:
499                    if (optlen<1)
500                            goto e_inval;
501                    if(val==-1)
502                            val = sysctl_ip_default_ttl;
```

```
503                         if(val<1||val>255)
504                                 goto e_inval;
505                         sk->protinfo.af_inet.ttl=val;
506                         break;
507                 case IP_HDRINCL:
508                         if(sk->type!=SOCK_RAW) {
509                                 err = -ENOPROTOOPT;
510                                 break;
511                         }
512                         sk->protinfo.af_inet.hdrincl=val?1:0;
513                         break;
514                 case IP_MTU_DISCOVER:
515                         if (val<0 || val>2)
516                                 goto e_inval;
517                         sk->protinfo.af_inet.pmtudisc = val;
518                         break;
519                 case IP_RECVERR:
520                         sk->protinfo.af_inet.recverr = !!val;
521                         if (!val)
522                                 skb_queue_purge(&sk->error_queue);
523                         break;
```

Multicast socket options:

Figure 6.97 IP socket glue—setsockopt entry for IP: linux/net/ipv4/ip_sockglue.c.

```
524                 case IP_MULTICAST_TTL:
525                         if (sk->type == SOCK_STREAM)
526                                 goto e_inval;
527                         if (optlen<1)
528                                 goto e_inval;
529                         if (val==-1)
530                                 val = 1;
531                         if (val < 0 || val > 255)
532                                 goto e_inval;
533                         sk->protinfo.af_inet.mc_ttl=val;
534                         break;
535                 case IP_MULTICAST_LOOP:
536                         if (optlen<1)
537                                 goto e_inval;
538                         sk->protinfo.af_inet.mc_loop = val ? 1 : 0;
539                         break;
```

Figure 6.98 IP socket glue—setsockopt entry for IP: linux/net/ipv4/ip_sockglue.c.

```
540                 case IP_MULTICAST_IF:
541                 {
542                         struct ip_mreqn mreq;
543                         struct net_device *dev = NULL;
544
```

```
		if (sk->type == SOCK_STREAM)
			goto e_inval;
		/*
		 *	Check the arguments are allowable
		 */

		err = -EFAULT;
		if (optlen >= sizeof(struct ip_mreqn)) {
			if (copy_from_user(&mreq,optval,sizeof(mreq)))
				break;
		} else {
			memset(&mreq, 0, sizeof(mreq));
			if (optlen >= sizeof(struct in_addr) &&
			    copy_from_user(&mreq.imr_address,optval,sizeof(struct in_addr)))
				break;
		}
```

Figure 6.99 IP socket glue—`setsockopt` entry for IP: `linux/net/ipv4/ip_sockglue.c`.

```
		if (!mreq.imr_ifindex) {
			if (mreq.imr_address.s_addr == INADDR_ANY) {
				sk->protinfo.af_inet.mc_index = 0;
				sk->protinfo.af_inet.mc_addr = 0;
				err = 0;
				break;
			}
			dev = ip_dev_find(mreq.imr_address.s_addr);
			if (dev) {
				mreq.imr_ifindex = dev->ifindex;
				dev_put(dev);
			}
		} else
			dev = __dev_get_by_index(mreq.imr_ifindex);


		err = -EADDRNOTAVAIL;
		if (!dev)
			break;

		err = -EINVAL;
		if (sk->bound_dev_if && mreq.imr_ifindex != sk->bound_dev_if)
			break;

		sk->protinfo.af_inet.mc_index = mreq.imr_ifindex;
		sk->protinfo.af_inet.mc_addr = mreq.imr_address.s_addr;
		err = 0;
		break;
	}
```

Figure 6.100 IP socket glue—setsockopt entry for IP: linux/net/ipv4/ip_sockglue.c.

```
592                  case IP_ADD_MEMBERSHIP:
593                  case IP_DROP_MEMBERSHIP:
594                  {
595                          struct ip_mreqn mreq;
596
597                          if (optlen < sizeof(struct ip_mreq))
598                                  goto e_inval;
599                          err = -EFAULT;
600                          if (optlen >= sizeof(struct ip_mreqn)) {
601                                  if(copy_from_user(&mreq,optval,sizeof(mreq)))
602                                          break;
603                          } else {
604                                  memset(&mreq, 0, sizeof(mreq));
605                                  if (copy_from_user(&mreq,optval,sizeof(struct ip_mreq)))
606                                          break;
607                          }
608
609                          if (optname == IP_ADD_MEMBERSHIP)
610                                  err = ip_mc_join_group(sk,&mreq);
611                          else
612                                  err = ip_mc_leave_group(sk,&mreq);
613                          break;
614                  }
615                  case IP_ROUTER_ALERT:
616                          err = ip_ra_control(sk, val ? 1 : 0, NULL);
617                          break;
618
619                  case IP_FREEBIND:
620                          if (optlen<1)
621                                  goto e_inval;
622                          sk->protinfo.af_inet.freebind = !!val;
623                          break;
624
625                  default:
626  #ifdef CONFIG_NETFILTER
627                          err = nf_setsockopt(sk, PF_INET, optname, optval,
628                                              optlen);
629  #else
630                          err = -ENOPROTOOPT;
631  #endif
632                          break;
633          }
634      release_sock(sk);
635      return err;
636
637  e_inval:
638      release_sock(sk);
639      return -EINVAL;
640  }
```

Getting Socket Options

Getting socket options is just the inverse of setting them:

Figure 6.101 IP socket glue—getsockopt entry for IP: linux/net/ipv4/ip_sockglue.c.

```
642   /*
643    *      Get the options. Note for future reference. The GET of IP options gets the
644    *      _received_ ones. The set sets the _sent_ ones.
645    */
646
647   int ip_getsockopt(struct sock *sk, int level, int optname, char *optval, int *optlen)
648   {
649           int val;
650           int len;
651
652           if(level!=SOL_IP)
653                   return -EOPNOTSUPP;
654
655   #ifdef CONFIG_IP_MROUTE
656           if(optname>=MRT_BASE && optname <=MRT_BASE+10)
657           {
658                   return ip_mroute_getsockopt(sk,optname,optval,optlen);
659           }
660   #endif
661
662           if(get_user(len,optlen))
663                   return -EFAULT;
664
665           lock_sock(sk);
```

Figure 6.102 IP socket glue—getsockopt entry for IP: linux/net/ipv4/ip_sockglue.c.

```
667           switch(optname) {
668                   case IP_OPTIONS:
669                           {
670                                   unsigned char optbuf[sizeof(struct ip_options)+40];
671                                   struct ip_options * opt = (struct ip_options*)optbuf;
672                                   opt->optlen = 0;
673                                   if (sk->protinfo.af_inet.opt)
674                                           memcpy(optbuf, sk->protinfo.af_inet.opt,
675                                                   sizeof(struct ip_options)+
676                                                   sk->protinfo.af_inet.opt->optlen);
677                                   release_sock(sk);
678
679                                   if (opt->optlen == 0)
680                                           return put_user(0, optlen);
681
682                                   ip_options_undo(opt);
683
684                                   len=min(len, opt->optlen);
```

```
                if(put_user(len, optlen))
                    return -EFAULT;
                if(copy_to_user(optval, opt->__data, len))
                    return -EFAULT;
                return 0;
            }
        case IP_PKTINFO:
            val = (sk->protinfo.af_inet.cmsg_flags & IP_CMSG_PKTINFO) != 0;
            break;
        case IP_RECVTTL:
            val = (sk->protinfo.af_inet.cmsg_flags & IP_CMSG_TTL) != 0;
            break;
        case IP_RECVTOS:
            val = (sk->protinfo.af_inet.cmsg_flags & IP_CMSG_TOS) != 0;
            break;
        case IP_RECVOPTS:
            val = (sk->protinfo.af_inet.cmsg_flags & IP_CMSG_RECVOPTS) != 0;
            break;
        case IP_RETOPTS:
            val = (sk->protinfo.af_inet.cmsg_flags & IP_CMSG_RETOPTS) != 0;
            break;
        case IP_TOS:
            val=sk->protinfo.af_inet.tos;
            break;
        case IP_TTL:
            val=sk->protinfo.af_inet.ttl;
            break;
        case IP_HDRINCL:
            val=sk->protinfo.af_inet.hdrincl;
            break;
```

Figure 6.103 IP socket glue—`getsockopt` entry for IP: `linux/net/ipv4/ip_sockglue.c`.

```
        case IP_MTU_DISCOVER:
            val=sk->protinfo.af_inet.pmtudisc;
            break;
        case IP_MTU:
        {
            struct dst_entry *dst;
            val = 0;
            dst = sk_dst_get(sk);
            if (dst) {
                val = dst->pmtu;
                dst_release(dst);
            }
            if (!val) {
                release_sock(sk);
                return -ENOTCONN;
            }
            break;
        }
        case IP_RECVERR:
            val=sk->protinfo.af_inet.recverr;
            break;
```

```
        case IP_MULTICAST_TTL:
                val=sk->protinfo.af_inet.mc_ttl;
                break;
        case IP_MULTICAST_LOOP:
                val=sk->protinfo.af_inet.mc_loop;
                break;
        case IP_MULTICAST_IF:
        {
                struct in_addr addr;
                len = min(len,sizeof(struct in_addr));
                addr.s_addr = sk->protinfo.af_inet.mc_addr;
                release_sock(sk);

                if(put_user(len, optlen))
                        return -EFAULT;
                if(copy_to_user((void *)optval, &addr, len))
                        return -EFAULT;
                return 0;
        }
```

Figure 6.104 IP socket glue—`getsockopt` entry for IP: `linux/net/ipv4/ip_sockglue.c`.

```
        case IP_PKTOPTIONS:
        {
                struct msghdr msg;

                release_sock(sk);

                if (sk->type != SOCK_STREAM)
                        return -ENOPROTOOPT;

                msg.msg_control = optval;
                msg.msg_controllen = len;
                msg.msg_flags = 0;

                if (sk->protinfo.af_inet.cmsg_flags&IP_CMSG_PKTINFO) {
                        struct in_pktinfo info;

                        info.ipi_addr.s_addr = sk->rcv_saddr;
                        info.ipi_spec_dst.s_addr = sk->rcv_saddr;
                        info.ipi_ifindex = sk->protinfo.af_inet.mc_index;
                        put_cmsg(&msg, SOL_IP, IP_PKTINFO, sizeof(info), &info);
                }
                if (sk->protinfo.af_inet.cmsg_flags&IP_CMSG_TTL) {
                        int hlim = sk->protinfo.af_inet.mc_ttl;
                        put_cmsg(&msg, SOL_IP, IP_TTL, sizeof(hlim), &hlim);
                }
                len -= msg.msg_controllen;
                return put_user(len, optlen);
        }
```

Figure 6.105 IP socket glue—getsockopt entry for IP: linux/net/ipv4/ip_sockglue.c.

```
783                    case IP_FREEBIND:
784                            val = sk->protinfo.af_inet.freebind;
785                            break;
786                    default:
787  #ifdef CONFIG_NETFILTER
788                            val = nf_getsockopt(sk, PF_INET, optname, optval,
789                                                &len);
790                            release_sock(sk);
791                            if (val >= 0)
792                                    val = put_user(len, optlen);
793                            return val;
794  #else
795                            release_sock(sk);
796                            return -ENOPROTOOPT;
797  #endif
798          }
799      release_sock(sk);
800
801      if (len < sizeof(int) && len > 0 && val>=0 && val<255) {
802              unsigned char ucval = (unsigned char)val;
803              len = 1;
804              if(put_user(len, optlen))
805                      return -EFAULT;
806              if(copy_to_user(optval,&ucval,1))
807                      return -EFAULT;
808      } else {
809              len=min(sizeof(int),len);
810              if(put_user(len, optlen))
811                      return -EFAULT;
812              if(copy_to_user(optval,&val,len))
813                      return -EFAULT;
814      }
815      return 0;
816  }
```

6.3 Addressing

Link and network addresses have specific finite lifetimes and scopes. In fact, so do names (as in domain names), and this means that we need to consider binding names to addresses from one level to the next.

Address data structures. We have the IP and link layer data structures.

Address formats. We have the specified formats for addresses as discussed earlier.

Configuration/management. We can override binding and scope rules through management.

ARP Management

Figure 6.106 ARP—data: `linux/net/ipv4/arp.c`.

```
70   /* RFC 1122 Status:
71      2.3.2.1 (ARP Cache Validation):
72        MUST provide mechanism to flush stale cache entries (OK)
73        SHOULD be able to configure cache timeout (OK)
74        MUST throttle ARP retransmits (OK)
75      2.3.2.2 (ARP Packet Queue):
76        SHOULD save at least one packet from each "conversation" with an
77          unresolved IP address. (OK)
78      950727 -- MS
79   */
```

Figure 6.107 ARP neighbor operations: `linux/net/ipv4/arp.c`.

```
127  /*
128   *       Interface to generic neighbour cache.
129   */
130  static u32 arp_hash(const void *pkey, const struct net_device *dev);
131  static int arp_constructor(struct neighbour *neigh);
132  static void arp_solicit(struct neighbour *neigh, struct sk_buff *skb);
133  static void arp_error_report(struct neighbour *neigh, struct sk_buff *skb);
134  static void parp_redo(struct sk_buff *skb);
135
136  static struct neigh_ops arp_generic_ops =
137  {
138        AF_INET,
139        NULL,
140        arp_solicit,
141        arp_error_report,
142        neigh_resolve_output,
143        neigh_connected_output,
144        dev_queue_xmit,
145        dev_queue_xmit
146  };
147
148  static struct neigh_ops arp_hh_ops =
149  {
150        AF_INET,
151        NULL,
152        arp_solicit,
153        arp_error_report,
154        neigh_resolve_output,
155        neigh_resolve_output,
156        dev_queue_xmit,
157        dev_queue_xmit
158  };
```

Figure 6.108 ARP neighbor operations: `linux/net/ipv4/arp.c`.

```
160    static struct neigh_ops arp_direct_ops =
161    {
162            AF_INET,
163            NULL,
164            NULL,
165            NULL,
166            dev_queue_xmit,
167            dev_queue_xmit,
168            dev_queue_xmit,
169            dev_queue_xmit
170    };
171
172    struct neigh_ops arp_broken_ops =
173    {
174            AF_INET,
175            NULL,
176            arp_solicit,
177            arp_error_report,
178            neigh_compat_output,
179            neigh_compat_output,
180            dev_queue_xmit,
181            dev_queue_xmit,
182    };
```

Figure 6.109 ARP table structure: `linux/net/ipv4/arp.c`.

```
184    struct neigh_table arp_tbl =
185    {
186            NULL,
187            AF_INET,
188            sizeof(struct neighbour) + 4,
189            4,
190            arp_hash,
191            arp_constructor,
192            NULL,
193            NULL,
194            parp_redo,
195            "arp_cache",
196            { NULL, NULL, &arp_tbl, 0, NULL, NULL,
197                    30*HZ, 1*HZ, 60*HZ, 30*HZ, 5*HZ, 3, 3, 0, 3, 1*HZ, (8*HZ)/10, 64, 1*HZ },
198            30*HZ, 128, 512, 1024,
199    };
```

Figure 6.110 ARP map MAC-type/IEEE-type: `linux/net/ipv4/arp.c`.

```
201    int arp_mc_map(u32 addr, u8 *haddr, struct net_device *dev, int dir)
202    {
203            switch (dev->type) {
204            case ARPHRD_ETHER:
```

```
205          case ARPHRD_FDDI:
206          case ARPHRD_IEEE802:
207                  ip_eth_mc_map(addr, haddr) ;
208                  return 0 ;
209          case ARPHRD_IEEE802_TR:
210                  ip_tr_mc_map(addr, haddr) ;
211                  return 0;
212          default:
213                  if (dir) {
214                          memcpy(haddr, dev->broadcast, dev->addr_len);
215                          return 0;
216                  }
217          }
218          return -EINVAL;
219  }
```

Figure 6.111 ARP hash function: `linux/net/ipv4/arp.c`.

```
222  static u32 arp_hash(const void *pkey, const struct net_device *dev)
223  {
224          u32 hash_val;
225
226          hash_val = *(u32*)pkey;
227          hash_val ^= (hash_val>>16);
228          hash_val ^= hash_val>>8;
229          hash_val ^= hash_val>>3;
230          hash_val = (hash_val^dev->ifindex)&NEIGH_HASHMASK;
231
232          return hash_val;
233  }
```

Figure 6.112 ARP build entry: `linux/net/ipv4/arp.c`.

```
235  static int arp_constructor(struct neighbour *neigh)
236  {
237          u32 addr = *(u32*)neigh->primary_key;
238          struct net_device *dev = neigh->dev;
239          struct in_device *in_dev = in_dev_get(dev);
240
241          if (in_dev == NULL)
242                  return -EINVAL;
243
244          neigh->type = inet_addr_type(addr);
245          if (in_dev->arp_parms)
246                  neigh->parms = in_dev->arp_parms;
247
248          in_dev_put(in_dev);
249
250          if (dev->hard_header == NULL) {
251                  neigh->nud_state = NUD_NOARP;
```

```
                neigh->ops = &arp_direct_ops;
                neigh->output = neigh->ops->queue_xmit;
        } else {
                /* Good devices (checked by reading texts, but only Ethernet is
                   tested)

                   ARPHRD_ETHER: (ethernet, apfddi)
                   ARPHRD_FDDI: (fddi)
                   ARPHRD_IEEE802: (tr)
                   ARPHRD_METRICOM: (strip)
                   ARPHRD_ARCNET:
                   etc. etc. etc.

                   ARPHRD_IPDDP will also work, if author repairs it.
                   I did not it, because this driver does not work even
                   in old paradigm.
                 */
```

Figure 6.113 ARP build entry: `linux/net/ipv4/arp.c`.

```
#if 1
                /* So... these "amateur" devices are hopeless.
                   The only thing, that I can say now:
                   It is very sad that we need to keep ugly obsolete
                   code to make them happy.

                   They should be moved to more reasonable state, now
                   they use rebuild_header INSTEAD OF hard_start_xmit!!!
                   Besides that, they are sort of out of date
                   (a lot of redundant clones/copies, useless in 2.1),
                   I wonder why people believe that they work.
                 */
                switch (dev->type) {
                default:
                        break;
                case ARPHRD_ROSE:
#if defined(CONFIG_AX25) || defined(CONFIG_AX25_MODULE)
                case ARPHRD_AX25:
#if defined(CONFIG_NETROM) || defined(CONFIG_NETROM_MODULE)
                case ARPHRD_NETROM:
#endif
                        neigh->ops = &arp_broken_ops;
                        neigh->output = neigh->ops->output;
                        return 0;
#endif
                ;}
#endif
                if (neigh->type == RTN_MULTICAST) {
                        neigh->nud_state = NUD_NOARP;
                        arp_mc_map(addr, neigh->ha, dev, 1);
                } else if (dev->flags&(IFF_NOARP|IFF_LOOPBACK)) {
                        neigh->nud_state = NUD_NOARP;
                        memcpy(neigh->ha, dev->dev_addr, dev->addr_len);
```

```
		} else if (neigh->type == RTN_BROADCAST || dev->flags&IFF_POINTOPOINT) {
			neigh->nud_state = NUD_NOARP;
			memcpy(neigh->ha, dev->broadcast, dev->addr_len);
		}
		if (dev->hard_header_cache)
			neigh->ops = &arp_hh_ops;
		else
			neigh->ops = &arp_generic_ops;
		if (neigh->nud_state&NUD_VALID)
			neigh->output = neigh->ops->connected_output;
		else
			neigh->output = neigh->ops->output;
	}
	return 0;
}
```

Figure 6.114 ARP error report: `linux/net/ipv4/arp.c`.

```
static void arp_error_report(struct neighbour *neigh, struct sk_buff *skb)
{
	dst_link_failure(skb);
	kfree_skb(skb);
}
```

ARP Solitication

Figure 6.115 ARP solicit (who has): `linux/net/ipv4/arp.c`.

```
static void arp_solicit(struct neighbour *neigh, struct sk_buff *skb)
{
	u32 saddr;
	u8  *dst_ha = NULL;
	struct net_device *dev = neigh->dev;
	u32 target = *(u32*)neigh->primary_key;
	int probes = atomic_read(&neigh->probes);

	if (skb && inet_addr_type(skb->nh.iph->saddr) == RTN_LOCAL)
		saddr = skb->nh.iph->saddr;
	else
		saddr = inet_select_addr(dev, target, RT_SCOPE_LINK);

	if ((probes -= neigh->parms->ucast_probes) < 0) {
		if (!(neigh->nud_state&NUD_VALID))
			printk(KERN_DEBUG "trying to ucast probe in NUD_INVALID\n");
		dst_ha = neigh->ha;
		read_lock_bh(&neigh->lock);
	} else if ((probes -= neigh->parms->app_probes) < 0) {
#ifdef CONFIG_ARPD
		neigh_app_ns(neigh);
```

```
#endif
                return;
        }

        arp_send(ARPOP_REQUEST, ETH_P_ARP, target, dev, saddr,
                 dst_ha, dev->dev_addr, NULL);
        if (dst_ha)
                read_unlock_bh(&neigh->lock);
}
```

Figure 6.116 ARP—even Russians have built-in obsolescence: `linux/net/ipv4/arp.c`.

```
/* OBSOLETE FUNCTIONS */

/*
 *      Find an arp mapping in the cache. If not found, post a request.
 *
 *      It is very UGLY routine: it DOES NOT use skb->dst->neighbour,
 *      even if it exists. It is supposed that skb->dev was mangled
 *      by a virtual device (eql, shaper). Nobody but broken devices
 *      is allowed to use this function, it is scheduled to be removed. --ANK
 */

static int arp_set_predefined(int addr_hint, unsigned char * haddr, u32 paddr, struct net_device * dev)
{
        switch (addr_hint) {
        case RTN_LOCAL:
                printk(KERN_DEBUG "ARP: arp called for own IP address\n");
                memcpy(haddr, dev->dev_addr, dev->addr_len);
                return 1;
        case RTN_MULTICAST:
                arp_mc_map(paddr, haddr, dev, 1);
                return 1;
        case RTN_BROADCAST:
                memcpy(haddr, dev->broadcast, dev->addr_len);
                return 1;
        }
        return 0;
}
```

Figure 6.117 ARP—even Russians have built-in obsolescence: `linux/net/ipv4/arp.c`.

```

int arp_find(unsigned char *haddr, struct sk_buff *skb)
{
        struct net_device *dev = skb->dev;
        u32 paddr;
        struct neighbour *n;

        if (!skb->dst) {
                printk(KERN_DEBUG "arp_find is called with dst==NULL\n");
```

```
393                      kfree_skb(skb);
394                      return 1;
395             }
396
397             paddr = ((struct rtable*)skb->dst)->rt_gateway;
398
399             if (arp_set_predefined(inet_addr_type(paddr), haddr, paddr, dev))
400                      return 0;
401
402             n = __neigh_lookup(&arp_tbl, &paddr, dev, 1);
403
404             if (n) {
405                      n->used = jiffies;
406                      if (n->nud_state&NUD_VALID || neigh_event_send(n, skb) == 0) {
407                              read_lock_bh(&n->lock);
408                              memcpy(haddr, n->ha, dev->addr_len);
409                              read_unlock_bh(&n->lock);
410                              neigh_release(n);
411                              return 0;
412                      }
413                      neigh_release(n);
414             } else
415                      kfree_skb(skb);
416             return 1;
417    }
418
419    /* END OF OBSOLETE FUNCTIONS */
```

Figure 6.118 ARP—bind address to neighbor: `linux/net/ipv4/arp.c`.

```
421    int arp_bind_neighbour(struct dst_entry *dst)
422    {
423             struct net_device *dev = dst->dev;
424             struct neighbour *n = dst->neighbour;
425
426             if (dev == NULL)
427                      return -EINVAL;
428             if (n == NULL) {
429                      u32 nexthop = ((struct rtable*)dst)->rt_gateway;
430                      if (dev->flags&(IFF_LOOPBACK|IFF_POINTOPOINT))
431                              nexthop = 0;
432                      n = __neigh_lookup_errno(
433    #ifdef CONFIG_ATM_CLIP
434                              dev->type == ARPHRD_ATM ? &clip_tbl :
435    #endif
436                              &arp_tbl, &nexthop, dev);
437                      if (IS_ERR(n))
438                              return PTR_ERR(n);
439                      dst->neighbour = n;
440             }
441             return 0;
442    }
```

Send an ARP

Figure 6.119 ARP—send an ARP message: `linux/net/ipv4/arp.c`.

```
/*
 *      Create and send an arp packet. If (dest_hw == NULL), we create a broadcast
 *      message.
 */

void arp_send(int type, int ptype, u32 dest_ip,
              struct net_device *dev, u32 src_ip,
              unsigned char *dest_hw, unsigned char *src_hw,
              unsigned char *target_hw)
{
        struct sk_buff *skb;
        struct arphdr *arp;
        unsigned char *arp_ptr;

        /*
         *      No arp on this interface.
         */

        if (dev->flags&IFF_NOARP)
                return;

        /*
         *      Allocate a buffer
         */

        skb = alloc_skb(sizeof(struct arphdr)+ 2*(dev->addr_len+4)
                                + dev->hard_header_len + 15, GFP_ATOMIC);
        if (skb == NULL)
                return;

        skb_reserve(skb, (dev->hard_header_len+15)&~15);
        skb->nh.raw = skb->data;
        arp = (struct arphdr *) skb_put(skb,sizeof(struct arphdr) + 2*(dev->addr_len+4));
        skb->dev = dev;
        skb->protocol = __constant_htons (ETH_P_ARP);
        if (src_hw == NULL)
                src_hw = dev->dev_addr;
        if (dest_hw == NULL)
                dest_hw = dev->broadcast;
```

Figure 6.120 ARP—send an ARP message: `linux/net/ipv4/arp.c`.

```
        /*
         *      Fill the device header for the ARP frame
         */
        if (dev->hard_header &&
            dev->hard_header(skb,dev,ptype,dest_hw,src_hw,skb->len) < 0)
                goto out;

```

```
        /*
         * Fill out the arp protocol part.
         *
         * The arp hardware type should match the device type, except for FDDI,
         * which (according to RFC 1390) should always equal 1 (Ethernet).
         */
        /*
         *      Exceptions everywhere. AX.25 uses the AX.25 PID value not the
         *      DIX code for the protocol. Make these device structure fields.
         */
        switch (dev->type) {
        default:
                arp->ar_hrd = htons(dev->type);
                arp->ar_pro = __constant_htons(ETH_P_IP);
                break;

#if defined(CONFIG_AX25) || defined(CONFIG_AX25_MODULE)
        case ARPHRD_AX25:
                arp->ar_hrd = __constant_htons(ARPHRD_AX25);
                arp->ar_pro = __constant_htons(AX25_P_IP);
                break;

#if defined(CONFIG_NETROM) || defined(CONFIG_NETROM_MODULE)
        case ARPHRD_NETROM:
                arp->ar_hrd = __constant_htons(ARPHRD_NETROM);
                arp->ar_pro = __constant_htons(AX25_P_IP);
                break;
#endif
#endif

#ifdef CONFIG_FDDI
        case ARPHRD_FDDI:
                arp->ar_hrd = __constant_htons(ARPHRD_ETHER);
                arp->ar_pro = __constant_htons(ETH_P_IP);
                break;
#endif
#ifdef CONFIG_TR
        case ARPHRD_IEEE802_TR:
                arp->ar_hrd = __constant_htons(ARPHRD_IEEE802);
                arp->ar_pro = __constant_htons(ETH_P_IP);
                break;
#endif
        }
```

Figure 6.121 ARP—send an ARP message: `linux/net/ipv4/arp.c`.

```
        arp->ar_hln = dev->addr_len;
        arp->ar_pln = 4;
        arp->ar_op = htons(type);

        arp_ptr=(unsigned char *)(arp+1);

        memcpy(arp_ptr, src_hw, dev->addr_len);
        arp_ptr+=dev->addr_len;
```

```
        memcpy(arp_ptr, &src_ip,4);
        arp_ptr+=4;
        if (target_hw != NULL)
              memcpy(arp_ptr, target_hw, dev->addr_len);
        else
              memset(arp_ptr, 0, dev->addr_len);
        arp_ptr+=dev->addr_len;
        memcpy(arp_ptr, &dest_ip, 4);
        skb->dev = dev;

        dev_queue_xmit(skb);
        return;

out:
        kfree_skb(skb);
}
```

ARP Reception

Figure 6.122 ARP—receive an ARP message: `linux/net/ipv4/arp.c`.

```
static void parp_redo(struct sk_buff *skb)
{
        arp_rcv(skb, skb->dev, NULL);
}

/*
 *      Receive an arp request by the device layer.
 */
```

Figure 6.123 ARP—receive an ARP message: `linux/net/ipv4/arp.c`.

```
int arp_rcv(struct sk_buff *skb, struct net_device *dev, struct packet_type *pt)
{
        struct arphdr *arp = skb->nh.arph;
        unsigned char *arp_ptr= (unsigned char *)(arp+1);
        struct rtable *rt;
        unsigned char *sha, *tha;
        u32 sip, tip;
        u16 dev_type = dev->type;
        int addr_type;
        struct in_device *in_dev = in_dev_get(dev);
        struct neighbour *n;

/*
 *      The hardware length of the packet should match the hardware length
 *      of the device. Similarly, the hardware types should match. The
 *      device should be ARP-able. Also, if pln is not 4, then the lookup
```

```
589    *      is not from an IP number. We can't currently handle this, so toss
590    *      it.
591    */
592           if (in_dev == NULL ||
593               arp->ar_hln != dev->addr_len ||
594               dev->flags & IFF_NOARP ||
595               skb->pkt_type == PACKET_OTHERHOST ||
596               skb->pkt_type == PACKET_LOOPBACK ||
597               arp->ar_pln != 4)
598                   goto out;
599
600           if ((skb = skb_share_check(skb, GFP_ATOMIC)) == NULL)
601                   goto out_of_mem;
```

Figure 6.124 ARP—receive an ARP message: `linux/net/ipv4/arp.c`.

```
603           switch (dev_type) {
604           default:
605                   if (arp->ar_pro != __constant_htons(ETH_P_IP))
606                           goto out;
607                   if (htons(dev_type) != arp->ar_hrd)
608                           goto out;
609                   break;
610    #ifdef CONFIG_NET_ETHERNET
611           case ARPHRD_ETHER:
612                   /*
613                    * ETHERNET devices will accept ARP hardware types of either
614                    * 1 (Ethernet) or 6 (IEEE 802.2).
615                    */
616                   if (arp->ar_hrd != __constant_htons(ARPHRD_ETHER) &&
617                       arp->ar_hrd != __constant_htons(ARPHRD_IEEE802))
618                           goto out;
619                   if (arp->ar_pro != __constant_htons(ETH_P_IP))
620                           goto out;
621                   break;
622    #endif
623    #ifdef CONFIG_TR
624           case ARPHRD_IEEE802_TR:
625                   /*
626                    * Token ring devices will accept ARP hardware types of either
627                    * 1 (Ethernet) or 6 (IEEE 802.2).
628                    */
629                   if (arp->ar_hrd != __constant_htons(ARPHRD_ETHER) &&
630                       arp->ar_hrd != __constant_htons(ARPHRD_IEEE802))
631                           goto out;
632                   if (arp->ar_pro != __constant_htons(ETH_P_IP))
633                           goto out;
634                   break;
635    #endif
```

Figure 6.125 ARP—receive an ARP message: `linux/net/ipv4/arp.c`.

```
636  #ifdef CONFIG_FDDI
637      case ARPHRD_FDDI:
638          /*
639           * According to RFC 1390, FDDI devices should accept ARP hardware types
640           * of 1 (Ethernet). However, to be more robust, we'll accept hardware
641           * types of either 1 (Ethernet) or 6 (IEEE 802.2).
642           */
643          if (arp->ar_hrd != __constant_htons(ARPHRD_ETHER) &&
644              arp->ar_hrd != __constant_htons(ARPHRD_IEEE802))
645                  goto out;
646          if (arp->ar_pro != __constant_htons(ETH_P_IP))
647                  goto out;
648          break;
649  #endif
650  #if defined(CONFIG_AX25) || defined(CONFIG_AX25_MODULE)
651      case ARPHRD_AX25:
652          if (arp->ar_pro != __constant_htons(AX25_P_IP))
653                  goto out;
654          if (arp->ar_hrd != __constant_htons(ARPHRD_AX25))
655                  goto out;
656          break;
657  #if defined(CONFIG_NETROM) || defined(CONFIG_NETROM_MODULE)
658      case ARPHRD_NETROM:
659          if (arp->ar_pro != __constant_htons(AX25_P_IP))
660                  goto out;
661          if (arp->ar_hrd != __constant_htons(ARPHRD_NETROM))
662                  goto out;
663          break;
664  #endif
665  #endif
666      }
```

Figure 6.126 ARP—receive an ARP message: `linux/net/ipv4/arp.c`.

```
668      /* Understand only these message types */
669
670      if (arp->ar_op != __constant_htons(ARPOP_REPLY) &&
671          arp->ar_op != __constant_htons(ARPOP_REQUEST))
672              goto out;
673
674  /*
675   *    Extract fields
676   */
677      sha=arp_ptr;
678      arp_ptr += dev->addr_len;
679      memcpy(&sip, arp_ptr, 4);
680      arp_ptr += 4;
681      tha=arp_ptr;
682      arp_ptr += dev->addr_len;
683      memcpy(&tip, arp_ptr, 4);
684  /*
```

```
 *      Check for bad requests for 127.x.x.x and requests for multicast
 *      addresses. If this is one such, delete it.
 */
        if (LOOPBACK(tip) || MULTICAST(tip))
                goto out;

/*
 * Process entry. The idea here is we want to send a reply if it is a
 * request for us or if it is a request for someone else that we hold
 * a proxy for. We want to add an entry to our cache if it is a reply
 * to us or if it is a request for our address.
 * (The assumption for this last is that if someone is requesting our
 * address, they are probably intending to talk to us, so it saves time
 * if we cache their address. Their address is also probably not in
 * our cache, since ours is not in their cache.)
 *
 * Putting this another way, we only care about replies if they are to
 * us, in which case we add them to the cache. For requests, we care
 * about those for us and those for our proxies. We reply to both,
 * and in the case of requests for us we add the requester to the arp
 * cache.
 */
```

Figure 6.127 ARP—receive an ARP message: `linux/net/ipv4/arp.c`.

```
        /* Special case: IPv4 duplicate address detection packet (RFC 2131) */
        if (sip == 0) {
                if (arp->ar_op == __constant_htons(ARPOP_REQUEST) &&
                    inet_addr_type(tip) == RTN_LOCAL)
                        arp_send(ARPOP_REPLY,ETH_P_ARP,tip,dev,tip,sha,dev->dev_addr,
                             dev->dev_addr);
                goto out;
        }

        if (arp->ar_op == __constant_htons(ARPOP_REQUEST) &&
            ip_route_input(skb, tip, sip, 0, dev) == 0) {

                rt = (struct rtable*)skb->dst;
                addr_type = rt->rt_type;

                if (addr_type == RTN_LOCAL) {
                        n = neigh_event_ns(&arp_tbl, sha, &sip, dev);
                        if (n) {
                                arp_send(ARPOP_REPLY,ETH_P_ARP,sip,dev,tip,sha,dev->dev_addr,sha);
                                neigh_release(n);
                        }
                        goto out;
                } else if (IN_DEV_FORWARD(in_dev)) {
                        if ((rt->rt_flags&RTCF_DNAT) ||
                            (addr_type == RTN_UNICAST && rt->u.dst.dev != dev &&
                             (IN_DEV_PROXY_ARP(in_dev) || pneigh_lookup(&arp_tbl, &tip, dev, 0)))){
                                n = neigh_event_ns(&arp_tbl, sha, &sip, dev);
```

```
                if (n)
                    neigh_release(n);

                if (skb->stamp.tv_sec == 0 ||
                    skb->pkt_type == PACKET_HOST ||
                    in_dev->arp_parms->proxy_delay == 0) {
                    arp_send(ARPOP_REPLY,ETH_P_ARP,sip,dev,tip,sha,dev->dev_addr
                        ,sha);
                } else {
                    pneigh_enqueue(&arp_tbl, in_dev->arp_parms, skb);
                    in_dev_put(in_dev);
                    return 0;
                }
                goto out;
            }
        }
    }
```

Figure 6.128 ARP—receive an ARP message: `linux/net/ipv4/arp.c`.

```
    /* Update our ARP tables */

    n = __neigh_lookup(&arp_tbl, &sip, dev, 0);

#ifdef CONFIG_IP_ACCEPT_UNSOLICITED_ARP
    /* Unsolicited ARP is not accepted by default.
       It is possible, that this option should be enabled for some
       devices (strip is candidate)
     */
    if (n == NULL &&
        arp->ar_op == __constant_htons(ARPOP_REPLY) &&
        inet_addr_type(sip) == RTN_UNICAST)
            n = __neigh_lookup(&arp_tbl, &sip, dev, -1);
#endif

    if (n) {
        int state = NUD_REACHABLE;
        int override = 0;

        /* If several different ARP replies follows back-to-back,
           use the FIRST one. It is possible, if several proxy
           agents are active. Taking the first reply prevents
           arp trashing and chooses the fastest router.
         */
        if (jiffies - n->updated >= n->parms->locktime)
            override = 1;

        /* Broadcast replies and request packets
           do not assert neighbour reachability.
         */
        if (arp->ar_op != __constant_htons(ARPOP_REPLY) ||
            skb->pkt_type != PACKET_HOST)
```

```
783                         state = NUD_STALE;
784                 neigh_update(n, sha, state, override, 1);
785                 neigh_release(n);
786         }
787
788 out:
789         kfree_skb(skb);
790         if (in_dev)
791                 in_dev_put(in_dev);
792 out_of_mem:
793         return 0;
794 }
```

ARP User Interface

Figure 6.129 ARP—user interface (proc, ioctl)—create a cache entry: linux/net/ipv4/arp.c.

```
798 /*
799  *      User level interface (ioctl, /proc)
800  */
801
802 /*
803  *      Set (create) an ARP cache entry.
804  */
805
806 int arp_req_set(struct arpreq *r, struct net_device * dev)
807 {
808         u32 ip = ((struct sockaddr_in *) &r->arp_pa)->sin_addr.s_addr;
809         struct neighbour *neigh;
810         int err;
811
812         if (r->arp_flags&ATF_PUBL) {
813                 u32 mask = ((struct sockaddr_in *) &r->arp_netmask)->sin_addr.s_addr;
814                 if (mask && mask != 0xFFFFFFFF)
815                         return -EINVAL;
816                 if (!dev && (r->arp_flags & ATF_COM)) {
817                         dev = dev_getbyhwaddr(r->arp_ha.sa_family, r->arp_ha.sa_data);
818                         if (!dev)
819                                 return -ENODEV;
820                 }
821                 if (mask) {
822                         if (pneigh_lookup(&arp_tbl, &ip, dev, 1) == NULL)
823                                 return -ENOBUFS;
824                         return 0;
825                 }
826                 if (dev == NULL) {
827                         ipv4_devconf.proxy_arp = 1;
828                         return 0;
829                 }
830                 if (__in_dev_get(dev)) {
```

```
831                      __in_dev_get(dev)->cnf.proxy_arp = 1;
832                      return 0;
833              }
834              return -ENXIO;
835      }
```

Figure 6.130 ARP—user interface (`proc`, `ioctl`)—create a cache entry: `linux/net/ipv4/arp.c`.

```
837          if (r->arp_flags & ATF_PERM)
838                  r->arp_flags |= ATF_COM;
839          if (dev == NULL) {
840                  struct rtable * rt;
841                  if ((err = ip_route_output(&rt, ip, 0, RTO_ONLINK, 0)) != 0)
842                          return err;
843                  dev = rt->u.dst.dev;
844                  ip_rt_put(rt);
845                  if (!dev)
846                          return -EINVAL;
847          }
848          if (r->arp_ha.sa_family != dev->type)
849                  return -EINVAL;
850
851          neigh = __neigh_lookup_errno(&arp_tbl, &ip, dev);
852          err = PTR_ERR(neigh);
853          if (!IS_ERR(neigh)) {
854                  unsigned state = NUD_STALE;
855                  if (r->arp_flags & ATF_PERM)
856                          state = NUD_PERMANENT;
857                  err = neigh_update(neigh, (r->arp_flags&ATF_COM) ?
858                                      r->arp_ha.sa_data : NULL, state, 1, 0);
859                  neigh_release(neigh);
860          }
861          return err;
862  }
```

Figure 6.131 ARP—user interface—change ARP entry flags: `linux/net/ipv4/arp.c`.

```
864  static unsigned arp_state_to_flags(struct neighbour *neigh)
865  {
866          unsigned flags = 0;
867          if (neigh->nud_state&NUD_PERMANENT)
868                  flags = ATF_PERM|ATF_COM;
869          else if (neigh->nud_state&NUD_VALID)
870                  flags = ATF_COM;
871          return flags;
872  }
```

Figure 6.132 ARP—user interface—get an ARP entry: `linux/net/ipv4/arp.c`.

```
878   static int arp_req_get(struct arpreq *r, struct net_device *dev)
879   {
880         u32 ip = ((struct sockaddr_in *) &r->arp_pa)->sin_addr.s_addr;
881         struct neighbour *neigh;
882         int err = -ENXIO;
883
884         neigh = neigh_lookup(&arp_tbl, &ip, dev);
885         if (neigh) {
886               read_lock_bh(&neigh->lock);
887               memcpy(r->arp_ha.sa_data, neigh->ha, dev->addr_len);
888               r->arp_flags = arp_state_to_flags(neigh);
889               read_unlock_bh(&neigh->lock);
890               r->arp_ha.sa_family = dev->type;
891               strncpy(r->arp_dev, dev->name, sizeof(r->arp_dev));
892               neigh_release(neigh);
893               err = 0;
894         }
895         return err;
896   }
```

Figure 6.133 ARP—user interface—delete an ARP entry: `linux/net/ipv4/arp.c`.

```
898   int arp_req_delete(struct arpreq *r, struct net_device * dev)
899   {
900         int err;
901         u32 ip = ((struct sockaddr_in *)&r->arp_pa)->sin_addr.s_addr;
902         struct neighbour *neigh;
903
904         if (r->arp_flags & ATF_PUBL) {
905               u32 mask = ((struct sockaddr_in *) &r->arp_netmask)->sin_addr.s_addr;
906               if (mask == 0xFFFFFFFF)
907                     return pneigh_delete(&arp_tbl, &ip, dev);
908               if (mask == 0) {
909                     if (dev == NULL) {
910                           ipv4_devconf.proxy_arp = 0;
911                           return 0;
912                     }
913                     if (__in_dev_get(dev)) {
914                           __in_dev_get(dev)->cnf.proxy_arp = 0;
915                           return 0;
916                     }
917                     return -ENXIO;
918               }
919               return -EINVAL;
920         }
```

Figure 6.134 ARP—user interface—delete an ARP entry: `linux/net/ipv4/arp.c`.

```
922              if (dev == NULL) {
923                      struct rtable * rt;
924                      if ((err = ip_route_output(&rt, ip, 0, RTO_ONLINK, 0)) != 0)
925                              return err;
926                      dev = rt->u.dst.dev;
927                      ip_rt_put(rt);
928                      if (!dev)
929                              return -EINVAL;
930              }
931              err = -ENXIO;
932              neigh = neigh_lookup(&arp_tbl, &ip, dev);
933              if (neigh) {
934                      if (neigh->nud_state&~NUD_NOARP)
935                              err = neigh_update(neigh, NULL, NUD_FAILED, 1, 0);
936                      neigh_release(neigh);
937              }
938              return err;
939      }
```

Figure 6.135 ARP—user interface—`ioctl` entry point: `linux/net/ipv4/arp.c`.

```
945      int arp_ioctl(unsigned int cmd, void *arg)
946      {
947              int err;
948              struct arpreq r;
949              struct net_device * dev = NULL;
950
951              switch(cmd) {
952                      case SIOCDARP:
953                      case SIOCSARP:
954                              if (!capable(CAP_NET_ADMIN))
955                                      return -EPERM;
956                      case SIOCGARP:
957                              err = copy_from_user(&r, arg, sizeof(struct arpreq));
958                              if (err)
959                                      return -EFAULT;
960                              break;
961                      default:
962                              return -EINVAL;
963              }
964
965              if (r.arp_pa.sa_family != AF_INET)
966                      return -EPFNOSUPPORT;
967
968              if (!(r.arp_flags & ATF_PUBL) &&
969                  (r.arp_flags & (ATF_NETMASK|ATF_DONTPUB)))
970                      return -EINVAL;
971              if (!(r.arp_flags & ATF_NETMASK))
972                      ((struct sockaddr_in *)&r.arp_netmask)->sin_addr.s_addr=__constant_htonl(0
                              xFFFFFFFFUL);
```

Figure 6.136 ARP—user interface—`ioctl` entry point: `linux/net/ipv4/arp.c`.

```
974        rtnl_lock();
975        if (r.arp_dev[0]) {
976                err = -ENODEV;
977                if ((dev = __dev_get_by_name(r.arp_dev)) == NULL)
978                        goto out;
979
980                /* Mmmm... It is wrong... ARPHRD_NETROM==0 */
981                if (!r.arp_ha.sa_family)
982                        r.arp_ha.sa_family = dev->type;
983                err = -EINVAL;
984                if ((r.arp_flags & ATF_COM) && r.arp_ha.sa_family != dev->type)
985                        goto out;
986        } else if (cmd == SIOCGARP) {
987                err = -ENODEV;
988                goto out;
989        }
990
991        switch(cmd) {
992        case SIOCDARP:
993                err = arp_req_delete(&r, dev);
994                break;
995        case SIOCSARP:
996                err = arp_req_set(&r, dev);
997                break;
998        case SIOCGARP:
999                err = arp_req_get(&r, dev);
1000                if (!err && copy_to_user(arg, &r, sizeof(r)))
1001                        err = -EFAULT;
1002                break;
1003        }
1004 out:
1005        rtnl_unlock();
1006        return err;
1007 }
```

Figure 6.137 ARP—user interface—`procfs` entry point—write table: `linux/net/ipv4/arp.c`.

```
1009 /*
1010  *      Write the contents of the ARP cache to a PROCfs file.
1011  */
1012 #ifndef CONFIG_PROC_FS
1013 static int arp_get_info(char *buffer, char **start, off_t offset, int length) { return 0; }
1014 #else
1015 #if defined(CONFIG_AX25) || defined(CONFIG_AX25_MODULE)
1016 static char *ax2asc2(ax25_address *a, char *buf);
1017 #endif
1018 #define HBUFFERLEN 30
1019
1020 static int arp_get_info(char *buffer, char **start, off_t offset, int length)
1021 {
```

```
1022        int len=0;
1023        off_t pos=0;
1024        int size;
1025        char hbuffer[HBUFFERLEN];
1026        int i,j,k;
1027        const char hexbuf[] = "0123456789ABCDEF";
1028
1029        size = sprintf(buffer,"IP address    HW type    Flags    HW address         Mask
               Device\n");
1030
1031        pos+=size;
1032        len+=size;
1033
1034        for(i=0; i<=NEIGH_HASHMASK; i++) {
1035                struct neighbour *n;
1036                read_lock_bh(&arp_tbl.lock);
1037                for (n=arp_tbl.hash_buckets[i]; n; n=n->next) {
1038                        struct net_device *dev = n->dev;
1039                        int hatype = dev->type;
1040
1041                        /* Do not confuse users "arp -a" with magic entries */
1042                        if (!(n->nud_state&~NUD_NOARP))
1043                                continue;
1044
1045                        read_lock(&n->lock);
```

Figure 6.138 ARP—user interface—`procfs` entry point—write table: `linux/net/ipv4/arp.c`.

```
1047    /*
1048     *      Convert hardware address to XX:XX:XX:XX ... form.
1049     */
1050    #if defined(CONFIG_AX25) || defined(CONFIG_AX25_MODULE)
1051                    if (hatype == ARPHRD_AX25 || hatype == ARPHRD_NETROM)
1052                            ax2asc2((ax25_address *)n->ha, hbuffer);
1053                    else {
1054    #endif
1055                    for (k=0,j=0;k<HBUFFERLEN-3 && j<dev->addr_len;j++) {
1056                            hbuffer[k++]=hexbuf[(n->ha[j]>>4)&15 ];
1057                            hbuffer[k++]=hexbuf[n->ha[j]&15 ];
1058                            hbuffer[k++]=':';
1059                    }
1060                    hbuffer[--k]=0;
1061
1062    #if defined(CONFIG_AX25) || defined(CONFIG_AX25_MODULE)
1063                    }
1064    #endif
1065
1066                    {
1067                            char tbuf[16];
1068                            sprintf(tbuf, "%u.%u.%u.%u", NIPQUAD(*(u32*)n->primary_key));
1069                            size = sprintf(buffer+len, "%-16s 0x%-10x0x%-10x%s"
```

```
                                        "     *       %s\n",
                                tbuf,
                                hatype,
                                arp_state_to_flags(n),
                                hbuffer,
                                dev->name);
                        }

                        read_unlock(&n->lock);

                        len += size;
                        pos += size;

                        if (pos <= offset)
                                len=0;
                        if (pos >= offset+length) {
                                read_unlock_bh(&arp_tbl.lock);
                                goto done;
                        }
                }
                read_unlock_bh(&arp_tbl.lock);
        }
```

Figure 6.139 ARP—user interface—procfs entry point—write table: linux/net/ipv4/arp.c.

```
        for (i=0; i<=PNEIGH_HASHMASK; i++) {
                struct pneigh_entry *n;
                for (n=arp_tbl.phash_buckets[i]; n; n=n->next) {
                        struct net_device *dev = n->dev;
                        int hatype = dev ? dev->type : 0;

                        {
                                char tbuf[16];
                                sprintf(tbuf, "%u.%u.%u.%u", NIPQUAD(*(u32*)n->key));
                                size = sprintf(buffer+len, "%-16s 0x%-10x0x%-10x%s"
                                        "     *       %s\n",
                                        tbuf,
                                        hatype,
                                        ATF_PUBL|ATF_PERM,
                                        "00:00:00:00:00:00",
                                        dev ? dev->name : "*");
                        }

                        len += size;
                        pos += size;

                        if (pos <= offset)
                                len=0;
                        if (pos >= offset+length)
                                goto done;
                }
        }

```

```
done:

        *start = buffer+len-(pos-offset);    /* Start of wanted data */
        len = pos-offset;                    /* Start slop */
        if (len>length)
                len = length;                /* Ending slop */
        if (len<0)
                len = 0;
        return len;
}
#endif
```

Figure 6.140 ARP—interface down: `linux/net/ipv4/arp.c`.

```
/* Note, that it is not on notifier chain.
   It is necessary, that this routine was called after route cache will be
   flushed.
 */
void arp_ifdown(struct net_device *dev)
{
        neigh_ifdown(&arp_tbl, dev);
}
```

ARP Initialization and Usage Example

Figure 6.141 ARP—initialize: `linux/net/ipv4/arp.c`.

```
static struct packet_type arp_packet_type =
{
        __constant_htons(ETH_P_ARP),
        NULL,           /* All devices */
        arp_rcv,
        (void*)1,
        NULL
};

void __init arp_init (void)
{
        neigh_table_init(&arp_tbl);

        dev_add_pack(&arp_packet_type);

        proc_net_create ("arp", 0, arp_get_info);

#ifdef CONFIG_SYSCTL
        neigh_sysctl_register(NULL, &arp_tbl.parms, NET_IPV4, NET_IPV4_NEIGH, "ipv4");
#endif
}
```

Figure 6.142 ARP—amateur radio X.25 ARP string address conversion: `linux/net/ipv4/arp.c`.

```
1170  #ifdef CONFIG_PROC_FS
1171  #if defined(CONFIG_AX25) || defined(CONFIG_AX25_MODULE)
1172
1173  /*
1174   *      ax25 -> ASCII conversion
1175   */
1176  char *ax2asc2(ax25_address *a, char *buf)
1177  {
1178          char c, *s;
1179          int n;
1180
1181          for (n = 0, s = buf; n < 6; n++) {
1182                  c = (a->ax25_call[n] >> 1) & 0x7F;
1183
1184                  if (c != ' ') *s++ = c;
1185          }
1186
1187          *s++ = '-';
1188
1189          if ((n = ((a->ax25_call[6] >> 1) & 0x0F)) > 9) {
1190                  *s++ = '1';
1191                  n -= 10;
1192          }
1193
1194          *s++ = n + '0';
1195          *s++ = '\0';
1196
1197          if (*buf == '\0' || *buf == '-')
1198             return "*";
1199
1200          return buf;
1201
1202  }
1203
1204  #endif
1205  #endif
```

6.4 Network-Level Debugging—ICMP

Figure 6.143 ICMP, host requirement conformance: `linux/net/ipv4/icmp.c`.

```
61   * RFC 1122 (Host Requirements -- Comm. Layer) Status:
62   * (boy, are there a lot of rules for ICMP)
63   * 3.2.2 (Generic ICMP stuff)
64   *   MUST discard messages of unknown type. (OK)
65   *   MUST copy at least the first 8 bytes from the offending packet
```

```
 *    when sending ICMP errors. (OBSOLETE -- see RFC 1812)
 *  MUST pass received ICMP errors up to protocol level. (OK)
 *  SHOULD send ICMP errors with TOS == 0. (OBSOLETE -- see RFC 1812)
 *  MUST NOT send ICMP errors in reply to:
 *    ICMP errors (OK)
 *    Broadcast/multicast datagrams (OK)
 *    MAC broadcasts (OK)
 *    Non-initial fragments (OK)
 *    Datagram with a source address that isn't a single host. (OK)
 * 3.2.2.1 (Destination Unreachable)
 *  All the rules govern the IP layer, and are dealt with in ip.c, not here.
 * 3.2.2.2 (Redirect)
 *  Host SHOULD NOT send ICMP_REDIRECTs. (OK)
 *  MUST update routing table in response to host or network redirects.
 *    (host OK, network OBSOLETE)
 *  SHOULD drop redirects if they're not from directly connected gateway
 *    (OK -- we drop it if it's not from our old gateway, which is close
 *     enough)
```

Figure 6.144 ICMP, host requirement conformance: `linux/net/ipv4/icmp.c`.

```
 * 3.2.2.3 (Source Quench)
 *  MUST pass incoming SOURCE_QUENCHs to transport layer (OK)
 *  Other requirements are dealt with at the transport layer.
 * 3.2.2.4 (Time Exceeded)
 *  MUST pass TIME_EXCEEDED to transport layer (OK)
 *  Other requirements dealt with at IP (generating TIME_EXCEEDED).
 * 3.2.2.5 (Parameter Problem)
 *  SHOULD generate these (OK)
 *  MUST pass received PARAMPROBLEM to transport layer (NOT YET)
 *     [Solaris 2.X seems to assert EPROTO when this occurs] -- AC
 * 3.2.2.6 (Echo Request/Reply)
 *  MUST reply to ECHO_REQUEST, and give app to do ECHO stuff (OK, OK)
 *  MAY discard broadcast ECHO_REQUESTs. (Configurable with a sysctl.)
 *  MUST reply using same source address as the request was sent to.
 *    We're OK for unicast ECHOs, and it doesn't say anything about
 *    how to handle broadcast ones, since it's optional.
 *  MUST copy data from REQUEST to REPLY (OK)
 *    unless it would require illegal fragmentation (OK)
 *  MUST pass REPLYs to transport/user layer (OK)
 *  MUST use any provided source route (reversed) for REPLY. (NOT YET)
 * 3.2.2.7 (Information Request/Reply)
 *  MUST NOT implement this. (I guess that means silently discard...?) (OK)
 * 3.2.2.8 (Timestamp Request/Reply)
 *  MAY implement (OK)
 *  SHOULD be in-kernel for "minimum variability" (OK)
 *  MAY discard broadcast REQUESTs. (OK, but see source for inconsistency)
 *  MUST reply using same source address as the request was sent to. (OK)
 *  MUST reverse source route, as per ECHO (NOT YET)
 *  MUST pass REPLYs to transport/user layer (requires RAW, just like
 *     ECHO) (OK)
 *  MUST update clock for timestamp at least 15 times/sec (OK)
```

```
 *   MUST be "correct within a few minutes" (OK)
 * 3.2.2.9 (Address Mask Request/Reply)
 *   MAY implement (OK)
 *   MUST send a broadcast REQUEST if using this system to set netmask
 *     (OK... we don't use it)
 *   MUST discard received REPLYs if not using this system (OK)
 *   MUST NOT send replies unless specifically made agent for this sort
 *     of thing. (OK)
```

Figure 6.145 ICMP, router requirement conformance: `linux/net/ipv4/icmp.c`.

```
 * RFC 1812 (IPv4 Router Requirements) Status (even longer):
 *  4.3.2.1 (Unknown Message Types)
 *   MUST pass messages of unknown type to ICMP user iface or silently discard
 *     them (OK)
 *  4.3.2.2 (ICMP Message TTL)
 *   MUST initialize TTL when originating an ICMP message (OK)
 *  4.3.2.3 (Original Message Header)
 *   SHOULD copy as much data from the offending packet as possible without
 *     the length of the ICMP datagram exceeding 576 bytes (OK)
 *   MUST leave original IP header of the offending packet, but we're not
 *     required to undo modifications made (OK)
 *  4.3.2.4 (Original Message Source Address)
 *   MUST use one of addresses for the interface the orig. packet arrived as
 *     source address (OK)
 *  4.3.2.5 (TOS and Precedence)
 *   SHOULD leave TOS set to the same value unless the packet would be
 *     discarded for that reason (OK)
 *   MUST use TOS=0 if not possible to leave original value (OK)
 *   MUST leave IP Precedence for Source Quench messages (OK -- not sent
 *      at all)
 *   SHOULD use IP Precedence = 6 (Internetwork Control) or 7 (Network Control)
 *     for all other error messages (OK, we use 6)
 *   MAY allow configuration of IP Precedence (OK -- not done)
 *   MUST leave IP Precedence and TOS for reply messages (OK)
 *  4.3.2.6 (Source Route)
 *   SHOULD use reverse source route UNLESS sending Parameter Problem on source
 *     routing and UNLESS the packet would be immediately discarded (NOT YET)
 *  4.3.2.7 (When Not to Send ICMP Errors)
 *   MUST NOT send ICMP errors in reply to:
 *     ICMP errors (OK)
 *     Packets failing IP header validation tests unless otherwise noted (OK)
 *     Broadcast/multicast datagrams (OK)
 *     MAC broadcasts (OK)
 *     Non-initial fragments (OK)
 *     Datagram with a source address that isn't a single host. (OK)
```

Figure 6.146 ICMP, router requirement conformance: `linux/net/ipv4/icmp.c`.

```
 * 4.3.2.8 (Rate Limiting)
 *  SHOULD be able to limit error message rate (OK)
 *  SHOULD allow setting of rate limits (OK, in the source)
 * 4.3.3.1 (Destination Unreachable)
 *  All the rules govern the IP layer, and are dealt with in ip.c, not here.
 * 4.3.3.2 (Redirect)
 *  MAY ignore ICMP Redirects if running a routing protocol or if forwarding
 *    is enabled on the interface (OK -- ignores)
 * 4.3.3.3 (Source Quench)
 *  SHOULD NOT originate SQ messages (OK)
 *  MUST be able to limit SQ rate if originates them (OK as we don't
 *     send them)
 *  MAY ignore SQ messages it receives (OK -- we don't)
 * 4.3.3.4 (Time Exceeded)
 *  Requirements dealt with at IP (generating TIME_EXCEEDED).
 * 4.3.3.5 (Parameter Problem)
 *  MUST generate these for all errors not covered by other messages (OK)
 *  MUST include original value of the value pointed by (OK)
```

Figure 6.147 ICMP, router requirement conformance: `linux/net/ipv4/icmp.c`.

```
 * 4.3.3.6 (Echo Request)
 *  MUST implement echo server function (OK)
 *  MUST process at ER of at least max(576, MTU) (OK)
 *  MAY reject broadcast/multicast ER's (We don't, but that's OK)
 *  SHOULD have a config option for silently ignoring ER's (OK)
 *  MUST have a default value for the above switch = NO (OK)
 *  MUST have application layer interface for Echo Request/Reply (OK)
 *  MUST reply using same source address as the request was sent to.
 *    We're OK for unicast ECHOs, and it doesn't say anything about
 *    how to handle broadcast ones, since it's optional.
 *  MUST copy data from Request to Reply (OK)
 *  SHOULD update Record Route / Timestamp options (??)
 *  MUST use reversed Source Route for Reply if possible (NOT YET)
 * 4.3.3.7 (Information Request/Reply)
 *  SHOULD NOT originate or respond to these (OK)
 * 4.3.3.8 (Timestamp / Timestamp Reply)
 *  MAY implement (OK)
 *  MUST reply to every Timestamp message received (OK)
 *  MAY discard broadcast REQUESTs. (OK, but see source for inconsistency)
 *  MUST reply using same source address as the request was sent to. (OK)
 *  MUST use reversed Source Route if possible (NOT YET)
 *  SHOULD update Record Route / Timestamp options (??)
 *  MUST pass REPLYs to transport/user layer (requires RAW, just like
 *     ECHO) (OK)
 *  MUST update clock for timestamp at least 16 times/sec (OK)
 *  MUST be "correct within a few minutes" (OK)
 * 4.3.3.9 (Address Mask Request/Reply)
 *  MUST have support for receiving AMRq and responding with AMRe (OK,
 *     but only as a compile-time option)
 *  SHOULD have option for each interface for AMRe's, MUST default to
```

```
 *      NO (NOT YET)
 *   MUST NOT reply to AMRq before knows the correct AM (OK)
 *   MUST NOT respond to AMRq with source address 0.0.0.0 on physical
 *      interfaces having multiple logical i-faces with different masks
 *      (NOT YET)
 *   SHOULD examine all AMRe's it receives and check them (NOT YET)
 *   SHOULD log invalid AMRe's (AM+sender) (NOT YET)
 *   MUST NOT use contents of AMRe to determine correct AM (OK)
 *   MAY broadcast AMRe's after having configured address masks (OK -- doesn't)
 *   MUST NOT do broadcast AMRe's if not set by extra option (OK, no option)
 *   MUST use the { <NetPrefix>, -1 } form of broadcast addresses (OK)
 * 4.3.3.10 (Router Advertisement and Solicitations)
 *   MUST support router part of Router Discovery Protocol on all networks we
 *     support broadcast or multicast addressing. (OK -- done by gated)
 *   MUST have all config parameters with the respective defaults (OK)
```

Figure 6.148 CMP, router requirement conformance: `linux/net/ipv4/icmp.c`.

```
 * 5.2.7.1 (Destination Unreachable)
 *   MUST generate DU's (OK)
 *   SHOULD choose a best-match response code (OK)
 *   SHOULD NOT generate Host Isolated codes (OK)
 *   SHOULD use Communication Administratively Prohibited when administratively
 *     filtering packets (NOT YET -- bug-to-bug compatibility)
 *   MAY include config option for not generating the above and silently
 *      discard the packets instead (OK)
 *   MAY include config option for not generating Precedence Violation and
 *     Precedence Cutoff messages (OK as we don't generate them at all)
 *   MUST use Host Unreachable or Dest. Host Unknown codes whenever other hosts
 *     on the same network might be reachable (OK -- no net unreach's at all)
 *   MUST use new form of Fragmentation Needed and DF Set messages (OK)
 * 5.2.7.2 (Redirect)
 *   MUST NOT generate network redirects (OK)
 *   MUST be able to generate host redirects (OK)
 *   SHOULD be able to generate Host+TOS redirects (NO as we don't use TOS)
 *   MUST have an option to use Host redirects instead of Host+TOS ones (OK as
 *     no Host+TOS Redirects are used)
 *   MUST NOT generate redirects unless forwarding to the same i-face and the
 *     dest. address is on the same subnet as the src. address and no source
 *     routing is in use. (OK)
 *   MUST NOT follow redirects when using a routing protocol (OK)
 *   MAY use redirects if not using a routing protocol (OK, compile-time option)
 *   MUST comply to Host Requirements when not acting as a router (OK)
 *  5.2.7.3 (Time Exceeded)
 *   MUST generate Time Exceeded Code 0 when discarding packet due to TTL=0 (OK)
 *   MAY have a per-interface option to disable origination of TE messages, but
 *     it MUST default to "originate" (OK -- we don't support it)
```

Now we look at the data associated with running ICMP.

Figure 6.149 ICMP global data: `linux/net/ipv4/icmp.c`.

```
struct icmp_mib icmp_statistics[NR_CPUS*2];

/* An array of errno for error messages from dest unreach. */
/* RFC 1122: 3.2.2.1 States that NET_UNREACH, HOS_UNREACH and SR_FAIELD MUST be considered '
        transient errs'. */

struct icmp_err icmp_err_convert[] = {
  { ENETUNREACH,      0 },    /*      ICMP_NET_UNREACH       */
  { EHOSTUNREACH,     0 },    /*      ICMP_HOST_UNREACH      */
  { ENOPROTOOPT,      1 },    /*      ICMP_PROT_UNREACH      */
  { ECONNREFUSED,     1 },    /*      ICMP_PORT_UNREACH      */
  { EMSGSIZE,         0 },    /*      ICMP_FRAG_NEEDED       */
  { EOPNOTSUPP,       0 },    /*      ICMP_SR_FAILED         */
  { ENETUNREACH,      1 },    /*      ICMP_NET_UNKNOWN       */
  { EHOSTDOWN,        1 },    /*      ICMP_HOST_UNKNOWN      */
  { ENONET,           1 },    /*      ICMP_HOST_ISOLATED     */
  { ENETUNREACH,      1 },    /*      ICMP_NET_ANO           */
  { EHOSTUNREACH,     1 },    /*      ICMP_HOST_ANO          */
  { ENETUNREACH,      0 },    /*      ICMP_NET_UNR_TOS       */
  { EHOSTUNREACH,     0 },    /*      ICMP_HOST_UNR_TOS      */
  { EHOSTUNREACH,     1 },    /*      ICMP_PKT_FILTERED      */
  { EHOSTUNREACH,     1 },    /*      ICMP_PREC_VIOLATION    */
  { EHOSTUNREACH,     1 }     /*      ICMP_PREC_CUTOFF       */
};

/* Control parameters for ECHO relies. */
int sysctl_icmp_echo_ignore_all = 0;
int sysctl_icmp_echo_ignore_broadcasts = 0;

/* Control parameter - ignore bogus broadcast responses? */
int sysctl_icmp_ignore_bogus_error_responses =0;
```

Figure 6.150 ICMP global data: `linux/net/ipv4/icmp.c`.

```
/*
 *      ICMP control array. This specifies what to do with each ICMP.
 */

struct icmp_control
{
        unsigned long *output;        /* Address to increment on output */
        unsigned long *input;         /* Address to increment on input */
        void (*handler)(struct icmphdr *icmph, struct sk_buff *skb, int len);
        short  error;          /* This ICMP is classed as an error message */
        int *timeout; /* Rate limit */
};

static struct icmp_control icmp_pointers[NR_ICMP_TYPES+1];
```

```

/*
 *      The ICMP socket. This is the most convenient way to flow control
 *      our ICMP output as well as maintain a clean interface throughout
 *      all layers. All Socketless IP sends will soon be gone.
 */

struct inode icmp_inode;
struct socket *icmp_socket=&icmp_inode.u.socket_i;

/* ICMPv4 socket is only a bit non-reenterable (unlike ICMPv6,
   which is strongly non-reenterable). A bit later it will be made
   reenterable and the lock may be removed then.
 */

static int icmp_xmit_holder = -1;
```

Figure 6.151 ICMP—transmit locks: `linux/net/ipv4/icmp.c`.

```
static int icmp_xmit_lock_bh(void)
{
        if (!spin_trylock(&icmp_socket->sk->lock.slock)) {
                if (icmp_xmit_holder == smp_processor_id())
                        return -EAGAIN;
                spin_lock(&icmp_socket->sk->lock.slock);
        }
        icmp_xmit_holder = smp_processor_id();
        return 0;
}

static __inline__ int icmp_xmit_lock(void)
{
        int ret;
        local_bh_disable();
        ret = icmp_xmit_lock_bh();
        if (ret)
                local_bh_enable();
        return ret;
}

static void icmp_xmit_unlock_bh(void)
{
        icmp_xmit_holder = -1;
        spin_unlock(&icmp_socket->sk->lock.slock);
}

static __inline__ void icmp_xmit_unlock(void)
{
        icmp_xmit_unlock_bh();
        local_bh_enable();
}
```

Figure 6.152 ICMP transmit rate limiter–token bucket: `linux/net/ipv4/icmp.c`.

```
/*
 *      Check transmit rate limitation for given message.
 *      The rate information is held in the destination cache now.
 *      This function is generic and could be used for other purposes
 *      too. It uses a Token bucket filter as suggested by Alexey Kuznetsov.
 *
 *      Note that the same dst_entry fields are modified by functions in
 *      route.c too, but these work for packet destinations while xrlim_allow
 *      works for icmp destinations. This means the rate limiting information
 *      for one "ip object" is shared.
 *
 *      Note that the same dst_entry fields are modified by functions in
 *      route.c too, but these work for packet destinations while xrlim_allow
 *      works for icmp destinations. This means the rate limiting information
 *      for one "ip object" is shared - and these ICMPs are twice limited:
 *      by source and by destination.
 *
 *      RFC 1812: 4.3.2.8 SHOULD be able to limit error message rate
 *                        SHOULD allow setting of rate limits
 *
 *      Shared between ICMPv4 and ICMPv6.
 */
#define XRLIM_BURST_FACTOR 6
int xrlim_allow(struct dst_entry *dst, int timeout)
{
        unsigned long now;

        now = jiffies;
        dst->rate_tokens += now - dst->rate_last;
        dst->rate_last = now;
        if (dst->rate_tokens > XRLIM_BURST_FACTOR*timeout)
                dst->rate_tokens = XRLIM_BURST_FACTOR*timeout;
        if (dst->rate_tokens >= timeout) {
                dst->rate_tokens -= timeout;
                return 1;
        }
        return 0;
}
```

Figure 6.153 ICMP transmit rate limit computation: `linux/net/ipv4/icmp.c`.

```
static inline int icmpv4_xrlim_allow(struct rtable *rt, int type, int code)
{
        struct dst_entry *dst = &rt->u.dst;

        if (type > NR_ICMP_TYPES || !icmp_pointers[type].timeout)
                return 1;

        /* Don't limit PMTU discovery. */
        if (type == ICMP_DEST_UNREACH && code == ICMP_FRAG_NEEDED)
                return 1;
```

```

        /* Redirect has its own rate limit mechanism */
        if (type == ICMP_REDIRECT)
                return 1;

        /* No rate limit on loopback */
        if (dst->dev && (dst->dev->flags&IFF_LOOPBACK))
                return 1;

        return xrlim_allow(dst, *(icmp_pointers[type].timeout));
}
```

Figure 6.154 ICMP/SNMP statistics counters: `linux/net/ipv4/icmp.c`.

```
/*
 *      Maintain the counters used in the SNMP statistics for outgoing ICMP
 */

static void icmp_out_count(int type)
{
        if (type>NR_ICMP_TYPES)
                return;
        (icmp_pointers[type].output)[(smp_processor_id()*2+!in_softirq())*sizeof(struct icmp_mib)
             /sizeof(unsigned long)]++;
        ICMP_INC_STATS(IcmpOutMsgs);
}
```

Figure 6.155 ICMP checksum: `linux/net/ipv4/icmp.c`.

```
 */

static void icmp_out_count(int type)
{
        if (type>NR_ICMP_TYPES)
                return;
        (icmp_pointers[type].output)[(smp_processor_id()*2+!in_softirq())*sizeof(struct icmp_mib)
             /sizeof(unsigned long)]++;
        ICMP_INC_STATS(IcmpOutMsgs);
}

/*
 *      Checksum each fragment, and on the first include the headers and final checksum.
 */

static int icmp_glue_bits(const void *p, char *to, unsigned int offset, unsigned int fraglen)
{
        struct icmp_bxm *icmp_param = (struct icmp_bxm *)p;
        struct icmphdr *icmph;
        unsigned long csum;

```

```
        if (offset) {
                icmp_param->csum=csum_partial_copy_nocheck(icmp_param->data_ptr+offset-sizeof(
                      struct icmphdr),
                                to, fraglen,icmp_param->csum);
                return 0;
        }

        /*
         *      First fragment includes header. Note that we've done
         *      the other fragments first, so that we get the checksum
         *      for the whole packet here.
         */
        csum = csum_partial_copy_nocheck((void *)&icmp_param->icmph,
                to, sizeof(struct icmphdr),
                icmp_param->csum);
        csum = csum_partial_copy_nocheck(icmp_param->data_ptr,
                to+sizeof(struct icmphdr),
                fraglen-sizeof(struct icmphdr), csum);
        icmph=(struct icmphdr *)to;
        icmph->checksum = csum_fold(csum);
        return 0;
}
```

Figure 6.156 ICMP reply: `linux/net/ipv4/icmp.c`.

```
void icmp_reply(struct icmp_bxm *icmp_param, struct sk_buff *skb)
{
        struct sock *sk=icmp_socket->sk;
        struct ipcm_cookie ipc;
        struct rtable *rt = (struct rtable*)skb->dst;
        u32 daddr;

        if (ip_options_echo(&icmp_param->replyopts, skb))
                return;

        if (icmp_xmit_lock_bh())
                return;

        icmp_param->icmph.checksum=0;
        icmp_param->csum=0;
        icmp_out_count(icmp_param->icmph.type);

        sk->protinfo.af_inet.tos = skb->nh.iph->tos;
        daddr = ipc.addr = rt->rt_src;
        ipc.opt = NULL;
        if (icmp_param->replyopts.optlen) {
                ipc.opt = &icmp_param->replyopts;
                if (ipc.opt->srr)
                        daddr = icmp_param->replyopts.faddr;
        }
        if (ip_route_output(&rt, daddr, rt->rt_spec_dst, RT_TOS(skb->nh.iph->tos), 0))
                goto out;
```

```
        if (icmpv4_xrlim_allow(rt, icmp_param->icmph.type,
                               icmp_param->icmph.code)) {
                ip_build_xmit(sk, icmp_glue_bits, icmp_param,
                        icmp_param->data_len+sizeof(struct icmphdr),
                        &ipc, rt, MSG_DONTWAIT);
        }
        ip_rt_put(rt);
out:
        icmp_xmit_unlock_bh();
}
```

Figure 6.157 ICMP send: `linux/net/ipv4/icmp.c`.

```
/*
 *      Send an ICMP message in response to a situation
 *
 *      RFC 1122: 3.2.2 MUST send at least the IP header and 8 bytes of header. MAY send more (we
        do).
 *                      MUST NOT change this header information.
 *                      MUST NOT reply to a multicast/broadcast IP address.
 *                      MUST NOT reply to a multicast/broadcast MAC address.
 *                      MUST reply to only the first fragment.
 */

void icmp_send(struct sk_buff *skb_in, int type, int code, unsigned long info)
{
        struct iphdr *iph;
        struct icmphdr *icmph;
        int room;
        struct icmp_bxm icmp_param;
        struct rtable *rt = (struct rtable*)skb_in->dst;
        struct ipcm_cookie ipc;
        u32 saddr;
        u8  tos;

        if (!rt)
                return;

        /*
         *      Find the original header
         */
        iph = skb_in->nh.iph;

        /*
         *      No replies to physical multicast/broadcast
         */
        if (skb_in->pkt_type!=PACKET_HOST)
                return;

        /*
         *      Now check at the protocol level
         */
```

```
	if (rt->rt_flags&(RTCF_BROADCAST|RTCF_MULTICAST))
		return;

	/*
	 *	Only reply to fragment 0. We byte re-order the constant
	 *	mask for efficiency.
	 */
	if (iph->frag_off&htons(IP_OFFSET))
		return;
```

Avoid recursive ICMP errors:

Figure 6.158 ICMP send: `linux/net/ipv4/icmp.c`.

```
	/*
	 *	If we send an ICMP error to an ICMP error a mess would result..
	 */
	if (icmp_pointers[type].error) {
		/*
		 *	We are an error, check if we are replying to an ICMP error
		 */
		if (iph->protocol==IPPROTO_ICMP) {
			icmph = (struct icmphdr *)((char *)iph + (iph->ihl<<2));
			/*
			 *	Assume any unknown ICMP type is an error. This isn't
			 *	specified by the RFC, but think about it..
			 */
			if (icmph->type>NR_ICMP_TYPES || icmp_pointers[icmph->type].error)
				return;
		}
	}


	if (icmp_xmit_lock())
		return;

	/*
	 *	Construct source address and options.
	 */

#ifdef CONFIG_IP_ROUTE_NAT
	/*
	 *	Restore original addresses if packet has been translated.
	 */
	if (rt->rt_flags&RTCF_NAT && IPCB(skb_in)->flags&IPSKB_TRANSLATED) {
		iph->daddr = rt->key.dst;
		iph->saddr = rt->key.src;
	}
#endif

	saddr = iph->daddr;
	if (!(rt->rt_flags & RTCF_LOCAL))
```

```
                saddr = 0;

        tos = icmp_pointers[type].error ?
                ((iph->tos & IPTOS_TOS_MASK) | IPTOS_PREC_INTERNETCONTROL) :
                        iph->tos;
```

Figure 6.159 ICMP send: `linux/net/ipv4/icmp.c`.

```
        /* XXX: use a more aggressive expire for routes created by
         * this call (not longer than the rate limit timeout).
         * It could be also worthwhile to not put them into ipv4
         * fast routing cache at first. Otherwise an attacker can
         * grow the routing table.
         */
        if (ip_route_output(&rt, iph->saddr, saddr, RT_TOS(tos), 0))
                goto out;

        if (ip_options_echo(&icmp_param.replyopts, skb_in))
                goto ende;


        /*
         *      Prepare data for ICMP header.
         */

        icmp_param.icmph.type=type;
        icmp_param.icmph.code=code;
        icmp_param.icmph.un.gateway = info;
        icmp_param.icmph.checksum=0;
        icmp_param.csum=0;
        icmp_param.data_ptr=iph;
        icmp_out_count(icmp_param.icmph.type);
        icmp_socket->sk->protinfo.af_inet.tos = tos;
        ipc.addr = iph->saddr;
        ipc.opt = &icmp_param.replyopts;
        if (icmp_param.replyopts.srr) {
                ip_rt_put(rt);
                if (ip_route_output(&rt, icmp_param.replyopts.faddr, saddr, RT_TOS(tos), 0))
                        goto out;
        }
```

Figure 6.160 ICMP send: `linux/net/ipv4/icmp.c`.

```
        if (!icmpv4_xrlim_allow(rt, type, code))
                goto ende;

        /* RFC says return as much as we can without exceeding 576 bytes. */

        room = rt->u.dst.pmtu;
        if (room > 576)
                room = 576;
```

```
	room -= sizeof(struct iphdr) + icmp_param.replyopts.optlen;
	room -= sizeof(struct icmphdr);

	icmp_param.data_len=(skb_in->tail-(u8*)iph);
	if (icmp_param.data_len > room)
		icmp_param.data_len = room;

	ip_build_xmit(icmp_socket->sk, icmp_glue_bits, &icmp_param,
		icmp_param.data_len+sizeof(struct icmphdr),
		&ipc, rt, MSG_DONTWAIT);

ende:
	ip_rt_put(rt);
out:
	icmp_xmit_unlock();
}
```

Handle unreachables correctly:

Figure 6.161 ICMP unreachables: `linux/net/ipv4/icmp.c`.

```
/*
 *	Handle ICMP_DEST_UNREACH, ICMP_TIME_EXCEED, and ICMP_QUENCH.
 */

static void icmp_unreach(struct icmphdr *icmph, struct sk_buff *skb, int len)
{
	struct iphdr *iph;
	int hash;
	struct inet_protocol *ipprot;
	unsigned char *dp;
	struct sock *raw_sk;

	/*
	 *	Incomplete header ?
	 *	Only checks for the IP header, there should be an
	 *	additional check for longer headers in upper levels.
	 */

	if(len<sizeof(struct iphdr)) {
		ICMP_INC_STATS_BH(IcmpInErrors);
		return;
	}

	iph = (struct iphdr *) (icmph + 1);
	dp = (unsigned char*)iph;
```

Figure 6.162 ICMP unreachables: `linux/net/ipv4/icmp.c`.

```
	if(icmph->type==ICMP_DEST_UNREACH) {
		switch(icmph->code & 15) {
			case ICMP_NET_UNREACH:
				break;
			case ICMP_HOST_UNREACH:
				break;
			case ICMP_PROT_UNREACH:
				break;
			case ICMP_PORT_UNREACH:
				break;
			case ICMP_FRAG_NEEDED:
				if (ipv4_config.no_pmtu_disc) {
					if (net_ratelimit())
						printk(KERN_INFO "ICMP: %u.%u.%u.%u: fragmentation
							needed and DF set.\n",
							NIPQUAD(iph->daddr));
				} else {
					unsigned short new_mtu;
					new_mtu = ip_rt_frag_needed(iph, ntohs(icmph->un.frag.mtu));
					if (!new_mtu)
						return;
					icmph->un.frag.mtu = htons(new_mtu);
				}
				break;
			case ICMP_SR_FAILED:
				if (net_ratelimit())
					printk(KERN_INFO "ICMP: %u.%u.%u.%u: Source Route Failed.\n
						", NIPQUAD(iph->daddr));
				break;
			default:
				break;
		}
		if (icmph->code>NR_ICMP_UNREACH)
			return;
	}
```

Figure 6.163 ICMP unreachables: `linux/net/ipv4/icmp.c`.

```
	/*
	 *	Throw it at our lower layers
	 *
	 *	RFC 1122: 3.2.2 MUST extract the protocol ID from the passed header.
	 *	RFC 1122: 3.2.2.1 MUST pass ICMP unreach messages to the transport layer.
	 *	RFC 1122: 3.2.2.2 MUST pass ICMP time expired messages to transport layer.
	 */

	/*
	 *	Check the other end isnt violating RFC 1122. Some routers send
	 *	bogus responses to broadcast frames. If you see this message
	 *	first check your netmask matches at both ends, if it does then
```

```
	 *	get the other vendor to fix their kit.
	 */

	if (!sysctl_icmp_ignore_bogus_error_responses)
	{

		if (inet_addr_type(iph->daddr) == RTN_BROADCAST)
		{
			if (net_ratelimit())
				printk(KERN_WARNING "%u.%u.%u.%u sent an invalid ICMP error to a
					broadcast.\n",
				NIPQUAD(skb->nh.iph->saddr));
			return;
		}
	}

	/*
	 *	Deliver ICMP message to raw sockets. Pretty useless feature?
	 */

	/* Note: See raw.c and net/raw.h, RAWV4_HTABLE_SIZE==MAX_INET_PROTOS */
	hash = iph->protocol & (MAX_INET_PROTOS - 1);
	read_lock(&raw_v4_lock);
	if ((raw_sk = raw_v4_htable[hash]) != NULL)
	{
		while ((raw_sk = __raw_v4_lookup(raw_sk, iph->protocol, iph->saddr,
						 iph->daddr, skb->dev->ifindex)) != NULL) {
			raw_err(raw_sk, skb);
			raw_sk = raw_sk->next;
		}
	}
	read_unlock(&raw_v4_lock);
```

Figure 6.164 ICMP unreachables: `linux/net/ipv4/icmp.c`.

```
	/*
	 *	This can't change while we are doing it.
	 *	Callers have obtained BR_NETPROTO_LOCK so
	 *	we are OK.
	 */

	ipprot = (struct inet_protocol *) inet_protos[hash];
	while(ipprot != NULL) {
		struct inet_protocol *nextip;

		nextip = (struct inet_protocol *) ipprot->next;

		/*
		 *	Pass it off to everyone who wants it.
		 */

```

```
807                    /* RFC 1122: OK. Passes appropriate ICMP errors to the */
808                    /* appropriate protocol layer (MUST), as per 3.2.2. */
809
810                    if (iph->protocol == ipprot->protocol && ipprot->err_handler)
811                            ipprot->err_handler(skb, dp, len);
812
813                    ipprot = nextip;
814            }
815    }
```

Figure 6.165 ICMP redirects: `linux/net/ipv4/icmp.c`.

```
822    static void icmp_redirect(struct icmphdr *icmph, struct sk_buff *skb, int len)
823    {
824            struct iphdr *iph;
825            unsigned long ip;
826
827            if (len < sizeof(struct iphdr)) {
828                    ICMP_INC_STATS_BH(IcmpInErrors);
829                    return;
830            }
831
832            /*
833             *      Get the copied header of the packet that caused the redirect
834             */
835
836            iph = (struct iphdr *) (icmph + 1);
837            ip = iph->daddr;
838
839            switch(icmph->code & 7) {
840                    case ICMP_REDIR_NET:
841                    case ICMP_REDIR_NETTOS:
842                            /*
843                             *      As per RFC recommendations now handle it as
844                             *      a host redirect.
845                             */
846
847                    case ICMP_REDIR_HOST:
848                    case ICMP_REDIR_HOSTTOS:
849                            ip_rt_redirect(skb->nh.iph->saddr, ip, icmph->un.gateway, iph->saddr, iph->
850                                    tos, skb->dev);
851                            break;
852                    default:
853                            break;
854            }
855    }
```

Figure 6.166 ICMP echo: `linux/net/ipv4/icmp.c`.

```
/*
 *      Handle ICMP_ECHO ("ping") requests.
 *
 *      RFC 1122: 3.2.2.6 MUST have an echo server that answers ICMP echo requests.
 *      RFC 1122: 3.2.2.6 Data received in the ICMP_ECHO request MUST be included in the reply.
 *      RFC 1812: 4.3.3.6 SHOULD have a config option for silently ignoring echo requests, MUST
        have default=NOT.
 *      See also WRT handling of options once they are done and working.
 */

static void icmp_echo(struct icmphdr *icmph, struct sk_buff *skb, int len)
{
        if (!sysctl_icmp_echo_ignore_all) {
                struct icmp_bxm icmp_param;

                icmp_param.icmph=*icmph;
                icmp_param.icmph.type=ICMP_ECHOREPLY;
                icmp_param.data_ptr=(icmph+1);
                icmp_param.data_len=len;
                icmp_reply(&icmp_param, skb);
        }
}
```

Figure 6.167 ICMP timestamp: `linux/net/ipv4/icmp.c`.

```
/*
 *      Handle ICMP Timestamp requests.
 *      RFC 1122: 3.2.2.8 MAY implement ICMP timestamp requests.
 *              SHOULD be in the kernel for minimum random latency.
 *              MUST be accurate to a few minutes.
 *              MUST be updated at least at 15Hz.
 */

static void icmp_timestamp(struct icmphdr *icmph, struct sk_buff *skb, int len)
{
        struct timeval tv;
        __u32 times[3];         /* So the new timestamp works on ALPHA's.. */
        struct icmp_bxm icmp_param;

        /*
         *      Too short.
         */

        if(len<12) {
                ICMP_INC_STATS_BH(IcmpInErrors);
                return;
        }

        /*
         *      Fill in the current time as ms since midnight UT:
         */

```

```
        do_gettimeofday(&tv);
        times[1] = htonl((tv.tv_sec % 86400) * 1000 + tv.tv_usec / 1000);
        times[2] = times[1];
        memcpy((void *)&times[0], icmph+1, 4);     /* Incoming stamp */
        icmp_param.icmph=*icmph;
        icmp_param.icmph.type=ICMP_TIMESTAMPREPLY;
        icmp_param.icmph.code=0;
        icmp_param.data_ptr=&times;
        icmp_param.data_len=12;
        icmp_reply(&icmp_param, skb);
}
```

Figure 6.168 ICMP address mask (not!): `linux/net/ipv4/icmp.c`.

```
/*
 *     Handle ICMP_ADDRESS_MASK requests. (RFC 950)
 *
 * RFC 1122 (3.2.2.9). A host MUST only send replies to
 * ADDRESS_MASK requests if it's been configured as an address mask
 * agent. Receiving a request doesn't constitute implicit permission to
 * act as one. Of course, implementing this correctly requires (SHOULD)
 * a way to turn the functionality on and off. Another one for sysctl(),
 * I guess. -- MS
 *
 * RFC 1812 (4.3.3.9). A router MUST implement it.
 *                     A router SHOULD have switch turning it on/off.
 *                     This switch MUST be ON by default.
 *
 * Gratuitous replies, zero-source replies are not implemented,
 * that complies with RFC. DO NOT implement them!!! All the idea
 * of broadcast addrmask replies as specified in RFC 950 is broken.
 * The problem is that it is not uncommon to have several prefixes
 * on one physical interface. Moreover, addrmask agent can even be
 * not aware of existing another prefixes.
 * If source is zero, addrmask agent cannot choose correct prefix.
 * Gratuitous mask announcements suffer from the same problem.
 * RFC 1812 explains it, but still allows to use ADDRMASK,
 * that is pretty silly. --ANK
 *
 * All these rules are so bizarre, that I removed kernel addrmask
 * support at all. It is wrong, it is obsolete, nobody uses it in
 * any case. --ANK
 *
 * Furthermore you can do it with a usermode address agent program
 * anyway...
 */

static void icmp_address(struct icmphdr *icmph, struct sk_buff *skb, int len)
{
#if 0
        if (net_ratelimit())
               printk(KERN_DEBUG "a guy asks for address mask. Who is it?\n");
#endif
}
```

Figure 6.169 ICMP address reply: `linux/net/ipv4/icmp.c`.

```
/*
 * RFC 1812 (4.3.3.9). A router SHOULD listen all replies, and complain
 *                loudly if an inconsistency is found.
 */

static void icmp_address_reply(struct icmphdr *icmph, struct sk_buff *skb, int len)
{
        struct rtable *rt = (struct rtable*)skb->dst;
        struct net_device *dev = skb->dev;
        struct in_device *in_dev;
        struct in_ifaddr *ifa;
        u32 mask;

        if (len < 4 || !(rt->rt_flags&RTCF_DIRECTSRC))
                return;

        in_dev = in_dev_get(dev);
        if (!in_dev)
                return;
        read_lock(&in_dev->lock);
        if (in_dev->ifa_list &&
            IN_DEV_LOG_MARTIANS(in_dev) &&
            IN_DEV_FORWARD(in_dev)) {

                mask = *(u32*)&icmph[1];
                for (ifa=in_dev->ifa_list; ifa; ifa = ifa->ifa_next) {
                        if (mask == ifa->ifa_mask && inet_ifa_match(rt->rt_src, ifa))
                                break;
                }
                if (!ifa && net_ratelimit()) {
                        printk(KERN_INFO "Wrong address mask %u.%u.%u.%u from %s/%u.%u.%u.%u\n",
                               NIPQUAD(mask), dev->name, NIPQUAD(rt->rt_src));
                }
        }
        read_unlock(&in_dev->lock);
        in_dev_put(in_dev);
}
```

Figure 6.170 ICMP discard: `linux/net/ipv4/icmp.c`.

```
static void icmp_discard(struct icmphdr *icmph, struct sk_buff *skb, int len)
{
}
```

Figure 6.171 ICMP receive general packet: `linux/net/ipv4/icmp.c`.

```
int icmp_rcv(struct sk_buff *skb, unsigned short len)
{
        struct icmphdr *icmph = skb->h.icmph;
        struct rtable *rt = (struct rtable*)skb->dst;

        ICMP_INC_STATS_BH(IcmpInMsgs);

        /*
         *      18 is the highest 'known' ICMP type. Anything else is a mystery
         *
         *      RFC 1122: 3.2.2 Unknown ICMP messages types MUST be silently discarded.
         */
        if(len < sizeof(struct icmphdr) ||
           ip_compute_csum((unsigned char *) icmph, len) ||
           icmph->type > NR_ICMP_TYPES)
                goto error;

        /*
         *      Parse the ICMP message
         */

        if (rt->rt_flags&(RTCF_BROADCAST|RTCF_MULTICAST)) {
                /*
                 *      RFC 1122: 3.2.2.6 An ICMP_ECHO to broadcast MAY be
                 *        silently ignored (we let user decide with a sysctl).
                 *      RFC 1122: 3.2.2.8 An ICMP_TIMESTAMP MAY be silently
                 *        discarded if to broadcast/multicast.
                 */
                if (icmph->type == ICMP_ECHO &&
                    sysctl_icmp_echo_ignore_broadcasts) {
                        goto error;
                }
                if (icmph->type != ICMP_ECHO &&
                    icmph->type != ICMP_TIMESTAMP &&
                    icmph->type != ICMP_ADDRESS &&
                    icmph->type != ICMP_ADDRESSREPLY) {
                        goto error;
                }
        }

        len -= sizeof(struct icmphdr);
        icmp_pointers[icmph->type].input[smp_processor_id()*2*sizeof(struct icmp_mib)/sizeof(
              unsigned long)]++;
        (icmp_pointers[icmph->type].handler)(icmph, skb, len);

drop:
        kfree_skb(skb);
        return 0;
error:
        ICMP_INC_STATS_BH(IcmpInErrors);
        goto drop;
}
```

Figure 6.172 ICMP statistics: `linux/net/ipv4/icmp.c`.

```
static unsigned long dummy;

/*
 *      Configurable rate limits.
 *      Someone should check if these default values are correct.
 *      Note that these values interact with the routing cache GC timeout.
 *      If you chose them too high they won't take effect, because the
 *      dst_entry gets expired too early. The same should happen when
 *      the cache grows too big.
 */
int sysctl_icmp_destunreach_time = 1*HZ;
int sysctl_icmp_timeexceed_time = 1*HZ;
int sysctl_icmp_paramprob_time = 1*HZ;
int sysctl_icmp_echoreply_time = 0; /* don't limit it per default. */
```

Figure 6.173 ICMP statistics: `linux/net/ipv4/icmp.c`.

```
/*
 *      This table is the definition of how we handle ICMP.
 */

static struct icmp_control icmp_pointers[NR_ICMP_TYPES+1] = {
/* ECHO REPLY (0) */
 { &icmp_statistics[0].IcmpOutEchoReps, &icmp_statistics[0].IcmpInEchoReps, icmp_discard, 0, &
      sysctl_icmp_echoreply_time},
 { &dummy, &icmp_statistics[0].IcmpInErrors, icmp_discard, 1, },
 { &dummy, &icmp_statistics[0].IcmpInErrors, icmp_discard, 1, },
/* DEST UNREACH (3) */
 { &icmp_statistics[0].IcmpOutDestUnreachs, &icmp_statistics[0].IcmpInDestUnreachs, icmp_unreach
      , 1, &sysctl_icmp_destunreach_time },
/* SOURCE QUENCH (4) */
 { &icmp_statistics[0].IcmpOutSrcQuenchs, &icmp_statistics[0].IcmpInSrcQuenchs, icmp_unreach
      , 1, },
/* REDIRECT (5) */
 { &icmp_statistics[0].IcmpOutRedirects, &icmp_statistics[0].IcmpInRedirects, icmp_redirect
      , 1, },
 { &dummy, &icmp_statistics[0].IcmpInErrors, icmp_discard, 1, },
 { &dummy, &icmp_statistics[0].IcmpInErrors, icmp_discard, 1, },
/* ECHO (8) */
 { &icmp_statistics[0].IcmpOutEchos, &icmp_statistics[0].IcmpInEchos, icmp_echo, 0, },
 { &dummy, &icmp_statistics[0].IcmpInErrors, icmp_discard, 1, },
 { &dummy, &icmp_statistics[0].IcmpInErrors, icmp_discard, 1, },
/* TIME EXCEEDED (11) */
 { &icmp_statistics[0].IcmpOutTimeExcds, &icmp_statistics[0].IcmpInTimeExcds, icmp_unreach, 1, &
      sysctl_icmp_timeexceed_time },
/* PARAMETER PROBLEM (12) */
 { &icmp_statistics[0].IcmpOutParmProbs, &icmp_statistics[0].IcmpInParmProbs, icmp_unreach, 1, &
      sysctl_icmp_paramprob_time },
/* TIMESTAMP (13) */
```

```
 { &icmp_statistics[0].IcmpOutTimestamps, &icmp_statistics[0].IcmpInTimestamps, icmp_timestamp, 0, },
/* TIMESTAMP REPLY (14) */
 { &icmp_statistics[0].IcmpOutTimestampReps, &icmp_statistics[0].IcmpInTimestampReps, icmp_discard, 0, },
/* INFO (15) */
 { &dummy, &dummy, icmp_discard, 0, },
/* INFO REPLY (16) */
 { &dummy, &dummy, icmp_discard, 0, },
/* ADDR MASK (17) */
 { &icmp_statistics[0].IcmpOutAddrMasks, &icmp_statistics[0].IcmpInAddrMasks, icmp_address, 0, },
/* ADDR MASK REPLY (18) */
 { &icmp_statistics[0].IcmpOutAddrMaskReps, &icmp_statistics[0].IcmpInAddrMaskReps, icmp_address_reply, 0, }
};
```

Figure 6.174 ICMP initialization: `linux/net/ipv4/icmp.c`.

```
void __init icmp_init(struct net_proto_family *ops)
{
	int err;

	icmp_inode.i_mode = S_IFSOCK;
	icmp_inode.i_sock = 1;
	icmp_inode.i_uid = 0;
	icmp_inode.i_gid = 0;
	init_waitqueue_head(&icmp_inode.i_wait);
	init_waitqueue_head(&icmp_inode.u.socket_i.wait);

	icmp_socket->inode = &icmp_inode;
	icmp_socket->state = SS_UNCONNECTED;
	icmp_socket->type=SOCK_RAW;

	if ((err=ops->create(icmp_socket, IPPROTO_ICMP))<0)
		panic("Failed to create the ICMP control socket.\n");
	icmp_socket->sk->allocation=GFP_ATOMIC;
	icmp_socket->sk->sndbuf = SK_WMEM_MAX*2;
	icmp_socket->sk->protinfo.af_inet.ttl = MAXTTL;

	/* Unhash it so that IP input processing does not even
	 * see it, we do not wish this socket to see incoming
	 * packets.
	 */
	icmp_socket->sk->prot->unhash(icmp_socket->sk);
}
```

6.5 Group Management—IGMP

A reasonable fraction of the Internet supports multicast, particularly in tier-one ISPs and in academic and research networks where the access networks are LANs. The host group membership system is managed through the host-router communications protocol, Internet Group Management Protocol (IGMP). The Linux implementation is covered here.

6.5.1 IGMP

In this section we take a tour around IP multicast support in Linux. Multicast is a tricky concept and is intimately bound up between host and router functions, so rather than defer the main discussion to the chapter on routing, we look through most of the code here. The rationale is also that UP multicast makes use of encapsulation (tunnels) which is also discussed here as it is part host and part router functionality.

Figure 6.175 IGMP—data: `linux/net/ipv4/igmp.c`.

```
#define IP_MAX_MEMBERSHIPS 20

#ifdef CONFIG_IP_MULTICAST


/* Parameter names and values are taken from igmp-v2-06 draft */

#define IGMP_V1_Router_Present_Timeout      (400*HZ)
#define IGMP_Unsolicited_Report_Interval    (10*HZ)
#define IGMP_Query_Response_Interval        (10*HZ)
#define IGMP_Unsolicited_Report_Count       2


#define IGMP_Initial_Report_Delay           (1*HZ)

/* IGMP_Initial_Report_Delay is not from IGMP specs!
 * IGMP specs require to report membership immediately after
 * joining a group, but we delay the first report by a
 * small interval. It seems more natural and still does not
 * contradict to specs provided this delay is small enough.
 */

#define IGMP_V1_SEEN(in_dev) ((in_dev)->mr_v1_seen && (long)(jiffies - (in_dev)->mr_v1_seen)
      < 0)

#endif
```

Figure 6.176 IGMP configure multicast interface: `linux/net/ipv4/igmp.c`.

```
static void ip_ma_put(struct ip_mc_list *im)
{
        if (atomic_dec_and_test(&im->refcnt)) {
                in_dev_put(im->interface);
                kfree(im);
        }
}
```

IGMP Timers to Manage State

Figure 6.177 IGMP timer management: `linux/net/ipv4/igmp.c`.

```
static __inline__ void igmp_stop_timer(struct ip_mc_list *im)
{
        spin_lock_bh(&im->lock);
        if (del_timer(&im->timer))
                atomic_dec(&im->refcnt);
        im->tm_running=0;
        im->reporter = 0;
        im->unsolicit_count = 0;
        spin_unlock_bh(&im->lock);
}

/* It must be called with locked im->lock */
static void igmp_start_timer(struct ip_mc_list *im, int max_delay)
{
        int tv=net_random() % max_delay;

        im->tm_running=1;
        if (!mod_timer(&im->timer, jiffies+tv+2))
                atomic_inc(&im->refcnt);
}

static void igmp_mod_timer(struct ip_mc_list *im, int max_delay)
{
        spin_lock_bh(&im->lock);
        im->unsolicit_count = 0;
        if (del_timer(&im->timer)) {
                if ((long)(im->timer.expires-jiffies) < max_delay) {
                        add_timer(&im->timer);
                        im->tm_running=1;
                        spin_unlock_bh(&im->lock);
                        return;
                }
                atomic_dec(&im->refcnt);
        }
        igmp_start_timer(im, max_delay);
        spin_unlock_bh(&im->lock);
}
```

Figure 6.178 IGMP timer expired: `linux/net/ipv4/igmp.c`.

```
static void igmp_timer_expire(unsigned long data)
{
	struct ip_mc_list *im=(struct ip_mc_list *)data;
	struct in_device *in_dev = im->interface;
	int err;

	spin_lock(&im->lock);
	im->tm_running=0;

	if (IGMP_V1_SEEN(in_dev))
		err = igmp_send_report(in_dev->dev, im->multiaddr, IGMP_HOST_MEMBERSHIP_REPORT);
	else
		err = igmp_send_report(in_dev->dev, im->multiaddr, IGMP_HOST_NEW_MEMBERSHIP_REPORT
			);

	/* Failed. Retry later. */
	if (err) {
		if (!in_dev->dead)
			igmp_start_timer(im, IGMP_Unsolicited_Report_Interval);
		goto out;
	}

	if (im->unsolicit_count) {
		im->unsolicit_count--;
		igmp_start_timer(im, IGMP_Unsolicited_Report_Interval);
	}
	im->reporter = 1;
out:
	spin_unlock(&im->lock);
	ip_ma_put(im);
}
```

IGMP Transmission

Figure 6.179 IGMP send report: `linux/net/ipv4/igmp.c`.

```
#define IGMP_SIZE (sizeof(struct igmphdr)+sizeof(struct iphdr)+4)

/* Don't just hand NF_HOOK skb->dst->output, in case netfilter hook
   changes route */
static inline int
output_maybe_reroute(struct sk_buff *skb)
{
	return skb->dst->output(skb);
}

static int igmp_send_report(struct net_device *dev, u32 group, int type)
{
	struct sk_buff *skb;
```

```
198          struct iphdr *iph;
199          struct igmphdr *ih;
200          struct rtable *rt;
201          u32    dst;
202
203          /* According to IGMPv2 specs, LEAVE messages are
204           * sent to all-routers group.
205           */
206          dst = group;
207          if (type == IGMP_HOST_LEAVE_MESSAGE)
208                  dst = IGMP_ALL_ROUTER;
209
210          if (ip_route_output(&rt, dst, 0, 0, dev->ifindex))
211                  return -1;
212          if (rt->rt_src == 0) {
213                  ip_rt_put(rt);
214                  return -1;
215          }
216
217          skb=alloc_skb(IGMP_SIZE+dev->hard_header_len+15, GFP_ATOMIC);
218          if (skb == NULL) {
219                  ip_rt_put(rt);
220                  return -1;
221          }
```

Figure 6.180 IGMP send report: `linux/net/ipv4/igmp.c`.

```
223          skb->dst = &rt->u.dst;
224
225          skb_reserve(skb, (dev->hard_header_len+15)&~15);
226
227          skb->nh.iph = iph = (struct iphdr *)skb_put(skb, sizeof(struct iphdr)+4);
228
229          iph->version = 4;
230          iph->ihl    = (sizeof(struct iphdr)+4)>>2;
231          iph->tos    = 0;
232          iph->frag_off = __constant_htons(IP_DF);
233          iph->ttl    = 1;
234          iph->daddr  = dst;
235          iph->saddr  = rt->rt_src;
236          iph->protocol = IPPROTO_IGMP;
237          iph->tot_len = htons(IGMP_SIZE);
238          ip_select_ident(iph, &rt->u.dst);
239          ((u8*)&iph[1])[0] = IPOPT_RA;
240          ((u8*)&iph[1])[1] = 4;
241          ((u8*)&iph[1])[2] = 0;
242          ((u8*)&iph[1])[3] = 0;
243          ip_send_check(iph);
244
245          ih = (struct igmphdr *)skb_put(skb, sizeof(struct igmphdr));
246          ih->type=type;
247          ih->code=0;
```

```
	ih->csum=0;
	ih->group=group;
	ih->csum=ip_compute_csum((void *)ih, sizeof(struct igmphdr));

	return NF_HOOK(PF_INET, NF_IP_LOCAL_OUT, skb, NULL, rt->u.dst.dev,
		       output_maybe_reroute);
}
```

IGMP Reception

Figure 6.181 IGMP heard a report: `linux/net/ipv4/igmp.c`.

```
static void igmp_heard_report(struct in_device *in_dev, u32 group)
{
	struct ip_mc_list *im;

	/* Timers are only set for non-local groups */

	if (group == IGMP_ALL_HOSTS)
		return;

	read_lock(&in_dev->lock);
	for (im=in_dev->mc_list; im!=NULL; im=im->next) {
		if (im->multiaddr == group) {
			igmp_stop_timer(im);
			break;
		}
	}
	read_unlock(&in_dev->lock);
}
```

Figure 6.182 IGMP heard a query: `linux/net/ipv4/igmp.c`.

```
static void igmp_heard_query(struct in_device *in_dev, unsigned char max_resp_time,
			     u32 group)
{
	struct ip_mc_list	*im;
	int			max_delay;

	max_delay = max_resp_time*(HZ/IGMP_TIMER_SCALE);

	if (max_resp_time == 0) {
		/* Alas, old v1 router presents here. */

		max_delay = IGMP_Query_Response_Interval;
		in_dev->mr_v1_seen = jiffies + IGMP_V1_Router_Present_Timeout;
		group = 0;
	}

```

```
323              /*
324               * - Start the timers in all of our membership records
325               *   that the query applies to for the interface on
326               *   which the query arrived excl. those that belong
327               *   to a "local" group (224.0.0.X)
328               * - For timers already running check if they need to
329               *   be reset.
330               * - Use the igmp->igmp_code field as the maximum
331               *   delay possible
332               */
333              read_lock(&in_dev->lock);
334              for (im=in_dev->mc_list; im!=NULL; im=im->next) {
335                      if (group && group != im->multiaddr)
336                              continue;
337                      if (im->multiaddr == IGMP_ALL_HOSTS)
338                              continue;
339                      igmp_mod_timer(im, max_delay);
340              }
341              read_unlock(&in_dev->lock);
342      }
```

Figure 6.183 IGMP receive: `linux/net/ipv4/igmp.c`.

```
344      int igmp_rcv(struct sk_buff *skb, unsigned short len)
345      {
346              /* This basically follows the spec line by line -- see RFC 1112 */
347              struct igmphdr *ih = skb->h.igmph;
348              struct in_device *in_dev = in_dev_get(skb->dev);
349
350              if (in_dev==NULL) {
351                      kfree_skb(skb);
352                      return 0;
353              }
354
355              if (len < sizeof(struct igmphdr) || ip_compute_csum((void *)ih, len)) {
356                      in_dev_put(in_dev);
357                      kfree_skb(skb);
358                      return 0;
359              }
360
361              switch (ih->type) {
362              case IGMP_HOST_MEMBERSHIP_QUERY:
363                      igmp_heard_query(in_dev, ih->code, ih->group);
364                      break;
365              case IGMP_HOST_MEMBERSHIP_REPORT:
366              case IGMP_HOST_NEW_MEMBERSHIP_REPORT:
367                      /* Is it our report looped back? */
368                      if (((struct rtable*)skb->dst)->key.iif == 0)
369                              break;
370                      igmp_heard_report(in_dev, ih->group);
371                      break;
372              case IGMP_PIM:
```

```
373    #ifdef CONFIG_IP_PIMSM_V1
374                    in_dev_put(in_dev);
375                    return pim_rcv_v1(skb, len);
376    #endif
377         case IGMP_DVMRP:
378         case IGMP_TRACE:
379         case IGMP_HOST_LEAVE_MESSAGE:
380         case IGMP_MTRACE:
381         case IGMP_MTRACE_RESP:
382              break;
383         default:
384              NETDEBUG(printk(KERN_DEBUG "New IGMP type=%d, why we do not know about it?\n", ih
                      ->type));
385         }
386         in_dev_put(in_dev);
387         kfree_skb(skb);
388         return 0;
389    }
```

6.5.2 Managing the Group/Interface State

Figure 6.184 IGMP add and delete filter from interface: `linux/net/ipv4/igmp.c`.

```
398    static void ip_mc_filter_add(struct in_device *in_dev, u32 addr)
399    {
400         char buf[MAX_ADDR_LEN];
401         struct net_device *dev = in_dev->dev;
402
403         /* Checking for IFF_MULTICAST here is WRONG-WRONG-WRONG.
404            We will get multicast token leakage, when IFF_MULTICAST
405            is changed. This check should be done in dev->set_multicast_list
406            routine. Something sort of:
407            if (dev->mc_list && dev->flags&IFF_MULTICAST) { do it; }
408            --ANK
409            */
410         if (arp_mc_map(addr, buf, dev, 0) == 0)
411              dev_mc_add(dev,buf,dev->addr_len,0);
412    }
413
414    /*
415     *    Remove a filter from a device
416     */
417
418    static void ip_mc_filter_del(struct in_device *in_dev, u32 addr)
419    {
420         char buf[MAX_ADDR_LEN];
421         struct net_device *dev = in_dev->dev;
422
423         if (arp_mc_map(addr, buf, dev, 0) == 0)
424              dev_mc_delete(dev,buf,dev->addr_len,0);
425    }
```

Figure 6.185 IGMP group added or dropped: `linux/net/ipv4/igmp.c`.

```
static void igmp_group_dropped(struct ip_mc_list *im)
{
#ifdef CONFIG_IP_MULTICAST
        int reporter;
#endif

        if (im->loaded) {
                im->loaded = 0;
                ip_mc_filter_del(im->interface, im->multiaddr);
        }

#ifdef CONFIG_IP_MULTICAST
        if (im->multiaddr == IGMP_ALL_HOSTS)
                return;

        reporter = im->reporter;
        igmp_stop_timer(im);

        if (reporter && !IGMP_V1_SEEN(im->interface))
                igmp_send_report(im->interface->dev, im->multiaddr, IGMP_HOST_LEAVE_MESSAGE);
#endif
}

static void igmp_group_added(struct ip_mc_list *im)
{
        if (im->loaded == 0) {
                im->loaded = 1;
                ip_mc_filter_add(im->interface, im->multiaddr);
        }

#ifdef CONFIG_IP_MULTICAST
        if (im->multiaddr == IGMP_ALL_HOSTS)
                return;

        spin_lock_bh(&im->lock);
        igmp_start_timer(im, IGMP_Initial_Report_Delay);
        spin_unlock_bh(&im->lock);
#endif
}
```

User/Group Management Layer

Figure 6.186 IGMP—socket joins group: `linux/net/ipv4/igmp.c`.

```
void ip_mc_inc_group(struct in_device *in_dev, u32 addr)
{
        struct ip_mc_list *im;

        ASSERT_RTNL();

```

```
483             for (im=in_dev->mc_list; im; im=im->next) {
484                     if (im->multiaddr == addr) {
485                             im->users++;
486                             goto out;
487                     }
488             }
489
490             im = (struct ip_mc_list *)kmalloc(sizeof(*im), GFP_KERNEL);
491             if (!im)
492                     goto out;
493
494             im->users=1;
495             im->interface=in_dev;
496             in_dev_hold(in_dev);
497             im->multiaddr=addr;
498             atomic_set(&im->refcnt, 1);
499             spin_lock_init(&im->lock);
500  #ifdef CONFIG_IP_MULTICAST
501             im->tm_running=0;
502             init_timer(&im->timer);
503             im->timer.data=(unsigned long)im;
504             im->timer.function=&igmp_timer_expire;
505             im->unsolicit_count = IGMP_Unsolicited_Report_Count;
506             im->reporter = 0;
507             im->loaded = 0;
508  #endif
509             write_lock_bh(&in_dev->lock);
510             im->next=in_dev->mc_list;
511             in_dev->mc_list=im;
512             write_unlock_bh(&in_dev->lock);
513             igmp_group_added(im);
514             if (in_dev->dev->flags & IFF_UP)
515                     ip_rt_multicast_event(in_dev);
516  out:
517             return;
518  }
```

Figure 6.187 IGMP socket leaves group: `linux/net/ipv4/igmp.c`.

```
524  int ip_mc_dec_group(struct in_device *in_dev, u32 addr)
525  {
526          int err = -ESRCH;
527          struct ip_mc_list *i, **ip;
528
529          ASSERT_RTNL();
530
531          for (ip=&in_dev->mc_list; (i=*ip)!=NULL; ip=&i->next) {
532                  if (i->multiaddr==addr) {
533                          if (--i->users == 0) {
534                                  write_lock_bh(&in_dev->lock);
535                                  *ip = i->next;
536                                  write_unlock_bh(&in_dev->lock);
```

```
537                                    igmp_group_dropped(i);
538
539                                    if (in_dev->dev->flags & IFF_UP)
540                                            ip_rt_multicast_event(in_dev);
541
542                                    ip_ma_put(i);
543                                    return 0;
544                            }
545                            err = 0;
546                            break;
547                    }
548            }
549            return -ESRCH;
550    }
```

Figure 6.188 IGMP joins socket to group: `linux/net/ipv4/igmp.c`.

```
630    int sysctl_igmp_max_memberships = IP_MAX_MEMBERSHIPS;
631
632    int ip_mc_join_group(struct sock *sk , struct ip_mreqn *imr)
633    {
634            int err;
635            u32 addr = imr->imr_multiaddr.s_addr;
636            struct ip_mc_socklist *iml, *i;
637            struct in_device *in_dev;
638            int count = 0;
639
640            if (!MULTICAST(addr))
641                    return -EINVAL;
642
643            rtnl_shlock();
644
645            if (!imr->imr_ifindex)
646                    in_dev = ip_mc_find_dev(imr);
647            else {
648                    in_dev = inetdev_by_index(imr->imr_ifindex);
649                    if (in_dev)
650                            __in_dev_put(in_dev);
651            }
652
653            if (!in_dev) {
654                    iml = NULL;
655                    err = -ENODEV;
656                    goto done;
657            }
```

Figure 6.189 IGMP joins socket to group: `linux/net/ipv4/igmp.c`.

```
659              iml = (struct ip_mc_socklist *)sock_kmalloc(sk, sizeof(*iml), GFP_KERNEL);
660
661              err = -EADDRINUSE;
662              for (i=sk->protinfo.af_inet.mc_list; i; i=i->next) {
663                      if (memcmp(&i->multi, imr, sizeof(*imr)) == 0) {
664                              /* New style additions are reference counted */
665                              if (imr->imr_address.s_addr == 0) {
666                                      i->count++;
667                                      err = 0;
668                              }
669                              goto done;
670                      }
671                      count++;
672              }
673              err = -ENOBUFS;
674              if (iml == NULL || count >= sysctl_igmp_max_memberships)
675                      goto done;
676              memcpy(&iml->multi, imr, sizeof(*imr));
677              iml->next = sk->protinfo.af_inet.mc_list;
678              iml->count = 1;
679              sk->protinfo.af_inet.mc_list = iml;
680              ip_mc_inc_group(in_dev, addr);
681              iml = NULL;
682              err = 0;
683
684      done:
685              rtnl_shunlock();
686              if (iml)
687                      sock_kfree_s(sk, iml, sizeof(*iml));
688              return err;
689      }
```

Figure 6.190 IGMP: `linux/net/ipv4/igmp.c`.

```
695      int ip_mc_leave_group(struct sock *sk, struct ip_mreqn *imr)
696      {
697              struct ip_mc_socklist *iml, **imlp;
698
699              rtnl_lock();
700              for (imlp=&sk->protinfo.af_inet.mc_list; (iml=*imlp)!=NULL; imlp=&iml->next) {
701                      if (iml->multi.imr_multiaddr.s_addr==imr->imr_multiaddr.s_addr &&
702                          iml->multi.imr_address.s_addr==imr->imr_address.s_addr &&
703                          (!imr->imr_ifindex || iml->multi.imr_ifindex==imr->imr_ifindex)) {
704                              struct in_device *in_dev;
705                              if (--iml->count) {
706                                      rtnl_unlock();
707                                      return 0;
708                              }
709
710                              *imlp = iml->next;
711
```

```
712                        in_dev = inetdev_by_index(iml->multi.imr_ifindex);
713                        if (in_dev) {
714                                ip_mc_dec_group(in_dev, imr->imr_multiaddr.s_addr);
715                                in_dev_put(in_dev);
716                        }
717                        rtnl_unlock();
718                        sock_kfree_s(sk, iml, sizeof(*iml));
719                        return 0;
720                }
721        }
722        rtnl_unlock();
723        return -EADDRNOTAVAIL;
724 }
```

Figure 6.191 IGMP—socket closing: `linux/net/ipv4/igmp.c`.

```
730 void ip_mc_drop_socket(struct sock *sk)
731 {
732        struct ip_mc_socklist *iml;
733
734        if (sk->protinfo.af_inet.mc_list == NULL)
735                return;
736
737        rtnl_lock();
738        while ((iml=sk->protinfo.af_inet.mc_list) != NULL) {
739                struct in_device *in_dev;
740                sk->protinfo.af_inet.mc_list = iml->next;
741
742                if ((in_dev = inetdev_by_index(iml->multi.imr_ifindex)) != NULL) {
743                        ip_mc_dec_group(in_dev, iml->multi.imr_multiaddr.s_addr);
744                        in_dev_put(in_dev);
745                }
746                sock_kfree_s(sk, iml, sizeof(*iml));
747
748        }
749        rtnl_unlock();
750 }
```

Device Events That Influence Group State

Figure 6.192 IGMP—device goes down or comes up: `linux/net/ipv4/igmp.c`.

```
554 void ip_mc_down(struct in_device *in_dev)
555 {
556        struct ip_mc_list *i;
557
558        ASSERT_RTNL();
559
560        for (i=in_dev->mc_list; i; i=i->next)
```

```
                igmp_group_dropped(i);

        ip_mc_dec_group(in_dev, IGMP_ALL_HOSTS);
}

/* Device going up */

void ip_mc_up(struct in_device *in_dev)
{
        struct ip_mc_list *i;

        ASSERT_RTNL();

        ip_mc_inc_group(in_dev, IGMP_ALL_HOSTS);

        for (i=in_dev->mc_list; i; i=i->next)
                igmp_group_added(i);
}
```

Figure 6.193 IGMP—destroy device: `linux/net/ipv4/igmp.c`.

```
void ip_mc_destroy_dev(struct in_device *in_dev)
{
        struct ip_mc_list *i;

        ASSERT_RTNL();

        write_lock_bh(&in_dev->lock);
        while ((i = in_dev->mc_list) != NULL) {
                in_dev->mc_list = i->next;
                write_unlock_bh(&in_dev->lock);

                igmp_group_dropped(i);
                ip_ma_put(i);

                write_lock_bh(&in_dev->lock);
        }
        write_unlock_bh(&in_dev->lock);
}
```

Figure 6.194 IGMP—find device: `linux/net/ipv4/igmp.c`.

```
static struct in_device * ip_mc_find_dev(struct ip_mreqn *imr)
{
        struct rtable *rt;
        struct net_device *dev = NULL;
        struct in_device *idev = NULL;

        if (imr->imr_address.s_addr) {
```

```
610                  dev = ip_dev_find(imr->imr_address.s_addr);
611                  if (!dev)
612                          return NULL;
613                  __dev_put(dev);
614          }
615
616          if (!dev && !ip_route_output(&rt, imr->imr_multiaddr.s_addr, 0, 0, 0)) {
617                  dev = rt->u.dst.dev;
618                  ip_rt_put(rt);
619          }
620          if (dev) {
621                  imr->imr_ifindex = dev->ifindex;
622                  idev = __in_dev_get(dev);
623          }
624          return idev;
625  }
```

Figure 6.195 IPMR—device notifier: `linux/net/ipv4/ipmr.c`.

```
1055  static int ipmr_device_event(struct notifier_block *this, unsigned long event, void *ptr)
1056  {
1057          struct vif_device *v;
1058          int ct;
1059          if (event != NETDEV_UNREGISTER)
1060                  return NOTIFY_DONE;
1061          v=&vif_table[0];
1062          for(ct=0;ct<maxvif;ct++,v++) {
1063                  if (v->dev==ptr)
1064                          vif_delete(ct);
1065          }
1066          return NOTIFY_DONE;
1067  }
1068
1069
1070  static struct notifier_block ip_mr_notifier={
1071          ipmr_device_event,
1072          NULL,
1073          0
1074  };
```

Figure 6.196 IGMP—check if address is in use on any interface: `linux/net/ipv4/igmp.c`.

```
752  int ip_check_mc(struct in_device *in_dev, u32 mc_addr)
753  {
754          struct ip_mc_list *im;
755
756          read_lock(&in_dev->lock);
757          for (im=in_dev->mc_list; im; im=im->next) {
758                  if (im->multiaddr == mc_addr) {
759                          read_unlock(&in_dev->lock);
```

```
                        return 1;
                }
        }
        read_unlock(&in_dev->lock);
        return 0;
}
```

Figure 6.197 IGMP—`procfs`—report membership, and so on: `linux/net/ipv4/igmp.c`.

```
int ip_mc_procinfo(char *buffer, char **start, off_t offset, int length)
{
        off_t pos=0, begin=0;
        struct ip_mc_list *im;
        int len=0;
        struct net_device *dev;

        len=sprintf(buffer,"Idx\tDevice : Count Querier\tGroup Users Timer\tReporter\n");

        read_lock(&dev_base_lock);
        for(dev = dev_base; dev; dev = dev->next) {
                struct in_device *in_dev = in_dev_get(dev);
                char   *querier = "NONE";

                if (in_dev == NULL)
                        continue;

                querier = IGMP_V1_SEEN(in_dev) ? "V1" : "V2";

                len+=sprintf(buffer+len,"%d\t%-10s: %5d %7s\n",
                             dev->ifindex, dev->name, dev->mc_count, querier);

                read_lock(&in_dev->lock);
```

Figure 6.198 IGMP—`procfs`—report membership, and so on: `linux/net/ipv4/igmp.c`.

```
                for (im = in_dev->mc_list; im; im = im->next) {
                        len+=sprintf(buffer+len,
                                     "\t\t\t\t%08lX %5d %d:%08lX\t\t%d\n",
                                     im->multiaddr, im->users,
                                     im->tm_running, im->timer.expires-jiffies, im->reporter);

                        pos=begin+len;
                        if(pos<offset)
                        {
                                len=0;
                                begin=pos;
                        }
                        if(pos>offset+length) {
                                read_unlock(&in_dev->lock);
```

```
                        in_dev_put(in_dev);
                        goto done;
                    }
                }
                read_unlock(&in_dev->lock);
                in_dev_put(in_dev);
        }
done:
        read_unlock(&dev_base_lock);

        *start=buffer+(offset-begin);
        len-=(offset-begin);
        if(len>length)
                len=length;
        if(len<0)
                len=0;
        return len;
}
```

6.5.3 Multicast Forwarding

Figure 6.199 Internet multicast routing support—data: `linux/net/ipv4/ipmr.c`.

```
#if defined(CONFIG_IP_PIMSM_V1) || defined(CONFIG_IP_PIMSM_V2)
#define CONFIG_IP_PIMSM 1
#endif

static struct sock *mroute_socket;


/* Big lock, protecting vif table, mrt cache and mroute socket state.
   Note that the changes are semaphored via rtnl_lock.
 */

static rwlock_t mrt_lock = RW_LOCK_UNLOCKED;

/*
 *      Multicast router control variables
 */

static struct vif_device vif_table[MAXVIFS];       /* Devices           */
static int maxvif;

#define VIF_EXISTS(idx) (vif_table[idx].dev != NULL)

int mroute_do_assert = 0;                           /* Set in PIM assert */
int mroute_do_pim = 0;

static struct mfc_cache *mfc_cache_array[MFC_LINES]; /* Forwarding cache */

```

```
static struct mfc_cache *mfc_unres_queue;          /* Queue of unresolved entries */
atomic_t cache_resolve_queue_len;                  /* Size of unresolved */

/* Special spinlock for queue of unresolved entries */
static spinlock_t mfc_unres_lock = SPIN_LOCK_UNLOCKED;
```

Figure 6.200 Internet multicast routing support—data: `linux/net/ipv4/ipmr.c`.

```
/* We return to original Alan's scheme. Hash table of resolved
   entries is changed only in process context and protected
   with weak lock mrt_lock. Queue of unresolved entries is protected
   with strong spinlock mfc_unres_lock.

   In this case data path is free of exclusive locks at all.
 */

kmem_cache_t *mrt_cachep;

static int ip_mr_forward(struct sk_buff *skb, struct mfc_cache *cache, int local);
static int ipmr_cache_report(struct sk_buff *pkt, vifi_t vifi, int assert);
static int ipmr_fill_mroute(struct sk_buff *skb, struct mfc_cache *c, struct rtmsg *rtm);

extern struct inet_protocol pim_protocol;

static struct timer_list ipmr_expire_timer;
```

Virtual Interface Support for Multicast

Figure 6.201 IPMR—new vif/tunnel: `linux/net/ipv4/ipmr.c`.

```
static
struct net_device *ipmr_new_tunnel(struct vifctl *v)
{
        struct net_device *dev;

        dev = __dev_get_by_name("tunl0");

        if (dev) {
                int err;
                struct ifreq ifr;
                mm_segment_t  oldfs;
                struct ip_tunnel_parm p;
                struct in_device *in_dev;

                memset(&p, 0, sizeof(p));
                p.iph.daddr = v->vifc_rmt_addr.s_addr;
                p.iph.saddr = v->vifc_lcl_addr.s_addr;
                p.iph.version = 4;
```

```
135                     p.iph.ihl = 5;
136                     p.iph.protocol = IPPROTO_IPIP;
137                     sprintf(p.name, "dvmrp%d", v->vifc_vifi);
138                     ifr.ifr_ifru.ifru_data = (void*)&p;
139
140                     oldfs = get_fs(); set_fs(KERNEL_DS);
141                     err = dev->do_ioctl(dev, &ifr, SIOCADDTUNNEL);
142                     set_fs(oldfs);
143
144                     dev = NULL;
145
146                     if (err == 0 && (dev = __dev_get_by_name(p.name)) != NULL) {
147                             dev->flags |= IFF_MULTICAST;
148
149                             in_dev = __in_dev_get(dev);
150                             if (in_dev == NULL && (in_dev = inetdev_init(dev)) == NULL)
151                                     goto failure;
152                             in_dev->cnf.rp_filter = 0;
153
154                             if (dev_open(dev))
155                                     goto failure;
156                     }
157             }
158             return dev;
159
160     failure:
161             unregister_netdevice(dev);
162             return NULL;
163     }
```

Figure 6.202 IPMR—register a vif: `linux/net/ipv4/ipmr.c`.

```
165     #ifdef CONFIG_IP_PIMSM
166
167     static int reg_vif_num = -1;
168
169     static int reg_vif_xmit(struct sk_buff *skb, struct net_device *dev)
170     {
171             read_lock(&mrt_lock);
172             ((struct net_device_stats*)dev->priv)->tx_bytes += skb->len;
173             ((struct net_device_stats*)dev->priv)->tx_packets++;
174             ipmr_cache_report(skb, reg_vif_num, IGMPMSG_WHOLEPKT);
175             read_unlock(&mrt_lock);
176             kfree_skb(skb);
177             return 0;
178     }
179
180     static struct net_device_stats *reg_vif_get_stats(struct net_device *dev)
181     {
182             return (struct net_device_stats*)dev->priv;
183     }
```

Figure 6.203 IPMR—register a vif: `linux/net/ipv4/ipmr.c`.

```
185    static
186    struct net_device *ipmr_reg_vif(struct vifctl *v)
187    {
188            struct net_device *dev;
189            struct in_device *in_dev;
190            int size;
191
192            size = sizeof(*dev) + sizeof(struct net_device_stats);
193            dev = kmalloc(size, GFP_KERNEL);
194            if (!dev)
195                    return NULL;
196
197            memset(dev, 0, size);
198
199            dev->priv = dev + 1;
200
201            strcpy(dev->name, "pimreg");
202
203            dev->type           = ARPHRD_PIMREG;
204            dev->mtu            = 1500 - sizeof(struct iphdr) - 8;
205            dev->flags          = IFF_NOARP;
206            dev->hard_start_xmit = reg_vif_xmit;
207            dev->get_stats      = reg_vif_get_stats;
208            dev->features       |= NETIF_F_DYNALLOC;
209
210            if (register_netdevice(dev)) {
211                    kfree(dev);
212                    return NULL;
213            }
214            dev->iflink = 0;
215
216            if ((in_dev = inetdev_init(dev)) == NULL)
217                    goto failure;
218
219            in_dev->cnf.rp_filter = 0;
220
221            if (dev_open(dev))
222                    goto failure;
223
224            return dev;
225
226    failure:
227            unregister_netdevice(dev);
228            return NULL;
229    }
230    #endif
```

Figure 6.204 IPMR—delete a vif: `linux/net/ipv4/ipmr.c`.

```
236    static int vif_delete(int vifi)
237    {
238            struct vif_device *v;
239            struct net_device *dev;
240            struct in_device *in_dev;
241
242            if (vifi < 0 || vifi >= maxvif)
243                    return -EADDRNOTAVAIL;
244
245            v = &vif_table[vifi];
246
247            write_lock_bh(&mrt_lock);
248            dev = v->dev;
249            v->dev = NULL;
250
251            if (!dev) {
252                    write_unlock_bh(&mrt_lock);
253                    return -EADDRNOTAVAIL;
254            }
255
256    #ifdef CONFIG_IP_PIMSM
257            if (vifi == reg_vif_num)
258                    reg_vif_num = -1;
259    #endif
260
261            if (vifi+1 == maxvif) {
262                    int tmp;
263                    for (tmp=vifi-1; tmp>=0; tmp--) {
264                            if (VIF_EXISTS(tmp))
265                                    break;
266                    }
267                    maxvif = tmp+1;
268            }
269
270            write_unlock_bh(&mrt_lock);
271
272            dev_set_allmulti(dev, -1);
273
274            if ((in_dev = __in_dev_get(dev)) != NULL) {
275                    in_dev->cnf.mc_forwarding--;
276                    ip_rt_multicast_event(in_dev);
277            }
278
279            if (v->flags&(VIFF_TUNNEL|VIFF_REGISTER))
280                    unregister_netdevice(dev);
281
282            dev_put(dev);
283            return 0;
284    }
```

Figure 6.205 IPMR—add a vif: `linux/net/ipv4/ipmr.c`.

```
static int vif_add(struct vifctl *vifc, int mrtsock)
{
	int vifi = vifc->vifc_vifi;
	struct vif_device *v = &vif_table[vifi];
	struct net_device *dev;
	struct in_device *in_dev;

	/* Is vif busy ? */
	if (VIF_EXISTS(vifi))
		return -EADDRINUSE;

	switch (vifc->vifc_flags) {
#ifdef CONFIG_IP_PIMSM
	case VIFF_REGISTER:
		/*
		 * Special Purpose VIF in PIM
		 * All the packets will be sent to the daemon
		 */
		if (reg_vif_num >= 0)
			return -EADDRINUSE;
		dev = ipmr_reg_vif(vifc);
		if (!dev)
			return -ENOBUFS;
		break;
#endif
	case VIFF_TUNNEL:
		dev = ipmr_new_tunnel(vifc);
		if (!dev)
			return -ENOBUFS;
		break;
	case 0:
		dev=ip_dev_find(vifc->vifc_lcl_addr.s_addr);
		if (!dev)
			return -EADDRNOTAVAIL;
		__dev_put(dev);
		break;
	default:
		return -EINVAL;
	}
```

Figure 6.206 IPMR—add a vif: `linux/net/ipv4/ipmr.c`.

```
	if ((in_dev = __in_dev_get(dev)) == NULL)
		return -EADDRNOTAVAIL;
	in_dev->cnf.mc_forwarding++;
	dev_set_allmulti(dev, +1);
	ip_rt_multicast_event(in_dev);

	/*
	 *	Fill in the VIF structures
	 */
```

```
426               v->rate_limit=vifc->vifc_rate_limit;
427               v->local=vifc->vifc_lcl_addr.s_addr;
428               v->remote=vifc->vifc_rmt_addr.s_addr;
429               v->flags=vifc->vifc_flags;
430               if (!mrtsock)
431                       v->flags |= VIFF_STATIC;
432               v->threshold=vifc->vifc_threshold;
433               v->bytes_in = 0;
434               v->bytes_out = 0;
435               v->pkt_in = 0;
436               v->pkt_out = 0;
437               v->link = dev->ifindex;
438               if (v->flags&(VIFF_TUNNEL|VIFF_REGISTER))
439                       v->link = dev->iflink;
440
441               /* And finish update writing critical data */
442               write_lock_bh(&mrt_lock);
443               dev_hold(dev);
444               v->dev=dev;
445  #ifdef CONFIG_IP_PIMSM
446               if (v->flags&VIFF_REGISTER)
447                       reg_vif_num = vifi;
448  #endif
449               if (vifi+1 > maxvif)
450                       maxvif = vifi+1;
451               write_unlock_bh(&mrt_lock);
452               return 0;
453  }
```

Figure 6.207 IPMR—clean up vifs after socket close: `linux/net/ipv4/ipmr.c`.

```
776  static void mroute_clean_tables(struct sock *sk)
777  {
778        int i;
779
780        /*
781         *       Shut down all active vif entries
782         */
783        for(i=0; i<maxvif; i++) {
784                if (!(vif_table[i].flags&VIFF_STATIC))
785                        vif_delete(i);
786        }
787
788        /*
789         *       Wipe the cache
790         */
791        for (i=0;i<MFC_LINES;i++) {
792                struct mfc_cache *c, **cp;
793
794                cp = &mfc_cache_array[i];
795                while ((c = *cp) != NULL) {
796                        if (c->mfc_flags&MFC_STATIC) {
```

```
                        cp = &c->next;
                        continue;
                    }
                    write_lock_bh(&mrt_lock);
                    *cp = c->next;
                    write_unlock_bh(&mrt_lock);

                    kmem_cache_free(mrt_cachep, c);
                }
        }

        if (atomic_read(&cache_resolve_queue_len) != 0) {
                struct mfc_cache *c;

                spin_lock_bh(&mfc_unres_lock);
                while (mfc_unres_queue != NULL) {
                        c = mfc_unres_queue;
                        mfc_unres_queue = c->next;
                        spin_unlock_bh(&mfc_unres_lock);

                        ipmr_destroy_unres(c);

                        spin_lock_bh(&mfc_unres_lock);
                }
                spin_unlock_bh(&mfc_unres_lock);
        }
}
```

Multicast Cache

Figure 6.208 IPMR—destroy stale cache entry: `linux/net/ipv4/ipmr.c`.

```
/* Destroy an unresolved cache entry, killing queued skbs
   and reporting error to netlink readers.
 */

static void ipmr_destroy_unres(struct mfc_cache *c)
{
        struct sk_buff *skb;

        atomic_dec(&cache_resolve_queue_len);

        while((skb=skb_dequeue(&c->mfc_un.unres.unresolved))) {
#ifdef CONFIG_RTNETLINK
                if (skb->nh.iph->version == 0) {
                        struct nlmsghdr *nlh = (struct nlmsghdr *)skb_pull(skb,
                              sizeof(struct iphdr));
                        nlh->nlmsg_type = NLMSG_ERROR;
                        nlh->nlmsg_len = NLMSG_LENGTH(sizeof(struct nlmsgerr));
                        skb_trim(skb, nlh->nlmsg_len);
                        ((struct nlmsgerr*)NLMSG_DATA(nlh))->error = -ETIMEDOUT;
                        netlink_unicast(rtnl, skb, NETLINK_CB(skb).dst_pid, MSG_DONTWAIT);
```

```
305                     } else
306  #endif
307                             kfree_skb(skb);
308         }
309
310         kmem_cache_free(mrt_cachep, c);
311  }
```

Figure 6.209 IPMR—timer process: `linux/net/ipv4/ipmr.c`.

```
314  /* Single timer process for all the unresolved queue. */
315
316  void ipmr_expire_process(unsigned long dummy)
317  {
318         unsigned long now;
319         unsigned long expires;
320         struct mfc_cache *c, **cp;
321
322         if (!spin_trylock(&mfc_unres_lock)) {
323                 mod_timer(&ipmr_expire_timer, jiffies+HZ/10);
324                 return;
325         }
326
327         if (atomic_read(&cache_resolve_queue_len) == 0)
328                 goto out;
329
330         now = jiffies;
331         expires = 10*HZ;
332         cp = &mfc_unres_queue;
333
334         while ((c=*cp) != NULL) {
335                 long interval = c->mfc_un.unres.expires - now;
336
337                 if (interval > 0) {
338                         if (interval < expires)
339                                 expires = interval;
340                         cp = &c->next;
341                         continue;
342                 }
343
344                 *cp = c->next;
345
346                 ipmr_destroy_unres(c);
347         }
348
349         if (atomic_read(&cache_resolve_queue_len))
350                 mod_timer(&ipmr_expire_timer, jiffies + expires);
351
352  out:
353         spin_unlock(&mfc_unres_lock);
354  }
```

Figure 6.210 IPMR—update output interface lists: `linux/net/ipv4/ipmr.c`.

```
/* Fill oifs list. It is called under write locked mrt_lock. */

static void ipmr_update_threshoulds(struct mfc_cache *cache, unsigned char *ttls)
{
	int vifi;

	cache->mfc_un.res.minvif = MAXVIFS;
	cache->mfc_un.res.maxvif = 0;
	memset(cache->mfc_un.res.ttls, 255, MAXVIFS);

	for (vifi=0; vifi<maxvif; vifi++) {
		if (VIF_EXISTS(vifi) && ttls[vifi] && ttls[vifi] < 255) {
			cache->mfc_un.res.ttls[vifi] = ttls[vifi];
			if (cache->mfc_un.res.minvif > vifi)
				cache->mfc_un.res.minvif = vifi;
			if (cache->mfc_un.res.maxvif <= vifi)
				cache->mfc_un.res.maxvif = vifi + 1;
		}
	}
}
```

Figure 6.211 IPMR—allocate cache entries: `linux/net/ipv4/ipmr.c`.

```
static struct mfc_cache *ipmr_cache_find(__u32 origin, __u32 mcastgrp)
{
	int line=MFC_HASH(mcastgrp,origin);
	struct mfc_cache *c;

	for (c=mfc_cache_array[line]; c; c = c->next) {
		if (c->mfc_origin==origin && c->mfc_mcastgrp==mcastgrp)
			break;
	}
	return c;
}

/*
 *	Allocate a multicast cache entry
 */
static struct mfc_cache *ipmr_cache_alloc(void)
{
	struct mfc_cache *c=kmem_cache_alloc(mrt_cachep, GFP_KERNEL);
	if(c==NULL)
		return NULL;
	memset(c, 0, sizeof(*c));
	c->mfc_un.res.minvif = MAXVIFS;
	return c;
}

```

```
static struct mfc_cache *ipmr_cache_alloc_unres(void)
{
        struct mfc_cache *c=kmem_cache_alloc(mrt_cachep, GFP_ATOMIC);
        if(c==NULL)
                return NULL;
        memset(c, 0, sizeof(*c));
        skb_queue_head_init(&c->mfc_un.unres.unresolved);
        c->mfc_un.unres.expires = jiffies + 10*HZ;
        return c;
}
```

Figure 6.212 IPMR—resolve cache entries: `linux/net/ipv4/ipmr.c`.

```
/*
 *      A cache entry has gone into a resolved state from queued
 */

static void ipmr_cache_resolve(struct mfc_cache *uc, struct mfc_cache *c)
{
        struct sk_buff *skb;

        /*
         *      Play the pending entries through our router
         */

        while((skb=__skb_dequeue(&uc->mfc_un.unres.unresolved))) {
#ifdef CONFIG_RTNETLINK
                if (skb->nh.iph->version == 0) {
                        int err;
                        struct nlmsghdr *nlh = (struct nlmsghdr *)skb_pull(skb, sizeof(struct iphdr));

                        if (ipmr_fill_mroute(skb, c, NLMSG_DATA(nlh)) > 0) {
                                nlh->nlmsg_len = skb->tail - (u8*)nlh;
                        } else {
                                nlh->nlmsg_type = NLMSG_ERROR;
                                nlh->nlmsg_len = NLMSG_LENGTH(sizeof(struct nlmsgerr));
                                skb_trim(skb, nlh->nlmsg_len);
                                ((struct nlmsgerr*)NLMSG_DATA(nlh))->error = -EMSGSIZE;
                        }
                        err = netlink_unicast(rtnl, skb, NETLINK_CB(skb).dst_pid, MSG_DONTWAIT);
                } else
#endif
                        ip_mr_forward(skb, c, 0);
        }
}
```

Figure 6.213 IPMR—multicast route cache query passed up to `mrouted`: `linux/net/ipv4/ipmr.c`.

```
/*
 *      Bounce a cache query up to mrouted. We could use netlink for this but mrouted
 *      expects the following bizarre scheme.
 *
 *      Called under mrt_lock.
 */

static int ipmr_cache_report(struct sk_buff *pkt, vifi_t vifi, int assert)
{
        struct sk_buff *skb;
        int ihl = pkt->nh.iph->ihl<<2;
        struct igmphdr *igmp;
        struct igmpmsg *msg;
        int ret;

#ifdef CONFIG_IP_PIMSM
        if (assert == IGMPMSG_WHOLEPKT)
                skb = skb_realloc_headroom(pkt, sizeof(struct iphdr));
        else
#endif
                skb = alloc_skb(128, GFP_ATOMIC);

        if(!skb)
                return -ENOBUFS;

#ifdef CONFIG_IP_PIMSM
        if (assert == IGMPMSG_WHOLEPKT) {
                /* Ugly, but we have no choice with this interface.
                   Duplicate old header, fix ihl, length etc.
                   And all this only to mangle msg->im_msgtype and
                   to set msg->im_mbz to "mbz" :-)
                 */
                msg = (struct igmpmsg*)skb_push(skb, sizeof(struct iphdr));
                skb->nh.raw = skb->h.raw = (u8*)msg;
                memcpy(msg, pkt->nh.raw, sizeof(struct iphdr));
                msg->im_msgtype = IGMPMSG_WHOLEPKT;
                msg->im_mbz = 0;
                msg->im_vif = reg_vif_num;
                skb->nh.iph->ihl = sizeof(struct iphdr) >> 2;
                skb->nh.iph->tot_len = htons(ntohs(pkt->nh.iph->tot_len) + sizeof(struct iphdr));
        } else
#endif
```

Figure 6.214 IPMR—multicast route cache query passed up to `mrouted`: `linux/net/ipv4/ipmr.c`.

```
        {

        /*
         *      Copy the IP header
         */
```

```

        skb->nh.iph = (struct iphdr *)skb_put(skb, ihl);
        memcpy(skb->data,pkt->data,ihl);
        skb->nh.iph->protocol = 0;              /* Flag to the kernel this is a route add */
        msg = (struct igmpmsg*)skb->nh.iph;
        msg->im_vif = vifi;
        skb->dst = dst_clone(pkt->dst);

        /*
         *      Add our header
         */

        igmp=(struct igmphdr *)skb_put(skb,sizeof(struct igmphdr));
        igmp->type     =
        msg->im_msgtype = assert;
        igmp->code     =      0;
        skb->nh.iph->tot_len=htons(skb->len);             /* Fix the length */
        skb->h.raw = skb->nh.raw;
        }

        if (mroute_socket == NULL) {
                kfree_skb(skb);
                return -EINVAL;
        }

        /*
         *      Deliver to mrouted
         */
        if ((ret=sock_queue_rcv_skb(mroute_socket,skb))<0) {
                if (net_ratelimit())
                        printk(KERN_WARNING "mroute: pending queue full, dropping entries.\n");
                kfree_skb(skb);
        }

        return ret;
}
```

Multicast Forwarding and Lookup

Figure 6.215 IPMR—queue a packet to send awaiting resolution: `linux/net/ipv4/ipmr.c`.

```
static int
ipmr_cache_unresolved(vifi_t vifi, struct sk_buff *skb)
{
        int err;
        struct mfc_cache *c;

        spin_lock_bh(&mfc_unres_lock);
        for (c=mfc_unres_queue; c; c=c->next) {
                if (c->mfc_mcastgrp == skb->nh.iph->daddr &&
```

```
621                    c->mfc_origin == skb->nh.iph->saddr)
622                        break;
623            }
624
625        if (c == NULL) {
626            /*
627             *      Create a new entry if allowable
628             */
629
630            if (atomic_read(&cache_resolve_queue_len)>=10 ||
631                (c=ipmr_cache_alloc_unres())==NULL) {
632                    spin_unlock_bh(&mfc_unres_lock);
633
634                    kfree_skb(skb);
635                    return -ENOBUFS;
636            }
637
638            /*
639             *      Fill in the new cache entry
640             */
641            c->mfc_parent=-1;
642            c->mfc_origin=skb->nh.iph->saddr;
643            c->mfc_mcastgrp=skb->nh.iph->daddr;
```

Figure 6.216 IPMR—queue a packet to send awaiting resolution: `linux/net/ipv4/ipmr.c`.

```
645            /*
646             *      Reflect first query at mrouted.
647             */
648            if ((err = ipmr_cache_report(skb, vifi, IGMPMSG_NOCACHE))<0) {
649                    /* If the report failed throw the cache entry
650                       out - Brad Parker
651                     */
652                    spin_unlock_bh(&mfc_unres_lock);
653
654                    kmem_cache_free(mrt_cachep, c);
655                    kfree_skb(skb);
656                    return err;
657            }
658
659            atomic_inc(&cache_resolve_queue_len);
660            c->next = mfc_unres_queue;
661            mfc_unres_queue = c;
662
663            mod_timer(&ipmr_expire_timer, c->mfc_un.unres.expires);
664        }
```

Figure 6.217 IPMR—queue a packet to send awaiting resolution: `linux/net/ipv4/ipmr.c`.

```
        /*
         *      See if we can append the packet
         */
        if (c->mfc_un.unres.unresolved.qlen>3) {
                kfree_skb(skb);
                err = -ENOBUFS;
        } else {
                skb_queue_tail(&c->mfc_un.unres.unresolved,skb);
                err = 0;
        }

        spin_unlock_bh(&mfc_unres_lock);
        return err;
}
```

User Management of Multicast Forwarding Cache

Figure 6.218 IPMR—user space calls MFC delete: `linux/net/ipv4/ipmr.c`.

```
int ipmr_mfc_delete(struct mfcctl *mfc)
{
        int line;
        struct mfc_cache *c, **cp;

        line=MFC_HASH(mfc->mfcc_mcastgrp.s_addr, mfc->mfcc_origin.s_addr);

        for (cp=&mfc_cache_array[line]; (c=*cp) != NULL; cp = &c->next) {
                if (c->mfc_origin == mfc->mfcc_origin.s_addr &&
                    c->mfc_mcastgrp == mfc->mfcc_mcastgrp.s_addr) {
                        write_lock_bh(&mrt_lock);
                        *cp = c->next;
                        write_unlock_bh(&mrt_lock);

                        kmem_cache_free(mrt_cachep, c);
                        return 0;
                }
        }
        return -ENOENT;
}
```

Figure 6.219 IPMR—user space calls MFC add: `linux/net/ipv4/ipmr.c`.

```
int ipmr_mfc_add(struct mfcctl *mfc, int mrtsock)
{
        int line;
        struct mfc_cache *uc, *c, **cp;

        line=MFC_HASH(mfc->mfcc_mcastgrp.s_addr, mfc->mfcc_origin.s_addr);

        for (cp=&mfc_cache_array[line]; (c=*cp) != NULL; cp = &c->next) {
                if (c->mfc_origin == mfc->mfcc_origin.s_addr &&
                    c->mfc_mcastgrp == mfc->mfcc_mcastgrp.s_addr)
                        break;
        }

        if (c != NULL) {
                write_lock_bh(&mrt_lock);
                c->mfc_parent = mfc->mfcc_parent;
                ipmr_update_threshoulds(c, mfc->mfcc_ttls);
                if (!mrtsock)
                        c->mfc_flags |= MFC_STATIC;
                write_unlock_bh(&mrt_lock);
                return 0;
        }

        if(!MULTICAST(mfc->mfcc_mcastgrp.s_addr))
                return -EINVAL;

        c=ipmr_cache_alloc();
        if (c==NULL)
                return -ENOMEM;

        c->mfc_origin=mfc->mfcc_origin.s_addr;
        c->mfc_mcastgrp=mfc->mfcc_mcastgrp.s_addr;
        c->mfc_parent=mfc->mfcc_parent;
        ipmr_update_threshoulds(c, mfc->mfcc_ttls);
        if (!mrtsock)
                c->mfc_flags |= MFC_STATIC;

        write_lock_bh(&mrt_lock);
        c->next = mfc_cache_array[line];
        mfc_cache_array[line] = c;
        write_unlock_bh(&mrt_lock);
```

Figure 6.220 IPMR—user space calls MFC add: `linux/net/ipv4/ipmr.c`.

```
        /*
         *      Check to see if we resolved a queued list. If so we
         *      need to send on the frames and tidy up.
         */
        spin_lock_bh(&mfc_unres_lock);
        for (cp = &mfc_unres_queue; (uc=*cp) != NULL;
             cp = &uc->next) {
```

```
                if (uc->mfc_origin == c->mfc_origin &&
                    uc->mfc_mcastgrp == c->mfc_mcastgrp) {
                        *cp = uc->next;
                        if (atomic_dec_and_test(&cache_resolve_queue_len))
                                del_timer(&ipmr_expire_timer);
                        break;
                }
        }
        spin_unlock_bh(&mfc_unres_lock);

        if (uc) {
                ipmr_cache_resolve(uc, c);
                kmem_cache_free(mrt_cachep, uc);
        }
        return 0;
}
```

Figure 6.221 IPMR—`mrouted` socket dies: `linux/net/ipv4/ipmr.c`.

```
static void mrtsock_destruct(struct sock *sk)
{
        rtnl_lock();
        if (sk == mroute_socket) {
                ipv4_devconf.mc_forwarding--;

                write_lock_bh(&mrt_lock);
                mroute_socket=NULL;
                write_unlock_bh(&mrt_lock);

                mroute_clean_tables(sk);
        }
        rtnl_unlock();
}
```

Multicast Socket Options

Figure 6.222 IPMR—`setsockopt` entry handler: `linux/net/ipv4/ipmr.c`.

```
/*
 *      Socket options and virtual interface manipulation. The whole
 *      virtual interface system is a complete heap, but unfortunately
 *      that's how BSD mrouted happens to think. Maybe one day with a proper
 *      MOSPF/PIM router set up we can clean this up.
 */

int ip_mroute_setsockopt(struct sock *sk,int optname,char *optval,int optlen)
{
        int ret;
```

```
	struct vifctl vif;
	struct mfcctl mfc;

	if(optname!=MRT_INIT)
	{
		if(sk!=mroute_socket && !capable(CAP_NET_ADMIN))
			return -EACCES;
	}

	switch(optname)
	{
		case MRT_INIT:
			if(sk->type!=SOCK_RAW || sk->num!=IPPROTO_IGMP)
				return -EOPNOTSUPP;
			if(optlen!=sizeof(int))
				return -ENOPROTOOPT;

			rtnl_lock();
			if (mroute_socket) {
				rtnl_unlock();
				return -EADDRINUSE;
			}

			ret = ip_ra_control(sk, 1, mrtsock_destruct);
			if (ret == 0) {
				write_lock_bh(&mrt_lock);
				mroute_socket=sk;
				write_unlock_bh(&mrt_lock);

				ipv4_devconf.mc_forwarding++;
			}
			rtnl_unlock();
			return ret;
		case MRT_DONE:
			if (sk!=mroute_socket)
				return -EACCES;
			return ip_ra_control(sk, 0, NULL);
```

Figure 6.223 IPMR—`setsockopt` entry handler: `linux/net/ipv4/ipmr.c`.

```
		case MRT_ADD_VIF:
		case MRT_DEL_VIF:
			if(optlen!=sizeof(vif))
				return -EINVAL;
			if (copy_from_user(&vif,optval,sizeof(vif)))
				return -EFAULT;
			if(vif.vifc_vifi >= MAXVIFS)
				return -ENFILE;
			rtnl_lock();
			if (optname==MRT_ADD_VIF) {
				ret = vif_add(&vif, sk==mroute_socket);
```

```
898                         } else {
899                                 ret = vif_delete(vif.vifc_vifi);
900                         }
901                         rtnl_unlock();
902                         return ret;
903
904             /*
905              *      Manipulate the forwarding caches. These live
906              *      in a sort of kernel/user symbiosis.
907              */
908             case MRT_ADD_MFC:
909             case MRT_DEL_MFC:
910                     if(optlen!=sizeof(mfc))
911                             return -EINVAL;
912                     if (copy_from_user(&mfc,optval, sizeof(mfc)))
913                             return -EFAULT;
914                     rtnl_lock();
915                     if (optname==MRT_DEL_MFC)
916                             ret = ipmr_mfc_delete(&mfc);
917                     else
918                             ret = ipmr_mfc_add(&mfc, sk==mroute_socket);
919                     rtnl_unlock();
920                     return ret;
921             /*
922              *      Control PIM assert.
923              */
924             case MRT_ASSERT:
925             {
926                     int v;
927                     if(get_user(v,(int *)optval))
928                             return -EFAULT;
929                     mroute_do_assert=(v)?1:0;
930                     return 0;
931             }
```

Figure 6.224 IPMR—setsockopt entry handler: linux/net/ipv4/ipmr.c.

```
932     #ifdef CONFIG_IP_PIMSM
933             case MRT_PIM:
934             {
935                     int v;
936                     if(get_user(v,(int *)optval))
937                             return -EFAULT;
938                     v = (v)?1:0;
939                     rtnl_lock();
940                     if (v != mroute_do_pim) {
941                             mroute_do_pim = v;
942                             mroute_do_assert = v;
943     #ifdef CONFIG_IP_PIMSM_V2
944                             if (mroute_do_pim)
945                                     inet_add_protocol(&pim_protocol);
```

```
946                            else
947                                    inet_del_protocol(&pim_protocol);
948   #endif
949                    }
950                    rtnl_unlock();
951                    return 0;
952            }
953   #endif
954            /*
955             *     Spurious command, or MRT_VERSION which you cannot
956             *     set.
957             */
958            default:
959                    return -ENOPROTOOPT;
960        }
961   }
```

Figure 6.225 IPMR—`getsockopt` entry handler: `linux/net/ipv4/ipmr.c`.

```
967   int ip_mroute_getsockopt(struct sock *sk,int optname,char *optval,int *optlen)
968   {
969         int olr;
970         int val;
971
972         if(optname!=MRT_VERSION &&
973   #ifdef CONFIG_IP_PIMSM
974           optname!=MRT_PIM &&
975   #endif
976           optname!=MRT_ASSERT)
977               return -ENOPROTOOPT;
978
979         if(get_user(olr, optlen))
980               return -EFAULT;
981
982         olr=min(olr,sizeof(int));
983         if(put_user(olr,optlen))
984               return -EFAULT;
985         if(optname==MRT_VERSION)
986               val=0x0305;
987   #ifdef CONFIG_IP_PIMSM
988         else if(optname==MRT_PIM)
989               val=mroute_do_pim;
990   #endif
991         else
992               val=mroute_do_assert;
993         if(copy_to_user(optval,&val,olr))
994               return -EFAULT;
995         return 0;
996   }
```

6.5.4 Multicast Transmission

Figure 6.226 IPMR: `linux/net/ipv4/ipmr.c`.

```
1002  int ipmr_ioctl(struct sock *sk, int cmd, unsigned long arg)
1003  {
1004          struct sioc_sg_req sr;
1005          struct sioc_vif_req vr;
1006          struct vif_device *vif;
1007          struct mfc_cache *c;
1008
1009          switch(cmd)
1010          {
1011                  case SIOCGETVIFCNT:
1012                          if (copy_from_user(&vr,(void *)arg,sizeof(vr)))
1013                                  return -EFAULT;
1014                          if(vr.vifi>=maxvif)
1015                                  return -EINVAL;
1016                          read_lock(&mrt_lock);
1017                          vif=&vif_table[vr.vifi];
1018                          if(VIF_EXISTS(vr.vifi)) {
1019                                  vr.icount=vif->pkt_in;
1020                                  vr.ocount=vif->pkt_out;
1021                                  vr.ibytes=vif->bytes_in;
1022                                  vr.obytes=vif->bytes_out;
1023                                  read_unlock(&mrt_lock);
1024
1025                                  if (copy_to_user((void *)arg,&vr,sizeof(vr)))
1026                                          return -EFAULT;
1027                                  return 0;
1028                          }
1029                          read_unlock(&mrt_lock);
1030                          return -EADDRNOTAVAIL;
1031                  case SIOCGETSGCNT:
1032                          if (copy_from_user(&sr,(void *)arg,sizeof(sr)))
1033                                  return -EFAULT;
1034
1035                          read_lock(&mrt_lock);
1036                          c = ipmr_cache_find(sr.src.s_addr, sr.grp.s_addr);
1037                          if (c) {
1038                                  sr.pktcnt = c->mfc_un.res.pkt;
1039                                  sr.bytecnt = c->mfc_un.res.bytes;
1040                                  sr.wrong_if = c->mfc_un.res.wrong_if;
1041                                  read_unlock(&mrt_lock);
1042
1043                                  if (copy_to_user((void *)arg,&sr,sizeof(sr)))
1044                                          return -EFAULT;
1045                                  return 0;
1046                          }
1047                          read_unlock(&mrt_lock);
1048                          return -EADDRNOTAVAIL;
1049                  default:
1050                          return -ENOIOCTLCMD;
1051          }
1052  }
```

Figure 6.227 IPMR—transmit encapsualted: `linux/net/ipv4/ipmr.c`.

```
/*
 *      Encapsulate a packet by attaching a valid IPIP header to it.
 *      This avoids tunnel drivers and other mess and gives us the speed so
 *      important for multicast video.
 */

static void ip_encap(struct sk_buff *skb, u32 saddr, u32 daddr)
{
        struct iphdr *iph = (struct iphdr *)skb_push(skb,sizeof(struct iphdr));

        iph->version    =       4;
        iph->tos        =       skb->nh.iph->tos;
        iph->ttl        =       skb->nh.iph->ttl;
        iph->frag_off   =       0;
        iph->daddr      =       daddr;
        iph->saddr      =       saddr;
        iph->protocol   =       IPPROTO_IPIP;
        iph->ihl        =       5;
        iph->tot_len    =       htons(skb->len);
        ip_select_ident(iph, skb->dst);
        ip_send_check(iph);

        skb->h.ipiph = skb->nh.iph;
        skb->nh.iph = iph;
#ifdef CONFIG_NETFILTER
        nf_conntrack_put(skb->nfct);
        skb->nfct = NULL;
#endif
}
```

Figure 6.228 IPMR—finish forwarding: `linux/net/ipv4/ipmr.c`.

```
static inline int ipmr_forward_finish(struct sk_buff *skb)
{
        struct dst_entry *dst = skb->dst;

        if (skb->len <= dst->pmtu)
                return dst->output(skb);
        else
                return ip_fragment(skb, dst->output);
}
```

Figure 6.229 IPMR—transmission handler: `linux/net/ipv4/ipmr.c`.

```
/*
 *      Processing handlers for ipmr_forward
 */

static void ipmr_queue_xmit(struct sk_buff *skb, struct mfc_cache *c,
```

```
1121                            int vifi, int last)
1122    {
1123            struct iphdr *iph = skb->nh.iph;
1124            struct vif_device *vif = &vif_table[vifi];
1125            struct net_device *dev;
1126            struct rtable *rt;
1127            int    encap = 0;
1128            struct sk_buff *skb2;
1129
1130            if (vif->dev == NULL)
1131                    return;
1132
1133    #ifdef CONFIG_IP_PIMSM
1134            if (vif->flags & VIFF_REGISTER) {
1135                    vif->pkt_out++;
1136                    vif->bytes_out+=skb->len;
1137                    ((struct net_device_stats*)vif->dev->priv)->tx_bytes += skb->len;
1138                    ((struct net_device_stats*)vif->dev->priv)->tx_packets++;
1139                    ipmr_cache_report(skb, vifi, IGMPMSG_WHOLEPKT);
1140                    return;
1141            }
1142    #endif
```

Figure 6.230 IPMR—transmission handler: `linux/net/ipv4/ipmr.c.`

```
1144            if (vif->flags&VIFF_TUNNEL) {
1145                    if (ip_route_output(&rt, vif->remote, vif->local, RT_TOS(iph->tos), vif->link))
1146                            return;
1147                    encap = sizeof(struct iphdr);
1148            } else {
1149                    if (ip_route_output(&rt, iph->daddr, 0, RT_TOS(iph->tos), vif->link))
1150                            return;
1151            }
1152
1153            dev = rt->u.dst.dev;
1154
1155            if (skb->len+encap > rt->u.dst.pmtu && (ntohs(iph->frag_off) & IP_DF)) {
1156                    /* Do not fragment multicasts. Alas, IPv4 does not
1157                       allow to send ICMP, so that packets will disappear
1158                       to blackhole.
1159                     */
1160
1161                    IP_INC_STATS_BH(IpFragFails);
1162                    ip_rt_put(rt);
1163                    return;
1164            }
1165
1166            encap += dev->hard_header_len;
1167
1168            if (skb_headroom(skb) < encap || skb_cloned(skb) || !last)
1169                    skb2 = skb_realloc_headroom(skb, (encap + 15)&~15);
1170            else if (atomic_read(&skb->users) != 1)
```

```
                skb2 = skb_clone(skb, GFP_ATOMIC);
        else {
                atomic_inc(&skb->users);
                skb2 = skb;
        }

        if (skb2 == NULL) {
                ip_rt_put(rt);
                return;
        }
```

Figure 6.231 IPMR—transmission handler: `linux/net/ipv4/ipmr.c`.

```
        vif->pkt_out++;
        vif->bytes_out+=skb->len;

        dst_release(skb2->dst);
        skb2->dst = &rt->u.dst;
        iph = skb2->nh.iph;
        ip_decrease_ttl(iph);

        /* FIXME: forward and output firewalls used to be called here.
         * What do we do with netfilter? -- RR */
        if (vif->flags & VIFF_TUNNEL) {
                ip_encap(skb2, vif->local, vif->remote);
                /* FIXME: extra output firewall step used to be here. --RR */
                ((struct ip_tunnel *)vif->dev->priv)->stat.tx_packets++;
                ((struct ip_tunnel *)vif->dev->priv)->stat.tx_bytes+=skb2->len;
        }

        IPCB(skb2)->flags |= IPSKB_FORWARDED;

        /*
         * RFC 1584 teaches, that DVMRP/PIM router must deliver packets locally
         * not only before forwarding, but after forwarding on all output
         * interfaces. It is clear, if mrouter runs a multicasting
         * program, it should receive packets not depending to what interface
         * program is joined.
         * If we will not make it, the program will have to join on all
         * interfaces. On the other hand, multihoming host (or router, but
         * not mrouter) cannot join to more than one interface - it will
         * result in receiving multiple packets.
         */
        NF_HOOK(PF_INET, NF_IP_FORWARD, skb2, skb->dev, dev,
                ipmr_forward_finish);
}
```

Figure 6.232 IPMR–find a vif by device: `linux/net/ipv4/ipmr.c`.

```
int ipmr_find_vif(struct net_device *dev)
{
        int ct;
        for (ct=maxvif-1; ct>=0; ct--) {
                if (vif_table[ct].dev == dev)
                        break;
        }
        return ct;
}
```

Figure 6.233 IPMR–forwarding: `linux/net/ipv4/ipmr.c`.

```
/* "local" means that we should preserve one skb (for local delivery) */

int ip_mr_forward(struct sk_buff *skb, struct mfc_cache *cache, int local)
{
        int psend = -1;
        int vif, ct;

        vif = cache->mfc_parent;
        cache->mfc_un.res.pkt++;
        cache->mfc_un.res.bytes += skb->len;

        /*
         * Wrong interface: drop packet and (maybe) send PIM assert.
         */
        if (vif_table[vif].dev != skb->dev) {
                int true_vifi;

                if (((struct rtable*)skb->dst)->key.iif == 0) {
                        /* It is our own packet, looped back.
                           Very complicated situation...

                           The best workaround until routing daemons will be
                           fixed is not to redistribute packet, if it was
                           send through wrong interface. It means, that
                           multicast applications WILL NOT work for
                           (S,G), which have default multicast route pointing
                           to wrong oif. In any case, it is not a good
                           idea to use multicasting applications on router.
                         */
                        goto dont_forward;
                }

                cache->mfc_un.res.wrong_if++;
                true_vifi = ipmr_find_vif(skb->dev);

                if (true_vifi >= 0 && mroute_do_assert &&
                    /* pimsm uses asserts, when switching from RPT to SPT,
                       so that we cannot check that packet arrived on an oif.
                       It is bad, but otherwise we would need to move pretty
```

```
                    large chunk of pimd to kernel. Ough... --ANK
                  */
                 (mroute_do_pim || cache->mfc_un.res.ttls[true_vifi] < 255) &&
                 jiffies - cache->mfc_un.res.last_assert > MFC_ASSERT_THRESH) {
                    cache->mfc_un.res.last_assert = jiffies;
                    ipmr_cache_report(skb, true_vifi, IGMPMSG_WRONGVIF);
                }
                goto dont_forward;
        }
```

Figure 6.234 IPMR—forwarding: `linux/net/ipv4/ipmr.c`.

```
        vif_table[vif].pkt_in++;
        vif_table[vif].bytes_in+=skb->len;

        /*
         *      Forward the frame
         */
        for (ct = cache->mfc_un.res.maxvif-1; ct >= cache->mfc_un.res.minvif; ct--) {
                if (skb->nh.iph->ttl > cache->mfc_un.res.ttls[ct]) {
                        if (psend != -1)
                                ipmr_queue_xmit(skb, cache, psend, 0);
                        psend=ct;
                }
        }
        if (psend != -1)
                ipmr_queue_xmit(skb, cache, psend, !local);

dont_forward:
        if (!local)
                kfree_skb(skb);
        return 0;
}
```

Figure 6.235 IPMR—handle multicast packets to be forwarded: `linux/net/ipv4/ipmr.c`.

```
/*
 *      Multicast packets for forwarding arrive here
 */

int ip_mr_input(struct sk_buff *skb)
{
        struct mfc_cache *cache;
        int local = ((struct rtable*)skb->dst)->rt_flags&RTCF_LOCAL;

        /* Packet is looped back after forward, it should not be
           forwarded second time, but still can be delivered locally.
         */
        if (IPCB(skb)->flags&IPSKB_FORWARDED)
                goto dont_forward;

```

```
1313            if (!local) {
1314                    if (IPCB(skb)->opt.router_alert) {
1315                            if (ip_call_ra_chain(skb))
1316                                    return 0;
1317                    } else if (skb->nh.iph->protocol == IPPROTO_IGMP){
1318                            /* IGMPv1 (and broken IGMPv2 implementations sort of
1319                               Cisco IOS <= 11.2(8)) do not put router alert
1320                               option to IGMP packets destined to routable
1321                               groups. It is very bad, because it means
1322                               that we can forward NO IGMP messages.
1323                             */
1324                            read_lock(&mrt_lock);
1325                            if (mroute_socket) {
1326                                    raw_rcv(mroute_socket, skb);
1327                                    read_unlock(&mrt_lock);
1328                                    return 0;
1329                            }
1330                            read_unlock(&mrt_lock);
1331                    }
1332            }
```

Figure 6.236 IPMR—handle multicast packets to be forwarded: `linux/net/ipv4/ipmr.c`.

```
1334            read_lock(&mrt_lock);
1335            cache = ipmr_cache_find(skb->nh.iph->saddr, skb->nh.iph->daddr);
1336
1337            /*
1338             *      No usable cache entry
1339             */
1340            if (cache==NULL) {
1341                    int vif;
1342
1343                    if (local) {
1344                            struct sk_buff *skb2 = skb_clone(skb, GFP_ATOMIC);
1345                            ip_local_deliver(skb);
1346                            if (skb2 == NULL) {
1347                                    read_unlock(&mrt_lock);
1348                                    return -ENOBUFS;
1349                            }
1350                            skb = skb2;
1351                    }
1352
1353                    vif = ipmr_find_vif(skb->dev);
1354                    if (vif >= 0) {
1355                            int err = ipmr_cache_unresolved(vif, skb);
1356                            read_unlock(&mrt_lock);
1357
1358                            return err;
1359                    }
1360                    read_unlock(&mrt_lock);
1361                    kfree_skb(skb);
1362                    return -ENODEV;
1363            }
1364
```

```
1365            ip_mr_forward(skb, cache, local);
1366
1367            read_unlock(&mrt_lock);
1368
1369            if (local)
1370                    return ip_local_deliver(skb);
1371
1372            return 0;
1373
1374  dont_forward:
1375            if (local)
1376                    return ip_local_deliver(skb);
1377            kfree_skb(skb);
1378            return 0;
1379  }
```

6.5.5 PIM Specifics

Figure 6.237 IPMR—PIM v1 input handler: `linux/net/ipv4/ipmr.c`.

```
1381  #ifdef CONFIG_IP_PIMSM_V1
1382  /*
1383   * Handle IGMP messages of PIMv1
1384   */
1385
1386  int pim_rcv_v1(struct sk_buff * skb, unsigned short len)
1387  {
1388            struct igmphdr *pim = (struct igmphdr*)skb->h.raw;
1389            struct iphdr  *encap;
1390            struct net_device *reg_dev = NULL;
1391
1392            if (!mroute_do_pim ||
1393                len < sizeof(*pim) + sizeof(*encap) ||
1394                pim->group != PIM_V1_VERSION || pim->code != PIM_V1_REGISTER) {
1395                    kfree_skb(skb);
1396                    return -EINVAL;
1397            }
1398
1399            encap = (struct iphdr*)(skb->h.raw + sizeof(struct igmphdr));
1400            /*
1401               Check that:
1402               a. packet is really destinted to a multicast group
1403               b. packet is not a NULL-REGISTER
1404               c. packet is not truncated
1405            */
1406            if (!MULTICAST(encap->daddr) ||
1407                ntohs(encap->tot_len) == 0 ||
1408                ntohs(encap->tot_len) + sizeof(*pim) > len) {
1409                    kfree_skb(skb);
1410                    return -EINVAL;
1411            }
```

Figure 6.238 IPMR—PIM v1 input handler: `linux/net/ipv4/ipmr.c`.

```
        read_lock(&mrt_lock);
        if (reg_vif_num >= 0)
              reg_dev = vif_table[reg_vif_num].dev;
        if (reg_dev)
              dev_hold(reg_dev);
        read_unlock(&mrt_lock);

        if (reg_dev == NULL) {
              kfree_skb(skb);
              return -EINVAL;
        }

        skb->mac.raw = skb->nh.raw;
        skb_pull(skb, (u8*)encap - skb->data);
        skb->nh.iph = (struct iphdr *)skb->data;
        skb->dev = reg_dev;
        memset(&(IPCB(skb)->opt), 0, sizeof(struct ip_options));
        skb->protocol = __constant_htons(ETH_P_IP);
        skb->ip_summed = 0;
        skb->pkt_type = PACKET_HOST;
        dst_release(skb->dst);
        skb->dst = NULL;
        ((struct net_device_stats*)reg_dev->priv)->rx_bytes += skb->len;
        ((struct net_device_stats*)reg_dev->priv)->rx_packets++;
#ifdef CONFIG_NETFILTER
        nf_conntrack_put(skb->nfct);
        skb->nfct = NULL;
#endif
        netif_rx(skb);
        dev_put(reg_dev);
        return 0;
}
```

Figure 6.239 IPMR—PIM v2 input handler: `linux/net/ipv4/ipmr.c`.

```
#ifdef CONFIG_IP_PIMSM_V2
int pim_rcv(struct sk_buff * skb, unsigned short len)
{
        struct pimreghdr *pim = (struct pimreghdr*)skb->h.raw;
        struct iphdr  *encap;
        struct net_device *reg_dev = NULL;

        if (len < sizeof(*pim) + sizeof(*encap) ||
            pim->type != ((PIM_VERSION<<4)|(PIM_REGISTER)) ||
            (pim->flags&PIM_NULL_REGISTER) ||
            (ip_compute_csum((void *)pim, sizeof(*pim)) != 0 &&
             ip_compute_csum((void *)pim, len))) {
              kfree_skb(skb);
              return -EINVAL;
        }
```

```

        /* check if the inner packet is destined to mcast group */
        encap = (struct iphdr*)(skb->h.raw + sizeof(struct pimreghdr));
        if (!MULTICAST(encap->daddr) ||
            ntohs(encap->tot_len) == 0 ||
            ntohs(encap->tot_len) + sizeof(*pim) > len) {
                kfree_skb(skb);
                return -EINVAL;
        }
```

Figure 6.240 IPMR—PIM v2 input handler: `linux/net/ipv4/ipmr.c`.

```
        read_lock(&mrt_lock);
        if (reg_vif_num >= 0)
                reg_dev = vif_table[reg_vif_num].dev;
        if (reg_dev)
                dev_hold(reg_dev);
        read_unlock(&mrt_lock);

        if (reg_dev == NULL) {
                kfree_skb(skb);
                return -EINVAL;
        }

        skb->mac.raw = skb->nh.raw;
        skb_pull(skb, (u8*)encap - skb->data);
        skb->nh.iph = (struct iphdr *)skb->data;
        skb->dev = reg_dev;
        memset(&(IPCB(skb)->opt), 0, sizeof(struct ip_options));
        skb->protocol = __constant_htons(ETH_P_IP);
        skb->ip_summed = 0;
        skb->pkt_type = PACKET_HOST;
        dst_release(skb->dst);
        ((struct net_device_stats*)reg_dev->priv)->rx_bytes += skb->len;
        ((struct net_device_stats*)reg_dev->priv)->rx_packets++;
        skb->dst = NULL;
#ifdef CONFIG_NETFILTER
        nf_conntrack_put(skb->nfct);
        skb->nfct = NULL;
#endif
        netif_rx(skb);
        dev_put(reg_dev);
        return 0;
}
```

Router User to Kernel Management

Figure 6.241 IPMR–RTNetlink fill route: `linux/net/ipv4/ipmr.c`.

```
static int
ipmr_fill_mroute(struct sk_buff *skb, struct mfc_cache *c, struct rtmsg *rtm)
{
        int ct;
        struct rtnexthop *nhp;
        struct net_device *dev = vif_table[c->mfc_parent].dev;
        u8 *b = skb->tail;
        struct rtattr *mp_head;

        if (dev)
                RTA_PUT(skb, RTA_IIF, 4, &dev->ifindex);

        mp_head = (struct rtattr*)skb_put(skb, RTA_LENGTH(0));

        for (ct = c->mfc_un.res.minvif; ct < c->mfc_un.res.maxvif; ct++) {
                if (c->mfc_un.res.ttls[ct] < 255) {
                        if (skb_tailroom(skb) < RTA_ALIGN(RTA_ALIGN(sizeof(*nhp)) + 4))
                                goto rtattr_failure;
                        nhp = (struct rtnexthop*)skb_put(skb, RTA_ALIGN(sizeof(*nhp)));
                        nhp->rtnh_flags = 0;
                        nhp->rtnh_hops = c->mfc_un.res.ttls[ct];
                        nhp->rtnh_ifindex = vif_table[ct].dev->ifindex;
                        nhp->rtnh_len = sizeof(*nhp);
                }
        }
        mp_head->rta_type = RTA_MULTIPATH;
        mp_head->rta_len = skb->tail - (u8*)mp_head;
        rtm->rtm_type = RTN_MULTICAST;
        return 1;

rtattr_failure:
        skb_trim(skb, b - skb->data);
        return -EMSGSIZE;
}
```

Figure 6.242 IPMR–RTNetlink get route: `linux/net/ipv4/ipmr.c`.

```
int ipmr_get_route(struct sk_buff *skb, struct rtmsg *rtm, int nowait)
{
        int err;
        struct mfc_cache *cache;
        struct rtable *rt = (struct rtable*)skb->dst;

        read_lock(&mrt_lock);
        cache = ipmr_cache_find(rt->rt_src, rt->rt_dst);

        if (cache==NULL) {
                struct net_device *dev;
```

```
                int vif;

                if (nowait) {
                        read_unlock(&mrt_lock);
                        return -EAGAIN;
                }

                dev = skb->dev;
                if (dev == NULL || (vif = ipmr_find_vif(dev)) < 0) {
                        read_unlock(&mrt_lock);
                        return -ENODEV;
                }
                skb->nh.raw = skb_push(skb, sizeof(struct iphdr));
                skb->nh.iph->ihl = sizeof(struct iphdr)>>2;
                skb->nh.iph->saddr = rt->rt_src;
                skb->nh.iph->daddr = rt->rt_dst;
                skb->nh.iph->version = 0;
                err = ipmr_cache_unresolved(vif, skb);
                read_unlock(&mrt_lock);
                return err;
        }

        if (!nowait && (rtm->rtm_flags&RTM_F_NOTIFY))
                cache->mfc_flags |= MFC_NOTIFY;
        err = ipmr_fill_mroute(skb, cache, rtm);
        read_unlock(&mrt_lock);
        return err;
}
```

Figure 6.243 IPMR—`procfs` vif reporting: `linux/net/ipv4/ipmr.c`.

```
static int ipmr_vif_info(char *buffer, char **start, off_t offset, int length)
{
        struct vif_device *vif;
        int len=0;
        off_t pos=0;
        off_t begin=0;
        int size;
        int ct;

        len += sprintf(buffer,
                 "Interface    BytesIn PktsIn BytesOut PktsOut Flags Local Remote\n");
        pos=len;

        read_lock(&mrt_lock);
        for (ct=0;ct<maxvif;ct++)
        {
                char *name = "none";
                vif=&vif_table[ct];
                if(!VIF_EXISTS(ct))
                        continue;
                if (vif->dev)
                        name = vif->dev->name;
```

```
1611            size = sprintf(buffer+len, "%2d %-10s %81d %71d %81d %71d %05X %08X %08X\n",
1612                    ct, name, vif->bytes_in, vif->pkt_in, vif->bytes_out, vif->pkt_out,
1613                    vif->flags, vif->local, vif->remote);
1614            len+=size;
1615            pos+=size;
1616            if(pos<offset)
1617            {
1618                    len=0;
1619                    begin=pos;
1620            }
1621            if(pos>offset+length)
1622                    break;
1623        }
1624        read_unlock(&mrt_lock);
1625
1626        *start=buffer+(offset-begin);
1627        len-=(offset-begin);
1628        if(len>length)
1629            len=length;
1630        if (len<0)
1631            len = 0;
1632        return len;
1633  }
```

Figure 6.244 IPMR—procfs mfc reporting: linux/net/ipv4/ipmr.c.

```
1635  static int ipmr_mfc_info(char *buffer, char **start, off_t offset, int length)
1636  {
1637        struct mfc_cache *mfc;
1638        int len=0;
1639        off_t pos=0;
1640        off_t begin=0;
1641        int size;
1642        int ct;
1643
1644        len += sprintf(buffer,
1645                "Group   Origin  Iif    Pkts    Bytes   Wrong Oifs\n");
1646        pos=len;
1647
1648        read_lock(&mrt_lock);
1649        for (ct=0;ct<MFC_LINES;ct++)
1650        {
1651            for(mfc=mfc_cache_array[ct]; mfc; mfc=mfc->next)
1652            {
1653                int n;
1654
1655                /*
1656                 *    Interface forwarding map
1657                 */
1658                size = sprintf(buffer+len, "%081X %081X %-3d %81d %81d %81d",
1659                    (unsigned long)mfc->mfc_mcastgrp,
1660                    (unsigned long)mfc->mfc_origin,
```

```
1661                              mfc->mfc_parent,
1662                              mfc->mfc_un.res.pkt,
1663                              mfc->mfc_un.res.bytes,
1664                              mfc->mfc_un.res.wrong_if);
1665                  for(n=mfc->mfc_un.res.minvif;n<mfc->mfc_un.res.maxvif;n++)
1666                  {
1667                      if(VIF_EXISTS(n) && mfc->mfc_un.res.ttls[n] < 255)
1668                          size += sprintf(buffer+len+size, " %2d:%-3d", n, mfc->mfc_un
                                  .res.ttls[n]);
1669                  }
1670                  size += sprintf(buffer+len+size, "\n");
1671                  len+=size;
1672                  pos+=size;
1673                  if(pos<offset)
1674                  {
1675                      len=0;
1676                      begin=pos;
1677                  }
1678                  if(pos>offset+length)
1679                      goto done;
1680              }
1681          }
```

Figure 6.245 IPMR—procfs mfc reporting: `linux/net/ipv4/ipmr.c`.

```
1683          spin_lock_bh(&mfc_unres_lock);
1684          for(mfc=mfc_unres_queue; mfc; mfc=mfc->next) {
1685              size = sprintf(buffer+len, "%08lX %08lX %-3d %8ld %8ld %8ld\n",
1686                              (unsigned long)mfc->mfc_mcastgrp,
1687                              (unsigned long)mfc->mfc_origin,
1688                              -1,
1689                              (long)mfc->mfc_un.unres.unresolved.qlen,
1690                              0L, 0L);
1691              len+=size;
1692              pos+=size;
1693              if(pos<offset)
1694              {
1695                  len=0;
1696                  begin=pos;
1697              }
1698              if(pos>offset+length)
1699                  break;
1700          }
1701          spin_unlock_bh(&mfc_unres_lock);
1702
1703  done:
1704          read_unlock(&mrt_lock);
1705          *start=buffer+(offset-begin);
1706          len-=(offset-begin);
1707          if(len>length)
1708              len=length;
```

```
        if (len < 0) {
                len = 0;
        }
        return len;
}
```

6.5.6 Starting Multicast

Figure 6.246 IPMR—initialize multicast routing: `linux/net/ipv4/ipmr.c`.

```
#ifdef CONFIG_IP_PIMSM_V2
struct inet_protocol pim_protocol =
{
        pim_rcv,                /* PIM handler       */
        NULL,                   /* PIM error control */
        NULL,                   /* next              */
        IPPROTO_PIM,            /* protocol ID       */
        0,                      /* copy              */
        NULL,                   /* data              */
        "PIM"                   /* name              */
};
#endif


/*
 *      Setup for IP multicast routing
 */

void __init ip_mr_init(void)
{
        printk(KERN_INFO "Linux IP multicast router 0.06 plus PIM-SM\n");
        mrt_cachep = kmem_cache_create("ip_mrt_cache",
                                       sizeof(struct mfc_cache),
                                       0, SLAB_HWCACHE_ALIGN,
                                       NULL, NULL);
        init_timer(&ipmr_expire_timer);
        ipmr_expire_timer.function=ipmr_expire_process;
        register_netdevice_notifier(&ip_mr_notifier);
#ifdef CONFIG_PROC_FS
        proc_net_create("ip_mr_vif",0,ipmr_vif_info);
        proc_net_create("ip_mr_cache",0,ipmr_mfc_info);
#endif
}
```

6.6 NATs, Tunnels, and Other Hacks

These three (NAT, IP in IP, and GRE) are very similar—note also that the multicast tunnel support is quite homomorphic, too. Network address translation is covered in more detail in Chapter 10.

6.7 Network Address Translation

Network address translation is popular wherever one has a shortage of addresses, and is frequently also used as part of simple site security, especially in conjunction with firewalls.

Figure 6.247 Internet Protocol—simple NAT: `linux/net/ipv4/ip_nat_dumb.c`.

```
int
ip_do_nat(struct sk_buff *skb)
{
        struct rtable *rt = (struct rtable*)skb->dst;
        struct iphdr *iph = skb->nh.iph;
        u32 odaddr = iph->daddr;
        u32 osaddr = iph->saddr;
        u16     check;

        IPCB(skb)->flags |= IPSKB_TRANSLATED;

        /* Rewrite IP header */
        iph->daddr = rt->rt_dst_map;
        iph->saddr = rt->rt_src_map;
        iph->check = 0;
        iph->check = ip_fast_csum((unsigned char *)iph, iph->ihl);
```

Figure 6.248 Internet Protocol—simple NAT: `linux/net/ipv4/ip_nat_dumb.c`.

```
        /* If it is the first fragment, rewrite protocol headers */

        if (!(iph->frag_off & htons(IP_OFFSET))) {
                u16     *cksum;

                switch(iph->protocol) {
                case IPPROTO_TCP:
                        cksum = (u16*)&((struct tcphdr*)(((char*)iph) + (iph->ihl<<2)))->check;
                        if ((u8*)(cksum+1) > skb->tail)
                                goto truncated;
                        check = csum_tcpudp_magic(iph->saddr, iph->daddr, 0, 0, ~(*cksum));
                        *cksum = csum_tcpudp_magic(~osaddr, ~odaddr, 0, 0, ~check);
                        break;
                case IPPROTO_UDP:
                        cksum = (u16*)&((struct udphdr*)(((char*)iph) + (iph->ihl<<2)))->check;
                        if ((u8*)(cksum+1) > skb->tail)
                                goto truncated;
                        if ((check = *cksum) != 0) {
                                check = csum_tcpudp_magic(iph->saddr, iph->daddr, 0, 0, ~check);
                                check = csum_tcpudp_magic(~osaddr, ~odaddr, 0, 0, ~check);
                                *cksum = check ? : 0xFFFF;
                        }
                        break;
```

Figure 6.249 Internet Protocol—simple NAT: `linux/net/ipv4/ip_nat_dumb.c`.

```
            case IPPROTO_ICMP:
            {
                   struct icmphdr *icmph = (struct icmphdr*)((char*)iph + (iph->ihl<<2));
                   struct  iphdr *ciph;
                   u32 idaddr, isaddr;
                   int updated;

                   if ((icmph->type != ICMP_DEST_UNREACH) &&
                       (icmph->type != ICMP_TIME_EXCEEDED) &&
                       (icmph->type != ICMP_PARAMETERPROB))
                          break;

                   ciph = (struct iphdr *) (icmph + 1);

                   if ((u8*)(ciph+1) > skb->tail)
                          goto truncated;

                   isaddr = ciph->saddr;
                   idaddr = ciph->daddr;
                   updated = 0;

                   if (rt->rt_flags&RTCF_DNAT && ciph->saddr == odaddr) {
                          ciph->saddr = iph->daddr;
                          updated = 1;
                   }
```

Figure 6.250 Internet Protocol—simple NAT: `linux/net/ipv4/ip_nat_dumb.c`.

```
                   if (rt->rt_flags&RTCF_SNAT) {
                          if (ciph->daddr != osaddr) {
                                 struct  fib_result res;
                                 struct  rt_key key;
                                 unsigned flags = 0;

                                 key.src = ciph->daddr;
                                 key.dst = ciph->saddr;
                                 key.iif = skb->dev->ifindex;
                                 key.oif = 0;
#ifdef CONFIG_IP_ROUTE_TOS
                                 key.tos = RT_TOS(ciph->tos);
#endif
#ifdef CONFIG_IP_ROUTE_FWMARK
                                 key.fwmark = 0;
#endif
                                 /* Use fib_lookup() until we get our own
                                  * hash table of NATed hosts -- Rani
                                  */
                                 if (fib_lookup(&key, &res) == 0) {
                                        if (res.r) {
                                               ciph->daddr = fib_rules_policy(ciph->daddr, &
                                                    res, &flags);
```

```
133                                          if (ciph->daddr != idaddr)
134                                                  updated = 1;
135                                  }
136                                  fib_res_put(&res);
137                          }
138                  } else {
139                          ciph->daddr = iph->saddr;
140                          updated = 1;
141                  }
142          }
143          if (updated) {
144                  cksum = &icmph->checksum;
145                  /* Using tcpudp primitive. Why not? */
146                  check = csum_tcpudp_magic(ciph->saddr, ciph->daddr, 0, 0, ~(*cksum)
                          );
147                  *cksum = csum_tcpudp_magic(~isaddr, ~idaddr, 0, 0, ~check);
148          }
149              break;
150          }
151      default:
152              break;
153      }
154  }
155  return NET_RX_SUCCESS;
156
157 truncated:
158      /* should be return NET_RX_BAD; */
159      return -EINVAL;
160 }
```

6.8 Tunnels

6.8.1 IP in IP Tunnels

Figure 6.251 IP in IP tunnel—opening remarks: `linux/net/ipv4/ipip.c`.

```
29  /* tunnel.c: an IP tunnel driver
30
31      The purpose of this driver is to provide an IP tunnel through
32      which you can tunnel network traffic transparently across subnets.
33
34      This was written by looking at Nick Holloway's dummy driver
35      Thanks for the great code!
36
37              -Sam Lantinga (slouken@cs.ucdavis.edu) 02/01/95
38
39      Minor tweaks:
40              Cleaned up the code a little and added some pre-1.3.0 tweaks.
41              dev->hard_header/hard_header_len changed to use no headers.
42              Comments/bracketing tweaked.
43              Made the tunnels use dev->name not tunnel: when error reporting.
```

```
		Added tx_dropped stat

		-Alan Cox	(Alan.Cox@linux.org) 21 March 95

	Reworked:
		Changed to tunnel to destination gateway in addition to the
			tunnel's pointopoint address
		Almost completely rewritten
		Note: There is currently no firewall or ICMP handling done.

		-Sam Lantinga (slouken@cs.ucdavis.edu) 02/13/96

*/
```

Figure 6.252 Internet Protocol—room for improvement: `linux/net/ipv4/ipip.c`.

```

/* Things I wish I had known when writing the tunnel driver:

	When the tunnel_xmit() function is called, the skb contains the
	packet to be sent (plus a great deal of extra info), and dev
	contains the tunnel device that _we_ are.

	When we are passed a packet, we are expected to fill in the
	source address with our source IP address.

	What is the proper way to allocate, copy and free a buffer?
	After you allocate it, it is a "0 length" chunk of memory
	starting at zero. If you want to add headers to the buffer
	later, you'll have to call "skb_reserve(skb, amount)" with
	the amount of memory you want reserved. Then, you call
	"skb_put(skb, amount)" with the amount of space you want in
	the buffer. skb_put() returns a pointer to the top (#0) of
	that buffer. skb->len is set to the amount of space you have
	"allocated" with skb_put(). You can then write up to skb->len
	bytes to that buffer. If you need more, you can call skb_put()
	again with the additional amount of space you need. You can
	find out how much more space you can allocate by calling
	"skb_tailroom(skb)".
	Now, to add header space, call "skb_push(skb, header_len)".
	This creates space at the beginning of the buffer and returns
	a pointer to this new space. If later you need to strip a
	header from a buffer, call "skb_pull(skb, header_len)".
	skb_headroom() will return how much space is left at the top
	of the buffer (before the main data). Remember, this headroom
	space must be reserved before the skb_put() function is called.
	*/

/*
   This version of net/ipv4/ipip.c is cloned of net/ipv4/ip_gre.c

   For comments look at net/ipv4/ip_gre.c --ANK
 */
```

Figure 6.253 IP in IP—data: `linux/net/ipv4/ipip.c`.

```
#define HASH_SIZE 16
#define HASH(addr) ((addr^(addr>>4))&0xF)

static int ipip_fb_tunnel_init(struct net_device *dev);
static int ipip_tunnel_init(struct net_device *dev);

static struct net_device ipip_fb_tunnel_dev = {
	"tunl0", 0x0, 0x0, 0x0, 0x0, 0, 0, 0, 0, 0, NULL, ipip_fb_tunnel_init,
};

static struct ip_tunnel ipip_fb_tunnel = {
	NULL, &ipip_fb_tunnel_dev, {0, }, 0, 0, 0, 0, 0, 0, 0, {"tunl0", }
};

static struct ip_tunnel *tunnels_r_l[HASH_SIZE];
static struct ip_tunnel *tunnels_r[HASH_SIZE];
static struct ip_tunnel *tunnels_l[HASH_SIZE];
static struct ip_tunnel *tunnels_wc[1];
static struct ip_tunnel **tunnels[4] = { tunnels_wc, tunnels_l, tunnels_r, tunnels_r_l };

static rwlock_t ipip_lock = RW_LOCK_UNLOCKED;
```

Figure 6.254 IP in IP—lookup tunnel based on local and remote addresses: `linux/net/ipv4/ipip.c`.

```
static struct ip_tunnel * ipip_tunnel_lookup(u32 remote, u32 local)
{
	unsigned h0 = HASH(remote);
	unsigned h1 = HASH(local);
	struct ip_tunnel *t;

	for (t = tunnels_r_l[h0^h1]; t; t = t->next) {
		if (local == t->parms.iph.saddr &&
		    remote == t->parms.iph.daddr && (t->dev->flags&IFF_UP))
			return t;
	}
	for (t = tunnels_r[h0]; t; t = t->next) {
		if (remote == t->parms.iph.daddr && (t->dev->flags&IFF_UP))
			return t;
	}
	for (t = tunnels_l[h1]; t; t = t->next) {
		if (local == t->parms.iph.saddr && (t->dev->flags&IFF_UP))
			return t;
	}
	if ((t = tunnels_wc[0]) != NULL && (t->dev->flags&IFF_UP))
		return t;
	return NULL;
}
```

Figure 6.255 IP in IP—tunnel hash bucket: `linux/net/ipv4/ipip.c`.

```
static struct ip_tunnel **ipip_bucket(struct ip_tunnel *t)
{
        u32 remote = t->parms.iph.daddr;
        u32 local = t->parms.iph.saddr;
        unsigned h = 0;
        int prio = 0;

        if (remote) {
                prio |= 2;
                h ^= HASH(remote);
        }
        if (local) {
                prio |= 1;
                h ^= HASH(local);
        }
        return &tunnels[prio][h];
}
```

Figure 6.256 IP in IP—unlink/link tunnel hash entry: `linux/net/ipv4/ipip.c`.

```
static void ipip_tunnel_unlink(struct ip_tunnel *t)
{
        struct ip_tunnel **tp;

        for (tp = ipip_bucket(t); *tp; tp = &(*tp)->next) {
                if (t == *tp) {
                        write_lock_bh(&ipip_lock);
                        *tp = t->next;
                        write_unlock_bh(&ipip_lock);
                        break;
                }
        }
}

static void ipip_tunnel_link(struct ip_tunnel *t)
{
        struct ip_tunnel **tp = ipip_bucket(t);

        t->next = *tp;
        write_lock_bh(&ipip_lock);
        *tp = t;
        write_unlock_bh(&ipip_lock);
}
```

Figure 6.257 IP in IP—locate a tunnel: `linux/net/ipv4/ipip.c`.

```
208  struct ip_tunnel * ipip_tunnel_locate(struct ip_tunnel_parm *parms, int create)
209  {
210          u32 remote = parms->iph.daddr;
211          u32 local = parms->iph.saddr;
212          struct ip_tunnel *t, **tp, *nt;
213          struct net_device *dev;
214          unsigned h = 0;
215          int prio = 0;
216
217          if (remote) {
218                  prio |= 2;
219                  h ^= HASH(remote);
220          }
221          if (local) {
222                  prio |= 1;
223                  h ^= HASH(local);
224          }
225          for (tp = &tunnels[prio][h]; (t = *tp) != NULL; tp = &t->next) {
226                  if (local == t->parms.iph.saddr && remote == t->parms.iph.daddr)
227                          return t;
228          }
229          if (!create)
230                  return NULL;
231
232          MOD_INC_USE_COUNT;
233          dev = kmalloc(sizeof(*dev) + sizeof(*t), GFP_KERNEL);
234          if (dev == NULL) {
235                  MOD_DEC_USE_COUNT;
236                  return NULL;
237          }
```

Figure 6.258 IP in IP—locate a tunnel: `linux/net/ipv4/ipip.c`.

```
239          dev->priv = (void*)(dev+1);
240          nt = (struct ip_tunnel*)dev->priv;
241          nt->dev = dev;
242          dev->init = ipip_tunnel_init;
243          dev->features |= NETIF_F_DYNALLOC;
244          memcpy(&nt->parms, parms, sizeof(*parms));
245          strcpy(dev->name, nt->parms.name);
246          if (dev->name[0] == 0) {
247                  int i;
248                  for (i=1; i<100; i++) {
249                          sprintf(dev->name, "tunl%d", i);
250                          if (__dev_get_by_name(dev->name) == NULL)
251                                  break;
252                  }
253                  if (i==100)
254                          goto failed;
255                  memcpy(parms->name, dev->name, IFNAMSIZ);
256          }
```

```
        if (register_netdevice(dev) < 0)
                goto failed;

        dev_hold(dev);
        ipip_tunnel_link(nt);
        /* Do not decrement MOD_USE_COUNT here. */
        return nt;

failed:
        kfree(dev);
        MOD_DEC_USE_COUNT;
        return NULL;
}
```

Figure 6.259 IP in IP—uninitialize and destroy a tunnel: `linux/net/ipv4/ipip.c`.

```
static void ipip_tunnel_destructor(struct net_device *dev)
{
        if (dev != &ipip_fb_tunnel_dev) {
                MOD_DEC_USE_COUNT;
        }
}

static void ipip_tunnel_uninit(struct net_device *dev)
{
        if (dev == &ipip_fb_tunnel_dev) {
                write_lock_bh(&ipip_lock);
                tunnels_wc[0] = NULL;
                write_unlock_bh(&ipip_lock);
                dev_put(dev);
        } else {
                ipip_tunnel_unlink((struct ip_tunnel*)dev->priv);
                dev_put(dev);
        }
}
```

ICMP in IP in IP Tunnels

Figure 6.260 IP in IP—ICMP error handling: `linux/net/ipv4/ipip.c`.

```
void ipip_err(struct sk_buff *skb, unsigned char *dp, int len)
{
#ifndef I_WISH_WORLD_WERE_PERFECT

/* It is not :-( All the routers (except for Linux) return only
   8 bytes of packet payload. It means, that precise relaying of
   ICMP in the real Internet is absolutely infeasible.
 */
        struct iphdr *iph = (struct iphdr*)dp;
        int type = skb->h.icmph->type;
```

```
301        int code = skb->h.icmph->code;
302        struct ip_tunnel *t;
303
304        if (len < sizeof(struct iphdr))
305                return;
306
307        switch (type) {
308        default:
309        case ICMP_PARAMETERPROB:
310                return;
```

Figure 6.261 IP in IP—ICMP error handling: `linux/net/ipv4/ipip.c`.

```
312        case ICMP_DEST_UNREACH:
313                switch (code) {
314                case ICMP_SR_FAILED:
315                case ICMP_PORT_UNREACH:
316                        /* Impossible event. */
317                        return;
318                case ICMP_FRAG_NEEDED:
319                        /* Soft state for pmtu is maintained by IP core. */
320                        return;
321                default:
322                        /* All others are translated to HOST_UNREACH.
323                           rfc2003 contains "deep thoughts" about NET_UNREACH,
324                           I believe they are just ether pollution. --ANK
325                         */
326                        break;
327                }
328                break;
329        case ICMP_TIME_EXCEEDED:
330                if (code != ICMP_EXC_TTL)
331                        return;
332                break;
333        }
334
335        read_lock(&ipip_lock);
336        t = ipip_tunnel_lookup(iph->daddr, iph->saddr);
337        if (t == NULL || t->parms.iph.daddr == 0)
338                goto out;
339        if (t->parms.iph.ttl == 0 && type == ICMP_TIME_EXCEEDED)
340                goto out;
341
342        if (jiffies - t->err_time < IPTUNNEL_ERR_TIMEO)
343                t->err_count++;
344        else
345                t->err_count = 1;
346        t->err_time = jiffies;
347 out:
348        read_unlock(&ipip_lock);
349        return;
350 #else
```

```
351        struct iphdr *iph = (struct iphdr*)dp;
352        int hlen = iph->ihl<<2;
353        struct iphdr *eiph;
354        int type = skb->h.icmph->type;
355        int code = skb->h.icmph->code;
356        int rel_type = 0;
357        int rel_code = 0;
358        int rel_info = 0;
359        struct sk_buff *skb2;
360        struct rtable *rt;
```

Figure 6.262 IP in IP—ICMP error handling: `linux/net/ipv4/ipip.c`.

```
362        if (len < hlen + sizeof(struct iphdr))
363               return;
364        eiph = (struct iphdr*)(dp + hlen);
365
366        switch (type) {
367        default:
368               return;
369        case ICMP_PARAMETERPROB:
370               if (skb->h.icmph->un.gateway < hlen)
371                     return;
372
373               /* So... This guy found something strange INSIDE encapsulated
374                  packet. Well, he is fool, but what can we do ?
375                */
376               rel_type = ICMP_PARAMETERPROB;
377               rel_info = skb->h.icmph->un.gateway - hlen;
378               break;
379
380        case ICMP_DEST_UNREACH:
381               switch (code) {
382               case ICMP_SR_FAILED:
383               case ICMP_PORT_UNREACH:
384                     /* Impossible event. */
385                     return;
386               case ICMP_FRAG_NEEDED:
387                     /* And it is the only really necesary thing :-) */
388                     rel_info = ntohs(skb->h.icmph->un.frag.mtu);
389                     if (rel_info < hlen+68)
390                            return;
391                     rel_info -= hlen;
392                     /* BSD 4.2 MORE DOES NOT EXIST IN NATURE. */
393                     if (rel_info > ntohs(eiph->tot_len))
394                            return;
395                     break;
396               default:
397                     /* All others are translated to HOST_UNREACH.
398                        rfc2003 contains "deep thoughts" about NET_UNREACH,
399                        I believe, it is just ether pollution. --ANK
400                      */
```

```
401                         rel_type = ICMP_DEST_UNREACH;
402                         rel_code = ICMP_HOST_UNREACH;
403                         break;
404             }
405             break;
```

Figure 6.263 IP in IP—ICMP error handling: `linux/net/ipv4/ipip.c`.

```
406         case ICMP_TIME_EXCEEDED:
407             if (code != ICMP_EXC_TTL)
408                 return;
409             break;
410     }
```

Figure 6.264 IP in IP—ICMP error handling: `linux/net/ipv4/ipip.c`.

```
412         /* Prepare fake skb to feed it to icmp_send */
413         skb2 = skb_clone(skb, GFP_ATOMIC);
414         if (skb2 == NULL)
415             return;
416         dst_release(skb2->dst);
417         skb2->dst = NULL;
418         skb_pull(skb2, skb->data - (u8*)eiph);
419         skb2->nh.raw = skb2->data;
420
421         /* Try to guess incoming interface */
422         if (ip_route_output(&rt, eiph->saddr, 0, RT_TOS(eiph->tos), 0)) {
423             kfree_skb(skb2);
424             return;
425         }
426         skb2->dev = rt->u.dst.dev;
427
428         /* route "incoming" packet */
429         if (rt->rt_flags&RTCF_LOCAL) {
430             ip_rt_put(rt);
431             rt = NULL;
432             if (ip_route_output(&rt, eiph->daddr, eiph->saddr, eiph->tos, 0) ||
433                 rt->u.dst.dev->type != ARPHRD_IPGRE) {
434                 ip_rt_put(rt);
435                 kfree_skb(skb2);
436                 return;
437             }
438         } else {
439             ip_rt_put(rt);
440             if (ip_route_input(skb2, eiph->daddr, eiph->saddr, eiph->tos, skb2->dev) ||
441                 skb2->dst->dev->type != ARPHRD_IPGRE) {
442                 kfree_skb(skb2);
443                 return;
444             }
445         }
```

Figure 6.265 IP in IP—ICMP error handling: `linux/net/ipv4/ipip.c`.

```
        /* change mtu on this route */
        if (type == ICMP_DEST_UNREACH && code == ICMP_FRAG_NEEDED) {
                if (rel_info > skb2->dst->pmtu) {
                        kfree_skb(skb2);
                        return;
                }
                skb2->dst->pmtu = rel_info;
                rel_info = htonl(rel_info);
        } else if (type == ICMP_TIME_EXCEEDED) {
                struct ip_tunnel *t = (struct ip_tunnel*)skb2->dev->priv;
                if (t->parms.iph.ttl) {
                        rel_type = ICMP_DEST_UNREACH;
                        rel_code = ICMP_HOST_UNREACH;
                }
        }

        icmp_send(skb2, rel_type, rel_code, rel_info);
        kfree_skb(skb2);
        return;
#endif
}
```

Figure 6.266 IP in IP—ECN handling: `linux/net/ipv4/ipip.c`.

```
static inline void ipip_ecn_decapsulate(struct iphdr *iph, struct sk_buff *skb)
{
        if (INET_ECN_is_ce(iph->tos) &&
            INET_ECN_is_not_ce(skb->nh.iph->tos))
                IP_ECN_set_ce(iph);
}
```

Data in IP in IP Tunnels

Figure 6.267 IP in IP—receive code: `linux/net/ipv4/ipip.c`.

```
int ipip_rcv(struct sk_buff *skb, unsigned short len)
{
        struct iphdr *iph;
        struct ip_tunnel *tunnel;

        iph = skb->nh.iph;
        skb->mac.raw = skb->nh.raw;
        skb->nh.raw = skb_pull(skb, skb->h.raw - skb->data);
        memset(&(IPCB(skb)->opt), 0, sizeof(struct ip_options));
        skb->protocol = __constant_htons(ETH_P_IP);
        skb->ip_summed = 0;
        skb->pkt_type = PACKET_HOST;

```

```
        read_lock(&ipip_lock);
        if ((tunnel = ipip_tunnel_lookup(iph->saddr, iph->daddr)) != NULL) {
                tunnel->stat.rx_packets++;
                tunnel->stat.rx_bytes += skb->len;
                skb->dev = tunnel->dev;
                dst_release(skb->dst);
                skb->dst = NULL;
#ifdef CONFIG_NETFILTER
                nf_conntrack_put(skb->nfct);
                skb->nfct = NULL;
#ifdef CONFIG_NETFILTER_DEBUG
                skb->nf_debug = 0;
#endif
#endif
                ipip_ecn_decapsulate(iph, skb);
                netif_rx(skb);
                read_unlock(&ipip_lock);
                return 0;
        }
        read_unlock(&ipip_lock);

        icmp_send(skb, ICMP_DEST_UNREACH, ICMP_PROT_UNREACH, 0);
        kfree_skb(skb);
        return 0;
}
```

Figure 6.268 IP in IP—Tx wrapper for NF hook: `linux/net/ipv4/ipip.c`.

```
/* Need this wrapper because NF_HOOK takes the function address */
static inline int do_ip_send(struct sk_buff *skb)
{
        return ip_send(skb);
}
```

Figure 6.269 IP in IP—transmit code: `linux/net/ipv4/ipip.c`.

```
/*
 *      This function assumes it is being called from dev_queue_xmit()
 *      and that skb is filled properly by that function.
 */

static int ipip_tunnel_xmit(struct sk_buff *skb, struct net_device *dev)
{
        struct ip_tunnel *tunnel = (struct ip_tunnel*)dev->priv;
        struct net_device_stats *stats = &tunnel->stat;
        struct iphdr *tiph = &tunnel->parms.iph;
        u8     tos = tunnel->parms.iph.tos;
        u16    df = tiph->frag_off;
        struct rtable *rt;                      /* Route to the other host */
        struct net_device *tdev;                        /* Device to other host */
        struct iphdr *old_iph = skb->nh.iph;
```

```
536        struct iphdr *iph;                  /* Our new IP header */
537        int    max_headroom;                /* The extra header space needed */
538        u32    dst = tiph->daddr;
539        int    mtu;
540
541        if (tunnel->recursion++) {
542                tunnel->stat.collisions++;
543                goto tx_error;
544        }
545
546        if (skb->protocol != __constant_htons(ETH_P_IP))
547                goto tx_error;
548
549        if (tos&1)
550                tos = old_iph->tos;
551
552        if (!dst) {
553                /* NBMA tunnel */
554                if ((rt = (struct rtable*)skb->dst) == NULL) {
555                        tunnel->stat.tx_fifo_errors++;
556                        goto tx_error;
557                }
558                if ((dst = rt->rt_gateway) == 0)
559                        goto tx_error_icmp;
560        }
```

Figure 6.270 IP in IP—transmit code: `linux/net/ipv4/ipip.c`.

```
562        if (ip_route_output(&rt, dst, tiph->saddr, RT_TOS(tos), tunnel->parms.link)) {
563                tunnel->stat.tx_carrier_errors++;
564                goto tx_error_icmp;
565        }
566        tdev = rt->u.dst.dev;
567
568        if (tdev == dev) {
569                ip_rt_put(rt);
570                tunnel->stat.collisions++;
571                goto tx_error;
572        }
573
574        mtu = rt->u.dst.pmtu - sizeof(struct iphdr);
575        if (mtu < 68) {
576                tunnel->stat.collisions++;
577                ip_rt_put(rt);
578                goto tx_error;
579        }
580        if (skb->dst && mtu < skb->dst->pmtu)
581                skb->dst->pmtu = mtu;
582
583        df |= (old_iph->frag_off&__constant_htons(IP_DF));
584
585        if ((old_iph->frag_off&__constant_htons(IP_DF)) && mtu < ntohs(old_iph->tot_len)) {
```

```
586              icmp_send(skb, ICMP_DEST_UNREACH, ICMP_FRAG_NEEDED, htonl(mtu));
587              ip_rt_put(rt);
588              goto tx_error;
589          }
590
591      if (tunnel->err_count > 0) {
592          if (jiffies - tunnel->err_time < IPTUNNEL_ERR_TIMEO) {
593                  tunnel->err_count--;
594                  dst_link_failure(skb);
595          } else
596                  tunnel->err_count = 0;
597      }
598
599      skb->h.raw = skb->nh.raw;
```

Figure 6.271 IP in IP—transmit code: `linux/net/ipv4/ipip.c`.

```
601      /*
602       * Okay, now see if we can stuff it in the buffer as-is.
603       */
604      max_headroom = (((tdev->hard_header_len+15)&~15)+sizeof(struct iphdr));
605
606      if (skb_headroom(skb) < max_headroom || skb_cloned(skb) || skb_shared(skb)) {
607              struct sk_buff *new_skb = skb_realloc_headroom(skb, max_headroom);
608              if (!new_skb) {
609                      ip_rt_put(rt);
610                      stats->tx_dropped++;
611                      dev_kfree_skb(skb);
612                      tunnel->recursion--;
613                      return 0;
614              }
615              if (skb->sk)
616                      skb_set_owner_w(new_skb, skb->sk);
617              dev_kfree_skb(skb);
618              skb = new_skb;
619      }
620
621      skb->nh.raw = skb_push(skb, sizeof(struct iphdr));
622      memset(&(IPCB(skb)->opt), 0, sizeof(IPCB(skb)->opt));
623      dst_release(skb->dst);
624      skb->dst = &rt->u.dst;
```

Figure 6.272 IP in IP—transmit code: `linux/net/ipv4/ipip.c`.

```
626      /*
627       *      Push down and install the IPIP header.
628       */
629
630      iph             =       skb->nh.iph;
631      iph->version    =       4;
632      iph->ihl        =       sizeof(struct iphdr)>>2;
```

```
633        iph->frag_off      =      df;
634        iph->protocol      =      IPPROTO_IPIP;
635        iph->tos           =      INET_ECN_encapsulate(tos, old_iph->tos);
636        iph->daddr         =      rt->rt_dst;
637        iph->saddr         =      rt->rt_src;
638
639        if ((iph->ttl = tiph->ttl) == 0)
640                iph->ttl   =      old_iph->ttl;
641
642 #ifdef CONFIG_NETFILTER
643        nf_conntrack_put(skb->nfct);
644        skb->nfct = NULL;
645 #ifdef CONFIG_NETFILTER_DEBUG
646        skb->nf_debug = 0;
647 #endif
648 #endif
649
650        IPTUNNEL_XMIT();
651        tunnel->recursion--;
652        return 0;
653
654 tx_error_icmp:
655        dst_link_failure(skb);
656 tx_error:
657        stats->tx_errors++;
658        dev_kfree_skb(skb);
659        tunnel->recursion--;
660        return 0;
661 }
```

Management of IP in IP Tunnels

Figure 6.273 IP in IP—ioctl entry: linux/net/ipv4/ipip.c.

```
663 static int
664 ipip_tunnel_ioctl (struct net_device *dev, struct ifreq *ifr, int cmd)
665 {
666        int err = 0;
667        struct ip_tunnel_parm p;
668        struct ip_tunnel *t;
669
670        MOD_INC_USE_COUNT;
671
672        switch (cmd) {
673        case SIOCGETTUNNEL:
674                t = NULL;
675                if (dev == &ipip_fb_tunnel_dev) {
676                        if (copy_from_user(&p, ifr->ifr_ifru.ifru_data, sizeof(p))) {
677                                err = -EFAULT;
678                                break;
679                        }
680                        t = ipip_tunnel_locate(&p, 0);
```

```
681                   }
682                   if (t == NULL)
683                         t = (struct ip_tunnel*)dev->priv;
684                   memcpy(&p, &t->parms, sizeof(p));
685                   if (copy_to_user(ifr->ifr_ifru.ifru_data, &p, sizeof(p)))
686                         err = -EFAULT;
687                   break;
```

Figure 6.274 IP in IP—`ioctl` entry: `linux/net/ipv4/ipip.c`.

```
689          case SIOCADDTUNNEL:
690          case SIOCCHGTUNNEL:
691                  err = -EPERM;
692                  if (!capable(CAP_NET_ADMIN))
693                         goto done;
694
695                  err = -EFAULT;
696                  if (copy_from_user(&p, ifr->ifr_ifru.ifru_data, sizeof(p)))
697                         goto done;
698
699                  err = -EINVAL;
700                  if (p.iph.version != 4 || p.iph.protocol != IPPROTO_IPIP ||
701                     p.iph.ihl != 5 || (p.iph.frag_off&__constant_htons(~IP_DF)))
702                         goto done;
703                  if (p.iph.ttl)
704                         p.iph.frag_off |= __constant_htons(IP_DF);
705
706                  t = ipip_tunnel_locate(&p, cmd == SIOCADDTUNNEL);
707
708                  if (dev != &ipip_fb_tunnel_dev && cmd == SIOCCHGTUNNEL &&
709                      t != &ipip_fb_tunnel) {
710                      if (t != NULL) {
711                              if (t->dev != dev) {
712                                    err = -EEXIST;
713                                    break;
714                              }
715                      } else {
716                              if (((dev->flags&IFF_POINTOPOINT) && !p.iph.daddr) ||
717                                 (!(dev->flags&IFF_POINTOPOINT) && p.iph.daddr)) {
718                                    err = -EINVAL;
719                                    break;
720                              }
721                              t = (struct ip_tunnel*)dev->priv;
722                              ipip_tunnel_unlink(t);
723                              t->parms.iph.saddr = p.iph.saddr;
724                              t->parms.iph.daddr = p.iph.daddr;
725                              memcpy(dev->dev_addr, &p.iph.saddr, 4);
726                              memcpy(dev->broadcast, &p.iph.daddr, 4);
727                              ipip_tunnel_link(t);
728                              netdev_state_change(dev);
729                      }
730                  }
```

Figure 6.275 IP in IP—`ioctl` entry: `linux/net/ipv4/ipip.c`.

```

		if (t) {
			err = 0;
			if (cmd == SIOCCHGTUNNEL) {
				t->parms.iph.ttl = p.iph.ttl;
				t->parms.iph.tos = p.iph.tos;
				t->parms.iph.frag_off = p.iph.frag_off;
			}
			if (copy_to_user(ifr->ifr_ifru.ifru_data, &t->parms, sizeof(p)))
				err = -EFAULT;
		} else
			err = (cmd == SIOCADDTUNNEL ? -ENOBUFS : -ENOENT);
		break;

	case SIOCDELTUNNEL:
		err = -EPERM;
		if (!capable(CAP_NET_ADMIN))
			goto done;

		if (dev == &ipip_fb_tunnel_dev) {
			err = -EFAULT;
			if (copy_from_user(&p, ifr->ifr_ifru.ifru_data, sizeof(p)))
				goto done;
			err = -ENOENT;
			if ((t = ipip_tunnel_locate(&p, 0)) == NULL)
				goto done;
			err = -EPERM;
			if (t == &ipip_fb_tunnel)
				goto done;
		}
		err = unregister_netdevice(dev);
		break;

	default:
		err = -EINVAL;
	}

done:
	MOD_DEC_USE_COUNT;
	return err;
}
```

Figure 6.276 IP in IP—stats: `linux/net/ipv4/ipip.c`.

```
static struct net_device_stats *ipip_tunnel_get_stats(struct net_device *dev)
{
	return &(((struct ip_tunnel*)dev->priv)->stat);
}

static int ipip_tunnel_change_mtu(struct net_device *dev, int new_mtu)
```

```
{
        if (new_mtu < 68 || new_mtu > 0xFFF8 - sizeof(struct iphdr))
                return -EINVAL;
        dev->mtu = new_mtu;
        return 0;
}
```

Figure 6.277 IP in IP—general initialization: `linux/net/ipv4/ipip.c`.

```
static void ipip_tunnel_init_gen(struct net_device *dev)
{
        struct ip_tunnel *t = (struct ip_tunnel*)dev->priv;

        dev->uninit             = ipip_tunnel_uninit;
        dev->destructor         = ipip_tunnel_destructor;
        dev->hard_start_xmit    = ipip_tunnel_xmit;
        dev->get_stats          = ipip_tunnel_get_stats;
        dev->do_ioctl           = ipip_tunnel_ioctl;
        dev->change_mtu         = ipip_tunnel_change_mtu;

        dev_init_buffers(dev);

        dev->type               = ARPHRD_TUNNEL;
        dev->hard_header_len    = LL_MAX_HEADER + sizeof(struct iphdr);
        dev->mtu                = 1500 - sizeof(struct iphdr);
        dev->flags              = IFF_NOARP;
        dev->iflink             = 0;
        dev->addr_len           = 4;
        memcpy(dev->dev_addr, &t->parms.iph.saddr, 4);
        memcpy(dev->broadcast, &t->parms.iph.daddr, 4);
}
```

Figure 6.278 IP in IP—initialize a tunnel: `linux/net/ipv4/ipip.c`.

```
static int ipip_tunnel_init(struct net_device *dev)
{
        struct net_device *tdev = NULL;
        struct ip_tunnel *tunnel;
        struct iphdr *iph;

        tunnel = (struct ip_tunnel*)dev->priv;
        iph = &tunnel->parms.iph;

        ipip_tunnel_init_gen(dev);

        if (iph->daddr) {
                struct rtable *rt;
                if (!ip_route_output(&rt, iph->daddr, iph->saddr, RT_TOS(iph->tos), tunnel->parms.
                        link)) {
                        tdev = rt->u.dst.dev;
```

```
                ip_rt_put(rt);
            }
            dev->flags |= IFF_POINTOPOINT;
        }

        if (!tdev && tunnel->parms.link)
            tdev = __dev_get_by_index(tunnel->parms.link);

        if (tdev) {
            dev->hard_header_len = tdev->hard_header_len + sizeof(struct iphdr);
            dev->mtu = tdev->mtu - sizeof(struct iphdr);
        }
        dev->iflink = tunnel->parms.link;

        return 0;
}
```

Figure 6.279 IP in IP—module setup/teardown: `linux/net/ipv4/ipip.c`.

```
#ifdef MODULE
static int ipip_fb_tunnel_open(struct net_device *dev)
{
        MOD_INC_USE_COUNT;
        return 0;
}

static int ipip_fb_tunnel_close(struct net_device *dev)
{
        MOD_DEC_USE_COUNT;
        return 0;
}
#endif
```

Figure 6.280 IP in IP—module init: `linux/net/ipv4/ipip.c`.

```
int __init ipip_fb_tunnel_init(struct net_device *dev)
{
        struct iphdr *iph;

        ipip_tunnel_init_gen(dev);
#ifdef MODULE
        dev->open               = ipip_fb_tunnel_open;
        dev->stop               = ipip_fb_tunnel_close;
#endif

        iph = &ipip_fb_tunnel.parms.iph;
        iph->version            = 4;
        iph->protocol           = IPPROTO_IPIP;
        iph->ihl                = 5;

```

```
        dev_hold(dev);
        tunnels_wc[0]         = &ipip_fb_tunnel;
        return 0;
}

static struct inet_protocol ipip_protocol = {
  ipip_rcv,            /* IPIP handler     */
  ipip_err,            /* TUNNEL error control */
  0,                   /* next             */
  IPPROTO_IPIP,        /* protocol ID      */
  0,                   /* copy             */
  NULL,                /* data             */
  "IPIP"               /* name             */
};
```

6.8.2 GRE Tunnels

Figure 6.281 GRE tunnels—opening salvo: `linux/net/ipv4/ip_gre.c`.

```
   Problems & solutions
   --------------------

   1. The most important issue is detecting local dead loops.
   They would cause complete host lockup in transmit, which
   would be "resolved" by stack overflow or, if queueing is enabled,
   with infinite looping in net_bh.

   We cannot track such dead loops during route installation,
   it is infeasible task. The most general solutions would be
   to keep skb->encapsulation counter (sort of local ttl),
   and silently drop packet when it expires. It is the best
   solution, but it supposes maintaing new variable in ALL
   skb, even if no tunneling is used.

   Current solution: t->recursion lock breaks dead loops. It looks
   like dev->tbusy flag, but I preferred new variable, because
   the semantics is different. One day, when hard_start_xmit
   will be multithreaded we will have to use skb->encapsulation.
```

Figure 6.282 GRE tunnels—opening salvo: `linux/net/ipv4/ip_gre.c`.

```
   2. Networking dead loops would not kill routers, but would really
   kill network. IP hop limit plays role of "t->recursion" in this case,
   if we copy it from packet being encapsulated to upper header.
   It is very good solution, but it introduces two problems:

   - Routing protocols, using packets with ttl=1 (OSPF, RIP2),
     do not work over tunnels.
```

```
   - traceroute does not work. I planned to relay ICMP from tunnel,
     so that this problem would be solved and traceroute output
     would even more informative. This idea appeared to be wrong:
     only Linux complies to rfc1812 now (yes, guys, Linux is the only
     true router now :-)), all routers (at least, in neighbourhood of mine)
     return only 8 bytes of payload. It is the end.

   Hence, if we want that OSPF worked or traceroute said something reasonable,
   we should search for another solution.

   One of them is to parse packet trying to detect inner encapsulation
   made by our node. It is difficult or even impossible, especially,
   taking into account fragmentation. TO be short, tt is not solution at all.

   Current solution: The solution was UNEXPECTEDLY SIMPLE.
   We force DF flag on tunnels with preconfigured hop limit,
   that is ALL. :-) Well, it does not remove the problem completely,
   but exponential growth of network traffic is changed to linear
   (branches, that exceed pmtu are pruned) and tunnel mtu
   fastly degrades to value <68, where looping stops.
   Yes, it is not good if there exists a router in the loop,
   which does not force DF, even when encapsulating packets have DF set.
   But it is not our problem! Nobody could accuse us, we made
   all that we could make. Even if it is your gated who injected
   fatal route to network, even if it were you who configured
   fatal static route: you are innocent. :-)



   3. Really, ipv4/ipip.c, ipv4/ip_gre.c and ipv6/sit.c contain
   practically identical code. It would be good to glue them
   together, but it is not very evident, how to make them modular.
   sit is integral part of IPv6, ipip and gre are naturally modular.
   We could extract common parts (hash table, ioctl etc)
   to a separate module (ip_tunnel.c).
```

Figure 6.283 GRE tunnel data: `linux/net/ipv4/ip_gre.c`.

```
static int ipgre_tunnel_init(struct net_device *dev);

/* Fallback tunnel: no source, no destination, no key, no options */

static int ipgre_fb_tunnel_init(struct net_device *dev);

static struct net_device ipgre_fb_tunnel_dev = {
        "gre0", 0x0, 0x0, 0x0, 0x0, 0, 0, 0, 0, 0, NULL, ipgre_fb_tunnel_init,
};

static struct ip_tunnel ipgre_fb_tunnel = {
        NULL, &ipgre_fb_tunnel_dev, {0, }, 0, 0, 0, 0, 0, 0, 0, {"gre0", }
};

```

```
/* Tunnel hash table */

/*
   4 hash tables:

   3: (remote,local)
   2: (remote,*)
   1: (*,local)
   0: (*,*)

   We require exact key match i.e. if a key is present in packet
   it will match only tunnel with the same key; if it is not present,
   it will match only keyless tunnel.

   All keysless packets, if not matched configured keyless tunnels
   will match fallback tunnel.
 */

#define HASH_SIZE 16
#define HASH(addr) ((addr^(addr>>4))&0xF)

static struct ip_tunnel *tunnels[4][HASH_SIZE];

#define tunnels_r_l   (tunnels[3])
#define tunnels_r     (tunnels[2])
#define tunnels_l     (tunnels[1])
#define tunnels_wc    (tunnels[0])

static rwlock_t ipgre_lock = RW_LOCK_UNLOCKED;
```

Figure 6.284 GRE tunnels—hash fucntion: `linux/net/ipv4/ip_gre.c`.

```
/* Given src, dst and key, find approriate for input tunnel. */

static struct ip_tunnel * ipgre_tunnel_lookup(u32 remote, u32 local, u32 key)
{
        unsigned h0 = HASH(remote);
        unsigned h1 = HASH(key);
        struct ip_tunnel *t;

        for (t = tunnels_r_l[h0^h1]; t; t = t->next) {
                if (local == t->parms.iph.saddr && remote == t->parms.iph.daddr) {
                        if (t->parms.i_key == key && (t->dev->flags&IFF_UP))
                                return t;
                }
        }
        for (t = tunnels_r[h0^h1]; t; t = t->next) {
                if (remote == t->parms.iph.daddr) {
                        if (t->parms.i_key == key && (t->dev->flags&IFF_UP))
                                return t;
                }
        }
```

```
        for (t = tunnels_l[h1]; t; t = t->next) {
                if (local == t->parms.iph.saddr ||
                    (local == t->parms.iph.daddr && MULTICAST(local))) {
                        if (t->parms.i_key == key && (t->dev->flags&IFF_UP))
                                return t;
                }
        }
        for (t = tunnels_wc[h1]; t; t = t->next) {
                if (t->parms.i_key == key && (t->dev->flags&IFF_UP))
                        return t;
        }
        if (ipgre_fb_tunnel_dev.flags&IFF_UP)
                return &ipgre_fb_tunnel;
        return NULL;
}
```

Figure 6.285 GRE tunnels—hash bucket: `linux/net/ipv4/ip_gre.c`.

```
static struct ip_tunnel **ipgre_bucket(struct ip_tunnel *t)
{
        u32 remote = t->parms.iph.daddr;
        u32 local = t->parms.iph.saddr;
        u32 key = t->parms.i_key;
        unsigned h = HASH(key);
        int prio = 0;

        if (local)
                prio |= 1;
        if (remote && !MULTICAST(remote)) {
                prio |= 2;
                h ^= HASH(remote);
        }

        return &tunnels[prio][h];
}
```

Figure 6.286 GRE tunnels—link/unlink hash entry: `linux/net/ipv4/ip_gre.c`.

```
static void ipgre_tunnel_link(struct ip_tunnel *t)
{
        struct ip_tunnel **tp = ipgre_bucket(t);

        t->next = *tp;
        write_lock_bh(&ipgre_lock);
        *tp = t;
        write_unlock_bh(&ipgre_lock);
}

static void ipgre_tunnel_unlink(struct ip_tunnel *t)
{
        struct ip_tunnel **tp;
```

```
227
228            for (tp = ipgre_bucket(t); *tp; tp = &(*tp)->next) {
229                    if (t == *tp) {
230                            write_lock_bh(&ipgre_lock);
231                            *tp = t->next;
232                            write_unlock_bh(&ipgre_lock);
233                            break;
234                    }
235            }
236    }
```

Figure 6.287 GRE tunnels—locate hash entry: `linux/net/ipv4/ip_gre.c`.

```
238    static struct ip_tunnel * ipgre_tunnel_locate(struct ip_tunnel_parm *parms, int create)
239    {
240            u32 remote = parms->iph.daddr;
241            u32 local = parms->iph.saddr;
242            u32 key = parms->i_key;
243            struct ip_tunnel *t, **tp, *nt;
244            struct net_device *dev;
245            unsigned h = HASH(key);
246            int prio = 0;
247
248            if (local)
249                    prio |= 1;
250            if (remote && !MULTICAST(remote)) {
251                    prio |= 2;
252                    h ^= HASH(remote);
253            }
254            for (tp = &tunnels[prio][h]; (t = *tp) != NULL; tp = &t->next) {
255                    if (local == t->parms.iph.saddr && remote == t->parms.iph.daddr) {
256                            if (key == t->parms.i_key)
257                                    return t;
258                    }
259            }
260            if (!create)
261                    return NULL;
262
263            MOD_INC_USE_COUNT;
```

Figure 6.288 GRE tunnels—uninitialize and destroy entry: `linux/net/ipv4/ip_gre.c`.

```
265            if (dev == NULL) {
266                    MOD_DEC_USE_COUNT;
267                    return NULL;
268            }
269            memset(dev, 0, sizeof(*dev) + sizeof(*t));
270            dev->priv = (void*)(dev+1);
271            nt = (struct ip_tunnel*)dev->priv;
272            nt->dev = dev;
273            dev->init = ipgre_tunnel_init;
```

```
274              dev->features |= NETIF_F_DYNALLOC;
275          memcpy(&nt->parms, parms, sizeof(*parms));
276          strcpy(dev->name, nt->parms.name);
277          if (dev->name[0] == 0) {
278                  int i;
279                  for (i=1; i<100; i++) {
280                          sprintf(dev->name, "gre%d", i);
281                          if (__dev_get_by_name(dev->name) == NULL)
282                                  break;
283                  }
284                  if (i==100)
285                          goto failed;
286                  memcpy(parms->name, dev->name, IFNAMSIZ);
287          }
288          if (register_netdevice(dev) < 0)
289                  goto failed;
290
291          dev_hold(dev);
292          ipgre_tunnel_link(nt);
293          /* Do not decrement MOD_USE_COUNT here. */
294          return nt;
295
296  failed:
297          kfree(dev);
298          MOD_DEC_USE_COUNT;
299          return NULL;
300  }
301
302  static void ipgre_tunnel_destructor(struct net_device *dev)
303  {
304          if (dev != &ipgre_fb_tunnel_dev) {
305                  MOD_DEC_USE_COUNT;
306          }
307  }
308
309  static void ipgre_tunnel_uninit(struct net_device *dev)
310  {
311          ipgre_tunnel_unlink((struct ip_tunnel*)dev->priv);
312          dev_put(dev);
313  }
```

Receive Data in GRE Tunnels

Figure 6.289 GRE tunnels—receive case: `linux/net/ipv4/ip_gre.c`.

```
562  int ipgre_rcv(struct sk_buff *skb, unsigned short len)
563  {
564          struct iphdr *iph = skb->nh.iph;
565          u8      *h = skb->h.raw;
566          u16     flags = *(u16*)h;
567          u16     csum = 0;
568          u32     key = 0;
```

```
        u32   seqno = 0;
        struct ip_tunnel *tunnel;
        int   offset = 4;

        if (flags&(GRE_CSUM|GRE_KEY|GRE_ROUTING|GRE_SEQ|GRE_VERSION)) {
                /* - Version must be 0.
                   - We do not support routing headers.
                 */
                if (flags&(GRE_VERSION|GRE_ROUTING))
                        goto drop_nolock;

                if (flags&GRE_CSUM) {
                        csum = ip_compute_csum(h, len);
                        offset += 4;
                }
                if (flags&GRE_KEY) {
                        key = *(u32*)(h + offset);
                        offset += 4;
                }
                if (flags&GRE_SEQ) {
                        seqno = ntohl(*(u32*)(h + offset));
                        offset += 4;
                }
        }

        read_lock(&ipgre_lock);
```

Figure 6.290 GRE tunnels—receive case: `linux/net/ipv4/ip_gre.c`.

```
        if ((tunnel = ipgre_tunnel_lookup(iph->saddr, iph->daddr, key)) != NULL) {
                skb->mac.raw = skb->nh.raw;
                skb->nh.raw = skb_pull(skb, h + offset - skb->data);
                memset(&(IPCB(skb)->opt), 0, sizeof(struct ip_options));
                skb->ip_summed = 0;
                skb->protocol = *(u16*)(h + 2);
                skb->pkt_type = PACKET_HOST;
#ifdef CONFIG_NET_IPGRE_BROADCAST
                if (MULTICAST(iph->daddr)) {
                        /* Looped back packet, drop it! */
                        if (((struct rtable*)skb->dst)->key.iif == 0)
                                goto drop;
                        tunnel->stat.multicast++;
                        skb->pkt_type = PACKET_BROADCAST;
                }
#endif

                if (((flags&GRE_CSUM) && csum) ||
                    (!(flags&GRE_CSUM) && tunnel->parms.i_flags&GRE_CSUM)) {
                        tunnel->stat.rx_crc_errors++;
                        tunnel->stat.rx_errors++;
                        goto drop;
                }
```

Figure 6.291 GRE tunnels—receive case: `linux/net/ipv4/ip_gre.c`.

```
                if (tunnel->parms.i_flags&GRE_SEQ) {
                        if (!(flags&GRE_SEQ) ||
                            (tunnel->i_seqno && (s32)(seqno - tunnel->i_seqno) < 0)) {
                                tunnel->stat.rx_fifo_errors++;
                                tunnel->stat.rx_errors++;
                                goto drop;
                        }
                        tunnel->i_seqno = seqno + 1;
                }
                tunnel->stat.rx_packets++;
                tunnel->stat.rx_bytes += skb->len;
                skb->dev = tunnel->dev;
                dst_release(skb->dst);
                skb->dst = NULL;
#ifdef CONFIG_NETFILTER
                nf_conntrack_put(skb->nfct);
                skb->nfct = NULL;
#ifdef CONFIG_NETFILTER_DEBUG
                skb->nf_debug = 0;
#endif
#endif
                ipgre_ecn_decapsulate(iph, skb);
                netif_rx(skb);
                read_unlock(&ipgre_lock);
                return(0);
        }
        icmp_send(skb, ICMP_DEST_UNREACH, ICMP_PROT_UNREACH, 0);

drop:
        read_unlock(&ipgre_lock);
drop_nolock:
        kfree_skb(skb);
        return(0);
}
```

Figure 6.292 GRE tunnels—Tx wrapper: `linux/net/ipv4/ip_gre.c`.

```
/* Need this wrapper because NF_HOOK takes the function address */
static inline int do_ip_send(struct sk_buff *skb)
{
        return ip_send(skb);
}
```

Transmit Data in GRE Tunnels

Figure 6.293 GRE tunnels—transmit case: `linux/net/ipv4/ip_gre.c`.

```
static int ipgre_tunnel_xmit(struct sk_buff *skb, struct net_device *dev)
{
        struct ip_tunnel *tunnel = (struct ip_tunnel*)dev->priv;
        struct net_device_stats *stats = &tunnel->stat;
        struct iphdr *old_iph = skb->nh.iph;
        struct iphdr *tiph;
        u8     tos;
        u16    df;
        struct rtable *rt;                      /* Route to the other host */
        struct net_device *tdev;                        /* Device to other host */
        struct iphdr *iph;                      /* Our new IP header */
        int    max_headroom;                    /* The extra header space needed */
        int    gre_hlen;
        u32    dst;
        int    mtu;

        if (tunnel->recursion++) {
                tunnel->stat.collisions++;
                goto tx_error;
        }

        if (dev->hard_header) {
                gre_hlen = 0;
                tiph = (struct iphdr*)skb->data;
        } else {
                gre_hlen = tunnel->hlen;
                tiph = &tunnel->parms.iph;
        }

        if ((dst = tiph->daddr) == 0) {
                /* NBMA tunnel */

                if (skb->dst == NULL) {
                        tunnel->stat.tx_fifo_errors++;
                        goto tx_error;
                }
```

Figure 6.294 GRE tunnels—transmit case: `linux/net/ipv4/ip_gre.c`.

```
                if (skb->protocol == __constant_htons(ETH_P_IP)) {
                        rt = (struct rtable*)skb->dst;
                        if ((dst = rt->rt_gateway) == 0)
                                goto tx_error_icmp;
                }
#ifdef CONFIG_IPV6
                else if (skb->protocol == __constant_htons(ETH_P_IPV6)) {
                        struct in6_addr *addr6;
                        int addr_type;
```

```
705                         struct neighbour *neigh = skb->dst->neighbour;
706
707                         if (neigh == NULL)
708                                 goto tx_error;
709
710                         addr6 = (struct in6_addr*)&neigh->primary_key;
711                         addr_type = ipv6_addr_type(addr6);
712
713                         if (addr_type == IPV6_ADDR_ANY) {
714                                 addr6 = &skb->nh.ipv6h->daddr;
715                                 addr_type = ipv6_addr_type(addr6);
716                         }
717
718                         if ((addr_type & IPV6_ADDR_COMPATv4) == 0)
719                                 goto tx_error_icmp;
720
721                         dst = addr6->s6_addr32[3];
722                 }
723 #endif
724         else
725                 goto tx_error;
726         }
727
728         tos = tiph->tos;
729         if (tos&1) {
730                 if (skb->protocol == __constant_htons(ETH_P_IP))
731                         tos = old_iph->tos;
732                 tos &= ~1;
733         }
734
735         if (ip_route_output(&rt, dst, tiph->saddr, RT_TOS(tos), tunnel->parms.link)) {
736                 tunnel->stat.tx_carrier_errors++;
737                 goto tx_error;
738         }
739         tdev = rt->u.dst.dev;
740
741         if (tdev == dev) {
742                 ip_rt_put(rt);
743                 tunnel->stat.collisions++;
744                 goto tx_error;
745         }
```

Figure 6.295 GRE tunnels—transmit case: `linux/net/ipv4/ip_gre.c`.

```
747         df = tiph->frag_off;
748         mtu = rt->u.dst.pmtu - tunnel->hlen;
749
750         if (skb->protocol == __constant_htons(ETH_P_IP)) {
751                 if (skb->dst && mtu < skb->dst->pmtu && mtu >= 68)
752                         skb->dst->pmtu = mtu;
753
754                 df |= (old_iph->frag_off&__constant_htons(IP_DF));
```

```
755
756                 if ((old_iph->frag_off&__constant_htons(IP_DF)) &&
757                     mtu < ntohs(old_iph->tot_len)) {
758                         icmp_send(skb, ICMP_DEST_UNREACH, ICMP_FRAG_NEEDED, htonl(mtu));
759                         ip_rt_put(rt);
760                         goto tx_error;
761                 }
762         }
763 #ifdef CONFIG_IPV6
764         else if (skb->protocol == __constant_htons(ETH_P_IPV6)) {
765                 struct rt6_info *rt6 = (struct rt6_info*)skb->dst;
766
767                 if (rt6 && mtu < rt6->u.dst.pmtu && mtu >= IPV6_MIN_MTU) {
768                         if ((tunnel->parms.iph.daddr && !MULTICAST(tunnel->parms.iph.daddr)) ||
769                             rt6->rt6i_dst.plen == 128) {
770                                 rt6->rt6i_flags |= RTF_MODIFIED;
771                                 skb->dst->pmtu = mtu;
772                         }
773                 }
774
775                 if (mtu >= IPV6_MIN_MTU && mtu < skb->len - tunnel->hlen + gre_hlen) {
776                         icmpv6_send(skb, ICMPV6_PKT_TOOBIG, 0, mtu, dev);
777                         ip_rt_put(rt);
778                         goto tx_error;
779                 }
780         }
781 #endif
```

Figure 6.296 GRE tunnels—transmit case: `linux/net/ipv4/ip_gre.c`.

```
783         if (tunnel->err_count > 0) {
784                 if (jiffies - tunnel->err_time < IPTUNNEL_ERR_TIMEO) {
785                         tunnel->err_count--;
786
787                         dst_link_failure(skb);
788                 } else
789                         tunnel->err_count = 0;
790         }
791
792         skb->h.raw = skb->nh.raw;
793
794         max_headroom = ((tdev->hard_header_len+15)&~15)+ gre_hlen;
795
796         if (skb_headroom(skb) < max_headroom || skb_cloned(skb) || skb_shared(skb)) {
797                 struct sk_buff *new_skb = skb_realloc_headroom(skb, max_headroom);
798                 if (!new_skb) {
799                         ip_rt_put(rt);
800                         stats->tx_dropped++;
801                         dev_kfree_skb(skb);
802                         tunnel->recursion--;
803                         return 0;
804                 }
```

```
		if (skb->sk)
			skb_set_owner_w(new_skb, skb->sk);
		dev_kfree_skb(skb);
		skb = new_skb;
	}

	skb->nh.raw = skb_push(skb, gre_hlen);
	memset(&(IPCB(skb)->opt), 0, sizeof(IPCB(skb)->opt));
	dst_release(skb->dst);
	skb->dst = &rt->u.dst;
```

Figure 6.297 GRE tunnels—transmit case: `linux/net/ipv4/ip_gre.c`.

```
	/*
	 *	Push down and install the IPIP header.
	 */

	iph			=	skb->nh.iph;
	iph->version		=	4;
	iph->ihl		=	sizeof(struct iphdr) >> 2;
	iph->frag_off		=	df;
	iph->protocol		=	IPPROTO_GRE;
	iph->tos		=	ipgre_ecn_encapsulate(tos, old_iph, skb);
	iph->daddr		=	rt->rt_dst;
	iph->saddr		=	rt->rt_src;

	if ((iph->ttl = tiph->ttl) == 0) {
		if (skb->protocol == __constant_htons(ETH_P_IP))
			iph->ttl = old_iph->ttl;
#ifdef CONFIG_IPV6
		else if (skb->protocol == __constant_htons(ETH_P_IPV6))
			iph->ttl = ((struct ipv6hdr*)old_iph)->hop_limit;
#endif
		else
			iph->ttl = sysctl_ip_default_ttl;
	}

	((u16*)(iph+1))[0] = tunnel->parms.o_flags;
	((u16*)(iph+1))[1] = skb->protocol;
```

Figure 6.298 GRE tunnels—transmit case: `linux/net/ipv4/ip_gre.c`.

```
	if (tunnel->parms.o_flags&(GRE_KEY|GRE_CSUM|GRE_SEQ)) {
		u32 *ptr = (u32*)(((u8*)iph) + tunnel->hlen - 4);

		if (tunnel->parms.o_flags&GRE_SEQ) {
			++tunnel->o_seqno;
			*ptr = htonl(tunnel->o_seqno);
			ptr--;
```

```
            }
            if (tunnel->parms.o_flags&GRE_KEY) {
                *ptr = tunnel->parms.o_key;
                ptr--;
            }
            if (tunnel->parms.o_flags&GRE_CSUM) {
                *ptr = 0;
                *(__u16*)ptr = ip_compute_csum((void*)(iph+1), skb->len - sizeof(struct
                    iphdr));
            }
        }

#ifdef CONFIG_NETFILTER
        nf_conntrack_put(skb->nfct);
        skb->nfct = NULL;
#ifdef CONFIG_NETFILTER_DEBUG
        skb->nf_debug = 0;
#endif
#endif

        IPTUNNEL_XMIT();
        tunnel->recursion--;
        return 0;

tx_error_icmp:
        dst_link_failure(skb);

tx_error:
        stats->tx_errors++;
        dev_kfree_skb(skb);
        tunnel->recursion--;
        return 0;
}
```

ICMP in GRE Tunnels

Care needs to be taken in mapping the causes of ICMP messages when they emanate within or outside a tunnel.

Figure 6.299 GRE tunnels—error/ICMP cases: `linux/net/ipv4/ip_gre.c`.

```
void ipgre_err(struct sk_buff *skb, unsigned char *dp, int len)
{
#ifndef I_WISH_WORLD_WERE_PERFECT

/* It is not :-( All the routers (except for Linux) return only
   8 bytes of packet payload. It means, that precise relaying of
   ICMP in the real Internet is absolutely infeasible.

   Moreover, Cisco "wise men" put GRE key to the third word
```

```
325          in GRE header. It makes impossible maintaining even soft state for keyed
326          GRE tunnels with enabled checksum. Tell them "thank you".
327
328          Well, I wonder, rfc1812 was written by Cisco employee,
329          what the hell these idiots break standrads established
330          by themself???
331      */
332
333              struct iphdr *iph = (struct iphdr*)dp;
334              u16        *p = (u16*)(dp+(iph->ihl<<2));
335              int grehlen = (iph->ihl<<2) + 4;
336              int type = skb->h.icmph->type;
337              int code = skb->h.icmph->code;
338              struct ip_tunnel *t;
339              u16 flags;
340
341              flags = p[0];
342              if (flags&(GRE_CSUM|GRE_KEY|GRE_SEQ|GRE_ROUTING|GRE_VERSION)) {
343                      if (flags&(GRE_VERSION|GRE_ROUTING))
344                              return;
345                      if (flags&GRE_KEY) {
346                              grehlen += 4;
347                              if (flags&GRE_CSUM)
348                                      grehlen += 4;
349                      }
350              }
351
352              /* If only 8 bytes returned, keyed message will be dropped here */
353              if (len < grehlen)
354                      return;
```

Figure 6.300 GRE tunnels—error/ICMP cases: `linux/net/ipv4/ip_gre.c`.

```
356              switch (type) {
357              default:
358              case ICMP_PARAMETERPROB:
359                      return;
360
361              case ICMP_DEST_UNREACH:
362                      switch (code) {
363                      case ICMP_SR_FAILED:
364                      case ICMP_PORT_UNREACH:
365                              /* Impossible event. */
366                              return;
367                      case ICMP_FRAG_NEEDED:
368                              /* Soft state for pmtu is maintained by IP core. */
369                              return;
370                      default:
371                              /* All others are translated to HOST_UNREACH.
372                                 rfc2003 contains "deep thoughts" about NET_UNREACH,
373                                 I believe they are just ether pollution. --ANK
374                               */
```

```
375                        break;
376                }
377            break;
378        case ICMP_TIME_EXCEEDED:
379                if (code != ICMP_EXC_TTL)
380                    return;
381            break;
382        }
```

Figure 6.301 GRE tunnels—error/ICMP cases: `linux/net/ipv4/ip_gre.c`.

```
384        read_lock(&ipgre_lock);
385        t = ipgre_tunnel_lookup(iph->daddr, iph->saddr, (flags&GRE_KEY) ? *(((u32*)p) + (grehlen
               >>2) - 1) : 0);
386        if (t == NULL || t->parms.iph.daddr == 0 || MULTICAST(t->parms.iph.daddr))
387            goto out;
388
389        if (t->parms.iph.ttl == 0 && type == ICMP_TIME_EXCEEDED)
390            goto out;
391
392        if (jiffies - t->err_time < IPTUNNEL_ERR_TIMEO)
393            t->err_count++;
394        else
395            t->err_count = 1;
396        t->err_time = jiffies;
397 out:
398        read_unlock(&ipgre_lock);
399        return;
400 #else
401        struct iphdr *iph = (struct iphdr*)dp;
402        struct iphdr *eiph;
403        u16       *p = (u16*)(dp+(iph->ihl<<2));
404        int type = skb->h.icmph->type;
405        int code = skb->h.icmph->code;
406        int rel_type = 0;
407        int rel_code = 0;
408        int rel_info = 0;
409        u16 flags;
410        int grehlen = (iph->ihl<<2) + 4;
411        struct sk_buff *skb2;
412        struct rtable *rt;
```

Figure 6.302 GRE tunnels—error/ICMP cases: `linux/net/ipv4/ip_gre.c`.

```
414        if (p[1] != __constant_htons(ETH_P_IP))
415            return;
416
417        flags = p[0];
418        if (flags&(GRE_CSUM|GRE_KEY|GRE_SEQ|GRE_ROUTING|GRE_VERSION)) {
419            if (flags&(GRE_VERSION|GRE_ROUTING))
```

```
420              return;
421          if (flags&GRE_CSUM)
422                  grehlen += 4;
423          if (flags&GRE_KEY)
424                  grehlen += 4;
425          if (flags&GRE_SEQ)
426                  grehlen += 4;
427      }
428      if (len < grehlen + sizeof(struct iphdr))
429              return;
430      eiph = (struct iphdr*)(dp + grehlen);
```

Figure 6.303 GRE tunnels—error/ICMP cases: `linux/net/ipv4/ip_gre.c`.

```
432          switch (type) {
433          default:
434                  return;
435          case ICMP_PARAMETERPROB:
436                  if (skb->h.icmph->un.gateway < (iph->ihl<<2))
437                          return;
438
439                  /* So... This guy found something strange INSIDE encapsulated
440                     packet. Well, he is fool, but what can we do ?
441                   */
442                  rel_type = ICMP_PARAMETERPROB;
443                  rel_info = skb->h.icmph->un.gateway - grehlen;
444                  break;
445
446          case ICMP_DEST_UNREACH:
447                  switch (code) {
448                  case ICMP_SR_FAILED:
449                  case ICMP_PORT_UNREACH:
450                          /* Impossible event. */
451                          return;
452                  case ICMP_FRAG_NEEDED:
453                          /* And it is the only really necesary thing :-) */
454                          rel_info = ntohs(skb->h.icmph->un.frag.mtu);
455                          if (rel_info < grehlen+68)
456                                  return;
457                          rel_info -= grehlen;
458                          /* BSD 4.2 MORE DOES NOT EXIST IN NATURE. */
459                          if (rel_info > ntohs(eiph->tot_len))
460                                  return;
461                          break;
462                  default:
463                          /* All others are translated to HOST_UNREACH.
464                             rfc2003 contains "deep thoughts" about NET_UNREACH,
465                             I believe, it is just ether pollution. --ANK
466                           */
467                          rel_type = ICMP_DEST_UNREACH;
468                          rel_code = ICMP_HOST_UNREACH;
469                          break;
```

```
470                    }
471                    break;
472            case ICMP_TIME_EXCEEDED:
473                    if (code != ICMP_EXC_TTL)
474                            return;
475                    break;
476            }
```

Figure 6.304 GRE tunnels—error/ICMP cases: `linux/net/ipv4/ip_gre.c`.

```
478            /* Prepare fake skb to feed it to icmp_send */
479            skb2 = skb_clone(skb, GFP_ATOMIC);
480            if (skb2 == NULL)
481                    return;
482            dst_release(skb2->dst);
483            skb2->dst = NULL;
484            skb_pull(skb2, skb->data - (u8*)eiph);
485            skb2->nh.raw = skb2->data;
486
487            /* Try to guess incoming interface */
488            if (ip_route_output(&rt, eiph->saddr, 0, RT_TOS(eiph->tos), 0)) {
489                    kfree_skb(skb2);
490                    return;
491            }
492            skb2->dev = rt->u.dst.dev;
```

Figure 6.305 GRE tunnels—error/ICMP cases: `linux/net/ipv4/ip_gre.c`.

```
494            /* route "incoming" packet */
495            if (rt->rt_flags&RTCF_LOCAL) {
496                    ip_rt_put(rt);
497                    rt = NULL;
498                    if (ip_route_output(&rt, eiph->daddr, eiph->saddr, eiph->tos, 0) ||
499                        rt->u.dst.dev->type != ARPHRD_IPGRE) {
500                            ip_rt_put(rt);
501                            kfree_skb(skb2);
502                            return;
503                    }
504            } else {
505                    ip_rt_put(rt);
506                    if (ip_route_input(skb2, eiph->daddr, eiph->saddr, eiph->tos, skb2->dev) ||
507                        skb2->dst->dev->type != ARPHRD_IPGRE) {
508                            kfree_skb(skb2);
509                            return;
510                    }
511            }
512
513            /* change mtu on this route */
```

```
        if (type == ICMP_DEST_UNREACH && code == ICMP_FRAG_NEEDED) {
                if (rel_info > skb2->dst->pmtu) {
                        kfree_skb(skb2);
                        return;
                }
                skb2->dst->pmtu = rel_info;
                rel_info = htonl(rel_info);
        } else if (type == ICMP_TIME_EXCEEDED) {
                struct ip_tunnel *t = (struct ip_tunnel*)skb2->dev->priv;
                if (t->parms.iph.ttl) {
                        rel_type = ICMP_DEST_UNREACH;
                        rel_code = ICMP_HOST_UNREACH;
                }
        }

        icmp_send(skb2, rel_type, rel_code, rel_info);
        kfree_skb(skb2);
#endif
}
```

Figure 6.306 GRE tunnels—ECN handling: `linux/net/ipv4/ip_gre.c`.

```
static inline void ipgre_ecn_decapsulate(struct iphdr *iph, struct sk_buff *skb)
{
        if (INET_ECN_is_ce(iph->tos)) {
                if (skb->protocol == __constant_htons(ETH_P_IP)) {
                        if (INET_ECN_is_not_ce(skb->nh.iph->tos))
                                IP_ECN_set_ce(skb->nh.iph);
                } else if (skb->protocol == __constant_htons(ETH_P_IPV6)) {
                        if (INET_ECN_is_not_ce(ip6_get_dsfield(skb->nh.ipv6h)))
                                IP6_ECN_set_ce(skb->nh.ipv6h);
                }
        }
}

static inline u8
ipgre_ecn_encapsulate(u8 tos, struct iphdr *old_iph, struct sk_buff *skb)
{
#ifdef CONFIG_INET_ECN
        u8 inner = 0;
        if (skb->protocol == __constant_htons(ETH_P_IP))
                inner = old_iph->tos;
        else if (skb->protocol == __constant_htons(ETH_P_IPV6))
                inner = ip6_get_dsfield((struct ipv6hdr*)old_iph);
        return INET_ECN_encapsulate(tos, inner);
#else
        return tos;
#endif
}
```

GRE *ioctl*

Figure 6.307 GRE tunnels—`ioctl` entry handler: `linux/net/ipv4/ip_gre.c`.

```
883    static int
884    ipgre_tunnel_ioctl (struct net_device *dev, struct ifreq *ifr, int cmd)
885    {
886            int err = 0;
887            struct ip_tunnel_parm p;
888            struct ip_tunnel *t;
889
890            MOD_INC_USE_COUNT;
891
892            switch (cmd) {
893            case SIOCGETTUNNEL:
894                    t = NULL;
895                    if (dev == &ipgre_fb_tunnel_dev) {
896                            if (copy_from_user(&p, ifr->ifr_ifru.ifru_data, sizeof(p))) {
897                                    err = -EFAULT;
898                                    break;
899                            }
900                            t = ipgre_tunnel_locate(&p, 0);
901                    }
902                    if (t == NULL)
903                            t = (struct ip_tunnel*)dev->priv;
904                    memcpy(&p, &t->parms, sizeof(p));
905                    if (copy_to_user(ifr->ifr_ifru.ifru_data, &p, sizeof(p)))
906                            err = -EFAULT;
907                    break;
```

Figure 6.308 GRE tunnels—`ioctl` entry handler: `linux/net/ipv4/ip_gre.c`.

```
909            case SIOCADDTUNNEL:
910            case SIOCCHGTUNNEL:
911                    err = -EPERM;
912                    if (!capable(CAP_NET_ADMIN))
913                            goto done;
914
915                    err = -EFAULT;
916                    if (copy_from_user(&p, ifr->ifr_ifru.ifru_data, sizeof(p)))
917                            goto done;
918
919                    err = -EINVAL;
920                    if (p.iph.version != 4 || p.iph.protocol != IPPROTO_GRE ||
921                        p.iph.ihl != 5 || (p.iph.frag_off&__constant_htons(~IP_DF)) ||
922                        ((p.i_flags|p.o_flags)&(GRE_VERSION|GRE_ROUTING)))
923                            goto done;
924                    if (p.iph.ttl)
925                            p.iph.frag_off |= __constant_htons(IP_DF);
926
927                    if (!(p.i_flags&GRE_KEY))
```

```
                p.i_key = 0;
        if (!(p.o_flags&GRE_KEY))
                p.o_key = 0;

        t = ipgre_tunnel_locate(&p, cmd == SIOCADDTUNNEL);
```

Figure 6.309 GRE tunnels—`ioctl` entry handler: `linux/net/ipv4/ip_gre.c`.

```
        if (dev != &ipgre_fb_tunnel_dev && cmd == SIOCCHGTUNNEL &&
            t != &ipgre_fb_tunnel) {
                if (t != NULL) {
                        if (t->dev != dev) {
                                err = -EEXIST;
                                break;
                        }
                } else {
                        unsigned nflags=0;

                        t = (struct ip_tunnel*)dev->priv;

                        if (MULTICAST(p.iph.daddr))
                                nflags = IFF_BROADCAST;
                        else if (p.iph.daddr)
                                nflags = IFF_POINTOPOINT;

                        if ((dev->flags^nflags)&(IFF_POINTOPOINT|IFF_BROADCAST)) {
                                err = -EINVAL;
                                break;
                        }
                        ipgre_tunnel_unlink(t);
                        t->parms.iph.saddr = p.iph.saddr;
                        t->parms.iph.daddr = p.iph.daddr;
                        t->parms.i_key = p.i_key;
                        t->parms.o_key = p.o_key;
                        memcpy(dev->dev_addr, &p.iph.saddr, 4);
                        memcpy(dev->broadcast, &p.iph.daddr, 4);
                        ipgre_tunnel_link(t);
                        netdev_state_change(dev);
                }
        }
```

Figure 6.310 GRE tunnels—`ioctl` entry handler: `linux/net/ipv4/ip_gre.c`.

```
        if (t) {
                err = 0;
                if (cmd == SIOCCHGTUNNEL) {
                        t->parms.iph.ttl = p.iph.ttl;
                        t->parms.iph.tos = p.iph.tos;
                        t->parms.iph.frag_off = p.iph.frag_off;
```

```
                        }
                        if (copy_to_user(ifr->ifr_ifru.ifru_data, &t->parms, sizeof(p)))
                                err = -EFAULT;
                } else
                        err = (cmd == SIOCADDTUNNEL ? -ENOBUFS : -ENOENT);
                break;

        case SIOCDELTUNNEL:
                err = -EPERM;
                if (!capable(CAP_NET_ADMIN))
                        goto done;

                if (dev == &ipgre_fb_tunnel_dev) {
                        err = -EFAULT;
                        if (copy_from_user(&p, ifr->ifr_ifru.ifru_data, sizeof(p)))
                                goto done;
                        err = -ENOENT;
                        if ((t = ipgre_tunnel_locate(&p, 0)) == NULL)
                                goto done;
                        err = -EPERM;
                        if (t == &ipgre_fb_tunnel)
                                goto done;
                }
                err = unregister_netdevice(dev);
                break;

        default:
                err = -EINVAL;
        }

done:
        MOD_DEC_USE_COUNT;
        return err;
}
```

GRE Broadcast

Figure 6.311 GRE tunnels—broadcast support: `linux/net/ipv4/ip_gre.c`.

```
#ifdef CONFIG_NET_IPGRE_BROADCAST
/* Nice toy. Unfortunately, useless in real life :-)
   It allows to construct virtual multiprotocol broadcast "LAN"
   over the Internet, provided multicast routing is tuned.


   I have no idea was this bicycle invented before me,
   so that I had to set ARPHRD_IPGRE to a random value.
   I have an impression, that Cisco could make something similar,
   but this feature is apparently missing in IOS<=11.2(8).

```

```
1033        I set up 10.66.66/24 and fec0:6666:6666::0/96 as virtual networks
1034        with broadcast 224.66.66.66. If you have access to mbone, play with me :-)
1035
1036        ping -t 255 224.66.66.66
1037
1038        If nobody answers, mbone does not work.
1039
1040        ip tunnel add Universe mode gre remote 224.66.66.66 local <Your_real_addr> ttl 255
1041        ip addr add 10.66.66.<somewhat>/24 dev Universe
1042        ifconfig Universe up
1043        ifconfig Universe add fe80::<Your_real_addr>/10
1044        ifconfig Universe add fec0:6666:6666::<Your_real_addr>/96
1045        ftp 10.66.66.66
1046        ...
1047        ftp fec0:6666:6666::193.233.7.65
1048        ...
1049
1050    */
```

Figure 6.312 GRE tunnels—broadcast support: `linux/net/ipv4/ip_gre.c`.

```
1052    static int ipgre_header(struct sk_buff *skb, struct net_device *dev, unsigned short type,
1053                        void *daddr, void *saddr, unsigned len)
1054    {
1055            struct ip_tunnel *t = (struct ip_tunnel*)dev->priv;
1056            struct iphdr *iph = (struct iphdr *)skb_push(skb, t->hlen);
1057            u16 *p = (u16*)(iph+1);
1058
1059            memcpy(iph, &t->parms.iph, sizeof(struct iphdr));
1060            p[0]            = t->parms.o_flags;
1061            p[1]            = htons(type);
1062
1063            /*
1064             *      Set the source hardware address.
1065             */
1066
1067            if (saddr)
1068                    memcpy(&iph->saddr, saddr, 4);
1069
1070            if (daddr) {
1071                    memcpy(&iph->daddr, daddr, 4);
1072                    return t->hlen;
1073            }
1074            if (iph->daddr && !MULTICAST(iph->daddr))
1075                    return t->hlen;
1076
1077            return -t->hlen;
1078    }
```

Figure 6.313 GRE tunnels—broadcast support: linux/net/ipv4/ip_gre.c.

```
1080   static int ipgre_open(struct net_device *dev)
1081   {
1082           struct ip_tunnel *t = (struct ip_tunnel*)dev->priv;
1083
1084           MOD_INC_USE_COUNT;
1085           if (MULTICAST(t->parms.iph.daddr)) {
1086                   struct rtable *rt;
1087                   if (ip_route_output(&rt, t->parms.iph.daddr,
1088                                           t->parms.iph.saddr, RT_TOS(t->parms.iph.tos),
1089                                           t->parms.link)) {
1090                           MOD_DEC_USE_COUNT;
1091                           return -EADDRNOTAVAIL;
1092                   }
1093                   dev = rt->u.dst.dev;
1094                   ip_rt_put(rt);
1095                   if (__in_dev_get(dev) == NULL) {
1096                           MOD_DEC_USE_COUNT;
1097                           return -EADDRNOTAVAIL;
1098                   }
1099                   t->mlink = dev->ifindex;
1100                   ip_mc_inc_group(__in_dev_get(dev), t->parms.iph.daddr);
1101           }
1102           return 0;
1103   }
1104
1105   static int ipgre_close(struct net_device *dev)
1106   {
1107           struct ip_tunnel *t = (struct ip_tunnel*)dev->priv;
1108           if (MULTICAST(t->parms.iph.daddr) && t->mlink) {
1109                   struct in_device *in_dev = inetdev_by_index(t->mlink);
1110                   if (in_dev) {
1111                           ip_mc_dec_group(in_dev, t->parms.iph.daddr);
1112                           in_dev_put(in_dev);
1113                   }
1114           }
1115           MOD_DEC_USE_COUNT;
1116           return 0;
1117   }
1118
1119   #endif
```

GRE Management and Initialization

Figure 6.314 GRE tunnels—stats: linux/net/ipv4/ip_gre.c.

```
1008   static struct net_device_stats *ipgre_tunnel_get_stats(struct net_device *dev)
1009   {
1010           return &(((struct ip_tunnel*)dev->priv)->stat);
1011   }
1012
1013   static int ipgre_tunnel_change_mtu(struct net_device *dev, int new_mtu)
```

```
{
        struct ip_tunnel *tunnel = (struct ip_tunnel*)dev->priv;
        if (new_mtu < 68 || new_mtu > 0xFFF8 - tunnel->hlen)
                return -EINVAL;
        dev->mtu = new_mtu;
        return 0;
}
```

Figure 6.315 GRE tunnels—general initialization: `linux/net/ipv4/ip_gre.c`.

```
static void ipgre_tunnel_init_gen(struct net_device *dev)
{
        struct ip_tunnel *t = (struct ip_tunnel*)dev->priv;

        dev->uninit           = ipgre_tunnel_uninit;
        dev->destructor       = ipgre_tunnel_destructor;
        dev->hard_start_xmit  = ipgre_tunnel_xmit;
        dev->get_stats        = ipgre_tunnel_get_stats;
        dev->do_ioctl         = ipgre_tunnel_ioctl;
        dev->change_mtu       = ipgre_tunnel_change_mtu;

        dev_init_buffers(dev);

        dev->type             = ARPHRD_IPGRE;
        dev->hard_header_len  = LL_MAX_HEADER + sizeof(struct iphdr) + 4;
        dev->mtu              = 1500 - sizeof(struct iphdr) - 4;
        dev->flags            = IFF_NOARP;
        dev->iflink           = 0;
        dev->addr_len         = 4;
        memcpy(dev->dev_addr, &t->parms.iph.saddr, 4);
        memcpy(dev->broadcast, &t->parms.iph.daddr, 4);
}
```

Figure 6.316 GRE tunnels—tunnel initialization: `linux/net/ipv4/ip_gre.c`.

```
static int ipgre_tunnel_init(struct net_device *dev)
{
        struct net_device *tdev = NULL;
        struct ip_tunnel *tunnel;
        struct iphdr *iph;
        int hlen = LL_MAX_HEADER;
        int mtu = 1500;
        int addend = sizeof(struct iphdr) + 4;

        tunnel = (struct ip_tunnel*)dev->priv;
        iph = &tunnel->parms.iph;

        ipgre_tunnel_init_gen(dev);

        /* Guess output device to choose reasonable mtu and hard_header_len */

        if (iph->daddr) {
```

```
1161                      struct rtable *rt;
1162                      if (!ip_route_output(&rt, iph->daddr, iph->saddr, RT_TOS(iph->tos), tunnel->parms.
                              link)) {
1163                            tdev = rt->u.dst.dev;
1164                            ip_rt_put(rt);
1165                      }
1166
1167                      dev->flags |= IFF_POINTOPOINT;
```

Figure 6.317 GRE tunnels—tunnel initialization: `linux/net/ipv4/ip_gre.c`.

```
1169    #ifdef CONFIG_NET_IPGRE_BROADCAST
1170                      if (MULTICAST(iph->daddr)) {
1171                            if (!iph->saddr)
1172                                  return -EINVAL;
1173                            dev->flags = IFF_BROADCAST;
1174                            dev->hard_header = ipgre_header;
1175                            dev->open = ipgre_open;
1176                            dev->stop = ipgre_close;
1177                      }
1178    #endif
1179          }
1180
1181          if (!tdev && tunnel->parms.link)
1182                tdev = __dev_get_by_index(tunnel->parms.link);
1183
1184          if (tdev) {
1185                hlen = tdev->hard_header_len;
1186                mtu = tdev->mtu;
1187          }
1188          dev->iflink = tunnel->parms.link;
1189
1190          /* Precalculate GRE options length */
1191          if (tunnel->parms.o_flags&(GRE_CSUM|GRE_KEY|GRE_SEQ)) {
1192                if (tunnel->parms.o_flags&GRE_CSUM)
1193                      addend += 4;
1194                if (tunnel->parms.o_flags&GRE_KEY)
1195                      addend += 4;
1196                if (tunnel->parms.o_flags&GRE_SEQ)
1197                      addend += 4;
1198          }
1199          dev->hard_header_len = hlen + addend;
1200          dev->mtu = mtu - addend;
1201          tunnel->hlen = addend;
1202          return 0;
1203    }
```

Figure 6.318 GRE tunnels—module initialization: `linux/net/ipv4/ip_gre.c`.

```
1205    #ifdef MODULE
1206    static int ipgre_fb_tunnel_open(struct net_device *dev)
1207    {
1208          MOD_INC_USE_COUNT;
```

```
1209            return 0;
1210    }
1211
1212    static int ipgre_fb_tunnel_close(struct net_device *dev)
1213    {
1214            MOD_DEC_USE_COUNT;
1215            return 0;
1216    }
1217    #endif
1218
1219    int __init ipgre_fb_tunnel_init(struct net_device *dev)
1220    {
1221            struct ip_tunnel *tunnel = (struct ip_tunnel*)dev->priv;
1222            struct iphdr *iph;
1223
1224            ipgre_tunnel_init_gen(dev);
1225    #ifdef MODULE
1226            dev->open              = ipgre_fb_tunnel_open;
1227            dev->stop              = ipgre_fb_tunnel_close;
1228    #endif
1229
1230            iph = &ipgre_fb_tunnel.parms.iph;
1231            iph->version           = 4;
1232            iph->protocol          = IPPROTO_GRE;
1233            iph->ihl               = 5;
1234            tunnel->hlen           = sizeof(struct iphdr) + 4;
1235
1236            dev_hold(dev);
1237            tunnels_wc[0]          = &ipgre_fb_tunnel;
1238            return 0;
1239    }
```

Figure 6.319 GRE tunnels—protocol setup: `linux/net/ipv4/ip_gre.c`.

```
1242    static struct inet_protocol ipgre_protocol = {
1243      ipgre_rcv,           /* GRE handler        */
1244      ipgre_err,           /* TUNNEL error control */
1245      0,                   /* next               */
1246      IPPROTO_GRE,         /* protocol ID        */
1247      0,                   /* copy               */
1248      NULL,                /* data               */
1249      "GRE"                /* name               */
1250    };
1251
1252
1253    /*
1254     *      And now the modules code and kernel interface.
1255     */
1256
1257    #ifdef MODULE
1258    int init_module(void)
1259    #else
1260    int __init ipgre_init(void)
1261    #endif
```

```
{
        printk(KERN_INFO "GRE over IPv4 tunneling driver\n");

        ipgre_fb_tunnel_dev.priv = (void*)&ipgre_fb_tunnel;
#ifdef MODULE
        register_netdev(&ipgre_fb_tunnel_dev);
#else
        rtnl_lock();
        register_netdevice(&ipgre_fb_tunnel_dev);
        rtnl_unlock();
#endif

        inet_add_protocol(&ipgre_protocol);
        return 0;
}

#ifdef MODULE

void cleanup_module(void)
{
        if ( inet_del_protocol(&ipgre_protocol) < 0 )
                printk(KERN_INFO "ipgre close: can't remove protocol\n");

        unregister_netdev(&ipgre_fb_tunnel_dev);
}

#endif
```

6.9 IP version 6

To a large extent, the IPv6 code is modeled on the IPv4 code, so we need only look at the salient places that it is different. IPv6 is both more complex and simpler. For example, its stateless autoconfiguration means that a lot of associated protocols are not required. On the other hand, this means that this built-in functionality is more complex.

6.9.1 IPv6 Header Definitions

Figure 6.320 IPv6 packet format: `linux/include/linux/ipv6.h`.

```
/*
 *      IPv6 fixed header
 *
 *      BEWARE, it is incorrect. The first 4 bits of flow_lbl
 *      are glued to priority now, forming "class".
 */
```

```
struct ipv6hdr {
#if defined(__LITTLE_ENDIAN_BITFIELD)
        __u8                    priority:4,
                                version:4;
#elif defined(__BIG_ENDIAN_BITFIELD)
        __u8                    version:4,
                                priority:4;
#else
#error "Please fix <asm/byteorder.h>"
#endif
        __u8                    flow_lbl[3];

        __u16                   payload_len;
        __u8                    nexthdr;
        __u8                    hop_limit;

        struct in6_addr         saddr;
        struct in6_addr         daddr;
};
```

IPv6 interface header definitions for the INET address family:

Figure 6.321 Next header types: `linux/include/net/ipv6.h`.

```
#define SIN6_LEN_RFC 2133   24

/*
 *      NextHeader field of IPv6 header
 */

#define NEXTHDR_HOP         0       /* Hop-by-hop option header. */
#define NEXTHDR_TCP         6       /* TCP segment. */
#define NEXTHDR_UDP         17      /* UDP message. */
#define NEXTHDR_IPV6        41      /* IPv6 in IPv6 */
#define NEXTHDR_ROUTING     43      /* Routing header. */
#define NEXTHDR_FRAGMENT    44      /* Fragmentation/reassembly header. */
#define NEXTHDR_ESP         50      /* Encapsulating security payload. */
#define NEXTHDR_AUTH        51      /* Authentication header. */
#define NEXTHDR_ICMP        58      /* ICMP for IPv6. */
#define NEXTHDR_NONE        59      /* No next header */
#define NEXTHDR_DEST        60      /* Destination options header. */

#define NEXTHDR_MAX         255
```

Figure 6.322 IPv6 address family information: `linux/include/net/ipv6.h`.

```
#define IPV6_DEFAULT_HOPLIMIT 64
#define IPV6_DEFAULT_MCASTHOPS 1

/*
 *      Addr type
 *
 *      type   -      unicast | multicast | anycast
 *      scope  -      local   | site      | global
 *      v4     -      compat
 *      v4mapped
 *      any
 *      loopback
 */

#define IPV6_ADDR_ANY         0x0000U

#define IPV6_ADDR_UNICAST     0x0001U
#define IPV6_ADDR_MULTICAST   0x0002U
#define IPV6_ADDR_ANYCAST     0x0004U

#define IPV6_ADDR_LOOPBACK    0x0010U
#define IPV6_ADDR_LINKLOCAL   0x0020U
#define IPV6_ADDR_SITELOCAL   0x0040U

#define IPV6_ADDR_COMPATv4    0x0080U

#define IPV6_ADDR_SCOPE_MASK 0x00f0U

#define IPV6_ADDR_MAPPED      0x1000U
#define IPV6_ADDR_RESERVED    0x2000U /* reserved address space */
```

Figure 6.323 IPv6 fragmentation header: `linux/include/net/ipv6.h`.

```
struct frag_hdr {
        unsigned char nexthdr;
        unsigned char reserved;
        unsigned short frag_off;
        __u32          identification;
};
```

Figure 6.324 IPv6 network interface structures: `linux/include/net/if_inet6.h`.

```
struct inet6_ifaddr
{
        struct in6_addr      addr;
        __u32                prefix_len;

        __u32                valid_lft;
        __u32                prefered_lft;
        unsigned long        tstamp;
        atomic_t             refcnt;
        spinlock_t           lock;

        __u8                 probes;
        __u8                 flags;

        __u16                scope;

        struct timer_list    timer;

        struct inet6_dev     *idev;

        struct inet6_ifaddr  *lst_next;     /* next addr in addr_lst */
        struct inet6_ifaddr  *if_next;      /* next addr in inet6_dev */

        int                  dead;
};
```

Figure 6.325 IPv6 multicast interface structures: `linux/include/net/if_inet6.h`.

```
struct ipv6_mc_socklist
{
        struct in6_addr      addr;
        int                  ifindex;
        struct ipv6_mc_socklist *next;
};

#define MAF_TIMER_RUNNING    0x01
#define MAF_LAST_REPORTER    0x02
#define MAF_LOADED           0x04

struct ifmcaddr6
{
        struct in6_addr      mca_addr;
        struct inet6_dev     *idev;
        struct ifmcaddr6     *next;
        struct timer_list    mca_timer;
        unsigned             mca_flags;
        int                  mca_users;
        atomic_t             mca_refcnt;
        spinlock_t           mca_lock;
};
```

Figure 6.326 IPv6 device configuration struct: `linux/include/net/if_inet6.h`.

```
72    #define IFA_HOST      IPV6_ADDR_LOOPBACK
73    #define IFA_LINK      IPV6_ADDR_LINKLOCAL
74    #define IFA_SITE      IPV6_ADDR_SITELOCAL
75    #define IFA_GLOBAL    0x0000U
76
77    struct ipv6_devconf
78    {
79          int           forwarding;
80          int           hop_limit;
81          int           mtu6;
82          int           accept_ra;
83          int           accept_redirects;
84          int           autoconf;
85          int           dad_transmits;
86          int           rtr_solicits;
87          int           rtr_solicit_interval;
88          int           rtr_solicit_delay;
89
90          void          *sysctl;
91    };
```

Figure 6.327 IPv6 device data: `linux/include/net/if_inet6.h`.

```
93    struct inet6_dev
94    {
95          struct net_device        *dev;
96
97          struct inet6_ifaddr   *addr_list;
98          struct ifmcaddr6      *mc_list;
99          rwlock_t              lock;
100         atomic_t              refcnt;
101         __u32                 if_flags;
102         int                   dead;
103
104         struct neigh_parms    *nd_parms;
105         struct inet6_dev      *next;
106         struct ipv6_devconf   cnf;
107   };
```

Figure 6.328 IPv6 example of Ethernet-to-IPv6 map: `linux/include/net/if_inet6.h`.

```
111   static inline void ipv6_eth_mc_map(struct in6_addr *addr, char *buf)
112   {
113         /*
114          *      +-------+-------+-------+-------+-------+-------+
115          *      |  33   |   33  | DST13 | DST14 | DST15 | DST16 |
116          *      +-------+-------+-------+-------+-------+-------+
117          */
```

```
118
119          buf[0]= 0x33;
120          buf[1]= 0x33;
121
122          memcpy(buf + 2, &addr->s6_addr32[3], sizeof(__u32));
123   }
```

6.9.2 IPv6 API

Figure 6.329 IPv6 API—address family: `linux/include/linux/in6.h`.

```
26   /*
27    *      IPv6 address structure
28    */
29
30   struct in6_addr
31   {
32          union
33          {
34                  __u8          u6_addr8[16];
35                  __u16         u6_addr16[8];
36                  __u32         u6_addr32[4];
37          } in6_u;
38   #define s6_addr             in6_u.u6_addr8
39   #define s6_addr16           in6_u.u6_addr16
40   #define s6_addr32           in6_u.u6_addr32
41   };
42
43   struct sockaddr_in6 {
44          unsigned short int  sin6_family;  /* AF_INET6 */
45          __u16               sin6_port;    /* Transport layer port # */
46          __u32               sin6_flowinfo; /* IPv6 flow information */
47          struct in6_addr     sin6_addr;    /* IPv6 address */
48          __u32               sin6_scope_id; /* scope id (new in RFC 2553) */
49   };
```

Figure 6.330 IPv6 API—multicast programmer interface: `linux/include/linux/in6.h`.

```
51   struct ipv6_mreq {
52          /* IPv6 multicast address of group */
53          struct in6_addr ipv6mr_multiaddr;
54
55          /* local IPv6 address of interface */
56          int            ipv6mr_ifindex;
57   };
```

Flow labels can be set by application programmers—doing this is described in the IProute2 documentation.

Figure 6.331 IPv6 API—flow label programmer interface structure: `linux/include/linux/in6.h`.

```
struct in6_flowlabel_req
{
        struct in6_addr flr_dst;
        __u32  flr_label;
        __u8   flr_action;
        __u8   flr_share;
        __u16  flr_flags;
        __u16  flr_expires;
        __u16  flr_linger;
        __u32  __flr_pad;
        /* Options in format of IPV6_PKTOPTIONS */
};

#define IPV6_FL_A_GET 0
#define IPV6_FL_A_PUT 1
#define IPV6_FL_A_RENEW 2

#define IPV6_FL_F_CREATE     1
#define IPV6_FL_F_EXCL       2

#define IPV6_FL_S_NONE       0
#define IPV6_FL_S_EXCL       1
#define IPV6_FL_S_PROCESS    2
#define IPV6_FL_S_USER       3
#define IPV6_FL_S_ANY        255
```

6.9.3 IPv6 Address (Auto)Configuration

Not surprisingly, the most complex part of IPv6 is the addressing, since that is where it has both more bits, and more ways of allocating them than its ancestor, IPv4.

An IPv6 address can have different scope, such as loopback, link local, site local, and so on.

Figure 6.332 IP address configurator—determine address type: `linux/net/ipv6/addrconf.c`.

```
int ipv6_addr_type(struct in6_addr *addr)
{
        u32 st;

        st = addr->s6_addr32[0];

        /* Consider all addresses with the first three bits different of
```

```
        000 and 111 as unicasts.
      */
     if ((st & __constant_htonl(0xE0000000)) != __constant_htonl(0x00000000) &&
         (st & __constant_htonl(0xE0000000)) != __constant_htonl(0xE0000000))
             return IPV6_ADDR_UNICAST;

     if ((st & __constant_htonl(0xFF000000)) == __constant_htonl(0xFF000000)) {
             int type = IPV6_ADDR_MULTICAST;

             switch((st & __constant_htonl(0x00FF0000))) {
                     case __constant_htonl(0x00010000):
                             type |= IPV6_ADDR_LOOPBACK;
                             break;

                     case __constant_htonl(0x00020000):
                             type |= IPV6_ADDR_LINKLOCAL;
                             break;

                     case __constant_htonl(0x00050000):
                             type |= IPV6_ADDR_SITELOCAL;
                             break;
             };
             return type;
     }
```

It can be unicast, multicast, or anycast. It can also be IPv4-compatible.

Figure 6.333 IP address configurator—determine address type: `linux/net/ipv6/addrconf.c`.

```
     if ((st & __constant_htonl(0xFFC00000)) == __constant_htonl(0xFE800000))
             return (IPV6_ADDR_LINKLOCAL | IPV6_ADDR_UNICAST);

     if ((st & __constant_htonl(0xFFC00000)) == __constant_htonl(0xFEC00000))
             return (IPV6_ADDR_SITELOCAL | IPV6_ADDR_UNICAST);

     if ((addr->s6_addr32[0] | addr->s6_addr32[1]) == 0) {
             if (addr->s6_addr32[2] == 0) {
                     if (addr->in6_u.u6_addr32[3] == 0)
                             return IPV6_ADDR_ANY;

                     if (addr->s6_addr32[3] == __constant_htonl(0x00000001))
                             return (IPV6_ADDR_LOOPBACK | IPV6_ADDR_UNICAST);

                     return (IPV6_ADDR_COMPATv4 | IPV6_ADDR_UNICAST);
             }

             if (addr->s6_addr32[2] == __constant_htonl(0x0000ffff))
                     return IPV6_ADDR_MAPPED;
     }

     return IPV6_ADDR_RESERVED;
}
```

Addresses need to be allocated when devices come up, and freed up when devices go offline.

When sending a packet, we also need to choose an address carefully.

Figure 6.334 Select IPv6 source address given destination to get to: `linux/net/ipv6/addrconf.c`.

```
/*
 *      Choose an apropriate source address
 *      should do:
 *      i)      get an address with an apropriate scope
 *      ii)     see if there is a specific route for the destination and use
 *              an address of the attached interface
 *      iii)    don't use deprecated addresses
 */
int ipv6_get_saddr(struct dst_entry *dst,
                   struct in6_addr *daddr, struct in6_addr *saddr)
{
        int scope;
        struct inet6_ifaddr *ifp = NULL;
        struct inet6_ifaddr *match = NULL;
        struct net_device *dev = NULL;
        struct inet6_dev *idev;
        struct rt6_info *rt;
        int err;

        rt = (struct rt6_info *) dst;
        if (rt)
                dev = rt->rt6i_dev;

        scope = ipv6_addr_scope(daddr);
        if (rt && (rt->rt6i_flags & RTF_ALLONLINK)) {
                /*
                 *      route for the "all destinations on link" rule
                 *      when no routers are present
                 */
                scope = IFA_LINK;
        }
```

Figure 6.335 Select IPv6 source address given destination to get to: `linux/net/ipv6/addrconf.c`.

```
         *      search dev and walk through dev addresses
         */

        if (dev) {
                if (dev->flags & IFF_LOOPBACK)
                        scope = IFA_HOST;

                read_lock(&addrconf_lock);
                idev = __in6_dev_get(dev);
                if (idev) {
                        read_lock_bh(&idev->lock);
```

```
            for (ifp=idev->addr_list; ifp; ifp=ifp->if_next) {
                if (ifp->scope == scope) {
                    if (!(ifp->flags & (IFA_F_DEPRECATED|IFA_F_TENTATIVE))) {
                        in6_ifa_hold(ifp);
                        read_unlock_bh(&idev->lock);
                        read_unlock(&addrconf_lock);
                        goto out;
                    }

                    if (!match && !(ifp->flags & IFA_F_TENTATIVE)) {
                        match = ifp;
                        in6_ifa_hold(ifp);
                    }
                }
            }
            read_unlock_bh(&idev->lock);
        }
        read_unlock(&addrconf_lock);
    }
```

Figure 6.336 Select IPv6 source address given destination to get to: `linux/net/ipv6/addrconf.c`.

```
    if (scope == IFA_LINK)
        goto out;

    /*
     *      dev == NULL or search failed for specified dev
     */

    read_lock(&dev_base_lock);
    read_lock(&addrconf_lock);
    for (dev = dev_base; dev; dev=dev->next) {
        idev = __in6_dev_get(dev);
        if (idev) {
            read_lock_bh(&idev->lock);
            for (ifp=idev->addr_list; ifp; ifp=ifp->if_next) {
                if (ifp->scope == scope) {
                    if (!(ifp->flags&(IFA_F_DEPRECATED|IFA_F_TENTATIVE))) {
                        in6_ifa_hold(ifp);
                        read_unlock_bh(&idev->lock);
                        goto out_unlock_base;
                    }

                    if (!match && !(ifp->flags&IFA_F_TENTATIVE)) {
                        match = ifp;
                        in6_ifa_hold(ifp);
                    }
                }
            }
            read_unlock_bh(&idev->lock);
        }
    }
```

Figure 6.337 Select IPv6 source address given destination to get to: `linux/net/ipv6/`
`addrconf.c`.

```
529   out_unlock_base:
530          read_unlock(&addrconf_lock);
531          read_unlock(&dev_base_lock);
532
533   out:
534          if (ifp == NULL) {
535                  ifp = match;
536                  match = NULL;
537          }
538
539          err = -EADDRNOTAVAIL;
540          if (ifp) {
541                  ipv6_addr_copy(saddr, &ifp->addr);
542                  err = 0;
543                  in6_ifa_put(ifp);
544          }
545          if (match)
546                  in6_ifa_put(match);
547
548          return err;
549   }
```

Deriving an IPv6 Address

Multicast address management is not so different from IPv4. There are also addresses for tunnels.

Typically we build an address from a LAN interface's MAC address and a route prefix.

Figure 6.338 Deriving EUI64 bits of IPv6 address: `linux/net/ipv6/addrconf.c`.

```
667   static int ipv6_generate_eui64(u8 *eui, struct net_device *dev)
668   {
669          switch (dev->type) {
670          case ARPHRD_ETHER:
671          case ARPHRD_FDDI:
672          case ARPHRD_IEEE802_TR:
673                  if (dev->addr_len != ETH_ALEN)
674                          return -1;
675                  memcpy(eui, dev->dev_addr, 3);
676                  memcpy(eui + 5, dev->dev_addr+3, 3);
677                  eui[3] = 0xFF;
678                  eui[4] = 0xFE;
679                  eui[0] ^= 2;
680                  return 0;
681          }
682          return -1;
683   }
```

The unicast address can start with the LAN device address. It can then have a route-based prefix added.

Figure 6.339 Adding prefix route: `linux/net/ipv6/addrconf.c`.

```
static void
addrconf_prefix_route(struct in6_addr *pfx, int plen, struct net_device *dev,
                    unsigned long expires, unsigned flags)
{
        struct in6_rtmsg rtmsg;

        memset(&rtmsg, 0, sizeof(rtmsg));
        memcpy(&rtmsg.rtmsg_dst, pfx, sizeof(struct in6_addr));
        rtmsg.rtmsg_dst_len = plen;
        rtmsg.rtmsg_metric = IP6_RT_PRIO_ADDRCONF;
        rtmsg.rtmsg_ifindex = dev->ifindex;
        rtmsg.rtmsg_info = expires;
        rtmsg.rtmsg_flags = RTF_UP|flags;
        rtmsg.rtmsg_type = RTMSG_NEWROUTE;

        /* Prevent useless cloning on PtP SIT.
           This thing is done here expecting that the whole
           class of non-broadcast devices need not cloning.
         */
        if (dev->type == ARPHRD_SIT && (dev->flags&IFF_POINTOPOINT))
                rtmsg.rtmsg_flags |= RTF_NONEXTHOP;

        ip6_route_add(&rtmsg);
}
```

Figure 6.340 Adding prefix route: `linux/net/ipv6/addrconf.c`.

```
void addrconf_prefix_rcv(struct net_device *dev, u8 *opt, int len)
{
        struct prefix_info *pinfo;
        struct rt6_info *rt;
        __u32 valid_lft;
        __u32 prefered_lft;
        int addr_type;
        unsigned long rt_expires;
        struct inet6_dev *in6_dev;

        pinfo = (struct prefix_info *) opt;

        if (len < sizeof(struct prefix_info)) {
                ADBG(("addrconf: prefix option too short\n"));
                return;
        }

```

```
/*
 *      Validation checks ([ADDRCONF], page 19)
 */

addr_type = ipv6_addr_type(&pinfo->prefix);

if (addr_type & (IPV6_ADDR_MULTICAST|IPV6_ADDR_LINKLOCAL))
        return;
```

Figure 6.341 Adding prefix route: `linux/net/ipv6/addrconf.c`.

```
valid_lft = ntohl(pinfo->valid);
prefered_lft = ntohl(pinfo->prefered);

if (prefered_lft > valid_lft) {
        printk(KERN_WARNING "addrconf: prefix option has invalid lifetime\n");
        return;
}

in6_dev = in6_dev_get(dev);

if (in6_dev == NULL) {
        printk(KERN_DEBUG "addrconf: device %s not configured\n", dev->name);
        return;
}
```

Figure 6.342 Adding prefix route: `linux/net/ipv6/addrconf.c`.

```
/*
 *      Two things going on here:
 *      1) Add routes for on-link prefixes
 *      2) Configure prefixes with the auto flag set
 */

/* Avoid arithemtic overflow. Really, we could
   save rt_expires in seconds, likely valid_lft,
   but it would require division in fib gc, that it
   not good.
 */
if (valid_lft >= 0x7FFFFFFF/HZ)
        rt_expires = 0;
else
        rt_expires = jiffies + valid_lft * HZ;

rt = rt6_lookup(&pinfo->prefix, NULL, dev->ifindex, 1);

if (rt && ((rt->rt6i_flags & (RTF_GATEWAY | RTF_DEFAULT)) == 0)) {
```

```
                if (rt->rt6i_flags&RTF_EXPIRES) {
                        if (pinfo->onlink == 0 || valid_lft == 0) {
                                ip6_del_rt(rt);
                                rt = NULL;
                        } else {
                                rt->rt6i_expires = rt_expires;
                        }
                }
        } else if (pinfo->onlink && valid_lft) {
                addrconf_prefix_route(&pinfo->prefix, pinfo->prefix_len,
                                      dev, rt_expires, RTF_ADDRCONF|RTF_EXPIRES);
        }
        if (rt)
                dst_release(&rt->u.dst);
```

Figure 6.343 Adding prefix route: `linux/net/ipv6/addrconf.c`.

```
        /* Try to figure out our local address for this prefix */

        if (pinfo->autoconf && in6_dev->cnf.autoconf) {
                struct inet6_ifaddr * ifp;
                struct in6_addr addr;
                int plen;

                plen = pinfo->prefix_len >> 3;

#ifdef CONFIG_IPV6_EUI64
                if (pinfo->prefix_len == 64) {
                        memcpy(&addr, &pinfo->prefix, 8);
                        if (ipv6_generate_eui64(addr.s6_addr + 8, dev) &&
                            ipv6_inherit_eui64(addr.s6_addr + 8, in6_dev)) {
                                in6_dev_put(in6_dev);
                                return;
                        }
                        goto ok;
                }
#endif
#ifndef CONFIG_IPV6_NO_PB
                if (pinfo->prefix_len == ((sizeof(struct in6_addr) - dev->addr_len)<<3)) {
                        memcpy(&addr, &pinfo->prefix, plen);
                        memcpy(addr.s6_addr + plen, dev->dev_addr,
                               dev->addr_len);
                        goto ok;
                }
#endif
                printk(KERN_DEBUG "IPv6 addrconf: prefix with wrong length %d\n", pinfo->
                     prefix_len);
                in6_dev_put(in6_dev);
                return;
```

Figure 6.344 Adding prefix route: `linux/net/ipv6/addrconf.c`.

```
ok:

            ifp = ipv6_get_ifaddr(&addr, dev);

            if (ifp == NULL && valid_lft) {
                  ifp = ipv6_add_addr(in6_dev, &addr, pinfo->prefix_len,
                                 addr_type&IPV6_ADDR_SCOPE_MASK, 0);

                  if (ifp == NULL) {
                        in6_dev_put(in6_dev);
                        return;
                  }

                  addrconf_dad_start(ifp);
            }

            if (ifp && valid_lft == 0) {
                  ipv6_del_addr(ifp);
                  ifp = NULL;
            }
```

Figure 6.345 Adding prefix route: `linux/net/ipv6/addrconf.c`.

```
            if (ifp) {
                  int flags;

                  spin_lock(&ifp->lock);
                  ifp->valid_lft = valid_lft;
                  ifp->prefered_lft = prefered_lft;
                  ifp->tstamp = jiffies;
                  flags = ifp->flags;
                  ifp->flags &= ~IFA_F_DEPRECATED;
                  spin_unlock(&ifp->lock);

                  if (!(flags&IFA_F_TENTATIVE))
                        ipv6_ifa_notify((flags&IFA_F_DEPRECATED) ?
                                    0 : RTM_NEWADDR, ifp);
                  in6_ifa_put(ifp);
            }
      }
      in6_dev_put(in6_dev);
}
```

IPv6 Address Management

Addresses are managed through timers, which limit their lifetime.

Addresses can also be managed manually. There are a bunch of parameters that can be controlled by the system:

Figure 6.346 IPv6 `addrconf sysctl: linux/net/ipv6/addrconf.c.`

```
1886    static struct addrconf_sysctl_table
1887    {
1888            struct ctl_table_header *sysctl_header;
1889            ctl_table addrconf_vars[11];
1890            ctl_table addrconf_dev[2];
1891            ctl_table addrconf_conf_dir[2];
1892            ctl_table addrconf_proto_dir[2];
1893            ctl_table addrconf_root_dir[2];
1894    } addrconf_sysctl = {
1895            NULL,
1896            {{NET_IPV6_FORWARDING, "forwarding",
1897             &ipv6_devconf.forwarding, sizeof(int), 0644, NULL,
1898             &addrconf_sysctl_forward},
1899
1900            {NET_IPV6_HOP_LIMIT, "hop_limit",
1901             &ipv6_devconf.hop_limit, sizeof(int), 0644, NULL,
1902             &proc_dointvec},
1903
1904            {NET_IPV6_MTU, "mtu",
1905             &ipv6_devconf.mtu6, sizeof(int), 0644, NULL,
1906             &proc_dointvec},
1907
1908            {NET_IPV6_ACCEPT_RA, "accept_ra",
1909             &ipv6_devconf.accept_ra, sizeof(int), 0644, NULL,
1910             &proc_dointvec},
```

Figure 6.347 IPv6 `addrconf sysctl: linux/net/ipv6/addrconf.c.`

```
1912            {NET_IPV6_ACCEPT_REDIRECTS, "accept_redirects",
1913             &ipv6_devconf.accept_redirects, sizeof(int), 0644, NULL,
1914             &proc_dointvec},
1915
1916            {NET_IPV6_AUTOCONF, "autoconf",
1917             &ipv6_devconf.autoconf, sizeof(int), 0644, NULL,
1918             &proc_dointvec},
1919
1920            {NET_IPV6_DAD_TRANSMITS, "dad_transmits",
1921             &ipv6_devconf.dad_transmits, sizeof(int), 0644, NULL,
1922             &proc_dointvec},
1923
1924            {NET_IPV6_RTR_SOLICITS, "router_solicitations",
1925             &ipv6_devconf.rtr_solicits, sizeof(int), 0644, NULL,
1926             &proc_dointvec},
1927
1928            {NET_IPV6_RTR_SOLICIT_INTERVAL, "router_solicitation_interval",
1929             &ipv6_devconf.rtr_solicit_interval, sizeof(int), 0644, NULL,
1930             &proc_dointvec_jiffies},
1931
1932            {NET_IPV6_RTR_SOLICIT_DELAY, "router_solicitation_delay",
1933             &ipv6_devconf.rtr_solicit_delay, sizeof(int), 0644, NULL,
```

```
1934            &proc_dointvec_jiffies},
1935
1936        {0}},
1937
1938        {{NET_PROTO_CONF_ALL, "all", NULL, 0, 0555, addrconf_sysctl.addrconf_vars},{0}},
1939        {{NET_IPV6_CONF, "conf", NULL, 0, 0555, addrconf_sysctl.addrconf_dev},{0}},
1940        {{NET_IPV6, "ipv6", NULL, 0, 0555, addrconf_sysctl.addrconf_conf_dir},{0}},
1941        {{CTL_NET, "net", NULL, 0, 0555, addrconf_sysctl.addrconf_proto_dir},{0}}
1942    };
```

6.9.4 IPv6 Neighbor Discovery

IPv6 is trying to be as free of manual configuration as possible. Thus it tries to discover from its environment any configuration necessary. One thing that needs finding is neighbors.

Figure 6.348 IPv6 neighbor discovery operations: `linux/net/ipv6/ndisc.c`.

```
86  static struct neigh_ops ndisc_generic_ops =
87  {
88          AF_INET6,
89          NULL,
90          ndisc_solicit,
91          ndisc_error_report,
92          neigh_resolve_output,
93          neigh_connected_output,
94          dev_queue_xmit,
95          dev_queue_xmit
96  };
97
98  static struct neigh_ops ndisc_hh_ops =
99  {
100         AF_INET6,
101         NULL,
102         ndisc_solicit,
103         ndisc_error_report,
104         neigh_resolve_output,
105         neigh_resolve_output,
106         dev_queue_xmit,
107         dev_queue_xmit
108 };
109
110
111 static struct neigh_ops ndisc_direct_ops =
112 {
113         AF_INET6,
114         NULL,
115         NULL,
116         NULL,
```

```
117            dev_queue_xmit,
118            dev_queue_xmit,
119            dev_queue_xmit,
120            dev_queue_xmit
121    };
```

Essentially, if a network supports broadcast, then this is used to propagate messages to find out who is out there. An example of such a message is the neighbor advertisement. It is like ARP, but uses the ICMPv6 message formats. We'll just look at this one—others are all similarly constructed.

Figure 6.349 IPv6 neighbor advertisement: `linux/net/ipv6/ndisc.c`.

```
317    /*
318     *      Send a Neighbour Advertisement
319     */
320
321    void ndisc_send_na(struct net_device *dev, struct neighbour *neigh,
322                    struct in6_addr *daddr, struct in6_addr *solicited_addr,
323                    int router, int solicited, int override, int inc_opt)
324    {
325            struct sock *sk = ndisc_socket->sk;
326            struct nd_msg *msg;
327            int len;
328            struct sk_buff *skb;
329            int err;
330
331            len = sizeof(struct icmp6hdr) + sizeof(struct in6_addr);
332
333            if (inc_opt) {
334                    if (dev->addr_len)
335                            len += NDISC_OPT_SPACE(dev->addr_len);
336                    else
337                            inc_opt = 0;
338            }
339
340            skb = sock_alloc_send_skb(sk, MAX_HEADER + len + dev->hard_header_len + 15,
341                                    0, 0, &err);
342
343            if (skb == NULL) {
344                    ND_PRINTK1("send_na: alloc skb failed\n");
345                    return;
346            }
347
348            if (ndisc_build_ll_hdr(skb, dev, daddr, neigh, len) == 0) {
349                    kfree_skb(skb);
350                    return;
351            }
352
353            ip6_nd_hdr(sk, skb, dev, solicited_addr, daddr, IPPROTO_ICMPV6, len);
```

```

        msg = (struct nd_msg *) skb_put(skb, len);

        msg->icmph.icmp6_type = NDISC_NEIGHBOUR_ADVERTISEMENT;
        msg->icmph.icmp6_code = 0;
        msg->icmph.icmp6_cksum = 0;
```

Figure 6.350 IPv6 neighbor advertisement: `linux/net/ipv6/ndisc.c`.

```
        msg->icmph.icmp6_unused = 0;
        msg->icmph.icmp6_router = router;
        msg->icmph.icmp6_solicited = solicited;
        msg->icmph.icmp6_override = !!override;

        /* Set the target address. */
        ipv6_addr_copy(&msg->target, solicited_addr);

        if (inc_opt)
                ndisc_fill_option((void*)&msg->opt, ND_OPT_TARGET_LL_ADDR, dev->dev_addr, dev->
                    addr_len);

        /* checksum */
        msg->icmph.icmp6_cksum = csum_ipv6_magic(solicited_addr, daddr, len,
                                                 IPPROTO_ICMPV6,
                                                 csum_partial((__u8 *) msg,
                                                              len, 0));

        dev_queue_xmit(skb);

        ICMP6_INC_STATS(Icmp6OutNeighborAdvertisements);
        ICMP6_INC_STATS(Icmp6OutMsgs);
}
```

Neighbor Discovery—Router Advertisement

Inbound messages may include router advertisements, for example:

Figure 6.351 IPv6 router discovery: `linux/net/ipv6/ndisc.c`.

```
static void ndisc_router_discovery(struct sk_buff *skb)
{
        struct ra_msg *ra_msg = (struct ra_msg *) skb->h.raw;
        struct neighbour *neigh;
        struct inet6_dev *in6_dev;
        struct rt6_info *rt;
        int lifetime;
        int optlen;

        __u8 * opt = (__u8 *)(ra_msg + 1);
```

```
        optlen = (skb->tail - skb->h.raw) - sizeof(struct ra_msg);

        if (skb->nh.ipv6h->hop_limit != 255) {
                printk(KERN_INFO
                       "NDISC: fake router advertisment received\n");
                return;
        }

        /*
         *      set the RA_RECV flag in the interface
         */

        in6_dev = in6_dev_get(skb->dev);
        if (in6_dev == NULL) {
                ND_PRINTK1("RA: can't find in6 device\n");
                return;
        }
        if (in6_dev->cnf.forwarding || !in6_dev->cnf.accept_ra) {
                in6_dev_put(in6_dev);
                return;
        }
```

Figure 6.352 IPv6 router discovery: `linux/net/ipv6/ndisc.c`.

```
        if (in6_dev->if_flags & IF_RS_SENT) {
                /*
                 *      flag that an RA was received after an RS was sent
                 *      out on this interface.
                 */
                in6_dev->if_flags |= IF_RA_RCVD;
        }

        lifetime = ntohs(ra_msg->icmph.icmp6_rt_lifetime);

        rt = rt6_get_dflt_router(&skb->nh.ipv6h->saddr, skb->dev);

        if (rt && lifetime == 0) {
                ip6_del_rt(rt);
                rt = NULL;
        }

        if (rt == NULL && lifetime) {
                ND_PRINTK2("ndisc_rdisc: adding default router\n");

                rt = rt6_add_dflt_router(&skb->nh.ipv6h->saddr, skb->dev);
                if (rt == NULL) {
                        ND_PRINTK1("route_add failed\n");
                        in6_dev_put(in6_dev);
                        return;
                }

                neigh = rt->rt6i_nexthop;
```

```
		if (neigh == NULL) {
			ND_PRINTK1("nd: add default router: null neighbour\n");
			dst_release(&rt->u.dst);
			in6_dev_put(in6_dev);
			return;
		}
		neigh->flags |= NTF_ROUTER;

		/*
		 *	If we where using an "all destinations on link" route
		 *	delete it
		 */

		rt6_purge_dflt_routers(RTF_ALLONLINK);
	}
```

Figure 6.353 IPv6 router discovery: `linux/net/ipv6/ndisc.c`.

```
	if (rt)
		rt->rt6i_expires = jiffies + (HZ * lifetime);

	if (ra_msg->icmph.icmp6_hop_limit)
		in6_dev->cnf.hop_limit = ra_msg->icmph.icmp6_hop_limit;

	/*
	 *	Update Reachable Time and Retrans Timer
	 */

	if (in6_dev->nd_parms) {
		__u32 rtime = ntohl(ra_msg->retrans_timer);

		if (rtime && rtime/1000 < MAX_SCHEDULE_TIMEOUT/HZ) {
			rtime = (rtime*HZ)/1000;
			if (rtime < HZ/10)
				rtime = HZ/10;
			in6_dev->nd_parms->retrans_time = rtime;
		}

		rtime = ntohl(ra_msg->reachable_time);
		if (rtime && rtime/1000 < MAX_SCHEDULE_TIMEOUT/(3*HZ)) {
			rtime = (rtime*HZ)/1000;

			if (rtime < HZ/10)
				rtime = HZ/10;

			if (rtime != in6_dev->nd_parms->base_reachable_time) {
				in6_dev->nd_parms->base_reachable_time = rtime;
				in6_dev->nd_parms->gc_staletime = 3 * rtime;
				in6_dev->nd_parms->reachable_time = neigh_rand_reach_time(rtime);
			}
		}
	}
```

Figure 6.354 IPv6 router discovery: `linux/net/ipv6/ndisc.c`.

```
681          /*
682           *      Process options.
683           */
684
685          while (optlen > 0) {
686                  int len = (opt[1] << 3);
687
688                  if (len == 0) {
689                          ND_PRINTK0("RA: opt has 0 len\n");
690                          break;
691                  }
692
693                  switch(*opt) {
694                  case ND_OPT_SOURCE_LL_ADDR:
695
696                          if (rt == NULL)
697                                  break;
698
699                          if ((neigh = rt->rt6i_nexthop) != NULL &&
700                              skb->dev->addr_len + 2 >= len)
701                                  neigh_update(neigh, opt+2, NUD_STALE, 1, 1);
702                          break;
703
704                  case ND_OPT_PREFIX_INFO:
705                          addrconf_prefix_rcv(skb->dev, opt, len);
706                          break;
```

Figure 6.355 IPv6 router discovery: `linux/net/ipv6/ndisc.c`.

```
708                  case ND_OPT_MTU:
709                  {
710                          int mtu;
711
712                          mtu = htonl(*(__u32 *)(opt+4));
713
714                          if (mtu < IPV6_MIN_MTU || mtu > skb->dev->mtu) {
715                                  ND_PRINTK0("NDISC: router "
716                                          "announcement with mtu = %d\n",
717                                          mtu);
718                                  break;
719                          }
720
721                          if (in6_dev->cnf.mtu6 != mtu) {
722                                  in6_dev->cnf.mtu6 = mtu;
723
724                                  if (rt)
725                                          rt->u.dst.pmtu = mtu;
726
727                                  rt6_mtu_change(skb->dev, mtu);
728                          }
729                  }
730                  break;
```

```

		case ND_OPT_TARGET_LL_ADDR:
		case ND_OPT_REDIRECT_HDR:
			ND_PRINTK0("got illegal option with RA");
			break;
		default:
			ND_PRINTK0("unkown option in RA\n");
		};
		optlen -= len;
		opt += len;
	}
	if (rt)
		dst_release(&rt->u.dst);
	in6_dev_put(in6_dev);
}
```

Other messages include redirects and errors.

6.9.5 IPv6 Input

As with IPv4, IPv6 input is called on demultiplexing a packet (see discussion in Chapters 3 and 4). This ends up here:

Figure 6.356 IPv6 receive: `linux/net/ipv6/ip6_input.c`.

```
int ipv6_rcv(struct sk_buff *skb, struct net_device *dev, struct packet_type *pt)
{
	struct ipv6hdr *hdr;
	u32		pkt_len;

	if (skb->pkt_type == PACKET_OTHERHOST)
		goto drop;

	IP6_INC_STATS_BH(Ip6InReceives);

	if ((skb = skb_share_check(skb, GFP_ATOMIC)) == NULL)
		goto out;

	/* Store incoming device index. When the packet will
	   be queued, we cannot refer to skb->dev anymore.
	 */
	((struct inet6_skb_parm *)skb->cb)->iif = dev->ifindex;

	hdr = skb->nh.ipv6h;

	if (skb->len < sizeof(struct ipv6hdr) || hdr->version != 6)
		goto err;

	pkt_len = ntohs(hdr->payload_len);
```

Figure 6.357 IPv6 receive: `linux/net/ipv6/ip6_input.c.`

```
        /* pkt_len may be zero if Jumbo payload option is present */
        if (pkt_len || hdr->nexthdr != NEXTHDR_HOP) {
                if (pkt_len + sizeof(struct ipv6hdr) > skb->len)
                        goto truncated;
                skb_trim(skb, pkt_len + sizeof(struct ipv6hdr));
        }

        if (hdr->nexthdr == NEXTHDR_HOP) {
                skb->h.raw = (u8*)(hdr+1);
                if (!ipv6_parse_hopopts(skb, &hdr->nexthdr)) {
                        IP6_INC_STATS_BH(Ip6InHdrErrors);
                        return 0;
                }
        }
        return NF_HOOK(PF_INET6,NF_IP6_PRE_ROUTING, skb, dev, NULL, ip6_rcv_finish);
truncated:
        IP6_INC_STATS_BH(Ip6InTruncatedPkts);
err:
        IP6_INC_STATS_BH(Ip6InHdrErrors);
drop:
        kfree_skb(skb);
out:
        return 0;
}
```

This ends up calling `ip6_rcv_finish()` via the Network Filter Hook again, which then routes the packet to the appropriate demultiplexing (e.g., forwarding, or local reception to a transport protocol) via the normal pattern:

Figure 6.358 IPv6 receive finish: `linux/net/ipv6/ip6_input.c.`

```
static inline int ip6_rcv_finish( struct sk_buff *skb)
{

        if (skb->dst == NULL)
                ip6_route_input(skb);

        return skb->dst->input(skb);
}
```

6.9.6 IPv6 Output

Output is pretty straightforward. As usual we have to go via the Network Filter Hook.

Figure 6.359 IPv6—output: `linux/net/ipv6/ip6_output.c.`

```
int ip6_output(struct sk_buff *skb)
{
        struct dst_entry *dst = skb->dst;
        struct net_device *dev = dst->dev;

        skb->protocol = __constant_htons(ETH_P_IPV6);
        skb->dev = dev;

        if (ipv6_addr_is_multicast(&skb->nh.ipv6h->daddr)) {
                if (!(dev->flags&IFF_LOOPBACK) &&
                    (skb->sk == NULL || skb->sk->net_pinfo.af_inet6.mc_loop) &&
                    ipv6_chk_mcast_addr(dev, &skb->nh.ipv6h->daddr)) {
                        struct sk_buff *newskb = skb_clone(skb, GFP_ATOMIC);

                        /* Do not check for IFF_ALLMULTI; multicast routing
                           is not supported in any case.
                         */
                        if (newskb)
                                NF_HOOK(PF_INET, NF_IP6_POST_ROUTING, newskb, NULL,
                                        newskb->dev,
                                        ip6_dev_loopback_xmit);

                        if (skb->nh.ipv6h->hop_limit == 0) {
                                kfree_skb(skb);
                                return 0;
                        }
                }

                IP6_INC_STATS(Ip6OutMcastPkts);
        }

        return NF_HOOK(PF_INET6, NF_IP6_POST_ROUTING, skb,NULL, skb->dev,ip6_output_finish);
}
```

Then the hard work is done in the actual transmit function.

Figure 6.360 IPv6—Xmit: `linux/net/ipv6/ip6_output.c.`

```
int ip6_xmit(struct sock *sk, struct sk_buff *skb, struct flowi *fl,
             struct ipv6_txoptions *opt)
{
        struct ipv6_pinfo * np = sk ? &sk->net_pinfo.af_inet6 : NULL;
        struct in6_addr *first_hop = fl->nl_u.ip6_u.daddr;
        struct dst_entry *dst = skb->dst;
        struct ipv6hdr *hdr;
        u8  proto = fl->proto;
        int seg_len = skb->len;
        int hlimit;

        if (opt) {
```

```
            int head_room;

            /* First: exthdrs may take lots of space (~8K for now)
               MAX_HEADER is not enough.
             */
            head_room = opt->opt_nflen + opt->opt_flen;
            seg_len += head_room;
            head_room += sizeof(struct ipv6hdr) + ((dst->dev->hard_header_len + 15)&~15);

            if (skb_headroom(skb) < head_room) {
                struct sk_buff *skb2 = skb_realloc_headroom(skb, head_room);
                kfree_skb(skb);
                skb = skb2;
                if (skb == NULL)
                    return -ENOBUFS;
                if (sk)
                    skb_set_owner_w(skb, sk);
            }
            if (opt->opt_flen)
                ipv6_push_frag_opts(skb, opt, &proto);
            if (opt->opt_nflen)
                ipv6_push_nfrag_opts(skb, opt, &proto, &first_hop);
        }

        hdr = skb->nh.ipv6h = (struct ipv6hdr*)skb_push(skb, sizeof(struct ipv6hdr));
```

Figure 6.361 IPv6—output: `linux/net/ipv6/ip6_output.c`.

```
        /*
         *      Fill in the IPv6 header
         */

        *(u32*)hdr = __constant_htonl(0x60000000) | fl->fl6_flowlabel;
        hlimit = -1;
        if (np)
            hlimit = np->hop_limit;
        if (hlimit < 0)
            hlimit = ((struct rt6_info*)dst)->rt6i_hoplimit;

        hdr->payload_len = htons(seg_len);
        hdr->nexthdr = proto;
        hdr->hop_limit = hlimit;

        ipv6_addr_copy(&hdr->saddr, fl->nl_u.ip6_u.saddr);
        ipv6_addr_copy(&hdr->daddr, first_hop);

        if (skb->len <= dst->pmtu) {
            IP6_INC_STATS(Ip6OutRequests);
            return NF_HOOK(PF_INET6, NF_IP6_LOCAL_OUT, skb, NULL, dst->dev,ip6_maybe_reroute);
        }

        printk(KERN_DEBUG "IPv6: sending pkt_too_big to self\n");
```

```
        icmpv6_send(skb, ICMPV6_PKT_TOOBIG, 0, dst->pmtu, skb->dev);
        kfree_skb(skb);
        return -EMSGSIZE;
}
```

The packet building is a little more complex due to the IPv6 option structures.

Figure 6.362 IPv6—output: `linux/net/ipv6/ip6_output.c`.

```
int ip6_build_xmit(struct sock *sk, inet_getfrag_t getfrag, const void *data,
```

Figure 6.363 IPv6—output: `linux/net/ipv6/ip6_output.c`.

```
        last_skb->dst = dst_clone(dst);

        skb_reserve(last_skb, (dst->dev->hard_header_len + 15) & ~15);

        hdr = ip6_bld_1(sk, last_skb, fl, hlimit, frag_len+unfrag_len);
        prev_hdr = &hdr->nexthdr;

        if (opt && opt->opt_nflen)
                prev_hdr = ipv6_build_nfrag_opts(last_skb, prev_hdr, opt, final_dst, 0);

        prev_hdr = ipv6_build_fraghdr(last_skb, prev_hdr, frag_off);
        fhdr_dist = prev_hdr - last_skb->data;

        err = getfrag(data, &hdr->saddr, last_skb->tail, data_off, last_len);

        if (!err) {
                while (nfrags--) {
                        struct sk_buff *skb;

                        struct frag_hdr *fhdr2;

                        skb = skb_copy(last_skb, sk->allocation);

                        if (skb == NULL) {
                                IP6_INC_STATS(Ip6FragFails);
                                kfree_skb(last_skb);
                                return -ENOMEM;
                        }

                        frag_off -= frag_len;
                        data_off -= frag_len;

                        fhdr2 = (struct frag_hdr *) (skb->data + fhdr_dist);

                        /* more flag on */
                        fhdr2->frag_off = htons(frag_off | 1);
```

```

                /* Write fragmentable exthdrs to the first chunk */
                if (nfrags == 0 && opt && opt->opt_flen) {
                        ipv6_build_frag_opts(skb, &fhdr2->nexthdr, opt);
                        frag_len -= opt->opt_flen;
                        data_off = 0;
                }

                err = getfrag(data, &hdr->saddr,skb_put(skb, frag_len),
                              data_off, frag_len);

                if (err) {
                        kfree_skb(skb);
                        break;
                }

                IP6_INC_STATS(Ip6FragCreates);
                IP6_INC_STATS(Ip6OutRequests);
                err = NF_HOOK(PF_INET6,NF_IP6_LOCAL_OUT, skb, NULL, dst->dev,
                     ip6_maybe_reroute);
                if (err) {
                        kfree_skb(last_skb);
                        return err;
                }
        }
    }

    if (err) {
        IP6_INC_STATS(Ip6FragFails);
        kfree_skb(last_skb);
        return -EFAULT;
    }

    hdr->payload_len = htons(unfrag_len + last_len - sizeof(struct ipv6hdr));

    /*
     *      update last_skb to reflect the getfrag we did
     *      on start.
     */

    skb_put(last_skb, last_len);

    IP6_INC_STATS(Ip6FragCreates);
    IP6_INC_STATS(Ip6FragOKs);
    IP6_INC_STATS(Ip6OutRequests);
    return NF_HOOK(PF_INET6, NF_IP6_LOCAL_OUT, last_skb, NULL,dst->dev, ip6_maybe_reroute);
}

int ip6_build_xmit(struct sock *sk, inet_getfrag_t getfrag, const void *data,
                   struct flowi *fl, unsigned length,
                   struct ipv6_txoptions *opt, int hlimit, int flags)
{
    struct ipv6_pinfo *np = &sk->net_pinfo.af_inet6;
    struct in6_addr *final_dst = NULL;
    struct dst_entry *dst;
```

```
        int err = 0;
        unsigned int pktlength, jumbolen, mtu;
        struct in6_addr saddr;

        if (opt && opt->srcrt) {
                struct rt0_hdr *rt0 = (struct rt0_hdr *) opt->srcrt;
                final_dst = fl->fl6_dst;
                fl->fl6_dst = rt0->addr;
        }

        if (!fl->oif && ipv6_addr_is_multicast(fl->nl_u.ip6_u.daddr))
                fl->oif = np->mcast_oif;

        dst = __sk_dst_check(sk, np->dst_cookie);
        if (dst) {
                struct rt6_info *rt = (struct rt6_info*)dst;

                        /* Yes, checking route validity in not connected
                           case is not very simple. Take into account,
                           that we do not support routing by source, TOS,
                           and MSG_DONTROUTE          --ANK (980726)

                           1. If route was host route, check that
                              cached destination is current.
                              If it is network route, we still may
                              check its validity using saved pointer
                              to the last used address: daddr_cache.
                              We do not want to save whole address now,
                              (because main consumer of this service
                               is tcp, which has not this problem),
                              so that the last trick works only on connected
                              sockets.
                           2. oif also should be the same.
                         */

                if (((rt->rt6i_dst.plen != 128 ||
                      ipv6_addr_cmp(fl->fl6_dst, &rt->rt6i_dst.addr))
                     && (np->daddr_cache == NULL ||
                        ipv6_addr_cmp(fl->fl6_dst, np->daddr_cache)))
                    || (fl->oif && fl->oif != dst->dev->ifindex)) {
                        dst = NULL;
                } else
                        dst_clone(dst);
        }
```

Figure 6.364 IPv6—output: `linux/net/ipv6/ip6_output.c`.

```
        if (dst == NULL)
                dst = ip6_route_output(sk, fl);

        if (dst->error) {
                IP6_INC_STATS(Ip6OutNoRoutes);
                dst_release(dst);
```

```
554                     return -ENETUNREACH;
555             }
556
557         if (fl->fl6_src == NULL) {
558                     err = ipv6_get_saddr(dst, fl->fl6_dst, &saddr);
559
560                     if (err) {
561 #if IP6_DEBUG >= 2
562                         printk(KERN_DEBUG "ip6_build_xmit: "
563                             "no availiable source address\n");
564 #endif
565                         goto out;
566                     }
567                     fl->fl6_src = &saddr;
568             }
569         pktlength = length;
570
571         if (hlimit < 0) {
572                 if (ipv6_addr_is_multicast(fl->fl6_dst))
573                     hlimit = np->mcast_hops;
574                 else
575                     hlimit = np->hop_limit;
576                 if (hlimit < 0)
577                     hlimit = ((struct rt6_info*)dst)->rt6i_hoplimit;
578             }
```

Figure 6.365 IPv6—output: `linux/net/ipv6/ip6_output.c`.

```
580         jumbolen = 0;
581
582         if (!sk->protinfo.af_inet.hdrincl) {
583                 pktlength += sizeof(struct ipv6hdr);
584                 if (opt)
585                     pktlength += opt->opt_flen + opt->opt_nflen;
586
587                 if (pktlength > 0xFFFF + sizeof(struct ipv6hdr)) {
588                     /* Jumbo datagram.
589                        It is assumed, that in the case of hdrincl
590                        jumbo option is supplied by user.
591                     */
592                     pktlength += 8;
593                     jumbolen = pktlength - sizeof(struct ipv6hdr);
594                 }
595             }
596
597         mtu = dst->pmtu;
598         if (np->frag_size < mtu) {
599                 if (np->frag_size)
600                     mtu = np->frag_size;
601                 else if (np->pmtudisc == IPV6_PMTUDISC_DONT)
602                     mtu = IPV6_MIN_MTU;
603             }
```

```

        /* Critical arithmetic overflow check.
           FIXME: may gcc optimize it out? --ANK (980726)
         */
        if (pktlength < length) {
                ipv6_local_error(sk, EMSGSIZE, fl, mtu);
                err = -EMSGSIZE;
                goto out;
        }

        if (flags&MSG_CONFIRM)
                dst_confirm(dst);
```

Figure 6.366 IPv6—output: `linux/net/ipv6/ip6_output.c`.

```
        if (pktlength <= mtu) {
                struct sk_buff *skb;
                struct ipv6hdr *hdr;
                struct net_device *dev = dst->dev;

                err = 0;
                if (flags&MSG_PROBE)
                        goto out;

                skb = sock_alloc_send_skb(sk, pktlength + 15 +
                                          dev->hard_header_len, 0,
                                          flags & MSG_DONTWAIT, &err);

                if (skb == NULL) {
                        IP6_INC_STATS(Ip6OutDiscards);
                        goto out;
                }

                skb->dst = dst_clone(dst);

                skb_reserve(skb, (dev->hard_header_len + 15) & ~15);

                hdr = (struct ipv6hdr *) skb->tail;
                skb->nh.ipv6h = hdr;

                if (!sk->protinfo.af_inet.hdrincl) {
                        ip6_bld_1(sk, skb, fl, hlimit,
                                  jumbolen ? sizeof(struct ipv6hdr) : pktlength);

                        if (opt || jumbolen) {
                                u8 *prev_hdr = &hdr->nexthdr;
                                prev_hdr = ipv6_build_nfrag_opts(skb, prev_hdr, opt, final_dst,
                                     jumbolen);
                                if (opt && opt->opt_flen)
                                        ipv6_build_frag_opts(skb, prev_hdr, opt);
                        }
                }
```

Figure 6.367 IPv6—output: `linux/net/ipv6/ip6_output.c`.

```
654                    skb_put(skb, length);
655                    err = getfrag(data, &hdr->saddr,
656                                  ((char *) hdr) + (pktlength - length),
657                                  0, length);
658
659                    if (!err) {
660                            IP6_INC_STATS(Ip6OutRequests);
661                            err = NF_HOOK(PF_INET6, NF_IP6_LOCAL_OUT, skb, NULL, dst->dev,
                                          ip6_maybe_reroute);
662                    } else {
663                            err = -EFAULT;
664                            kfree_skb(skb);
665                    }
666            } else {
667                    if (sk->protinfo.af_inet.hdrincl || jumbolen ||
668                        np->pmtudisc == IPV6_PMTUDISC_DO) {
669                            ipv6_local_error(sk, EMSGSIZE, fl, mtu);
670                            err = -EMSGSIZE;
671                            goto out;
672                    }
673
674                    err = ip6_frag_xmit(sk, getfrag, data, dst, fl, opt, final_dst, hlimit,
675                                        flags, longth, mtu);
676            }
677
678            /*
679             *     cleanup
680             */
681    out:
682            ip6_dst_store(sk, dst, fl->nl_u.ip6_u.daddr == &np->daddr ? &np->daddr : NULL);
683            if (err > 0)
684                    err = np->recverr ? net_xmit_errno(err) : 0;
685            return err;
686    }
```

6.9.7 IPv6 Forward Function

Figure 6.368 IPv6—forward: `linux/net/ipv6/ip6_output.c`.

```
720    int ip6_forward(struct sk_buff *skb)
721    {
722            struct dst_entry *dst = skb->dst;
723            struct ipv6hdr *hdr = skb->nh.ipv6h;
724            struct inet6_skb_parm *opt =(struct inet6_skb_parm*)skb->cb;
725
726            if (ipv6_devconf.forwarding == 0 && opt->srcrt == 0)
727                    goto drop;
728
```

```
	/*
	 *	We DO NOT make any processing on
	 *	RA packets, pushing them to user level AS IS
	 *	without ane WARRANTY that application will be able
	 *	to interpret them. The reason is that we
	 *	cannot make anything clever here.
	 *
	 *	We are not end-node, so that if packet contains
	 *	AH/ESP, we cannot make anything.
	 *	Defragmentation also would be mistake, RA packets
	 *	cannot be fragmented, because there is no warranty
	 *	that different fragments will go along one path. --ANK
	 */
	if (opt->ra) {
		u8 *ptr = skb->nh.raw + opt->ra;
		if (ip6_call_ra_chain(skb, (ptr[2]<<8) + ptr[3]))
			return 0;
	}

	/*
	 *	check and decrement ttl
	 */
	if (hdr->hop_limit <= 1) {
		/* Force OUTPUT device used as source address */
		skb->dev = dst->dev;
		icmpv6_send(skb, ICMPV6_TIME_EXCEED, ICMPV6_EXC_HOPLIMIT,
			    0, skb->dev);

		kfree_skb(skb);
		return -ETIMEDOUT;
	}
```

Figure 6.369 IPv6—forward: `linux/net/ipv6/ip6_output.c.`

```

	/* IPv6 specs say nothing about it, but it is clear that we cannot
	   send redirects to source routed frames.
	 */
	if (skb->dev == dst->dev && dst->neighbour && opt->srcrt == 0) {
		struct in6_addr *target = NULL;
		struct rt6_info *rt;
		struct neighbour *n = dst->neighbour;

		/*
		 *	incoming and outgoing devices are the same
		 *	send a redirect.
		 */

		rt = (struct rt6_info *) dst;
		if ((rt->rt6i_flags & RTF_GATEWAY))
			target = (struct in6_addr*)&n->primary_key;
		else
```

```
			target = &hdr->daddr;

		/* Limit redirects both by destination (here)
		   and by source (inside ndisc_send_redirect)
		 */
		if (xrlim_allow(dst, 1*HZ))
			ndisc_send_redirect(skb, n, target);
	} else if (ipv6_addr_type(&hdr->saddr)&(IPV6_ADDR_MULTICAST|IPV6_ADDR_LOOPBACK
						|IPV6_ADDR_LINKLOCAL)) {
		/* This check is security critical. */
		goto drop;
	}
```

Figure 6.370 IPv6—forward: `linux/net/ipv6/ip6_output.c`.

```
	if (skb->len > dst->pmtu) {
		/* Again, force OUTPUT device used as source address */
		skb->dev = dst->dev;
		icmpv6_send(skb, ICMPV6_PKT_TOOBIG, 0, dst->pmtu, skb->dev);
		IP6_INC_STATS_BH(Ip6InTooBigErrors);
		kfree_skb(skb);
		return -EMSGSIZE;
	}

	if ((skb = skb_cow(skb, dst->dev->hard_header_len)) == NULL)
		return 0;

	hdr = skb->nh.ipv6h;

	/* Mangling hops number delayed to point after skb COW */

	hdr->hop_limit--;

	IP6_INC_STATS_BH(Ip6OutForwDatagrams);
	return NF_HOOK(PF_INET6,NF_IP6_FORWARD, skb, skb->dev, dst->dev, ip6_forward_finish);

drop:
	IP6_INC_STATS_BH(Ip6InAddrErrors);
	kfree_skb(skb);
	return -EINVAL;
}
```

6.9.8 IPv6 Socket Glue

The socket glue code is slightly different from IPv4 because the socket options are slightly different, as you would expect. Here is an excerpt:

Figure 6.371 IPv6—socket glue set socket options: `linux/net/ipv6/ipv6_sockglue.c`.

```
int ipv6_setsockopt(struct sock *sk, int level, int optname, char *optval,
                    int optlen)
{
        struct ipv6_pinfo *np = &sk->net_pinfo.af_inet6;
        int val, valbool;
        int retv = -ENOPROTOOPT;

        if(level==SOL_IP && sk->type != SOCK_RAW)
                return udp_prot.setsockopt(sk, level, optname, optval, optlen);

        if(level!=SOL_IPV6)
                goto out;

        if (optval == NULL)
                val=0;
        else if (get_user(val, (int *) optval))
                return -EFAULT;

        valbool = (val!=0);

        lock_sock(sk);

        switch (optname) {
```

Addressing:

Figure 6.372 IPv6—socket glue set socket options: `linux/net/ipv6/ipv6_sockglue.c`.

```
        case IPV6_ADDRFORM:
                if (val == PF_INET) {
                        struct ipv6_txoptions *opt;
                        struct sk_buff *pktopt;

                        if (sk->protocol != IPPROTO_UDP &&
                            sk->protocol != IPPROTO_TCP)
                                break;

                        if (sk->state != TCP_ESTABLISHED) {
                                retv = -ENOTCONN;
                                break;
                        }

                        if (!(ipv6_addr_type(&np->daddr) & IPV6_ADDR_MAPPED)) {
                                retv = -EADDRNOTAVAIL;
                                break;
                        }

                        fl6_free_socklist(sk);
                        ipv6_sock_mc_close(sk);
```

```
167
168                          if (sk->protocol == IPPROTO_TCP) {
169                                  struct tcp_opt *tp = &(sk->tp_pinfo.af_tcp);
170
171                                  local_bh_disable();
172                                  sock_prot_dec_use(sk->prot);
173                                  sock_prot_inc_use(&tcp_prot);
174                                  local_bh_enable();
175                                  sk->prot = &tcp_prot;
176                                  tp->af_specific = &ipv4_specific;
177                                  sk->socket->ops = &inet_stream_ops;
178                                  sk->family = PF_INET;
179                                  tcp_sync_mss(sk, tp->pmtu_cookie);
180                          } else {
181                                  local_bh_disable();
182                                  sock_prot_dec_use(sk->prot);
183                                  sock_prot_inc_use(&udp_prot);
184                                  local_bh_enable();
185                                  sk->prot = &udp_prot;
186                                  sk->socket->ops = &inet_dgram_ops;
187                                  sk->family = PF_INET;
188                          }
189                          opt = xchg(&np->opt, NULL);
190                          if (opt)
191                                  sock_kfree_s(sk, opt, opt->tot_len);
192                          pktopt = xchg(&np->pktoptions, NULL);
193                          if (pktopt)
194                                  kfree_skb(pktopt);
195
196                          sk->destruct = inet_sock_destruct;
197 #ifdef INET_REFCNT_DEBUG
198                          atomic_dec(&inet6_sock_nr);
199 #endif
200                          MOD_DEC_USE_COUNT;
201                          retv = 0;
202                          break;
203                  }
204          goto e_inval;
```

Figure 6.373 IPv6—socket glue set socket options: `linux/net/ipv6/ipv6_sockglue.c`.

```
206          case IPV6_PKTINFO:
207                  np->rxopt.bits.rxinfo = valbool;
208                  retv = 0;
209                  break;
210
211          case IPV6_HOPLIMIT:
212                  np->rxopt.bits.rxhlim = valbool;
213                  retv = 0;
214                  break;
215
216          case IPV6_RTHDR:
```

```
217                       if (val < 0 || val > 2)
218                               goto e_inval;
219                       np->rxopt.bits.srcrt = val;
220                       retv = 0;
221                       break;
222
223               case IPV6_HOPOPTS:
224                       np->rxopt.bits.hopopts = valbool;
225                       retv = 0;
226                       break;
227
228               case IPV6_AUTHHDR:
229                       np->rxopt.bits.authhdr = valbool;
230                       retv = 0;
231                       break;
232
233               case IPV6_DSTOPTS:
234                       np->rxopt.bits.dstopts = valbool;
235                       retv = 0;
236                       break;
237
238               case IPV6_FLOWINFO:
239                       np->rxopt.bits.rxflow = valbool;
240                       retv = 0;
241                       break;
```

Packet options:

Figure 6.374 IPv6—socket glue set socket options: `linux/net/ipv6/ipv6_sockglue.c`.

```
243               case IPV6_PKTOPTIONS:
244               {
245                       struct ipv6_txoptions *opt = NULL;
246                       struct msghdr msg;
247                       struct flowi fl;
248                       int junk;
249
250                       fl.fl6_flowlabel = 0;
251                       fl.oif = sk->bound_dev_if;
252
253                       if (optlen == 0)
254                               goto update;
255
256                       opt = sock_kmalloc(sk, sizeof(*opt) + optlen, GFP_KERNEL);
257                       retv = -ENOBUFS;
258                       if (opt == NULL)
259                               break;
260
261                       memset(opt, 0, sizeof(*opt));
262                       opt->tot_len = sizeof(*opt) + optlen;
263                       retv = -EFAULT;
264                       if (copy_from_user(opt+1, optval, optlen))
```

```
265                       goto done;
266
267               msg.msg_controllen = optlen;
268               msg.msg_control = (void*)(opt+1);
269
270               retv = datagram_send_ctl(&msg, &fl, opt, &junk);
271               if (retv)
272                       goto done;
273   update:
274               retv = 0;
275               if (sk->type == SOCK_STREAM) {
276                       if (opt) {
277                               struct tcp_opt *tp = &sk->tp_pinfo.af_tcp;
278                               if (!((1<<sk->state)&(TCPF_LISTEN|TCPF_CLOSE))
279                                   && sk->daddr != LOOPBACK4_IPV6) {
280                                       tp->ext_header_len = opt->opt_flen + opt->opt_nflen;
281                                       tcp_sync_mss(sk, tp->pmtu_cookie);
282                               }
283                       }
284                       opt = xchg(&np->opt, opt);
285                       sk_dst_reset(sk);
286               } else {
287                       write_lock(&sk->dst_lock);
288                       opt = xchg(&np->opt, opt);
289                       write_unlock(&sk->dst_lock);
290                       sk_dst_reset(sk);
291               }
292
293   done:
294               if (opt)
295                       sock_kfree_s(sk, opt, opt->tot_len);
296               break;
297       }
```

Multicast parameters:

Figure 6.375 IPv6—socket glue set socket options: `linux/net/ipv6/ipv6_sockglue.c`.

```
298       case IPV6_UNICAST_HOPS:
299               if (val > 255 || val < -1)
300                       goto e_inval;
301               np->hop_limit = val;
302               retv = 0;
303               break;
304
305       case IPV6_MULTICAST_HOPS:
306               if (sk->type == SOCK_STREAM)
307                       goto e_inval;
308               if (val > 255 || val < -1)
309                       goto e_inval;
310               np->mcast_hops = val;
311               retv = 0;
```

```
			break;

		case IPV6_MULTICAST_LOOP:
			np->mc_loop = valbool;
			retv = 0;
			break;

		case IPV6_MULTICAST_IF:
			if (sk->type == SOCK_STREAM)
				goto e_inval;
			if (sk->bound_dev_if && sk->bound_dev_if != val)
				goto e_inval;

			if (__dev_get_by_index(val) == NULL) {
				retv = -ENODEV;
				break;
			}
			np->mcast_oif = val;
			retv = 0;
			break;
```

Multicast membership:

Figure 6.376 IPv6—socket glue set socket options: `linux/net/ipv6/ipv6_sockglue.c`.

```
		case IPV6_ADD_MEMBERSHIP:
		case IPV6_DROP_MEMBERSHIP:
		{
			struct ipv6_mreq mreq;

			retv = -EFAULT;
			if (copy_from_user(&mreq, optval, sizeof(struct ipv6_mreq)))
				break;

			if (optname == IPV6_ADD_MEMBERSHIP)
				retv = ipv6_sock_mc_join(sk, mreq.ipv6mr_ifindex, &mreq.ipv6mr_multiaddr);
			else
				retv = ipv6_sock_mc_drop(sk, mreq.ipv6mr_ifindex, &mreq.ipv6mr_multiaddr);
			break;
		}
```

Path parameters:

Figure 6.377 IPv6—socket glue set socket options: `linux/net/ipv6/ipv6_sockglue.c`.

```
		case IPV6_ROUTER_ALERT:
			retv = ip6_ra_control(sk, val, NULL);
			break;
		case IPV6_MTU_DISCOVER:
```

```
351                 if (val<0 || val>2)
352                         goto e_inval;
353                 np->pmtudisc = val;
354                 retv = 0;
355                 break;
356         case IPV6_MTU:
357                 if (val && val < IPV6_MIN_MTU)
358                         goto e_inval;
359                 np->frag_size = val;
360                 retv = 0;
361                 break;
362         case IPV6_RECVERR:
363                 np->recverr = valbool;
364                 if (!val)
365                         skb_queue_purge(&sk->error_queue);
366                 retv = 0;
367                 break;
368         case IPV6_FLOWINFO_SEND:
369                 np->sndflow = valbool;
370                 retv = 0;
371                 break;
372         case IPV6_FLOWLABEL_MGR:
373                 retv = ipv6_flowlabel_opt(sk, optval, optlen);
374                 break;
375
376 #ifdef CONFIG_NETFILTER
377         default:
378                 retv = nf_setsockopt(sk, PF_INET6, optname, optval,
379                                         optlen);
380                 break;
381 #endif
382
383         }
384         release_sock(sk);
385
386 out:
387         return retv;
388
389 e_inval:
390         release_sock(sk);
391         return -EINVAL;
392 }
```

6.9.9 IPv6 Flow Label

Flow labels are a unique feature of IPv6 that can be used as fast routing table indexes. They may refer to a session at a higher level (hence the name *flow*), and thus also index flow state such as differentiated or integrated services, as discussed in Chapter 9.

Here is an excerpt of the flow label management code:

Figure 6.378 IPv6 flow label creation: `linux/net/ipv6/ip6_flowlabel.c`.

```
274  static struct ip6_flowlabel *
275  fl_create(struct in6_flowlabel_req *freq, char *optval, int optlen, int *err_p)
276  {
277          struct ip6_flowlabel *fl;
278          int olen;
279          int addr_type;
280          int err;
281
282          err = -ENOMEM;
283          fl = kmalloc(sizeof(*fl), GFP_KERNEL);
284          if (fl == NULL)
285                  goto done;
286          memset(fl, 0, sizeof(*fl));
```

Figure 6.379 IPv6 flow label creation: `linux/net/ipv6/ip6_flowlabel.c`.

```
288          olen = optlen - CMSG_ALIGN(sizeof(*freq));
289          if (olen > 0) {
290                  struct msghdr msg;
291                  struct flowi flowi;
292                  int junk;
293
294                  err = -ENOMEM;
295                  fl->opt = kmalloc(sizeof(*fl->opt) + olen, GFP_KERNEL);
296                  if (fl->opt == NULL)
297                          goto done;
298
299                  memset(fl->opt, 0, sizeof(*fl->opt));
300                  fl->opt->tot_len = sizeof(*fl->opt) + olen;
301                  err = -EFAULT;
302                  if (copy_from_user(fl->opt+1, optval+CMSG_ALIGN(sizeof(*freq)), olen))
303                          goto done;
304
305                  msg.msg_controllen = olen;
306                  msg.msg_control = (void*)(fl->opt+1);
307                  flowi.oif = 0;
308
309                  err = datagram_send_ctl(&msg, &flowi, fl->opt, &junk);
310                  if (err)
311                          goto done;
312                  err = -EINVAL;
313                  if (fl->opt->opt_flen)
314                          goto done;
315                  if (fl->opt->opt_nflen == 0) {
316                          kfree(fl->opt);
317                          fl->opt = NULL;
318                  }
319          }
```

Figure 6.380 IPv6 flow label creation: `linux/net/ipv6/ip6_flowlabel.c`.

```
        fl->expires = jiffies;
        err = fl6_renew(fl, freq->flr_linger, freq->flr_expires);
        if (err)
                goto done;
        fl->share = freq->flr_share;
        addr_type = ipv6_addr_type(&freq->flr_dst);
        if ((addr_type&IPV6_ADDR_MAPPED)
           || addr_type == IPV6_ADDR_ANY)
                goto done;
        ipv6_addr_copy(&fl->dst, &freq->flr_dst);
        atomic_set(&fl->users, 1);
        switch (fl->share) {
        case IPV6_FL_S_EXCL:
        case IPV6_FL_S_ANY:
                break;
        case IPV6_FL_S_PROCESS:
                fl->owner = current->pid;
                break;
        case IPV6_FL_S_USER:
                fl->owner = current->euid;
                break;
        default:
                err = -EINVAL;
                goto done;
        }
        return fl;

done:
        if (fl)
                fl_free(fl);
        *err_p = err;
        return NULL;
}
```

6.9.10 Extension Headers

IPv6 has a number of extension headers—to illustrate what may be present, let's look at the function used to skip them for ICMP, which doesn't want to consider them at all:

Figure 6.381 IPv6 extension headers: `linux/net/ipv6/exthdrs.c`.

```
/*
 * Skip any extension headers. This is used by the ICMP module.
 *
 * Note that strictly speaking this conflicts with RFC 1883 4.0:
 * ...The contents and semantics of each extension header determine whether
 * or not to proceed to the next header. Therefore, extension headers must
 * be processed strictly in the order they appear in the packet; a
```

```
 * receiver must not, for example, scan through a packet looking for a
 * particular kind of extension header and process that header prior to
 * processing all preceding ones.
 *
 * We do exactly this. This is a protocol bug. We can't decide after a
 * seeing an unknown discard-with-error flavour TLV option if it's a
 * ICMP error message or not (errors should never be send in reply to
 * ICMP error messages).
 *
 * But I see no other way to do this. This might need to be reexamined
 * when Linux implements ESP (and maybe AUTH) headers.
 * --AK
 *
 * This function parses (probably truncated) exthdr set "hdr"
 * of length "len". "nexthdrp" initially points to some place,
 * where type of the first header can be found.
 *
 * It skips all well-known exthdrs, and returns pointer to the start
 * of unparsable area i.e. the first header with unknown type.
 * If it is not NULL *nexthdr is updated by type/protocol of this header.
 *
 * NOTES: - if packet terminated with NEXTHDR_NONE it returns NULL.
 *        - it may return pointer pointing beyond end of packet,
 *          if the last recognized header is truncated in the middle.
 *        - if packet is truncated, so that all parsed headers are skipped,
 *          it returns NULL.
 *        - First fragment header is skipped, not-first ones
 *          are considered as unparsable.
 *        - ESP is unparsable for now and considered like
 *          normal payload protocol.
 *        - Note also special handling of AUTH header. Thanks to IPsec wizards.
 *
 * --ANK (980726)
 */
```

Figure 6.382 IPv6 extension headers: `linux/net/ipv6/exthdrs.c`.

```
u8 *ipv6_skip_exthdr(struct ipv6_opt_hdr *hdr, u8 *nexthdrp, int len)
{
        u8 nexthdr = *nexthdrp;

        while (ipv6_ext_hdr(nexthdr)) {
                int hdrlen;

                if (len < sizeof(struct ipv6_opt_hdr))
                        return NULL;
                if (nexthdr == NEXTHDR_NONE)
                        return NULL;
                if (nexthdr == NEXTHDR_FRAGMENT) {
                        struct frag_hdr *fhdr = (struct frag_hdr *) hdr;
                        if (ntohs(fhdr->frag_off) & ~0x7)
                                break;
```

```
                        hdrlen = 8;
                } else if (nexthdr == NEXTHDR_AUTH)
                        hdrlen = (hdr->hdrlen+2)<<2;
                else
                        hdrlen = ipv6_optlen(hdr);

                nexthdr = hdr->nexthdr;
                hdr = (struct ipv6_opt_hdr *) ((u8*)hdr + hdrlen);
                len -= hdrlen;
        }

        *nexthdrp = nexthdr;
        return (u8*)hdr;
}
```

6.9.11 Simple Internet Transition

SIT is like a GRE tunnel:

Figure 6.383 SIT: `linux/net/ipv6/sit.c`.

```
/*
   This version of net/ipv6/sit.c is cloned of net/ipv4/ip_gre.c

   For comments look at net/ipv4/ip_gre.c --ANK
 */

#define HASH_SIZE 16
#define HASH(addr) ((addr^(addr>>4))&0xF)

static int ipip6_fb_tunnel_init(struct net_device *dev);
static int ipip6_tunnel_init(struct net_device *dev);

static struct net_device ipip6_fb_tunnel_dev = {
        "sit0", 0x0, 0x0, 0x0, 0x0, 0, 0, 0, 0, 0, NULL, ipip6_fb_tunnel_init,
};

static struct ip_tunnel ipip6_fb_tunnel = {
        NULL, &ipip6_fb_tunnel_dev, {0, }, 0, 0, 0, 0, 0, 0, 0, {"sit0", }
};

static struct ip_tunnel *tunnels_r_l[HASH_SIZE];
static struct ip_tunnel *tunnels_r[HASH_SIZE];
static struct ip_tunnel *tunnels_l[HASH_SIZE];
static struct ip_tunnel *tunnels_wc[1];
static struct ip_tunnel **tunnels[4] = { tunnels_wc, tunnels_l, tunnels_r, tunnels_r_l };
```

Figure 6.384 SIT: `linux/net/ipv6/sit.c`.

```
static struct ip_tunnel * ipip6_tunnel_lookup(u32 remote, u32 local)
{
        unsigned h0 = HASH(remote);
        unsigned h1 = HASH(local);
        struct ip_tunnel *t;

        for (t = tunnels_r_l[h0^h1]; t; t = t->next) {
                if (local == t->parms.iph.saddr &&
                    remote == t->parms.iph.daddr && (t->dev->flags&IFF_UP))
                        return t;
        }
        for (t = tunnels_r[h0]; t; t = t->next) {
                if (remote == t->parms.iph.daddr && (t->dev->flags&IFF_UP))
                        return t;
        }
        for (t = tunnels_l[h1]; t; t = t->next) {
                if (local == t->parms.iph.saddr && (t->dev->flags&IFF_UP))
                        return t;
        }
        if ((t = tunnels_wc[0]) != NULL && (t->dev->flags&IFF_UP))
                return t;
        return NULL;
}
```

6.9.12 Effect on Transport of IPv6 of Note

In general, IPv6 has as little impact on transport and above as possible. The TCP and UDP pseudoheaders used for checksums have to be modified since they include parts of the IP header (including addresses). The modules `linux/net/ipv6/tcp_ipv6.c` and `linux/net/ipv6/udp.c` incorporate the relevant changes. These are relatively minor.

6.10 Summary

In this chapter, we looked at the implementation of the Internet infrastructure. The network is built out of links that carry IP packets. IP packets have to be framed for transmission and reception, so we looked at the Ethernet Local Area Network as an example of this, and covered a specific driver. IP addresses need to be translated into link layer addresses, so we looked at the Address Resolution Protocol. IP packets cause problems, and these must be reported from time to time, so we looked at the ICMP protocol. Penultimately, there are some things that require additional levels of encapsulation, so we looked at tunnels. Finally, IP is running out of address space, so a replacement, IPv6, has been designed and implemented, so we looked at the Linux implementation of that.

In the next chapter, we look at end-to-end protocols such as TCP, UDP, and RTP, which run over this infrastructure.

CHAPTER 7

Transport

7.1 Roadmap

This chapter talks about end-to-end transfer of data across IP networks. The Internet provides a number of different transport mechanisms. The most common ones are TCP (Transmission Control Protocol) and UDP (User Datagram Protocol).[1] TCP provides a connection-oriented, reliable, stream-based transport, and UDP an unreliable connectionless datagram-based one. RTP is a newer protocol designed for the transport of real-time streams such as video and audio. In this chapter we will examine the workings of UDP, TCP, and RTP, and their implementations in Linux.

The services transport protocols have to cover a wide range of services, including:

- Multiplexing
- Reliability
- Flow control
- Congestion control
- Framing
- Synchronization

[1] As with most acronyms on the Internet, the abbreviation is more important and well-known than the expansion.

This chapter covers the UDP protocol, by analysis of its use in the anatomy of a DNS lookup, and the TCP protocol, including the anatomy of flow providing service to HTTP, for a single Web page download. We also take a brief look at RTP.

7.2 Introduction

Transport protocols handle the end-to-end transfer of data between two IP-connected hosts. Each packet created by the transport layer is addressed to the destination host, and transported by the network layer. Higher-layer protocols and services will make use of the transport layer to transport their protocols. Recall from Chapter 6 that the network layer (and below) devices, such as switches and routers, store no state about the connections established or flows traversing through them. So any state information needed to maintain communication must be stored by the end system hosts.

7.3 UDP—User Datagram Protocol

UDP is much simpler than TCP, so we will discuss its operation first.

7.3.1 Introduction

UDP is a connectionless, unreliable datagram service. This means that there is no connection information maintained and therefore each packet carries its own addressing information. By unreliable we mean:

- That there is no guarantee that the data will be received by the destination process.
- That if it is received it may contain errors.
- That packets may arrive out of sequence, i.e., in a different order from the one in which they were transmitted.

UDP provides a multiplexing service over the basic IP functionality, and a simple form of error detection.

7.3.2 Multiplexing

Although most people will refer to hosts communicating over a network (such as the Internet), in reality it is software processes that communicate. Devices in the network layer (such as routers) will use the IP address information to route the packets to hosts. The host must then process the packet and eventually route the data carried to the appropriate software process. In the same way that a sailing ship needs to know both the country of its destination and the port of disembarkation, a port is used to identify the process that the data is destined for. Ports are transport layer information. In the TCP/IP suite, port numbers are 16-bit quantities.

Many hosts provide a set of server software processes such as Web servers. These servers listen for potential data packets or connections on so-called well-known ports. A mapping between service names and port numbers is in the `/etc/services` file. A sample is shown in Figure 7.1. Each line consists of a service name such as `ftp`, followed by a port number and protocol.

Figure 7.1 A sample from the /etc/services file.

```
tcpmux      1/tcp                       # TCP port service multiplexer
echo        7/tcp
echo        7/udp
discard     9/tcp      sink null
discard     9/udp      sink null
systat      11/tcp     users
daytime     13/tcp
daytime     13/udp
netstat     15/tcp
qotd        17/tcp     quote
msp         18/tcp                      # message send protocol
msp         18/udp                      # message send protocol
chargen     19/tcp     ttytst source
chargen     19/udp     ttytst source
ftp-data    20/tcp
ftp         21/tcp
fsp         21/udp     fspd
ssh         22/tcp                      # SSH Remote Login Protocol
ssh         22/udp                      # SSH Remote Login Protocol
telnet      23/tcp
```

7.3.3 UDP Packet Header Anatomy

The UDP datagram contains an 8-byte header and is carried within an IP datagram. When carrying UDP data, the IP protocol field is set to 17. The UDP header is shown in Figure 7.1a.

Figure 7.1a UDP header.

```
 0      7 8     15 16    23 24     31
+--------+--------+--------+--------+
|     Source      |   Destination   |
|      port       |      port       |
+--------+--------+--------+--------+
|                 |                 |
|     Length      |    Checksum     |
+--------+--------+--------+--------+
|
|          Data octets ...
+---------------- ...
```

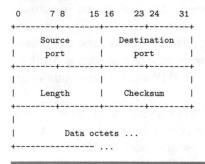

Figure 7.2 Linkage structures and functions (i).

```
struct proto_ops inet_stream_ops = {
       family:         PF_INET,

       release:        inet_release,
       bind:           inet_bind,
       connect:        inet_stream_connect,
       socketpair:     sock_no_socketpair,
       accept:         inet_accept,
       getname:        inet_getname,
       poll:           tcp_poll,
       ioctl:          inet_ioctl,
       listen:         inet_listen,
       shutdown:       inet_shutdown,
       setsockopt:     inet_setsockopt,
       getsockopt:     inet_getsockopt,
       sendmsg:        inet_sendmsg,
       recvmsg:        inet_recvmsg,
       mmap:           sock_no_mmap,
       sendpage:       tcp_sendpage
};

struct proto_ops inet_dgram_ops = {
```

The only transport layer facilities that UDP provides over and above that of the IP datagram layer are those of multiplexing and a checksum for rudimentary error checking.

Not only does UDP offer the disadvantage of no reliability in transmission, but also it cannot adapt to the network conditions. If the network is too highly loaded for the communication to take place, the UDP connection will be poor, and also have an adverse effect on other traffic on the network. The TCP transport described later in this chapter provides this extra functionality.

7.3.4 Transport Layer Linkage

This section describes the functions that link the transport layer to the socket layer above and the network layer below.

Socket to Transport Layer

A socket's life is one of create, operate on, and close. This section describes how the user space calls are passed through to kernel functions. We will use the example of socket creation to show this.

Socket state information is maintained in a number of structures:

- `struct socket`, which is a protocol-independent structure.
- `struct sock`, which contains transport layer information. In most of the functions, the current socket's `sock` structure is called `sk`.

The main socket code is in `net/socket.c`. Functions in this file are coded to call functions specific to the type of socket created.

When a socket is created (`socket` call) there is a call to `sys_socket`. This calls `sock_create` and then maps the socket to a file descriptor. This descriptor is passed back to the user process for future operations on the socket. `sock_create` allocates the socket and then calls the `create` function for the family of sockets being created (in the case of an IP network socket `PF_INET`).

Here reference is made to the `net_families` array, so we now need to travel to the initialization code for the Linux networking in order to see how this and other structures are initialized.

The `net_families` array is initialized when the kernel is booted in the `inet_init` function in `net/ipv4/af_inet.c`. This function is part of the code run at boot-up as can be seen from the printed message at the start of the function. One of the first operations in `inet_init` is to register the inet family of sockets with the socket functionality. Then the protocols are added to a hash table of protocols. These functions are in `protocol.c`.

The inet family is registered with the `sock_register` call, which is a function in `socket.c` that stores the family operations structure. This structure contains the family name and a create function for the socket family—`inet_create`.

The create function for `PF_INET` sockets is `inet_create`, which is the function called as `net_families[family]->create` in `sock_create`. `inet_create` allocates and initializes the sock structure. An important part of the initialization is the assignment of the socket operations structure to the ops field. The two main types of IP socket (`SOCK_STREAM` and `SOCK_DGRAM`) each have a set of functions associated with their operations. These are `inet_stream_ops` and `inet_dgram_ops`, which are statically initialized in `net/ipv4/af_inet.c`.

A further important structure to be initialized is the `prot` structure that contains specific functions for each protocol type. `udp_prot` and `tcp_prot` are static structures in net/ipv4/udp.c and net/ipv4/tcp_ipv4.c. This use of sets of function pointers allows for a greater use of generic code in the socket and inet functions. When the socket is created, there is a call to prot->init to initialize the socket.

To summarize the above, on startup the protocol family (PF_INET) is first registered. Each socket created has a set of socket operations (either inet_stream _ops or inet_dgram_ops). Each protocol, TCP or UDP, has a set of protocol functions (tcp_prot or udp_prot). Throughout the code, calls are made to these functions.

The first operation on most sockets after creation will be a connect call. This appears in the kernel as sys_connect in net/ipv4/socket.c. Here the socket is found (by looking up its file descriptor) and the memory block containing the address this socket is to be connected to is moved to the kernel. Then the the connect function out of sock->ops is called. For UDP this will be inet_dgram_connect (in af_inet.c), which itself calls connect in the sk->prot structure, which for UDP will be udp_connect. Other socket operations are passed through to the relevant function in this way.

Figure 7.3 Linkage structures and functions (ii).

```
struct proto udp_prot = {
        name:           "UDP",
        close:          udp_close,
        connect:        udp_connect,
        disconnect:     udp_disconnect,
        ioctl:          udp_ioctl,
        setsockopt:     ip_setsockopt,
        getsockopt:     ip_getsockopt,
        sendmsg:        udp_sendmsg,
        recvmsg:        udp_recvmsg,
        backlog_rcv:    udp_queue_rcv_skb,
        hash:           udp_v4_hash,
        unhash:         udp_v4_unhash,
        get_port:       udp_v4_get_port,
};
    . . .

struct proto tcp_prot = {
        name:           "TCP",
        close:          tcp_close,
        connect:        tcp_v4_connect,
        disconnect:     tcp_disconnect,
        accept:         tcp_accept,
        ioctl:          tcp_ioctl,
        init:           tcp_v4_init_sock,
        destroy:        tcp_v4_destroy_sock,
        shutdown:       tcp_shutdown,
        setsockopt:     tcp_setsockopt,
        getsockopt:     tcp_getsockopt,
        sendmsg:        tcp_sendmsg,
```

```
        recvmsg:        tcp_recvmsg,
        backlog_rcv:    tcp_v4_do_rcv,
        hash:           tcp_v4_hash,
        unhash:         tcp_unhash,
        get_port:       tcp_v4_get_port,
};
```

```
struct tcp_func ipv4_specific = {
        ip_queue_xmit,
        tcp_v4_send_check,
        tcp_v4_rebuild_header,
        tcp_v4_conn_request,
        tcp_v4_syn_recv_sock,
        tcp_v4_hash_connecting,
        tcp_v4_remember_stamp,
        sizeof(struct iphdr),

        ip_setsockopt,
        ip_getsockopt,
        v4_addr2sockaddr,
        sizeof(struct sockaddr_in)
};
```

Figure 7.4 Start of the sock structure `linux{2.4.4/include/net/sock.h.`

```
struct sock {
        /* Socket demultiplex comparisons on incoming packets. */
        __u32               daddr;        /* Foreign IPv4 addr              */
        __u32               rcv_saddr;    /* Bound local IPv4 addr          */
        __u16               dport;        /* Destination port               */
        unsigned short      num;          /* Local port                     */
        int                 bound_dev_if; /* Bound device index if != 0     */

        /* Main hash linkage for various protocol lookup tables. */
        struct sock         *next;
        struct sock         **pprev;
        struct sock         *bind_next;
        struct sock         **bind_pprev;
```

IP Layer Linkage

The `af_specific` structure contains functions that pass data to and from the network layer. This is set to `ipv4_specific` when the socket is initialized. See Figure 7.3.

Figure 7.5 Strace of a DNS lookup.

```
1  socket(PF_INET, SOCK_DGRAM, IPPROTO_IP) = 3
2  connect(3, {sin_family=AF_INET, sin_port=htons(53), sin_addr=inet_addr("xxx.xxx.xxx.xxx")}}, 28)
       = 0
3  send(3, "xE\1\0\0\1\0\0\0\0\0\0\3www\5lboro\2ac\2uk\0\0\1\0"..., 33, 0) = 33
4  gettimeofday({986376794, 91755}, NULL) = 0
5  poll([{fd=3, events=POLLIN, revents=POLLIN}], 1, 5000) = 1
6  recvfrom(3, "xE\205\200\0\1\0\2\0\5\0\4\3www\5lboro\2ac\2uk\0\0\1\0"..., 1024, 0, {sin_family=
       AF_INET, sin_port=htons(53), sin_addr=inet_addr("xxx.xxx.xxx.xxx")}}, [16]) = 255
7  close(3)
```

7.3.5 The `sock` Structure

The `sock` structure holds information relevant to a particular socket. This information includes values such as the port numbers, destination address, and so on. It is declared in `linux/include/net/sock.h` (see Figure 7.4 for the part of the structure that stores the source and destination addresses and ports). Whenever a socket option is changed or queried, the kernel stores the value of the option in this structure. The `tp_pinfo` union contains a `struct tcp_opt`, which itself contains important TCP information, which we will cover in the TCP section following.

Socket structures are allocated by the `sk_alloc` call. Each socket maintains a reference count. When this reaches zero, the socket can be freed from memory (`sk_free`). The `sock_hold` and `sock_put` increment and decrement the reference counts. These are implemented in `linux/net/sock.c` and `linux/net/sock.h`.

Figure 7.6 UDP connect function `linux{2.4.4/net/ipv4/udp.c`.

```
int udp_connect(struct sock *sk, struct sockaddr *uaddr, int addr_len)
{
        struct sockaddr_in *usin = (struct sockaddr_in *) uaddr;
        struct rtable *rt;
        int err;


        if (addr_len < sizeof(*usin))
                return -EINVAL;

        if (usin->sin_family != AF_INET)
                return -EAFNOSUPPORT;

        sk_dst_reset(sk);

        err = ip_route_connect(&rt, usin->sin_addr.s_addr, sk->saddr,
                        sk->protinfo.af_inet.tos|sk->localroute, sk->bound_dev_if);
```

```
        if (err)
              return err;
        if ((rt->rt_flags&RTCF_BROADCAST) && !sk->broadcast) {
              ip_rt_put(rt);
              return -EACCES;
        }
        if(!sk->saddr)
              sk->saddr = rt->rt_src;       /* Update source address */
        if(!sk->rcv_saddr)
              sk->rcv_saddr = rt->rt_src;
        sk->daddr = rt->rt_dst;
        sk->dport = usin->sin_port;
        sk->state = TCP_ESTABLISHED;
        sk->protinfo.af_inet.id = jiffies ;

        sk_dst_set(sk, &rt->u.dst);
        return(0);
}
```

7.3.6 DNS Lookup

The Domain Name Service (DNS) is responsible for converting names to addresses on the Internet. The actual service is not described in this chapter, but we will use a DNS lookup as an example of an application that uses a UDP transport. In C, the function `gethostbyname` is the programming interface to this protocol. If we take a simple program that performs a lookup and simply outputs it to the screen, we observe the strace output in Figure 7.5. This output has been edited to only show the information appropriate to the DNS request and response. Here a call to `socket` creates a datagram (i.e., UDP) socket and connects it to the DNS server. As UDP is a datagram-based protocol, this connect simply updates structures in the operating system rather than generating network traffic. Any datagrams sent to this socket that are unaddressed will be forwarded using this connection information. A DNS packet is then formed and sent. The program must now wait for a reply and also be ready to time out if a reply is not forthcoming. Eventually a message is available and the `recvfrom` call allows it to be read. The socket is then closed.

Figure 7.7 UDP lookup disconnect function `linux{2.4.4/net/ipv4/udp.c.`

```
int udp_disconnect(struct sock *sk, int flags)
{
        /*
         *      1003.1g - break association.
         */

        sk->state = TCP_CLOSE;
```

```
        sk->daddr = 0;
        sk->dport = 0;
        sk->bound_dev_if = 0;
        if (!(sk->userlocks&SOCK_BINDADDR_LOCK)) {
                sk->rcv_saddr = 0;
                sk->saddr = 0;
#if defined(CONFIG_IPV6) || defined(CONFIG_IPV6_MODULE)
                memset(&sk->net_pinfo.af_inet6.saddr, 0, 16);
                memset(&sk->net_pinfo.af_inet6.rcv_saddr, 0, 16);
#endif
        }
        if (!(sk->userlocks&SOCK_BINDPORT_LOCK)) {
                sk->prot->unhash(sk);
                sk->sport = 0;
        }
        sk_dst_reset(sk);
        return 0;
}
```

We can now trace the path of this request through the Linux kernel to the IP layer, and then the response from the IP layer back to the application.

The socket is first created and then connected (`udp_connect`, see Figure 7.6), which as this is a datagram socket, doesn't result in any traffic across the network, but a modification of the kernel structures. Specifically, a routing table entry is created for this destination address and this entry is added to the socket structure.

The application library now builds a DNS request packet and passes this to the kernel with the `sendmsg` call. This is passed on by `socket.c` to `udp_send` in `net/ipv4/udp.c`. One of the operations of `sendmsg` is the calculation of the UDP checksum. This checksum provides for some rudimentary error checking at the receiver, and is calculated over the entire UDP packet and also some fields from the IP layer (a fake header) (see RFC 768). The checksum value is the one's complement of the sum of all the 16-bit words to be checked. This is inserted into the checksum field. At the receiver, the stack can simply add the values together, and an all ones sum indicates a correct packet. The packet is passed to the datagram (IP) layer via the `ip_build_xmit()` call. Note that the call to `ip_build_xmit()` call's second parameter is a function pointer. This pointer can take one of two values depending on whether the packet's checksum is to be calculated or not. In either case, the purpose of this function is to copy the data from user space to the IP layer directly, and if necessary calculate the checksum as the data are copied. A further optimization here would be to copy the data from user space directly to the interface adapter card. Figure 7.8 shows the building of the UDP header and the eventual transmission of the packet.

The request traverses the Internet to one or many servers and eventually a response is received. This is processed by the infrastructure protocols and buffered. The packet arrives at the UDP layer via a call to `udp_rcv`. This function is the handler function stored in the `inet_protocol` structure (see Chapter 4). `udp_rcv` first validates the packet (`udp_checksum_init`). If this check is passed and the packet is a multicast or broadcast packet, then it is delivered using `udp_v4_mcast_deliver`. Otherwise, the packet's socket is searched for (`udp_v4_lookup`). This function is shown in Figure 7.9.

If the socket is found then the data is queued. If a socket is not found then this could be due either to an errored packet, or an attempted communication to a port without a bound process. If the former case, the checksum failure will cause the packet to be silently dropped, and in the latter, an ICMP port unreachable message is returned to the sender (see Figure 7.10).

UDP (and TCP) checksums are performed over the entire segment and an additional pseudoheader, which includes some IP layer fields (addresses, protocol type, length, and so on). This provides some extra integrity if the IP checksum has failed to catch errored packets. For reasons of performance, the checksums are calculated as the packets are copied from user space to the kernel (see `linux/net/core/iovec.c`).

When the application is ready to receive a message it calls `recv`, `recvfrom`, or `recvmsg`, which arrive in `udp.c` as a call `udp_recvmsg()`. Here, if a datagram is available, it is taken from the datagram layer (`skb_recv_datagram`) and copied to user space. As with transmit, a checksum calculation is done as the data are copied and if this fails then an error is returned. After this, the source address of the datagram is placed into a `sockaddr` structure for copying to the parameter of a `recvfrom` or `recvmsg` call.

When the application has finished using the socket, `close` will be called. This passes to the kernel as `sock_release`, which then calls the release operation for the protocol—`inet_release`. This in turn calls the close operation, `udp_close`, which in turn calls `inet_sock_release`. Here the resources used by the socket begin to be released back to the system. A point to note is that although this machine has finished with the socket and its communication, there may be packets in the network still arriving. The system is left in a state to handle these.

Figure 7.8 Building and sending a UDP packet (from `udp_sendmsg`).

```
        ufh.saddr = rt->rt_src;
        if (!ipc.addr)
                ufh.daddr = ipc.addr = rt->rt_dst;
        ufh.uh.len = htons(ulen);
        ufh.uh.check = 0;
        ufh.iov = msg->msg_iov;
        ufh.wcheck = 0;

        /* RFC1122: OK. Provides the checksumming facility (MUST) as per */
        /* 4.1.3.4. It's configurable by the application via setsockopt() */
```

```
545              /* (MAY) and it defaults to on (MUST). */
546
547          err = ip_build_xmit(sk,
548                            (sk->no_check == UDP_CSUM_NOXMIT ?
549                             udp_getfrag_nosum :
550                             udp_getfrag),
551                            &ufh, ulen, &ipc, rt, msg->msg_flags);
552
553  out:
554          ip_rt_put(rt);
555          if (free)
556                  kfree(ipc.opt);
557          if (!err) {
558                  UDP_INC_STATS_USER(UdpOutDatagrams);
559                  return len;
560          }
561          return err;
562
563  do_confirm:
```

Figure 7.9 UDP lookup socket function `linux{2.4.4/net/ipv4/udp.c`.

```
211  struct sock *udp_v4_lookup_longway(u32 saddr, u16 sport, u32 daddr, u16 dport, int dif)
212  {
213          struct sock *sk, *result = NULL;
214          unsigned short hnum = ntohs(dport);
215          int badness = -1;
216
217          for(sk = udp_hash[hnum & (UDP_HTABLE_SIZE - 1)]; sk != NULL; sk = sk->next) {
218                  if(sk->num == hnum) {
219                          int score = 0;
220                          if(sk->rcv_saddr) {
221                                  if(sk->rcv_saddr != daddr)
222                                          continue;
223                                  score++;
224                          }
225                          if(sk->daddr) {
226                                  if(sk->daddr != saddr)
227                                          continue;
228                                  score++;
229                          }
230                          if(sk->dport) {
231                                  if(sk->dport != sport)
232                                          continue;
233                                  score++;
234                          }
235                          if(sk->bound_dev_if) {
236                                  if(sk->bound_dev_if != dif)
237                                          continue;
238                                  score++;
239                          }
240                          if(score == 4) {
241                                  result = sk;
```

```
242                          break;
243                   } else if(score > badness) {
244                          result = sk;
245                          badness = score;
246                   }
247             }
248      }
249      return result;
250 }
```

Figure 7.10 UDP actions after lookup `linux{2.4.4/net/ipv4/udp.c`.

```
899 if (udp_checksum_init(skb, uh, ulen, saddr, daddr) < 0)
900             goto csum_error;
901
902      if(rt->rt_flags & (RTCF_BROADCAST|RTCF_MULTICAST))
903             return udp_v4_mcast_deliver(skb, uh, saddr, daddr);
904
905      sk = udp_v4_lookup(saddr, uh->source, daddr, uh->dest, skb->dev->ifindex);
906
907      if (sk != NULL) {
908             udp_queue_rcv_skb(sk, skb);
909             sock_put(sk);
910             return 0;
911      }
912
913      /* No socket. Drop packet silently, if checksum is wrong */
914      if (udp_checksum_complete(skb))
915             goto csum_error;
916
917      UDP_INC_STATS_BH(UdpNoPorts);
918      icmp_send(skb, ICMP_DEST_UNREACH, ICMP_PORT_UNREACH, 0);
919
920      /*
921       * Hmm. We got an UDP packet to a port to which we
922       * don't wanna listen. Ignore it.
923       */
924      kfree_skb(skb);
925      return(0);
```

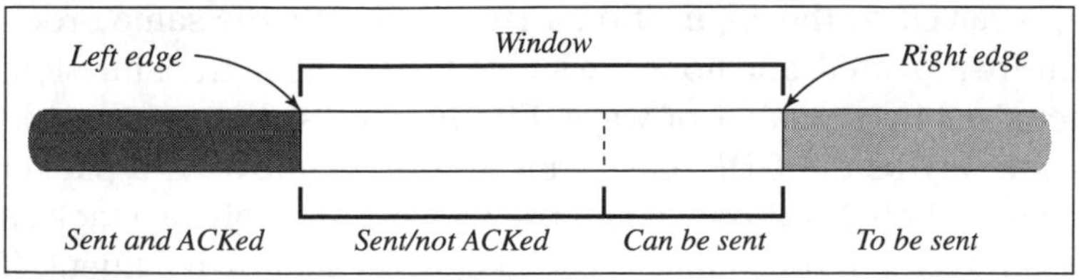

Figure 7.11 Sliding window operation.

Figure 7.12 Strace output from a Web browse with Lynx.

```
...
connect(3, {sin_family=AF_INET, sin_port=htons(80), sin_addr=inet_addr("x.x.x.x")}}, 16) = 0
ioctl(3, FIONBIO, [0])              = 0
write(3, "GET /test/index.html HTTP/1.0\r\nH"..., 1140) = 1140
gettimeofday({990094476, 833725}, NULL) = 0
time(NULL)                          = 990094476
select(1024, [3], NULL, NULL, {0, 100000}) = 1 (in [3], left {0, 90000})
read(3, "HTTP/1.1 200 OK\r\nDate: Thu, 17 M"..., 1535) = 450
gettimeofday({990094476, 838885}, NULL) = 0
brk(0x8196000)                      = 0x8196000
brk(0x8198000)                      = 0x8198000
brk(0x819b000)                      = 0x819b000
brk(0x81a0000)                      = 0x81a0000
gettimeofday({990094476, 840321}, NULL) = 0
time(NULL)                          = 990094476
select(1024, [3], NULL, NULL, {0, 100000}) = 1 (in [3], left {0, 100000})
read(3, "", 4096)                   = 0
close(3)                            = 0
fstat64(1, {st_mode=S_IFCHR|0666, st_rdev=makedev(3, 2), ...}) = 0
mmap2(NULL, 4096, PROT_READ|PROT_WRITE, MAP_PRIVATE|MAP_ANONYMOUS, -1, 0) = 0x402f2000
ioctl(1, TCGETS, {B38400 opost isig icanon echo ...}) = 0
write(1, "\n", 1)                   = 1
write(1, "                              "..., 47) = 47
write(1, "\n", 1)                   = 1
write(1, "  Here is an image [test.png]\n", 31) = 31
...
```

7.4 TCP—Transmission Control Protocol

In addition to muliplexing, TCP provides other transport layer services to the application layer. These are reliability, flow control, and congestion control. These are described here and followed by a description of the TCP packet header and the stack implementation in Linux.

7.4.1 TCP Transport Functionality

Reliability

The data sent and received by the application arrive in exactly the same order, none are lost, none are repeated, and none are subject to errors in transmission. These aims are acheived in a number of ways. Firstly, each segment is check-summed in the same way as the UDP checksum described above. If a packet fails the checksum test, then it is dropped and treated by the receiving stack as a loss. Secondly, each segment transmitted is subject to an acknowledgment. If the acknowledgment does not arrive after a predetermined time interval then the segment may be retransmitted. The calculation of the optimum time-out interval is important for efficiency, and the estimator functionality is described later in this chapter. Thirdly, each packet is given a sequence number. If two packets arrive with the same value, then a duplicate has been detected and the second may be discarded. Sequence numbering also provides for detection of out-of-order arrivals and allows the receiving stack to reorder these, saving on retransmissions.

Connection-Oriented

As the IP layer is a simple datagram, only the TCP layer adds the concept of a connection at the transport layer. There is a handshake between the sender and the receiver at the start of a communication in order for each end to agree on whether they wish to communicate, and also some specific communication parameters.

TCP is also a streaming protocol, rather than the datagram-based UDP. This means that two processes communicating with TCP are connected simply by a pipe, where data are sent in one end and received out of the other. There is no relationship between the size of the data blocks sent into this pipe, the size of the datablocks read from the pipe, and the size of the data blocks as they are sent over the network.

Flow Control

In the simple case, the sender could wait for every packet sent to be acknowledged or timeout before sending the next packet. This, while being relatively easy to implement, is rather inefficient on bandwidth use.

For example, a 100 Mbps pipe between two geographically separate end points with a round trip time of say 5 ms, will only allow one new packet every 5 ms, if an acknowledgment has to be awaited between packets. For 1,000 byte packets this will be an effective bandwidth use of only $(1000 \times 8)/0.005 = 1.6$ Mbps, that is, 1.6 percent of the available bandwidth.

On the other hand, a sending stack cannot simply send the data as fast as possible or else there will be problems in both the network and the receiving system. If a fast sender is sending to a slow receiver then the data may all arrive, but not be processed fast enough. This can lead to the situation where data are completing their journey across the network, but being dropped at their destination. In order to prevent this, TCP uses *flow control*.

Flow control employs a mechanism called a sliding window (see Figure 7.11). All data falls into one of the following categories:

- Data that have been sent and acknowledged.
- Data that have been sent but not acknowledged.
- Data that can be sent but haven't been yet.
- Data that can't yet be sent.

The data in the center two categories represent those data that the receiver is willing to receive. These data are encompassed by a window—the sliding window. As acknowledgments are received for data at the left-hand edge of the window, the whole window can slide to the right bringing further data into the category of data that can be sent.

Figure 7.13 tcpflow output from a Web browsing session.

From client to server

```
GET /test/test.html HTTP/1.0
Host: server
Accept: text/html, text/plain, application/mac-binhex40, application/msword, application/pdf,
     application/vnd.ms-excel, application/postscript, application/x-dvi, application/frame-
     idraw, audio/mod, image/*, video/*, video/mpeg, application/pgp
Accept: application/pgp, application/pdf, message/partial, message/external-body, application/
     postscript, x-be2, application/andrew-inset, text/richtext, text/enriched, x-sun-attachment
     , audio-file, postscript-file, default, mail-file
Accept: sun-deskset-message, application/x-metamail-patch, application/msword, text/sgml, video/
     mpeg, image/jpeg, image/tiff, image/x-rgb, image/png, image/x-xbitmap, image/x-xbm, image/
     gif, application/postscript, */*;q=0.01
Accept-Encoding: gzip, compress
Accept-Language: en
User-Agent: Lynx/2.8.4dev.16 libwww-FM/2.14 SSL-MM/1.4.1 OpenSSL/0.9.6
```

From server to client

```
HTTP/1.1 200 OK
Date: Thu, 17 May 2001 10:15:15 GMT
Server: Apache/1.3.12 (Unix) (Red Hat/Linux) mod_ssl/2.6.6 OpenSSL/0.9.5a DAV/1.0.1 PHP/4.0.1pl2
      mod_perl/1.24
Last-Modified: Thu, 17 May 2001 09:22:34 GMT
ETag: "7c1c3-79-3b03985a"
Accept-Ranges: bytes
Content-Length: 121
Connection: close
Content-Type: text/html

<html>
<head>
</head>
<body>

<h1> Test HTML page</h1>

<p>Here is an image

<img src="test.png"></img>

</body>
</html>
```

```
1  browser.42978 > server.http: S 799139388:799139388(0) win 5840 <mss 1460,sackOK,timestamp
       69053329 0,nop,wscale 0> (DF)
2  server.http > browser.42978: S 846949739:846949739(0) ack 799139389 win 32120 <mss 1460,sackOK,
      timestamp 188746286 69053329,nop,wscale 0> (DF)
3  browser.42978 > server.http: . 1:1(0) ack 1 win 5840 <nop,nop,timestamp 69053329 188746286> (DF)
4  browser.42978 > server.http: P 1:1141(1140) ack 1 win 5840 <nop,nop,timestamp
       69053329 188746286> (DF)
5  server.http > browser.42978: . 1:1(0) ack 1141 win 32120 <nop,nop,timestamp
       188746286 69053329> (DF)
6  server.http > browser.42978: P 1:451(450) ack 1141 win 32120 <nop,nop,timestamp
       188746286 69053329> (DF)
7  browser.42978 > server.http: . 1141:1141(0) ack 451 win 6432 <nop,nop,timestamp
       69053330 188746286> (DF)
8  server.http > browser.42978: F 451:451(0) ack 1141 win 32120 <nop,nop,timestamp
       188746287 69053329> (DF)
9  browser.42978 > server.http: F 1141:1141(0) ack 452 win 6432 <nop,nop,timestamp
       69053330 188746287> (DF)
10 server.http > browser.42978: . 452:452(0) ack 1142 win 32120 <nop,nop,timestamp
       188746287 69053330> (DF)
```

Congestion Control

In the preceding discussion of flow control, we recall that there can be network-related problems to senders sending too fast. If a sender with a high bandwidth connection to its network is sending to a receiver, and at some point in the path there is a lower bandwidth link, then as soon as the sender starts sending too fast for the lower bandwidth link there will be loss. This is called congestion. Congestion can also occur when a number of connections are sharing a link and each is trying to make as much use as possible of the available bandwidth. TCP congestion control makes sure that a TCP connection in either of the two preceding cases receives a fair share of the available bandwidth. Definition of fair in these cases is generally a contentious issue.

Congestion control employs another window in the data to be transmitted. This window is called a congestion window and controls the amount of data that can be sent into the network unacknowledged. The congestion window increases in size while the network is uncongested and decreases when congestion is detected. Currently congestion is detected by detection of a lost packet. Explicit Congestion Notification (ECN) is a technique where congestion in the network is detected and the sending sites informed by the setting of a TCP header bit in the returning data stream.

The increases and decreases in the congestion window size are specified in RFC 2581. A TCP connection can be in one of two states: slow start or congestion avoidance. In slow start, the congestion window increases in size by doubling after an amount of data equal to the congestion window's size has been sent, until a threshold is reached. After this, congestion avoidance is entered when the congestion window increases by the value of the maximum segment size (MSS). If at any point loss is detected, then the threshold is set to half the current congestion window size and the congestion window size is set to the MSS. The connection returns to slow start. This is TCP TAHOE. TCP RENO is an enhancement where at the onset of congestion the connection reduces the threshold as before, but sets the congestion window to the threshold and enters congestion avoidance.

7.4.2 HTTP Request

We will use the example of an HTTP request to illustrate the operations of TCP in the Linux protocol stack. The request is a single HTML page from a local Web server. Figure 7.12 showed an edited version of the strace output from the Web browser (`lynx` in this case). Figure 7.13 showed the output from `tcpflow`, which is a program that prints out application layer data from snooped packets. Figure 7.16 shows the output from `tcpdump` for this operation.

Figure 7.14 Strace of a server process.

```
...
socket(PF_INET, SOCK_STREAM, IPPROTO_TCP) = 3
setsockopt(3, SOL_SOCKET, SO_REUSEADDR, [1], 4) = 0
bind(3, {sin_family=AF_INET, sin_port=htons(5656), sin_addr=inet_addr("0.0.0.0")}}, 16) = 0
listen(3, 1)                          = 0
rt_sigaction(SIGALRM, {SIG_IGN}, {SIG_DFL}, 8) = 0
alarm(0)                              = 0
accept(3, {sin_family=AF_INET, sin_port=htons(43036), sin_addr=inet_addr("127.0.0.1")}}, [16])
    = 4
rt_sigaction(SIGALRM, {SIG_IGN}, {SIG_IGN}, 8) = 0
alarm(0)                              = 0
close(3)                              = 0
getsockname(4, {sin_family=AF_INET, sin_port=htons(5656), sin_addr=inet_addr("127.0.0.1")
      }}, [16]) = 0
select(16, [0 4], NULL, NULL, NULL) = 1 (in [4])
read(4, "", 8192)                     = 0
close(4)                              = 0
...
```

Figure 7.15 The TCP header.

```
0                   1                   2                   3
0 1 2 3 4 5 6 7 8 9 0 1 2 3 4 5 6 7 8 9 0 1 2 3 4 5 6 7 8 9 0 1
+-+-+-+-+-+-+-+-+-+-+-+-+-+-+-+-+-+-+-+-+-+-+-+-+-+-+-+-+-+-+-+-+
|          Source port          |       Destination port        |
+-+-+-+-+-+-+-+-+-+-+-+-+-+-+-+-+-+-+-+-+-+-+-+-+-+-+-+-+-+-+-+-+
|                        Sequence number                        |
+-+-+-+-+-+-+-+-+-+-+-+-+-+-+-+-+-+-+-+-+-+-+-+-+-+-+-+-+-+-+-+-+
|                    Acknowledgment number                      |
+-+-+-+-+-+-+-+-+-+-+-+-+-+-+-+-+-+-+-+-+-+-+-+-+-+-+-+-+-+-+-+-+
|  Data |           |U|A|P|R|S|F|                               |
| offset| Reserved  |R|C|S|S|Y|I|            Window             |
|       |           |G|K|H|T|N|N|                               |
+-+-+-+-+-+-+-+-+-+-+-+-+-+-+-+-+-+-+-+-+-+-+-+-+-+-+-+-+-+-+-+-+
|           Checksum            |         Urgent pointer        |
+-+-+-+-+-+-+-+-+-+-+-+-+-+-+-+-+-+-+-+-+-+-+-+-+-+-+-+-+-+-+-+-+
|                    Options                    |    Padding    |
+-+-+-+-+-+-+-+-+-+-+-+-+-+-+-+-+-+-+-+-+-+-+-+-+-+-+-+-+-+-+-+-+
|                             Data                              |
+-+-+-+-+-+-+-+-+-+-+-+-+-+-+-+-+-+-+-+-+-+-+-+-+-+-+-+-+-+-+-+-+
```

Figure 7.16 TCP states (from RFC 793).

```
LISTEN - represents waiting for a connection request from any remote TCP and port.

SYN-SENT - represents waiting for a matching connection request after having
sent a connection request.

SYN-RECEIVED - represents waiting for a confirming connection request acknowledgment
after having both received and sent a connection request.

ESTABLISHED - represents an open connection, data received can be delivered to
the user.  The normal state for the data transfer phase of the connection.

FIN-WAIT-1 - represents waiting for a connection termination request from the remote
TCP, or an acknowledgment of the connection termination request previously sent.

FIN-WAIT-2 - represents waiting for a connection termination request from the
remote TCP.

CLOSE-WAIT - represents waiting for a connection termination request from the
local user.

CLOSING - represents waiting for a connection termination request acknowledgment
from the remote TCP.

LAST-ACK - represents waiting for an acknowledgment of the connection termination
request previously sent to the remote TCP (which includes an acknowledgment
of its connection termination request).

TIME-WAIT - represents waiting for enough time to pass to be sure the remote TCP
received the acknowledgment of its connection termination request.

CLOSED - represents no connection state at all.
```

In order to see the strace of execution on a server process, we will employ the nc program. First we set up nc as a TCP listener on port 5656 and connect to it using a Telnet session. The session is then closed down. The resultant strace on the nc session is shown in Figure 7.17.

Figure 7.17 The TCP connection creation state diagram (from RFC 793).

```
                             +---------+ ---------\      active OPEN
                             |  CLOSED |            \    -----------
                             +---------+<---------\   \   create TCB
                               |     ^              \   \  snd SYN
                  passive OPEN |     |   CLOSE        \   \
                  ------------ |     | ----------       \   \
                   create TCB  |     | delete TCB         \   \
                               V     |                      \   \
                             +---------+            CLOSE    |    \
                             |  LISTEN |          ---------- |     |
                             +---------+          delete TCB |     |
                  rcv SYN      |     |     SEND              |     |
                 -----------   |     |    -------            |     V
+---------+      snd SYN,ACK  /       \   snd SYN          +---------+
|         |<-----------------           ------------------>|         |
|   SYN   |                    rcv SYN                     |   SYN   |
|   RCVD  |<-----------------------------------------------|   SENT  |
|         |                    snd ACK                     |         |
|         |------------------           -------------------|         |
+---------+   rcv ACK of SYN  \       /  rcv SYN,ACK       +---------+
  |           --------------   |     |   -----------
  |                  x         |     |     snd ACK
  |                            V     V
  |  CLOSE                   +---------+
  | -------                  |  ESTAB  |
  | snd FIN                  +---------+
  |                   CLOSE    |     |    rcv FIN
  V                  -------   |     |    -------
+---------+          snd FIN  /       \   snd ACK          +---------+
|  FIN    |<-----------------           ------------------>|  CLOSE  |
| WAIT-1  |------------------                              |   WAIT  |
+---------+          rcv FIN  \                            +---------+
  | rcv ACK of FIN   -------   |                            CLOSE  |
  | --------------   snd ACK   |                           ------- |
  V        x                   V                           snd FIN V
+---------+                  +---------+                   +---------+
|FINWAIT-2|                  | CLOSING |                   | LAST-ACK|
+---------+                  +---------+                   +---------+
  |                rcv ACK of FIN |                 rcv ACK of FIN |
  |  rcv FIN       -------------- |    Timeout=2MSL -------------- |
  |  -------              x       V    ------------        x       V
   \ snd ACK                 +---------+delete TCB         +---------+
    ------------------------>|TIME WAIT|------------------>| CLOSED  |
                             +---------+                   +---------+
```

Examining Figure 7.17 closely we can see that the first three packets are the connection setup three-way handshake, the next four are the data transfer, one packet in each direction and their acknowledgments, and the final three the connection close-down. Note that the acknowledgment of the first FIN packet is piggybacked onto the client's FIN.

From the strace output in Figure 7.12, we can see that the sequence of significant operations on the socket is connect, write, read, and close (the socket will already have been created by this point).

On the server side (see Figure 7.14), the significant operations are socket, bind, listen, accept, read, and close. Most servers will also write in response to a read.

7.4.3 TCP Header

The TCP header has a large number of fields and is shown in Figure 7.15.

Figure 7.18 Assignment to `tp`.

```
struct tcp_opt *tp = &(sk->tp_pinfo.af_tcp);
```

7.4.4 TCP Implementation

The TCP stack has to respond to a number of externally and internally generated events. These are:

User requests. These come through the socket layer as `connect`, `send`, `recv`, `close`, and other calls.

Network events. These come from the network layer as datagrams arrive.

Time events. These come via interrupts from timers running in the kernel.

files linux/net/ipv4/tcp.c*

Unlike UDP, TCP needs to maintain state about each connection. With UDP, the message to be sent passes through the kernel into a single (possibly fragmented) datagram on its own. With TCP, because reliability, flow, and congestion control need to be maintained, the data have to be buffered and information concerning the current state of the connection stored. This is done in the Process Control Block.

7.4.5 TCP States

TCP can be in a number of states. These are listed in Figure 7.16. The process of connection setup and teardown is controlled as in the state transition diagram shown in Figure 7.17. This is copied directly from RFC 793, which details the transition between these states.

Figure 7.19 tcp_opt (i).

```
struct tcp_opt {
        int     tcp_header_len; /* Bytes of tcp header to send     */

/*
 *      Header prediction flags
 *      0x5?10 << 16 + snd_wnd in net byte order
 */
        __u32  pred_flags;

/*
 *      RFC793 variables by their proper names. This means you can
 *      read the code and the spec side by side (and laugh ...)
 *      See RFC793 and RFC1122. The RFC writes these in capitals.
 */
        __u32  rcv_nxt;        /* What we want to receive next      */
        __u32  snd_nxt;        /* Next sequence we send             */

        __u32  snd_una;        /* First byte we want an ack for     */
        __u32  snd_sml;        /* Last byte of the most recently transmitted small packet */
        __u32  rcv_tstamp;     /* timestamp of last received ACK (for keepalives) */
        __u32  lsndtime;       /* timestamp of last sent data packet (for restart window) */

        /* Delayed ACK control data */
        struct {
                __u8   pending;        /* ACK is pending */
                __u8   quick;          /* Scheduled number of quick acks  */
                __u8   pingpong;       /* The session is interactive      */
                __u8   blocked;        /* Delayed ACK was blocked by socket lock*/
                __u32  ato;            /* Predicted tick of soft clock            */
                unsigned long timeout; /* Currently scheduled timeout     */
                __u32  lrcvtime;       /* timestamp of last received data packet*/
                __u16  last_seg_size;  /* Size of last incoming segment   */
                __u16  rcv_mss;        /* MSS used for delayed ACK decisions */
        } ack;

        /* Data for direct copy to user */
        struct {
                struct sk_buff_head  prequeue;
                int                  memory;
                struct task_struct   *task;
```

Figure 7.20 `tcp_opt` (ii).

```
                struct iovec            *iov;
                int                     len;
        } ucopy;

        __u32   snd_wl1;        /* Sequence for window update       */
        __u32   snd_wnd;        /* The window we expect to receive */
        __u32   max_window;     /* Maximal window ever seen from peer */
        __u32   pmtu_cookie;    /* Last pmtu seen by socket         */
        __u16   mss_cache;      /* Cached effective mss, not including SACKS */
        __u16   mss_clamp;      /* Maximal mss, negotiated at connection setup */
        __u16   ext_header_len; /* Network protocol overhead (IP/IPv6 options) */
        __u8    ca_state;       /* State of fast-retransmit machine  */
        __u8    retransmits;    /* Number of unrecovered RTO timeouts.    */

        __u8    reordering;   /* Packet reordering metric.         */
        __u8    queue_shrunk; /* Write queue has been shrunk recently.*/
        __u8    defer_accept; /* User waits for some data after accept() */

/* RTT measurement */
        __u8    backoff;      /* backoff                          */
        __u32   srtt;         /* smothed round trip time << 3     */
        __u32   mdev;         /* medium deviation                 */
        __u32   mdev_max;     /* maximal mdev for the last rtt period */
        __u32   rttvar;       /* smoothed mdev_max                */
        __u32   rtt_seq;      /* sequence number to update rttvar */
        __u32   rto;          /* retransmit timeout               */

        __u32   packets_out;  /* Packets which are "in flight"    */
        __u32   left_out;     /* Packets which leaved network     */
        __u32   retrans_out;  /* Retransmitted packets out        */


/*
 *      Slow start and congestion control (see also Nagle, and Karn & Partridge)
 */
        __u32   snd_ssthresh; /* Slow start size threshold        */
        __u32   snd_cwnd;     /* Sending congestion window        */
        __u16   snd_cwnd_cnt; /* Linear increase counter          */
        __u16   snd_cwnd_clamp; /* Do not allow snd_cwnd to grow above this */
        __u32   snd_cwnd_used;
```

7.4.6 TCP Structures

These are all coordinated per TCP connection through the Transmission Control Block data structure. The values are described in RFC 793, and key values will be illustrated in the following text. The `sock` structure is a large structure where these values are held. This contains a number of other structures, including a `struct tcp_opt` called `af_tcp` in the union `tp_pinfo`. This structure is usually refered to as tp, by an assignment at the start of each function that uses it (see Figure 7.18).

Figure 7.21 tcp_opt (iii).

```
        __u32  snd_cwnd_stamp;

        /* Two commonly used timers in both sender and receiver paths. */
        unsigned long           timeout;
        struct timer_list       retransmit_timer;       /* Resend (no ack)      */
        struct timer_list       delack_timer;           /* Ack delay            */

        struct sk_buff_head     out_of_order_queue; /* Out of order segments go here */

        struct tcp_func         *af_specific;   /* Operations which are AF_INET{4,6} specific */
        struct sk_buff          *send_head;     /* Front of stuff to transmit              */
        struct page             *sndmsg_page;   /* Cached page for sendmsg                 */
        u32                     sndmsg_off;     /* Cached offset for sendmsg               */

        __u32  rcv_wnd;         /* Current receiver window          */
        __u32  rcv_wup;         /* rcv_nxt on last window update sent */
        __u32  write_seq;       /* Tail(+1) of data held in tcp send buffer */
        __u32  pushed_seq;      /* Last pushed seq, required to talk to windows */
        __u32  copied_seq;      /* Head of yet unread data          */
/*
 *      Options received (usually on last packet, some only on SYN packets).
 */
        char   tstamp_ok,       /* TIMESTAMP seen on SYN packet     */
               wscale_ok,       /* Wscale seen on SYN packet        */
               sack_ok;         /* SACK seen on SYN packet          */
        char   saw_tstamp;      /* Saw TIMESTAMP on last packet     */
        __u8   snd_wscale;      /* Window scaling received from sender */
        __u8   rcv_wscale;      /* Window scaling to send to receiver */
        __u8   nonagle;         /* Disable Nagle algorithm?         */
        __u8   keepalive_probes; /* num of allowed keep alive probes */

/*      PAWS/RTTM data */
        __u32  rcv_tsval;         /* Time stamp value               */
        __u32  rcv_tsecr;         /* Time stamp echo reply          */
        __u32  ts_recent;         /* Time stamp to echo next        */
        long   ts_recent_stamp;/* Time we stored ts_recent (for aging) */

/*      SACKs data     */
        __u16  user_mss;          /* mss requested by user in ioctl */
        __u8   dsack;             /* D-SACK is scheduled                 */
```

Figure 7.22 tcp_opt (iv).

```
        __u8   eff_sacks;         /* Size of SACK array to send with next packet */
        struct tcp_sack_block duplicate_sack[1]; /* D-SACK block */
        struct tcp_sack_block selective_acks[4]; /* The SACKS themselves*/

        __u32  window_clamp;      /* Maximal window to advertise          */
```

```
        __u32  rcv_ssthresh;   /* Current window clamp                  */
        __u8   probes_out;     /* unanswered 0 window probes       */
        __u8   num_sacks;      /* Number of SACK blocks            */
        __u16  advmss;         /* Advertised MSS                   */

        __u8   syn_retries;    /* num of allowed syn retries */
        __u8   ecn_flags;      /* ECN status bits.                 */
        __u16  prior_ssthresh; /* ssthresh saved at recovery start */
        __u32  lost_out;       /* Lost packets                          */
        __u32  sacked_out;     /* SACK'd packets                   */
        __u32  fackets_out;    /* FACK'd packets                   */
        __u32  high_seq;       /* snd_nxt at onset of congestion */

        __u32  retrans_stamp;  /* Timestamp of the last retransmit,
                                * also used in SYN-SENT to remember stamp of
                                * the first SYN. */
        __u32  undo_marker;    /* tracking retrans started here. */
        int    undo_retrans;   /* number of undoable retransmissions. */
        __u32  urg_seq;        /* Seq of received urgent pointer */
        __u16  urg_data;       /* Saved octet of OOB data and control flags */
        __u8   pending;        /* Scheduled timer event    */
        __u8   urg_mode;       /* In urgent mode           */
        __u32  snd_up;         /* Urgent pointer           */

        /* The syn_wait_lock is necessary only to avoid tcp_get_info having
         * to grab the main lock sock while browsing the listening hash
         * (otherwise it's deadlock prone).
         * This lock is acquired in read mode only from tcp_get_info() and
         * it's acquired in write mode _only_ from code that is actively
         * changing the syn_wait_queue. All readers that are holding
         * the master sock lock don't need to grab this lock in read mode
         * too as the syn_wait_queue writes are always protected from
         * the main sock lock.
         */
        rwlock_t               syn_wait_lock;
```

Figure 7.23 tcp_opt (v).

```
        struct tcp_listen_opt *listen_opt;

        /* FIFO of established children */
        struct open_request   *accept_queue;
        struct open_request   *accept_queue_tail;

        int                    write_pending; /* A write to socket waits to start. */

        unsigned int           keepalive_time; /* time before keep alive takes place */
        unsigned int           keepalive_intvl; /* time interval between keep alive probes */
        int                    linger2;
};
```

Figure 7.24 `tcp_skb_cb` **structure.**

```
/* This is what the send packet queueing engine uses to pass
 * TCP per-packet control information to the transmission
 * code. We also store the host-order sequence numbers in
 * here too. This is 36 bytes on 32-bit architectures,
 * 40 bytes on 64-bit machines, if this grows please adjust
 * skbuff.h:skbuff->cb[xxx] size appropriately.
 */
struct tcp_skb_cb {
       union {
               struct inet_skb_parm  h4;
#if defined(CONFIG_IPV6) || defined (CONFIG_IPV6_MODULE)
               struct inet6_skb_parm h6;
#endif
       } header;      /* For incoming frames       */
       __u32          seq;          /* Starting sequence number */
       __u32          end_seq;      /* SEQ + FIN + SYN + datalen */
       __u32          when;         /* used to compute rtt's     */
       __u8           flags;        /* TCP header flags.         */

       /* NOTE: These must match up to the flags byte in a
        *      real TCP header.
        */
#define TCPCB_FLAG_FIN       0x01
#define TCPCB_FLAG_SYN       0x02
#define TCPCB_FLAG_RST       0x04
#define TCPCB_FLAG_PSH       0x08
#define TCPCB_FLAG_ACK       0x10
#define TCPCB_FLAG_URG       0x20
#define TCPCB_FLAG_ECE       0x40
#define TCPCB_FLAG_CWR       0x80

       __u8           sacked;       /* State flags for SACK/FACK. */
#define TCPCB_SACKED_ACKED   0x01   /* SKB ACK'd by a SACK block */
#define TCPCB_SACKED_RETRANS 0x02   /* SKB retransmitted         */
#define TCPCB_LOST           0x04   /* SKB is lost               */
#define TCPCB_TAGBITS        0x07   /* All tag bits              */

#define TCPCB_EVER_RETRANS   0x80   /* Ever retransmitted frame  */
#define TCPCB_RETRANS        (TCPCB_SACKED_RETRANS|TCPCB_EVER_RETRANS)

#define TCPCB_URG            0x20   /* Urgent pointer advenced here */

#define TCPCB_AT_TAIL        (TCPCB_URG)

       __u16          urg_ptr;      /* Valid w/URG flags is set. */
       __u32          ack_seq;      /* Sequence number ACK'd     */
};
```

Figure 7.25 Start of `tcp_sendmsg`.

```
1008  int tcp_sendmsg(struct sock *sk, struct msghdr *msg, int size)
1009  {
1010      struct iovec *iov;
1011      struct tcp_opt *tp;
1012      struct sk_buff *skb;
1013      int iovlen, flags;
1014      int mss_now;
1015      int err, copied;
1016      long timeo;
1017
1018      tp = &(sk->tp_pinfo.af_tcp);
1019
1020      lock_sock(sk);
1021      TCP_CHECK_TIMER(sk);
1022
1023      flags = msg->msg_flags;
1024      timeo = sock_sndtimeo(sk, flags&MSG_DONTWAIT);
1025
1026      /* Wait for a connection to finish. */
1027      if ((1 << sk->state) & ~(TCPF_ESTABLISHED | TCPF_CLOSE_WAIT))
1028          if((err = wait_for_tcp_connect(sk, flags, &timeo)) != 0)
1029              goto out_err;
1030
1031      /* This should be in poll */
1032      clear_bit(SOCK_ASYNC_NOSPACE, &sk->socket->flags);
1033
1034      mss_now = tcp_current_mss(sk);
1035
1036      /* Ok commence sending. */
1037      iovlen = msg->msg_iovlen;
1038      iov = msg->msg_iov;
1039      copied = 0;
1040
1041      err = -EPIPE;
1042      if (sk->err || (sk->shutdown&SEND_SHUTDOWN))
1043          goto do_error;
```

Figure 7.26 Determine MSS.

```
892  /* Compute the current effective MSS, taking SACKs and IP options,
893   * and even PMTU discovery events into account.
894   */
895
896  static __inline__ unsigned int tcp_current_mss(struct sock *sk)
897  {
898      struct tcp_opt *tp = &sk->tp_pinfo.af_tcp;
899      struct dst_entry *dst = __sk_dst_get(sk);
900      int mss_now = tp->mss_cache;
901
```

```
902            if (dst && dst->pmtu != tp->pmtu_cookie)
903                    mss_now = tcp_sync_mss(sk, dst->pmtu);
904
905            if (tp->eff_sacks)
906                    mss_now -= (TCPOLEN_SACK_BASE_ALIGNED +
907                              (tp->eff_sacks * TCPOLEN_SACK_PERBLOCK));
908            return mss_now;
909   }
```

The `tcp_skb_cb` structure contains information about the current TCP connection on a per segment basis. Access to this structure is via the `TCP_SKB_CB` (see Figure 7.27).

Figure 7.27 Start of send loop.

```
1045          while (--iovlen >= 0) {
1046                  int seglen=iov->iov_len;
1047                  unsigned char * from=iov->iov_base;
1048
1049                  iov++;
1050
1051                  while (seglen > 0) {
1052                          int copy;
1053
1054                          skb = sk->write_queue.prev;
1055
1056                          if (tp->send_head == NULL ||
1057                              (copy = mss_now - skb->len) <= 0) {
1058
1059   new_segment:
1060                                  /* Allocate new segment. If the interface is SG,
1061                                   * allocate skb fitting to single page.
1062                                   */
1063                                  if (!tcp_memory_free(sk))
1064                                          goto wait_for_sndbuf;
1065
1066                                  skb = tcp_alloc_pskb(sk, select_size(sk, tp), 0, sk->allocation);
1067                                  if (skb == NULL)
1068                                          goto wait_for_memory;
1069
1070                                  skb_entail(sk, tp, skb);
1071                                  copy = mss_now;
1072                          }
1073
1074                          /* Try to append data to the end of skb. */
1075                          if (copy > seglen)
1076                                  copy = seglen;
```

7.4.7 TCP Code

This section takes a walk through the salient features of the TCP stack. The order is intuitive of the typical TCP operations, rather than architectural or procedural. We initially look at connection setup from a server and client perspective and the demultiplexing of individual segments to their socket owners. Then we go on to cover tear down, which will complete a look at the state machine in the preceding figures. The next stage to examine is the sending of data, the actions taken on receiving segments, and what to do in the event of timeouts. Finally we look at other features of TCP, including congestion control, PAWS (Protection Against Wrapped Sequence numbers), window scaling, and SACK (Selective Acknowledgments).

Connection Setup

The client side of connection setup causes a call to `tcp_connect`. Here various fields in the `tcp_opt` structure are initialized and a socket buffer for the SYN segment is filled. This is transmitted at the end of the function.

Meanwhile the server has created a socket, bound it to a port (`bind`), and has called `listen` to wait for a connection. This changes the state of the socket to listening. The `tcp_rcv_state_process` function processes the incoming data.

When the server replies with its own SYNACK packet, this will be processed by `tcp_rcv_synsent_state_process`.

TCP Demultiplexing

The socket structures for listening and establishing connections are stored for searching in the `tcp_hashinfo` structure. This is searched on the arrival of a segment to determine which socket is required. This search, which is done by `__tcp_v4_lookup` (and other functions with similar names), is for established connections based on a hash value of the source and destination addresses and ports—`tcp_hashfn`. For listening connections, the hash value, calculated by `tcp_lhashfn`, is simply based on the listening port number.

Send and Receive

The application sends data by writing to the socket. This passes through the socket linkage and becomes a call to `tcp_sendmsg` in `linux/net/tcp.c` (see Figure 7.25). The current MSS is determined. The data to be sent is within the `msg` structure and assigned to `iov`, which is an array of `iovlen` blocks. If the socket is not in an errored state or a half shutdown state then transmission can begin.

Figure 7.28 Finding space to copy the data to (i).

```
1078                        /* Where to copy to? */
1079                        if (skb_tailroom(skb) > 0) {
1080                                /* We have some space in skb head. Superb! */
1081                                if (copy > skb_tailroom(skb))
1082                                        copy = skb_tailroom(skb);
1083                                if ((err = skb_add_data(skb, from, copy)) != 0)
1084                                        goto do_fault;
1085                        } else {
1086                                int merge = 0;
1087                                int i = skb_shinfo(skb)->nr_frags;
1088                                struct page *page = TCP_PAGE(sk);
1089                                int off = TCP_OFF(sk);
1090
1091                                if (can_coalesce(skb, i, page, off) && off != PAGE_SIZE) {
1092                                        /* We can extend the last page fragment. */
1093                                        merge = 1;
1094                                } else if (i == MAX_SKB_FRAGS ||
1095                                        (i == 0 && !(sk->route_caps&NETIF_F_SG))) {
1096                                        /* Need to add new fragment and cannot
1097                                         * do this because interface is non-SG,
1098                                         * or because all the page slots are busy.
1099                                         */
1100                                        tcp_mark_push(tp, skb);
1101                                        goto new_segment;
1102                                } else if (page) {
1103                                        /* If page is cached, align
1104                                         * offset to L1 cache boundary
1105                                         */
1106                                        off = (off+L1_CACHE_BYTES-1)&~(L1_CACHE_BYTES-1);
1107                                        if (off == PAGE_SIZE) {
1108                                                put_page(page);
1109                                                TCP_PAGE(sk) = page = NULL;
1110                                        }
1111                                }
1112
1113                                if (!page) {
1114                                        /* Allocate new cache page. */
1115                                        if (!(page=tcp_alloc_page(sk)))
1116                                                goto wait_for_memory;
1117                                        off = 0;
```

Figure 7.29 Finding space to copy the data to (ii).

```
1118                                }
1119
1120                                if (copy > PAGE_SIZE-off)
1121                                        copy = PAGE_SIZE-off;
1122
1123                                /* Time to copy data. We are close to the end! */
1124                                err = tcp_copy_to_page(sk, from, skb, page, off, copy);
1125                                if (err)
```

```
1126                                      goto do_error;
1127
1128                        /* Update the skb. */
1129                        if (merge) {
1130                                skb_shinfo(skb)->frags[i-1].size += copy;
1131                        } else {
1132                                fill_page_desc(skb, i, page, off, copy);
1133                                if (TCP_PAGE(sk)) {
1134                                        get_page(page);
1135                                } else if (off + copy < PAGE_SIZE) {
1136                                        get_page(page);
1137                                        TCP_PAGE(sk) = page;
1138                                }
1139                        }
1140
1141                        TCP_OFF(sk) = off+copy;
1142                }
```

We now loop though the message blocks and build segments. As TCP is byte-oriented, the blocks can be divided and joined in order to achieve full segments where possible. First the socket buffer at the end of the write queue is examined. If this doesn't exist (say because it has been transmitted and acknowledged) or it is full, then a new socket buffer is allocated. If there is room, then the space left is calculated. By the end of Figure 7.27, copy contains the number of bytes that can be added to this sk_buff.

Figure 7.30 Rest of tcp_send.

```
1144                        if (!copied)
1145                                TCP_SKB_CB(skb)->flags &= ~TCPCB_FLAG_PSH;
1146
1147                        tp->write_seq += copy;
1148                        TCP_SKB_CB(skb)->end_seq += copy;
1149
1150                        from += copy;
1151                        copied += copy;
1152                        seglen -= copy;
1153
1154                        if (skb->len != mss_now || (flags&MSG_OOB))
1155                                continue;
1156
1157                        if (forced_push(tp)) {
1158                                tcp_mark_push(tp, skb);
1159                                __tcp_push_pending_frames(sk, tp, mss_now, 1);
1160                        } else if (skb == tp->send_head)
1161                                tcp_push_one(sk, mss_now);
1162                        continue;
1163
1164    wait_for_sndbuf:
```

```
1165                        set_bit(SOCK_NOSPACE, &sk->socket->flags);
1166  wait_for_memory:
1167                  if (copied)
1168                        tcp_push(sk, tp, flags&~MSG_MORE, mss_now, 1);
1169
1170                  if ((err = wait_for_tcp_memory(sk, &timeo)) != 0)
1171                        goto do_error;
1172
1173                  mss_now = tcp_current_mss(sk);
1174              }
1175          }
1176
1177  out:
1178      if (copied)
1179          tcp_push(sk, tp, flags, mss_now, tp->nonagle);
1180      TCP_CHECK_TIMER(sk);
1181      release_sock(sk);
1182      return copied;
```

This data now needs to be copied into the socket buffer. Some memory may need to be found. Data is copied from the user using the csum_and_copy_from_user function, called either from skb_add_data() or tcp_copy_to_page() (see Figures 7.27–7.29).

Figure 7.31 Rest of tcp_send.

```
1184  do_fault:
1185      if (skb->len==0) {
1186          if (tp->send_head == skb) {
1187              tp->send_head = skb->prev;
1188              if (tp->send_head == (struct sk_buff*)&sk->write_queue)
1189                  tp->send_head = NULL;
1190          }
1191          __skb_unlink(skb, skb->list);
1192          tcp_free_skb(sk, skb);
1193      }
1194
1195  do_error:
1196      if (copied)
1197          goto out;
1198  out_err:
1199      err = tcp_error(sk, flags, err);
1200      TCP_CHECK_TIMER(sk);
1201      release_sock(sk);
1202      return err;
1203  }
```

Figure 7.32 Writing socket buffers to the network.

```
/* This routine writes packets to the network. It advances the
 * send_head. This happens as incoming acks open up the remote
 * window for us.
 *
 * Returns 1, if no segments are in flight and we have queued segments, but
 * cannot send anything now because of SWS or another problem.
 */
int tcp_write_xmit(struct sock *sk)
{
        struct tcp_opt *tp = &(sk->tp_pinfo.af_tcp);
        unsigned int mss_now;

        /* If we are closed, the bytes will have to remain here.
         * In time closedown will finish, we empty the write queue and all
         * will be happy.
         */
        if(sk->state != TCP_CLOSE) {
                struct sk_buff *skb;
                int sent_pkts = 0;

                /* Account for SACKS, we may need to fragment due to this.
                 * It is just like the real MSS changing on us midstream.
                 * We also handle things correctly when the user adds some
                 * IP options mid-stream. Silly to do, but cover it.
                 */
                mss_now = tcp_current_mss(sk);

                while((skb = tp->send_head) &&
                      tcp_snd_test(tp, skb, mss_now, tcp_skb_is_last(sk, skb) ? tp->nonagle : 1)) {
                        if (skb->len > mss_now) {
                                if (tcp_fragment(sk, skb, mss_now))
                                        break;
                        }

                        TCP_SKB_CB(skb)->when = tcp_time_stamp;
                        if (tcp_transmit_skb(sk, skb_clone(skb, GFP_ATOMIC)))
                                break;
                        /* Advance the send_head. This one is sent out. */
                        update_send_head(sk, tp, skb);
                        tcp_minshall_update(tp, mss_now, skb);
                        sent_pkts = 1;
                }

                if (sent_pkts) {
                        tcp_cwnd_validate(sk, tp);
                        return 0;
                }

                return !tp->packets_out && tp->send_head;
        }
        return 0;
}
```

The rest of the function is shown in Figures 7.30–7.32. If the length of the data in this socket buffer is still not as big as the MSS then the loop is continued.

Figure 7.33 Should we send.

```
/* This checks if the data bearing packet SKB (usually tp->send_head)
 * should be put on the wire right now.
 */
static __inline__ int tcp_snd_test(struct tcp_opt *tp, struct sk_buff *skb,
                                   unsigned cur_mss, int nonagle)
{
        /*      RFC 1122 - section 4.2.3.4
         *
         *      We must queue if
         *
         *      a) The right edge of this frame exceeds the window
         *      b) There are packets in flight and we have a small segment
         *         [SWS avoidance and Nagle algorithm]
         *         (part of SWS is done on packetization)
         *         Minshall version sounds: there are no _small_
         *         segments in flight. (tcp_nagle_check)
         *      c) We have too many packets 'in flight'
         *
         *      Don't use the nagle rule for urgent data (or
         *      for the final FIN -DaveM).
         *
         *      Also, Nagle rule does not apply to frames, which
         *      sit in the middle of queue (they have no chances
         *      to get new data) and if room at tail of skb is
         *      not enough to save something seriously (<32 for now).
         */

        /* Don't be strict about the congestion window for the
         * final FIN frame. -DaveM
         */
        return ((nonagle==1 || tp->urg_mode
                 || !tcp_nagle_check(tp, skb, cur_mss, nonagle)) &&
                ((tcp_packets_in_flight(tp) < tp->snd_cwnd) ||
                 (TCP_SKB_CB(skb)->flags & TCPCB_FLAG_FIN)) &&
                !after(TCP_SKB_CB(skb)->end_seq, tp->snd_una + tp->snd_wnd));
}
```

Figure 7.34 Building a TCP header (i).

```
/* This routine actually transmits TCP packets queued in by
 * tcp_do_sendmsg(). This is used by both the initial
 * transmission and possible later retransmissions.
 * All SKB's seen here are completely headerless. It is our
 * job to build the TCP header, and pass the packet down to
 * IP so it can do the same plus pass the packet off to the
 * device.
 *
 * We are working here with either a clone of the original
```

```
 * SKB, or a fresh unique copy made by the retransmit engine.
 */
int tcp_transmit_skb(struct sock *sk, struct sk_buff *skb)
{
	if(skb != NULL) {
		struct tcp_opt *tp = &(sk->tp_pinfo.af_tcp);
		struct tcp_skb_cb *tcb = TCP_SKB_CB(skb);
		int tcp_header_size = tp->tcp_header_len;
		struct tcphdr *th;
		int sysctl_flags;
		int err;

#define SYSCTL_FLAG_TSTAMPS	0x1
#define SYSCTL_FLAG_WSCALE	0x2
#define SYSCTL_FLAG_SACK	0x4

		sysctl_flags = 0;
		if (tcb->flags & TCPCB_FLAG_SYN) {
			tcp_header_size = sizeof(struct tcphdr) + TCPOLEN_MSS;
			if(sysctl_tcp_timestamps) {
				tcp_header_size += TCPOLEN_TSTAMP_ALIGNED;
				sysctl_flags |= SYSCTL_FLAG_TSTAMPS;
			}
			if(sysctl_tcp_window_scaling) {
				tcp_header_size += TCPOLEN_WSCALE_ALIGNED;
				sysctl_flags |= SYSCTL_FLAG_WSCALE;
			}
			if(sysctl_tcp_sack) {
				sysctl_flags |= SYSCTL_FLAG_SACK;
				if(!(sysctl_flags & SYSCTL_FLAG_TSTAMPS))
					tcp_header_size += TCPOLEN_SACKPERM_ALIGNED;
			}
		} else if (tp->eff_sacks) {
			/* A SACK is 2 pad bytes, a 2 byte header, plus
			 * 2 32-bit sequence numbers for each SACK block.
			 */
			tcp_header_size += (TCPOLEN_SACK_BASE_ALIGNED +
					    (tp->eff_sacks * TCPOLEN_SACK_PERBLOCK));
		}
		th = (struct tcphdr *) skb_push(skb, tcp_header_size);
		skb->h.th = th;
```

The socket buffer is sent to the network layer with `tcp_transmit_skb`, which at this stage is either called via `tcp_push_one`, or `__tcp_push_pending_frames` and `tcp_write_xmit`. This latter function attempts to send each packet in the send queue (see Figure 7.34). Prior to transmission of a packet there is a call to `tcp_snd_test` (see Figure 7.33). Note that `TCP_SKB_CB(skb)->end_seq` is the sequence number of the last byte in the socket buffer, `tp->snd_una` is the next expected acknowledgment number, and `tp->snd_wnd` is the current advertised receive window from the other end of the connection. This is the sliding window protocol in action.

Figure 7.35 Building a TCP header (ii).

```
skb_set_owner_w(skb, sk);

/* Build TCP header and checksum it. */
th->source              = sk->sport;
th->dest                = sk->dport;
th->seq                 = htonl(tcb->seq);
th->ack_seq             = htonl(tp->rcv_nxt);
*(((__u16 *)th) + 6)    = htons(((tcp_header_size >> 2) << 12) | tcb->flags);
if (tcb->flags & TCPCB_FLAG_SYN) {
        /* RFC1323: The window in SYN & SYN/ACK segments
         * is never scaled.
         */
        th->window      = htons(tp->rcv_wnd);
} else {
        th->window      = htons(tcp_select_window(sk));
}
th->check               = 0;
th->urg_ptr             = 0;

if (tp->urg_mode &&
    between(tp->snd_up, tcb->seq+1, tcb->seq+0xFFFF)) {
        th->urg_ptr             = htons(tp->snd_up-tcb->seq);
        th->urg                 = 1;
}

if (tcb->flags & TCPCB_FLAG_SYN) {
        tcp_syn_build_options((__u32 *)(th + 1),
                              tcp_advertise_mss(sk),
                              (sysctl_flags & SYSCTL_FLAG_TSTAMPS),
                              (sysctl_flags & SYSCTL_FLAG_SACK),
                              (sysctl_flags & SYSCTL_FLAG_WSCALE),
                              tp->rcv_wscale,
                              tcb->when,
                              tp->ts_recent);
} else {
        tcp_build_and_update_options((__u32 *)(th + 1),
                                     tp, tcb->when);

        TCP_ECN_send(sk, tp, skb, tcp_header_size);
}
tp->af_specific->send_check(sk, th, skb->len, skb);

if (tcb->flags & TCPCB_FLAG_ACK)
        tcp_event_ack_sent(sk);

if (skb->len != tcp_header_size)
        tcp_event_data_sent(tp, skb);

TCP_INC_STATS(TcpOutSegs);
```

Figure 7.36 Building a TCP header (iii).

```
                err = tp->af_specific->queue_xmit(skb);
                if (err <= 0)
                        return err;

                tcp_enter_cwr(tp);

                /* NET_XMIT_CN is special. It does not guarantee,
                 * that this packet is lost. It tells that device
                 * is about to start to drop packets or already
                 * drops some packets of the same priority and
                 * invokes us to send less aggressively.
                 */
                return err == NET_XMIT_CN ? 0 : err;
        }
        return -ENOBUFS;
#undef SYSCTL_FLAG_TSTAMPS
#undef SYSCTL_FLAG_WSCALE
#undef SYSCTL_FLAG_SACK
}
```

`tcp_transmit_skb` is the function that builds the TCP header, including any option fields, eventually checksumming the packet via the `tp->af_specific->send_check()` call, which maps to `tcp_v4_send_check`, and transmitting the buffer with `tp->af_specific->queue_xmit(skb)`, which is actually `ip_queue_xmit`. Note that a clone of the buffer i passed, which means that the original is saved in the case of a retransmission being required.

Figure 7.37 Checksumming TCP packets.

```
/* This routine computes an IPv4 TCP checksum. */
void tcp_v4_send_check(struct sock *sk, struct tcphdr *th, int len,
                          struct sk_buff *skb)
{
        if (skb->ip_summed == CHECKSUM_HW) {
                th->check = ~tcp_v4_check(th, len, sk->saddr, sk->daddr, 0);
                skb->csum = offsetof(struct tcphdr, check);
        } else {
                th->check = tcp_v4_check(th, len, sk->saddr, sk->daddr,
                                         csum_partial((char *)th, th->doff<<2, skb->csum));
        }
}
```

Figure 7.38 Receiving a packet by the TCP layer (i).

```
1592    int tcp_v4_rcv(struct sk_buff *skb)
1593    {
1594            struct tcphdr *th;
1595            struct sock *sk;
1596            int ret;
1597
1598            if (skb->pkt_type!=PACKET_HOST)
1599                    goto discard_it;
1600
1601            /* Count it even if it's bad */
1602            TCP_INC_STATS_BH(TcpInSegs);
1603
1604            if (!pskb_may_pull(skb, sizeof(struct tcphdr)))
1605                    goto discard_it;
1606
1607            th = skb->h.th;
1608
1609            if (th->doff < sizeof(struct tcphdr)/4)
1610                    goto bad_packet;
1611            if (!pskb_may_pull(skb, th->doff*4))
1612                    goto discard_it;
1613
1614            /* An explanation is required here, I think.
1615             * Packet length and doff are validated by header prediction,
1616             * provided case of th->doff==0 is elimineted.
1617             * So, we defer the checks. */
1618            if ((skb->ip_summed != CHECKSUM_UNNECESSARY &&
1619                 tcp_v4_checksum_init(skb) < 0))
1620                    goto bad_packet;
1621
1622            th = skb->h.th;
1623            TCP_SKB_CB(skb)->seq = ntohl(th->seq);
1624            TCP_SKB_CB(skb)->end_seq = (TCP_SKB_CB(skb)->seq + th->syn + th->fin +
1625                                    skb->len - th->doff*4);
1626            TCP_SKB_CB(skb)->ack_seq = ntohl(th->ack_seq);
1627            TCP_SKB_CB(skb)->when = 0;
1628            TCP_SKB_CB(skb)->flags = skb->nh.iph->tos;
1629            TCP_SKB_CB(skb)->sacked = 0;
1630
1631            sk = __tcp_v4_lookup(skb->nh.iph->saddr, th->source,
1632                                    skb->nh.iph->daddr, ntohs(th->dest), tcp_v4_iif(skb));
1633
1634            if (!sk)
1635                    goto no_tcp_socket;
1636
1637    process:
1638            if(!ipsec_sk_policy(sk,skb))
1639                    goto discard_and_relse;
1640
1641            if (sk->state == TCP_TIME_WAIT)
1642                    goto do_time_wait;
1643
1644            skb->dev = NULL;
1645
1646            bh_lock_sock(sk);
```

Figure 7.39 Receiving a packet by the TCP layer (ii).

```
        ret = 0;
        if (!sk->lock.users) {
                if (!tcp_prequeue(sk, skb))
                        ret = tcp_v4_do_rcv(sk, skb);
        } else
                sk_add_backlog(sk, skb);
        bh_unlock_sock(sk);

        sock_put(sk);

        return ret;

no_tcp_socket:
        if (skb->len < (th->doff<<2) || tcp_checksum_complete(skb)) {
bad_packet:
                TCP_INC_STATS_BH(TcpInErrs);
        } else {
                tcp_v4_send_reset(skb);
        }

discard_it:
        /* Discard frame. */
        kfree_skb(skb);
        return 0;

discard_and_relse:
        sock_put(sk);
        goto discard_it;

do_time_wait:
        if (skb->len < (th->doff<<2) || tcp_checksum_complete(skb)) {
                TCP_INC_STATS_BH(TcpInErrs);
                goto discard_and_relse;
        }
        switch(tcp_timewait_state_process((struct tcp_tw_bucket *)sk,
                                          skb, th, skb->len)) {
        case TCP_TW_SYN:
        {
                struct sock *sk2;

                sk2 = tcp_v4_lookup_listener(skb->nh.iph->daddr, ntohs(th->dest),
                    tcp_v4_ii(skb));
                if (sk2 != NULL) {
                        tcp_tw_deschedule((struct tcp_tw_bucket *)sk);
                        tcp_timewait_kill((struct tcp_tw_bucket *)sk);
                        tcp_tw_put((struct tcp_tw_bucket *)sk);
                        sk = sk2;
                        goto process;
                }
                /* Fall through to ACK */
        }
        case TCP_TW_ACK:
                tcp_v4_timewait_ack(sk, skb);
```

```
1699                    break;
1700            case TCP_TW_RST:
1701                    goto no_tcp_socket;
1702            case TCP_TW_SUCCESS:;
1703            }
1704            goto discard_it;
1705    }
```

Figure 7.40 An optimization.

```
1309    /* Packet is added to VJ-style prequeue for processing in process
1310     * context, if a reader task is waiting. Apparently, this exciting
1311     * idea (VJ's mail "Re: query about TCP header on tcp-ip" of 07 Sep 93)
1312     * failed somewhere. Latency? Burstiness? Well, at least now we will
1313     * see, why it failed. 8)8)                        --ANK
1314     *
1315     * NOTE: is this not too big to inline?
1316     */
1317    static __inline__ int tcp_prequeue(struct sock *sk, struct sk_buff *skb)
1318    {
1319            struct tcp_opt *tp = &sk->tp_pinfo.af_tcp;
1320
1321            if (tp->ucopy.task) {
1322                    __skb_queue_tail(&tp->ucopy.prequeue, skb);
1323                    tp->ucopy.memory += skb->truesize;
1324                    if (tp->ucopy.memory > sk->rcvbuf) {
1325                            struct sk_buff *skb1;
1326
1327                            if (sk->lock.users) BUG();
1328
1329                            while ((skb1 = __skb_dequeue(&tp->ucopy.prequeue)) != NULL) {
1330                                    sk->backlog_rcv(sk, skb1);
1331                                    NET_INC_STATS_BH(TCPPrequeueDropped);
1332                            }
1333
1334                            tp->ucopy.memory = 0;
1335                    } else if (skb_queue_len(&tp->ucopy.prequeue) == 1) {
1336                            wake_up_interruptible(sk->sleep);
1337                            if (!tcp_ack_scheduled(tp))
1338                                    tcp_reset_xmit_timer(sk, TCP_TIME_DACK, (3*TCP_RTO_MIN)/4);
1339                    }
1340                    return 1;
1341            }
1342            return 0;
1343    }
```

We now consider the receiving of data at the other end of the connection. Packets are received by the IP layer and forwarded to the TCP layer via the `tcp_v4_rcv`, which is part of the `net_family` structure for TCP (see Figures 7.38–7.39).

Figure 7.41 Receiving a socket buffer on an established connection (i).

```
/*
 *      TCP receive function for the ESTABLISHED state.
 *
 *      It is split into a fast path and a slow path. The fast path is
 *      disabled when:
 *      - A zero window was announced from us - zero window probing
 *        is only handled properly in the slow path.
 *      - Out of order segments arrived.
 *      - Urgent data is expected.
 *      - There is no buffer space left
 *      - Unexpected TCP flags/window values/header lengths are received
 *        (detected by checking the TCP header against pred_flags)
 *      - Data is sent in both directions. Fast path only supports pure senders
 *        or pure receivers (this means either the sequence number or the ack
 *        value must stay constant)
 *      - Unexpected TCP option.
 *
 *      When these conditions are not satisfied it drops into a standard
 *      receive procedure patterned after RFC793 to handle all cases.
 *      The first three cases are guaranteed by proper pred_flags setting,
 *      the rest is checked inline. Fast processing is turned on in
 *      tcp_data_queue when everything is OK.
 */
int tcp_rcv_established(struct sock *sk, struct sk_buff *skb,
                        struct tcphdr *th, unsigned len)
{
        struct tcp_opt *tp = &(sk->tp_pinfo.af_tcp);

        /*
         *      Header prediction.
         *      The code losely follows the one in the famous
         *      "30 instruction TCP receive" Van Jacobson mail.
         *
         *      Van's trick is to deposit buffers into socket queue
         *      on a device interrupt, to call tcp_recv function
         *      on the receive process context and checksum and copy
         *      the buffer to user space. smart...
         *
         *      Our current scheme is not silly either but we take the
         *      extra cost of the net_bh soft interrupt processing...
         *      We do checksum and copy also but from device to kernel.
         */

        tp->saw_tstamp = 0;

        /*      pred_flags is 0xS?10 << 16 + snd_wnd
         *      if header_predition is to be made
         *      'S' will always be tp->tcp_header_len >> 2
         *      '?' will be 0 for the fast path, otherwise pred_flags is 0 to
         *  turn it off (when there are holes in the receive
```

Figure 7.42 Receiving a socket buffer on an established connection (ii).

```
3250          *      space for instance)
3251          *      PSH flag is ignored.
3252          */
3253
3254          if ((tcp_flag_word(th) & TCP_HP_BITS) == tp->pred_flags &&
3255                  TCP_SKB_CB(skb)->seq == tp->rcv_nxt) {
3256                  int tcp_header_len = tp->tcp_header_len;
3257
3258                  /* Timestamp header prediction: tcp_header_len
3259                   * is automatically equal to th->doff*4 due to pred_flags
3260                   * match.
3261                   */
3262
3263                  /* Check timestamp */
3264                  if (tcp_header_len == sizeof(struct tcphdr) + TCPOLEN_TSTAMP_ALIGNED) {
3265                          __u32 *ptr = (__u32 *)(th + 1);
3266
3267                          /* No? Slow path! */
3268                          if (*ptr != __constant_ntohl((TCPOPT_NOP << 24) | (TCPOPT_NOP << 16)
3269                                                      | (TCPOPT_TIMESTAMP << 8) | TCPOLEN_TIMESTAMP))
3270                                  goto slow_path;
3271
3272                          tp->saw_tstamp = 1;
3273                          ++ptr;
3274                          tp->rcv_tsval = ntohl(*ptr);
3275                          ++ptr;
3276                          tp->rcv_tsecr = ntohl(*ptr);
3277
3278                          /* If PAWS failed, check it more carefully in slow path */
3279                          if ((s32)(tp->rcv_tsval - tp->ts_recent) < 0)
3280                                  goto slow_path;
3281
3282                          /* Predicted packet is in window by definition.
3283                           * seq == rcv_nxt and rcv_wup <= rcv_nxt.
3284                           * Hence, check seq<=rcv_wup reduces to:
3285                           */
3286                          if (tp->rcv_nxt == tp->rcv_wup)
3287                                  tcp_store_ts_recent(tp);
3288                  }
3289
3290                  if (len <= tcp_header_len) {
3291                          /* Bulk data transfer: sender */
3292                          if (len == tcp_header_len) {
3293                                  /* We know that such packets are checksummed
3294                                   * on entry.
3295                                   */
3296                                  tcp_ack(sk, skb, 0);
3297                                  __kfree_skb(skb);
3298                                  tcp_data_snd_check(sk);
3299                                  return 0;
```

First the packet's header information (from `th->`) is copied to the socket buffers TCP_SKB_CB block. Then the packet's socket is found (see Section 7.4.7). Now the socket buffer is either added to the socket backlog, for future processing, or passed to `tcp_v4_do_rcv`. The `fig:tcppreque` provides for an optimization if the current user process is the one owning the socket (see Figure 7.40).

Figure 7.43 Receiving a socket buffer on an established connection (iii).

```
3300                    } else { /* Header too small */
3301                            TCP_INC_STATS_BH(TcpInErrs);
3302                            goto discard;
3303                    }
3304            } else {
3305                    int eaten = 0;
3306
3307                    if (tp->ucopy.task == current &&
3308                        tp->copied_seq == tp->rcv_nxt &&
3309                        len - tcp_header_len <= tp->ucopy.len &&
3310                        sk->lock.users) {
3311                            eaten = 1;
3312
3313                            NET_INC_STATS_BH(TCPHPHitsToUser);
3314
3315                            __set_current_state(TASK_RUNNING);
3316
3317                            if (tcp_copy_to_iovec(sk, skb, tcp_header_len))
3318                                    goto csum_error;
3319
3320                            __skb_pull(skb,tcp_header_len);
3321
3322                            tp->rcv_nxt = TCP_SKB_CB(skb)->end_seq;
3323                    } else {
3324                            if (tcp_checksum_complete_user(sk, skb))
3325                                    goto csum_error;
3326
3327                            if ((int)skb->truesize > sk->forward_alloc)
3328                                    goto step5;
3329
3330                            NET_INC_STATS_BH(TCPHPHits);
3331
3332                            /* Bulk data transfer: receiver */
3333                            __skb_pull(skb,tcp_header_len);
3334                            __skb_queue_tail(&sk->receive_queue, skb);
3335                            tcp_set_owner_r(skb, sk);
3336                            tp->rcv_nxt = TCP_SKB_CB(skb)->end_seq;
3337                    }
3338
3339                    tcp_event_data_recv(sk, tp, skb);
3340
3341                    if (TCP_SKB_CB(skb)->ack_seq != tp->snd_una) {
3342                            /* Well, only one small jumplet in fast path... */
3343                            tcp_ack(sk, skb, FLAG_DATA);
3344                            tcp_data_snd_check(sk);
```

```
3345                          if (!tcp_ack_scheduled(tp))
3346                                  goto no_ack;
3347                  }
3348
3349                  if (eaten) {
```

tcp_v4_do_rcv (see Figure 7.41) in the connection setup section fast-paths
if the socket is in an established state to tcp_rcv_established, this being the
most common state, and also that which requires fastest processing.

Figure 7.44 Receiving a socket buffer on an established connection (iv).

```
3350                          if (tcp_in_quickack_mode(tp)) {
3351                                  tcp_send_ack(sk);
3352                          } else {
3353                                  tcp_send_delayed_ack(sk);
3354                          }
3355                  } else {
3356                          __tcp_ack_snd_check(sk, 0);
3357                  }
3358
3359  no_ack:
3360                  if (eaten)
3361                          __kfree_skb(skb);
3362                  else
3363                          sk->data_ready(sk, 0);
3364                  return 0;
3365          }
3366      }
3367
3368  slow_path:
3369      if (len < (th->doff<<2) || tcp_checksum_complete_user(sk, skb))
3370              goto csum_error;
3371
3372      /*
3373       * RFC 1323: H1. Apply PAWS check first.
3374       */
3375      if (tcp_fast_parse_options(skb, th, tp) && tp->saw_tstamp &&
3376         tcp_paws_discard(tp, skb)) {
3377          if (!th->rst) {
3378                  NET_INC_STATS_BH(PAWSEstabRejected);
3379                  tcp_send_dupack(sk, skb);
3380                  goto discard;
3381          }
3382          /* Resets are accepted even if PAWS failed.
3383
3384             ts_recent update must be made after we are sure
3385             that the packet is in window.
3386           */
3387      }
3388
3389      /*
```

```
3390            *      Standard slow path.
3391            */
3392
3393       if (!tcp_sequence(tp, TCP_SKB_CB(skb)->seq, TCP_SKB_CB(skb)->end_seq)) {
3394               /* RFC 793, page 37: "In all states except SYN-SENT, all reset
3395                * (RST) segments are validated by checking their SEQ-fields."
3396                * And page 69: "If an incoming segment is not acceptable,
3397                * an acknowledgment should be sent in reply (unless the RST bit
3398                * is set, if so drop the segment and return)".
3399                */
```

Figure 7.45 Receiving a socket buffer on an established connection (v).

```
3400                  if (!th->rst)
3401                        tcp_send_dupack(sk, skb);
3402                  goto discard;
3403           }
3404
3405       if(th->rst) {
3406               tcp_reset(sk);
3407               goto discard;
3408       }
3409
3410       tcp_replace_ts_recent(tp, TCP_SKB_CB(skb)->seq);
3411
3412       if (th->syn && !before(TCP_SKB_CB(skb)->seq, tp->rcv_nxt)) {
3413               TCP_INC_STATS_BH(TcpInErrs);
3414               NET_INC_STATS_BH(TCPAbortOnSyn);
3415               tcp_reset(sk);
3416               return 1;
3417       }
3418
3419 step5:
3420       if(th->ack)
3421               tcp_ack(sk, skb, FLAG_SLOWPATH);
3422
3423       /* Process urgent data. */
3424       tcp_urg(sk, skb, th);
3425
3426       /* step 7: process the segment text */
3427       tcp_data_queue(sk, skb);
3428
3429       tcp_data_snd_check(sk);
3430       tcp_ack_snd_check(sk);
3431       return 0;
3432
3433 csum_error:
3434       TCP_INC_STATS_BH(TcpInErrs);
3435
3436 discard:
3437       __kfree_skb(skb);
3438       return 0;
3439 }
```

Figure 7.46 TCP sequence number check.

```
/* Check segment sequence number for validity.
 *
 * Segment controls are considered valid, if the segment
 * fits to the window after truncation to the window. Acceptability
 * of data (and SYN, FIN, of course) is checked separately.
 * See tcp_data_queue(), for example.
 *
 * Also, controls (RST is main one) are accepted using RCV.WUP instead
 * of RCV.NXT. Peer still did not advance his SND.UNA when we
 * delayed ACK, so that hisSND.UNA<=ourRCV.WUP.
 * (borrowed from freebsd)
 */

static inline int tcp_sequence(struct tcp_opt *tp, u32 seq, u32 end_seq)
{
        return !before(end_seq, tp->rcv_wup) &&
              !after(seq, tp->rcv_nxt + tcp_receive_window(tp));
}
```

Figure 7.47 TCP receive window determination.

```
/* Compute the actual receive window we are currently advertising.
 * Rcv_nxt can be after the window if our peer push more data
 * than the offered window.
 */
static __inline__ u32 tcp_receive_window(struct tcp_opt *tp)
{
        s32 win = tp->rcv_wup + tp->rcv_wnd - tp->rcv_nxt;

        if (win < 0)
              win = 0;
        return (u32) win;
}
```

Figure 7.48 ACK sending code.

```
/*
 * Check if sending an ack is needed.
 */
static __inline__ void __tcp_ack_snd_check(struct sock *sk, int ofo_possible)
{
        struct tcp_opt *tp = &(sk->tp_pinfo.af_tcp);

            /* More than one full frame received... */
        if (((tp->rcv_nxt - tp->rcv_wup) > tp->ack.rcv_mss
             /* ... and right edge of window advances far enough.
              * (tcp_recvmsg() will send ACK otherwise). Or...
              */
             && __tcp_select_window(sk) >= tp->rcv_wnd) ||
            /* We ACK each frame or... */
```

```
            tcp_in_quickack_mode(tp) ||
            /* We have out of order data. */
            (ofo_possible &&
             skb_peek(&tp->out_of_order_queue) != NULL)) {
                /* Then ack it now */
                tcp_send_ack(sk);
        } else {
                /* Else, send delayed ack. */
                tcp_send_delayed_ack(sk);
        }
}

static __inline__ void tcp_ack_snd_check(struct sock *sk)
{
        struct tcp_opt *tp = &(sk->tp_pinfo.af_tcp);
        if (!tcp_ack_scheduled(tp)) {
                /* We sent a data segment already. */
                return;
        }
        __tcp_ack_snd_check(sk, 1);
}
```

The fast path in this function uses the header prediction in RFC 1323, that is, the expected sequence number is the same as that of the incoming packet. Here the timestamp option, if present, is decoded, and PAWS (see later) is checked. If the packet is empty, then we call `tcp_ack`. If it is too small then it is discarded, and if it contains data then it is queued for the owning socket. There is another optimization here if the current process is the task that owns the socket, as the data can be copied directly to the `iovec`. The checksum is checked in this function, and the `tcp->rcv_nxt` value updated.

In the slow path, first PAWS is checked (see later). Then whether the packet is in sequence is checked with the `tcp_sequence` function (see Figures 7.46–7.47).

Figure 7.49 Processing an acknowledgment (i).

```
/* This routine deals with incoming acks, but not outgoing ones. */
static int tcp_ack(struct sock *sk, struct sk_buff *skb, int flag)
{
        struct tcp_opt *tp = &(sk->tp_pinfo.af_tcp);
        u32 prior_snd_una = tp->snd_una;
        u32 ack_seq = TCP_SKB_CB(skb)->seq;
        u32 ack = TCP_SKB_CB(skb)->ack_seq;
        u32 prior_in_flight;
        int prior_packets;

        /* If the ack is newer than sent or older than previous acks
         * then we can probably ignore it.
         */
        if (after(ack, tp->snd_nxt))
                goto uninteresting_ack;
```

```

        if (before(ack, prior_snd_una))
                goto old_ack;

        if (!(flag&FLAG_SLOWPATH) && after(ack, prior_snd_una)) {
                /* Window is constant, pure forward advance.
                 * No more checks are required.
                 * Note, we use the fact that SND.UNA>=SND.WL2.
                 */
                tcp_update_wl(tp, ack, ack_seq);
                tp->snd_una = ack;
                flag |= FLAG_WIN_UPDATE;

                NET_INC_STATS_BH(TCPHPAcks);
        } else {
                if (ack_seq != TCP_SKB_CB(skb)->end_seq)
                        flag |= FLAG_DATA;
                else
                        NET_INC_STATS_BH(TCPPureAcks);

                flag |= tcp_ack_update_window(sk, tp, skb, ack, ack_seq);

                if (TCP_SKB_CB(skb)->sacked)
                        flag |= tcp_sacktag_write_queue(sk, skb, prior_snd_una);

                if (TCP_ECN_rcv_ecn_echo(tp, skb->h.th))
                        flag |= FLAG_ECE;
        }

        /* We passed data and got it acked, remove any soft error
         * log. Something worked...
         */
        sk->err_soft = 0;
        tp->rcv_tstamp = tcp_time_stamp;
        if ((prior_packets = tp->packets_out) == 0)
                goto no_queue;
```

Figure 7.50 Processing an acknowledgment (ii).

```
                !((1<<tp->ca_state)&(TCPF_CA_Recovery|TCPF_CA_CWR));
}

/* Check that window update is acceptable.
 * The function assumes that snd_una<=ack<=snd_next.
 */
static __inline__ int
tcp_may_update_window(struct tcp_opt *tp, u32 ack, u32 ack_seq, u32 nwin)
{
        return (after(ack, tp->snd_una) ||
                after(ack_seq, tp->snd_wl1) ||
                (ack_seq == tp->snd_wl1 && nwin > tp->snd_wnd));
}

```

```
1862    /* Update our send window.
1863     *
1864     * Window update algorithm, described in RFC793/RFC1122 (used in linux-2.2
1865     * and in FreeBSD. NetBSD's one is even worse.) is wrong.
1866     */
1867    static int tcp_ack_update_window(struct sock *sk, struct tcp_opt *tp,
1868                            struct sk_buff *skb, u32 ack, u32 ack_seq)
1869    {
1870            int flag = 0;
1871            u32 nwin = ntohs(skb->h.th->window) << tp->snd_wscale;
1872
1873            if (tcp_may_update_window(tp, ack, ack_seq, nwin)) {
1874                    flag |= FLAG_WIN_UPDATE;
1875                    tcp_update_wl(tp, ack, ack_seq);
1876
1877                    if (tp->snd_wnd != nwin) {
1878                            tp->snd_wnd = nwin;
1879
1880                            /* Note, it is the only place, where
1881                             * fast path is recovered for sending TCP.
1882                             */
1883                            tcp_fast_path_check(sk, tp);
1884
1885                            if (nwin > tp->max_window) {
1886                                    tp->max_window = nwin;
1887                                    tcp_sync_mss(sk, tp->pmtu_cookie);
1888                            }
1889                    }
1890            }
1891
1892            tp->snd_una = ack;
1893
1894            return flag;
1895    }
1896
1897    /* This routine deals with incoming acks, but not outgoing ones. */
1898    static int tcp_ack(struct sock *sk, struct sk_buff *skb, int flag)
1899    {
1900            struct tcp_opt *tp = &(sk->tp_pinfo.af_tcp);
1901            u32 prior_snd_una = tp->snd_una;
1902            u32 ack_seq = TCP_SKB_CB(skb)->seq;
1903            u32 ack = TCP_SKB_CB(skb)->ack_seq;
1904            u32 prior_in_flight;
1905            int prior_packets;
1906
1907            /* If the ack is newer than sent or older than previous acks
1908             * then we can probably ignore it.
1909             */
1910            if (after(ack, tp->snd_nxt))
1911                    goto uninteresting_ack;
1912
1913            if (before(ack, prior_snd_una))
1914                    goto old_ack;
1915
1916            if (!(flag&FLAG_SLOWPATH) && after(ack, prior_snd_una)) {
```

```
1917                    /* Window is constant, pure forward advance.
1918                     * No more checks are required.
1919                     * Note, we use the fact that SND.UNA>=SND.WL2.
1920                     */
1921                    tcp_update_wl(tp, ack, ack_seq);
1922                    tp->snd_una = ack;
1923                    flag |= FLAG_WIN_UPDATE;
1924
1925                    NET_INC_STATS_BH(TCPHPAcks);
1926            } else {
1927                    if (ack_seq != TCP_SKB_CB(skb)->end_seq)
1928                            flag |= FLAG_DATA;
1929                    else
1930                            NET_INC_STATS_BH(TCPPureAcks);
1931
1932                    flag |= tcp_ack_update_window(sk, tp, skb, ack, ack_seq);
1933
1934                    if (TCP_SKB_CB(skb)->sacked)
1935                            flag |= tcp_sacktag_write_queue(sk, skb, prior_snd_una);
1936
1937                    if (TCP_ECN_rcv_ecn_echo(tp, skb->h.th))
1938                            flag |= FLAG_ECE;
1939            }
1940
1941            /* We passed data and got it acked, remove any soft error
1942             * log. Something worked...
1943             */
1944            sk->err_soft = 0;
1945            tp->rcv_tstamp = tcp_time_stamp;
1946            if ((prior_packets = tp->packets_out) == 0)
1947                    goto no_queue;
1948
1949            prior_in_flight = tcp_packets_in_flight(tp);
1950
1951            /* See if we can take anything off of the retransmit queue. */
1952            flag |= tcp_clean_rtx_queue(sk);
1953
1954            if (tcp_ack_is_dubious(tp, flag)) {
1955                    /* Advanve CWND, if state allows this. */
1956                    if ((flag&FLAG_DATA_ACKED) && prior_in_flight >= tp->snd_cwnd &&
1957                        tcp_may_raise_cwnd(tp, flag))
1958                            tcp_cong_avoid(tp);
1959                    tcp_fastretrans_alert(sk, prior_snd_una, prior_packets, flag);
1960            } else {
1961                    if ((flag&FLAG_DATA_ACKED) && prior_in_flight >= tp->snd_cwnd)
1962                            tcp_cong_avoid(tp);
1963            }
1964
1965            if ((flag & FLAG_FORWARD_PROGRESS) || !(flag&FLAG_NOT_DUP))
1966                    dst_confirm(sk->dst_cache);
1967
1968            return 1;
1969
1970    no_queue:
1971            tp->probes_out = 0;
```

```
1972
1973            /* If this ack opens up a zero window, clear backoff. It was
1974             * being used to time the probes, and is probably far higher than
1975             * it needs to be for normal retransmission.
1976             */
1977            if (tp->send_head)
1978                    tcp_ack_probe(sk);
1979            return 1;
1980
1981    old_ack:
1982            if (TCP_SKB_CB(skb)->sacked)
1983                    tcp_sacktag_write_queue(sk, skb, prior_snd_una);
1984
1985    uninteresting_ack:
1986            SOCK_DEBUG(sk, "Ack %u out of %u:%u\n", ack, tp->snd_una, tp->snd_nxt);
1987            return 0;
1988    }
```

If an out-of-sequence packet occurs, then a duplicate ACK is sent, with a call to tcp_send_dupack(). If successful, a call to tcp_ack_snd_check (and __tcp_ack_snd_check) will send an immediate ACK or schedule a delayed ACK (see Figure 7.48).

Figure 7.51 Processing and queuing incoming data (i).

```
2524    static void tcp_data_queue(struct sock *sk, struct sk_buff *skb)
2525    {
2526            struct tcphdr *th = skb->h.th;
2527            struct tcp_opt *tp = &(sk->tp_pinfo.af_tcp);
2528            int eaten = -1;
2529
2530            th = skb->h.th;
2531            __skb_pull(skb, th->doff*4);
2532
2533            if (skb->len == 0 && !th->fin)
2534                    goto drop;
2535
2536            TCP_ECN_accept_cwr(tp, skb);
2537
2538            if (tp->dsack) {
2539                    tp->dsack = 0;
2540                    tp->eff_sacks = min(tp->num_sacks, 4-tp->tstamp_ok);
2541            }
2542
2543            /* Queue data for delivery to the user.
2544             * Packets in sequence go to the receive queue.
2545             * Out of sequence packets to the out_of_order_queue.
2546             */
2547            if (TCP_SKB_CB(skb)->seq == tp->rcv_nxt) {
2548                    if (tcp_receive_window(tp) == 0)
2549                            goto out_of_window;
2550
```

```
2551                    /* Ok. In sequence. In window. */
2552                    if (tp->ucopy.task == current &&
2553                        tp->copied_seq == tp->rcv_nxt &&
2554                        tp->ucopy.len &&
2555                        sk->lock.users &&
2556                        !tp->urg_data) {
2557                            int chunk = min(skb->len, tp->ucopy.len);
2558
2559                            __set_current_state(TASK_RUNNING);
2560
2561                            local_bh_enable();
2562                            if (skb_copy_datagram_iovec(skb, 0, tp->ucopy.iov, chunk)) {
2563                                    sk->err = EFAULT;
2564                                    sk->error_report(sk);
2565                            }
2566                            local_bh_disable();
2567                            tp->ucopy.len -= chunk;
2568                            tp->copied_seq += chunk;
2569                            eaten = (chunk == skb->len && !th->fin);
2570                    }
2571
2572            if (eaten <= 0) {
2573  queue_and_out:
2574                    if (eaten < 0 &&
2575                        (atomic_read(&sk->rmem_alloc) > sk->rcvbuf ||
2576                         !tcp_rmem_schedule(sk, skb))) {
2577                            if (tcp_prune_queue(sk) < 0 || !tcp_rmem_schedule(sk, skb))
2578                                    goto drop;
```

When an acknowledgment packet is received, a call is made to tcp_ack (see Figures 7.49–7.50).

Figure 7.52 Processing and queuing incoming data (ii).

```
2579                    }
2580                    tcp_set_owner_r(skb, sk);
2581                    __skb_queue_tail(&sk->receive_queue, skb);
2582            }
2583            tp->rcv_nxt = TCP_SKB_CB(skb)->end_seq;
2584            if(skb->len)
2585                    tcp_event_data_recv(sk, tp, skb);
2586            if(th->fin)
2587                    tcp_fin(skb, sk, th);
2588
2589            if (skb_queue_len(&tp->out_of_order_queue)) {
2590                    tcp_ofo_queue(sk);
2591
2592                    /* RFC 2581. 4.2. SHOULD send immediate ACK, when
2593                     * gap in queue is filled.
2594                     */
2595                    if (skb_queue_len(&tp->out_of_order_queue) == 0)
2596                            tp->ack.pingpong = 0;
2597            }
```

```
2598
2599                    if(tp->num_sacks)
2600                            tcp_sack_remove(tp);
2601
2602                    tcp_fast_path_check(sk, tp);
2603
2604                    if (eaten > 0) {
2605                            __kfree_skb(skb);
2606                    } else if (!sk->dead)
2607                            sk->data_ready(sk, 0);
2608                    return;
2609            }
2610
2611            if (!after(TCP_SKB_CB(skb)->end_seq, tp->rcv_nxt)) {
2612                    /* A retransmit, 2nd most common case. Force an immediate ack. */
2613                    NET_INC_STATS_BH(DelayedACKLost);
2614                    tcp_enter_quickack_mode(tp);
2615                    tcp_dsack_set(tp, TCP_SKB_CB(skb)->seq, TCP_SKB_CB(skb)->end_seq);
2616
2617 out_of_window:
2618                    tcp_schedule_ack(tp);
2619 drop:
2620                    __kfree_skb(skb);
2621                    return;
2622            }
2623
2624            /* Out of window. F.e. zero window probe. */
2625            if (!before(TCP_SKB_CB(skb)->seq, tp->rcv_nxt+tcp_receive_window(tp)))
2626                    goto out_of_window;
2627
2628            tcp_enter_quickack_mode(tp);
2629
2630            if (before(TCP_SKB_CB(skb)->seq, tp->rcv_nxt)) {
2631                    /* Partial packet, seq < rcv_next < end_seq */
2632                    SOCK_DEBUG(sk, "partial packet: rcv_next %X seq %X - %X\n",
2633                            tp->rcv_nxt, TCP_SKB_CB(skb)->seq,
```

Figure 7.53 Processing and queuing incoming data (iii).

```
2634                            TCP_SKB_CB(skb)->end_seq);
2635
2636                    tcp_dsack_set(tp, TCP_SKB_CB(skb)->seq, tp->rcv_nxt);
2637
2638                    /* If window is closed, drop tail of packet. But after
2639                     * remembering D-SACK for its head made in previous line.
2640                     */
2641                    if (!tcp_receive_window(tp))
2642                            goto out_of_window;
2643                    goto queue_and_out;
2644            }
2645
2646            TCP_ECN_check_ce(tp, skb);
2647
```

```
2648            if (atomic_read(&sk->rmem_alloc) > sk->rcvbuf ||
2649                !tcp_rmem_schedule(sk, skb)) {
2650                    if (tcp_prune_queue(sk) < 0 || !tcp_rmem_schedule(sk, skb))
2651                        goto drop;
2652            }
2653
2654            /* Disable header prediction. */
2655            tp->pred_flags = 0;
2656            tcp_schedule_ack(tp);
2657
2658            SOCK_DEBUG(sk, "out of order segment: rcv_next %X seq %X - %X\n",
2659                    tp->rcv_nxt, TCP_SKB_CB(skb)->seq, TCP_SKB_CB(skb)->end_seq);
2660
2661            tcp_set_owner_r(skb, sk);
2662
2663            if (skb_peek(&tp->out_of_order_queue) == NULL) {
2664                    /* Initial out of order segment, build 1 SACK. */
2665                    if(tp->sack_ok) {
2666                            tp->num_sacks = 1;
2667                            tp->dsack = 0;
2668                            tp->eff_sacks = 1;
2669                            tp->selective_acks[0].start_seq = TCP_SKB_CB(skb)->seq;
2670                            tp->selective_acks[0].end_seq = TCP_SKB_CB(skb)->end_seq;
2671                    }
2672                    __skb_queue_head(&tp->out_of_order_queue,skb);
2673            } else {
2674                    struct sk_buff *skb1=tp->out_of_order_queue.prev;
2675                    u32 seq = TCP_SKB_CB(skb)->seq;
2676                    u32 end_seq = TCP_SKB_CB(skb)->end_seq;
2677
2678                    if (seq == TCP_SKB_CB(skb1)->end_seq) {
2679                            __skb_append(skb1, skb);
2680
2681                            if (tp->num_sacks == 0 ||
2682                                tp->selective_acks[0].end_seq != seq)
2683                                    goto add_sack;
2684
2685                            /* Common case: data arrive in order after hole. */
2686                            tp->selective_acks[0].end_seq = end_seq;
2687                            return;
2688                    }
```

At the end of tcp_rcv_established, tcp_data_queue is called. This is shown in Figures 7.51–7.54. Here the fast path is the most common packet, that is, in sequence and in the current window. Again there is an optimization if the current task is that owning the socket, otherwise memory must be reserved and the socket buffer queued. The rcv_nxt variable can be updated for the current connection, and if the socket buffer contained some data, then tcp_event_data_recv is called to schedule an ACK. If there are packets on the out-of-order queue, then this segment may have filled a gap, in which case an immmediate ACK should be scheduled. Eventually the socket buffer can be freed if the data has already been copied (i.e. `eaten > 0`); otherwise the `sk->data_ready` is called, which causes the task owning the socket to awake.

The next-fastest path is receipt of a retransmitted packet, which is indicated to the sender and then dropped.

The next-fastest is a zero window probe.

The remaining part of the function deals with out-of-order arrivals.

Figure 7.54 Processing and queuing incoming data (iv).

```
2689
2690                    /* Find place to insert this segment. */
2691                    do {
2692                            if (!after(TCP_SKB_CB(skb1)->seq, seq))
2693                                    break;
2694                    } while ((skb1=skb1->prev) != (struct sk_buff*)&tp->out_of_order_queue);
2695
2696                    /* Do skb overlap to previous one? */
2697                    if (skb1 != (struct sk_buff*)&tp->out_of_order_queue &&
2698                        before(seq, TCP_SKB_CB(skb1)->end_seq)) {
2699                            if (!after(end_seq, TCP_SKB_CB(skb1)->end_seq)) {
2700                                    /* All the bits are present. Drop. */
2701                                    __kfree_skb(skb);
2702                                    tcp_dsack_set(tp, seq, end_seq);
2703                                    goto add_sack;
2704                            }
2705                            if (after(seq, TCP_SKB_CB(skb1)->seq)) {
2706                                    /* Partial overlap. */
2707                                    tcp_dsack_set(tp, seq, TCP_SKB_CB(skb1)->end_seq);
2708                            } else {
2709                                    skb1 = skb1->prev;
2710                            }
2711                    }
2712                    __skb_insert(skb, skb1, skb1->next, &tp->out_of_order_queue);
2713
2714                    /* And clean segments covered by new one as whole. */
2715                    while ((skb1 = skb->next) != (struct sk_buff*)&tp->out_of_order_queue &&
2716                            after(end_seq, TCP_SKB_CB(skb1)->seq)) {
2717                            if (before(end_seq, TCP_SKB_CB(skb1)->end_seq)) {
2718                                    tcp_dsack_extend(tp, TCP_SKB_CB(skb1)->seq, end_seq);
2719                                    break;
2720                            }
2721                            __skb_unlink(skb1, skb1->list);
2722                            tcp_dsack_extend(tp, TCP_SKB_CB(skb1)->seq, TCP_SKB_CB(skb1)->end_seq);
2723                            __kfree_skb(skb1);
2724                    }
2725
2726  add_sack:
2727                    if (tp->sack_ok)
2728                            tcp_sack_new_ofo_skb(sk, seq, end_seq);
2729            }
2730  }
```

Figure 7.55 Timer initialization.

```
40   /*
41    * Using different timers for retransmit, delayed acks and probes
42    * We may wish use just one timer maintaining a list of expire jiffies
43    * to optimize.
44    */
45
46   void tcp_init_xmit_timers(struct sock *sk)
47   {
48           struct tcp_opt *tp = &sk->tp_pinfo.af_tcp;
49
50           init_timer(&tp->retransmit_timer);
51           tp->retransmit_timer.function=&tcp_write_timer;
52           tp->retransmit_timer.data = (unsigned long) sk;
53           tp->pending = 0;
54
55           init_timer(&tp->delack_timer);
56           tp->delack_timer.function=&tcp_delack_timer;
57           tp->delack_timer.data = (unsigned long) sk;
58           tp->ack.pending = 0;
59
60           init_timer(&sk->timer);
61           sk->timer.function=&tcp_keepalive_timer;
62           sk->timer.data = (unsigned long) sk;
63   }
```

Figure 7.56 TCP congestion avoidance.

```
1699   /* This is Jacobson's slow start and congestion avoidance.
1700    * SIGCOMM '88, p. 328.
1701    */
1702   static __inline__ void tcp_cong_avoid(struct tcp_opt *tp)
1703   {
1704           if (tp->snd_cwnd <= tp->snd_ssthresh) {
1705                   /* In "safe" area, increase. */
1706                   if (tp->snd_cwnd < tp->snd_cwnd_clamp)
1707                           tp->snd_cwnd++;
1708           } else {
1709                   /* In dangerous area, increase slowly.
1710                    * In theory this is tp->snd_cwnd += 1 / tp->snd_cwnd
1711                    */
1712                   if (tp->snd_cwnd_cnt >= tp->snd_cwnd) {
1713                           if (tp->snd_cwnd < tp->snd_cwnd_clamp)
1714                                   tp->snd_cwnd++;
1715                           tp->snd_cwnd_cnt=0;
1716                   } else
1717                           tp->snd_cwnd_cnt++;
1718           }
1719           tp->snd_cwnd_stamp = tcp_time_stamp;
1720   }
```

Figure 7.57 Recording the need to selectively acknowledge an out-of-order segment (i).

```
2397    static void tcp_sack_new_ofo_skb(struct sock *sk, u32 seq, u32 end_seq)
2398    {
2399            struct tcp_opt *tp = &(sk->tp_pinfo.af_tcp);
2400            struct tcp_sack_block *sp = &tp->selective_acks[0];
2401            int cur_sacks = tp->num_sacks;
2402            int this_sack;
2403
2404            if (!cur_sacks)
2405                    goto new_sack;
2406
2407            for (this_sack=0; this_sack<cur_sacks; this_sack++, sp++) {
2408                    if (tcp_sack_extend(sp, seq, end_seq)) {
2409                            /* Rotate this_sack to the first one. */
2410                            for (; this_sack>0; this_sack--, sp--)
2411                                    tcp_sack_swap(sp, sp-1);
2412                            if (cur_sacks > 1)
2413                                    tcp_sack_maybe_coalesce(tp);
2414                            return;
2415                    }
2416            }
2417
2418            /* Could not find an adjacent existing SACK, build a new one,
2419             * put it at the front, and shift everyone else down. We
2420             * always know there is at least one SACK present already here.
2421             *
2422             * If the sack array is full, forget about the last one.
2423             */
2424            if (this_sack >= 4) {
2425                    this_sack--;
2426                    tp->num_sacks--;
2427                    sp--;
2428            }
2429            for(; this_sack > 0; this_sack--, sp--)
2430                    *sp = *(sp-1);
2431
2432    new_sack:
2433            /* Build the new head SACK, and we're done. */
2434            sp->start_seq = seq;
2435            sp->end_seq = end_seq;
2436            tp->num_sacks++;
2437            tp->eff_sacks = min(tp->num_sacks+tp->dsack, 4-tp->tstamp_ok);
2438    }

            . . .

2298    static __inline__ int
2299    tcp_sack_extend(struct tcp_sack_block *sp, u32 seq, u32 end_seq)
2300    {
2301            if (!after(seq, sp->end_seq) && !after(sp->start_seq, end_seq)) {
2302                    if (before(seq, sp->start_seq))
2303                            sp->start_seq = seq;
2304                    if (after(end_seq, sp->end_seq))
2305                            sp->end_seq = end_seq;
2306                    return 1;
2307            }
2308            return 0;
2309    }
```

TCP is generally driven by receiving ACKs from the far end of the connection or data from the user. However, there will be situations where timers are needed to keep things going. There are three main timers in TCP:

- The retransmission timer—used if a packet is unacknowledged to cause a retransmission, this is also used if the receive window from the other end is zero to keep probing and give the opportunity for the window to grow again.

- The delayed ACK timer—used to send a delayed ACK, if it hasn't been sent for another reason.

- The keep-alive timer—used to keep a very low level of traffic over an idle connection.

These functions are in `tcp_timer.c` (see Figure 7.55).

Figure 7.58 Recording the need to selectively acknowledge an out-of-order segment (ii).

```
2355   /* These routines update the SACK block as out-of-order packets arrive or
2356    * in-order packets close up the sequence space.
2357    */
2358   static void tcp_sack_maybe_coalesce(struct tcp_opt *tp)
2359   {
2360           int this_sack;
2361           struct tcp_sack_block *sp = &tp->selective_acks[0];
2362           struct tcp_sack_block *swalk = sp+1;
2363
2364           /* See if the recent change to the first SACK eats into
2365            * or hits the sequence space of other SACK blocks, if so coalesce.
2366            */
2367           for (this_sack = 1; this_sack < tp->num_sacks; ){
2368                   if (tcp_sack_extend(sp, swalk->start_seq, swalk->end_seq)) {
2369                           int i;
2370
2371                           /* Zap SWALK, by moving every further SACK up by one slot.
2372                            * Decrease num_sacks.
2373                            */
2374                           tp->num_sacks--;
2375                           tp->eff_sacks = min(tp->num_sacks+tp->dsack, 4-tp->tstamp_ok);
2376                           for(i=this_sack; i < tp->num_sacks; i++)
2377                                   sp[i] = sp[i+1];
2378                           continue;
2379                   }
2380                   this_sack++, swalk++;
2381           }
2382   }
2383
2384   static __inline__ void tcp_sack_swap(struct tcp_sack_block *sack1, struct tcp_sack_block *sack2)
2385   {
2386           __u32 tmp;
2387
2388           tmp = sack1->start_seq;
```

```
        sack1->start_seq = sack2->start_seq;
        sack2->start_seq = tmp;

        tmp = sack1->end_seq;
        sack1->end_seq = sack2->end_seq;
        sack2->end_seq = tmp;
}
```

Congestion Control

The sender's congestion window is stored in the `tcp_opt` structure as `snd_cwnd`. This is initialized in `tcp_init_metrics` either on receipt of a SYN segment (for a host receiving a connection) in `tcp_rcv_state_process`, or on acknowledgment of a sent SYN segment (for a host initiating a connection) in `tcp_rcv_state_process`.

The congestion window is checked, along with other things, as a buffer is sent.

If the connection window is smaller than the slow-start threshold (`ssthresh`), the connection is in *slow start* state. If larger, then it is in *congestion avoidance*. The size of the congestion window increases in different ways depending on this state. Figure 7.56 shows the increase in the congestion window. This is called once per ACK from `tcp_ack`.

Figure 7.59 Recording the need to send a `dsack`.

```
static __inline__ void tcp_dsack_set(struct tcp_opt *tp, u32 seq, u32 end_seq)
{
        if (tp->sack_ok && sysctl_tcp_dsack) {
                if (before(seq, tp->rcv_nxt))
                        NET_INC_STATS_BH(TCPDSACKOldSent);
                else
                        NET_INC_STATS_BH(TCPDSACKOfoSent);

                tp->dsack = 1;
                tp->duplicate_sack[0].start_seq = seq;
                tp->duplicate_sack[0].end_seq = end_seq;
                tp->eff_sacks = min(tp->num_sacks+1, 4-tp->tstamp_ok);
        }
}

static __inline__ void tcp_dsack_extend(struct tcp_opt *tp, u32 seq, u32 end_seq)
{
        if (!tp->dsack)
                tcp_dsack_set(tp, seq, end_seq);
        else
                tcp_sack_extend(tp->duplicate_sack, seq, end_seq);
}
```

Selective Acknowledgment—SACK

Modern TCP/IP implementations such as the one described in this book employ a selective acknowledgment mechanism known as SACK (RFC 2018). SACK employs a TCP options field to indicate received segments that cannot be simply ACKed, as there would be gaps in the ACKed stream. The tcp_opt structure uses the following variables in SACK:

- eff_sacks—to indicate the number of sacks to send with the next packet.
- selective_acks—an array of sack blocks (each sack block is simply the sequence number of the beginning and end of the block).
- dsack—to indicate a duplicate sack should be sent.
- duplicate_sack—information about this D-SACK.

These are set by the TCP receive data functions (see Figures 7.57–7.59) and used to add options to generated packets (see Figure 7.60).

Figure 7.60 Building TCP option fields (timestamp and sack).

```
1406  static __inline__ void tcp_build_and_update_options(__u32 *ptr, struct tcp_opt *tp,
          __u32 tstamp)
1407  {
1408          if (tp->tstamp_ok) {
1409                  *ptr++ = __constant_htonl((TCPOPT_NOP << 24) |
1410                                            (TCPOPT_NOP << 16) |
1411                                            (TCPOPT_TIMESTAMP << 8) |
1412                                            TCPOLEN_TIMESTAMP);
1413                  *ptr++ = htonl(tstamp);
1414                  *ptr++ = htonl(tp->ts_recent);
1415          }
1416          if (tp->eff_sacks) {
1417                  struct tcp_sack_block *sp = tp->dsack ? tp->duplicate_sack : tp->selective_acks;
1418                  int this_sack;
1419
1420                  *ptr++ = __constant_htonl((TCPOPT_NOP << 24) |
1421                                            (TCPOPT_NOP << 16) |
1422                                            (TCPOPT_SACK << 8) |
1423                                            (TCPOLEN_SACK_BASE +
1424                                             (tp->eff_sacks * TCPOLEN_SACK_PERBLOCK)));
1425                  for(this_sack = 0; this_sack < tp->eff_sacks; this_sack++) {
1426                          *ptr++ = htonl(sp[this_sack].start_seq);
1427                          *ptr++ = htonl(sp[this_sack].end_seq);
1428                  }
1429                  if (tp->dsack) {
1430                          tp->dsack = 0;
1431                          tp->eff_sacks--;
1432                  }
1433          }
1434  }
```

Figure 7.61 Checking for a sack-reneging receiver.

```
static int tcp_check_sack_reneging(struct sock *sk, struct tcp_opt *tp)
{
        struct sk_buff *skb;

        /* If ACK arrived pointing to a remembered SACK,
         * it means that our remembered SACKs do not reflect
         * real state of receiver i.e.
         * receiver _host_ is heavily congested (or buggy).
         * Do processing similar to RTO timeout.
         */
        if ((skb = skb_peek(&sk->write_queue)) != NULL &&
            (TCP_SKB_CB(skb)->sacked & TCPCB_SACKED_ACKED)) {
                NET_INC_STATS_BH(TCPSACKReneging);

                tcp_enter_loss(sk, 1);
                tp->retransmits++;
                tcp_retransmit_skb(sk, skb_peek(&sk->write_queue));
                tcp_reset_xmit_timer(sk, TCP_TIME_RETRANS, tp->rto);
                return 1;
        }
        return 0;
}
```

Figure 7.62 PAWS checking.

```
static inline int tcp_paws_check(struct tcp_opt *tp, int rst)
{
        if ((s32)(tp->rcv_tsval - tp->ts_recent) >= 0)
                return 0;
        if (xtime.tv_sec >= tp->ts_recent_stamp + TCP_PAWS_24DAYS)
                return 0;

        /* RST segments are not recommended to carry timestamp,
           and, if they do, it is recommended to ignore PAWS because
           "their cleanup function should take precedence over timestamps."
           Certainly, it is mistake. It is necessary to understand the reasons
           of this constraint to relax it: if peer reboots, clock may go
           out-of-sync and half-open connections will not be reset.
           Actually, the problem would be not existing if all
           the implementations followed draft about maintaining clock
           via reboots. Linux-2.2 DOES NOT!

           However, we can relax time bounds for RST segments to MSL.
         */
        if (rst && xtime.tv_sec >= tp->ts_recent_stamp + TCP_PAWS_MSL)
                return 0;
        return 1;
}
```

Figure 7.63 Round-trip estimation (i).

```
/* Called to compute a smoothed rtt estimate. The data fed to this
 * routine either comes from timestamps, or from segments that were
 * known _not_ to have been retransmitted [see Karn/Partridge
 * Proceedings SIGCOMM 87]. The algorithm is from the SIGCOMM 88
 * piece by Van Jacobson.
 * NOTE: the next three routines used to be one big routine.
 * To save cycles in the RFC 1323 implementation it was better to break
 * it up into three procedures. -- erics
 */
static __inline__ void tcp_rtt_estimator(struct tcp_opt *tp, __u32 mrtt)
{
	long m = mrtt; /* RTT */

	/*	The following amusing code comes from Jacobson's
	 *	article in SIGCOMM '88. Note that rtt and mdev
	 *	are scaled versions of rtt and mean deviation.
	 *	This is designed to be as fast as possible
	 *	m stands for "measurement".
	 *
	 *	On a 1990 paper the rto value is changed to:
	 *	RTO = rtt + 4 * mdev
	 *
	 * Funny. This algorithm seems to be very broken.
	 * These formulae increase RTO, when it should be decreased, increase
	 * too slowly, when it should be incresed fastly, decrease too fastly
	 * etc. I guess in BSD RTO takes ONE value, so that it is absolutely
	 * does not matter how to _calculate_ it. Seems, it was trap
	 * that VJ failed to avoid. 8)
	 */
```

When a SACK option comes in, the relevant socket buffer is marked as received and not retransmitted. A receiver still has the option to drop the packet (an act known as reneging) (see Figure 7.61).

Figure 7.64 Round-trip estimation (ii).

```
	if(m == 0)
		m = 1;
	if (tp->srtt != 0) {
		m -= (tp->srtt >> 3); /* m is now error in rtt est */
		tp->srtt += m;		/* rtt = 7/8 rtt + 1/8 new */
		if (m < 0) {
			m = -m;		/* m is now abs(error) */
			m -= (tp->mdev >> 2); /* similar update on mdev */
			/* This is similar to one of Eifel findings.
			 * Eifel blocks mdev updates when rtt decreases.
			 * This solution is a bit different: we use finer gain
			 * for mdev in this case (alpha*beta).
			 * Like Eifel it also prevents growth of rto,
```

```
			 * but also it limits too fast rto decreases,
			 * happening in pure Eifel.
			 */
			if (m > 0)
				m >>= 3;
		} else {
			m -= (tp->mdev >> 2); /* similar update on mdev */
		}
		tp->mdev += m;		/* mdev = 3/4 mdev + 1/4 new */
		if (tp->mdev > tp->mdev_max) {
			tp->mdev_max = tp->mdev;
			if (tp->mdev_max > tp->rttvar)
				tp->rttvar = tp->mdev_max;
		}
		if (after(tp->snd_una, tp->rtt_seq)) {
			if (tp->mdev_max < tp->rttvar)
				tp->rttvar -= (tp->rttvar-tp->mdev_max)>>2;
			tp->rtt_seq = tp->snd_una;
			tp->mdev_max = TCP_RTO_MIN;
		}
	} else {
		/* no previous measure. */
		tp->srtt = m<<3;	/* take the measured time to be rtt */
		tp->mdev = m<<2;	/* make sure rto = 3*rtt */
		tp->mdev_max = tp->rttvar = max(tp->mdev, TCP_RTO_MIN);
		tp->rtt_seq = tp->snd_nxt;
	}
}
```

When a segment is acknowledged by the usual TCP acknowledgment mechanism, the fact that they have been SACKed needs no longer be recorded.

Protection Against Wrapped Sequence Numbers—PAWS

This is a high-performance extension to TCP described in RFC 1323. On high-bandwidth long-distance links there is a danger that the sequence count will wrap-round while there are still valid older segments in the network. The PAWS algorithm prevents this by using a timestamp option, which carries a non-decreasing integer. The basic idea is that a segment can be discarded if its timestamp is less than some other recently received timestamp. The following variables in `tcp_opt` are used:

- `rcv_tsval`—the timestamp in this segment
- `ts_recent`—the most recently received timestamp
- `ts_recent_stamp`—the time `ts_recent` became valid

Figure 7.65 Round-trip estimation (iii).

```

/* Calculate rto without backoff. This is the second half of Van Jacobson's
 * routine referred to above.
 */
static __inline__ void tcp_set_rto(struct tcp_opt *tp)
{
	/* Old crap is replaced with new one. 8)
	 *
	 * More seriously:
	 * 1. If rtt variance happened to be less 50msec, it is hallucination.
	 *    It cannot be less due to utterly erratic ACK generation made
	 *    at least by solaris and freebsd. "Erratic ACKs" has _nothing_
	 *    to do with delayed acks, because at cwnd>2 true delack timeout
	 *    is invisible. Actually, Linux-2.4 also generates erratic
	 *    ACKs in some curcumstances.
	 */
	tp->rto = (tp->srtt >> 3) + tp->rttvar;

	/* 2. Fixups made earlier cannot be right.
	 *    If we do not estimate RTO correctly without them,
	 *    all the algo is pure shit and should be replaced
	 *    with correct one. It is exaclty, which we pretend to do.
	 */
}

/* NOTE: clamping at TCP_RTO_MIN is not required, current algo
 * guarantees that rto is higher.
 */
static __inline__ void tcp_bound_rto(struct tcp_opt *tp)
{
	if (tp->rto > TCP_RTO_MAX)
		tp->rto = TCP_RTO_MAX;
}
```

Round-Trip Estimation

In order to get the most out of a TCP connection in terms of bandwidth utilization, an accurate method to determine the round-trip time for timeout purposes is needed. The mechanism is described in Stevens [8], and shown implemented in Figures 7.63–7.64.

Figure 7.66 Building options on SYN packets.

```
/* Construct a tcp options header for a SYN or SYN_ACK packet.
 * If this is every changed make sure to change the definition of
 * MAX_SYN_SIZE to match the new maximum number of options that you
 * can generate.
 */
```

```
static inline void tcp_syn_build_options(__u32 *ptr, int mss, int ts, int sack,
                                         int offer_wscale, int wscale, __u32 tstamp, __u32
                                                ts_recent)
{
        /* We always get an MSS option.
         * The option bytes which will be seen in normal data
         * packets should timestamps be used, must be in the MSS
         * advertised. But we subtract them from tp->mss_cache so
         * that calculations in tcp_sendmsg are simpler etc.
         * So account for this fact here if necessary. If we
         * don't do this correctly, as a receiver we won't
         * recognize data packets as being full sized when we
         * should, and thus we won't abide by the delayed ACK
         * rules correctly.
         * SACKs don't matter, we never delay an ACK when we
         * have any of those going out.
         */
        *ptr++ = htonl((TCPOPT_MSS << 24) | (TCPOLEN_MSS << 16) | mss);
        if (ts) {
                if(sack)
                        *ptr++ = __constant_htonl((TCPOPT_SACK_PERM << 24) | (TCPOLEN_SACK_PERM
                                                  << 16) |
                                                  (TCPOPT_TIMESTAMP << 8) | TCPOLEN_TIMESTAMP);
                else
                        *ptr++ = __constant_htonl((TCPOPT_NOP << 24) | (TCPOPT_NOP << 16) |
                                                  (TCPOPT_TIMESTAMP << 8) | TCPOLEN_TIMESTAMP);
                *ptr++ = htonl(tstamp);         /* TSVAL */
                *ptr++ = htonl(ts_recent);      /* TSECR */
        } else if(sack)
                *ptr++ = __constant_htonl((TCPOPT_NOP << 24) | (TCPOPT_NOP << 16) |
                                          (TCPOPT_SACK_PERM << 8) | TCPOLEN_SACK_PERM);
        if (offer_wscale)
                *ptr++ = htonl((TCPOPT_NOP << 24) | (TCPOPT_WINDOW << 16) | (TCPOLEN_WINDOW << 8)
                               | (wscale));
}
```

Figure 7.67 Parsing the WINDOW option.

```
if (!after(seq, sp->end_seq) && !after(sp->start_seq, end_seq)) {
```

Window Scaling

The TCP header allows for 16 bits to indicate the received window size. With ever-increasing bandwidth and distance this is no longer sufficient to keep efficiency. The TCP window scale option on synchronization allows for this value to be scaled. This is described in RFC 1323. The option is sent only in SYN packets, as it is only these that can be guaranteed to be carried to the receiver (see Figures 7.66–7.67).

7.4.8 TCP Behavior

Looking in some detail at TCP, latest theory and measurement by Padhye et al. (1998), shows how it really behaves:

$$B = \min\left(\frac{W_m}{RTT}, \frac{1}{RTT\sqrt{\frac{2bp}{3}} + T_0 \min(1, 3\sqrt{\frac{3bp}{8}})\,p(1+32p^2)}\right) \quad (7.1)$$

This equation is for long-lived transfers. There is more recent work by Cardwell and others on short-lived transfers (which the majority of Web usage consists of today). However, just looking at this equation, we can see a lot of single-instance specific parameters that affect the performance radically. For example, W_m, and the range of T_0 and b in implementations, could be quite large. Another problem here that we should consider when thinking about pricing is the range of values for RTT—in some theoretical work, RTT is used as a measure of resource use. However, it is actually a real value measured from the path delay, and as such, is suspect when used for comparability of, for example, satellite versus terrestrial hops. Another problem with such proposals is that the loss rate p is considered as congestion feedback, and therefore as a proportional resource utilization indication. However, it depends on the instantaneous load in the queue seen by a single packet, not the average over some period. Loss is also due to interference on wireless networks, and so is a very noisy signal. Proposed Internet replacements for loss such as Explicit Congestion Notification also need specifying with regard to the sampling interval; if a switch measures congestion over some interval, this must be known to the sources that receive congestion feedback, out of band, so that they can estimate the significance of some number of packets arriving with the ECN bit set.

Reliable multicast protocols (for games, share dealing, and software and news distribution), such as the family of protocols using Handley and Floyd's TCP Friendly Multicast Congestion Control, use similar adaptation techniques to that which TCP employs. However, one additional level of complexity is that

Table 7.1 Terms in the Padhye TCP Equation

W_m	maximum advertised receive window
T_0	initial timeout value
RTT	the round trip time
b	the number of packets acknowledged by one ACK
p	the mean packet loss probability
B	the throughput achieved by a TCP flow

these protocols also have self-organizing-repair server mechanisms. These will alter the traffic patterns again.

Similar evolution is occurring in the streamed multimedia traffic flows that emanate from Internet radio and TV sites, with TCP-like adaptation being the apparent goal for RealAudio and Video, the most commonly used products for such services in the Internet.

7.5 Management

The following commands on Linux can be used to monitor the transport layer:

- `Netstat`—can display active connections; for example `netstat -a` will display all active and listening connections.
- `Tcpdump`—can trace packets on wire by putting system into *promiscuous* mode at driver level (says "recognize all frames as *for me*") and passing up through a filter to an application that can further process or dump to a screen.
- `ethereal` (www.ethereal.com)—will provide a graphical display of network traffic.

7.6 TCP vs. UDP

As we have seen, TCP overcomes many of the problems with UDP, but at what cost? TCP is a much more heavyweight protocol than UDP. Indeed, it can be seen simply from the number of pages of this book how much more effort is needed in its description and implementation. However, there are some circumstances where UDP is the better transport mechanism. These include situations where memory and resources are limited, such as initial boot-off-network operations on diskless workstations where a full TFTP (Trivial File Transfer Protocol) implemenation, which runs over UDP, can be implemented in a few bytes of ROM code and minimal RAM requirements. Other times where use of UDP may benefit the situation are when the light weight nature can provide a performance advantage. An example here is DNS over a LAN, when a quick name resolution is required, and in a LAN environment there are often enough resources to be relatively assured of a successful communication. UDP can also be used when another mechanism is responsible for portioning out the bandwidth, for example communication over RSVP-established sessions. The Real-Time Protocol (RTP) is a protocol designed to carry real-time traffic, such as video and audio, over the Internet. It uses UDP as its transport mechanism.

7.7 RTP—Real-Time Protocol

The Real-Time protocol is designed to carry multimedia flows over the Internet. Whether RTP is a transport layer protocol or an application layer protocol is a commonly debated point. For the argument that RTP is an application layer protocol are the facts that RTP data packets are carried in UDP segments (a transport layer service), and RTP is usually implemented in user space. For the contrary argument is the fact that RTP provides a number of additional services to the application layer: these are syncronization and framing. RFC 1889 describes RTP and a number of other RFCs describe different payload formats for particular media types. RTP is generally implemented as a user library and not in the kernel, so is beyond the scope of this work.

7.8 Writing a New Transport Layer

If you are developing a new transport layer that uses IP as its networking layer and sockets as the application API, then linking it with the existing protocol suites becomes simply a matter of writing the appropriate linkage functions and filling in the function holding structures (see Section 7.3.4).

7.9 Summary

This chapter examined transport protocols and their implementation. The facilities provided by the transport layer, that is, multiplexing, reliability, flow and congestion control, synchronization, and framing, have each been examined and their implementations detailed. A comparison of popular transport protocols TCP, UDP, and RTP, has been made and instructions on writing your own transport layer given.

CHAPTER 8

Routing

"I'm not sure that the ability to create routing diagrams similar to pretzels with Mad Cow disease is actually a marketable skill."

—Steve Levin

8.1 Roadmap

This chapter is about Internet plumbing and path finding. Here we discuss how we interconnect links of different types, and having done so, how we find our way from A to B across a complex topology. Linux supports a variety of routing protocols; and Linux systems, running on PCs or other hardware platforms, are in widespread use as low-cost solutions for low- to medium-performance routers (though not entirely modest—up to 100 BaseT local and OC3 wide area links are easily supported, and there are no obvious reasons not to build up to a Gbps router).

There are two main components to a router: forwarding and routing. The forwarding task is carried out on each and every packet and involves looking up the destination (and possibly other data from the packet) in a forwarding table, and using the result to decide which interface to transmit the packet on. This is a kernel procedure. The routing task involves the business of building and maintaining the forwarding table, and is carried out asynchronously, usually by a user space process. There are a variety of routing protocols that are used in the Internet, but the basic tasks are the same.

In this chapter, we review the components of the routing system, and then look at Linux kernel support for the forwarding information base and control of it from routing protocols in user space.

8.2 Introduction

An IP routing system takes the work of finding a path away from end systems. As with the postal service, end users and systems need only know the location (address) of a recipient to get information there. An end system discovers an address by being given it. Typically, an end user uses a DNS name, which is looked up in the name server system, and results in the application software being given an IP address. The end system software then uses this address as the handle for communication with the *far end*. The infrastructure of the Internet protocol layer, in end systems routers and links, conspires to deliver the packets to the right place, based on the destination address in IP packets. The routing system may optionally consult other fields in the IP header to provide enhanced services.

To do all this, routers have to consult maps. The maps have to be constructed somehow, and there are a variety of approaches to doing this.

Forwarding decision frequency. The forwarding decision is taken most often. We can decide which route a packet will take separately for each packet, or we might fix our decision for a number of packets in a row, or even for a number of packets for a given user, perhaps for some configured amount of time. Whichever way a forwarding system works, it seems that we do not want to carry out any complex calculation, and we especially want to avoid any exchange of information with any other routers just so as to be able to forward one packet.

Information about the world cannot be distributed infinitely quickly. In a physical transport system (e.g., the postal service, or a freeway system for cars) where information can be sent about remote conditions by radio in a communications network, the state of a link some ways away can only be learned as quickly as the users' own data can travel. In other words, our information about the rest of the world is out of date. This means that it does not make sense to change what route we use too often. At one extreme, we can fix the route taken by packets manually, via some configuration tool or through network management. In fact, it is quite common to do this effectively in parts of the network where there are no choices anyhow—this is called setting up a default route. As one looks further into the network, this does not make sense, since there are alternative possible paths through the network, and it would seem a shame not to be able to use them if our main (default) choice link or path fails. Thus it is usual to configure fixed, or even default routes only on end systems or non-multihomed site access routers.

Routing calculation frequency. We could recalculate routes every time there was a new flow (e.g., a new TCP session or a new Web download). This might make sesnse if flows lasted a long time, since we might also be able to carry out some clever load balancing, provided we were able to tell the rest of the world about our new flow and which paths we were considering for it. In practice, on the Internet, flows are short lived, so most current routing protocols do not consider recalculating routes simply based on short-term information. It is more common to carry out a routing calculation based on one of two factors:

1. *Topology change*—a link outage, repair, or new link installation triggers an update. Of course it may be necessary to dampen down the trigger if a link has an intermittent status, to avoid putting too much traffic load (and computational effort) onto other routers.
2. *Long-term traffic change*—a long-term traffic monitoring system may input data into the route computation; currently, this is regarded as somewhat of a black art (also known as a research topic).

It is also usual to have periodic exchanges (*soft state* refreshes) to make sure that everyone has a consistent view of the world.

Routing update data sources. The input data for a routing calculation can be delivered from a central monitoring system to each router, or from the router's neighbors, hop-by-hop, or distributed by each router flooding information to all the other routers in an area. Each approach has its advantages. Central systems may fail, depriving the routers of updates, but a centralized system takes this load off the routers. A hop-by-hop advertisement is simple, but leads to potential inconsistency. A flooding approach can lead to a consistent view, but requires some traffic control for the route updates.

Routing update data distribution. The way the routing data is distributed is partly a consequence of the sources of data for routing calculation. However, in general, routing data is high priority, since without it, user data is unlikely to be delivered to the right place, or via the right path. Routing data may flow over different channels than the users' data. If so, it is important for a routing protocol to maintain status information about the users' actual data path, since it is no longer implicit in the reception of routing update data over a link that the users' data will travel so easily.

If a flooding approach is used to distribute routing data, from or to a management node, or from each router to all others in an area, the flood must be constrained not to loop. This may entail a simplified baseline routing computation (e.g., building a spanning tree amongst all the routers) first.

Routing calculation location. Having accumulated information about the state of the network, we need to compute the best routes. This might be done at a central node that would then distribute actual path information to each and every router, or, more realistically, can be done autonomously at each router. CPU power is cheap. Memory is reasonably cheap. Thus it makes sense to gain the advantage of timeliness and independence from failure of other nodes, by distributing (and to some extent, effectively replicating) the computation of the routes at every router.

Routing update data semantics. Route updates carry link status information. At its simplest, this is a binary up/down indication. However, increasingly network operators wish to select routes based on more complex *metrics*. These measurements can include propagation delay, current mean queuing delay, link capacity, monetary cost, loss statistics, and many other possibilities.

In special circumstances, other counterintuitive approaches have been taken in the design of routing systems. For example, in ad hoc radio networks, random routing is sometimes used. In systems with very limited computational resources (e.g., CPU, memory), hot potato routing is used, where packets are forwarded based only on current local information, such as choosing the output link with the shortest current queue.

In practice, at the moment, Internet routing is largely distributed and adaptive. Forwarding decisions (frequent) are largely decoupled from routing calculations (occasional). These design choices make the forwarding task relatively simple, but the routing protocol and map computation task Routing Information Base (RIB) and Forwarding Information Base (FIB) relatively complex. A few other tasks need to be accomplished:

Neighbor discovery. A router starts out either configured with information about who is down the end of them there links or else has to find it out by probing or listening.

Status. A router maintains some idea of the state of its neighbors, typically by periodically saying hello—this will sometimes be authenticated. The exact details for this operation are part of a specific routing protocol.

Distribution. Routers collaborate. They exchange views with each other about the state of the network as well as each other. There are actually two fundamentally different approaches to the actual details of this. The common, cheap and cheerful way is called *distance-vector*. Each router tells its neighbors everything it knows and has learned so far. This is discussed later in this chapter. The more respectable method is called *link-state*. Here, each router *floods* reports about the state of links that it looks after to all the other routers in a domain or area.

Scaling. As the Internet grows, the potential load on the links, router CPU, and memory systems also grows. Since network growth in the last two decades has been exponential, this would not bode well for network service providers or operators. Luckily, several techniques exist to reduce the load on the network routing and forwarding system.

- *Hierarchical addressing.* Most networks employ some kind of hierarchical addressing. In many networks, such as the postal system and the telephone network, addresses in use are variable in length. Only as much of an address as neccessary need be quoted to make it unique for the area within which it is being used. When constructing routes for the whole world, however, the full address must be used. Thus when sending a letter to someone else in the same city, the author doesn't have to quote the city name or country name; when the post offices of the world construct their routing tables to be able to deliver letters to anywhere in the world, they need to be able to distinguish `10 Downing St., London`, from `10 Downing St., Cambridge`, and both of these from `10 Downing St., New York, NY, USA`.

  In the Internet, addresses are fixed in length, but a technique called classless interdomain routing is used to provide the hierarchical addresses within a fixed-length field. This relies on associating a variable length mask with an address in use in a routing area, and exchanging the mask as well as the address when building up maps of the world. We look at this more below.

- *Hierarchical routing.* In large networks, it is generally the case that different regions in the network have more or less connectivity. If a region is connected to the rest of the world only via a single link (*single homed*), then it seems unnecessary to bother the rest of the world with the details of the internal topology of the region.

  It is also the case that we often deploy new routing protocols in part of the network at a time rather than having a flag day when we upgrade (or downgrade) the entire network.

  Thus it is important to separate routing into regions. This is done in two different ways in Internet routing. Firstly, routing protocols are divided into *intradomain* and *interdomain*. Here, the term domain refers to the autonomous management of routing, and not any other aspect of networking. Intradomain routing domains are separated from each other by interdomain routing protocols. In IP networks, these are known as Interior Gateway Protocol (IGP) and Exterior Gateway Protocol (EGP). Secondly, within a domain, a routing protocol may have explicit configuration management mechanisms for dividing routers and links into subdomains. In the Internet, there are several examples of this, ranging from subnet routing, up to area routing (in Open Shortest Path First (OSPF) and Intermediate System-Intermedia System (IS-IS)). We will revisit this briefly at the end of this chapter.

Routing table construction. It is an internal matter for a routing daemon how it constructs its routing information base. The entries will essentially list all the peer routers, and typically all possible destination prefixes, as well as some destinations known about but currently unreachable. The most general data structure for this would be a graph of nodes (routers) and edges (links), with the edges labeled with the various metrics for making route (or forwarding) decisions. Associated with any node and edge would be the source of the information about it, and the time that the last information was received. Of course, in practice, given all information arrives either from or via neighbors, this data could be built around a smaller data structure, such as a list of neighbors and the list of updates, with a single entry for the last update time—it really depends on the granularity of information in the routing protocol.

Forwarding table computation. At the end of each update epoch, a computation is carried out by the routing daemon to derive the new forwarding information base (FIB). This is then downloaded into the forwarding engine—in Linux terms, the kernel FIB is updated by the routing process. This can and often is manual, of course.

In distance-vector algorithms, the data distribution *is* the computation. A router receives a vector of destinations and metrics from a neighbor, and simply replaces the forwarding entry for the next hop with the new value, if the new value is better.

In link state protocols, a more complex procedure is needed to derive the forwarding table from the set of route updates. At the end of the route update flooding epoch, the network graph is built, simply by adding all the updates together in a jigsaw puzzle. Subsequently, Dijkstra's well-known graph-walking algorithm can be used to carry out a forward search from the current router to all other routers (and the networks attached to those routers). This finds the path from here to there with the lowest metric. If paths with different metrics need to be considered (or multiple alternate paths for load balancing or instant failover), then the algorithm can be called multiple times.

Typically, we can imagine that this only occurs for the entire routing system very occasionally. Most updates may result in local parts of the graph being changes, and there are several techniques for incrementally computing a Dijkstra, and keeping the CPU cost to a minimum.

Forwarding is simple. However, the lookup of an entry is complicated by the fact that the procedure typically involves an algorithm called *longest match* due to classless interdomain routing. There are a variety of data structures that have been used to keep this procedure fast and also to keep the associated forwarding tables small, and we describe the one currently used in Linux in this chapter.

The rest of this chapter discusses simple forwarding and routing in Linux. More complex routing protocols are not part of any standard release, but are rather separate products that are available from the networking community (e.g., GateD). In the future, we hope this may change, as Open Source produces some high-quality routing protocol daemons.

A complete discussion of routing protocol design is outside the scope of this book.

In the next section, we take a look at the Linux kernel support for forwarding information.

8.3 Forwarding Table Computation

8.3.1 IP Addressing

Each packet arrives with some information in it about where it wants to go and how it wants to be treated. The simplest data we can lookup in our forwarding table in an IPv4 data packet is the destination address.

IPv4 addresses are 32 bits long. This makes a simple table lookup somewhat unrealistic. Even if each entry in the table just had the 32-bit IP address of the next hop (ignoring other important information), we would need $4 * 2^{32}$ bytes of memory in every router (16 Gbytes of memory)! In other network protocol worlds, such as connection-oriented packet networks, this approach is taken, since the number of entries used for forwarding each packet is limited to the maximum number of concurrent connections, and this is typically a smaller number. In fact, we will see later how multi-protocol label switching (MPLS) can make use of this idea. It has the added bonus of being efficient (a single-access cycle time to return the data). This means it has potential for low-cost hardware implementation. If we know that we are building hardware with a limited number of flows and a limited number of interfaces that the next hop can be reached on, we can limit the table size to something quite tractable. However, this would not be in line with the Internet philosophy of generality, flexibility, or software implementations, which is what we are mainly concerned with here.

Staying with the idea of a flat (i.e., unstructured) 32-bit address, a programmer's first thought when confronted with this type of problem is to look at a *hash table.*

Hash tables rely on some knowledge that the distribution of *used* entries is relatively sparse, and relatively evenly scattered in some sense. With some knowledge of the distribution of actually assigned IP addresses, a *hash function*

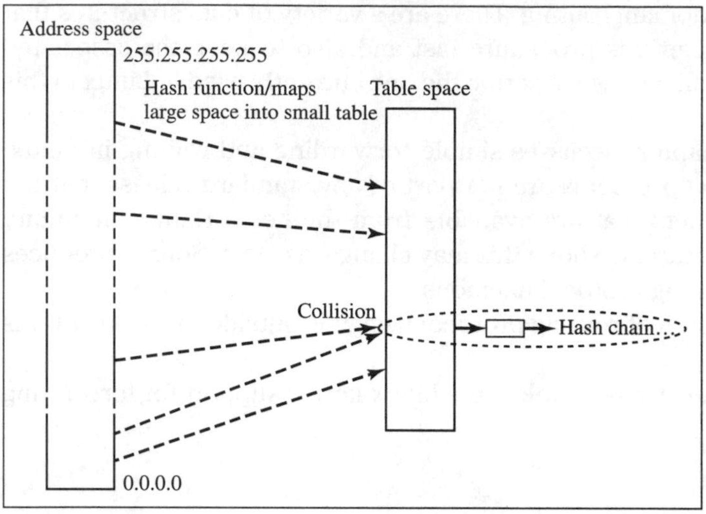

Figure 8.1 Hash tables.

can be designed which *maps* the address, from a possible 32-bit value, or 2^{32} entries, into a smaller identifier space. For example, if we know that there are only 65,536 assigned Net numbers in the world, we could have a table with a mere 100,000 entries (a few spare to be on the safe side), and choose the hash function to be `modulo`, in this case, `modulo` 2^{16}.

IP addresses are not assigned in a perfect, uniform random distribution, so this will lead almost inevitably to *collisions* or clashes in entries in the hash table (see Figure 8.1). These are dealt with by *chaining* a linked list from the entries that collide. This also needs a marker to say if the entry *is* an entry, or is part of a chain.

The hash function takes somewhat longer to compute than a table offset. It then subsequently requires a table offset in any case, and typically, this results in a possible linked list search, too. This is considerably more costly in CPU than in memory. However, the relative costs of CPU and memory are in favor of this kind of approach as a basis for modern route lookups for IP-like networks. Considering trends in current memory performance and prices, it would be a decade or more before we could consider direct route lookup. If you consider IPv6 addresses, which are 128 bits long, any likely full table is completely out of the question.

Of course, life is more complex than this; IP addresses are effectively structured into several parts. IPv4 unicast addresses are in two parts. IPv6 addresses may have more components depending on the scheme in use. IP multicast addresses are yet another kettle of fish, and we look at IP multicast later in this chapter.

For now, let's just consider IPv4. IPv4 has a *network* part and a *host* part, together making up the full 32 bits. Historically, a site was allocated an IPv4 network address taken from one of three *classes* of the address space. The idea was that there were typically three different-size networks: the core networks such as ARPANET and SATNET—these would be given 8-bit network addresses (class A), and there could be only ever up to 256 of them; the site networks such as Berkeley, MIT, UCLA, and UCL—these were given 16-bit network numbers (class B) and there could be 65,536 of them, each with 65,536 hosts on; finally, there would be small local networks, with only 256 hosts on them—but there could be up to 2^{24} of these, that is 16,777,216 class C network numbers.

There are two big problems with this approach. Firstly, not only does "one size fits all" not apply, but in fact three sizes didn't fit all either; many networks have a topology that allows more than 256 hosts to be attached locally, but if given a class C network, not all these hosts would be reachable; conversely, many networks only attached 100 hosts to a class B network. More critically, the routing system had to know about all the addresses, yet in practice (and this is not unrelated to the first point), many sites had a single way to reach the whole world, even when they had several networks internally.

The first step away from a globally visible network numbering system was the introduction of *subnet addressing*. The second step away from a globally visible topology was the hierarchical allocation of addresses to organizations. Consideration of the size and topological location of an organization would lead to the assignment of a network number, together with a mask, which indicates how many bits of the address are actually free to be used for allocation to hosts, and how many are for advertising the network as reachable to the next level of the topology (see Figure 8.2).

The downside of this is that it leads to the requirement for hosts, routers, and routing protocols to know or discover the mask associated with their region of the network. The upside is that it leads to the possibilitiy that address prefixes may now be hierarchically aggregated. In other words, on the edge of the network, we only care about routes towards the core, while in the core of the network, we only need now about the highest levels of aggregation. Hopefully, these would usually be long masks, or shorter network prefixes, leading to a reduction in routing table requirements.

The scheme has worked very well for local and global routing table management for several years. Recent trends in multihoming have emerged from the requirement for sites to have high availability. If multihoming for a site is done transparently, this requires network providers to advertize the site prefix through at lease one path along which the address is not aggregatable.

An important consideration for implementors of classless interdomain routing is that a router must now compare destination addresses in packets with multiple possible routing entries. Which routing entry is the correct one to pick? Clearly, the *most specific* entry is the one nearest the destination. Given the way that addresses are now hierarchically allocated and assigned, this means that the best match is the *longest* match, or in other words the one with the longest

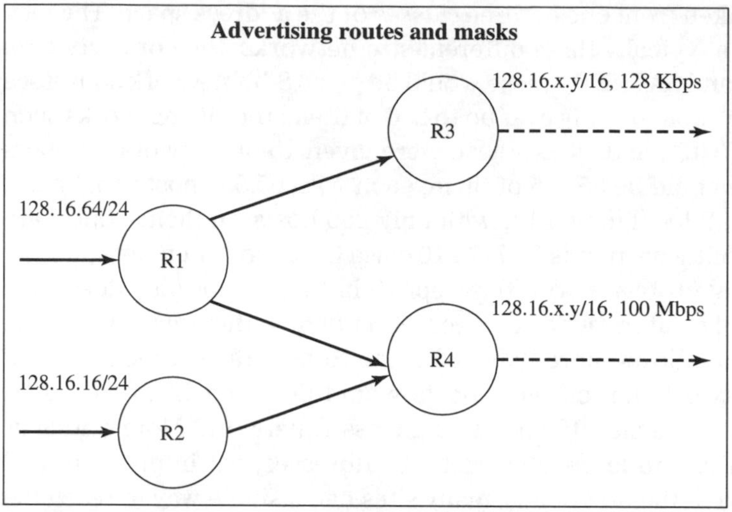

Figure 8.2 IP addresses, masks, and route advertisements: `linux{2.4.4/net/ipv4/tcp_input.c`.

number of bits matching in the prefix in the destination address and the routing entry address after the routing entry mask has been applied.

A naive approach to implementation might be to carry out a linear search of the routing table. This may be all right in local routers, but in the routers nearer the core of the Internet, we find tens of thousands of route entries. If a single hash table is used, we do not know the order with which entries with different length prefixes will occur. Other solutions are required, otherwise we end up with a linear search, which results in the same order of number of lookups *for every single packet to be forwarded* as there are route entries, which can be very large.

Trees and tries. The old BSD UNIX approach to the forwarding table was to keep three levels of information: host, route, and default. The search involved hashing into the host table, and if a miss occurred, hashing into the route table, and then finally, if that failed, searching the list of default gateways. Later, in BSD UNIX 4.3 radix trees were developed. These are a form of Patricia Trie–a trie is just a name for the type of tree data structure that stored information at each internal node as well as at the leaves. The BSD UNIX 4.3 radix tree is a binary tree, which, starting at the root, stores the prefix address and mask so far. As you move down the tree, more bits are matched going one way down the tree. If they don't match, the other branch holds the entry required. This sort of data structure can result in efficient average performance for forwarding table lookup times, on the order of *ln*(number of entries), which for large routing tables is quite a gain (e.g., for 65,536 route entries, an average of about 16 comparisons). Of course, the worst-case performance is the length of the address, or 32 comparisons for an IPv4 address.

Caches. The next stage in the evolution of forwarding table lookup schemes was the idea of adding a cache of most-recently-used routes in front of the standard FIB. Before looking in the standard FIB, the forwarding code will look up a destination in a route cache, which is hopefully a smaller table and can be searched more quickly. This idea sounds good until you realize that the performance advantage of caching depends on the pattern of access over time. Specifically, caching relies on temporal locality—this means that if a sequence of lookups resulting do in fact tend to reference the same subset of destinations, and this subset only changes much slower than the rate of actual packets arriving, then a cache can be a big win. In practice, it depends where you are in the Net whether this is true or not—certainly, according to measurements made my some experts for core routers, there doesn't appear to be a great deal of temporal locality. The Internet is "all over the place" [14]. On the other hand, a given site router may see packets go by with a very focused set of destinations.

Multiple hash tables. It was observed that one could have a hash table for each possible prefix length. A refinement of this is to see that, rather than searching all of these different tables linearly, one can do a binary search by prefix lengths, starting with the most common [12]. This is straightforward computing. Even with an IPv6 address of 128 bits, this will take eight hash lookups to find the longest matching entry.

Trie compression. A still more recent approach is to try to improve over the radix tree by compressing the trie in some way [13]. This scheme involves reducing the number of levels in the trie by increasing the degree of the nodes.

Content-addressable memory—CAMs. A CAM is a custom piece of hardware that is addressed by its content—a 32-bit-wide CAM would be a device that is accessed by presenting it with an input value (e.g., the IP destination), and returns another value (i.e., the next hop) if the input value is in its contents. Generally CAMs get expensive if the width is large, and require an exact match. Due to the interest in fast IP packet forwarding (and therefore fast lookup), there are a number of refinements to these devices, such as *ternary CAMs*. Ternary CAMs allow three values for each input bit, including a *don't care*. This allows multiple matches to be done in parallel—the order of the results typically implies preference.

8.3.2 FIB Purpose

Forwarding tables are consulted for every packet to be sent from a system. An entry is indexed by IP destination address, and has to store this and the associated mask, as well as information that may be used to time out an entry, and metrics. The returned value from looking up an entry will typically be the next hop IP router. Local routing (i.e., link level mechanisms) are then used to deliver a packet to the next IP hop.

The forwarding table data structures in Linux are pretty sophisticated, as well as being close to state-of-the art in efficiency.

8.3.3 FIB Implementation

The diagram below illustrates how the FIB data is stored in the Linux 2.4 kernel.

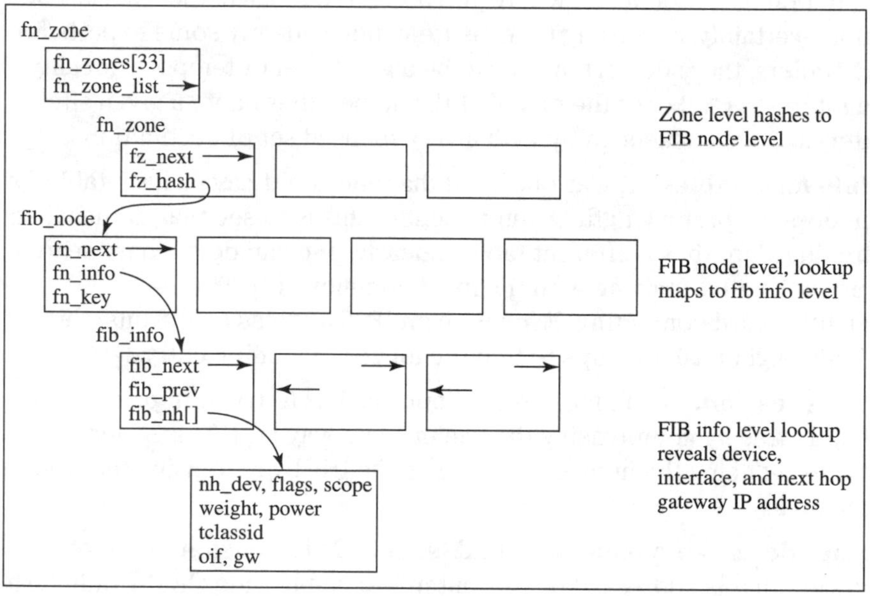

Figure 8.3 The FIB.

8.3.4 FIB Interface

In the `rtattr` data structure (see Figure 8.4), we can see the generality of information that could be added in the FIB. In principle, we have source- and destination-based routing, input and output interfaces, priority, multipath, protocol-based information, and so on.

The fields are typically added into an FIB entry by a call via the RTNetlink socket, from a routing daemon, or from the superuser running the `IP` command, which we look at later.

Figure 8.4 FIB route table attribute entry: `linux/include/net/ip_fib.h`.

```
21  struct kern_rta
22  {
23          void        *rta_dst;
24          void        *rta_src;
25          int         *rta_iif;
26          int         *rta_oif;
27          void        *rta_gw;
28          u32         *rta_priority;
29          void        *rta_prefsrc;
30          struct rtattr *rta_mx;
31          struct rtattr *rta_mp;
32          unsigned char *rta_protoinfo;
33          unsigned char *rta_flow;
34          struct rta_cacheinfo *rta_ci;
35  };
```

As described before, the final result after the long smart haul of looking up a forwarding information base entry is the *next hop*. This data structure (see Figure 8.5) is relatively simple; either we are told the IP address of the next hop gateway, or output device (or both)—the output device is all that is needed if we have a point-to-point link, for example, where the actual IP address of the next hop is irrelevant. Linux also supports multipath routing, where we can load balance traffic across several links. It also indicates the distance (*scope*) to the destination.

Figure 8.5 FIB next hop data structure: `linux/include/net/ip_fib.h`.

```
37  struct fib_nh
38  {
39          struct net_device       *nh_dev;
40          unsigned                nh_flags;
41          unsigned char           nh_scope;
42  #ifdef CONFIG_IP_ROUTE_MULTIPATH
43          int                     nh_weight;
44          int                     nh_power;
45  #endif
46  #ifdef CONFIG_NET_CLS_ROUTE
47          __u32                   nh_tclassid;
48  #endif
49          int                     nh_oif;
50          u32                     nh_gw;
51  };
```

FIB information is not just a single next hop. There is other data, as shown in Figure 8.6. This includes the possibility of multipath, source-based preferences, and some entry maintenance data that we'll look at later.

Figure 8.6 The main FIB structure: `linux/include/net/ip_fib.h`.

```
struct fib_info
{
        struct fib_info         *fib_next;
        struct fib_info         *fib_prev;
        int                     fib_treeref;
        atomic_t                fib_clntref;
        int                     fib_dead;
        unsigned                fib_flags;
        int                     fib_protocol;
        u32                     fib_prefsrc;
        u32                     fib_priority;
        unsigned                fib_metrics[RTAX_MAX];
#define fib_mtu fib_metrics[RTAX_MTU-1]
#define fib_window fib_metrics[RTAX_WINDOW-1]
#define fib_rtt fib_metrics[RTAX_RTT-1]
#define fib_advmss fib_metrics[RTAX_ADVMSS-1]
        int                     fib_nhs;
#ifdef CONFIG_IP_ROUTE_MULTIPATH
        int                     fib_power;
#endif
        struct fib_nh           fib_nh[0];
#define fib_dev         fib_nh[0].nh_dev
};
```

As described before, the lookup in the FIB essentially returns one or more next hops—the case for multiple next hops is generally currently only when we have multipath routing operating, when traffic is being balanced over more than one link. We can see the different metrics and other parameters that need to be matched for some types of lookup, such as protocol, preference, and priority, and then there are a number of internal management fields, such as the tree reference, client reference, liveness (`fib_dead`), and flags fields.

Figure 8.7 FIB lookup result structure: `linux/include/net/ip_fib.h`.

```
struct fib_result
{
        unsigned char prefixlen;
        unsigned char nh_sel;
        unsigned char type;
        unsigned char scope;
        struct fib_info *fi;
#ifdef CONFIG_IP_MULTIPLE_TABLES
        struct fib_rule *r;
#endif
};
```

The overall structure (see Figure 8.6) is complex. Usually, FIB-related functions return the `fib_result` type (see Figure 8.7) as a reference parameter, with the `fib_info *fi` field pointing at the appropriate entry.

The `fib_table` structure is a more generic interface to the FIB, including pointers to the various FIB access functions, so that new FIB functions can be written per routing system. Currently, only the set of lookup functions in the `fib_hash` module are defined, so the pointers are only initialled to point at the respective `fn_` functions.

Figure 8.8 FIB generic interface: `linux/include/net/ip_fib.h`.

```
struct fib_table
{
        unsigned char tb_id;
        unsigned      tb_stamp;
        int           (*tb_lookup)(struct fib_table *tb, const struct rt_key *key, struct
                                   fib_result *res);
        int           (*tb_insert)(struct fib_table *table, struct rtmsg *r,
                                   struct kern_rta *rta, struct nlmsghdr *n,
                                   struct netlink_skb_parms *req);
        int           (*tb_delete)(struct fib_table *table, struct rtmsg *r,
                                   struct kern_rta *rta, struct nlmsghdr *n,
                                   struct netlink_skb_parms *req);
        int           (*tb_dump)(struct fib_table *table, struct sk_buff *skb,
                                   struct netlink_callback *cb);
        int           (*tb_flush)(struct fib_table *table);
        int           (*tb_get_info)(struct fib_table *table, char *buf,
                                     int first, int count);
        void          (*tb_select_default)(struct fib_table *table,
                                           const struct rt_key *key, struct fib_result *res);

        unsigned char tb_data[0];
};
```

8.3.5 FIB Code

The FIB implementation is split into four main parts. There is a front end (`fib_frontend`), which is the externally visible interface to the FIB. Then there is the `fib_rules` module, which implements the set of ways that we pick a next hop—we need to discriminate one from another potentially by policy or metric, as well as simply on longest match. Thirdly, we have the `fib_semantics` module, which deals with the arcane definitions of what `nexthop` really means—this is well described in the comment in Figure 8.37. Finally, there is the `fib_hash` module, which implements the set of hash functions described earlier in this chapter.

The Front End

Figure 8.9 FIB front end i—setting up the table: `linux/net/ipv4/fib_frontend.c`.

```
struct fib_table *local_table;
struct fib_table *main_table;

#else

#define RT_TABLE_MIN 1

struct fib_table *fib_tables[RT_TABLE_MAX+1];

struct fib_table *__fib_new_table(int id)
{
        struct fib_table *tb;

        tb = fib_hash_init(id);
        if (!tb)
                return NULL;
        fib_tables[id] = tb;
        return tb;
}
```

Figure 8.10 FIB front end i—flushing table: `linux/net/ipv4/fib_frontend.c`.

```
void fib_flush(void)
{
        int flushed = 0;
#ifdef CONFIG_IP_MULTIPLE_TABLES
        struct fib_table *tb;
        int id;

        for (id = RT_TABLE_MAX; id>0; id--) {
                if ((tb = fib_get_table(id))==NULL)
                        continue;
                flushed += tb->tb_flush(tb);
        }
#else /* CONFIG_IP_MULTIPLE_TABLES */
        flushed += main_table->tb_flush(main_table);
        flushed += local_table->tb_flush(local_table);
#endif /* CONFIG_IP_MULTIPLE_TABLES */

        if (flushed)
                rt_cache_flush(-1);
}
```

Figure 8.11 FIB front end PROC FS interface: `linux/net/ipv4/fib_frontend.c`.

```
100    #ifdef CONFIG_PROC_FS
101
102    /*
103     *      Called from the PROCfs module. This outputs /proc/net/route.
104     *
105     *      It always works in backward compatibility mode.
106     *      The format of the file is not supposed to be changed.
107     */
108
109    static int
110    fib_get_procinfo(char *buffer, char **start, off_t offset, int length)
111    {
112            int first = offset/128;
113            char *ptr = buffer;
114            int count = (length+127)/128;
115            int len;
116
117            *start = buffer + offset%128;
118
119            if (--first < 0) {
120                    sprintf(buffer, "%-127s\n", "Iface\tDestination\tGateway \tFlags\tRefCnt\tUse\
                              tMetric\tMask\t\tMTU\tWindow\tIRTT");
121                    --count;
122                    ptr += 120;
123                    first = 0;
124            }
125
126            if (main_table && count > 0) {
127                    int n = main_table->tb_get_info(main_table, ptr, first, count);
128                    count -= n;
129                    ptr += n*128;
130            }
131            len = ptr - *start;
132            if (len >= length)
133                    return length;
134            if (len >= 0)
135                    return len;
136            return 0;
137    }
138
139    #endif /* CONFIG_PROC_FS */
```

Figure 8.12 FIB front end—find device by address: `linux/net/ipv4/fib_frontend.c`.

```
141    /*
142     *      Find the first device with a given source address.
143     */
144
145    struct net_device * ip_dev_find(u32 addr)
146    {
147            struct rt_key key;
```

```
148              struct fib_result res;
149              struct net_device *dev = NULL;
150
151              memset(&key, 0, sizeof(key));
152              key.dst = addr;
153     #ifdef CONFIG_IP_MULTIPLE_TABLES
154              res.r = NULL;
155     #endif
156
157              if (!local_table || local_table->tb_lookup(local_table, &key, &res)) {
158                      return NULL;
159              }
160              if (res.type != RTN_LOCAL)
161                      goto out;
162              dev = FIB_RES_DEV(res);
163              if (dev)
164                      atomic_inc(&dev->refcnt);
165
166     out:
167              fib_res_put(&res);
168              return dev;
169     }
```

Figure 8.13 FIB front end—find by address type: `linux/net/ipv4/fib_frontend.c`.

```
171     unsigned inet_addr_type(u32 addr)
172     {
173              struct rt_key        key;
174              struct fib_result    res;
175              unsigned ret = RTN_BROADCAST;
176
177              if (ZERONET(addr) || BADCLASS(addr))
178                      return RTN_BROADCAST;
179              if (MULTICAST(addr))
180                      return RTN_MULTICAST;
181
182              memset(&key, 0, sizeof(key));
183              key.dst = addr;
184     #ifdef CONFIG_IP_MULTIPLE_TABLES
185              res.r = NULL;
186     #endif
187
188              if (local_table) {
189                      ret = RTN_UNICAST;
190                      if (local_table->tb_lookup(local_table, &key, &res) == 0) {
191                              ret = res.type;
192                              fib_res_put(&res);
193                      }
194              }
195              return ret;
196     }
```

Figure 8.14 FIB front end—check address makes sense i: `linux/net/ipv4/fib_frontend.c`.

```
198   /* Given (packet source, input interface) and optional (dst, oif, tos):
199      - (main) check, that source is valid i.e. not broadcast or our local
200        address.
201      - figure out what "logical" interface this packet arrived
202        and calculate "specific destination" address.
203      - check, that packet arrived from expected physical interface.
204    */
205
206   int fib_validate_source(u32 src, u32 dst, u8 tos, int oif,
207                           struct net_device *dev, u32 *spec_dst, u32 *itag)
208   {
209         struct in_device *in_dev;
210         struct rt_key key;
211         struct fib_result res;
212         int no_addr, rpf;
213         int ret;
214
215         key.dst = src;
216         key.src = dst;
217         key.tos = tos;
218         key.oif = 0;
219         key.iif = oif;
220         key.scope = RT_SCOPE_UNIVERSE;
221
222         no_addr = rpf = 0;
223         read_lock(&inetdev_lock);
224         in_dev = __in_dev_get(dev);
225         if (in_dev) {
226                 no_addr = in_dev->ifa_list == NULL;
227                 rpf = IN_DEV_RPFILTER(in_dev);
228         }
229         read_unlock(&inetdev_lock);
230
231         if (in_dev == NULL)
232                 goto e_inval;
233
234         if (fib_lookup(&key, &res))
235                 goto last_resort;
236         if (res.type != RTN_UNICAST)
237                 goto e_inval_res;
```

Figure 8.15 FIB front end—check address makes sense ii: `linux/net/ipv4/fib_frontend.c`.

```
238         *spec_dst = FIB_RES_PREFSRC(res);
239         if (itag)
240                 fib_combine_itag(itag, &res);
241   #ifdef CONFIG_IP_ROUTE_MULTIPATH
242         if (FIB_RES_DEV(res) == dev || res.fi->fib_nhs > 1)
243   #else
244         if (FIB_RES_DEV(res) == dev)
```

```
245    #endif
246          {
247                  ret = FIB_RES_NH(res).nh_scope >= RT_SCOPE_HOST;
248                  fib_res_put(&res);
249                  return ret;
250          }
251          fib_res_put(&res);
252          if (no_addr)
253                  goto last_resort;
254          if (rpf)
255                  goto e_inval;
256          key.oif = dev->ifindex;
257
258          ret = 0;
259          if (fib_lookup(&key, &res) == 0) {
260                  if (res.type == RTN_UNICAST) {
261                          *spec_dst = FIB_RES_PREFSRC(res);
262                          ret = FIB_RES_NH(res).nh_scope >= RT_SCOPE_HOST;
263                  }
264                  fib_res_put(&res);
265          }
266          return ret;
267
268    last_resort:
269          if (rpf)
270                  goto e_inval;
271          *spec_dst = inet_select_addr(dev, 0, RT_SCOPE_UNIVERSE);
272          *itag = 0;
273          return 0;
274
275    e_inval_res:
276          fib_res_put(&res);
277    e_inval:
278          return -EINVAL;
279    }
```

Figure 8.16 FIB front end—`ioctl` handler: `linux/net/ipv4/fib_frontend.c`.

```
283    /*
284     *     Handle IP routing ioctl calls. These are used to manipulate the routing tables
285     */
286
287    int ip_rt_ioctl(unsigned int cmd, void *arg)
288    {
289          int err;
290          struct kern_rta rta;
291          struct rtentry r;
292          struct {
293                  struct nlmsghdr nlh;
294                  struct rtmsg   rtm;
295          } req;
296
```

```
        switch (cmd) {
        case SIOCADDRT:         /* Add a route */
        case SIOCDELRT:         /* Delete a route */
                if (!capable(CAP_NET_ADMIN))
                        return -EPERM;
                if (copy_from_user(&r, arg, sizeof(struct rtentry)))
                        return -EFAULT;
                rtnl_lock();
                err = fib_convert_rtentry(cmd, &req.nlh, &req.rtm, &rta, &r);
                if (err == 0) {
                        if (cmd == SIOCDELRT) {
                                struct fib_table *tb = fib_get_table(req.rtm.rtm_table);
                                err = -ESRCH;
                                if (tb)
                                        err = tb->tb_delete(tb, &req.rtm, &rta, &req.nlh, NULL);
                        } else {
                                struct fib_table *tb = fib_new_table(req.rtm.rtm_table);
                                err = -ENOBUFS;
                                if (tb)
                                        err = tb->tb_insert(tb, &req.rtm, &rta, &req.nlh, NULL);
                        }
                        if (rta.rta_mx)
                                kfree(rta.rta_mx);
                }
                rtnl_unlock();
                return err;
        }
        return -EINVAL;
}
```

Figure 8.17 FIB front end route—find/add/delete: `linux/net/ipv4/fib_frontend.c`.

```
static int inet_check_attr(struct rtmsg *r, struct rtattr **rta)
{
        int i;

        for (i=1; i<=RTA_MAX; i++) {
                struct rtattr *attr = rta[i-1];
                if (attr) {
                        if (RTA_PAYLOAD(attr) < 4)
                                return -EINVAL;
                        if (i != RTA_MULTIPATH && i != RTA_METRICS)
                                rta[i-1] = (struct rtattr*)RTA_DATA(attr);
                }
        }
        return 0;
}

int inet_rtm_delroute(struct sk_buff *skb, struct nlmsghdr* nlh, void *arg)
{
        struct fib_table * tb;
        struct rtattr **rta = arg;
```

```
        struct rtmsg *r = NLMSG_DATA(nlh);

        if (inet_check_attr(r, rta))
                return -EINVAL;

        tb = fib_get_table(r->rtm_table);
        if (tb)
                return tb->tb_delete(tb, r, (struct kern_rta*)rta, nlh, &NETLINK_CB(skb));
        return -ESRCH;
}

int inet_rtm_newroute(struct sk_buff *skb, struct nlmsghdr* nlh, void *arg)
{
        struct fib_table * tb;
        struct rtattr **rta = arg;
        struct rtmsg *r = NLMSG_DATA(nlh);

        if (inet_check_attr(r, rta))
                return -EINVAL;

        tb = fib_new_table(r->rtm_table);
        if (tb)
                return tb->tb_insert(tb, r, (struct kern_rta*)rta, nlh, &NETLINK_CB(skb));
        return -ENOBUFS;
}
```

Accessing FIB Statistics

Figure 8.18 FIB front end—dump FIB: `linux/net/ipv4/fib_frontend.c`.

```
int inet_dump_fib(struct sk_buff *skb, struct netlink_callback *cb)
{
        int t;
        int s_t;
        struct fib_table *tb;

        if (NLMSG_PAYLOAD(cb->nlh, 0) >= sizeof(struct rtmsg) &&
            ((struct rtmsg*)NLMSG_DATA(cb->nlh))->rtm_flags&RTM_F_CLONED)
                return ip_rt_dump(skb, cb);

        s_t = cb->args[0];
        if (s_t == 0)
                s_t = cb->args[0] = RT_TABLE_MIN;

        for (t=s_t; t<=RT_TABLE_MAX; t++) {
                if (t < s_t) continue;
                if (t > s_t)
                        memset(&cb->args[1], 0, sizeof(cb->args)-sizeof(cb->args[0]));
                if ((tb = fib_get_table(t))==NULL)
                        continue;
                if (tb->tb_dump(tb, skb, cb) < 0)
                        break;
        }
```

```
        cb->args[0] = t;

        return skb->len;
}
```

Figure 8.19 FIB front end—intrakernel route message: `linux/net/ipv4/fib_frontend.c`.

```
/* Prepare and feed intra-kernel routing request.
   Really, it should be netlink message, but :-( netlink
   can be not configured, so that we feed it directly
   to fib engine. It is legal, because all events occur
   only when netlink is already locked.
 */
```

Figure 8.20 FIB front end—intrakernel route message: `linux/net/ipv4/fib_frontend.c`.

```
static void fib_magic(int cmd, int type, u32 dst, int dst_len, struct in_ifaddr *ifa)
{
        struct fib_table * tb;
        struct {
                struct nlmsghdr nlh;
                struct rtmsg    rtm;
        } req;
        struct kern_rta rta;

        memset(&req.rtm, 0, sizeof(req.rtm));
        memset(&rta, 0, sizeof(rta));

        if (type == RTN_UNICAST)
                tb = fib_new_table(RT_TABLE_MAIN);
        else
                tb = fib_new_table(RT_TABLE_LOCAL);

        if (tb == NULL)
                return;

        req.nlh.nlmsg_len = sizeof(req);
        req.nlh.nlmsg_type = cmd;
        req.nlh.nlmsg_flags = NLM_F_REQUEST|NLM_F_CREATE|NLM_F_APPEND;
        req.nlh.nlmsg_pid = 0;
        req.nlh.nlmsg_seq = 0;

        req.rtm.rtm_dst_len = dst_len;
        req.rtm.rtm_table = tb->tb_id;
        req.rtm.rtm_protocol = RTPROT_KERNEL;
        req.rtm.rtm_scope = (type != RTN_LOCAL ? RT_SCOPE_LINK : RT_SCOPE_HOST);
        req.rtm.rtm_type = type;
```

Figure 8.21 FIB front end–intrakernel route message: `linux/net/ipv4/fib_frontend.c`.

```
        rta.rta_dst = &dst;
        rta.rta_prefsrc = &ifa->ifa_local;
        rta.rta_oif = &ifa->ifa_dev->dev->ifindex;

        if (cmd == RTM_NEWROUTE)
              tb->tb_insert(tb, &req.rtm, &rta, &req.nlh, NULL);
        else
              tb->tb_delete(tb, &req.rtm, &rta, &req.nlh, NULL);
}
```

Figure 8.22 FIB front end–add entry by interface address: `linux/net/ipv4/fib_frontend.c`.

```
static void fib_add_ifaddr(struct in_ifaddr *ifa)
{
        struct in_device *in_dev = ifa->ifa_dev;
        struct net_device *dev = in_dev->dev;
        struct in_ifaddr *prim = ifa;
        u32 mask = ifa->ifa_mask;
        u32 addr = ifa->ifa_local;
        u32 prefix = ifa->ifa_address&mask;

        if (ifa->ifa_flags&IFA_F_SECONDARY) {
              prim = inet_ifa_byprefix(in_dev, prefix, mask);
              if (prim == NULL) {
                    printk(KERN_DEBUG "fib_add_ifaddr: bug: prim == NULL\n");
                    return;
              }
        }

        fib_magic(RTM_NEWROUTE, RTN_LOCAL, addr, 32, prim);

        if (!(dev->flags&IFF_UP))
              return;

        /* Add broadcast address, if it is explicitly assigned. */
        if (ifa->ifa_broadcast && ifa->ifa_broadcast != 0xFFFFFFFF)
              fib_magic(RTM_NEWROUTE, RTN_BROADCAST, ifa->ifa_broadcast, 32, prim);

        if (!ZERONET(prefix) && !(ifa->ifa_flags&IFA_F_SECONDARY) &&
            (prefix != addr || ifa->ifa_prefixlen < 32)) {
              fib_magic(RTM_NEWROUTE, dev->flags&IFF_LOOPBACK ? RTN_LOCAL :
                           RTN_UNICAST, prefix, ifa->ifa_prefixlen, prim);

              /* Add network specific broadcasts, when it takes a sense */
              if (ifa->ifa_prefixlen < 31) {
                    fib_magic(RTM_NEWROUTE, RTN_BROADCAST, prefix, 32, prim);
                    fib_magic(RTM_NEWROUTE, RTN_BROADCAST, prefix|~mask, 32, prim);
              }
        }
}
```

Figure 8.23 FIB front end—delete entry by interface address i: `linux/net/ipv4/fib_frontend.c`.

```
static void fib_del_ifaddr(struct in_ifaddr *ifa)
{
        struct in_device *in_dev = ifa->ifa_dev;
        struct net_device *dev = in_dev->dev;
        struct in_ifaddr *ifa1;
        struct in_ifaddr *prim = ifa;
        u32 brd = ifa->ifa_address|~ifa->ifa_mask;
        u32 any = ifa->ifa_address&ifa->ifa_mask;
#define LOCAL_OK        1
#define BRD_OK          2
#define BRD0_OK         4
#define BRD1_OK         8
        unsigned ok = 0;

        if (!(ifa->ifa_flags&IFA_F_SECONDARY))
                fib_magic(RTM_DELROUTE, dev->flags&IFF_LOOPBACK ? RTN_LOCAL :
                          RTN_UNICAST, any, ifa->ifa_prefixlen, prim);
        else {
                prim = inet_ifa_byprefix(in_dev, any, ifa->ifa_mask);
                if (prim == NULL) {
                        printk(KERN_DEBUG "fib_del_ifaddr: bug: prim == NULL\n");
                        return;
                }
        }

        /* Deletion is more complicated than add.
           We should take care of not to delete too much :-)

           Scan address list to be sure that addresses are really gone.
         */

        for (ifa1 = in_dev->ifa_list; ifa1; ifa1 = ifa1->ifa_next) {
                if (ifa->ifa_local == ifa1->ifa_local)
                        ok |= LOCAL_OK;
                if (ifa->ifa_broadcast == ifa1->ifa_broadcast)
                        ok |= BRD_OK;
                if (brd == ifa1->ifa_broadcast)
                        ok |= BRD1_OK;
                if (any == ifa1->ifa_broadcast)
                        ok |= BRD0_OK;
        }
```

Figure 8.24 FIB front end—delete entry by interface address ii: `linux/net/ipv4/fib_frontend.c`.

```
        if (!(ok&BRD_OK))
                fib_magic(RTM_DELROUTE, RTN_BROADCAST, ifa->ifa_broadcast, 32, prim);
        if (!(ok&BRD1_OK))
                fib_magic(RTM_DELROUTE, RTN_BROADCAST, brd, 32, prim);
        if (!(ok&BRD0_OK))
                fib_magic(RTM_DELROUTE, RTN_BROADCAST, any, 32, prim);
        if (!(ok&LOCAL_OK)) {
```

```
552                     fib_magic(RTM_DELROUTE, RTN_LOCAL, ifa->ifa_local, 32, prim);
553
554                     /* Check, that this local address finally disappeared. */
555                     if (inet_addr_type(ifa->ifa_local) != RTN_LOCAL) {
556                             /* And the last, but not the least thing.
557                                We must flush stray FIB entries.
558
559                                First of all, we scan fib_info list searching
560                                for stray nexthop entries, then ignite fib_flush.
561                             */
562                             if (fib_sync_down(ifa->ifa_local, NULL, 0))
563                                     fib_flush();
564                     }
565             }
566     #undef LOCAL_OK
567     #undef BRD_OK
568     #undef BRD0_OK
569     #undef BRD1_OK
570     }
```

FIB Event Handler

Figure 8.25 FIB front end event handler: `linux/net/ipv4/fib_frontend.c`.

```
572     static void fib_disable_ip(struct net_device *dev, int force)
573     {
574             if (fib_sync_down(0, dev, force))
575                     fib_flush();
576             rt_cache_flush(0);
577             arp_ifdown(dev);
578     }
```

Figure 8.26 FIB front end event handler: `linux/net/ipv4/fib_frontend.c`.

```
580     static int fib_inetaddr_event(struct notifier_block *this, unsigned long event, void *ptr)
581     {
582             struct in_ifaddr *ifa = (struct in_ifaddr*)ptr;
583
584             switch (event) {
585             case NETDEV_UP:
586                     fib_add_ifaddr(ifa);
587                     rt_cache_flush(-1);
588                     break;
589             case NETDEV_DOWN:
590                     if (ifa->ifa_dev && ifa->ifa_dev->ifa_list == NULL) {
591                             /* Last address was deleted from this interface.
592                                Disable IP.
```

```
593                                  */
594                          fib_disable_ip(ifa->ifa_dev->dev, 1);
595                  } else {
596                          fib_del_ifaddr(ifa);
597                          rt_cache_flush(-1);
598                  }
599                  break;
600          }
601          return NOTIFY_DONE;
602  }
```

Figure 8.27 FIB front end event handler: `linux/net/ipv4/fib_frontend.c`.

```
604  static int fib_netdev_event(struct notifier_block *this, unsigned long event, void *ptr)
605  {
606          struct net_device *dev = ptr;
607          struct in_device *in_dev = __in_dev_get(dev);
608
609          if (!in_dev)
610                  return NOTIFY_DONE;
611
612          switch (event) {
613          case NETDEV_UP:
614                  for_ifa(in_dev) {
615                          fib_add_ifaddr(ifa);
616                  } endfor_ifa(in_dev);
617  #ifdef CONFIG_IP_ROUTE_MULTIPATH
618                  fib_sync_up(dev);
619  #endif
620                  rt_cache_flush(-1);
621                  break;
622          case NETDEV_DOWN:
623                  fib_disable_ip(dev, 0);
624                  break;
625          case NETDEV_UNREGISTER:
626                  fib_disable_ip(dev, 1);
627                  break;
628          case NETDEV_CHANGEMTU:
629          case NETDEV_CHANGE:
630                  rt_cache_flush(0);
631                  break;
632          }
633          return NOTIFY_DONE;
634  }
```

Figure 8.28 FIB front end initialization: `linux/net/ipv4/fib_frontend.c.`

```

void __init ip_fib_init(void)
{
#ifdef CONFIG_PROC_FS
       proc_net_create("route",0,fib_get_procinfo);
#endif        /* CONFIG_PROC_FS */

#ifndef CONFIG_IP_MULTIPLE_TABLES
       local_table = fib_hash_init(RT_TABLE_LOCAL);
       main_table = fib_hash_init(RT_TABLE_MAIN);
#else
       fib_rules_init();
#endif

       register_netdevice_notifier(&fib_netdev_notifier);
       register_inetaddr_notifier(&fib_inetaddr_notifier);
}
```

Semantics—What It All Means

Figure 8.29 FIB semantics–looping macros over FIB entries : `linux/net/ipv4/fib_semantics.c.`

```
static struct fib_info  *fib_info_list;
static rwlock_t fib_info_lock = RW_LOCK_UNLOCKED;
int fib_info_cnt;

#define for_fib_info() { struct fib_info *fi; \
       for (fi = fib_info_list; fi; fi = fi->fib_next)

#define endfor_fib_info() }

#ifdef CONFIG_IP_ROUTE_MULTIPATH

#define for_nexthops(fi) { int nhsel; const struct fib_nh * nh; \
for (nhsel=0, nh = (fi)->fib_nh; nhsel < (fi)->fib_nhs; nh++, nhsel++)

#define change_nexthops(fi) { int nhsel; struct fib_nh * nh; \
for (nhsel=0, nh = (struct fib_nh*)((fi)->fib_nh); nhsel < (fi)->fib_nhs; nh++, nhsel++)

#else /* CONFIG_IP_ROUTE_MULTIPATH */

/* Hope, that gcc will optimize it to get rid of dummy loop */

#define for_nexthops(fi) { int nhsel=0; const struct fib_nh * nh = (fi)->fib_nh; \
for (nhsel=0; nhsel < 1; nhsel++)

#define change_nexthops(fi) { int nhsel=0; struct fib_nh * nh = (struct fib_nh*)
     ((fi)->fib_nh); \
for (nhsel=0; nhsel < 1; nhsel++)
```

```
74
75   #endif /* CONFIG_IP_ROUTE_MULTIPATH */
76
77   #define endfor_nexthops(fi) }
```

Figure 8.30 FIB semantics—initial route attribute properties: `linux/net/ipv4/fib_`
`semantics.c`.

```
80   static struct
81   {
82          int    error;
83          u8     scope;
84   } fib_props[RTA_MAX+1] = {
85          { 0, RT_SCOPE_NOWHERE},        /* RTN_UNSPEC */
86          { 0, RT_SCOPE_UNIVERSE},       /* RTN_UNICAST */
87          { 0, RT_SCOPE_HOST},           /* RTN_LOCAL */
88          { 0, RT_SCOPE_LINK},           /* RTN_BROADCAST */
89          { 0, RT_SCOPE_LINK},           /* RTN_ANYCAST */
90          { 0, RT_SCOPE_UNIVERSE},       /* RTN_MULTICAST */
91          { -EINVAL, RT_SCOPE_UNIVERSE}, /* RTN_BLACKHOLE */
92          { -EHOSTUNREACH, RT_SCOPE_UNIVERSE},/* RTN_UNREACHABLE */
93          { -EACCES, RT_SCOPE_UNIVERSE}, /* RTN_PROHIBIT */
94          { -EAGAIN, RT_SCOPE_UNIVERSE}, /* RTN_THROW */
95   #ifdef CONFIG_IP_ROUTE_NAT
96          { 0, RT_SCOPE_HOST},           /* RTN_NAT */
97   #else
98          { -EINVAL, RT_SCOPE_NOWHERE}, /* RTN_NAT */
99   #endif
100         { -EINVAL, RT_SCOPE_NOWHERE} /* RTN_XRESOLVE */
101  };
```

Figure 8.31 FIB semantics—find and release next hop info: `linux/net/ipv4/fib_`
`semantics.c`.

```
104  /* Release a nexthop info record */
105
106  void free_fib_info(struct fib_info *fi)
107  {
108         if (fi->fib_dead == 0) {
109                printk("Freeing alive fib_info %p\n", fi);
110                return;
111         }
112         change_nexthops(fi) {
113                if (nh->nh_dev)
114                       dev_put(nh->nh_dev);
115                nh->nh_dev = NULL;
116         } endfor_nexthops(fi);
117         fib_info_cnt--;
118         kfree(fi);
119  }
120
121  void fib_release_info(struct fib_info *fi)
```

```
{
        write_lock(&fib_info_lock);
        if (fi && --fi->fib_treeref == 0) {
                if (fi->fib_next)
                        fi->fib_next->fib_prev = fi->fib_prev;
                if (fi->fib_prev)
                        fi->fib_prev->fib_next = fi->fib_next;
                if (fi == fib_info_list)
                        fib_info_list = fi->fib_next;
                fi->fib_dead = 1;
                fib_info_put(fi);
        }
        write_unlock(&fib_info_lock);
}
```

Figure 8.32 FIB semantics—lookup: `linux/net/ipv4/fib_semantics.c`.

```
extern __inline__ int nh_comp(const struct fib_info *fi, const struct fib_info *ofi)
{
        const struct fib_nh *onh = ofi->fib_nh;

        for_nexthops(fi) {
                if (nh->nh_oif != onh->nh_oif ||
                    nh->nh_gw != onh->nh_gw ||
                    nh->nh_scope != onh->nh_scope ||
#ifdef CONFIG_IP_ROUTE_MULTIPATH
                    nh->nh_weight != onh->nh_weight ||
#endif
#ifdef CONFIG_NET_CLS_ROUTE
                    nh->nh_tclassid != onh->nh_tclassid ||
#endif
                    ((nh->nh_flags^onh->nh_flags)&~RTNH_F_DEAD))
                        return -1;
                onh++;
        } endfor_nexthops(fi);
        return 0;
}

extern __inline__ struct fib_info * fib_find_info(const struct fib_info *nfi)
{
        for_fib_info() {
                if (fi->fib_nhs != nfi->fib_nhs)
                        continue;
                if (nfi->fib_protocol == fi->fib_protocol &&
                    nfi->fib_prefsrc == fi->fib_prefsrc &&
                    nfi->fib_priority == fi->fib_priority &&
                    memcmp(nfi->fib_metrics, fi->fib_metrics, sizeof(fi->fib_metrics)) == 0 &&
                    ((nfi->fib_flags^fi->fib_flags)&~RTNH_F_DEAD) == 0 &&
                    (nfi->fib_nhs == 0 || nh_comp(fi, nfi) == 0))
                        return fi;
        } endfor_fib_info();
        return NULL;
}
```

Figure 8.33 FIB semantics—set defaults: `linux/net/ipv4/fib_semantics.c`.

```
/* Check, that the gateway is already configured.
  Used only by redirect accept routine.
 */

int ip_fib_check_default(u32 gw, struct net_device *dev)
{
        read_lock(&fib_info_lock);
        for_fib_info() {
                if (fi->fib_flags & RTNH_F_DEAD)
                        continue;
                for_nexthops(fi) {
                        if (nh->nh_dev == dev && nh->nh_gw == gw &&
                            !(nh->nh_flags&RTNH_F_DEAD)) {
                                read_unlock(&fib_info_lock);
                                return 0;
                        }
                } endfor_nexthops(fi);
        } endfor_fib_info();
        read_unlock(&fib_info_lock);
        return -1;
}

#ifdef CONFIG_IP_ROUTE_MULTIPATH

static u32 fib_get_attr32(struct rtattr *attr, int attrlen, int type)
{
        while (RTA_OK(attr,attrlen)) {
                if (attr->rta_type == type)
                        return *(u32*)RTA_DATA(attr);
                attr = RTA_NEXT(attr, attrlen);
```

Figure 8.34 FIB semantics—add up next hops and get nhs: `linux/net/ipv4/fib_semantics.c`.

```
        return 0;
}

static int
fib_count_nexthops(struct rtattr *rta)
{
        int nhs = 0;
        struct rtnexthop *nhp = RTA_DATA(rta);
        int nhlen = RTA_PAYLOAD(rta);

        while (nhlen >= (int)sizeof(struct rtnexthop)) {
                if ((nhlen -= nhp->rtnh_len) < 0)
                        return 0;
                nhs++;
                nhp = RTNH_NEXT(nhp);
        };
        return nhs;
```

```
}

static int
fib_get_nhs(struct fib_info *fi, const struct rtattr *rta, const struct rtmsg *r)
{
        struct rtnexthop *nhp = RTA_DATA(rta);
        int nhlen = RTA_PAYLOAD(rta);

        change_nexthops(fi) {
                int attrlen = nhlen - sizeof(struct rtnexthop);
                if (attrlen < 0 || (nhlen -= nhp->rtnh_len) < 0)
                        return -EINVAL;
                nh->nh_flags = (r->rtm_flags&~0xFF) | nhp->rtnh_flags;
                nh->nh_oif = nhp->rtnh_ifindex;
                nh->nh_weight = nhp->rtnh_hops + 1;
                if (attrlen) {
                        nh->nh_gw = fib_get_attr32(RTNH_DATA(nhp), attrlen, RTA_GATEWAY);
#ifdef CONFIG_NET_CLS_ROUTE
                        nh->nh_tclassid = fib_get_attr32(RTNH_DATA(nhp), attrlen, RTA_FLOW);
#endif
                }
                nhp = RTNH_NEXT(nhp);
        } endfor_nexthops(fi);
        return 0;
}
```

What Is a Next Hop?

Figure 8.35 FIB semantics—next hops match: `linux/net/ipv4/fib_semantics.c`.

```
int fib_nh_match(struct rtmsg *r, struct nlmsghdr *nlh, struct kern_rta *rta,
                 struct fib_info *fi)
{
#ifdef CONFIG_IP_ROUTE_MULTIPATH
        struct rtnexthop *nhp;
        int nhlen;
#endif

        if (rta->rta_priority &&
            *rta->rta_priority != fi->fib_priority)
                return 1;

        if (rta->rta_oif || rta->rta_gw) {
                if ((!rta->rta_oif || *rta->rta_oif == fi->fib_nh->nh_oif) &&
                    (!rta->rta_gw || memcmp(rta->rta_gw, &fi->fib_nh->nh_gw, 4) == 0))
                        return 0;
                return 1;
        }
```

Figure 8.36 FIB semantics—next hops match: `linux/net/ipv4/fib_semantics.c`.

```
#ifdef CONFIG_IP_ROUTE_MULTIPATH
        if (rta->rta_mp == NULL)
                return 0;
        nhp = RTA_DATA(rta->rta_mp);
        nhlen = RTA_PAYLOAD(rta->rta_mp);

        for_nexthops(fi) {
                int attrlen = nhlen - sizeof(struct rtnexthop);
                u32 gw;

                if (attrlen < 0 || (nhlen -= nhp->rtnh_len) < 0)
                        return -EINVAL;
                if (nhp->rtnh_ifindex && nhp->rtnh_ifindex != nh->nh_oif)
                        return 1;
                if (attrlen) {
                        gw = fib_get_attr32(RTNH_DATA(nhp), attrlen, RTA_GATEWAY);
                        if (gw && gw != nh->nh_gw)
                                return 1;
#ifdef CONFIG_NET_CLS_ROUTE
                        gw = fib_get_attr32(RTNH_DATA(nhp), attrlen, RTA_FLOW);
                        if (gw && gw != nh->nh_tclassid)
                                return 1;
#endif
                }
                nhp = RTNH_NEXT(nhp);
        } endfor_nexthops(fi);
#endif
        return 0;
}
```

The FIB Big Picture

The comment below goes a long way to explaining how this works:

Figure 8.37 FIB semantics—the big picture: `linux/net/ipv4/fib_semantics.c`.

```
/*
   Picture
   -------

   Semantics of nexthop is very messy by historical reasons.
   We have to take into account, that:
   a) gateway can be actually local interface address,
      so that gatewayed route is direct.
   b) gateway must be on-link address, possibly
      described not by an ifaddr, but also by a direct route.
   c) If both gateway and interface are specified, they should not
      contradict.
   d) If we use tunnel routes, gateway could be not on-link.
```

```

   Attempt to reconcile all of these (alas, self-contradictory) conditions
   results in pretty ugly and hairy code with obscure logic.

   I choosed to generalized it instead, so that the size
   of code does not increase practically, but it becomes
   much more general.
   Every prefix is assigned a "scope" value: "host" is local address,
   "link" is direct route,
   [ ... "site" ... "interior" ... ]
   and "universe" is true gateway route with global meaning.

   Every prefix refers to a set of "nexthop"s (gw, oif),
   where gw must have narrower scope. This recursion stops
   when gw has LOCAL scope or if "nexthop" is declared ONLINK,
   which means that gw is forced to be on link.

   Code is still hairy, but now it is apparently logically
   consistent and very flexible. F.e. as by-product it allows
   to co-exists in peace independent exterior and interior
   routing processes.

   Normally it looks as following.

   {universe prefix} -> (gw, oif) [scope link]
                         |
                         |-> {link prefix} -> (gw, oif) [scope local]
                                               |
                                               |-> {local prefix} (terminal node)
 */
```

Checking for Next Hop

Figure 8.38 FIB semantics—check next hop: `linux/net/ipv4/fib_semantics.c`.

```
static int fib_check_nh(const struct rtmsg *r, struct fib_info *fi, struct fib_nh *nh)
{
	int err;

	if (nh->nh_gw) {
		struct rt_key key;
		struct fib_result res;

#ifdef CONFIG_IP_ROUTE_PERVASIVE
		if (nh->nh_flags&RTNH_F_PERVASIVE)
			return 0;
#endif
		if (nh->nh_flags&RTNH_F_ONLINK) {
			struct net_device *dev;

			if (r->rtm_scope >= RT_SCOPE_LINK)
				return -EINVAL;
```

```
361                          if (inet_addr_type(nh->nh_gw) != RTN_UNICAST)
362                                  return -EINVAL;
363                          if ((dev = __dev_get_by_index(nh->nh_oif)) == NULL)
364                                  return -ENODEV;
365                          if (!(dev->flags&IFF_UP))
366                                  return -ENETDOWN;
367                      nh->nh_dev = dev;
368                      atomic_inc(&dev->refcnt);
369                      nh->nh_scope = RT_SCOPE_LINK;
370                      return 0;
371                  }
372              memset(&key, 0, sizeof(key));
373              key.dst = nh->nh_gw;
374              key.oif = nh->nh_oif;
375              key.scope = r->rtm_scope + 1;
```

Figure 8.39 FIB semantics—check next hop: linux/net/ipv4/fib_semantics.c.

```
377              /* It is not necessary, but requires a bit of thinking */
378              if (key.scope < RT_SCOPE_LINK)
379                      key.scope = RT_SCOPE_LINK;
380
381              if ((err = fib_lookup(&key, &res)) != 0)
382                      return err;
383              nh->nh_scope = res.scope;
384              nh->nh_oif = FIB_RES_OIF(res);
385              nh->nh_dev = FIB_RES_DEV(res);
386              if (nh->nh_dev)
387                      atomic_inc(&nh->nh_dev->refcnt);
388              fib_res_put(&res);
389          } else {
390              struct in_device *in_dev;
391
392              if (nh->nh_flags&(RTNH_F_PERVASIVE|RTNH_F_ONLINK))
393                      return -EINVAL;
394
395              in_dev = inetdev_by_index(nh->nh_oif);
396              if (in_dev == NULL)
397                      return -ENODEV;
398              if (!(in_dev->dev->flags&IFF_UP)) {
399                      in_dev_put(in_dev);
400                      return -ENETDOWN;
401              }
402              nh->nh_dev = in_dev->dev;
403              atomic_inc(&nh->nh_dev->refcnt);
404              nh->nh_scope = RT_SCOPE_HOST;
405              in_dev_put(in_dev);
406          }
407      return 0;
408  }
```

Creating a New FIB Entry

Figure 8.40 FIB semantics—create FIB entry i: `linux/net/ipv4/fib_semantics.c`.

```
struct fib_info *
fib_create_info(const struct rtmsg *r, struct kern_rta *rta,
                const struct nlmsghdr *nlh, int *errp)
{
        int err;
        struct fib_info *fi = NULL;
        struct fib_info *ofi;
#ifdef CONFIG_IP_ROUTE_MULTIPATH
        int nhs = 1;
#else
        const int nhs = 1;
#endif

        /* Fast check to catch the most weird cases */
        if (fib_props[r->rtm_type].scope > r->rtm_scope)
                goto err_inval;

#ifdef CONFIG_IP_ROUTE_MULTIPATH
        if (rta->rta_mp) {
                nhs = fib_count_nexthops(rta->rta_mp);
                if (nhs == 0)
                        goto err_inval;
        }
#endif
```

Figure 8.41 FIB semantics—create FIB entry i: `linux/net/ipv4/fib_semantics.c`.

```
        fi = kmalloc(sizeof(*fi)+nhs*sizeof(struct fib_nh), GFP_KERNEL);
        err = -ENOBUFS;
        if (fi == NULL)
                goto failure;
        fib_info_cnt++;
        memset(fi, 0, sizeof(*fi)+nhs*sizeof(struct fib_nh));

        fi->fib_protocol = r->rtm_protocol;
        fi->fib_nhs = nhs;
        fi->fib_flags = r->rtm_flags;
        if (rta->rta_priority)
                fi->fib_priority = *rta->rta_priority;
        if (rta->rta_mx) {
                int attrlen = RTA_PAYLOAD(rta->rta_mx);
                struct rtattr *attr = RTA_DATA(rta->rta_mx);

                while (RTA_OK(attr, attrlen)) {
                        unsigned flavor = attr->rta_type;
                        if (flavor) {
                                if (flavor > RTAX_MAX)
                                        goto err_inval;
                                fi->fib_metrics[flavor-1] = *(unsigned*)RTA_DATA(attr);
                        }
```

```
458                     attr = RTA_NEXT(attr, attrlen);
459                 }
460         }
461         if (rta->rta_prefsrc)
462                 memcpy(&fi->fib_prefsrc, rta->rta_prefsrc, 4);
```

Figure 8.42 FIB semantics—create FIB entry ii: `linux/net/ipv4/fib_semantics.c`.

```
464         if (rta->rta_mp) {
465 #ifdef CONFIG_IP_ROUTE_MULTIPATH
466                 if ((err = fib_get_nhs(fi, rta->rta_mp, r)) != 0)
467                         goto failure;
468                 if (rta->rta_oif && fi->fib_nh->nh_oif != *rta->rta_oif)
469                         goto err_inval;
470                 if (rta->rta_gw && memcmp(&fi->fib_nh->nh_gw, rta->rta_gw, 4))
471                         goto err_inval;
472 #ifdef CONFIG_NET_CLS_ROUTE
473                 if (rta->rta_flow && memcmp(&fi->fib_nh->nh_tclassid, rta->rta_flow, 4))
474                         goto err_inval;
475 #endif
476 #else
477                 goto err_inval;
478 #endif
479         } else {
480                 struct fib_nh *nh = fi->fib_nh;
481                 if (rta->rta_oif)
482                         nh->nh_oif = *rta->rta_oif;
483                 if (rta->rta_gw)
484                         memcpy(&nh->nh_gw, rta->rta_gw, 4);
485 #ifdef CONFIG_NET_CLS_ROUTE
486                 if (rta->rta_flow)
487                         memcpy(&nh->nh_tclassid, rta->rta_flow, 4);
488 #endif
489                 nh->nh_flags = r->rtm_flags;
490 #ifdef CONFIG_IP_ROUTE_MULTIPATH
491                 nh->nh_weight = 1;
492 #endif
493         }
494
495 #ifdef CONFIG_IP_ROUTE_NAT
496         if (r->rtm_type == RTN_NAT) {
497                 if (rta->rta_gw == NULL || nhs != 1 || rta->rta_oif)
498                         goto err_inval;
499                 memcpy(&fi->fib_nh->nh_gw, rta->rta_gw, 4);
500                 goto link_it;
501         }
502 #endif
503
504         if (fib_props[r->rtm_type].error) {
505                 if (rta->rta_gw || rta->rta_oif || rta->rta_mp)
506                         goto err_inval;
507                 goto link_it;
508         }
```

Figure 8.43 FIB semantics—create FIB entry iii: `linux/net/ipv4/fib_semantics.c`.

```
510          if (r->rtm_scope > RT_SCOPE_HOST)
511                  goto err_inval;
512
513          if (r->rtm_scope == RT_SCOPE_HOST) {
514                  struct fib_nh *nh = fi->fib_nh;
515
516                  /* Local address is added. */
517                  if (nhs != 1 || nh->nh_gw)
518                          goto err_inval;
519                  nh->nh_scope = RT_SCOPE_NOWHERE;
520                  nh->nh_dev = dev_get_by_index(fi->fib_nh->nh_oif);
521                  err = -ENODEV;
522                  if (nh->nh_dev == NULL)
523                          goto failure;
524          } else {
525                  change_nexthops(fi) {
526                          if ((err = fib_check_nh(r, fi, nh)) != 0)
527                                  goto failure;
528                  } endfor_nexthops(fi)
529          }
530
531          if (fi->fib_prefsrc) {
532                  if (r->rtm_type != RTN_LOCAL || rta->rta_dst == NULL ||
533                      memcmp(&fi->fib_prefsrc, rta->rta_dst, 4))
534                          if (inet_addr_type(fi->fib_prefsrc) != RTN_LOCAL)
535                                  goto err_inval;
536          }
```

Figure 8.44 FIB semantics—create FIB entry iv: `linux/net/ipv4/fib_semantics.c`.

```
538   link_it:
539          if ((ofi = fib_find_info(fi)) != NULL) {
540                  fi->fib_dead = 1;
541                  free_fib_info(fi);
542                  ofi->fib_treeref++;
543                  return ofi;
544          }
545
546          fi->fib_treeref++;
547          atomic_inc(&fi->fib_clntref);
548          write_lock(&fib_info_lock);
549          fi->fib_next = fib_info_list;
550          fi->fib_prev = NULL;
551          if (fib_info_list)
552                  fib_info_list->fib_prev = fi;
553          fib_info_list = fi;
554          write_unlock(&fib_info_lock);
555          return fi;
556
557   err_inval:
```

```
558            err = -EINVAL;
559
560  failure:
561            *errp = err;
562            if (fi) {
563                    fi->fib_dead = 1;
564                    free_fib_info(fi);
565            }
566            return NULL;
567  }
```

Looking Up a FIB Entry

Figure 8.45 FIB semantics—meaningful match?: `linux/net/ipv4/fib_semantics.c`.

```
569  int
570  fib_semantic_match(int type, struct fib_info *fi, const struct rt_key *key, struct fib_result *
         res)
571  {
572            int err = fib_props[type].error;
573
574            if (err == 0) {
575                    if (fi->fib_flags&RTNH_F_DEAD)
576                            return 1;
577
578                    res->fi = fi;
579
580                    switch (type) {
581  #ifdef CONFIG_IP_ROUTE_NAT
582                    case RTN_NAT:
583                            FIB_RES_RESET(*res);
584                            atomic_inc(&fi->fib_clntref);
585                            return 0;
586  #endif
587                    case RTN_UNICAST:
588                    case RTN_LOCAL:
589                    case RTN_BROADCAST:
590                    case RTN_ANYCAST:
591                    case RTN_MULTICAST:
592                            for_nexthops(fi) {
593                                    if (nh->nh_flags&RTNH_F_DEAD)
594                                            continue;
595                                    if (!key->oif || key->oif == nh->nh_oif)
596                                            break;
597                            }
```

Figure 8.46 FIB semantics—meaningful match?: `linux/net/ipv4/fib_semantics.c`.

```
598    #ifdef CONFIG_IP_ROUTE_MULTIPATH
599                    if (nhsel < fi->fib_nhs) {
600                            res->nh_sel = nhsel;
601                            atomic_inc(&fi->fib_clntref);
602                            return 0;
603                    }
604    #else
605                    if (nhsel < 1) {
606                            atomic_inc(&fi->fib_clntref);
607                            return 0;
608                    }
609    #endif
610                    endfor_nexthops(fi);
611                    res->fi = NULL;
612                    return 1;
613            default:
614                    res->fi = NULL;
615                    printk(KERN_DEBUG "impossible 102\n");
616                    return -EINVAL;
617            }
618        }
619        return err;
620    }
```

Accessing More FIB Statistics

Figure 8.47 FIB semantics—dump utilities i: `linux/net/ipv4/fib_semantics.c`.

```
622    /* Find appropriate source address to this destination */
623
624    u32 __fib_res_prefsrc(struct fib_result *res)
625    {
626            return inet_select_addr(FIB_RES_DEV(*res), FIB_RES_GW(*res), res->scope);
627    }
```

Figure 8.48 FIB semantics—dump utilities ii: `linux/net/ipv4/fib_semantics.c`.

```
631    int
632    fib_dump_info(struct sk_buff *skb, u32 pid, u32 seq, int event,
633                u8 tb_id, u8 type, u8 scope, void *dst, int dst_len, u8 tos,
634                struct fib_info *fi)
635    {
636        struct rtmsg *rtm;
637        struct nlmsghdr *nlh;
638        unsigned char  *b = skb->tail;
639
```

```
        nlh = NLMSG_PUT(skb, pid, seq, event, sizeof(*rtm));
        rtm = NLMSG_DATA(nlh);
        rtm->rtm_family = AF_INET;
        rtm->rtm_dst_len = dst_len;
        rtm->rtm_src_len = 0;
        rtm->rtm_tos = tos;
        rtm->rtm_table = tb_id;
        rtm->rtm_type = type;
        rtm->rtm_flags = fi->fib_flags;
        rtm->rtm_scope = scope;
        if (rtm->rtm_dst_len)
                RTA_PUT(skb, RTA_DST, 4, dst);
        rtm->rtm_protocol = fi->fib_protocol;
        if (fi->fib_priority)
                RTA_PUT(skb, RTA_PRIORITY, 4, &fi->fib_priority);
#ifdef CONFIG_NET_CLS_ROUTE
        if (fi->fib_nh[0].nh_tclassid)
                RTA_PUT(skb, RTA_FLOW, 4, &fi->fib_nh[0].nh_tclassid);
#endif
        if (rtnetlink_put_metrics(skb, fi->fib_metrics) < 0)
                goto rtattr_failure;
        if (fi->fib_prefsrc)
                RTA_PUT(skb, RTA_PREFSRC, 4, &fi->fib_prefsrc);
        if (fi->fib_nhs == 1) {
                if (fi->fib_nh->nh_gw)
                        RTA_PUT(skb, RTA_GATEWAY, 4, &fi->fib_nh->nh_gw);
                if (fi->fib_nh->nh_oif)
                        RTA_PUT(skb, RTA_OIF, sizeof(int), &fi->fib_nh->nh_oif);
        }
```

Figure 8.49 FIB semantics—dump utilities iii: `linux/net/ipv4/fib_semantics.c`.

```
#ifdef CONFIG_IP_ROUTE_MULTIPATH
        if (fi->fib_nhs > 1) {
                struct rtnexthop *nhp;
                struct rtattr *mp_head;
                if (skb_tailroom(skb) <= RTA_SPACE(0))
                        goto rtattr_failure;
                mp_head = (struct rtattr*)skb_put(skb, RTA_SPACE(0));

                for_nexthops(fi) {
                        if (skb_tailroom(skb) < RTA_ALIGN(RTA_ALIGN(sizeof(*nhp)) + 4))
                                goto rtattr_failure;
                        nhp = (struct rtnexthop*)skb_put(skb, RTA_ALIGN(sizeof(*nhp)));
                        nhp->rtnh_flags = nh->nh_flags & 0xFF;
                        nhp->rtnh_hops = nh->nh_weight-1;
                        nhp->rtnh_ifindex = nh->nh_oif;
                        if (nh->nh_gw)
                                RTA_PUT(skb, RTA_GATEWAY, 4, &nh->nh_gw);
                        nhp->rtnh_len = skb->tail - (unsigned char*)nhp;
                } endfor_nexthops(fi);
```

```
                mp_head->rta_type = RTA_MULTIPATH;
                mp_head->rta_len = skb->tail - (u8*)mp_head;
        }
#endif
        nlh->nlmsg_len = skb->tail - b;
        return skb->len;

nlmsg_failure:
rtattr_failure:
        skb_trim(skb, b - skb->data);
        return -1;
}
```

Taking an RTNetlink Request

Figure 8.50 FIB semantics—convert RT request: `linux/net/ipv4/fib_semantics.c`.

```
int
fib_convert_rtentry(int cmd, struct nlmsghdr *nl, struct rtmsg *rtm,
                      struct kern_rta *rta, struct rtentry *r)
{
        int    plen;
        u32    *ptr;

        memset(rtm, 0, sizeof(*rtm));
        memset(rta, 0, sizeof(*rta));

        if (r->rt_dst.sa_family != AF_INET)
                return -EAFNOSUPPORT;

        /* Check mask for validity:
           a) it must be contiguous.
           b) destination must have all host bits clear.
           c) if application forgot to set correct family (AF_INET),
              reject request unless it is absolutely clear i.e.
              both family and mask are zero.
         */
        plen = 32;
        ptr = &((struct sockaddr_in*)&r->rt_dst)->sin_addr.s_addr;
        if (!(r->rt_flags&RTF_HOST)) {
                u32 mask = ((struct sockaddr_in*)&r->rt_genmask)->sin_addr.s_addr;
                if (r->rt_genmask.sa_family != AF_INET) {
                        if (mask || r->rt_genmask.sa_family)
                                return -EAFNOSUPPORT;
                }
                if (bad_mask(mask, *ptr))
                        return -EINVAL;
                plen = inet_mask_len(mask);
        }

        nl->nlmsg_flags = NLM_F_REQUEST;
```

```
739        nl->nlmsg_pid = 0;
740        nl->nlmsg_seq = 0;
741        nl->nlmsg_len = NLMSG_LENGTH(sizeof(*rtm));
742        if (cmd == SIOCDELRT) {
743                nl->nlmsg_type = RTM_DELROUTE;
744                nl->nlmsg_flags = 0;
745        } else {
746                nl->nlmsg_type = RTM_NEWROUTE;
747                nl->nlmsg_flags = NLM_F_REQUEST|NLM_F_CREATE;
748                rtm->rtm_protocol = RTPROT_BOOT;
749        }
```

Figure 8.51 FIB semantics—export to RT entry i : linux/net/ipv4/fib_semantics.c.

```
751        rtm->rtm_dst_len = plen;
752        rta->rta_dst = ptr;
753
754        if (r->rt_metric) {
755                *(u32*)&r->rt_pad3 = r->rt_metric - 1;
756                rta->rta_priority = (u32*)&r->rt_pad3;
757        }
758        if (r->rt_flags&RTF_REJECT) {
759                rtm->rtm_scope = RT_SCOPE_HOST;
760                rtm->rtm_type = RTN_UNREACHABLE;
761                return 0;
762        }
763        rtm->rtm_scope = RT_SCOPE_NOWHERE;
764        rtm->rtm_type = RTN_UNICAST;
765
766        if (r->rt_dev) {
767                char *colon;
768                struct net_device *dev;
769                char  devname[IFNAMSIZ];
770
771                if (copy_from_user(devname, r->rt_dev, IFNAMSIZ-1))
772                        return -EFAULT;
773                devname[IFNAMSIZ-1] = 0;
774                colon = strchr(devname, ':');
775                if (colon)
776                        *colon = 0;
777                dev = __dev_get_by_name(devname);
778                if (!dev)
779                        return -ENODEV;
780                rta->rta_oif = &dev->ifindex;
781                if (colon) {
782                        struct in_ifaddr *ifa;
783                        struct in_device *in_dev = __in_dev_get(dev);
784                        if (!in_dev)
785                                return -ENODEV;
786                        *colon = ':';
787                        for (ifa = in_dev->ifa_list; ifa; ifa = ifa->ifa_next)
788                                if (strcmp(ifa->ifa_label, devname) == 0)
```

```
                        break;
                if (ifa == NULL)
                        return -ENODEV;
                rta->rta_prefsrc = &ifa->ifa_local;
        }
}
```

Figure 8.52 FIB semantics—export to RT entry ii: `linux/net/ipv4/fib_semantics.c`.

```
ptr = &((struct sockaddr_in*)&r->rt_gateway)->sin_addr.s_addr;
if (r->rt_gateway.sa_family == AF_INET && *ptr) {
        rta->rta_gw = ptr;
        if (r->rt_flags&RTF_GATEWAY && inet_addr_type(*ptr) == RTN_UNICAST)
                rtm->rtm_scope = RT_SCOPE_UNIVERSE;
}

if (cmd == SIOCDELRT)
        return 0;

if (r->rt_flags&RTF_GATEWAY && rta->rta_gw == NULL)
        return -EINVAL;

if (rtm->rtm_scope == RT_SCOPE_NOWHERE)
        rtm->rtm_scope = RT_SCOPE_LINK;

if (r->rt_flags&(RTF_MTU|RTF_WINDOW|RTF_IRTT)) {
        struct rtattr *rec;
        struct rtattr *mx = kmalloc(RTA_LENGTH(3*RTA_LENGTH(4)), GFP_KERNEL);
        if (mx == NULL)
                return -ENOMEM;
        rta->rta_mx = mx;
        mx->rta_type = RTA_METRICS;
        mx->rta_len = RTA_LENGTH(0);
        if (r->rt_flags&RTF_MTU) {
                rec = (void*)((char*)mx + RTA_ALIGN(mx->rta_len));
                rec->rta_type = RTAX_ADVMSS;
                rec->rta_len = RTA_LENGTH(4);
                mx->rta_len += RTA_LENGTH(4);
                *(u32*)RTA_DATA(rec) = r->rt_mtu - 40;
        }
        if (r->rt_flags&RTF_WINDOW) {
                rec = (void*)((char*)mx + RTA_ALIGN(mx->rta_len));
                rec->rta_type = RTAX_WINDOW;
                rec->rta_len = RTA_LENGTH(4);
                mx->rta_len += RTA_LENGTH(4);
                *(u32*)RTA_DATA(rec) = r->rt_window;
        }
        if (r->rt_flags&RTF_IRTT) {
                rec = (void*)((char*)mx + RTA_ALIGN(mx->rta_len));
                rec->rta_type = RTAX_RTT;
                rec->rta_len = RTA_LENGTH(4);
                mx->rta_len += RTA_LENGTH(4);
```

```
                        *(u32*)RTA_DATA(rec) = r->rt_irtt<<3;
                }
        }
        return 0;
}
```

Interface State Changes, Update Relevant FIB

Figure 8.53 FIB semantics—update FIB if address or interface down i: `linux/net/ipv4/fib_semantics.c`.

```
/*
   Update FIB if:
   - local address disappeared -> we must delete all the entries
     referring to it.
   - device went down -> we must shutdown all nexthops going via it.
 */
```

Figure 8.54 FIB semantics—update FIB if address or interface down ii: `linux/net/ipv4/fib_semantics.c`.

```
int fib_sync_down(u32 local, struct net_device *dev, int force)
{
        int ret = 0;
        int scope = RT_SCOPE_NOWHERE;

        if (force)
                scope = -1;

        for_fib_info() {
                if (local && fi->fib_prefsrc == local) {
                        fi->fib_flags |= RTNH_F_DEAD;
                        ret++;
                } else if (dev && fi->fib_nhs) {
                        int dead = 0;

                        change_nexthops(fi) {
                                if (nh->nh_flags&RTNH_F_DEAD)
                                        dead++;
                                else if (nh->nh_dev == dev &&
                                         nh->nh_scope != scope) {
                                        nh->nh_flags |= RTNH_F_DEAD;
#ifdef CONFIG_IP_ROUTE_MULTIPATH
                                        fi->fib_power -= nh->nh_power;
                                        nh->nh_power = 0;
#endif
                                        dead++;
```

```
880                            }
881                    } endfor_nexthops(fi)
882                    if (dead == fi->fib_nhs) {
883                            fi->fib_flags |= RTNH_F_DEAD;
884                            ret++;
885                    }
886            }
887    } endfor_fib_info();
888    return ret;
889 }
```

Figure 8.55 FIB semantics—update FIB if address or interface up: `linux/net/ipv4/fib_`
`semantics.c`.

```
893 /*
894    Dead device goes up. We wake up dead nexthops.
895    It takes sense only on multipath routes.
896  */
897
898 int fib_sync_up(struct net_device *dev)
899 {
900        int ret = 0;
901
902        if (!(dev->flags&IFF_UP))
903                return 0;
904
905        for_fib_info() {
906                int alive = 0;
907
908                change_nexthops(fi) {
909                        if (!(nh->nh_flags&RTNH_F_DEAD)) {
910                                alive++;
911                                continue;
912                        }
913                        if (nh->nh_dev == NULL || !(nh->nh_dev->flags&IFF_UP))
914                                continue;
915                        if (nh->nh_dev != dev || __in_dev_get(dev) == NULL)
916                                continue;
917                        alive++;
918                        nh->nh_power = 0;
919                        nh->nh_flags &= ~RTNH_F_DEAD;
920                } endfor_nexthops(fi)
921
922                if (alive > 0) {
923                        fi->fib_flags &= ~RTNH_F_DEAD;
924                        ret++;
925                }
926        } endfor_fib_info();
927        return ret;
928 }
```

Multipath Routing

Figure 8.56 FIB semantics—multipath case i: `linux/net/ipv4/fib_semantics.c`.

```
930  /*
931     The algorithm is suboptimal, but it provides really
932     fair weighted route distribution.
933  */
934
935  void fib_select_multipath(const struct rt_key *key, struct fib_result *res)
936  {
937          struct fib_info *fi = res->fi;
938          int w;
939
940          if (fi->fib_power <= 0) {
941                  int power = 0;
942                  change_nexthops(fi) {
943                          if (!(nh->nh_flags&RTNH_F_DEAD)) {
944                                  power += nh->nh_weight;
945                                  nh->nh_power = nh->nh_weight;
946                          }
947                  } endfor_nexthops(fi);
948                  fi->fib_power = power;
949  #if 1
950                  if (power <= 0) {
951                          printk(KERN_CRIT "impossible 777\n");
952                          return;
953                  }
954  #endif
955          }
956
957
958          /* w should be random number [0..fi->fib_power-1],
959             it is pretty bad approximation.
960           */
961
962          w = jiffies % fi->fib_power;
```

Figure 8.57 FIB semantics—multipath case ii: `linux/net/ipv4/fib_semantics.c`.

```
964          change_nexthops(fi) {
965                  if (!(nh->nh_flags&RTNH_F_DEAD) && nh->nh_power) {
966                          if ((w -= nh->nh_power) <= 0) {
967                                  nh->nh_power--;
968                                  fi->fib_power--;
969                                  res->nh_sel = nhsel;
970                                  return;
971                          }
972                  }
973          } endfor_nexthops(fi);
974
```

```
#if 1
        printk(KERN_CRIT "impossible 888\n");
#endif
        return;
}
```

FIB Proc FS

As well as RTNetlink, we also have the `proc fs` interface to modules:

Figure 8.58 FIB semantics—PROC FS interface: `linux/net/ipv4/fib_semantics.c.`

```
static unsigned fib_flag_trans(int type, int dead, u32 mask, struct fib_info *fi)
{
        static unsigned type2flags[RTN_MAX+1] = {
                0, 0, 0, 0, 0, 0, 0, RTF_REJECT, RTF_REJECT, 0, 0, 0
        };
        unsigned flags = type2flags[type];

        if (fi && fi->fib_nh->nh_gw)
                flags |= RTF_GATEWAY;
        if (mask == 0xFFFFFFFF)
                flags |= RTF_HOST;
        if (!dead)
                flags |= RTF_UP;
        return flags;
}

void fib_node_get_info(int type, int dead, struct fib_info *fi, u32 prefix, u32 mask, char * buffer)
{
        int len;
        unsigned flags = fib_flag_trans(type, dead, mask, fi);

        if (fi) {
                len = sprintf(buffer, "%s\t%08X\t%08X\t%04X\t%d\t%u\t%d\t%08X\t%d\t%u\t%u",
                              fi->fib_dev ? fi->fib_dev->name : "*", prefix,
                              fi->fib_nh->nh_gw, flags, 0, 0, fi->fib_priority,
                              mask, fi->fib_advmss+40, fi->fib_window, fi->fib_rtt>>3);
        } else {
                len = sprintf(buffer, "*\t%08X\t%08X\t%04X\t%d\t%u\t%d\t%08X\t%d\t%u\t%u",
                              prefix, 0,
                              flags, 0, 0, 0,
                              mask, 0, 0, 0);
        }
        memset(buffer+len, ' ', 127-len);
        buffer[127] = '\n';
}
```

Rules Is Rules

Now we can look at the rules for forwarding:

Figure 8.59 FIB rules—globals: `linux/net/ipv4/fib_rules.c`.

```
struct fib_rule
{
        struct fib_rule *r_next;
        atomic_t        r_clntref;
        u32             r_preference;
        unsigned char r_table;
        unsigned char r_action;
        unsigned char r_dst_len;
        unsigned char r_src_len;
        u32             r_src;
        u32             r_srcmask;
        u32             r_dst;
        u32             r_dstmask;
        u32             r_srcmap;
        u8              r_flags;
        u8              r_tos;
#ifdef CONFIG_IP_ROUTE_FWMARK
        u32             r_fwmark;
#endif
        int             r_ifindex;
#ifdef CONFIG_NET_CLS_ROUTE
        __u32           r_tclassid;
#endif
        char            r_ifname[IFNAMSIZ];
        int             r_dead;
};

static struct fib_rule default_rule = { NULL, ATOMIC_INIT(2), 0x7FFF, RT_TABLE_DEFAULT,
                                         RTN_UNICAST, };
static struct fib_rule main_rule = { &default_rule, ATOMIC_INIT(2), 0x7FFE, RT_TABLE_MAIN,
                                      RTN_UNICAST, };
static struct fib_rule local_rule = { &main_rule, ATOMIC_INIT(2), 0, RT_TABLE_LOCAL,
                                       RTN_UNICAST, };

static struct fib_rule *fib_rules = &local_rule;
static rwlock_t fib_rules_lock = RW_LOCK_UNLOCKED;
```

Figure 8.60 FIB rules i: `linux/net/ipv4/fib_rules.c`.

```
int inet_rtm_delrule(struct sk_buff *skb, struct nlmsghdr* nlh, void *arg)
{
        struct rtattr **rta = arg;
        struct rtmsg *rtm = NLMSG_DATA(nlh);
        struct fib_rule *r, **rp;
        int err = -ESRCH;

        for (rp=&fib_rules; (r=*rp) != NULL; rp=&r->r_next) {
```

```
94                  if ((!rta[RTA_SRC-1] || memcmp(RTA_DATA(rta[RTA_SRC-1]), &r->r_src, 4) == 0) &&
95                      rtm->rtm_src_len == r->r_src_len &&
96                      rtm->rtm_dst_len == r->r_dst_len &&
97                      (!rta[RTA_DST-1] || memcmp(RTA_DATA(rta[RTA_DST-1]), &r->r_dst, 4) == 0) &&
98                      rtm->rtm_tos == r->r_tos &&
99  #ifdef CONFIG_IP_ROUTE_FWMARK
100                     (!rta[RTA_PROTOINFO-1] || memcmp(RTA_DATA(rta[RTA_PROTOINFO-1]),
                            &r->r_fwmark, 4) == 0) &&
101 #endif
102                     (!rtm->rtm_type || rtm->rtm_type == r->r_action) &&
103                     (!rta[RTA_PRIORITY-1] || memcmp(RTA_DATA(rta[RTA_PRIORITY-1]), &r->
                            r_preference, 4) == 0) &&
104                     (!rta[RTA_IIF-1] || strcmp(RTA_DATA(rta[RTA_IIF-1]), r->r_ifname) == 0) &&
105                     (!rtm->rtm_table || (r && rtm->rtm_table == r->r_table))) {
106                         err = -EPERM;
107                         if (r == &local_rule)
108                             break;
109
110                         write_lock_bh(&fib_rules_lock);
111                         *rp = r->r_next;
112                         r->r_dead = 1;
113                         write_unlock_bh(&fib_rules_lock);
114                         fib_rule_put(r);
115                         err = 0;
116                         break;
117                 }
118         }
119         return err;
120 }
```

Figure 8.61 FIB rules—utils: `linux/net/ipv4/fib_rules.c`.

```
122 /* Allocate new unique table id */
123
124 static struct fib_table *fib_empty_table(void)
125 {
126         int id;
127
128         for (id = 1; id <= RT_TABLE_MAX; id++)
129                 if (fib_tables[id] == NULL)
130                         return __fib_new_table(id);
131         return NULL;
132 }
133
134 void fib_rule_put(struct fib_rule *r)
135 {
136         if (atomic_dec_and_test(&r->r_clntref)) {
137                 if (r->r_dead)
138                         kfree(r);
139                 else
140                         printk("Freeing alive rule %p\n", r);
141         }
142 }
```

Figure 8.62 FIB rules—new rule: `linux/net/ipv4/fib_rules.c`.

```
int inet_rtm_newrule(struct sk_buff *skb, struct nlmsghdr* nlh, void *arg)
{
        struct rtattr **rta = arg;
        struct rtmsg *rtm = NLMSG_DATA(nlh);
        struct fib_rule *r, *new_r, **rp;
        unsigned char table_id;

        if (rtm->rtm_src_len > 32 || rtm->rtm_dst_len > 32 ||
            (rtm->rtm_tos & ~IPTOS_TOS_MASK))
                return -EINVAL;

        if (rta[RTA_IIF-1] && RTA_PAYLOAD(rta[RTA_IIF-1]) > IFNAMSIZ)
                return -EINVAL;

        table_id = rtm->rtm_table;
        if (table_id == RT_TABLE_UNSPEC) {
                struct fib_table *table;
                if (rtm->rtm_type == RTN_UNICAST || rtm->rtm_type == RTN_NAT) {
                        if ((table = fib_empty_table()) == NULL)
                                return -ENOBUFS;
                        table_id = table->tb_id;
                }
        }
```

Figure 8.63 FIB rules—new rule: `linux/net/ipv4/fib_rules.c`.

```
        new_r = kmalloc(sizeof(*new_r), GFP_KERNEL);
        if (!new_r)
                return -ENOMEM;
        memset(new_r, 0, sizeof(*new_r));
        if (rta[RTA_SRC-1])
                memcpy(&new_r->r_src, RTA_DATA(rta[RTA_SRC-1]), 4);
        if (rta[RTA_DST-1])
                memcpy(&new_r->r_dst, RTA_DATA(rta[RTA_DST-1]), 4);
        if (rta[RTA_GATEWAY-1])
                memcpy(&new_r->r_srcmap, RTA_DATA(rta[RTA_GATEWAY-1]), 4);
        new_r->r_src_len = rtm->rtm_src_len;
        new_r->r_dst_len = rtm->rtm_dst_len;
        new_r->r_srcmask = inet_make_mask(rtm->rtm_src_len);
        new_r->r_dstmask = inet_make_mask(rtm->rtm_dst_len);
        new_r->r_tos = rtm->rtm_tos;
#ifdef CONFIG_IP_ROUTE_FWMARK
        if (rta[RTA_PROTOINFO-1])
                memcpy(&new_r->r_fwmark, RTA_DATA(rta[RTA_PROTOINFO-1]), 4);
#endif
        new_r->r_action = rtm->rtm_type;
        new_r->r_flags = rtm->rtm_flags;
        if (rta[RTA_PRIORITY-1])
                memcpy(&new_r->r_preference, RTA_DATA(rta[RTA_PRIORITY-1]), 4);
        new_r->r_table = table_id;
        if (rta[RTA_IIF-1]) {
```

```
                struct net_device *dev;
                memcpy(new_r->r_ifname, RTA_DATA(rta[RTA_IIF-1]), IFNAMSIZ);
                new_r->r_ifname[IFNAMSIZ-1] = 0;
                new_r->r_ifindex = -1;
                dev = __dev_get_by_name(new_r->r_ifname);
                if (dev)
                        new_r->r_ifindex = dev->ifindex;
        }
#ifdef CONFIG_NET_CLS_ROUTE
        if (rta[RTA_FLOW-1])
                memcpy(&new_r->r_tclassid, RTA_DATA(rta[RTA_FLOW-1]), 4);
#endif
```

Figure 8.64 FIB rules—new rule: `linux/net/ipv4/fib_rules.c.`

```
        rp = &fib_rules;
        if (!new_r->r_preference) {
                r = fib_rules;
                if (r && (r = r->r_next) != NULL) {
                        rp = &fib_rules->r_next;
                        if (r->r_preference)
                                new_r->r_preference = r->r_preference - 1;
                }
        }

        while ( (r = *rp) != NULL ){
                if (r->r_preference > new_r->r_preference)
                        break;
                rp = &r->r_next;
        }

        new_r->r_next = r;
        atomic_inc(&new_r->r_clntref);
        write_lock_bh(&fib_rules_lock);
        *rp = new_r;
        write_unlock_bh(&fib_rules_lock);
        return 0;
}
```

Figure 8.65 FIB rules—more utils: `linux/net/ipv4/fib_rules.c.`

```
u32 fib_rules_map_destination(u32 daddr, struct fib_result *res)
{
        u32 mask = inet_make_mask(res->prefixlen);
        return (daddr&~mask)|res->fi->fib_nh->nh_gw;
}

u32 fib_rules_policy(u32 saddr, struct fib_result *res, unsigned *flags)
{
        struct fib_rule *r = res->r;

        if (r->r_action == RTN_NAT) {
```

```
			int addrtype = inet_addr_type(r->r_srcmap);

			if (addrtype == RTN_NAT) {
				/* Packet is from translated source; remember it */
				saddr = (saddr&~r->r_srcmask)|r->r_srcmap;
				*flags |= RTCF_SNAT;
			} else if (addrtype == RTN_LOCAL || r->r_srcmap == 0) {
				/* Packet is from masqueraded source; remember it */
				saddr = r->r_srcmap;
				*flags |= RTCF_MASQ;
			}
		}
		return saddr;
}
```

Figure 8.66 FIB rules—attach and detach rule: `linux/net/ipv4/fib_rules.c`.

```
#ifdef CONFIG_NET_CLS_ROUTE
u32 fib_rules_tclass(struct fib_result *res)
{
		if (res->r)
			return res->r->r_tclassid;
		return 0;
}
#endif


static void fib_rules_detach(struct net_device *dev)
{
		struct fib_rule *r;

		for (r=fib_rules; r; r=r->r_next) {
			if (r->r_ifindex == dev->ifindex) {
				write_lock_bh(&fib_rules_lock);
				r->r_ifindex = -1;
				write_unlock_bh(&fib_rules_lock);
			}
		}
}

static void fib_rules_attach(struct net_device *dev)
{
		struct fib_rule *r;

		for (r=fib_rules; r; r=r->r_next) {
			if (r->r_ifindex == -1 && strcmp(dev->name, r->r_ifname) == 0) {
				write_lock_bh(&fib_rules_lock);
				r->r_ifindex = dev->ifindex;
				write_unlock_bh(&fib_rules_lock);
			}
		}
}
```

Figure 8.67 FIB rules—lookup rule: `linux/net/ipv4/fib_rules.c`.

```
int fib_lookup(const struct rt_key *key, struct fib_result *res)
{
        int err;
        struct fib_rule *r, *policy;
        struct fib_table *tb;

        u32 daddr = key->dst;
        u32 saddr = key->src;

FRprintk("Lookup: %u.%u.%u.%u <- %u.%u.%u.%u ",
        NIPQUAD(key->dst), NIPQUAD(key->src));
        read_lock(&fib_rules_lock);
        for (r = fib_rules; r; r=r->r_next) {
                if (((saddr^r->r_src) & r->r_srcmask) ||
                    ((daddr^r->r_dst) & r->r_dstmask) ||
#ifdef CONFIG_IP_ROUTE_TOS
                    (r->r_tos && r->r_tos != key->tos) ||
#endif
#ifdef CONFIG_IP_ROUTE_FWMARK
                    (r->r_fwmark && r->r_fwmark != key->fwmark) ||
#endif
                    (r->r_ifindex && r->r_ifindex != key->iif))
                        continue;

FRprintk("tb %d r %d ", r->r_table, r->r_action);
                switch (r->r_action) {
                case RTN_UNICAST:
                case RTN_NAT:
                        policy = r;
                        break;
                case RTN_UNREACHABLE:
                        read_unlock(&fib_rules_lock);
                        return -ENETUNREACH;
                default:
                case RTN_BLACKHOLE:
                        read_unlock(&fib_rules_lock);
                        return -EINVAL;
                case RTN_PROHIBIT:
                        read_unlock(&fib_rules_lock);
                        return -EACCES;
                }
```

Figure 8.68 FIB rules—lookup rule: `linux/net/ipv4/fib_rules.c`.

```
                if ((tb = fib_get_table(r->r_table)) == NULL)
                        continue;
                err = tb->tb_lookup(tb, key, res);
                if (err == 0) {
                        res->r = policy;
                        if (policy)
                                atomic_inc(&policy->r_clntref);
                        read_unlock(&fib_rules_lock);
                        return 0;
                }
                if (err < 0 && err != -EAGAIN) {
                        read_unlock(&fib_rules_lock);
                        return err;
                }
        }
FRprintk("FAILURE\n");
        read_unlock(&fib_rules_lock);
        return -ENETUNREACH;
}
```

Figure 8.69 FIB rules events: `linux/net/ipv4/fib_rules.c`.

```
void fib_select_default(const struct rt_key *key, struct fib_result *res)
{
        if (res->r && res->r->r_action == RTN_UNICAST &&
            FIB_RES_GW(*res) && FIB_RES_NH(*res).nh_scope == RT_SCOPE_LINK) {
                struct fib_table *tb;
                if ((tb = fib_get_table(res->r->r_table)) != NULL)
                        tb->tb_select_default(tb, key, res);
        }
}

static int fib_rules_event(struct notifier_block *this, unsigned long event, void *ptr)
{
        struct net_device *dev = ptr;

        if (event == NETDEV_UNREGISTER)
                fib_rules_detach(dev);
        else if (event == NETDEV_REGISTER)
                fib_rules_attach(dev);
        return NOTIFY_DONE;
}


struct notifier_block fib_rules_notifier = {
        fib_rules_event,
        NULL,
        0
};
```

Figure 8.70 FIB rules—initialization: `linux/net/ipv4/fib_rules.c`.

```
extern __inline__ int inet_fill_rule(struct sk_buff *skb,
                                      struct fib_rule *r,
                                      struct netlink_callback *cb)
{
        struct rtmsg *rtm;
        struct nlmsghdr *nlh;
        unsigned char  *b = skb->tail;

        nlh = NLMSG_PUT(skb, NETLINK_CREDS(cb->skb)->pid, cb->nlh->nlmsg_seq, RTM_NEWRULE, sizeof
                  (*rtm));
        rtm = NLMSG_DATA(nlh);
        rtm->rtm_family = AF_INET;
        rtm->rtm_dst_len = r->r_dst_len;
        rtm->rtm_src_len = r->r_src_len;
        rtm->rtm_tos = r->r_tos;
#ifdef CONFIG_IP_ROUTE_FWMARK
        if (r->r_fwmark)
                RTA_PUT(skb, RTA_PROTOINFO, 4, &r->r_fwmark);
#endif
        rtm->rtm_table = r->r_table;
        rtm->rtm_protocol = 0;
        rtm->rtm_scope = 0;
        rtm->rtm_type = r->r_action;
        rtm->rtm_flags = r->r_flags;

        if (r->r_dst_len)
                RTA_PUT(skb, RTA_DST, 4, &r->r_dst);
        if (r->r_src_len)
                RTA_PUT(skb, RTA_SRC, 4, &r->r_src);
        if (r->r_ifname[0])
                RTA_PUT(skb, RTA_IIF, IFNAMSIZ, &r->r_ifname);
        if (r->r_preference)
                RTA_PUT(skb, RTA_PRIORITY, 4, &r->r_preference);
        if (r->r_srcmap)
                RTA_PUT(skb, RTA_GATEWAY, 4, &r->r_srcmap);
#ifdef CONFIG_NET_CLS_ROUTE
        if (r->r_tclassid)
                RTA_PUT(skb, RTA_FLOW, 4, &r->r_tclassid);
#endif
        nlh->nlmsg_len = skb->tail - b;
        return skb->len;

nlmsg_failure:
rtattr_failure:
        skb_put(skb, b - skb->tail);
        return -1;
}
```

Figure 8.71 FIB rules—initialization: `linux/net/ipv4/fib_rules.c`.

```
431    int inet_dump_rules(struct sk_buff *skb, struct netlink_callback *cb)
432    {
433            int idx;
434            int s_idx = cb->args[0];
435            struct fib_rule *r;
436
437            read_lock(&fib_rules_lock);
438            for (r=fib_rules, idx=0; r; r = r->r_next, idx++) {
439                    if (idx < s_idx)
440                            continue;
441                    if (inet_fill_rule(skb, r, cb) < 0)
442                            break;
443            }
444            read_unlock(&fib_rules_lock);
445            cb->args[0] = idx;
446
447            return skb->len;
448    }
449
450    #endif /* CONFIG_RTNETLINK */
451
452    void __init fib_rules_init(void)
453    {
454            register_netdevice_notifier(&fib_rules_notifier);
455    }
```

Lookup—Making It All Go Fast!

Figure 8.72 Fast accessing of the FIB through hashing—types i: `linux/net/ipv4/fib_hash.c`.

```
51    static kmem_cache_t * fn_hash_kmem;
52
53    /*
54      These bizarre types are just to force strict type checking.
55      When I reversed order of bytes and changed to natural mask lengths,
56      I forgot to make fixes in several places. Now I am lazy to return
57      it back.
58     */
59
60    typedef struct {
61            u32     datum;
62    } fn_key_t;
63
64    typedef struct {
65            u32     datum;
66    } fn_hash_idx_t;
67
68    struct fib_node
69    {
```

```
        struct fib_node         *fn_next;
        struct fib_info         *fn_info;
#define FIB_INFO(f)   ((f)->fn_info)
        fn_key_t                fn_key;
        u8                      fn_tos;
        u8                      fn_type;
        u8                      fn_scope;
        u8                      fn_state;
};

#define FN_S_ZOMBIE   1
#define FN_S_ACCESSED 2

static int fib_hash_zombies;
```

Figure 8.73 Fast accessing of the FIB through hashing–types ii: `linux/net/ipv4/fib_hash.c`.

```
struct fn_zone
{
        struct fn_zone *fz_next;      /* Next not empty zone */
        struct fib_node **fz_hash;    /* Hash table pointer */
        int             fz_nent;      /* Number of entries */

        int             fz_divisor;   /* Hash divisor        */
        u32             fz_hashmask;  /* (1<<fz_divisor) - 1 */
#define FZ_HASHMASK(fz) ((fz)->fz_hashmask)

        int             fz_order;     /* Zone order          */
        u32             fz_mask;
#define FZ_MASK(fz)   ((fz)->fz_mask)
};

/* NOTE. On fast computers evaluation of fz_hashmask and fz_mask
   can be cheaper than memory lookup, so that FZ_* macros are used.
 */

struct fn_hash
{
        struct fn_zone *fn_zones[33];
        struct fn_zone *fn_zone_list;
};
```

Figure 8.74 Fast accessing of the FIB through hashing–inline functions i: `linux/net/ipv4/fib_hash.c`.

```
static __inline__ fn_hash_idx_t fn_hash(fn_key_t key, struct fn_zone *fz)
{
        u32 h = ntohl(key.datum)>>(32 - fz->fz_order);
        h ^= (h>>20);
        h ^= (h>>10);
```

```
        h ^= (h>>5);
        h &= FZ_HASHMASK(fz);
        return *(fn_hash_idx_t*)&h;
}

#define fz_key_0(key)           ((key).datum = 0)
#define fz_prefix(key,fz)       ((key).datum)

static __inline__ fn_key_t fz_key(u32 dst, struct fn_zone *fz)
{
        fn_key_t k;
        k.datum = dst & FZ_MASK(fz);
        return k;
}

static __inline__ struct fib_node ** fz_chain_p(fn_key_t key, struct fn_zone *fz)
{
        return &fz->fz_hash[fn_hash(key, fz).datum];
}

static __inline__ struct fib_node * fz_chain(fn_key_t key, struct fn_zone *fz)
{
        return fz->fz_hash[fn_hash(key, fz).datum];
}

extern __inline__ int fn_key_eq(fn_key_t a, fn_key_t b)
{
        return a.datum == b.datum;
}

extern __inline__ int fn_key_leq(fn_key_t a, fn_key_t b)
{
        return a.datum <= b.datum;
}

static rwlock_t fib_hash_lock = RW_LOCK_UNLOCKED;

#define FZ_MAX_DIVISOR 1024
```

Figure 8.75 Fast accessing of the FIB through hashing–inline functions ii: `linux/net/ipv4/fib_hash.c`.

```
#ifdef CONFIG_IP_ROUTE_LARGE_TABLES

/* The fib hash lock must be held when this is called. */
static __inline__ void fn_rebuild_zone(struct fn_zone *fz,
                                       struct fib_node **old_ht,
                                       int old_divisor)
{
        int i;
        struct fib_node *f, **fp, *next;

```

```
164             for (i=0; i<old_divisor; i++) {
165                     for (f=old_ht[i]; f; f=next) {
166                             next = f->fn_next;
167                             for (fp = fz_chain_p(f->fn_key, fz);
168                                     *fp && fn_key_leq((*fp)->fn_key, f->fn_key);
169                                     fp = &(*fp)->fn_next)
170                                             /* NONE */;
171                             f->fn_next = *fp;
172                             *fp = f;
173                     }
174             }
175     }
```

Figure 8.76 Fast accessing of the FIB through hashing—inline functions iii: linux/net/ipv4/fib_hash.c.

```
177     static void fn_rehash_zone(struct fn_zone *fz)
178     {
179             struct fib_node **ht, **old_ht;
180             int old_divisor, new_divisor;
181             u32 new_hashmask;
182
183             old_divisor = fz->fz_divisor;
184
185             switch (old_divisor) {
186             case 16:
187                     new_divisor = 256;
188                     new_hashmask = 0xFF;
189                     break;
190             case 256:
191                     new_divisor = 1024;
192                     new_hashmask = 0x3FF;
193                     break;
194             default:
195                     printk(KERN_CRIT "route.c: bad divisor %d!\n", old_divisor);
196                     return;
197             }
198     #if RT_CACHE_DEBUG >= 2
199             printk("fn_rehash_zone: hash for zone %d grows from %d\n", fz->fz_order, old_divisor);
200     #endif
201
202             ht = kmalloc(new_divisor*sizeof(struct fib_node*), GFP_KERNEL);
203
204             if (ht) {
205                     memset(ht, 0, new_divisor*sizeof(struct fib_node*));
206                     write_lock_bh(&fib_hash_lock);
207                     old_ht = fz->fz_hash;
208                     fz->fz_hash = ht;
209                     fz->fz_hashmask = new_hashmask;
210                     fz->fz_divisor = new_divisor;
211                     fn_rebuild_zone(fz, old_ht, old_divisor);
```

```
212                 write_unlock_bh(&fib_hash_lock);
213                 kfree(old_ht);
214         }
215 }
216 #endif /* CONFIG_IP_ROUTE_LARGE_TABLES */
```

Zone Information

Next we need to look for the right zone:

Figure 8.77 Fast accessing of the FIB through hashing—zone lookup functions: linux/net/ipv4/fib_hash.c.

```
218 static void fn_free_node(struct fib_node * f)
219 {
220         fib_release_info(FIB_INFO(f));
221         kmem_cache_free(fn_hash_kmem, f);
222 }
223
224
225 static struct fn_zone *
226 fn_new_zone(struct fn_hash *table, int z)
227 {
228         int i;
229         struct fn_zone *fz = kmalloc(sizeof(struct fn_zone), GFP_KERNEL);
230         if (!fz)
231                 return NULL;
232
233         memset(fz, 0, sizeof(struct fn_zone));
234         if (z) {
235                 fz->fz_divisor = 16;
236                 fz->fz_hashmask = 0xF;
237         } else {
238                 fz->fz_divisor = 1;
239                 fz->fz_hashmask = 0;
240         }
241         fz->fz_hash = kmalloc(fz->fz_divisor*sizeof(struct fib_node*), GFP_KERNEL);
242         if (!fz->fz_hash) {
243                 kfree(fz);
244                 return NULL;
245         }
246         memset(fz->fz_hash, 0, fz->fz_divisor*sizeof(struct fib_node*));
247         fz->fz_order = z;
248         fz->fz_mask = inet_make_mask(z);
249
250         /* Find the first not empty zone with more specific mask */
251         for (i=z+1; i<=32; i++)
252                 if (table->fn_zones[i])
253                         break;
```

```
	write_lock_bh(&fib_hash_lock);
	if (i>32) {
		/* No more specific masks, we are the first. */
		fz->fz_next = table->fn_zone_list;
		table->fn_zone_list = fz;
	} else {
		fz->fz_next = table->fn_zones[i]->fz_next;
		table->fn_zones[i]->fz_next = fz;
	}
	table->fn_zones[z] = fz;
	write_unlock_bh(&fib_hash_lock);
	return fz;
}
```

Then we look for the actual entry:

Figure 8.78 Fast accessing of the FIB through hashing—hash lookup function: `linux/net/ipv4/fib_hash.c`.

```
static int
fn_hash_lookup(struct fib_table *tb, const struct rt_key *key, struct fib_result *res)
{
	int err;
	struct fn_zone *fz;
	struct fn_hash *t = (struct fn_hash*)tb->tb_data;

	read_lock(&fib_hash_lock);
	for (fz = t->fn_zone_list; fz; fz = fz->fz_next) {
		struct fib_node *f;
		fn_key_t k = fz_key(key->dst, fz);

		for (f = fz_chain(k, fz); f; f = f->fn_next) {
			if (!fn_key_eq(k, f->fn_key)) {
				if (fn_key_leq(k, f->fn_key))
					break;
				else
					continue;
			}
#ifdef CONFIG_IP_ROUTE_TOS
			if (f->fn_tos && f->fn_tos != key->tos)
				continue;
#endif
			f->fn_state |= FN_S_ACCESSED;

			if (f->fn_state&FN_S_ZOMBIE)
				continue;
			if (f->fn_scope < key->scope)
				continue;
```

```
			err = fib_semantic_match(f->fn_type, FIB_INFO(f), key, res);
			if (err == 0) {
				res->type = f->fn_type;
				res->scope = f->fn_scope;
				res->prefixlen = fz->fz_order;
				goto out;
			}
			if (err < 0)
				goto out;
		}
	}
	err = 1;
out:
	read_unlock(&fib_hash_lock);
	return err;
}
```

Or find a dead one:

Figure 8.79 Fast accessing of the FIB through hashing—dead entry: `linux/net/ipv4/fib_hash.c`.

```
static int fn_hash_last_dflt=-1;

static int fib_detect_death(struct fib_info *fi, int order,
				struct fib_info **last_resort, int *last_idx)
{
	struct neighbour *n;
	int state = NUD_NONE;

	n = neigh_lookup(&arp_tbl, &fi->fib_nh[0].nh_gw, fi->fib_dev);
	if (n) {
		state = n->nud_state;
		neigh_release(n);
	}
	if (state==NUD_REACHABLE)
		return 0;
	if ((state&NUD_VALID) && order != fn_hash_last_dflt)
		return 0;
	if ((state&NUD_VALID) ||
	    (*last_idx<0 && order > fn_hash_last_dflt)) {
		*last_resort = fi;
		*last_idx = order;
	}
	return 1;
}
```

Or a default:

Figure 8.80 Fast accessing of the FIB through hashing—select default entry: `linux/net/ipv4/fib_hash.c`.

```
static void
fn_hash_select_default(struct fib_table *tb, const struct rt_key *key, struct fib_result *res)
{
        int order, last_idx;
        struct fib_node *f;
        struct fib_info *fi = NULL;
        struct fib_info *last_resort;
        struct fn_hash *t = (struct fn_hash*)tb->tb_data;
        struct fn_zone *fz = t->fn_zones[0];

        if (fz == NULL)
                return;

        last_idx = -1;
        last_resort = NULL;
        order = -1;

        read_lock(&fib_hash_lock);
        for (f = fz->fz_hash[0]; f; f = f->fn_next) {
                struct fib_info *next_fi = FIB_INFO(f);

                if ((f->fn_state&FN_S_ZOMBIE) ||
                    f->fn_scope != res->scope ||
                    f->fn_type != RTN_UNICAST)
                        continue;

                if (next_fi->fib_priority > res->fi->fib_priority)
                        break;
                if (!next_fi->fib_nh[0].nh_gw || next_fi->fib_nh[0].nh_scope != RT_SCOPE_LINK)
                        continue;
                f->fn_state |= FN_S_ACCESSED;

                if (fi == NULL) {
                        if (next_fi != res->fi)
                                break;
                } else if (!fib_detect_death(fi, order, &last_resort, &last_idx)) {
                        if (res->fi)
                                fib_info_put(res->fi);
                        res->fi = fi;
                        atomic_inc(&fi->fib_clntref);
                        fn_hash_last_dflt = order;
                        goto out;
                }
                fi = next_fi;
                order++;
        }
```

Figure 8.81 Fast accessing of the FIB through hashing—select default entry: `linux/net/ipv4/fib_hash.c`.

```
        if (order<=0 || fi==NULL) {
                fn_hash_last_dflt = -1;
                goto out;
        }

        if (!fib_detect_death(fi, order, &last_resort, &last_idx)) {
                if (res->fi)
                        fib_info_put(res->fi);
                res->fi = fi;
                atomic_inc(&fi->fib_clntref);
                fn_hash_last_dflt = order;
                goto out;
        }

        if (last_idx >= 0) {
                if (res->fi)
                        fib_info_put(res->fi);
                res->fi = last_resort;
                if (last_resort)
                        atomic_inc(&last_resort->fib_clntref);
        }
        fn_hash_last_dflt = last_idx;
out:
        read_unlock(&fib_hash_lock);
}
```

Adding a FIB Entry

Now we look at the case of adding (updating) entries.

Figure 8.82 Fast accessing of the FIB through hashing—insert entry i: `linux/net/ipv4/fib_hash.c`.

```
#define FIB_SCAN(f, fp) \
for ( ; ((f) = *(fp)) != NULL; (fp) = &(f)->fn_next)

#define FIB_SCAN_KEY(f, fp, key) \
for ( ; ((f) = *(fp)) != NULL && fn_key_eq((f)->fn_key, (key)); (fp) = &(f)->fn_next)

#ifndef CONFIG_IP_ROUTE_TOS
#define FIB_SCAN_TOS(f, fp, key, tos) FIB_SCAN_KEY(f, fp, key)
#else
#define FIB_SCAN_TOS(f, fp, key, tos) \
for ( ; ((f) = *(fp)) != NULL && fn_key_eq((f)->fn_key, (key)) && \
     (f)->fn_tos == (tos) ; (fp) = &(f)->fn_next)
#endif

```

```
427
428   #ifdef CONFIG_RTNETLINK
429   static void rtmsg_fib(int, struct fib_node*, int, int,
430                         struct nlmsghdr *n,
431                         struct netlink_skb_parms *);
432   #else
433   #define rtmsg_fib(a, b, c, d, e, f)
434   #endif
435
436
437   static int
438   fn_hash_insert(struct fib_table *tb, struct rtmsg *r, struct kern_rta *rta,
439                  struct nlmsghdr *n, struct netlink_skb_parms *req)
440   {
441         struct fn_hash *table = (struct fn_hash*)tb->tb_data;
442         struct fib_node *new_f, *f, **fp, **del_fp;
443         struct fn_zone *fz;
444         struct fib_info *fi;
445
446         int z = r->rtm_dst_len;
447         int type = r->rtm_type;
448   #ifdef CONFIG_IP_ROUTE_TOS
449         u8 tos = r->rtm_tos;
450   #endif
451         fn_key_t key;
452         int err;
```

Figure 8.83 Fast accessing of the FIB through hashing—insert entry ii: `linux/net/ipv4/fib_hash.c`.

```
454   FTprint("tb(%d)_insert: %d %08x/%d %d %08x\n", tb->tb_id, r->rtm_type, rta->rta_dst ?
455   *(u32*)rta->rta_dst : 0, z, rta->rta_oif ? *rta->rta_oif : -1,
456   rta->rta_prefsrc ? *(u32*)rta->rta_prefsrc : 0);
457         if (z > 32)
458               return -EINVAL;
459         fz = table->fn_zones[z];
460         if (!fz && !(fz = fn_new_zone(table, z)))
461               return -ENOBUFS;
462
463         fz_key_0(key);
464         if (rta->rta_dst) {
465               u32 dst;
466               memcpy(&dst, rta->rta_dst, 4);
467               if (dst & ~FZ_MASK(fz))
468                     return -EINVAL;
469               key = fz_key(dst, fz);
470         }
471
472         if ((fi = fib_create_info(r, rta, n, &err)) == NULL)
473               return err;
474
475   #ifdef CONFIG_IP_ROUTE_LARGE_TABLES
```

```
        if (fz->fz_nent > (fz->fz_divisor<<2) &&
            fz->fz_divisor < FZ_MAX_DIVISOR &&
            (z==32 || (1<<z) > fz->fz_divisor))
                fn_rehash_zone(fz);
#endif

        fp = fz_chain_p(key, fz);


        /*
         * Scan list to find the first route with the same destination
         */
        FIB_SCAN(f, fp) {
                if (fn_key_leq(key,f->fn_key))
                        break;
        }

#ifdef CONFIG_IP_ROUTE_TOS
        /*
         * Find route with the same destination and tos.
         */
        FIB_SCAN_KEY(f, fp, key) {
                if (f->fn_tos <= tos)
                        break;
        }
#endif
```

Figure 8.84 Fast accessing of the FIB through hashing—insert entry iii: `linux/net/ipv4/fib_hash.c`.

```
        del_fp = NULL;

        if (f && (f->fn_state&FN_S_ZOMBIE) &&
#ifdef CONFIG_IP_ROUTE_TOS
            f->fn_tos == tos &&
#endif
            fn_key_eq(f->fn_key, key)) {
                del_fp = fp;
                fp = &f->fn_next;
                f = *fp;
                goto create;
        }

        FIB_SCAN_TOS(f, fp, key, tos) {
                if (fi->fib_priority <= FIB_INFO(f)->fib_priority)
                        break;
        }
```

Figure 8.85 Fast accessing of the FIB through hashing—insert entry iv: `linux/net/ipv4/`
`fib_hash.c`.

```
521            /* Now f==*fp points to the first node with the same
522               keys [prefix,tos,priority], if such key already
523               exists or to the node, before which we will insert new one.
524            */
525
526            if (f &&
527    #ifdef CONFIG_IP_ROUTE_TOS
528               f->fn_tos == tos &&
529    #endif
530               fn_key_eq(f->fn_key, key) &&
531               fi->fib_priority == FIB_INFO(f)->fib_priority) {
532                   struct fib_node **ins_fp;
533
534                   err = -EEXIST;
535                   if (n->nlmsg_flags&NLM_F_EXCL)
536                           goto out;
537
538                   if (n->nlmsg_flags&NLM_F_REPLACE) {
539                           del_fp = fp;
540                           fp = &f->fn_next;
541                           f = *fp;
542                           goto replace;
543                   }
544
545                   ins_fp = fp;
546                   err = -EEXIST;
547
548                   FIB_SCAN_TOS(f, fp, key, tos) {
549                           if (fi->fib_priority != FIB_INFO(f)->fib_priority)
550                                   break;
551                           if (f->fn_type == type && f->fn_scope == r->rtm_scope
552                               && FIB_INFO(f) == fi)
553                                   goto out;
554                   }
555
556                   if (!(n->nlmsg_flags&NLM_F_APPEND)) {
557                           fp = ins_fp;
558                           f = *fp;
559                   }
560            }
```

Figure 8.86 Fast accessing of the FIB through hashing—insert entry v: `linux/net/ipv4/`
`fib_hash.c`.

```
562    create:
563            err = -ENOENT;
564            if (!(n->nlmsg_flags&NLM_F_CREATE))
565                    goto out;
566
567    replace:
```

```
568              err = -ENOBUFS;
569              new_f = kmem_cache_alloc(fn_hash_kmem, SLAB_KERNEL);
570              if (new_f == NULL)
571                      goto out;
572
573              memset(new_f, 0, sizeof(struct fib_node));
574
575              new_f->fn_key = key;
576    #ifdef CONFIG_IP_ROUTE_TOS
577              new_f->fn_tos = tos;
578    #endif
579              new_f->fn_type = type;
580              new_f->fn_scope = r->rtm_scope;
581              FIB_INFO(new_f) = fi;
582
583              /*
584               * Insert new entry to the list.
585               */
586
587              new_f->fn_next = f;
588              write_lock_bh(&fib_hash_lock);
589              *fp = new_f;
590              write_unlock_bh(&fib_hash_lock);
591              fz->fz_nent++;
```

Figure 8.87 Fast accessing of the FIB through hashing—insert entry vi: linux/net/ipv4/
fib_hash.c.

```
593              if (del_fp) {
594                      f = *del_fp;
595                      /* Unlink replaced node */
596                      write_lock_bh(&fib_hash_lock);
597                      *del_fp = f->fn_next;
598                      write_unlock_bh(&fib_hash_lock);
599
600                      if (!(f->fn_state&FN_S_ZOMBIE))
601                              rtmsg_fib(RTM_DELROUTE, f, z, tb->tb_id, n, req);
602                      if (f->fn_state&FN_S_ACCESSED)
603                              rt_cache_flush(-1);
604                      fn_free_node(f);
605                      fz->fz_nent--;
606              } else {
607                      rt_cache_flush(-1);
608              }
609              rtmsg_fib(RTM_NEWROUTE, new_f, z, tb->tb_id, n, req);
610              return 0;
611
612    out:
613              fib_release_info(fi);
614              return err;
615    }
```

Deleting a FIB Entry

Figure 8.88 Fast accessing of the FIB through hashing—delete entry i: `linux/net/ipv4/fib_hash.c`.

```
static int
fn_hash_delete(struct fib_table *tb, struct rtmsg *r, struct kern_rta *rta,
                struct nlmsghdr *n, struct netlink_skb_parms *req)
{
        struct fn_hash *table = (struct fn_hash*)tb->tb_data;
        struct fib_node **fp, **del_fp, *f;
        int z = r->rtm_dst_len;
        struct fn_zone *fz;
        fn_key_t key;
        int matched;
#ifdef CONFIG_IP_ROUTE_TOS
        u8 tos = r->rtm_tos;
#endif

FTprint("tb(%d)_delete: %d %08x/%d %d\n", tb->tb_id, r->rtm_type, rta->rta_dst ?
       *(u32*)rta->rta_dst : 0, z, rta->rta_oif ? *rta->rta_oif : -1);
        if (z > 32)
                return -EINVAL;
        if ((fz = table->fn_zones[z]) == NULL)
                return -ESRCH;

        fz_key_0(key);
        if (rta->rta_dst) {
                u32 dst;
                memcpy(&dst, rta->rta_dst, 4);
                if (dst & ~FZ_MASK(fz))
                        return -EINVAL;
                key = fz_key(dst, fz);
        }

        fp = fz_chain_p(key, fz);


        FIB_SCAN(f, fp) {
                if (fn_key_eq(f->fn_key, key))
                        break;
                if (fn_key_leq(key, f->fn_key)) {
                        return -ESRCH;
                }
        }
```

Figure 8.89 Fast accessing of the FIB through hashing—delete entry ii: `linux/net/ipv4/fib_hash.c`.

```
#ifdef CONFIG_IP_ROUTE_TOS
        FIB_SCAN_KEY(f, fp, key) {
                if (f->fn_tos == tos)
                        break;
        }
```

```
663    #endif
664
665         matched = 0;
666         del_fp = NULL;
667         FIB_SCAN_TOS(f, fp, key, tos) {
668                 struct fib_info * fi = FIB_INFO(f);
669
670                 if (f->fn_state&FN_S_ZOMBIE) {
671                         return -ESRCH;
672                 }
673                 matched++;
674
675                 if (del_fp == NULL &&
676                     (!r->rtm_type || f->fn_type == r->rtm_type) &&
677                     (r->rtm_scope == RT_SCOPE_NOWHERE || f->fn_scope == r->rtm_scope) &&
678                     (!r->rtm_protocol || fi->fib_protocol == r->rtm_protocol) &&
679                     fib_nh_match(r, n, rta, fi) == 0)
680                         del_fp = fp;
681         }
```

Figure 8.90 Fast accessing of the FIB through hashing—delete entry iii: linux/net/ipv4/ fib_hash.c.

```
683         if (del_fp) {
684                 f = *del_fp;
685                 rtmsg_fib(RTM_DELROUTE, f, z, tb->tb_id, n, req);
686
687                 if (matched != 1) {
688                         write_lock_bh(&fib_hash_lock);
689                         *del_fp = f->fn_next;
690                         write_unlock_bh(&fib_hash_lock);
691
692                         if (f->fn_state&FN_S_ACCESSED)
693                                 rt_cache_flush(-1);
694                         fn_free_node(f);
695                         fz->fz_nent--;
696                 } else {
697                         f->fn_state |= FN_S_ZOMBIE;
698                         if (f->fn_state&FN_S_ACCESSED) {
699                                 f->fn_state &= ~FN_S_ACCESSED;
700                                 rt_cache_flush(-1);
701                         }
702                         if (++fib_hash_zombies > 128)
703                                 fib_flush();
704                 }
705
706                 return 0;
707         }
708         return -ESRCH;
709    }
```

Figure 8.91 Fast accessing of the FIB through hashing—flush entries: `linux/net/ipv4/`
`fib_hash.c`.

```
711   extern __inline__ int
712   fn_flush_list(struct fib_node ** fp, int z, struct fn_hash *table)
713   {
714           int found = 0;
715           struct fib_node *f;
716
717           while ((f = *fp) != NULL) {
718                   struct fib_info *fi = FIB_INFO(f);
719
720                   if (fi && ((f->fn_state&FN_S_ZOMBIE) || (fi->fib_flags&RTNH_F_DEAD))) {
721                           write_lock_bh(&fib_hash_lock);
722                           *fp = f->fn_next;
723                           write_unlock_bh(&fib_hash_lock);
724
725                           fn_free_node(f);
726                           found++;
727                           continue;
728                   }
729                   fp = &f->fn_next;
730           }
731           return found;
732   }
733
734   static int fn_hash_flush(struct fib_table *tb)
735   {
736           struct fn_hash *table = (struct fn_hash*)tb->tb_data;
737           struct fn_zone *fz;
738           int found = 0;
739
740           fib_hash_zombies = 0;
741           for (fz = table->fn_zone_list; fz; fz = fz->fz_next) {
742                   int i;
743                   int tmp = 0;
744                   for (i=fz->fz_divisor-1; i>=0; i--)
745                           tmp += fn_flush_list(&fz->fz_hash[i], fz->fz_order, table);
746                   fz->fz_nent -= tmp;
747                   found += tmp;
748           }
749           return found;
750   }
```

Management

Figure 8.92 Accessing the FIB—PROC FS access : `linux/net/ipv4/fib_hash.c`.

```
755   static int fn_hash_get_info(struct fib_table *tb, char *buffer, int first, int count)
756   {
757           struct fn_hash *table = (struct fn_hash*)tb->tb_data;
758           struct fn_zone *fz;
759           int pos = 0;
```

```
760          int n = 0;
761
762          read_lock(&fib_hash_lock);
763          for (fz=table->fn_zone_list; fz; fz = fz->fz_next) {
764                  int i;
765                  struct fib_node *f;
766                  int maxslot = fz->fz_divisor;
767                  struct fib_node **fp = fz->fz_hash;
768
769                  if (fz->fz_nent == 0)
770                          continue;
771
772                  if (pos + fz->fz_nent <= first) {
773                          pos += fz->fz_nent;
774                          continue;
775                  }
776
777                  for (i=0; i < maxslot; i++, fp++) {
778                          for (f = *fp; f; f = f->fn_next) {
779                                  if (++pos <= first)
780                                          continue;
781                                  fib_node_get_info(f->fn_type,
782                                                  f->fn_state&FN_S_ZOMBIE,
783                                                  FIB_INFO(f),
784                                                  fz_prefix(f->fn_key, fz),
785                                                  FZ_MASK(fz), buffer);
786                                  buffer += 128;
787                                  if (++n >= count)
788                                          goto out;
789                          }
790                  }
791          }
792 out:
793          read_unlock(&fib_hash_lock);
794          return n;
795 }
```

Figure 8.93 Accessing the FIB—RT access i: linux/net/ipv4/fib_hash.c.

```
801 extern __inline__ int
802 fn_hash_dump_bucket(struct sk_buff *skb, struct netlink_callback *cb,
803                  struct fib_table *tb,
804                  struct fn_zone *fz,
805                  struct fib_node *f)
806 {
807      int i, s_i;
808
809      s_i = cb->args[3];
810      for (i=0; f; i++, f=f->fn_next) {
811              if (i < s_i) continue;
812              if (f->fn_state&FN_S_ZOMBIE) continue;
813              if (fib_dump_info(skb, NETLINK_CB(cb->skb).pid, cb->nlh->nlmsg_seq,
```

```
814                         RTM_NEWROUTE,
815                         tb->tb_id, (f->fn_state&FN_S_ZOMBIE) ? 0 : f->fn_type,
                                f->fn_scope,
816                         &f->fn_key, fz->fz_order, f->fn_tos,
817                         f->fn_info) < 0) {
818                     cb->args[3] = i;
819                     return -1;
820              }
821          }
822          cb->args[3] = i;
823          return skb->len;
824  }
```

Figure 8.94 Accessing the FIB—RT access ii: linux/net/ipv4/fib_hash.c.

```
826  extern __inline__ int
827  fn_hash_dump_zone(struct sk_buff *skb, struct netlink_callback *cb,
828                    struct fib_table *tb,
829                    struct fn_zone *fz)
830  {
831      int h, s_h;
832
833      s_h = cb->args[2];
834      for (h=0; h < fz->fz_divisor; h++) {
835          if (h < s_h) continue;
836          if (h > s_h)
837              memset(&cb->args[3], 0, sizeof(cb->args) - 3*sizeof(cb->args[0]));
838          if (fz->fz_hash == NULL || fz->fz_hash[h] == NULL)
839              continue;
840          if (fn_hash_dump_bucket(skb, cb, tb, fz, fz->fz_hash[h]) < 0) {
841              cb->args[2] = h;
842              return -1;
843          }
844      }
845      cb->args[2] = h;
846      return skb->len;
847  }
```

Figure 8.95 Accessing the FIB—RT access iii: linux/net/ipv4/fib_hash.c.

```
849  static int fn_hash_dump(struct fib_table *tb, struct sk_buff *skb, struct netlink_callback *cb)
850  {
851      int m, s_m;
852      struct fn_zone *fz;
853      struct fn_hash *table = (struct fn_hash*)tb->tb_data;
854
855      s_m = cb->args[1];
856      read_lock(&fib_hash_lock);
857      for (fz = table->fn_zone_list, m=0; fz; fz = fz->fz_next, m++) {
858          if (m < s_m) continue;
```

```
                if (m > s_m)
                        memset(&cb->args[2], 0, sizeof(cb->args) - 2*sizeof(cb->args[0]));
                if (fn_hash_dump_zone(skb, cb, tb, fz) < 0) {
                        cb->args[1] = m;
                        read_unlock(&fib_hash_lock);
                        return -1;
                }
        }
        read_unlock(&fib_hash_lock);
        cb->args[1] = m;
        return skb->len;
}
```

Figure 8.96 Accessing the FIB—RT access iv: `linux/net/ipv4/fib_hash.c`.

```
static void rtmsg_fib(int event, struct fib_node* f, int z, int tb_id,
                         struct nlmsghdr *n, struct netlink_skb_parms *req)
{
        struct sk_buff *skb;
        u32 pid = req ? req->pid : 0;
        int size = NLMSG_SPACE(sizeof(struct rtmsg)+256);

        skb = alloc_skb(size, GFP_KERNEL);
        if (!skb)
                return;

        if (fib_dump_info(skb, pid, n->nlmsg_seq, event, tb_id,
                          f->fn_type, f->fn_scope, &f->fn_key, z, f->fn_tos,
                          FIB_INFO(f)) < 0) {
                kfree_skb(skb);
                return;
        }
        NETLINK_CB(skb).dst_groups = RTMGRP_IPV4_ROUTE;
        if (n->nlmsg_flags&NLM_F_ECHO)
                atomic_inc(&skb->users);
        netlink_broadcast(rtnl, skb, pid, RTMGRP_IPV4_ROUTE, GFP_KERNEL);
        if (n->nlmsg_flags&NLM_F_ECHO)
                netlink_unicast(rtnl, skb, pid, MSG_DONTWAIT);
}
```

Starting It All Up

Figure 8.97 Accessing the FIB—initialization: `linux/net/ipv4/fib_hash.c`.

```
#ifdef CONFIG_IP_MULTIPLE_TABLES
struct fib_table * fib_hash_init(int id)
#else
struct fib_table * __init fib_hash_init(int id)
#endif
{
```

```
        struct fib_table *tb;

        if (fn_hash_kmem == NULL)
                fn_hash_kmem = kmem_cache_create("ip_fib_hash",
                                                 sizeof(struct fib_node),
                                                 0, SLAB_HWCACHE_ALIGN,
                                                 NULL, NULL);

        tb = kmalloc(sizeof(struct fib_table) + sizeof(struct fn_hash), GFP_KERNEL);
        if (tb == NULL)
                return NULL;

        tb->tb_id = id;
        tb->tb_lookup = fn_hash_lookup;
        tb->tb_insert = fn_hash_insert;
        tb->tb_delete = fn_hash_delete;
        tb->tb_flush = fn_hash_flush;
        tb->tb_select_default = fn_hash_select_default;
#ifdef CONFIG_RTNETLINK
        tb->tb_dump = fn_hash_dump;
#endif
#ifdef CONFIG_PROC_FS
        tb->tb_get_info = fn_hash_get_info;
#endif
        memset(tb->tb_data, 0, sizeof(struct fn_hash));
        return tb;
}
```

8.4 Multicast

The IP protocol supports one-to-all, one-to-many, and many-to-many delivery of packets. Linux supports these facilities through normal host support for broadcast and multicast addressing and through multicast forwarding support in the kernel. Again, as with unicast routing, if you want a routing daemon, you have to currently go elsewhere (GateD has support for most of the common multicast routing protocols).

The Internet standard multicast service provides what some people refer to as *any-to-many* delivery of IP packets. In the same way that anyone can send a normal IP packet to any IP unicast destination address, anyone can send an IP multicast-addressed packet to any group.

A group is defined by an IP multicast address and the current set of receivers that have expressed an interest in the group. As we discussed in Chapter 6, membership is achieved via the Internet Group Management Protocol (IGMP) (see Figure 8.98).

Many applications exist for which there is a single sender and many recipients. So long as the number of recipients is less than the number of hosts at a site or on a network, then multicast is useful. Some applications exist where there are also several senders (usually, in fact almost always, these senders are also receivers).

A group is defined in terms of a set of hosts. The effect of multicast routing is that a single transmission results in reception at many receivers—that is, it optimizes transmissions and reduces duplications.

Multicast addresses, at least in IPv4, are class D and are denoted in the dotted decimal notation, in the range `224.0.0.0`–`239.255.255.255`, as discussed in Chapters 1 and 5. Instead of referring to a host interface, an IP multicast address refers to a group of interfaces. IGMP and the socket API allows applications to indicate their membership of groups. Some addresses are reserved for internal management of multicast (e.g., for IGMP messages and for multicast routing messages).

There's a wide variety of applications for multicast. Many are single-source, but there are a few important ones that have multiple senders. For example, voice and multimedia conferencing is quite often touted as a good example of a many-to-many application, although some higher-level systems implement it as a set of point-to-point flows between clients and a distribution server that uses a one-to-many IP multicast channel back to all the clients.

Classic single-source applications include software update and distribution, and news distribution.

Other multiple-sender applications may in the future include multiplayer games and distributed simulations. Currently, though, most of these are server-based.

IP multicast support can be separated into three components: local network support, wide area Internet router support, and general traffic management, including scoped transmission using the IP TTL header field and other facilities.

Features of IP multicast are that a group of hosts is identified by a class D address. Applications use a transport protocol (*not* TCP, but something usually based on UDP, or else some novel transport protocol such as PGM) to carry out any higher-level end-to-end functions required over IP multicast (reliability, synchronization, session management, and so on).

Multicast systems can be divided into leaf nodes (hosts) and intermediate nodes (routers). The routing system conspires to construct delivery *trees*, rather than simple paths. It is critical to understand that IP multicast supports dynamic membership with a leaf-initiated join paradigm. This means that there is a lot of potential control traffic as hosts join and leave a multicast group. Another (typical, in line with the Internet design philosophy) feature is that a non-group member can send to group (subject to any firewalls, and so on).

Most IP routers in the world are multicast capable. However, not all of the Internet is multicast enabled—particularly true in dial-up and other low-bandwidth access links.

As described in Chapter 6, IGMP is used to coordinate group membership between hosts and *first hop* routers on the local network. On a given local link,

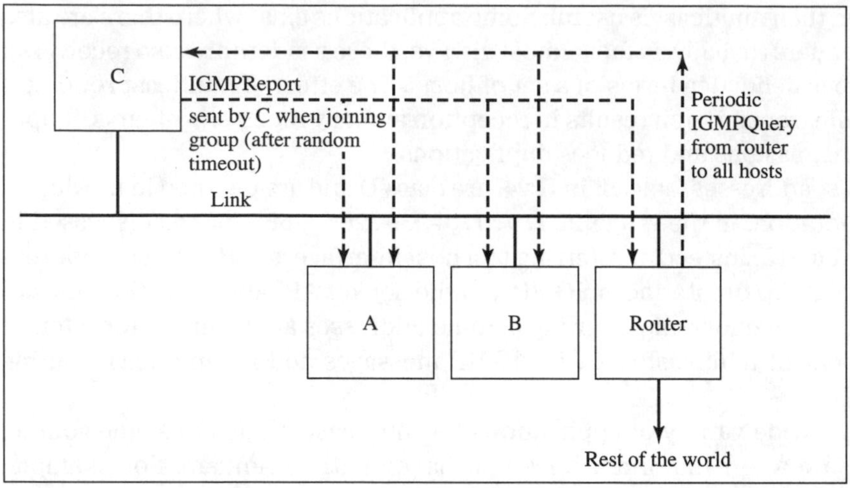

Figure 8.98 IGMP.

just as with IP unicast, there is a need to translate or map IP addresses to MAC address. For a point-to-point link this is trivial, but for an IEEE 802-type network, there's a bit more to it: unlike unicast addresses where ARP is typically used, IP multicast employs algorithmic resolution from layer 3 to layer 2 addresses since it is quick, easy, and distributed, and doesn't read to any of the broadcast storms associated with misconfigured ARP services.

The MAC address format is illustrated in Table 8.1. The IANA has carried out a MAC address allocation, and the algorithm is to take the last 23 bits of a class D address, and superimpose these on the MAC prefix assigned. Note that unfortunately, this is not a one-to-one mapping, which means that potentially, several IP multicast addresses may share a given MAC address—the mapping is designed to make this unlikely, but in this event, host filtering is required at the IP layer to recognize addresses for which the host *does* have receivers. In fact, due to hardware limitations in many LAN cards, it is quite likely that a host that is a member of more than a few groups will have to do this filtering in any case—this is because the only way to receive multicast to more groups than the LAN card can recognize is to enable promiscuous reception of *all* multicast

Table 8.1 Multicast Addressing

IPv4 multicast address; 224.20.5.1 = 1110 0000 0001 0100 0001 0100 0000 0001
IANA MAC address prefix; = 0000 0001 0000 0000 0101 1110 0– –
Final Ethernet multicast address; 0000 0001 0000 0000 0101 1110 0100 0001 0100 0000 0001

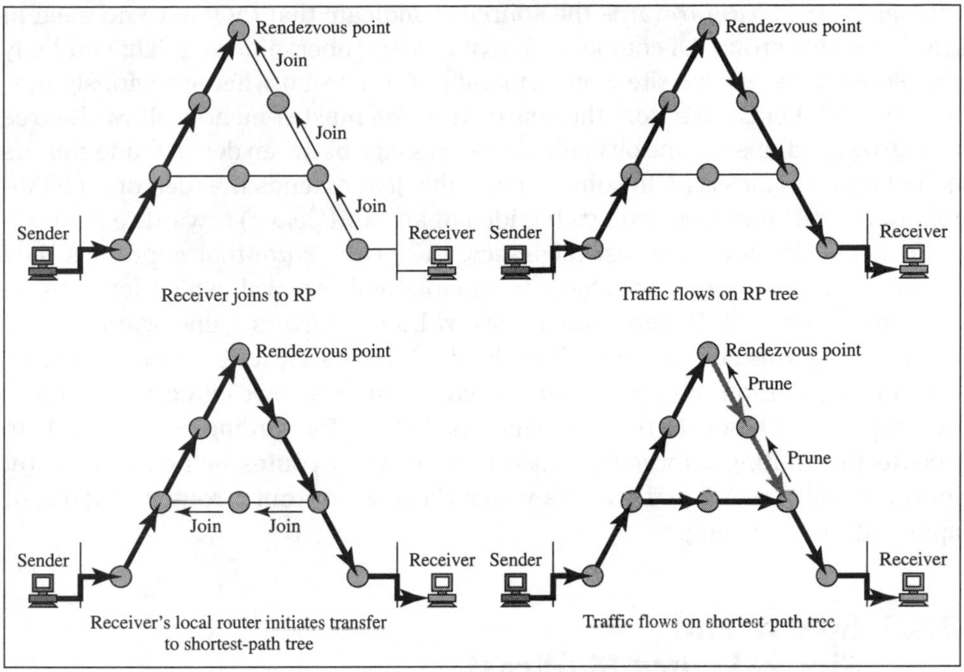

Figure 8.99 PIM SM.

(or in the worst case, all frames). In this case, the IP level maintains a list of active groups and rejects silently all other packets addressed to other groups. Of course, this represents a load on the host processor.

8.4.1 Dense Mode, Data-Driven Multicast Routing

The routers conspire to deliver packets to sites where there are members. In the simplest routing approach, not something used much nowadays, but illustrative of a neat idea, the path from sender to receivers is built in a *data-driven* manner. As soon as someone sends an IP multicast destined packet, the routers deliver it out all interfaces except the shortest path back towards the sender (i.e., the interface it came in, although an RPF check can be performed to elimate loops for packets that traverse a network while the routing is settling down after a change). In this approach, the packets would flood everywhere in the Internet, which is pretty big nowadays. If there were more than a very modest number of multicast data sources, this would be a very bad idea indeed. Thus the multicast scheme described here then employs another trick: networks with no group members are *pruned* from the tree. Routers with no site members send routing messages *up-stream* towards the source to indicate that they have no need of traffic for this group. Of course, with dynamic membership, we might suddenly find someone at such a site gains a member for a group where previously they had pruned themselves from the source tree. We must somehow allow the tree to regrow, and this is done by using a new message between dense mode routers called a *prune* message. In some senses, this just extends the idea of an IGMP join (as a graft message extends the idea of an IGMP leave) towards a source.

To keep life safe from lost messages, the *prune state* that supresses data distribution is periodically subject to timeout and removal, which leads to re-flooding of the data. Downstream nodes without receivers prune again.

Of course, this scheme doesn't scale at all. However, it illustrates the basic idea of distribution trees and state management. It also resulted in a modest, but important change to routing, which is that the forwarding engine needs to update the routing information base as a result of routes being installed (at least for multicast) data driven, as well as because of router-router updates, or applications signalling.

8.4.2 Sparse and Single-Source Multicast

The now widely used alternatives to dense-mode multicast are sparse mode and single source. These both leverage off the idea of an explicit graft message flowing from downstream nodes to join a tree up towards a distribution point, known as the rendezvous point (RP). In the latter case, the rendezvous point is at the source (i.e., single-only) source itself. In both cases the data-driven nature of flooding and pruning is avoided entirely, but the distribution trees may be suboptimal—switching from an RP to a source-based tree is a configuration option once the rendezvous with a receiver has been made.

8.5 QoS Routing

Traditional routing involves selection by destination address only. This means that it is hard to load balance or provide sensible choices of path or route to accord with non-default performance requirements. Traditional routers have one optimal path to destination, and the routing metrics are single values. For QoS routing, multiple paths would be possible, and alternative paths would have different QoS properties. Routing updates need to include QoS parameter information, and the route selection must use destination address, source address, ToS, and so on. The whole integrated services system, and to a lesser extent differentiated services, require some way to inform routers about these extra requirements.

Note that data-driven route update leads to a kernel-to-user signal or upcall requirement.

8.6 Routing Table Construction

Currently, there is no standard open source user space routing protocol for Linux. There are a number of projects that have produced routing protocol daemons that are widely used. The most prominent full-specification system is the GateD package from Merit.

8.6.1 GateD

GateD is a large system that implements a significant fraction of the Internet routing protocol suite. Currently, it consists of three main pieces, comprising a core set of common code, a routing database system, and a collection of protocol modules that implement the following standards:

- RIPv1 and RIPv2—RIP is the Routing Information Protocol. It is a distance vector protocol. RIPv2 incorporates masks in the routing updates, and so can support classless interdomain routing properly. It is useful mainly in small site networks.
- OSPFv1 and OSPv2—OSPF is the Open Shortest Path First routing protocol. This is a full, industrial, strength, hierarchical link-state routing system, and scales quite well to large corporate intranets, or modest-sized ISPs.
- IS-IS—IS-IS is the Intermediate System-Intermedia System protocol, derived from DECnet routing, and then, via the International Organization for Standardization (ISO), introduced into the IETF as a multiprotocol link-state hierarchical routing protocol. It has very similar properties to OSPF, although how it is defined (the packet headers) is a little more general. Some operators claim it scales a little better. Others disagree. It is probably a matter of implementation detail (the devil is always in the details).
- EGPv2—EGP is the Exterior Gateway Protocol, the original interdomain reachability mechanism in the 1980s.
- BGP2, BGP3, BGP4, and BGP+—BGP4 is the state-of-the-art Border Gateway Protocol that supports a path vector routing algorithm, and allows ISPs to claim which destination they advertise as reachable across their border (whether for ingress, egress, or transit). It provides unilateral and bilateral policy control, but not multilateral control. A path

vector algorithm is like a distance vector algorithm with the entire path spelled out in the update rather than merely listing the destination and a single metric. The BGP3-to-BGP4 evolution included the update to provide Classless Inter-Domain Routing (CIDR).

- DVMRP—DVMRP is the Distance Vector Multicast Routing Protocol, now largely a historic milestone in the evolution of multicast. It is a dense mode (flood and prune) mechanism, and so is rather a dangerous beast to let loose outside of a small site network. In fact, its probably fairly dangerous anywhere except on a broadcast medium subnet.
- PIM, MSDP—PIM is the Protocol Independent Multicast routing protocol. It provides dense mode, sparse mode, and single-source multicast routing. PIM DM (dense mode) is like DVMRP, but without its own unicast routing computation to derive the reverse paths from. Instead, it depends on the existence of unicast routing in some other form, and uses some API to extract the reverse paths from the RIB or FIB. PIM SM (sparse mode) is similar, but oriented around a rendezvous point, as described earlier in this chapter.

  MSDP is the Multicast Source Distribution Protocol, which is the nearest thing we have to a multicast interdomain routing protocol right now. It distributed between designated routers in a domain, the existence (liveliness) of a source in one domain, for receivers in another. It does not have good scaling properties.
- RIPv6—RIPv6 is RIP re-engineered to support the larger address space and address allocation schemes in IPv6.
- ICMP and IGMP—GateD supports ICMP and IGMP, but then if it runs on a Linux box, these are native to the kernel in any case.

GateD (Gateway Daemon) was implemented at a time when the U.S. federal agency, the National Science Foundation, funded and operated a U.S. continent-wide research and education network as part of the Internet. At that time, state-of-the art routers did not really support the line speeds or full range of protocols needed for such a complex system, so it was necessary for the agency to commission its own. GateD is *not* part of the open source world, and as such, we will not discuss it in great detail here. However, it is fairly comprehensive, and has been used as the basis for further development by a number of folks, so is worth of attention. It runs on most common platforms including Linux.

A similar package called Zebra is also available—this supports BGP4 protocol as described in RFC 1771, as well as RIPv1, RIPv2 and OSPFv2. While previously under the GPL, at the time of writing, the status of this system was unclear.

There are a number of good books on IP routing which we refer the reader to [15] for details.

8.6.2 Route Control and Traffic Control Maintenance

A routing protocol on Linux runs in user space. In some senses it is an application that makes use of a transport protocol (UDP for some routing protocols, TCP for others, e.g., BGP) to exchange messages with peers.[1]

However, the fortunate side-effect of a routing protocol is to compute a forwarding information base (FIB) from the routing information base (RIB) that it gleans from its exchanges with its peers.

As far as the interface between the routing daemon and other routing remote peer daemons, normal socket programming is just fine. Whether the daemon is multithreaded or not is of no interest here.

Management tools such as routing daemons need a control channel to access the forwarding information base. This channel is also needed for traffic control tools to be able to configure packet classifiers for customizing forwarding treatments, as discussed in the next chapter, as well as for setting up filters for security and access control, as discussed in Chapter 10.

Let's review communication between user space and the kernel. In Chapter 1 we had a look at how system calls allow user processes to use kernel services. However, the kernel is really a conduit through which the user process accesses an external resource (filesystems, communications with other computers, input/output to the user, and so on).

What is different here is that Linux does not use a simple map of the kernel memory the way that other UNIX systems have done. While it does provide a `/proc` file system, which is a lot more convenient than earlier schemes such as reading `/dev/kmem`, there is a requirement for a *protocol* to communicate in both directions between the kernel and user space. The scheme is part of a history starting with a mechanism called `cmsg`, which allows applications to look at ancillary data associated with a packet or a socket, but which are not from parts of the socket payload. For example, the normal socket interface (as described in Chapters 4 and 9) does not allow access to the TTL field of the IP header of an inbound packet, yet for some applications this is important, or at least useful. Subsequent to this, a more general mechanism called `netlink` was developed, which allows a new type of socket, `PF_NETLINK`, to be created for communication between application spaces (e.g., a routing daemon such as *GateD*) and kernel space. This provides an unreliable message protocol, on top of which a particular application must build its own level of reliability (and flow and resource control). It also has the beginnings of support for callbacks. Finally, the current interface is `rtnetlink`.

[1]In fact, routing protocols are the best example of a peer-to-peer application. Almost all other applications, until the recent emergence of gnutella, have been client-server based. Routing is the most inherently fundamentally distributed application.

rtnetlink API

All `rtnetlink` messages consist of a netlink message header and appended attributes. There is a set of convenient macros for accessing the attributes.

```
rtnetlink_socket =
        socket(PF_NETLINK,  int  socket_type, NETLINK_ROUTE);

       int RTA_OK(struct rtattr *rta, int rtabuflen);
       void *RTA_DATA(struct rtattr *rta);
       unsigned int RTA_PAYLOAD(struct rtattr *rta);
       struct rtattr *RTA_NEXT(struct rtattr *rta,  unsigned  int
       rtabuflen);
       unsigned int RTA_LENGTH(unsigned int length);
       unsigned int RTA_SPACE(unsigned int length);
```

Here is an example of the use of creating a `rtnetlink` message to set an MTU of a device:

```
 struct {
struct nlmsghdr nh;
struct ifinfomsg   if;
char           attrbuf[512];
 } req;

 struct rtattr *rta;
 unsigned int mtu = 1000;
 int rtnetlink_sk = socket(PF_NETLINK, SOCK_DGRAM, NETLINK_ROUTE);
 memset(&req, 0, sizeof(req));
 req.nh.nlmsg_len = NLMSG_LENGTH(sizeof(struct ifinfomsg));
 req.nh.nlmsg_flags = NLM_F_REQUEST;
 req.nh.nlmsg_type = RTML_NEWLINK;
 req.if.ifi_family = AF_UNSPEC;
 req.if.ifi_index = INTERFACE_INDEX;
 req.if.ifi_change = 0xffffffff; /* ???*/
 rta = (struct rtattr *)(((char *) &req) + NLMSG_ALIGN(n->nlmsg_len));
 rta->rta_type = IFLA_MTU;
 rta->rta_len = sizeof(unsigned int);
 req.n.nlmsg_len = NLMSG_ALIGN(req.n.nlmsg_len) + RTA_LENGTH(sizeof(mtu));
 memcpy(RTA_DATA(rta), &mtu, sizeof (mtu));
 send(rtnetlink_sk, &req, req.n.nlmsg_len);
```

Some `rtnetlink` messages have optional attributes after the initial header:

```
struct rtattr
{
    unsigned short rta_len;      /* Length of option */
    unsigned short rta_type;     /* Type of option */
    /* Data follows */
};
```

These attributes should be only manipulated using the `RTA_*` macros or libnetlink. Here are all the message types:

`RTM_NEWLINK`, `RTM_DELLINK`, `RTM_GETLINK`. Create, remove, or get information about a specific network interface.

`RTM_NEWADDR`, `RTM_DELADDR`, `RTM_GETADDR`. Add, remove, or receive information about an IP address associated with an interface.

`RTM_NEWROUTE`, `RTM_DELROUTE`, `RTM_GETROUTE`. Create, remove, or receive information about a network route.

`RTM_NEWNEIGH`, `RTM_DELNEIGH`, `RTM_GETNEIGH`. Add, remove, or receive information about a neighbor table entry.

`RTM_NEWRULE`, `RTM_DELRULE`, `RTM_GETRULE`. Add, delete, or retrieve a routing rule.

`RTM_NEWQDISC`, `RTM_DELQDISC`, `RTM_GETQDISC`. Add, remove, or get a queuing discipline.

`RTM_NEWTCLASS`, `RTM_DELTCLASS`, `RTM_GETTCLASS`. Add, remove, or get a traffic class.

`RTM_NEWTFILTER`, `RTM_DELTFILTER`, `RTM_GETTFILTER`. Add, remove, or receive information about a traffic filter.

The Code That Handles RTNetlink Calls

Figure 8.100 The route interface i: `linux/include/net/route.h`.

```

#define RTO_ONLINK      0x01
#define RTO_TPROXY      0x80000000

#define RTO_CONN        0

struct rt_key
{
        __u32                   dst;
        __u32                   src;
        int                     iif;
        int                     oif;
#ifdef CONFIG_IP_ROUTE_FWMARK
        __u32                   fwmark;
#endif
        __u8                    tos;
        __u8                    scope;
};

struct inet_peer;
```

Figure 8.101 The route interface ii: `linux/include/net/route.h`.

```
56   struct rtable
57   {
58          union
59          {
60                  struct dst_entry      dst;
61                  struct rtable         *rt_next;
62          } u;
63
64          unsigned              rt_flags;
65          unsigned              rt_type;
66
67          __u32                 rt_dst; /* Path destination */
68          __u32                 rt_src; /* Path source      */
69          int                   rt_iif;
70
71          /* Info on neighbour */
72          __u32                 rt_gateway;
73
74          /* Cache lookup keys */
75          struct rt_key         key;
76
77          /* Miscellaneous cached information */
78          __u32                 rt_spec_dst; /* RFC1122 specific destination */
79          struct inet_peer      *peer; /* long-living peer info */
80
81   #ifdef CONFIG_IP_ROUTE_NAT
82          __u32                 rt_src_map;
83          __u32                 rt_dst_map;
84   #endif
85   };
```

Figure 8.102 The route interface iii: `linux/include/net/route.h`.

```
87   struct ip_rt_acct
88   {
89          __u32  o_bytes;
90          __u32  o_packets;
91          __u32  i_bytes;
92          __u32  i_packets;
93   };
94
95   extern struct ip_rt_acct *ip_rt_acct;
96
97   struct in_device;
98   extern void          ip_rt_init(void);
99   extern void          ip_rt_redirect(u32 old_gw, u32 dst, u32 new_gw,
100                                u32 src, u8 tos, struct net_device *dev);
101  extern void          ip_rt_advice(struct rtable **rp, int advice);
102  extern void          rt_cache_flush(int how);
103  extern int           ip_route_output_key(struct rtable **, const struct rt_key *key);
104  extern int           ip_route_input(struct sk_buff*, u32 dst, u32 src, u8 tos, struct net_device
                                 *devin);
```

```
extern unsigned short ip_rt_frag_needed(struct iphdr *iph, unsigned short new_mtu);
extern void           ip_rt_update_pmtu(struct dst_entry *dst, unsigned mtu);
extern void           ip_rt_send_redirect(struct sk_buff *skb);

extern unsigned       inet_addr_type(u32 addr);
extern void           ip_rt_multicast_event(struct in_device *);
extern int            ip_rt_ioctl(unsigned int cmd, void *arg);
extern void           ip_rt_get_source(u8 *src, struct rtable *rt);
extern int            ip_rt_dump(struct sk_buff *skb, struct netlink_callback *cb);

/* Deprecated: use ip_route_output_key directly */
```

Figure 8.103 Basic route maintenance: `linux/net/ipv4/route.c`.

```
#define IP_MAX_MTU    0xFFF0

#define RT_GC_TIMEOUT (300*HZ)

int ip_rt_min_delay = 2*HZ;
int ip_rt_max_delay = 10*HZ;
int ip_rt_max_size;
int ip_rt_gc_timeout = RT_GC_TIMEOUT;
int ip_rt_gc_interval = 60*HZ;
int ip_rt_gc_min_interval = 5*HZ;
int ip_rt_redirect_number = 9;
int ip_rt_redirect_load = HZ/50;
int ip_rt_redirect_silence = ((HZ/50) << (9+1));
int ip_rt_error_cost = HZ;
int ip_rt_error_burst = 5*HZ;
int ip_rt_gc_elasticity = 8;
int ip_rt_mtu_expires = 10*60*HZ;
int ip_rt_min_pmtu = 512+20+20;
int ip_rt_min_advmss = 536;

static unsigned long rt_deadline;

#define RTprint(a...) printk(KERN_DEBUG a)

static struct timer_list rt_flush_timer;
static struct timer_list rt_periodic_timer;

/*
 *      Interface to generic destination cache.
 */

static struct dst_entry * ipv4_dst_check(struct dst_entry * dst, u32);
static struct dst_entry * ipv4_dst_reroute(struct dst_entry * dst,
                                           struct sk_buff *);
static void               ipv4_dst_destroy(struct dst_entry * dst);
static struct dst_entry * ipv4_negative_advice(struct dst_entry *);
static void               ipv4_link_failure(struct sk_buff *skb);
static int rt_garbage_collect(void);
```

Figure 8.104 Basic route maintenance ops: `linux/net/ipv4/route.c`.

```
struct dst_ops ipv4_dst_ops =
{
        AF_INET,
        __constant_htons(ETH_P_IP),
        0,

        rt_garbage_collect,
        ipv4_dst_check,
        ipv4_dst_reroute,
        ipv4_dst_destroy,
        ipv4_negative_advice,
        ipv4_link_failure,
        sizeof(struct rtable),
};

#ifdef CONFIG_INET_ECN
#define ECN_OR_COST(class)   TC_PRIO_##class
#else
#define ECN_OR_COST(class)   TC_PRIO_FILLER
#endif

__u8 ip_tos2prio[16] = {
        TC_PRIO_BESTEFFORT,
        ECN_OR_COST(FILLER),
        TC_PRIO_BESTEFFORT,
        ECN_OR_COST(BESTEFFORT),
        TC_PRIO_BULK,
        ECN_OR_COST(BULK),
        TC_PRIO_BULK,
        ECN_OR_COST(BULK),
        TC_PRIO_INTERACTIVE,
        ECN_OR_COST(INTERACTIVE),
        TC_PRIO_INTERACTIVE,
        ECN_OR_COST(INTERACTIVE),
        TC_PRIO_INTERACTIVE_BULK,
        ECN_OR_COST(INTERACTIVE_BULK),
        TC_PRIO_INTERACTIVE_BULK,
        ECN_OR_COST(INTERACTIVE_BULK)
};
```

Figure 8.105 API for route maintenance: `linux/net/core/rtnetlink.c`.

```
DECLARE_MUTEX(rtnl_sem);

void rtnl_lock(void)
{
        rtnl_shlock();
        rtnl_exlock();
}

void rtnl_unlock(void)
```

```
62  {
63          rtnl_exunlock();
64          rtnl_shunlock();
65  }
```

8.7 Host Routing

A Linux end system host needs to choose a route over which to send packets, but we do not really wish to incur the whole lookup overhead that is associated with the complex control for a full-blown router. Thus there is another level API to the routing system that keeps a cache of recently used routes—this would not be efficient for a forwarding engine unless its workload showed remarkable locality of reference, but is likely to work well for client and server machines where the length, number, and locality of flows means that many packets will hit the cache. The cache is maintained in the kernel and linked to and from the socket structure (as described in Chapter 5). It is looked up by a simple hash key, which is matched in the table itself.

Figure 8.106 The route API hash key: `linux/include/net/route.h`.

```
42  struct rt_key
43  {
44          __u32               dst;
45          __u32               src;
46          int                 iif;
47          int                 oif;
48  #ifdef CONFIG_IP_ROUTE_FWMARK
49          __u32               fwmark;
50  #endif
51          __u8                tos;
52          __u8                scope;
53  };
```

The table is as shown in the following figures.

Figure 8.107 The route API table: `linux/include/net/route.h`.

```
56  struct rtable
57  {
58          union
59          {
60                  struct dst_entry    dst;
61                  struct rtable       *rt_next;
62          } u;
63
```

```
        unsigned                rt_flags;
        unsigned                rt_type;

        __u32                   rt_dst; /* Path destination  */
        __u32                   rt_src; /* Path source       */
        int                     rt_iif;

        /* Info on neighbour */
        __u32                   rt_gateway;

        /* Cache lookup keys */
        struct rt_key           key;

        /* Miscellaneous cached information */
        __u32                   rt_spec_dst; /* RFC1122 specific destination */
        struct inet_peer        *peer; /* long-living peer info */

#ifdef CONFIG_IP_ROUTE_NAT
        __u32                   rt_src_map;
        __u32                   rt_dst_map;
#endif
};
```

Figure 8.108 Route output lookup: `linux/net/ipv4/route.c`.

```
int ip_route_output_key(struct rtable **rp, const struct rt_key *key)
{
        unsigned hash;
        struct rtable *rth;

        hash = rt_hash_code(key->dst, key->src^(key->oif<<5), key->tos);

        read_lock_bh(&rt_hash_table[hash].lock);
        for (rth=rt_hash_table[hash].chain; rth; rth=rth->u.rt_next) {
                if (rth->key.dst == key->dst &&
                    rth->key.src == key->src &&
                    rth->key.iif == 0 &&
                    rth->key.oif == key->oif &&
#ifdef CONFIG_IP_ROUTE_FWMARK
                    rth->key.fwmark == key->fwmark &&
#endif
                    !((rth->key.tos^key->tos)&(IPTOS_RT_MASK|RTO_ONLINK)) &&
                    ((key->tos&RTO_TPROXY) || !(rth->rt_flags&RTCF_TPROXY))
                ) {
                        rth->u.dst.lastuse = jiffies;
                        dst_hold(&rth->u.dst);
                        rth->u.dst.__use++;
                        read_unlock_bh(&rt_hash_table[hash].lock);
                        *rp = rth;
                        return 0;
                }
        }
```

```
1920            read_unlock_bh(&rt_hash_table[hash].lock);
1921
1922            return ip_route_output_slow(rp, key);
1923    }
```

Figure 8.109 Route lookup i: `linux/net/ipv4/route.c`.

```
1613    int ip_route_output_slow(struct rtable **rp, const struct rt_key *oldkey)
1614    {
1615            struct rt_key key;
1616            struct fib_result res;
1617            unsigned flags = 0;
1618            struct rtable *rth;
1619            struct net_device *dev_out = NULL;
1620            unsigned hash;
1621            int free_res = 0;
1622            int err;
1623            u32 tos;
1624
1625            tos = oldkey->tos & (IPTOS_RT_MASK|RTO_ONLINK);
1626            key.dst = oldkey->dst;
1627            key.src = oldkey->src;
1628            key.tos = tos&IPTOS_RT_MASK;
1629            key.iif = loopback_dev.ifindex;
1630            key.oif = oldkey->oif;
1631    #ifdef CONFIG_IP_ROUTE_FWMARK
1632            key.fwmark = oldkey->fwmark;
1633    #endif
1634            key.scope = (tos&RTO_ONLINK) ? RT_SCOPE_LINK : RT_SCOPE_UNIVERSE;
1635            res.fi = NULL;
1636    #ifdef CONFIG_IP_MULTIPLE_TABLES
1637            res.r = NULL;
1638    #endif
```

Figure 8.110 Route lookup ii—source case: `linux/net/ipv4/route.c`.

```
1640            if (oldkey->src) {
1641                    if (MULTICAST(oldkey->src)
1642                        || BADCLASS(oldkey->src)
1643                        || ZERONET(oldkey->src))
1644                            return -EINVAL;
1645
1646                    /* It is equivalent to inet_addr_type(saddr) == RTN_LOCAL */
1647                    dev_out = ip_dev_find(oldkey->src);
1648                    if (dev_out == NULL)
1649                            return -EINVAL;
1650
1651                    /* I removed check for oif == dev_out->oif here.
1652                       It was wrong by three reasons:
1653                       1. ip_dev_find(saddr) can return wrong iface, if saddr is
1654                          assigned to multiple interfaces.
```

```
                2. Moreover, we are allowed to send packets with saddr
                   of another iface. --ANK
              */

             if (oldkey->oif == 0
                 && (MULTICAST(oldkey->dst) || oldkey->dst == 0xFFFFFFFF)) {
                     /* Special hack: user can direct multicasts
                        and limited broadcast via necessary interface
                        without fiddling with IP_MULTICAST_IF or IP_PKTINFO.
                        This hack is not just for fun, it allows
                        vic,vat and friends to work.
                        They bind socket to loopback, set ttl to zero
                        and expect that it will work.
                        From the viewpoint of routing cache they are broken,
                        because we are not allowed to build multicast path
                        with loopback source addr (look, routing cache
                        cannot know, that ttl is zero, so that packet
                        will not leave this host and route is valid).
                        Luckily, this hack is good workaround.
                      */

                     key.oif = dev_out->ifindex;
                     goto make_route;
             }
             if (dev_out)
                     dev_put(dev_out);
             dev_out = NULL;
     }
```

Figure 8.111 Route lookup iii—oif case: `linux/net/ipv4/route.c`.

```
     if (oldkey->oif) {
             dev_out = dev_get_by_index(oldkey->oif);
             if (dev_out == NULL)
                     return -ENODEV;
             if (__in_dev_get(dev_out) == NULL) {
                     dev_put(dev_out);
                     return -ENODEV; /* Wrong error code */
             }

             if (LOCAL_MCAST(oldkey->dst) || oldkey->dst == 0xFFFFFFFF) {
                     if (!key.src)
                             key.src = inet_select_addr(dev_out, 0, RT_SCOPE_LINK);
                     goto make_route;
             }
             if (!key.src) {
                     if (MULTICAST(oldkey->dst))
                             key.src = inet_select_addr(dev_out, 0, key.scope);
                     else if (!oldkey->dst)
                             key.src = inet_select_addr(dev_out, 0, RT_SCOPE_HOST);
             }
     }
```

Figure 8.112 Route lookup—loopback case: `linux/net/ipv4/route.c`.

```
1705        if (!key.dst) {
1706                key.dst = key.src;
1707                if (!key.dst)
1708                        key.dst = key.src = htonl(INADDR_LOOPBACK);
1709                if (dev_out)
1710                        dev_put(dev_out);
1711                dev_out = &loopback_dev;
1712                dev_hold(dev_out);
1713                key.oif = loopback_dev.ifindex;
1714                res.type = RTN_LOCAL;
1715                flags |= RTCF_LOCAL;
1716                goto make_route;
1717        }
```

Figure 8.113 Route lookup—need a full FIB lookup: `linux/net/ipv4/route.c`.

```
1719        if (fib_lookup(&key, &res)) {
1720                res.fi = NULL;
1721                if (oldkey->oif) {
1722                        /* Apparently, routing tables are wrong. Assume,
1723                           that the destination is on link.
1724
1725                           WHY? DW.
1726                           Because we are allowed to send to iface
1727                           even if it has NO routes and NO assigned
1728                           addresses. When oif is specified, routing
1729                           tables are looked up with only one purpose:
1730                           to catch if destination is gatewayed, rather than
1731                           direct. Moreover, if MSG_DONTROUTE is set,
1732                           we send packet, ignoring both routing tables
1733                           and ifaddr state. --ANK
1734
1735
1736                           We could make it even if oif is unknown,
1737                           likely IPv6, but we do not.
1738                         */
1739
1740                        if (key.src == 0)
1741                                key.src = inet_select_addr(dev_out, 0, RT_SCOPE_LINK);
1742                        res.type = RTN_UNICAST;
1743                        goto make_route;
1744                }
1745                if (dev_out)
1746                        dev_put(dev_out);
1747                return -ENETUNREACH;
1748        }
```

Figure 8.114 Route lookup—corner cases: `linux/net/ipv4/route.c`.

```
        free_res = 1;

        if (res.type == RTN_NAT)
                goto e_inval;

        if (res.type == RTN_LOCAL) {
                if (!key.src)
                        key.src = key.dst;
                if (dev_out)
                        dev_put(dev_out);
                dev_out = &loopback_dev;
                dev_hold(dev_out);
                key.oif = dev_out->ifindex;
                if (res.fi)
                        fib_info_put(res.fi);
                res.fi = NULL;
                flags |= RTCF_LOCAL;
                goto make_route;
        }

#ifdef CONFIG_IP_ROUTE_MULTIPATH
        if (res.fi->fib_nhs > 1 && key.oif == 0)
                fib_select_multipath(&key, &res);
        else
#endif
        if (res.prefixlen==0 && res.type == RTN_UNICAST && key.oif == 0)
                fib_select_default(&key, &res);

        if (!key.src)
                key.src = FIB_RES_PREFSRC(res);

        if (dev_out)
                dev_put(dev_out);
        dev_out = FIB_RES_DEV(res);
        dev_hold(dev_out);
        key.oif = dev_out->ifindex;
```

Figure 8.115 Route lookup route request: `linux/net/ipv4/route.c`.

```
make_route:
        if (LOOPBACK(key.src) && !(dev_out->flags&IFF_LOOPBACK))
                goto e_inval;

        if (key.dst == 0xFFFFFFFF)
                res.type = RTN_BROADCAST;
        else if (MULTICAST(key.dst))
                res.type = RTN_MULTICAST;
        else if (BADCLASS(key.dst) || ZERONET(key.dst))
                goto e_inval;

```

```
	if (dev_out->flags&IFF_LOOPBACK)
		flags |= RTCF_LOCAL;

	if (res.type == RTN_BROADCAST) {
		flags |= RTCF_BROADCAST|RTCF_LOCAL;
		if (res.fi) {
			fib_info_put(res.fi);
			res.fi = NULL;
		}
	} else if (res.type == RTN_MULTICAST) {
		flags |= RTCF_MULTICAST|RTCF_LOCAL;
		read_lock(&inetdev_lock);
		if (!__in_dev_get(dev_out) || !ip_check_mc(__in_dev_get(dev_out), oldkey->dst))
			flags &= ~RTCF_LOCAL;
		read_unlock(&inetdev_lock);
		/* If multicast route do not exist use
		   default one, but do not gateway in this case.
		   Yes, it is hack.
		 */
		if (res.fi && res.prefixlen < 4) {
			fib_info_put(res.fi);
			res.fi = NULL;
		}
	}

	rth = dst_alloc(&ipv4_dst_ops);
	if (!rth)
		goto e_nobufs;

	atomic_set(&rth->u.dst.__refcnt, 1);
	rth->u.dst.flags= DST_HOST;
	rth->key.dst	= oldkey->dst;
	rth->key.tos	= tos;
	rth->key.src	= oldkey->src;
	rth->key.iif	= 0;
	rth->key.oif	= oldkey->oif;
```

Figure 8.116 Route lookup route request—tidy up refs (put): linux/net/ipv4/route.c.

```
#ifdef CONFIG_IP_ROUTE_FWMARK
	rth->key.fwmark = oldkey->fwmark;
#endif
	rth->rt_dst	= key.dst;
	rth->rt_src	= key.src;
#ifdef CONFIG_IP_ROUTE_NAT
	rth->rt_dst_map = key.dst;
	rth->rt_src_map = key.src;
#endif
	rth->rt_iif	= oldkey->oif ? : dev_out->ifindex;
	rth->u.dst.dev = dev_out;
	dev_hold(dev_out);
	rth->rt_gateway = key.dst;
```

```
1846          rth->rt_spec_dst= key.src;
1847
1848          rth->u.dst.output=ip_output;
1849
1850          if (flags&RTCF_LOCAL) {
1851                  rth->u.dst.input = ip_local_deliver;
1852                  rth->rt_spec_dst = key.dst;
1853          }
```

Figure 8.117 Route lookup route request—tidy up refs (put): linux/net/ipv4/route.c.

```
1854          if (flags&(RTCF_BROADCAST|RTCF_MULTICAST)) {
1855                  rth->rt_spec_dst = key.src;
1856                  if (flags&RTCF_LOCAL && !(dev_out->flags&IFF_LOOPBACK))
1857                          rth->u.dst.output = ip_mc_output;
1858  #ifdef CONFIG_IP_MROUTE
1859                  if (res.type == RTN_MULTICAST) {
1860                          struct in_device *in_dev = in_dev_get(dev_out);
1861                          if (in_dev) {
1862                                  if (IN_DEV_MFORWARD(in_dev) && !LOCAL_MCAST(oldkey->dst)) {
1863                                          rth->u.dst.input = ip_mr_input;
1864                                          rth->u.dst.output = ip_mc_output;
1865                                  }
1866                                  in_dev_put(in_dev);
1867                          }
1868                  }
1869  #endif
1870          }
1871
1872          rt_set_nexthop(rth, &res, 0);
1873
1874          rth->rt_flags = flags;
1875
1876          hash = rt_hash_code(oldkey->dst, oldkey->src^(oldkey->oif<<5), tos);
1877          err = rt_intern_hash(hash, rth, rp);
1878  done:
1879          if (free_res)
1880                  fib_res_put(&res);
1881          if (dev_out)
1882                  dev_put(dev_out);
1883          return err;
1884
1885  e_inval:
1886          err = -EINVAL;
1887          goto done;
1888  e_nobufs:
1889          err = -ENOBUFS;
1890          goto done;
1891  }
```

8.8 Managing IP-Level State Information—the IP Command

From user space, the ip command acts to glue all the rtnetlink API calls together into a single application for manual configuration or access to statistics. For those familiar with BSD-like UNIX, this command incorporates the combined functionality of the ifconfig, route, netstat, arp and other applications. Many of the things managed by this command have been covered in Chapter 6.

The command is well documented in the system releases, so we just summarize its capabilities here.

```
ip [ Options ] Object [ Command ] [ Arguments ]]
```

Options. -V, -s, -f, -r, for version, statistics, family (inet, inet6, or link), and use DNS instead of IP addresses.

Object. This is what we are trying to manage—each corresponds roughly to a separate command on other systems, with the exception of firewalls and traffic control, which are managed through separate commands that we discuss in Chapter 9 and Chapter 10 respectively. This can be *link*, *address*, *neighbor*, *route*, *multicast address*, *multicast route*, or *tunnel*.

Command. Takes some action on the object named, typically, add, delete, set, show, or some other object-specific command.

Now we look at these in more detail:

link. Basically manage link device level information.

For example, `ip link set { dev <name> | [up|down] | arp [on|off] | multicast [on|off] | dynamic [on|off] | txqlen <n> | mtu <n> | address <link address> | broadcast link broadcast address> } or ip link show`

The latter command can produce a lot of output, for example:

```
1: lo: <LOOPBACK,UP> mtu 3856 qdisc noqueue
    link/loopback 00:00:00:00:00:00 brd 00:00:00:00:00:00
2: eth0: <BROADCAST,MULTICAST,UP> mtu 1500 qdisc pfifo_fast qlen 100
    link/ether 00:c0:4f:d3:db:c3 brd ff:ff:ff:ff:ff:ff
3: tap0: <BROADCAST,MULTICAST,NOARP> mtu 1500 qdisc noqueue
    link/ether fe:fd:00:00:00:00 brd ff:ff:ff:ff:ff:ff
4: teql0: <NOARP> mtu 1500 qdisc noop qlen 100
    link/void
5: dummy0: <BROADCAST,NOARP> mtu 1500 qdisc noop
    link/ether 00:00:00:00:00:00 brd ff:ff:ff:ff:ff:ff
6: bond0: <BROADCAST,MULTICAST,MASTER> mtu 1500 qdisc noqueue
    link/ether 00:00:00:00:00:00 brd ff:ff:ff:ff:ff:ff
```

```
7: eql: <MASTER> mtu 576 qdisc noop qlen 5
    link/slip
8: tunl0@NONE: <NOARP> mtu 1480 qdisc noop
    link/ipip 0.0.0.0 brd 0.0.0.0
9: gre0@NONE: <NOARP> mtu 1476 qdisc noop
    link/gre 0.0.0.0 brd 0.0.0.0
10: sit0@NONE: <NOARP> mtu 1480 qdisc noop
    link/sit 0.0.0.0 brd 0.0.0.0
```

The output shows the interface name and index, the device link operation mode (e.g., LOOPBACK, BROADCAST, MULTICAST) and status, the maximum transfer unit size in the operation, the queuing discipline in use (if any, with queue length configured), the MAC address type, value, and broadcast value, and so on.

Another example of this is if we run `ip-s link show eth0` on the machine above:

```
2: eth0: <BROADCAST,MULTICAST,UP> mtu 1500 qdisc pfifo_fast qlen 100
    link/ether 00:c0:4f:d3:db:c3 brd ff:ff:ff:ff:ff:ff
    RX: bytes  packets  errors  dropped overrun mcast
    2805243643 31255469 28      0       28      0
    TX: bytes  packets  errors  dropped carrier collsns
    1423998005 15674317 0       0       1       815994
```

Here we can see the packet level statistics seen by the devive. This shows link level specific properties, too, such as collisions, overruns, and carrier-lost counts. For Ethernets and for a SLIP interface this would also show compressed packets.

address. Configure or list address(es) of an interface/device.

This can be used as `ip address add { [dev <name>| local <address>] | peer <address> [default] | broadcast <address>| label <name> | scope <scope value>] }`

Here the only new value is `scope`, which can be `global, site, link or host.`

neighbor. Setup or examine an ARP entry or neighbor discovery cache information.

For example, `ip neighbor add {to <address> | dev <name> | nud <state> }`. Here the only non-obvious parameter is `nud`, which refers to a "neighbor unreachable detection" and allows you to configure the way in which the system decides (or doesn't decide) a neighbor has become unreachable.

route. Look at or add routing entries.

Here we can set route attributes and types as well as just configuring entries. Types of routes include `unicast, unreachable, blackhole,` `prohibit, local, broadcast, throw, nat, anycast`, and `multicast`. NAT is explained in Chapter 10.

```
ip route add {to <prefix>| to <type> <prefix> | tos <TOS> | <dsfield TOS> |
metric <n> | preference <n> | table <table id> | dev <name> | via <address>
| src <address> | realm <realm id> | mtu <n> | window <n> | rtt <n> | rttvar
<n> | ssthresh <n> | cwnd <n> | advmss <n> | nexthop <next hop> | scope
<scope val> | protocol <rtproto> | onlink | equalize }
```

The only new things here are `rtproto`, which describes whether a route is acquired by redirect, from kernel autoconfiguration, at boot time, through static addition, or by router discovery, and the multipath parameter, `equalization`.

maddress. Manage multicast addresses.

mroute. Manage multicast routing cache entities. These two are similar to the unicast address and route management command options.

tunnel. Manage tunnel entries.

rule. Manage tunnel entries. These last two are covered in more detail in Chapter 10.

8.9 Summary

In this chapter, we have looked at routing and the forwarding lookup support needed in a modern sysem, for fast packet processing. We will see later on that there are other ways in which packet headers need to be matched. In particular, in Chapter 10, we take a look at firewall protection, where filters can be defined to exclude (or exclusively include) packets of certain patterns.

In the next chapter, we look at another part of the forwarding process, that of providing specified performance (*treatments*) to different packet flows.

CHAPTER 9

Forwarding

"Sometimes in order to be correct an implementation must meet certain performance constraints."

—Radia Perlman, 1998

9.1 Roadmap

This chapter is about how traffic is controlled in the Internet. The key concept associated with Internet traffic is the idea of a *flow*. A flow is a sequence of packets from a source or related set of sources to a receiver or set of receivers. The simplest instance of a flow is a single TCP connection. A more complex flow might be a virtual private network, which might be implemented as a collection of paths from a collection of sites requiring some overall resources (minimum rate) but no specific treatment for any particular packet or TCP connection.

There are three main models for traffic management in general:

End-to-end. End-to-end traffic management is either adaptive or nonadaptive—adaptive applications and users employ congestion avoidance, as implemented by TCP, for example, as described in Chapter 7. TCP reacts to congestion signals from packet loss, or from explicit congestion notification. These signals are generated by routers through queue management procedures that we look at in this chapter.

Nonadaptive applications and users simply send what they have when they have it—usually video, audio, and gaming applications are nonadaptive, and employ UDP (usually with RTP above it) to carry packets. These applications require some type of network path that is engineered for their requirements. This can be done by provisioning the path well enough when it is installed, or by some type of dynamic resource reservation near the time the path is needed. Resource reservation requires traffic to be given some type of preferential scheduling in routers. We'll look at this too in this chapter. Resource reservation is carried out using some type of signaling protocol such as RSVP, or else is done out-of-band by phone call, fax, or email to the network provider who then uses network management to configure routers along the relevant path or paths. This installs *state* in these routers associated with the sources and destinations requiring this preferential treatment.

Edge-to-edge. It is currently common for networks to have plenty of capacity in the core, but be limited in the access (dial-up and network access points). In this sort of situation it is possible to manage traffic in many places in the networks in large *aggregations*. This type of traffic management is called *differentiated services* and is the subject of much work in the Internet today. As discussed in the previous chapter, routers already aggregate table entries for the basic forwarding task. It is possible that preferential performance requirements for traffic for many sets of sources and sinks follow similar aggregation patterns, in which case the *state* associated with giving this traffic different scheduling and forwarding treatment can be kept in small tables. If this is not the case, and one needs this information for specific flows, then this is usually referred to as *integrated services*.

Hop-by-hop. The basic building block that implements different treatment for different flows is the actual forwarding treatment within a given hop or router. A router can apply a variety of different scheduling or queuing algorithms to a sequence of packets. The default schedule is FIFO, or *first in, first out*. The default queue management procedure is to drop packets that arrive at a full queue.

There are lots of ways the queues can be implemented. For example, routers can queue on input or output, or a hybrid mixture can occur. Most systems, Linux included, are output queued. There are other procedures required to monitor the queue occupancy, to decide what to do on overload, to mark or drop traffic that has behaved badly, to recondition a sequence of packets to reduce its burstiness (*shaping*), and to coordinate these actions with other routers to provide a consistent and fair service.

This chapter covers those preceding aspects of the forwarding treatments described currently in the Linux 2.4 kernel.

9.2 Introduction

The problem with vanilla IP is that it provides merely a best-effort service. When we say best effort, what we really mean is that the service offers no guarantees. The word best is misleading. In practice, a network path made out of arbitrary links and routers, with an arbitrary mix of traffic, has unpredictable performance. The available capacity (whether in bits per second, or packets per second) will vary packet by packet. The delay experienced at each hop, and end to end, will vary packet by packet. The chances of a packet being lost due to noise or congestion will vary moment by moment.

In practice, the situation is not that terrible. While the performance is unpredictable, most applications use TCP for end-to-end services, which provides reliability and carries out congestion avoidance and control, as described in Chapter 7. There are two main contributions to traffic variation, which will influence the network resources available to a given IP flow, and therefore the performance seen by a user: firstly, when TCP connections start, they expand the rate they send at fairly quickly; secondly, at some times of the day, there are a large number of connections starting (or finishing) at roughly the same time (e.g., start of day, or just after a new Web page is announced at a site or on a popular email list). Connection durations vary—most of the Internet traffic is normally Web downloads, and Web pages follow a Zipf distribution of page size. Having said that, we should allow for Web page popularity as well. Most of the time, there is a mix of shorter and longer TCP connections, known colloquially as *mice* and *elephants*, with the total number of connections varying relatively slowly. This means that traffic in the center of the network varies relatively slowly, unless there are correlated events. Actually characterizing the behavior of a mix of TCP flows is quite a large topic of research, and well outside the scope of this book. To make matters more complex, there are a number of applications emerging based on UDP that do not generally respond to congestion signals necessarily. If traffic from these grows, then best effort may become even less predictable.

Traditionally then, IP data transfer has followed the view that datagrams are strictly individual packets, with no relationship between one packet and the next. There was no recognition of flows; the fact that a sequence of packets with some fields constant might be recognized, or even externally classified and specified as belonging to some session or set of sessions that want consistent treatment and some kind of performance guarantees, was overlooked. In fact, the requirement for this sort of specification is present not only for reasons of performance, but also for security, as we will see in Chapter 10.

Thus the spirit of the connectionless network, with no signalling, was preserved for over two decades on the Internet. This enabled very simple-minded implementation of the forwarding task in a router, based on per-datagram forwarding, with extremely simple table lookups. We saw in the previous chapter that the sole basis for figuring out what to do with a packet is normally just the destination address of the packet. We also saw in Chapter 3 that the simplest way that a packet can be forwarded is to append the buffer to an output queue. In this scenario, there is no examination of the type of traffic. This means that there can be special treatment, or no priority traffic. Of course, in an underloaded network, as each packet is appended to a queue, the packet from the head of the queue is being transmitted, or has already been sent, so the variation in delay can be quite low. Also, the available capacity to a given flow is, by definition, more than adequate in an over-provisioned network—supply exceeds demand.

In practice, most links in the Internet are not over-provisioned. Some core networks may be, but simple economics mean that access links are always close to what is affordable. Even in wealthy parts of the world, given that we often provision links on quite long intervals (e.g., months or years) and demand keeps growing, it's likely that near the end of any provisioning period a link is overloaded. Dial-up and other slow links are always lower capacity than any modern computer system can transmit at. TCP sources will always attempt to fill up such links.

Another facet of the Internet that leads to unpredictable performance is also a result of a design strength. The Internet routing system is opportunistic. What this means is that almost as soon as a better route appears (perhaps because a new link is installed, or a broken one repaired), the routing system may alter the path taken by packets from source to destination, leading to a step up (or down) in performance, for example, in delay, throughput, or errors.

Dynamic routing changes occur reasonably frequently in today's Internet. Given that a typical route can only route packets for a given destination to a single next hop at any one time, this means that we do not see fixed paths. The consequence of this is that we also see no fixed quality of service (QoS). QoS is a much overused term—what we really mean is not quality, but quantitative performance guarantees, which may be absolute, or relative percentage of capacity, or delay, or may be expressed in terms of statistics (averages and chances of deviations).

As we imply above, the combination of source behavior (whether TCP- or UDP-based), the traffic patterns made by the collection of active sources and the destinations they talk to, and the dynamic routing behavior of the network, leads to the performance seen by any given flow being highly variable. At the level of a given hop, this is because the packets are being mixed together, after the routing decision has been made, into a single, first-in, first-out (FIFO) queue.

We can start bottom up to fix this by adding more sophisticated scheduling in the routers. Rather than FIFO queues, which offer a first come, first served (FCFS) model and no examination of the type of traffic, we could start to offer some differentiation in the way that we *treat* different packets belonging to different flows.

At the most intuitive level, we can think of the problem as being the lack of priority for traffic. When a link is busy, who gets to go next? Do packets form a simple *fair* queue behind each other, or do we think in terms of keeping some history about whose packets are whose, and make sure that flows get a fair share of a link? If we don't do this, some source sending packets twice as fast will get twice the chance at the link. Another consideration is that we may *wish* to give packets an advantage over others. If so, how do we mark packets to indicate priority?

Luckily, a field in the IP packet header was set aside early on for indicating the type of service. Although this was not widely used across the Internet in early implementations of host and router software, it is now seeing a new surge of interest.

From some users' perspective, the requirement is not to give priority or fair service simply to a single flow. It is often more immediately important to offer some service guarantees to aggregations of traffic. For example, an organization may need some minimum throughput for all the traffic from a particular source but to any destination, or all traffic to a particular destination but from any source, or both from and to specified sources and destinations.

The IP FIB holds data for figuring out where to send traffic next based only on the destination IP prefix, which is one form of aggregate. What other indication of aggregation might be useful? Over the last decade there have been many attempts to answer the following questions:

- Can we do better than best effort?
- What support do real-time flows need in the network?
- What support can we provide in the network?
- Are there alternatives to FCFS?

At the same time, the Internet community has also been adding facilities for mobility and many-to-many communication, which should not be excluded from enjoying any enhanced service models. To access these enhanced services, we need to consider end system application-level interfaces, remote access to router level support through in-band signaling, out-of-band signaling, or management. Above all, no new mechanism should threaten the scalability of the Internet too much to be worth offering. The other side of the QoS coin is that there must be incentives or pricing schemes for services that control use.

In practice, IP runs on links, and there are many different link-level technologies employed in the Internet. In their native form, these link-layer technologies offer a wide range of different capabilities in terms of performance guarantees. For example, a naked Ethernet LAN has non-deterministic delay. On the other hand, a point-to-point serial line has a well-known delay made from two components: the time to serialize a packet, and the propagation time for the packet over the distance the link traverses.

The Internet is inherently heterogeneous (aggresively so!). There is no common layer 2, thus there is no well-defined support for QoS without defining the mapping between any IP level mechanism and each and every link layer in use on any path that is to offer an enhanced service over best effort.

9.2.1 Integrated Services

One of the great debates in the Internet community has been about QoS requirements. It is certainly not well understood what users will use (and pay for). In the early days, the first steps towards enhanced services was the definition of the Integrated Services Packet Network (ISPN). Here a standard set of QoS service levels was defined, with detailed service type descriptions. The service interface includes a complex signalling protocol called RSVP, which we look at briefly later. This is out-of-band in the sense that it is sent separately from users' data packets. In telecom terms it is *in-band,* in that it travels down the same wires as the users' data, but it is additional to the users' data. Such a signalling protocol is assumed to be the interface to a network-level mechanism called *admission control.* Admission control is basically a decision function that uses the information from a signaled request, together with current and recent information about the conditions in the network, to compute whether the service requested can be satisfied. If so, the reservation, or *call,* is accepted or admitted; otherwise it will be rejected. In IP networks, if a reservation is rejected, this does not stop someone sending packets. It merely means that they will only be forwarded with best effort. If a reservation is accepted, then all the routers along a path must respect the new service level for the traffic—in other words, they all have to be able to recognize the traffic belonging to the reservation (call or flow—all the terms are interchangable). If the reservation needs preferential treatment, all the routers along the path need to apply the appropriate scheduling rules to packets from the flow, offering prioritization and differentiation of its traffic.

As we will see later in this chapter, Linux offers a very sophisticated choice of scheduling mechanisms to achieve this.

This a QoS service level is associated with quite a lot of additional functionality, including application flow description, traffic description, packet handling, as well as policing to make sure users or applications don't misuse their reservation.

The service interface for integrated services has a set of common procedures, data structures, and parameters, including a signalling protocol, the admission control function to check that a request can be honored, scheduling systems, and a packet classification to provide prioritization of traffic as well as queue management.

9.2.2 Admission Test for Integrated Services Guaranteed Service

$$d = \frac{b}{g} + (N-1)\frac{P_F}{g} + N\frac{P_N}{r} \tag{9.1}$$

One example of this requirement is illustrated in Figure 9.1, which plots the capacity needed for typical 64 Kbps PCM-coded voice calls packetized using RTP and a range of typical Internet line speeds, a delay bound as needed for interactive voice, and the over-allocation needed. Note the presence of hop count as part of the equation.

Table 9.1 Terms in the Parekh TCP Equation

d	worst-case delay
b	token bucket size
g	allocated rate
N	hopcount
P_F	this flow maximum packet size
P_N	network's maximum packet size
r	link speed

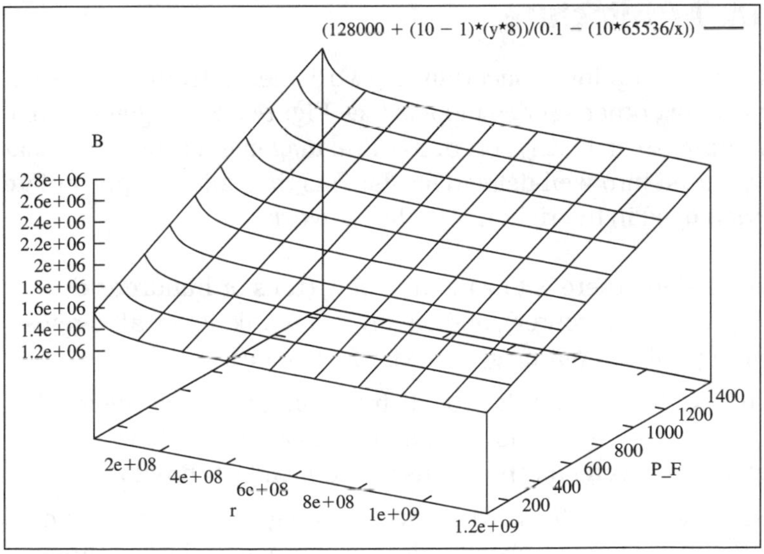

Figure 9.1 Guaranteed bounded delay and utilization.

The problems with this equation-based source specification are many and various. Some include the following:

Bucket rate. An application can choose to send at many different rates—audio, video, gaming, and data applications can all be configured to correspond loosely to some user-perceived quality. However, this correspondence has to be characterized for each and every application, and for a wide range of values of the data rate. As new coding and compression techniques emerge rapidly, this means that it is very hard for the user to choose a meaningful number here.

Burstiness. Just as the rate is hard to assess, the burstiness is even harder—this is also dependent on content as well as implementation.

Packet size. The packet size, and other parameters of note, are an artifact of the network design as well as host computer software. Why should the user be concerned with choosing or setting these?

One problem with this type of source model is that it is overspecified. Another more serious problem is that it appears to be oriented more towards optimizing for the network provider, not the user. Lastly, asking the user to state parameters including network-specific ones requires the provider to reveal internal factors about their network—this may undermine their competitive edge with other providers.

9.2.3 Network Architecture

There are quite a few assumptions concerning network hierarchy in the Internet standard work on adding other service models (see Figure 9.2). In general, one of the main assumptions to make any sort of traffic management tractable is that the network is organized into well-defined levels. This then allows appropriate techniques to be deployed in the right tier of the network.

Access network. Here, there is low multiplexing (tens or hundreds of flows at any given link or router), and on any given link, low traffic rates (compared to typical computing systems performance).

Distribution network. Here, ISPs provide interconnectivity at the local level, and traffic rates are medium. Again, there is a low level of multiplexing on any given link (hundreds or thousands of flows).

Core network backbone. This is where we see a high volume of traffic, and very high degrees of multiplexing. Here is where in today's Internet, we see systems approaching the limits of electronics (and pure hardware switching), let alone those of software systems.

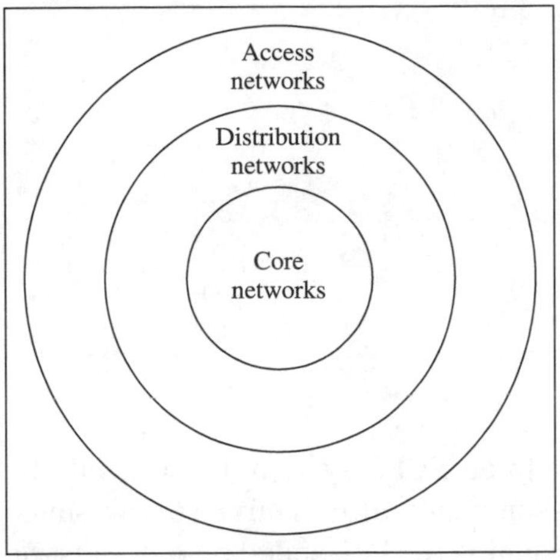

Figure 9.2 Network hierarchy.

Between these various tiers, we see administrative boundaries. Each tier is known as an *autonomous system* (AS). This simply means that it is managed irrespective of the management rules internal to the other systems. Typically, an AS makes its own choices of intradomain routing schemes, internal policies for security, and traffic engineering, including routing metrics and link preferences. Intradomain protocols might be RIPv2, OSPFv2, or ISIS.

Between these domains, we provide interconnection of ASs via interdomain routing. Here, interconnectivity information is exchanged (and constrained) using the Border Gateway Protocol (BGP).

When enhancing services over best effort, the hierarchy and structure of the network interconnect, differences in considerations at different levels, and intra- versus interdomain, all have to be understood and respected.

In general, resource reservation (sitting above, or *after* routing), and traffic engineering (sitting below, or *before* routing) are complex research topics.

9.3 Mixing Traffic onto the Wire

In a better-than-best-effort Internet, different applications will expect different performance. First we have to understand what different applications offer in terms of traffic (generation) profiles. This can be captured by looking at the packet-size distributions, and interdeparture times for packets from a source. We then need to understand how these timings should be reproduced at the far end so as to meet traffic timing constraints.

Routers that use FCFS queues have no knowledge of applications, and no knowledge of traffic patterns. If different traffic types share the same network path, we can see what occurs by considering three different applications, as illustrated in Figure 9.3.

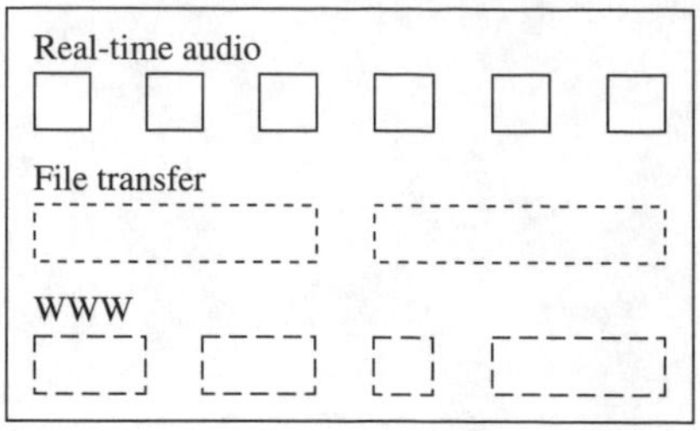

Figure 9.3 Mixing traffic onto one wire.

At the router, we see three input lines. In an FCFS system, these would be serviced round-robin at the router. Let's assume the traffic is mixed onto a single output line with a single output buffer. Assuming the line speed on output is the sum of input line speeds, we can see what happens to the traffic. The steady audio rate at the source ends up being severly disrupted by the variable rates and larger packet sizes of the other applications, even though the average rate of all the applications is respected. This is a scenario without any congestion. If there was any overload, we would also incur loss, which could be very bad for an audio application.

If we chose to consider different output line speeds, it would not affect the pattern of the relative spacing of packets—just the absolute spacing. At one extreme, the line speed could be so fast that the largest packet possible takes less time to serialize and transmit than the smallest packet on the input lines. In this case, the second (and other) audio packets would work ahead of where they should be.

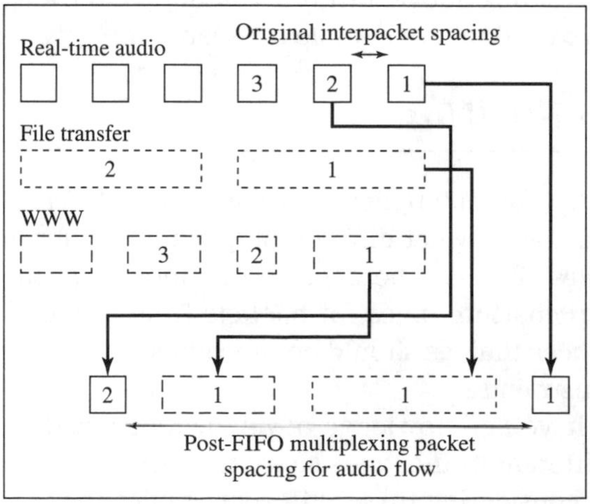

Figure 9.4 FIFO sharing.

In a full network, we need to consider these sorts of pictures, but with the overall traffic pattern. Different applications have different source models, and the receive side expects some similar arrival pattern. There is also the possibility that there are many uses of an application (some email users even expect near real-time turnaround of email responses, while some audio users do not mind long delays before audio response or playout).

The rules for traffic aggregation as you move through the tiers in the network hierarchy are not obvious. One might expect life to be easy if the network traffic follows the hierarchy. In other words, provided we see more multiplexing as we view the network from access towards the core, then perhaps the chances of disruption caused to one flow by others might decrease. However, it is very hard to model this. In fact, it is not at all obvious that this is right except in very simple, and from experience, rare circumstances. The Internet has a habit of forming hot spots that move with alarming frequency—this makes such assumptions frequently invalid.

9.3.1 Performance Parameters

We can take a top-down view of how to improve over best-effort service by thinking about user needs, instead of just router mechanisms. There are some obvious performance parameters we need to consider. Some of these are inputs to the performance decision process, others are results of it:

Packet sizes. A large packet size is good for general data, since it amortizes the packet header overhead (and packet handling overheads) efficiently over a lot of data. It is router-friendly, but leads to higher chances of slow down for real-time traffic.

On the other hand, a small packet size is good for real-time data since it entails less delay at the source (collecting audio or video samples, or text input), and lower hop-by-hop serialization times that lead to less end-to-end delay. For a given stream of flow, small packets also have a better tolerance to loss. They will possibly lead to less jitter. However, they are less efficient in terms of header overhead, and not router-friendly (in terms of input interrupts/packet processing time).

Delays. The end-to-end delay, the delay a user is concerned with, is made of several components: the propagation time (at the speed-of-light, or close to it); the transmission time, made from the data rate and the network elements' (router, switch) contributions, including buffering (queuing), processing, and so on, as well as pure end system processing, which will be application specific.

Delay bounds. Could an enhanced service include a possible delay bound? Well, there is no choice in the speed of light! Also, in today's Internet, paths are not known by the end user in advance, and are subject to change due to dynamic routing. The influence of other traffic and varying traffic patterns, including localized traffic and time-of-day effects, means that deterministic delay is often impractical, but not impossible.

Delay variation and end-to-end jitter. Variation in delay is the per-packet delay change. It can be contributed to by effects at the receiver, such as variable packet arrival rate and variable data rate for flow. For non-real-time applications, this does not represent a problem. For real-time applications, a receiving application may need jitter compensation.

Causes of jitter include media access (LAN and modem access delays for asymmetric codec lines) and FIFO queuing, where there is no notion of a flow. For traffic aggregation, a mix of different applications, the variation in load on routers due to localized load/congestion, and dynamic path changes can all lead to jitter.

Loss. End-to-end loss can be compensated for by non-real-time retransmission, for example, TCP. For real-time applications, it is possible to mask loss by using forward error correction and redundant encoding. This can also be achieved via media-specific fill-in at the receiver. If packet loss persists, this can often be taken as an indication of congestion. Many newer real-time applications are adaptive: they adjust flow construction and the resulting output rate according to a *TCP-rate-equivalent* formula, so that they look to a network provider like a smoothly varying TCP source.

Causes of loss include packet drop at routers due to short-, medium-, or long-term congestion, or traffic contract violations caused by misbehaving sources. More systemic, but less sinister, causes of problems can be source synchronization, excessive load due to failure in another part of the network, or simply abnormal traffic patterns, for example, new downloads.

Note that packet reordering, due to misbehavior of a load balancing scheme, misconfiguration of routers, or odd interactions between retransmission and rerouting, may be seen as loss by some receivers.

Throughput. Throughput is also often referred to as bandwidth—wrongly, but we're stuck with that.

The end-to-end data rate is subject to short-term changes, during the life-time of a flow over, say, seconds (on the order of round-trip times), as well as long-term changes during the course of a day on the order of hours.

This is partly a result of protocol behavior such as TCP congestion control and flow control, partly because of human reactions to perceived performance, and partly because of the normal daily patterns of life and Internet usage.

Changes to the data rate available on a path occur for several specific reasons. Different connectivity may become available, the dynamic routing system may then choose different paths, and it may even do so in response to router-based measurements of loss and/or delay.

9.3.2 Probing or Measurement-Based Admission Control?

Can we use probes to detect delay, jitter loss, and data rate?

There is of course a well-known set of network tools such as `ping`, `traceroute`, and `pathchar`, which will report the current end-to-end delay and loss statistics, the delay hop by hop along a path, and even estimate the link capacity on all the hops on a path.

Probes load the network, and therefore they affect the system being measured. Measurement is tricky. They are useful for medium- to long-term diagnostics, and will give some indication of whether a particular application will get its required network performance for the near-term future. However, they don't offer any differentiation or protection against vaguaries of other people's behavior.

9.4 Elastic and Inelastic Applications—Tolerance for Variation?

We can broadly partition applications into these two classes:

Elastic. Examples of elastic applications include: email, which is asynchronous (in the very general, user-centered meaning of the term)—a message is not real-time and delivery in several minutes is acceptable; file transfer, which is an interactive service and requires quick transfer, but a slower transfer may be acceptable; network file service, which is an interactive service, similar to file transfer, and where a fast response is required (usually over LAN); the WWW, which is interactive, and is really a combination of a user interface and a file access mechanism, and where a fast response is required. In the latter case, of course, one might

Table 9.2 Elastic Applications

Interactive: Telnet, X-Windows
Interactive bulk: FTP, HTTP
Asynchronous: email, voice mail

Table 9.3 Inelastic Applications

Tolerant: adaptive, delay adaptive
Tolerant: adaptive, rate adaptive
Intolerant: adaptive
Intolerant: non-adaptive

switch to a different model when QoS-sensitive content exists on WWW pages.

Inelastic. Examples of inelastic applications (impatient!) include: streaming music, video, and voice, which are not interactive, and where end-to-end delay is not important, end-to-end jitter is not important, and the data rate and loss *are* very important; and real-time voice, which is person-to-person and interactive, and where it is extremely important to control the end-to-end delay, the end-to-end jitter, the end-to-end loss, and the end-to-end data rate.

We can fill in some of the detail for these sets of application (and usage) requirements by specifying the parameters for QoS for them:

Delay. As we discussed earlier, it isn't really realistic to request the maximum delay value because there is no simple user control over the end-to-end network path in IP. It *is* possible to find actual values for the maximum end-to-end delay, DMAX in some cases, as well as the minimum end-to-end delay, DMIN.

Jitter. It is not possible in general to request the end-to-end jitter value, since this would essentially be equivalent to turning a packet-switched network into a time division multiplexing system, with all the associated inefficiencies. However, we can approximate the maximum jitter from DMAX and DMIN. We can evaluate DMIN dynamically, and choose some sensible statistical bound for DMAX, for example the 99th percentile. The jitter value has a contribution from the transport level and below, so protocols there have to convey this information (see the discussion on RTCP in Chapter 6), as well as a contribution from the application level.

Loss. Loss is not really a QoS parameter for IP networks. It is not something you really want to request as such, it is more something you want to avoid. How would a router honor a request for a specified loss level? Loss is in any case related to the data rate. It is very hard to guarantee. Probabilistic loss levels may be feasible. As better understanding of the relationship between loss and the congestion feedback signal emerge for

TCP and TCP-like transport protocols, we can imagine using loss (e.g., via RED; see Section 9.10) to provide some level of control of best effort, achieving more scalable and accurate traffic management and congestion control.

Packet size. Path MTU discovery (see Chapter 6) reveals the smallest maximum transfer unit that the links on a given route support. The application may use smaller packets, but using larger packet sizes than the MTU (and incurring fragmentation) is regarded as a bad idea. The users' packet size choice, and the path MTU, may be used by routers to help with buffer allocation, and are also vital parameters to the delay evaluation process in admission control.

Data rate. This is the key performance parameter, but how can we specify this for applications that are not a fixed (constant bit) rate? Data applications are inherently bursty. Voice and other multimedia sources use variable-rate compression and silence suppression, so they do not send at a single rate. How do we capture the rate information?

We can specify the mean data rate, and the peak rate, and the length of time a source spends sending traffic at the peak rate. How do we then allocate resources? If we allocate at peak rate, we waste resources when an application sends slower. If we allocate less resources, we take a risk.

Real-time flows may be a constant bit rate, but can also be a variable bit rate. A given application level flow is made up of a number of application data units (ADU) and we can specify a rate in terms of these. We would like the API for this to be both application-friendly as well as technology-neutral.

9.4.1 Network Source Behavior Characterization: Leaky and Token Buckets

The most common ways to capture the definition of traffic source behavior is via a leaky or token bucket specification:

Leaky bucket. This has two parameters:

$$B : bucketsize\ [Bytes] L : leakrate\ [B/s or b/s] \qquad (9.2)$$

Data pours into the bucket and is leaked out, with traffic always constrained to rate L. B/L is the maximum latency at transmission.

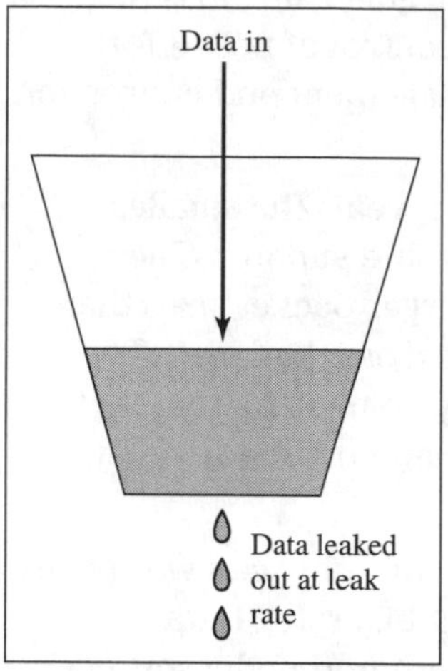

Figure 9.5 Leaky bucket description.

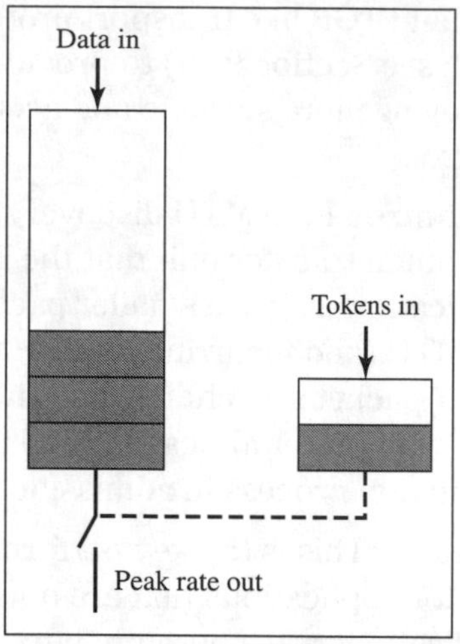

Figure 9.6 Token bucket description.

Token bucket. This has three parameters:

$$b : bucket\ size\ [B] r : bucketrate\ [B/sorb/s] p : peak\ rate\ [B/sorb/s] \tag{9.3}$$

The bucket fills with tokens at rate r, start full. The presence of tokens allows data transmission, and a burst is allowed at rate p, while the amount of data sent is limited to $< rt + b$.

9.5 Packet-Forward Scheduling and Queue Management

Linux has complex support for scheduling and queue management. Let's start out by looking at these in the abstract.

In the simple router schematic in Figure 9.4, we see a router with a number of input lines. These have no input buffering (at least nothing outside of what is on the actual network interface card, (NIC)). We see a packet classifier, which can employ information from policy-based classification to select the correct output queue once the forwarding/routing tables have indicated the right output interface. Between the input network interface card and output network interface card, there is a switching fabric. Of course, on a PC platform this is nothing so grand—it's a PCI bus. Packets are taken from the output buffer (queue) by a scheduler, which chooses which packet from the output queue is to be serviced next. The packet scheduler (in Linux) is driven from interrupts, of which we'll say more later.

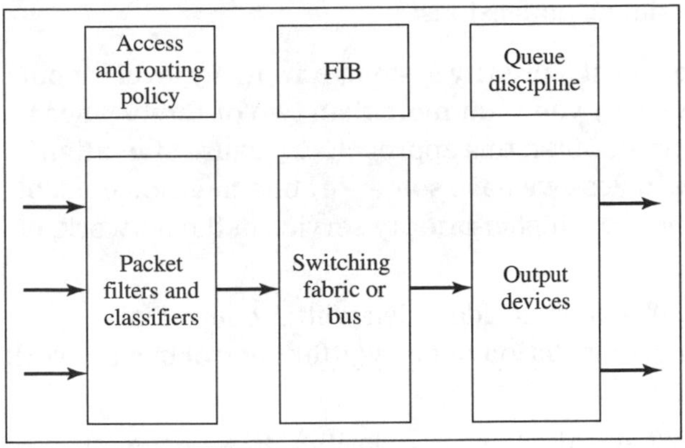

Figure 9.7 Router schematic.

9.6 Queuing Disciplines

The default, simplest queuing discipline we can imagine is probably FIFO (first in, first out), or FCFS (first come, first served).

This employs a null packet classifier. Packets are queued to outputs in the order they arrive, and there is no packet differentiation. There is no history or state, and as a result, no notion of flows of packets. Anytime a packet arrives, it is serviced as soon as possible. FCFS is what is called a *work-conserving* scheduler. This is defined as a scheduler that is never idle as long as any packets are waiting. Work conserving schedulers have the property that if you wish to reduce the delay of one flow, you necessarily increase the delay of one or more other flows. An interesting useful result to remember is that we cannot give all flows a lower delay than they would get under FCFS with any other scheduling scheme.

One can imagine *non-work-conserving* disciplines. These are schedulers that can be idle even if there are packets waiting. In principle, this allows for some possible smoothing of packet flows. Instead of serving a packet as soon as it arrives, we wait until the packet is eligible for transmission. This eligibility could be defined by a fixed time per router, or a fixed time across the network. The result of this (for a given flow) is less jitter. It makes the downstream traffic more predictable, and the output flow is controlled, leading to less bursty traffic. Another consequence is that we need less buffer space. In the router, work-conserving schedulers require less buffer in output queues, and the reduction in jitter means that end systems need little or no de-jitter buffering. However, it necessarily leads (for the same network) to higher end-to-end delay, and can be complex in practice, possibly requiring clock synchronization at routers. In fact, at one extreme, a time division multiplex (digital circuit switched network) is an example of this approach.

There are a number of scheduling dimensions:

Priority levels. If we implement a priority system, how many levels should there be? It is not obvious why you want more than two or three. Since a higher-priority queues services first, this approach can cause starvation for lower-priority queues, unless we have some sort of admission control for the overall occupancy of the higher-priority service in the network, or on any given path.

Work-conserving or not. We must decide if delay/jitter control is required. Is the cost of implementation of delay/jitter control in a network acceptable? In practice it isn't.

Degree of aggregation. What is the flow granularity? Do we have per-application flow, or per-user or per-end system? It is a question of tradeoff between the cost of implementation of the scheduling system (in terms of state, state setup messages, classification frequency, and complexity) and the granularity of control.

Servicing within a queue. Can we get away with FCFS within a queue? Should we check for other parameters? What other added processing overhead may there be (e.g., network management/logging). What kind of queue management do we need in an emergency?

9.6.1 Common Scheduling Disciplines

Let's now look at some of the more common systems for picking which packet to send next, and when to send it.

Priority queuing. We have K queues: $1 <= k <= K$. Queue $k + 1$ has greater priority than queue k. In other words, higher-priority queues are serviced first. This is very simple to implement and has a low processing overhead. It offers relative priority in practice (assuming we keep no history), and this offers no deterministic performance bounds. In terms of fairness and protection, it is not max-min fair and it hazards the risk of starvation of lower-priority queues.

Generalized processor sharing (GPS). This is a work-conserving scheme, and on paper it serves an infinitesimally small amount of data from flow i and then visits the next flows round robin. This provides a max-min fair share to each flow. It can provide a weighted max-min fair share, however in practice it is not directly implementable. Instead, it is used as a baseline abstract reference for comparing other schedulers.

Weighted round robin. This is the simplest attempt at an implementable approximation to GPS. The queues are visited round robin in proportion to weights assigned. Since different flows have different mean packet sizes, the weight has to be divided by mean packet size for each queue. Because mean packet size is unpredictable, this may cause unfairness.

The service is max-min fair over long time scales. We must have more than one visit to each flow/queue. This means that there are deviations from fairness for short-lived flows.

Deficit round robin (DRR). DRR does not need to know the mean packet size. Each queue has a deficit counter (*dc*); initially, this is set to zero. The DRR scheduler attempts to serve one quantum of data from a non-empty queue:

```
if size <= quantum + dc
packet at head served
dc = quantum + dc - size
else
dc += quantum
```

Queues that are not served during a round build up credits. The quantum is normally set to be the maximum expected packet size. This ensures that one packet is served per round per non-empty queue: $RFB : 3T/r(T = maxpktservicetime, r = linkrate)$. It works best for flows with small packet sizes and is fine for a small number of flows.

Weighted fair queuing (WFQ). The WFQ scheduler is also based on GPS. It is effectively a GPS emulation that is designed to produce finish numbers for packets in the queue. The simplification is that the scheme is a packet time scale instead of the GPS time scale that serves packets bit by bit round robin. The finish number is the time that a packet would have completed service, under the ideal (bit-by-bit) GPS. Packets are tagged with the finish number, then the smallest finish number across the queues is served first in the next round.

The round is a cycle of execution defined by an idealized bit-by-bit round-robin server. The finish number is calculated from the round number. If the queue is empty, the finish number is the *number of bits in packet + round-number*. If the queue non-empty, the finish number is *highest current finish number for queue + number of bits in packet.*

When a flow completes (empty queue), there is one less flow in the round, so R increases more quickly. Thus, as more flows complete, R increases more quickly, and so on. Because of this, WFQ needs to evaluate R each time a packet arrives or leaves, which can be a significant processing overhead.

In addition to the schedule, r, we have to have a buffer-drop policy to handle overloads. If packets arrive at full queue, we can drop packets already queued in order of decreasing finish numbers, for example. This can be used for best-effort queuing, or for providing a guaranteed data rate and deterministic end-to-end delay. WFQ is used in the real world, as is DRR. There are several alternatives also available, including self-clocked fair queuing (SCFQ), worst-case fair-weighted fair queuing (WF2Q), and a neat statistical approximation, stochastic fairness queuing (SFQ).

9.6.2 Class-Based Queuing

As well as organizing scheduling with a traffic class, we need to have a way of managing a set of different traffic classes, potentially with a range of different, appropriate scheduling algorithms. There are two specific approaches to this commonly today, and Linux supports both within a more general framework, as we shall see later. One is class-based queuing (CBQ), and the other is the so-called Clark/Shenker/Zhang architecture (after the three well-known researchers who devised it).

What is needed is a framework for organizing hierarchical link sharing. Firstly, link capacity is shared between organizations, with differing levels of aggregation. There is no reason to suppose that the scheduler and aggregation level follow the same hierarchy, so it is necessary to support both class-based allocation and policy-based class selection. Since the Internet is all about sharing resources, it should be possible, within the constraints of policy, to use the class hierarchy to assign capacity/priority to each node, but also to allow a node to borrow any spare capacity from a parent. Fine-grained flows are possible. CBQ is a queuing mechanism that employs a set of schedulers with the classification framework, as illustrated in Figure 9.8.

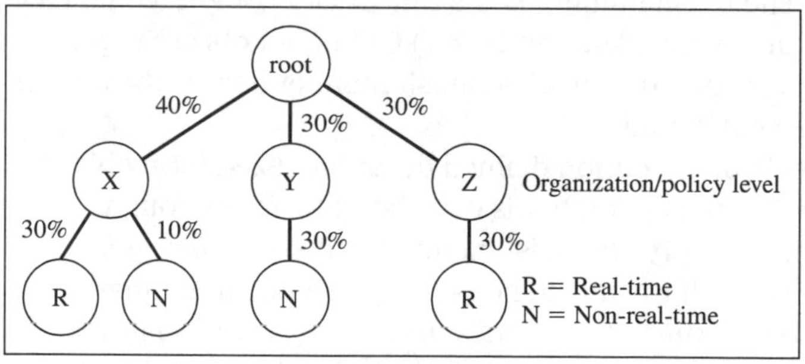

Figure 9.8 Class-based queuing.

9.7 Queue Management

Having revised scheduling, which addresses the problems of which output queue to visit and which packet to transmit from the output queue, let's now take a look at queue management.

Queue management entails the tasks of ensuring buffers are available, using memory management to look after resources, and deals with the details of organizing packets within a queue, and especially packet dropping when a queue is full, for example when triggering congestion control.

Congestion is typically caused (as we have seen previously) by a range of misfortunes, including misbehaving sources, source synchronization, routing instability, and network failure causing rerouting.

Congestion could hurt many flows, so we need to manage it somehow. Typically, we drop packets. We can also mark packets with the newly defined *explicit congestion notification* bit. Key questions are: Do we drop new packets until the queue clears, or do we admit new packets and drop existing packets in the queue? How much history, explicitly or implicitly, concerning misbehaving flows, do we keep?

Packet drop mechanisms include:

Drop from tail. Given a FIFO queue, tail-drop is clearly easy to implement. Of course, delayed packets within a queue may expire.

Drop from head. This may be harder to implement (especially if some of a transmit queue is no longer owned by the IP level, but is in the buffer owned by (or even on) the NIC. The idea here is that old packets are purged first, and this ought to be good for real time, and even better for TCP. In practice, it's not widely implemented.

Random drop. Random drop, especially in its random early detection guise, is popular. If the random number is chosen carefully to be uniform (proportional to the queue length), this is in some senses fair, since if all sources are behaving correctly, they are equally likely to see the drop; if there are misbehaving sources, then they will be proportionally more heavily penalized.

Flush queue. When a queue is overloaded, there is also the option to drop all packets in the queue. This is simple, and would mean that all the flows that are adaptive should back off. However it is inefficient, and possibly unsafe, since all the backed-off flows will start up again in a synchronized fashion, unlike random drop.

Intelligent drop. Various fair drop mechanisms have been proposed, sometimes based on level 4 (transport-specific) information such as port numbers. These may need a lot of state information, although it should be possible to make them fairer.

The reaction to packet drops is well defined for non-real-time applications using TCP. Packet drop is to be interpreted as congestion that leads to a slow down in transmission rate, as described in Chapter 7 ("Slow Start and Congestion Avoidance"). This leads to a happy network.

Real-time UDP flows have less obvious choices. For transient loss, packet drop can be concealed by an application-specific fill-in at receiver. However, we still need to employ an application-level congestion control. Nonetheless, flow data rate adaptation may not be suited to audio/video. Real-time flows may not adapt, but then this hurts adaptive flows. Queue management could protect adaptive flows, so perhaps smart queue management is required.

9.7.1 Random Early Detection

Random early detection is a refinement of simple random drop. The intention is to spot congestion before it happens. The idea is that a dropped packet can be used to provide a preemptive congestion signal. Since this means that the source slows down, it prevents real congestion. Which packets to drop? Well, we can monitor flows specifically, but that leads to a high cost in state and processing overhead versus overall performance of the network.

The probability of packet drop is related to queue length. If we monitor the queue length value using an exponential average, we smooth the RED process reaction to small bursts. This punishes sustained heavy traffic. Packets can be dropped or marked as offending, via ECN. RED-aware routers are more likely to drop offending packets. The source must be adaptive. Setting RED parameters is quite complex.

9.8 Linux Forwarding Treatment Architecture

The bulk of the code in the Linux implementation is by Alexey Kuznetsov, and is an excellent example of the use of C for both low-level efficiency and high-level clarity. Much along the lines previously discussed, the code provides comprehensive support for best effort, differentiated and integrated services forwarding, as well as clean interfaces for adding experimental facilities.

The code is heavily oriented around an *object-oriented* structure, which can be confusing since the word class is used in a special way in QoS; for example, consider the terms quality of service, class of service, and grade of service.

We'll refrain from using strict object-oriented programming terminology when talking about this code (especially since it is actually written in C). However, it is useful to bear it in mind if you have been trained that way.

9.8.1 Output Interface

The way that the sequence of queuing disciplines is invoked in Linux is illustrated in Figure 9.9. Once the route has been decided for a packet, the output interface

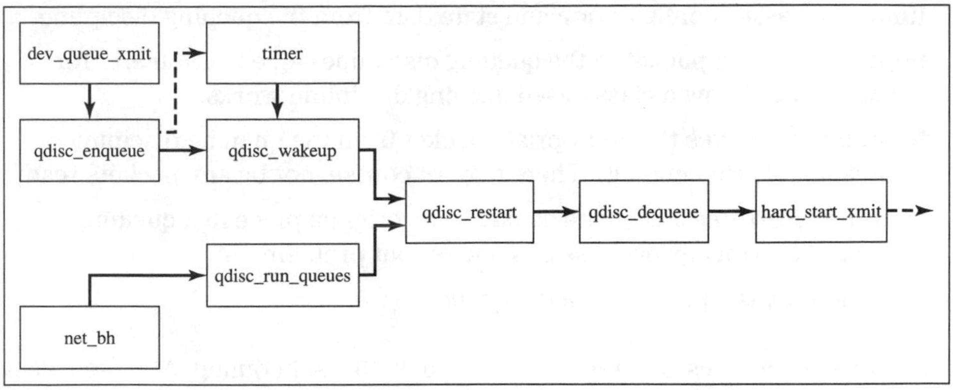

Figure 9.9 `qdisc` call graph structure.

is known. Then the packet is queued for output on the device by calling the `enqueue` function for the device. This invokes the `wakeup` function in an effort to send the packet just sent. Of course it is entirely possible that there are earlier packets queued that were too early, or that this packet is too early. So the next step is that `wakeup` calls `restart`, which attempts to find any packet from the queuing discipline for the device that is ready. If there are any, `restart` calls the device specific `hard_start_xmit` function to transmit the packet. If there are output failures, the packet is put back in the pool of packets ready to go by calling `requeue`.

There are (as is typical in networking code) two other ways that a packet may get pulled out of its queue and put through this process. Firstly, a timer-based event may fire that will call `wakeup`. Certain queuing disciplines require this, as we've seen previously. Secondly, the `net_bh` will invoke `wakeup` anytime it has finished processing any packets that it queues. These two together make sure that we never forget any packets in the queue.

9.8.2 Queue Discipline

Any queuing discipline involves a standard collection of functions. The actual specifics depend on the disciplines, which we have described previously and will list and walk through below. Here we just describe the generic `Qdisc_ops` interface:

init. Initializes the queuing discipline.

destroy. Tears down and removes the queuing discipline, clearing the classes, filters, and events, and freeing up associated resources.

reset. Clears all queues in a discipline, cancels all timers, and restores it to a pristine condition.

dump. Accesses configuration and state data from the queuing discipline.

enqueue. Adds a packet to the queuing discipline—see Section 9.11 for a discussion of how a class-based queuing discipline works.

dequeue. Removes the appropriate packet from the queuing discipline (presumably for sending). There may, of course, not be any packets ready.

requeue. Restores a dequeue packet to its original place in a queuing discipline, typically because of some output problem.

drop. Removes a packet from the queue.

Queuing disciplines are registered through the scheduling API (see Section 9.11), or they register themselves if they start as modules. There is an interface between the route attribute structure (`rtattr`) and the queuing disciplines that allows information to be exchanged via the `rtnetlink` interface to traffic management applications in an analogous way to the way that routing table data is exchanged between user space routing daemons and the kernel forwarding tables (FIBs, described in the previous chapter).

9.8.3 Class/Type

One of the really nice things about the Linux traffic management facilities is the flexibility of the queuing disciplines. Part of this is due to the facility to have *class-based queuing* disciplines. A queuing discipline can assign its own class, or the class can be defined by a user. Essentially, the class identifier space is normally used to create a classification hierarchy (although arbitrary graphs of classes of queues would in some sense be possible—its meaning, on the other hand, would be hard to ascertain).

graft. Adds a new queuing discipline to a class.

delete. Makes sure no one is using the class, and then removes it.

change. Modifies the properties of the class.

dump_class. The analog of dumping a queuing discipline—it returns class data.

get. Looks up a class based on its class identifier and returns the internal identifier—it increments the usage count for a class.

put. Decrements the usage count for a class—if it reaches zero, the class may be removed.

walk. Iterates over the classes of a queuing discipline and returns diagnostic data for all the classes in the queuing discipline.

bind_tcf. Associates or *binds* an instance of a filter to a class.

unbind_tcf. Removes an instance of a filter from a `class`, `bind` and `unbind` are similar to `get` and `put` (see the code in Section 9.9).

tcf_chain. Returns the head of a list of filters for a class.

9.8.4 Filter, or Classifier

Packets that are enqueued for a class-based queuing discipline need to be classified before the correct queue can be chosen to put them on.

There are two main ways that this can happen. Firstly, a packet may be classified by the user, using the `skb->priority` field to fold a class identifier (see the table from a local application via a `setsockopt()` call). Normally, `enqueue` calls `tc_classifiy()` to find the correct classification.

This works by walking the list of filters associated with the class-based queuing discipline.

Filter functions:

init. Initializes a filter.

delete. Removes a filter.

dump. Returns state information for a filter or filter element.

get. Looks up a filter.

put. Remove a filter.

change. Modifies filter properties.

walk. Iterates over all elements of a filter and call.

classify. Classifies a packet according to a filter.

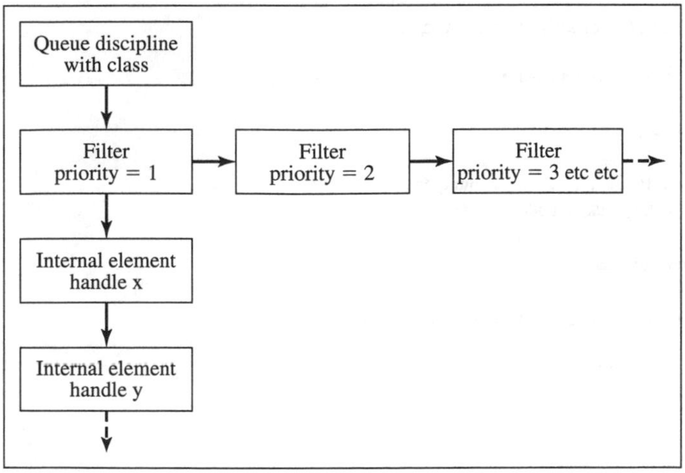

Figure 9.10 Queuing discipline fine-grain structure—classification via filters.

Filters are also structured by IP protocol (skb->protocol).

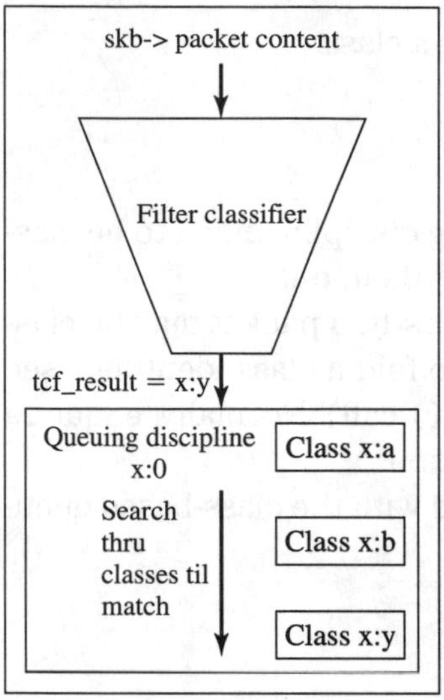

Figure 9.11 Queuing discipline applying a filter.

9.9 The Classifier Code

9.9.1 Classifiers

Linux has a rich mechanism for classifying packets in the various queuing disciplines. First we look at the API to this system.

Figure 9.12 Classifier: linux/net/sched/cls_api.c.

```
/* The list of all installed classifier types */

static struct tcf_proto_ops *tcf_proto_base;

/* Protects list of registered TC modules. It is pure SMP lock. */
static rwlock_t cls_mod_lock = RW_LOCK_UNLOCKED;

/* Find classifier type by string name */

struct tcf_proto_ops * tcf_proto_lookup_ops(struct rtattr *kind)
{
        struct tcf_proto_ops *t = NULL;

        if (kind) {
                read_lock(&cls_mod_lock);
                for (t = tcf_proto_base; t; t = t->next) {
                        if (rtattr_strcmp(kind, t->kind) == 0)
```

```
                        break;
                }
                read_unlock(&cls_mod_lock);
        }
        return t;
}
```

Figure 9.13 Classifier i: `linux/net/sched/cls_api.c`.

```
/* Register(unregister) new classifier type */

int register_tcf_proto_ops(struct tcf_proto_ops *ops)
{
        struct tcf_proto_ops *t, **tp;

        write_lock(&cls_mod_lock);
        for (tp = &tcf_proto_base; (t=*tp) != NULL; tp = &t->next) {
                if (strcmp(ops->kind, t->kind) == 0) {
                        write_unlock(&cls_mod_lock);
                        return -EEXIST;
                }
        }

        ops->next = NULL;
        *tp = ops;
        write_unlock(&cls_mod_lock);
        return 0;
}
```

Figure 9.14 Classifier ii: `linux/net/sched/cls_api.c`.

```
int unregister_tcf_proto_ops(struct tcf_proto_ops *ops)
{
        struct tcf_proto_ops *t, **tp;

        write_lock(&cls_mod_lock);
        for (tp = &tcf_proto_base; (t=*tp) != NULL; tp = &t->next)
                if (t == ops)
                        break;

        if (!t) {
                write_unlock(&cls_mod_lock);
                return -ENOENT;
        }
        *tp = t->next;
        write_unlock(&cls_mod_lock);
        return 0;
}
```

Figure 9.15 Classifier iii: `linux/net/sched/cls_api.c`.

```
#ifdef CONFIG_RTNETLINK

static int tfilter_notify(struct sk_buff *oskb, struct nlmsghdr *n,
                          struct tcf_proto *tp, unsigned long fh, int event);


/* Select new prio value from the range, managed by kernel. */

static __inline__ u32 tcf_auto_prio(struct tcf_proto *tp)
{
        u32 first = TC_H_MAKE(0xC0000000U,0U);

        if (tp)
                first = tp->prio-1;

        return first;
}
```

Figure 9.16 Classifier iv: `linux/net/sched/cls_api.c`.

```
/* Add/change/delete/get a filter node */

static int tc_ctl_tfilter(struct sk_buff *skb, struct nlmsghdr *n, void *arg)
{
        struct rtattr **tca = arg;
        struct tcmsg *t = NLMSG_DATA(n);
        u32 protocol = TC_H_MIN(t->tcm_info);
        u32 prio = TC_H_MAJ(t->tcm_info);
        u32 nprio = prio;
        u32 parent = t->tcm_parent;
        struct net_device *dev;
        struct Qdisc *q;
        struct tcf_proto **back, **chain;
        struct tcf_proto *tp = NULL;
        struct tcf_proto_ops *tp_ops;
        struct Qdisc_class_ops *cops;
        unsigned long cl = 0;
        unsigned long fh;
        int err;

        if (prio == 0) {
                /* If no priority is given, user wants we allocated it. */
                if (n->nlmsg_type != RTM_NEWTFILTER || !(n->nlmsg_flags&NLM_F_CREATE))
                        return -ENOENT;
                prio = TC_H_MAKE(0x80000000U,0U);
        }

        /* Find head of filter chain. */

        /* Find link */
        if ((dev = __dev_get_by_index(t->tcm_ifindex)) == NULL)
                return -ENODEV;
```

Figure 9.17 Classifier v: `linux/net/sched/cls_api.c`.

```
        /* Find qdisc */
        if (!parent) {
                q = dev->qdisc_sleeping;
                parent = q->handle;
        } else if ((q = qdisc_lookup(dev, TC_H_MAJ(t->tcm_parent))) == NULL)
                return -EINVAL;

        /* Is it classful? */
        if ((cops = q->ops->cl_ops) == NULL)
                return -EINVAL;

        /* Do we search for filter, attached to class? */
        if (TC_H_MIN(parent)) {
                cl = cops->get(q, parent);
                if (cl == 0)
                        return -ENOENT;
        }

        /* And the last stroke */
        chain = cops->tcf_chain(q, cl);
        err = -EINVAL;
        if (chain == NULL)
                goto errout;
```

Figure 9.18 Classifier vi: `linux/net/sched/cls_api.c`.

```
        /* Check the chain for existence of proto-tcf with this priority */
        for (back = chain; (tp=*back) != NULL; back = &tp->next) {
                if (tp->prio >= prio) {
                        if (tp->prio == prio) {
                                if (!nprio || (tp->protocol != protocol && protocol))
                                        goto errout;
                        } else
                                tp = NULL;
                        break;
                }
        }

        if (tp == NULL) {
                /* Proto-tcf does not exist, create new one */

                if (tca[TCA_KIND-1] == NULL || !protocol)
                        goto errout;

                err = -ENOENT;
                if (n->nlmsg_type != RTM_NEWTFILTER || !(n->nlmsg_flags&NLM_F_CREATE))
                        goto errout;
```

```
		/* Create new proto tcf */

		err = -ENOBUFS;
		if ((tp = kmalloc(sizeof(*tp), GFP_KERNEL)) == NULL)
			goto errout;
```

Figure 9.19 Classifier vii: `linux/net/sched/cls_api.c`.

```
		tp_ops = tcf_proto_lookup_ops(tca[TCA_KIND-1]);
#ifdef CONFIG_KMOD
		if (tp_ops==NULL && tca[TCA_KIND-1] != NULL) {
			struct rtattr *kind = tca[TCA_KIND-1];
			char module_name[4 + IFNAMSIZ + 1];

			if (RTA_PAYLOAD(kind) <= IFNAMSIZ) {
				sprintf(module_name, "cls_%s", (char*)RTA_DATA(kind));
				request_module (module_name);
				tp_ops = tcf_proto_lookup_ops(kind);
			}
		}
#endif
		if (tp_ops == NULL) {
			err = -EINVAL;
			kfree(tp);
			goto errout;
		}
		memset(tp, 0, sizeof(*tp));
		tp->ops = tp_ops;
		tp->protocol = protocol;
		tp->prio = nprio ? : tcf_auto_prio(*back);
		tp->q = q;
		tp->classify = tp_ops->classify;
		tp->classid = parent;
		err = tp_ops->init(tp);
		if (err) {
			kfree(tp);
			goto errout;
		}
		write_lock(&qdisc_tree_lock);
		spin_lock_bh(&dev->queue_lock);
		tp->next = *back;
		*back = tp;
		spin_unlock_bh(&dev->queue_lock);
		write_unlock(&qdisc_tree_lock);
	} else if (tca[TCA_KIND-1] && rtattr_strcmp(tca[TCA_KIND-1], tp->ops->kind))
		goto errout;
```

Figure 9.20 Classifier viii: `linux/net/sched/cls_api.c`.

```
242          fh = tp->ops->get(tp, t->tcm_handle);
243
244          if (fh == 0) {
245                  if (n->nlmsg_type == RTM_DELTFILTER && t->tcm_handle == 0) {
246                          write_lock(&qdisc_tree_lock);
247                          spin_lock_bh(&dev->queue_lock);
248                          *back = tp->next;
249                          spin_unlock_bh(&dev->queue_lock);
250                          write_unlock(&qdisc_tree_lock);
251
252                          tp->ops->destroy(tp);
253                          kfree(tp);
254                          err = 0;
255                          goto errout;
256                  }
257
258                  err = -ENOENT;
259                  if (n->nlmsg_type != RTM_NEWTFILTER || !(n->nlmsg_flags&NLM_F_CREATE))
260                          goto errout;
261          } else {
262                  switch (n->nlmsg_type) {
263                  case RTM_NEWTFILTER:
264                          err = -EEXIST;
265                          if (n->nlmsg_flags&NLM_F_EXCL)
266                                  goto errout;
267                          break;
268                  case RTM_DELTFILTER:
269                          err = tp->ops->delete(tp, fh);
270                          goto errout;
271                  case RTM_GETTFILTER:
272                          err = tfilter_notify(skb, n, tp, fh, RTM_NEWTFILTER);
273                          goto errout;
274                  default:
275                          err = -EINVAL;
276                          goto errout;
277                  }
278          }
```

Figure 9.21 Classifier ix: `linux/net/sched/cls_api.c`.

```
280          err = tp->ops->change(tp, cl, t->tcm_handle, tca, &fh);
281          if (err == 0)
282                  tfilter_notify(skb, n, tp, fh, RTM_NEWTFILTER);
283
284  errout:
285          if (cl)
286                  cops->put(q, cl);
287          return err;
288  }
```

Figure 9.22 Classifier x: linux/net/sched/cls_api.c.

```
290   static int
291   tcf_fill_node(struct sk_buff *skb, struct tcf_proto *tp, unsigned long fh,
292                   u32 pid, u32 seq, unsigned flags, int event)
293   {
294         struct tcmsg *tcm;
295         struct nlmsghdr *nlh;
296         unsigned char   *b = skb->tail;
297
298         nlh = NLMSG_PUT(skb, pid, seq, event, sizeof(*tcm));
299         nlh->nlmsg_flags = flags;
300         tcm = NLMSG_DATA(nlh);
301         tcm->tcm_family = AF_UNSPEC;
302         tcm->tcm_ifindex = tp->q->dev->ifindex;
303         tcm->tcm_parent = tp->classid;
304         tcm->tcm_handle = 0;
305         tcm->tcm_info = TC_H_MAKE(tp->prio, tp->protocol);
306         RTA_PUT(skb, TCA_KIND, IFNAMSIZ, tp->ops->kind);
307         if (tp->ops->dump && tp->ops->dump(tp, fh, skb, tcm) < 0)
308                 goto rtattr_failure;
309         nlh->nlmsg_len = skb->tail - b;
310         return skb->len;
311
312   nlmsg_failure:
313   rtattr_failure:
314         skb_trim(skb, b - skb->data);
315         return -1;
316   }
```

Figure 9.23 Classifier xi: linux/net/sched/cls_api.c.

```
318   static int tfilter_notify(struct sk_buff *oskb, struct nlmsghdr *n,
319                           struct tcf_proto *tp, unsigned long fh, int event)
320   {
321         struct sk_buff *skb;
322         u32 pid = oskb ? NETLINK_CB(oskb).pid : 0;
323
324         skb = alloc_skb(NLMSG_GOODSIZE, GFP_KERNEL);
325         if (!skb)
326                 return -ENOBUFS;
327
328         if (tcf_fill_node(skb, tp, fh, pid, n->nlmsg_seq, 0, event) <= 0) {
329                 kfree_skb(skb);
330                 return -EINVAL;
331         }
332
333         return rtnetlink_send(skb, pid, RTMGRP_TC, n->nlmsg_flags&NLM_F_ECHO);
334   }
```

Classifier Statistics

Figure 9.24 Classifier–dump output: `linux/net/sched/cls_api.c`.

```
struct tcf_dump_args
{
        struct tcf_walker w;
        struct sk_buff *skb;
        struct netlink_callback *cb;
};

static int tcf_node_dump(struct tcf_proto *tp, unsigned long n, struct tcf_walker *arg)
{
        struct tcf_dump_args *a = (void*)arg;

        return tcf_fill_node(a->skb, tp, n, NETLINK_CB(a->cb->skb).pid,
                             a->cb->nlh->nlmsg_seq, NLM_F_MULTI, RTM_NEWTFILTER);
}
```

Figure 9.25 Classifier–dump output: `linux/net/sched/cls_api.c`.

```
static int tc_dump_tfilter(struct sk_buff *skb, struct netlink_callback *cb)
{
        int t;
        int s_t;
        struct net_device *dev;
        struct Qdisc *q;
        struct tcf_proto *tp, **chain;
        struct tcmsg *tcm = (struct tcmsg*)NLMSG_DATA(cb->nlh);
        unsigned long cl = 0;
        struct Qdisc_class_ops *cops;
        struct tcf_dump_args arg;

        if (cb->nlh->nlmsg_len < NLMSG_LENGTH(sizeof(*tcm)))
                return skb->len;
        if ((dev = dev_get_by_index(tcm->tcm_ifindex)) == NULL)
                return skb->len;

        read_lock(&qdisc_tree_lock);
        if (!tcm->tcm_parent)
                q = dev->qdisc_sleeping;
        else
                q = qdisc_lookup(dev, TC_H_MAJ(tcm->tcm_parent));
        if (q == NULL) {
                read_unlock(&qdisc_tree_lock);
                dev_put(dev);
                return skb->len;
        }
        if ((cops = q->ops->cl_ops) == NULL)
                goto errout;
        if (TC_H_MIN(tcm->tcm_parent)) {
                cl = cops->get(q, tcm->tcm_parent);
                if (cl == 0)
```

```
                        goto errout;
        }
        chain = cops->tcf_chain(q, cl);
        if (chain == NULL)
                goto errout;

        s_t = cb->args[0];
```

Figure 9.26 Classifier—dump output: `linux/net/sched/cls_api.c`.

```
        for (tp=*chain, t=0; tp; tp = tp->next, t++) {
                if (t < s_t) continue;
                if (TC_H_MAJ(tcm->tcm_info) &&
                    TC_H_MAJ(tcm->tcm_info) != tp->prio)
                        continue;
                if (TC_H_MIN(tcm->tcm_info) &&
                    TC_H_MIN(tcm->tcm_info) != tp->protocol)
                        continue;
                if (t > s_t)
                        memset(&cb->args[1], 0, sizeof(cb->args)-sizeof(cb->args[0]));
                if (cb->args[1] == 0) {
                        if (tcf_fill_node(skb, tp, 0, NETLINK_CB(cb->skb).pid,
                                          cb->nlh->nlmsg_seq, NLM_F_MULTI, RTM_NEWTFILTER) <= 0) {
                                break;
                        }
                        cb->args[1] = 1;
                }
                if (tp->ops->walk == NULL)
                        continue;
                arg.w.fn = tcf_node_dump;
                arg.skb = skb;
```

Figure 9.27 Classifier—initialization: `linux/net/sched/cls_api.c`.

```
int __init tc_filter_init(void)
{
#ifdef CONFIG_RTNETLINK
        struct rtnetlink_link *link_p = rtnetlink_links[PF_UNSPEC];

        /* Setup rtnetlink links. It is made here to avoid
           exporting large number of public symbols.
         */

        if (link_p) {
                link_p[RTM_NEWTFILTER-RTM_BASE].doit = tc_ctl_tfilter;
                link_p[RTM_DELTFILTER-RTM_BASE].doit = tc_ctl_tfilter;
                link_p[RTM_GETTFILTER-RTM_BASE].doit = tc_ctl_tfilter;
                link_p[RTM_GETTFILTER-RTM_BASE].dumpit = tc_dump_tfilter;
        }
#endif
```

```
#define INIT_TC_FILTER(name) { \
        extern struct tcf_proto_ops cls_##name##_ops; \
        register_tcf_proto_ops(&cls_##name##_ops); \
      }

#ifdef CONFIG_NET_CLS_U32
      INIT_TC_FILTER(u32);
#endif
#ifdef CONFIG_NET_CLS_ROUTE4
      INIT_TC_FILTER(route4);
#endif
#ifdef CONFIG_NET_CLS_FW
      INIT_TC_FILTER(fw);
#endif
#ifdef CONFIG_NET_CLS_RSVP
      INIT_TC_FILTER(rsvp);
#endif
#ifdef CONFIG_NET_CLS_TCINDEX
      INIT_TC_FILTER(tcindex);
#endif
#ifdef CONFIG_NET_CLS_RSVP6
      INIT_TC_FILTER(rsvp6);
#endif
      return 0;
}
```

Universal Classifiers

The u32 classifier is such a common thing to need that it has its own form.

Figure 9.28 Universal 32-bit classifier API—global data: `linux/net/sched/cls_u32.c`.

```
struct tc_u_knode
{
      struct tc_u_knode    *next;
      u32                  handle;
      struct tc_u_hnode    *ht_up;
#ifdef CONFIG_NET_CLS_POLICE
      struct tcf_police    *police;
#endif
      struct tcf_result    res;
      struct tc_u_hnode    *ht_down;
      struct tc_u32_sel    sel;
};

struct tc_u_hnode
{
      struct tc_u_hnode    *next;
      u32                  handle;
      struct tc_u_common   *tp_c;
      int                  refcnt;
```

```
75              unsigned            divisor;
76              u32                 hgenerator;
77              struct tc_u_knode   *ht[1];
78      };
79
80      struct tc_u_common
81      {
82              struct tc_u_common  *next;
83              struct tc_u_hnode   *hlist;
84              struct Qdisc        *q;
85              int                 refcnt;
86              u32                 hgenerator;
87      };
88
89      static struct tc_u_common *u32_list;
90
91      static __inline__ unsigned u32_hash_fold(u32 key, struct tc_u32_sel *sel)
92      {
93              unsigned h = key & sel->hmask;
94
95              h ^= h>>16;
96              h ^= h>>8;
97              return h;
98      }
```

Figure 9.29 u32 API—the classifier i: `linux/net/sched/cls_u32.c`.

```
101     {
102             struct {
103                     struct tc_u_knode *knode;
104                     u8              *ptr;
105             } stack[TC_U32_MAXDEPTH];
106
107             struct tc_u_hnode *ht = (struct tc_u_hnode*)tp->root;
108             u8 *ptr = skb->nh.raw;
109             struct tc_u_knode *n;
110             int sdepth = 0;
111             int off2 = 0;
112             int sel = 0;
113             int i;
114
115     #if !defined(__i386__) && !defined(__mc68000__)
116             if ((unsigned long)ptr & 3)
117                     return -1;
118     #endif
119
120     next_ht:
121             n = ht->ht[sel];
122
123     next_knode:
124             if (n) {
125                     struct tc_u32_key *key = n->sel.keys;
126
```

```
127                     for (i = n->sel.nkeys; i>0; i--, key++) {
128                             if ((*(u32*)(ptr+key->off+(off2&key->offmask))^key->val)&key->mask) {
129                                     n = n->next;
130                                     goto next_knode;
131                             }
132                     }
133                     if (n->ht_down == NULL) {
134     check_terminal:
135                             if (n->sel.flags&TC_U32_TERMINAL) {
136                                     *res = n->res;
137     #ifdef CONFIG_NET_CLS_POLICE
138                                     if (n->police) {
139                                             int pol_res = tcf_police(skb, n->police);
140                                             if (pol_res >= 0)
141                                                     return pol_res;
142                                     } else
143     #endif
144                                             return 0;
145                             }
146                             n = n->next;
147                             goto next_knode;
148                     }
149
150                     /* PUSH */
151                     if (sdepth >= TC_U32_MAXDEPTH)
152                             goto deadloop;
```

Figure 9.30 u32 API—the classifier ii: `linux/net/sched/cls_u32.c`.

```
153                     stack[sdepth].knode = n;
154                     stack[sdepth].ptr = ptr;
155                     sdepth++;
156
157                     ht = n->ht_down;
158                     sel = 0;
159                     if (ht->divisor)
160                             sel = ht->divisor&u32_hash_fold(*(u32*)(ptr+n->sel.hoff), &n->sel);
161
162                     if (!(n->sel.flags&(TC_U32_VAROFFSET|TC_U32_OFFSET|TC_U32_EAT)))
163                             goto next_ht;
164
165                     if (n->sel.flags&(TC_U32_EAT|TC_U32_VAROFFSET)) {
166                             off2 = n->sel.off + 3;
167                             if (n->sel.flags&TC_U32_VAROFFSET)
168                                     off2 += ntohs(n->sel.offmask & *(u16*)(ptr+n->sel.offoff)) >>n->sel.
                                              offshift;
169                             off2 &= ~3;
170                     }
171                     if (n->sel.flags&TC_U32_EAT) {
172                             ptr += off2;
173                             off2 = 0;
174                     }
175
```

```
176                      if (ptr < skb->tail)
177                              goto next_ht;
178              }
179
180              /* POP */
181              if (sdepth--) {
182                      n = stack[sdepth].knode;
183                      ht = n->ht_up;
184                      ptr = stack[sdepth].ptr;
185                      goto check_terminal;
186              }
187              return -1;
188
189      deadloop:
190              if (net_ratelimit())
191                      printk("cls_u32: dead loop\n");
192              return -1;
193      }
```

There are lookup and other functions.

Figure 9.31 u32 API—lookup functions: `linux/net/sched/cls_u32.c`.

```
195      static __inline__ struct tc_u_hnode *
196      u32_lookup_ht(struct tc_u_common *tp_c, u32 handle)
197      {
198              struct tc_u_hnode *ht;
199
200              for (ht = tp_c->hlist; ht; ht = ht->next)
201                      if (ht->handle == handle)
202                              break;
203
204              return ht;
205      }
206
207      static __inline__ struct tc_u_knode *
208      u32_lookup_key(struct tc_u_hnode *ht, u32 handle)
209      {
210              unsigned sel;
211              struct tc_u_knode *n;
212
213              sel = TC_U32_HASH(handle);
214              if (sel > ht->divisor)
215                      return 0;
216
217              for (n = ht->ht[sel]; n; n = n->next)
218                      if (n->handle == handle)
219                              return n;
220
221              return NULL;
222      }
```

Figure 9.32 u32 API—miscellaneous support: `linux/net/sched/cls_u32.c`.

```
static unsigned long u32_get(struct tcf_proto *tp, u32 handle)
{
	struct tc_u_hnode *ht;
	struct tc_u_common *tp_c = tp->data;

	if (TC_U32_HTID(handle) == TC_U32_ROOT)
		ht = tp->root;
	else
		ht = u32_lookup_ht(tp_c, TC_U32_HTID(handle));

	if (!ht)
		return 0;

	if (TC_U32_KEY(handle) == 0)
		return (unsigned long)ht;

	return (unsigned long)u32_lookup_key(ht, handle);
}

static void u32_put(struct tcf_proto *tp, unsigned long f)
{
}

static u32 gen_new_htid(struct tc_u_common *tp_c)
{
	int i = 0x800;

	do {
		if (++tp_c->hgenerator == 0x7FF)
			tp_c->hgenerator = 1;
	} while (i>0 && u32_lookup_ht(tp_c, (tp_c->hgenerator|0x800)<<20));

	return i > 0 ? (tp_c->hgenerator|0x800)<<20 : 0;
}
```

Starting Up the Classifier System

Figure 9.33 u32 API—initialization: `linux/net/sched/cls_u32.c`.

```
static int u32_init(struct tcf_proto *tp)
{
	struct tc_u_hnode *root_ht;
	struct tc_u_common *tp_c;

	MOD_INC_USE_COUNT;

	for (tp_c = u32_list; tp_c; tp_c = tp_c->next)
		if (tp_c->q == tp->q)
			break;

	root_ht = kmalloc(sizeof(*root_ht), GFP_KERNEL);
```

```
272            if (root_ht == NULL) {
273                    MOD_DEC_USE_COUNT;
274                    return -ENOBUFS;
275            }
276            memset(root_ht, 0, sizeof(*root_ht));
277            root_ht->divisor = 0;
278            root_ht->refcnt++;
279            root_ht->handle = tp_c ? gen_new_htid(tp_c) : 0x80000000;
280
281            if (tp_c == NULL) {
282                    tp_c = kmalloc(sizeof(*tp_c), GFP_KERNEL);
283                    if (tp_c == NULL) {
284                            kfree(root_ht);
285                            MOD_DEC_USE_COUNT;
286                            return -ENOBUFS;
287                    }
288                    memset(tp_c, 0, sizeof(*tp_c));
289                    tp_c->q = tp->q;
290                    tp_c->next = u32_list;
291                    u32_list = tp_c;
292            }
293
294            tp_c->refcnt++;
295            root_ht->next = tp_c->hlist;
296            tp_c->hlist = root_ht;
297            root_ht->tp_c = tp_c;
298
299            tp->root = root_ht;
300            tp->data = tp_c;
301            return 0;
302    }
```

Figure 9.34 u32 API—destroy/delete key: `linux/net/sched/cls_u32.c`.

```
304    static int u32_destroy_key(struct tcf_proto *tp, struct tc_u_knode *n)
305    {
306            unsigned long cl;
307
308            if ((cl = __cls_set_class(&n->res.class, 0)) != 0)
309                    tp->q->ops->cl_ops->unbind_tcf(tp->q, cl);
310    #ifdef CONFIG_NET_CLS_POLICE
311            tcf_police_release(n->police);
312    #endif
313            if (n->ht_down)
314                    n->ht_down->refcnt--;
315            kfree(n);
316            return 0;
317    }
318
319    static int u32_delete_key(struct tcf_proto *tp, struct tc_u_knode* key)
320    {
321            struct tc_u_knode **kp;
322            struct tc_u_hnode *ht = key->ht_up;
```

```
323
324        if (ht) {
325            for (kp = &ht->ht[TC_U32_HASH(key->handle)]; *kp; kp = &(*kp)->next) {
326                if (*kp == key) {
327                    tcf_tree_lock(tp);
328                    *kp = key->next;
329                    tcf_tree_unlock(tp);
330
331                    u32_destroy_key(tp, key);
332                    return 0;
333                }
334            }
335        }
336        BUG_TRAP(0);
337        return 0;
338 }
339
340 static void u32_clear_hnode(struct tcf_proto *tp, struct tc_u_hnode *ht)
341 {
342        struct tc_u_knode *n;
343        unsigned h;
344
345        for (h=0; h<=ht->divisor; h++) {
346            while ((n = ht->ht[h]) != NULL) {
347                ht->ht[h] = n->next;
348
349                u32_destroy_key(tp, n);
350            }
351        }
352 }
```

Figure 9.35 u32 API—destroy/delete classifier: `linux/net/sched/cls_u32.c`.

```
354 static int u32_destroy_hnode(struct tcf_proto *tp, struct tc_u_hnode *ht)
355 {
356        struct tc_u_common *tp_c = tp->data;
357        struct tc_u_hnode **hn;
358
359        BUG_TRAP(!ht->refcnt);
360
361        u32_clear_hnode(tp, ht);
362
363        for (hn = &tp_c->hlist; *hn; hn = &(*hn)->next) {
364            if (*hn == ht) {
365                *hn = ht->next;
366                kfree(ht);
367                return 0;
368            }
369        }
370
371        BUG_TRAP(0);
372        return -ENOENT;
373 }
```

```
374
375    static void u32_destroy(struct tcf_proto *tp)
376    {
377            struct tc_u_common *tp_c = tp->data;
378            struct tc_u_hnode *root_ht = xchg(&tp->root, NULL);
379
380            BUG_TRAP(root_ht != NULL);
381
382            if (root_ht && --root_ht->refcnt == 0)
383                    u32_destroy_hnode(tp, root_ht);
384
385            if (--tp_c->refcnt == 0) {
386                    struct tc_u_hnode *ht;
387                    struct tc_u_common **tp_cp;
388
389                    for (tp_cp = &u32_list; *tp_cp; tp_cp = &(*tp_cp)->next) {
390                            if (*tp_cp == tp_c) {
391                                    *tp_cp = tp_c->next;
392                                    break;
393                            }
394                    }
395
396                    for (ht=tp_c->hlist; ht; ht = ht->next)
397                            u32_clear_hnode(tp, ht);
398
399                    while ((ht = tp_c->hlist) != NULL) {
400                            tp_c->hlist = ht->next;
401
402                            BUG_TRAP(ht->refcnt == 0);
403
404                            kfree(ht);
405                    };
406
407                    kfree(tp_c);
408            }
409
410            MOD_DEC_USE_COUNT;
411            tp->data = NULL;
412    }
```

Figure 9.36 u32 API—new key ID: `linux/net/sched/cls_u32.c`.

```
414    static int u32_delete(struct tcf_proto *tp, unsigned long arg)
415    {
416            struct tc_u_hnode *ht = (struct tc_u_hnode*)arg;
417
418            if (ht == NULL)
419                    return 0;
420
421            if (TC_U32_KEY(ht->handle))
422                    return u32_delete_key(tp, (struct tc_u_knode*)ht);
423
424            if (tp->root == ht)
```

```
425              return -EINVAL;
426
427        if (--ht->refcnt == 0)
428                u32_destroy_hnode(tp, ht);
429
430        return 0;
431 }
432
433 static u32 gen_new_kid(struct tc_u_hnode *ht, u32 handle)
434 {
435        struct tc_u_knode *n;
436        unsigned i = 0x7FF;
437
438        for (n=ht->ht[TC_U32_HASH(handle)]; n; n = n->next)
439                if (i < TC_U32_NODE(n->handle))
440                        i = TC_U32_NODE(n->handle);
441        i++;
442
443        return handle|(i>0xFFF ? 0xFFF : i);
444 }
```

Figure 9.37 u32 API—set parameters: `linux/net/sched/cls_u32.c`.

```
446 static int u32_set_parms(struct Qdisc *q, unsigned long base,
447                         struct tc_u_hnode *ht,
448                         struct tc_u_knode *n, struct rtattr **tb,
449                         struct rtattr *est)
450 {
451        if (tb[TCA_U32_LINK-1]) {
452                u32 handle = *(u32*)RTA_DATA(tb[TCA_U32_LINK-1]);
453                struct tc_u_hnode *ht_down = NULL;
454
455                if (TC_U32_KEY(handle))
456                        return -EINVAL;
457
458                if (handle) {
459                        ht_down = u32_lookup_ht(ht->tp_c, handle);
460
461                        if (ht_down == NULL)
462                                return -EINVAL;
463                        ht_down->refcnt++;
464                }
465
466                sch_tree_lock(q);
467                ht_down = xchg(&n->ht_down, ht_down);
468                sch_tree_unlock(q);
469
470                if (ht_down)
471                        ht_down->refcnt--;
472        }
473        if (tb[TCA_U32_CLASSID-1]) {
474                unsigned long cl;
475
```

```
			n->res.classid = *(u32*)RTA_DATA(tb[TCA_U32_CLASSID-1]);
			sch_tree_lock(q);
			cl = __cls_set_class(&n->res.class, q->ops->cl_ops->bind_tcf(q, base, n->res.classid));
			sch_tree_unlock(q);
			if (cl)
				q->ops->cl_ops->unbind_tcf(q, cl);
		}
#ifdef CONFIG_NET_CLS_POLICE
		if (tb[TCA_U32_POLICE-1]) {
			struct tcf_police *police = tcf_police_locate(tb[TCA_U32_POLICE-1], est);

			sch_tree_lock(q);
			police = xchg(&n->police, police);
			sch_tree_unlock(q);

			tcf_police_release(police);
		}
#endif
		return 0;
}
```

Figure 9.38 u32 API—change parameters: `linux/net/sched/cls_u32.c`.

```
static int u32_change(struct tcf_proto *tp, unsigned long base, u32 handle,
			struct rtattr **tca,
			unsigned long *arg)
{
	struct tc_u_common *tp_c = tp->data;
	struct tc_u_hnode *ht;
	struct tc_u_knode *n;
	struct tc_u32_sel *s;
	struct rtattr *opt = tca[TCA_OPTIONS-1];
	struct rtattr *tb[TCA_U32_MAX];
	u32 htid;
	int err;

	if (opt == NULL)
		return handle ? -EINVAL : 0;

	if (rtattr_parse(tb, TCA_U32_MAX, RTA_DATA(opt), RTA_PAYLOAD(opt)) < 0)
		return -EINVAL;

	if ((n = (struct tc_u_knode*)*arg) != NULL) {
		if (TC_U32_KEY(n->handle) == 0)
			return -EINVAL;

		return u32_set_parms(tp->q, base, n->ht_up, n, tb, tca[TCA_RATE-1]);
	}

	if (tb[TCA_U32_DIVISOR-1]) {
		unsigned divisor = *(unsigned*)RTA_DATA(tb[TCA_U32_DIVISOR-1]);

		if (--divisor > 0x100)
```

```
                return -EINVAL;
            if (TC_U32_KEY(handle))
                return -EINVAL;
            if (handle == 0) {
                handle = gen_new_htid(tp->data);
                if (handle == 0)
                    return -ENOMEM;
            }
            ht = kmalloc(sizeof(*ht) + divisor*sizeof(void*), GFP_KERNEL);
            if (ht == NULL)
                return -ENOBUFS;
            memset(ht, 0, sizeof(*ht) + divisor*sizeof(void*));
            ht->tp_c = tp_c;
            ht->refcnt = 0;
            ht->divisor = divisor;
            ht->handle = handle;
            ht->next = tp_c->hlist;
            tp_c->hlist = ht;
            *arg = (unsigned long)ht;
            return 0;
    }
```

Figure 9.39 u32 API—change parameters: `linux/net/sched/cls_u32.c`.

```
    if (tb[TCA_U32_HASH-1]) {
        htid = *(unsigned*)RTA_DATA(tb[TCA_U32_HASH-1]);
        if (TC_U32_HTID(htid) == TC_U32_ROOT) {
            ht = tp->root;
            htid = ht->handle;
        } else {
            ht = u32_lookup_ht(tp->data, TC_U32_HTID(htid));
            if (ht == NULL)
                return -EINVAL;
        }
    } else {
        ht = tp->root;
        htid = ht->handle;
    }

    if (ht->divisor < TC_U32_HASH(htid))
        return -EINVAL;

    if (handle) {
        if (TC_U32_HTID(handle) && TC_U32_HTID(handle^htid))
            return -EINVAL;
        handle = htid | TC_U32_NODE(handle);
    } else
        handle = gen_new_kid(ht, htid);

    if (tb[TCA_U32_SEL-1] == 0 ||
       RTA_PAYLOAD(tb[TCA_U32_SEL-1]) < sizeof(struct tc_u32_sel))
        return -EINVAL;

    s = RTA_DATA(tb[TCA_U32_SEL-1]);
```

```
579        n = kmalloc(sizeof(*n) + s->nkeys*sizeof(struct tc_u32_key), GFP_KERNEL);
580        if (n == NULL)
581                return -ENOBUFS;
582        memset(n, 0, sizeof(*n) + s->nkeys*sizeof(struct tc_u32_key));
583        memcpy(&n->sel, s, sizeof(*s) + s->nkeys*sizeof(struct tc_u32_key));
584        n->ht_up = ht;
585        n->handle = handle;
586        err = u32_set_parms(tp->q, base, ht, n, tb, tca[TCA_RATE-1]);
587        if (err == 0) {
588                struct tc_u_knode **ins;
589                for (ins = &ht->ht[TC_U32_HASH(handle)]; *ins; ins = &(*ins)->next)
590                        if (TC_U32_NODE(handle) < TC_U32_NODE((*ins)->handle))
591                                break;
592
593                n->next = *ins;
594                wmb();
595                *ins = n;
596
597                *arg = (unsigned long)n;
598                return 0;
599        }
600        kfree(n);
601        return err;
602 }
```

The next three code fragments manage the classifier, including walking a classification tree and calling a given callback (e.g., to dump out statistics):

Figure 9.40 u32 API—walk tree: `linux/net/sched/cls_u32.c`.

```
604 static void u32_walk(struct tcf_proto *tp, struct tcf_walker *arg)
605 {
606        struct tc_u_common *tp_c = tp->data;
607        struct tc_u_hnode *ht;
608        struct tc_u_knode *n;
609        unsigned h;
610
611        if (arg->stop)
612                return;
613
614        for (ht = tp_c->hlist; ht; ht = ht->next) {
615                if (arg->count >= arg->skip) {
616                        if (arg->fn(tp, (unsigned long)ht, arg) < 0) {
617                                arg->stop = 1;
618                                return;
619                        }
620                }
621                arg->count++;
622                for (h = 0; h <= ht->divisor; h++) {
623                        for (n = ht->ht[h]; n; n = n->next) {
624                                if (arg->count < arg->skip) {
625                                        arg->count++;
```

```
626                                 continue;
627                         }
628                         if (arg->fn(tp, (unsigned long)n, arg) < 0) {
629                                 arg->stop = 1;
630                                 return;
631                         }
632                         arg->count++;
633                 }
634         }
635     }
636 }
```

Figure 9.41 u32 API—RTNetlink comms: `linux/net/sched/cls_u32.c`.

```
639 static int u32_dump(struct tcf_proto *tp, unsigned long fh,
640                     struct sk_buff *skb, struct tcmsg *t)
641 {
642         struct tc_u_knode *n = (struct tc_u_knode*)fh;
643         unsigned char   *b = skb->tail;
644         struct rtattr *rta;
645
646         if (n == NULL)
647                 return skb->len;
648
649         t->tcm_handle = n->handle;
650
651         rta = (struct rtattr*)b;
652         RTA_PUT(skb, TCA_OPTIONS, 0, NULL);
653
654         if (TC_U32_KEY(n->handle) == 0) {
655                 struct tc_u_hnode *ht = (struct tc_u_hnode*)fh;
656                 u32 divisor = ht->divisor+1;
657                 RTA_PUT(skb, TCA_U32_DIVISOR, 4, &divisor);
658         } else {
659                 RTA_PUT(skb, TCA_U32_SEL,
660                         sizeof(n->sel) + n->sel.nkeys*sizeof(struct tc_u32_key),
661                         &n->sel);
662                 if (n->ht_up) {
663                         u32 htid = n->handle & 0xFFFFF000;
664                         RTA_PUT(skb, TCA_U32_HASH, 4, &htid);
665                 }
666                 if (n->res.classid)
667                         RTA_PUT(skb, TCA_U32_CLASSID, 4, &n->res.classid);
668                 if (n->ht_down)
669                         RTA_PUT(skb, TCA_U32_LINK, 4, &n->ht_down->handle);
670 #ifdef CONFIG_NET_CLS_POLICE
671                 if (n->police) {
672                         struct rtattr * p_rta = (struct rtattr*)skb->tail;
673
674                         RTA_PUT(skb, TCA_U32_POLICE, 0, NULL);
675
676                         if (tcf_police_dump(skb, n->police) < 0)
677                                 goto rtattr_failure;
678
```

```
679                         p_rta->rta_len = skb->tail - (u8*)p_rta;
680                 }
681  #endif
682         }
683
684         rta->rta_len = skb->tail - b;
685  #ifdef CONFIG_NET_CLS_POLICE
686         if (TC_U32_KEY(n->handle) && n->police) {
687                 if (qdisc_copy_stats(skb, &n->police->stats))
688                         goto rtattr_failure;
689         }
690  #endif
691         return skb->len;
692
693  rtattr_failure:
694         skb_trim(skb, b - skb->data);
695         return -1;
696  }
```

Figure 9.42 u32 API—TCF operation: linux/net/sched/Registration: `linux/net/sched/` `cls_u32.c`.

```
698
699  struct tcf_proto_ops cls_u32_ops = {
700         NULL,
701         "u32",
702         u32_classify,
703         u32_init,
704         u32_destroy,
705
706         u32_get,
707         u32_put,
708         u32_change,
709         u32_delete,
710         u32_walk,
711  #ifdef CONFIG_RTNETLINK
712         u32_dump
713  #else
714         NULL
715  #endif
716  };
717
718  #ifdef MODULE
719  int init_module(void)
720  {
721         return register_tcf_proto_ops(&cls_u32_ops);
722  }
723
724  void cleanup_module(void)
725  {
726         unregister_tcf_proto_ops(&cls_u32_ops);
727  }
```

RSVP

Figure 9.43 RSVP classifier interface—opening comment: `linux/net/sched/cls_rsvp.h`.

```
/*
  Comparing to general packet classification problem,
  RSVP needs only sevaral relatively simple rules:

  * (dst, protocol) are always specified,
    so that we are able to hash them.
  * src may be exact, or may be wildcard, so that
    we can keep a hash table plus one wildcard entry.
  * source port (or flow label) is important only if src is given.

  IMPLEMENTATION.

  We use a two level hash table: The top level is keyed by
  destination address and protocol ID, every bucket contains a list
  of "rsvp sessions", identified by destination address, protocol and
  DPI(="Destination Port ID"): triple (key, mask, offset).

  Every bucket has a smaller hash table keyed by source address
  (cf. RSVP flowspec) and one wildcard entry for wildcard reservations.
  Every bucket is again a list of "RSVP flows", selected by
  source address and SPI(="Source Port ID" here rather than
  "security parameter index"): triple (key, mask, offset).


  NOTE 1. All the packets with IPv6 extension headers (but AH and ESP)
  and all fragmented packets go to the best-effort traffic class.


  NOTE 2. Two "port id"'s seems to be redundant, rfc2207 requires
  only one "Generalized Port Identifier". So that for classic
  ah, esp (and udp,tcp) both *pi should coincide or one of them
  should be wildcard.

  At first sight, this redundancy is just a waste of CPU
  resources. But DPI and SPI add the possibility to assign different
  priorities to GPIs. Look also at note 4 about tunnels below.


  NOTE 3. One complication is the case of tunneled packets.
  We implement it as following: if the first lookup
  matches a special session with "tunnelhdr" value not zero,
  flowid doesn't contain the true flow ID, but the tunnel ID (1...255).
  In this case, we pull tunnelhdr bytes and restart lookup
  with tunnel ID added to the list of keys. Simple and stupid 8)8)
  It's enough for PIMREG and IPIP.


  NOTE 4. Two GPIs make it possible to parse even GRE packets.
  F.e. DPI can select ETH_P_IP (and necessary flags to make
  tunnelhdr correct) in GRE protocol field and SPI matches
  GRE key. Is it not nice? 8)8)
```

```
   Well, as result, despite its simplicity, we get a pretty
   powerful classification engine. */
```

Figure 9.44 RSVP—structures: `linux/net/sched/cls_rsvp.h`.

```
struct rsvp_head
{
        u32                     tmap[256/32];
        u32                     hgenerator;
        u8                      tgenerator;
        struct rsvp_session     *ht[256];
};

struct rsvp_session
{
        struct rsvp_session     *next;
        u32                     dst[RSVP_DST_LEN];
        struct tc_rsvp_gpi      dpi;
        u8                      protocol;
        u8                      tunnelid;
        /* 16 (src,sport) hash slots, and one wildcard source slot */
        struct rsvp_filter      *ht[16+1];
};


struct rsvp_filter
{
        struct rsvp_filter      *next;
        u32                     src[RSVP_DST_LEN];
        struct tc_rsvp_gpi      spi;
        u8                      tunnelhdr;

        struct tcf_result       res;
#ifdef CONFIG_NET_CLS_POLICE
        struct tcf_police       *police;
#endif

        u32                     handle;
        struct rsvp_session     *sess;
};
```

Figure 9.45 RSVP—police function: `linux/net/sched/cls_rsvp.h`.

```
static __inline__ unsigned hash_dst(u32 *dst, u8 protocol, u8 tunnelid)
{
        unsigned h = dst[RSVP_DST_LEN-1];
        h ^= h>>16;
        h ^= h>>8;
```

```
111          return (h ^ protocol ^ tunnelid) & 0xFF;
112  }
113
114  static __inline__ unsigned hash_src(u32 *src)
115  {
116          unsigned h = src[RSVP_DST_LEN-1];
117          h ^= h>>16;
118          h ^= h>>8;
119          h ^= h>>4;
120          return h & 0xF;
121  }
122
123  #ifdef CONFIG_NET_CLS_POLICE
124  #define RSVP_POLICE() \
125  if (f->police) { \
126          int pol_res = tcf_police(skb, f->police); \
127          if (pol_res < 0) continue; \
128          if (pol_res) return pol_res; \
129  }
130  #else
131  #define RSVP_POLICE()
132  #endif
```

Figure 9.46 RSVP—classifier function i: `linux/net/sched/cls_rsvp.h`.

```
135  static int rsvp_classify(struct sk_buff *skb, struct tcf_proto *tp,
136                      struct tcf_result *res)
137  {
138          struct rsvp_session **sht = ((struct rsvp_head*)tp->root)->ht;
139          struct rsvp_session *s;
140          struct rsvp_filter *f;
141          unsigned h1, h2;
142          u32 *dst, *src;
143          u8 protocol;
144          u8 tunnelid = 0;
145          u8 *xprt;
146  #if RSVP_DST_LEN == 4
147          struct ipv6hdr *nhptr = skb->nh.ipv6h;
148  #else
149          struct iphdr *nhptr = skb->nh.iph;
150  #endif
151
152  #if !defined( __i386__) && !defined(__mc68000__)
153          if ((unsigned long)nhptr & 3)
154                  return -1;
155  #endif
156
157  restart:
158
159  #if RSVP_DST_LEN == 4
160          src = &nhptr->saddr.s6_addr32[0];
161          dst = &nhptr->daddr.s6_addr32[0];
162          protocol = nhptr->nexthdr;
```

```
163            xprt = ((u8*)nhptr) + sizeof(struct ipv6hdr);
164   #else
165            src = &nhptr->saddr;
166            dst = &nhptr->daddr;
167            protocol = nhptr->protocol;
168            xprt = ((u8*)nhptr) + (nhptr->ihl<<2);
169            if (nhptr->frag_off&__constant_htons(IP_MF|IP_OFFSET))
170                    return -1;
171   #endif
```

Figure 9.47 RSVP—classifier function ii: `linux/net/sched/cls_rsvp.h`.

```
173            h1 = hash_dst(dst, protocol, tunnelid);
174            h2 = hash_src(src);
175
176            for (s = sht[h1]; s; s = s->next) {
177                    if (dst[RSVP_DST_LEN-1] == s->dst[RSVP_DST_LEN-1] &&
178                        protocol == s->protocol &&
179                        !(s->dpi.mask & (*(u32*)(xprt+s->dpi.offset)^s->dpi.key))
180   #if RSVP_DST_LEN == 4
181                        && dst[0] == s->dst[0]
182                        && dst[1] == s->dst[1]
183                        && dst[2] == s->dst[2]
184   #endif
185                        && tunnelid == s->tunnelid) {
186
187                            for (f = s->ht[h2]; f; f = f->next) {
188                                    if (src[RSVP_DST_LEN-1] == f->src[RSVP_DST_LEN-1] &&
189                                        !(f->spi.mask & (*(u32*)(xprt+f->spi.offset)^f->spi.key))
190   #if RSVP_DST_LEN == 4
191                                        && src[0] == f->src[0]
192                                        && src[1] == f->src[1]
193                                        && src[2] == f->src[2]
194   #endif
195                                        ) {
196                                            *res = f->res;
197
198                                            RSVP_POLICE();
199
200   matched:
201                                            if (f->tunnelhdr == 0)
202                                                    return 0;
203
204                                            tunnelid = f->res.classid;
205                                            nhptr = (void*)(xprt + f->tunnelhdr - sizeof(*nhptr));
206                                            goto restart;
207                                    }
208                            }
209
210                            /* And wildcard bucket... */
211                            for (f = s->ht[16]; f; f = f->next) {
```

```
212                              *res = f->res;
213                              RSVP_POLICE();
214                              goto matched;
215                          }
216                      return -1;
217                  }
218          }
219      return -1;
220  }
```

Figure 9.48 RSVP—miscellaneous functions: `linux/net/sched/cls_rsvp.h`.

```
222  static unsigned long rsvp_get(struct tcf_proto *tp, u32 handle)
223  {
224      struct rsvp_session **sht = ((struct rsvp_head*)tp->root)->ht;
225      struct rsvp_session *s;
226      struct rsvp_filter *f;
227      unsigned h1 = handle&0xFF;
228      unsigned h2 = (handle>>8)&0xFF;
229
230      if (h2 > 16)
231          return 0;
232
233      for (s = sht[h1]; s; s = s->next) {
234          for (f = s->ht[h2]; f; f = f->next) {
235              if (f->handle == handle)
236                  return (unsigned long)f;
237          }
238      }
239      return 0;
240  }
241
242  static void rsvp_put(struct tcf_proto *tp, unsigned long f)
243  {
244  }
245
246  static int rsvp_init(struct tcf_proto *tp)
247  {
248      struct rsvp_head *data;
249
250      MOD_INC_USE_COUNT;
251      data = kmalloc(sizeof(struct rsvp_head), GFP_KERNEL);
252      if (data) {
253          memset(data, 0, sizeof(struct rsvp_head));
254          tp->root = data;
255          return 0;
256      }
257      MOD_DEC_USE_COUNT;
258      return -ENOBUFS;
259  }
```

Figure 9.49 RSVP—delete: linux/net/sched/cls_rsvp.h.

```
261    static void rsvp_destroy(struct tcf_proto *tp)
262    {
263            struct rsvp_head *data = xchg(&tp->root, NULL);
264            struct rsvp_session **sht;
265            int h1, h2;
266
267            if (data == NULL)
268                    return;
269
270            sht = data->ht;
271
272            for (h1=0; h1<256; h1++) {
273                    struct rsvp_session *s;
274
275                    while ((s = sht[h1]) != NULL) {
276                            sht[h1] = s->next;
277
278                            for (h2=0; h2<=16; h2++) {
279                                    struct rsvp_filter *f;
280
281                                    while ((f = s->ht[h2]) != NULL) {
282                                            unsigned long cl;
283
284                                            s->ht[h2] = f->next;
285                                            if ((cl = __cls_set_class(&f->res.class, 0)) != 0)
286                                                    tp->q->ops->cl_ops->unbind_tcf(tp->q, cl);
287    #ifdef CONFIG_NET_CLS_POLICE
288                                            tcf_police_release(f->police);
289    #endif
290                                            kfree(f);
291                                    }
292                            }
293                            kfree(s);
294                    }
295            }
296            kfree(data);
297            MOD_DEC_USE_COUNT;
298    }
```

Figure 9.50 RSVP—destroy: linux/net/sched/cls_rsvp.h.

```
300    static int rsvp_delete(struct tcf_proto *tp, unsigned long arg)
301    {
302            struct rsvp_filter **fp, *f = (struct rsvp_filter*)arg;
303            unsigned h = f->handle;
304            struct rsvp_session **sp;
305            struct rsvp_session *s = f->sess;
306            int i;
307
308            for (fp = &s->ht[(h>>8)&0xFF]; *fp; fp = &(*fp)->next) {
309                    if (*fp == f) {
```

```
310                      unsigned long cl;
311
312
313                      tcf_tree_lock(tp);
314                      *fp = f->next;
315                      tcf_tree_unlock(tp);
316
317                      if ((cl = cls_set_class(tp, &f->res.class, 0)) != 0)
318                              tp->q->ops->cl_ops->unbind_tcf(tp->q, cl);
319
320  #ifdef CONFIG_NET_CLS_POLICE
321                      tcf_police_release(f->police);
322  #endif
323
324                      kfree(f);
325
326                      /* Strip tree */
327
328                      for (i=0; i<=16; i++)
329                              if (s->ht[i])
330                                      return 0;
331
332                      /* OK, session has no flows */
333                      for (sp = &((struct rsvp_head*)tp->root)->ht[h&0xFF];
334                          *sp; sp = &(*sp)->next) {
335                          if (*sp == s) {
336                                  tcf_tree_lock(tp);
337                                  *sp = s->next;
338                                  tcf_tree_unlock(tp);
339
340                                  kfree(s);
341                                  return 0;
342                          }
343                      }
344
345                      return 0;
346              }
347          }
348      return 0;
349  }
```

Figure 9.51 RSVP—general bits: `linux/net/sched/cls_rsvp.h`.

```
351  static unsigned gen_handle(struct tcf_proto *tp, unsigned salt)
352  {
353      struct rsvp_head *data = tp->root;
354      int i = 0xFFFF;
355
356      while (i-- > 0) {
357          u32 h;
358          if ((data->hgenerator += 0x10000) == 0)
359                  data->hgenerator = 0x10000;
360          h = data->hgenerator|salt;
```

```
361                 if (rsvp_get(tp, h) == 0)
362                     return h;
363         }
364         return 0;
365 }
366
367 static int tunnel_bts(struct rsvp_head *data)
368 {
369         int n = data->tgenerator>>5;
370         u32 b = 1<<(data->tgenerator&0x1F);
371
372         if (data->tmap[n]&b)
373             return 0;
374         data->tmap[n] |= b;
375         return 1;
376 }
```

Figure 9.52 RSVP—recycle or generate tunnel: `linux/net/sched/cls_rsvp.h`.

```
378 static void tunnel_recycle(struct rsvp_head *data)
379 {
380         struct rsvp_session **sht = data->ht;
381         u32 tmap[256/32];
382         int h1, h2;
383
384         memset(tmap, 0, sizeof(tmap));
385
386         for (h1=0; h1<256; h1++) {
387             struct rsvp_session *s;
388             for (s = sht[h1]; s; s = s->next) {
389                 for (h2=0; h2<=16; h2++) {
390                     struct rsvp_filter *f;
391
392                     for (f = s->ht[h2]; f; f = f->next) {
393                         if (f->tunnelhdr == 0)
394                             continue;
395                         data->tgenerator = f->res.classid;
396                         tunnel_bts(data);
397                     }
398                 }
399             }
400         }
401
402         memcpy(data->tmap, tmap, sizeof(tmap));
403 }
404
405 static u32 gen_tunnel(struct rsvp_head *data)
406 {
407         int i, k;
408
409         for (k=0; k<2; k++) {
410             for (i=255; i>0; i--) {
411                 if (++data->tgenerator == 0)
```

```
                        data->tgenerator = 1;
                if (tunnel_bts(data))
                        return data->tgenerator;
        }
        tunnel_recycle(data);
    }
    return 0;
}
```

Figure 9.53 RSVP—change parameters i: `linux/net/sched/cls_rsvp.h`.

```
static int rsvp_change(struct tcf_proto *tp, unsigned long base,
                       u32 handle,
                       struct rtattr **tca,
                       unsigned long *arg)
{
        struct rsvp_head *data = tp->root;
        struct rsvp_filter *f, **fp;
        struct rsvp_session *s, **sp;
        struct tc_rsvp_pinfo *pinfo = NULL;
        struct rtattr *opt = tca[TCA_OPTIONS-1];
        struct rtattr *tb[TCA_RSVP_MAX];
        unsigned h1, h2;
        u32 *dst;
        int err;

        if (opt == NULL)
                return handle ? -EINVAL : 0;

        if (rtattr_parse(tb, TCA_RSVP_MAX, RTA_DATA(opt), RTA_PAYLOAD(opt)) < 0)
                return -EINVAL;
```

Figure 9.54 RSVP—change parameters ii: `linux/net/sched/cls_rsvp.h`.

```
        if ((f = (struct rsvp_filter*)*arg) != NULL) {
                /* Node exists: adjust only classid */

                if (f->handle != handle && handle)
                        return -EINVAL;
                if (tb[TCA_RSVP_CLASSID-1]) {
                        unsigned long cl;

                        f->res.classid = *(u32*)RTA_DATA(tb[TCA_RSVP_CLASSID-1]);
                        cl = cls_set_class(tp, &f->res.class, tp->q->ops->cl_ops->bind_tcf(tp->q,
                                              base, f->res.classid));
                        if (cl)
                                tp->q->ops->cl_ops->unbind_tcf(tp->q, cl);
                }
#ifdef CONFIG_NET_CLS_POLICE
                if (tb[TCA_RSVP_POLICE-1]) {
```

```
                        struct tcf_police *police = tcf_police_locate(tb[TCA_RSVP_POLICE-1],
                            tca[TCA_RATE-1]);

                        tcf_tree_lock(tp);
                        police = xchg(&f->police, police);
                        tcf_tree_unlock(tp);

                        tcf_police_release(police);
                }
#endif
                return 0;
        }

        /* Now more serious part... */
        if (handle)
                return -EINVAL;
        if (tb[TCA_RSVP_DST-1] == NULL)
                return -EINVAL;

        f = kmalloc(sizeof(struct rsvp_filter), GFP_KERNEL);
        if (f == NULL)
                return -ENOBUFS;
```

Figure 9.55 RSVP—change parameters iii: `linux/net/sched/cls_rsvp.h`.

```
        memset(f, 0, sizeof(*f));
        h2 = 16;
        if (tb[TCA_RSVP_SRC-1]) {
                err = -EINVAL;
                if (RTA_PAYLOAD(tb[TCA_RSVP_SRC-1]) != sizeof(f->src))
                        goto errout;
                memcpy(f->src, RTA_DATA(tb[TCA_RSVP_SRC-1]), sizeof(f->src));
                h2 = hash_src(f->src);
        }
        if (tb[TCA_RSVP_PINFO-1]) {
                err = -EINVAL;
                if (RTA_PAYLOAD(tb[TCA_RSVP_PINFO-1]) < sizeof(struct tc_rsvp_pinfo))
                        goto errout;
                pinfo = RTA_DATA(tb[TCA_RSVP_PINFO-1]);
                f->spi = pinfo->spi;
                f->tunnelhdr = pinfo->tunnelhdr;
        }
        if (tb[TCA_RSVP_CLASSID-1]) {
                err = -EINVAL;
                if (RTA_PAYLOAD(tb[TCA_RSVP_CLASSID-1]) != 4)
                        goto errout;
                f->res.classid = *(u32*)RTA_DATA(tb[TCA_RSVP_CLASSID-1]);
        }

        err = -EINVAL;
        if (RTA_PAYLOAD(tb[TCA_RSVP_DST-1]) != sizeof(f->src))
```

```
505                   goto errout;
506             dst = RTA_DATA(tb[TCA_RSVP_DST-1]);
507             h1 = hash_dst(dst, pinfo ? pinfo->protocol : 0, pinfo ? pinfo->tunnelid : 0);
508
509             err = -ENOMEM;
510             if ((f->handle = gen_handle(tp, h1 | (h2<<8))) == 0)
511                   goto errout;
```

Figure 9.56 RSVP—change parameters iv: linux/net/sched/cls_rsvp.h.

```
513             if (f->tunnelhdr) {
514                   err = -EINVAL;
515                   if (f->res.classid > 255)
516                         goto errout;
517
518                   err = -ENOMEM;
519                   if (f->res.classid == 0 &&
520                       (f->res.classid = gen_tunnel(data)) == 0)
521                         goto errout;
522             }
523
524             for (sp = &data->ht[h1]; (s=*sp) != NULL; sp = &s->next) {
525                   if (dst[RSVP_DST_LEN-1] == s->dst[RSVP_DST_LEN-1] &&
526                       pinfo->protocol == s->protocol &&
527                       memcmp(&pinfo->dpi, &s->dpi, sizeof(s->dpi)) == 0
528  #if RSVP_DST_LEN == 4
529                       && dst[0] == s->dst[0]
530                       && dst[1] == s->dst[1]
531                       && dst[2] == s->dst[2]
532  #endif
533                       && pinfo->tunnelid == s->tunnelid) {
534
535  insert:
536                         /* OK, we found appropriate session */
537
538                         fp = &s->ht[h2];
539
540                         f->sess = s;
541                         if (f->tunnelhdr == 0)
542                               cls_set_class(tp, &f->res.class, tp->q->ops->cl_ops->bind_tcf
                                            (tp->q, base, f->res.classid));
543  #ifdef CONFIG_NET_CLS_POLICE
544                         if (tb[TCA_RSVP_POLICE-1])
545                               f->police = tcf_police_locate(tb[TCA_RSVP_POLICE-1],
                                          tca[TCA_RATE-1]);
546  #endif
547
548                         for (fp = &s->ht[h2]; *fp; fp = &(*fp)->next)
549                               if (((*fp)->spi.mask&f->spi.mask) != f->spi.mask)
550                                     break;
551                         f->next = *fp;
```

```
552                         wmb();
553                         *fp = f;
554
555                         *arg = (unsigned long)f;
556                         return 0;
557                 }
558         }
```

Figure 9.57 RSVP—change parameters v: `linux/net/sched/cls_rsvp.h`.

```
560         /* No session found. Create new one. */
561
562         err = -ENOBUFS;
563         s = kmalloc(sizeof(struct rsvp_session), GFP_KERNEL);
564         if (s == NULL)
565                 goto errout;
566         memset(s, 0, sizeof(*s));
567         memcpy(s->dst, dst, sizeof(s->dst));
568         s->dpi = pinfo->dpi;
569         s->protocol = pinfo->protocol;
570         s->tunnelid = pinfo->tunnelid;
571         for (sp = &data->ht[h1]; *sp; sp = &(*sp)->next) {
572                 if (((*sp)->dpi.mask&s->dpi.mask) != s->dpi.mask)
573                         break;
574         }
575         s->next = *sp;
576         wmb();
577         *sp = s;
578
579         goto insert;
580
581 errout:
582         if (f)
583                 kfree(f);
584         return err;
585 }
```

Figure 9.58 RSVP—walk RSVP tree: `linux/net/sched/cls_rsvp.h`.

```
587 static void rsvp_walk(struct tcf_proto *tp, struct tcf_walker *arg)
588 {
589         struct rsvp_head *head = tp->root;
590         unsigned h, h1;
591
592         if (arg->stop)
593                 return;
594
595         for (h = 0; h < 256; h++) {
596                 struct rsvp_session *s;
597
598                 for (s = head->ht[h]; s; s = s->next) {
```

```
                        for (h1 = 0; h1 <= 16; h1++) {
                                struct rsvp_filter *f;

                                for (f = s->ht[h1]; f; f = f->next) {
                                        if (arg->count < arg->skip) {
                                                arg->count++;
                                                continue;
                                        }
                                        if (arg->fn(tp, (unsigned long)f, arg) < 0) {
                                                arg->stop = 1;
                                                break;
                                        }
                                        arg->count++;
                                }
                        }
                }
        }
}
```

Why oh why (alexey?) is all this in the header file not the C file:

Figure 9.59 RSVP classifier API: `linux/net/sched/cls_rsvp.c`.

```
#include "cls_rsvp.h"
```

This file merely includes the header above.

Route Classifiers

This type of classifier works by recognizing the *route* that this packet is taking:

Figure 9.60 Route classifier API—structures: `linux/net/sched/cls_route.c`.

```
/*
   1. For now we assume that route tags < 256.
      It allows to use direct table lookups, instead of hash tables.
   2. For now we assume that "from TAG" and "fromdev DEV" statements
      are mutually exclusive.
   3. "to TAG from ANY" has higher priority, than "to ANY from XXX"
 */

struct route4_fastmap
{
        struct route4_filter  *filter;
        u32                   id;
        int                   iif;
};

```

```
struct route4_head
{
        struct route4_fastmap fastmap[16];
        struct route4_bucket  *table[256+1];
};

struct route4_bucket
{
        struct route4_filter  *ht[16+16+1];
};

struct route4_filter
{
        struct route4_filter  *next;
        u32                   id;
        int                   iif;

        struct tcf_result     res;
#ifdef CONFIG_NET_CLS_POLICE
        struct tcf_police     *police;
#endif

        u32                   handle;
        struct route4_bucket  *bkt;
};

#define ROUTE4_FAILURE ((struct route4_filter*)(-1L))
```

Figure 9.61 Route classifier API—functions including policer: `linux/net/sched/cls_route.c`.

```
static __inline__ int route4_fastmap_hash(u32 id, int iif)
{
        return id&0xF;
}

static void route4_reset_fastmap(struct net_device *dev, struct route4_head *head, u32 id)
{
        spin_lock_bh(&dev->queue_lock);
        memset(head->fastmap, 0, sizeof(head->fastmap));
        spin_unlock_bh(&dev->queue_lock);
}

static void __inline__
route4_set_fastmap(struct route4_head *head, u32 id, int iif,
                   struct route4_filter *f)
{
        int h = route4_fastmap_hash(id, iif);
        head->fastmap[h].id = id;
        head->fastmap[h].iif = iif;
        head->fastmap[h].filter = f;
}

```

```
103    static __inline__ int route4_hash_to(u32 id)
104    {
105            return id&0xFF;
106    }
107
108    static __inline__ int route4_hash_from(u32 id)
109    {
110            return (id>>16)&0xF;
111    }
112
113    static __inline__ int route4_hash_iif(int iif)
114    {
115            return 16 + ((iif>>16)&0xF);
116    }
117
118    static __inline__ int route4_hash_wild(void)
119    {
120            return 32;
121    }
122
123    #ifdef CONFIG_NET_CLS_POLICE
124    #define IF_ROUTE_POLICE \
125    if (f->police) { \
126            int pol_res = tcf_police(skb, f->police); \
127            if (pol_res >= 0) return pol_res; \
128            dont_cache = 1; \
129            continue; \
130    } \
131    if (!dont_cache)
132    #else
133    #define IF_ROUTE_POLICE
134    #endif
```

Figure 9.62 Route classifier API—classifier function i: `linux/net/sched/cls_route.c`.

```
137    static int route4_classify(struct sk_buff *skb, struct tcf_proto *tp,
138                               struct tcf_result *res)
139    {
140            struct route4_head *head = (struct route4_head*)tp->root;
141            struct dst_entry *dst;
142            struct route4_bucket *b;
143            struct route4_filter *f;
144    #ifdef CONFIG_NET_CLS_POLICE
145            int dont_cache = 0;
146    #endif
147            u32 id, h;
148            int iif;
149
150            if ((dst = skb->dst) == NULL)
151                    goto failure;
152
153            id = dst->tclassid;
154            if (head == NULL)
```

```
155                    goto old_method;
156
157         iif = ((struct rtable*)dst)->key.iif;
158
159         h = route4_fastmap_hash(id, iif);
160         if (id == head->fastmap[h].id &&
161             iif == head->fastmap[h].iif &&
162             (f = head->fastmap[h].filter) != NULL) {
163                    if (f == ROUTE4_FAILURE)
164                          goto failure;
165
166                    *res = f->res;
167                    return 0;
168         }
169
170         h = route4_hash_to(id);
```

Figure 9.63 Route classifier API—classifier function ii: `linux/net/sched/cls_route.c`.

```
172  restart:
173         if ((b = head->table[h]) != NULL) {
174                f = b->ht[route4_hash_from(id)];
175
176                for ( ; f; f = f->next) {
177                       if (f->id == id) {
178                             *res = f->res;
179                             IF_ROUTE_POLICE route4_set_fastmap(head, id, iif, f);
180                             return 0;
181                       }
182                }
183
184                for (f = b->ht[route4_hash_iif(iif)]; f; f = f->next) {
185                       if (f->iif == iif) {
186                             *res = f->res;
187                             IF_ROUTE_POLICE route4_set_fastmap(head, id, iif, f);
188                             return 0;
189                       }
190                }
191
192                for (f = b->ht[route4_hash_wild()]; f; f = f->next) {
193                       *res = f->res;
194                       IF_ROUTE_POLICE route4_set_fastmap(head, id, iif, f);
195                       return 0;
196                }
197
198         }
199         if (h < 256) {
200                h = 256;
201                id &= ~0xFFFF;
202                goto restart;
203         }
```

Figure 9.64 Route classifier API—classifier function iii: `linux/net/sched/cls_route.c`.

```
#ifdef CONFIG_NET_CLS_POLICE
        if (!dont_cache)
#endif
                route4_set_fastmap(head, id, iif, ROUTE4_FAILURE);
failure:
        return -1;

old_method:
        if (id && (TC_H_MAJ(id) == 0 ||
                   !(TC_H_MAJ(id^tp->q->handle)))) {
                res->classid = id;
                res->class = 0;
                return 0;
        }
        return -1;
}
```

Figure 9.65 Route classifier API—miscellaneous: `linux/net/sched/cls_route.c`.

```
static u32 to_hash(u32 id)
{
        u32 h = id&0xFF;
        if (id&0x8000)
                h += 256;
        return h;
}

static u32 from_hash(u32 id)
{
        id &= 0xFFFF;
        if (id == 0xFFFF)
                return 32;
        if (!(id & 0x8000)) {
                if (id > 255)
                        return 256;
                return id&0xF;
        }
        return 16 + (id&0xF);
}

static unsigned long route4_get(struct tcf_proto *tp, u32 handle)
{
        struct route4_head *head = (struct route4_head*)tp->root;
        struct route4_bucket *b;
        struct route4_filter *f;
        unsigned h1, h2;

        if (!head)
                return 0;

```

```
253             h1 = to_hash(handle);
254             if (h1 > 256)
255                     return 0;
256
257             h2 = from_hash(handle>>16);
258             if (h2 > 32)
259                     return 0;
260
261             if ((b = head->table[h1]) != NULL) {
262                     for (f = b->ht[h2]; f; f = f->next)
263                             if (f->handle == handle)
264                                     return (unsigned long)f;
265             }
266             return 0;
267     }
268
269     static void route4_put(struct tcf_proto *tp, unsigned long f)
270     {
271     }
272
273     static int route4_init(struct tcf_proto *tp)
274     {
275             MOD_INC_USE_COUNT;
276             return 0;
277     }
```

Figure 9.66 Route classifier API—destroy route classifier: `linux/net/sched/cls_`
`route.c`.

```
279     static void route4_destroy(struct tcf_proto *tp)
280     {
281             struct route4_head *head = xchg(&tp->root, NULL);
282             int h1, h2;
283
284             if (head == NULL) {
285                     MOD_DEC_USE_COUNT;
286                     return;
287             }
288
289             for (h1=0; h1<=256; h1++) {
290                     struct route4_bucket *b;
291
292                     if ((b = head->table[h1]) != NULL) {
293                             for (h2=0; h2<=32; h2++) {
294                                     struct route4_filter *f;
295
296                                     while ((f = b->ht[h2]) != NULL) {
297                                             unsigned long cl;
298
299                                             b->ht[h2] = f->next;
300                                             if ((cl = __cls_set_class(&f->res.class, 0)) != 0)
301                                                     tp->q->ops->cl_ops->unbind_tcf(tp->q, cl);
302     #ifdef CONFIG_NET_CLS_POLICE
```

```
303                               tcf_police_release(f->police);
304  #endif
305                          kfree(f);
306                     }
307                }
308           kfree(b);
309        }
310   }
311   kfree(head);
312   MOD_DEC_USE_COUNT;
313  }
```

Figure 9.67 Route classifier API—delete entry: `linux/net/sched/cls_route.c`.

```
315  static int route4_delete(struct tcf_proto *tp, unsigned long arg)
316  {
317        struct route4_head *head = (struct route4_head*)tp->root;
318        struct route4_filter **fp, *f = (struct route4_filter*)arg;
319        unsigned h = f->handle;
320        struct route4_bucket *b;
321        int i;
322
323        if (!head || !f)
324             return -EINVAL;
325
326        b = f->bkt;
327
328        for (fp = &b->ht[from_hash(h>>16)]; *fp; fp = &(*fp)->next) {
329             if (*fp == f) {
330                  unsigned long cl;
331
332                  tcf_tree_lock(tp);
333                  *fp = f->next;
334                  tcf_tree_unlock(tp);
335
336                  route4_reset_fastmap(tp->q->dev, head, f->id);
337
338                  if ((cl = cls_set_class(tp, &f->res.class, 0)) != 0)
339                       tp->q->ops->cl_ops->unbind_tcf(tp->q, cl);
340
341  #ifdef CONFIG_NET_CLS_POLICE
342                  tcf_police_release(f->police);
343  #endif
344                  kfree(f);
345
346                  /* Strip tree */
347
348                  for (i=0; i<=32; i++)
349                       if (b->ht[i])
350                            return 0;
351
352                  /* OK, session has no flows */
353                  tcf_tree_lock(tp);
```

```
                        head->table[to_hash(h)] = NULL;
                        tcf_tree_unlock(tp);

                        kfree(b);
                        return 0;
                }
        }
        return 0;
}
```

Firewall Classifiers

This classifier is based on a firewall rule.

Figure 9.68 Firewall classifier API—structures: `linux/net/sched/cls_fw.c.`

```
struct fw_head
{
        struct fw_filter *ht[256];
};

struct fw_filter
{
        struct fw_filter        *next;
        u32                     id;
        struct tcf_result       res;
#ifdef CONFIG_NET_CLS_POLICE
        struct tcf_police       *police;
#endif
};

static __inline__ int fw_hash(u32 handle)
{
        return handle&0xFF;
}
```

Figure 9.69 Firewall classifier API—classifier: `linux/net/sched/cls_fw.c.`

```
static int fw_classify(struct sk_buff *skb, struct tcf_proto *tp,
                          struct tcf_result *res)
{
        struct fw_head *head = (struct fw_head*)tp->root;
        struct fw_filter *f;
#ifdef CONFIG_NETFILTER
        u32 id = skb->nfmark;
#else
        u32 id = 0;
#endif

```

```
74          if (head == NULL)
75                  goto old_method;
76
77          for (f=head->ht[fw_hash(id)]; f; f=f->next) {
78                  if (f->id == id) {
79                          *res = f->res;
80  #ifdef CONFIG_NET_CLS_POLICE
81                          if (f->police)
82                                  return tcf_police(skb, f->police);
83  #endif
84                          return 0;
85                  }
86          }
87          return -1;
88
89  old_method:
90          if (id && (TC_H_MAJ(id) == 0 ||
91                  !(TC_H_MAJ(id^tp->q->handle)))) {
92                  res->classid = id;
93                  res->class = 0;
94                  return 0;
95          }
96          return -1;
97  }
```

Figure 9.70 Firewall classifier API—miscellaneous: `linux/net/sched/cls_fw.c`.

```
99   static unsigned long fw_get(struct tcf_proto *tp, u32 handle)
100  {
101          struct fw_head *head = (struct fw_head*)tp->root;
102          struct fw_filter *f;
103
104          if (head == NULL)
105                  return 0;
106
107          for (f=head->ht[fw_hash(handle)]; f; f=f->next) {
108                  if (f->id == handle)
109                          return (unsigned long)f;
110          }
111          return 0;
112  }
113
114  static void fw_put(struct tcf_proto *tp, unsigned long f)
115  {
116  }
117
118  static int fw_init(struct tcf_proto *tp)
119  {
120          MOD_INC_USE_COUNT;
121          return 0;
122  }
```

Figure 9.71 Firewall classifier API—destroy classifier: `linux/net/sched/cls_fw.c`.

```
124    static void fw_destroy(struct tcf_proto *tp)
125    {
126            struct fw_head *head = (struct fw_head*)xchg(&tp->root, NULL);
127            struct fw_filter *f;
128            int h;
129
130            if (head == NULL) {
131                    MOD_DEC_USE_COUNT;
132                    return;
133            }
134
135            for (h=0; h<256; h++) {
136                    while ((f=head->ht[h]) != NULL) {
137                            unsigned long cl;
138                            head->ht[h] = f->next;
139
140                            if ((cl = __cls_set_class(&f->res.class, 0)) != 0)
141                                    tp->q->ops->cl_ops->unbind_tcf(tp->q, cl);
142    #ifdef CONFIG_NET_CLS_POLICE
143                            tcf_police_release(f->police);
144    #endif
145                            kfree(f);
146                    }
147            }
148            kfree(head);
149            MOD_DEC_USE_COUNT;
150    }
```

Figure 9.72 Firewall classifier API—delete classifier: `linux/net/sched/cls_fw.c`.

```
152    static int fw_delete(struct tcf_proto *tp, unsigned long arg)
153    {
154            struct fw_head *head = (struct fw_head*)tp->root;
155            struct fw_filter *f = (struct fw_filter*)arg;
156            struct fw_filter **fp;
157
158            if (head == NULL || f == NULL)
159                    return -EINVAL;
160
161            for (fp=&head->ht[fw_hash(f->id)]; *fp; fp = &(*fp)->next) {
162                    if (*fp == f) {
163                            unsigned long cl;
164
165                            tcf_tree_lock(tp);
166                            *fp = f->next;
167                            tcf_tree_unlock(tp);
168
169                            if ((cl = cls_set_class(tp, &f->res.class, 0)) != 0)
170                                    tp->q->ops->cl_ops->unbind_tcf(tp->q, cl);
171    #ifdef CONFIG_NET_CLS_POLICE
172                            tcf_police_release(f->police);
```

```
#endif
                        kfree(f);
                        return 0;
                }
        }
        return -EINVAL;
}
```

Changing the Classifier

Figure 9.73 Firewall classifier API—change classifier i: `linux/net/sched/cls_fw.c`.

```
static int fw_change(struct tcf_proto *tp, unsigned long base,
                       u32 handle,
                       struct rtattr **tca,
                       unsigned long *arg)
{
        struct fw_head *head = (struct fw_head*)tp->root;
        struct fw_filter *f;
        struct rtattr *opt = tca[TCA_OPTIONS-1];
        struct rtattr *tb[TCA_FW_MAX];
        int err;

        if (!opt)
                return handle ? -EINVAL : 0;

        if (rtattr_parse(tb, TCA_FW_MAX, RTA_DATA(opt), RTA_PAYLOAD(opt)) < 0)
                return -EINVAL;
```

Figure 9.74 Firewall classifier API—change classifier ii: `linux/net/sched/cls_fw.c`.

```

        if ((f = (struct fw_filter*)*arg) != NULL) {
                /* Node exists: adjust only classid */

                if (f->id != handle && handle)
                        return -EINVAL;
                if (tb[TCA_FW_CLASSID-1]) {
                        unsigned long cl;

                        f->res.classid = *(u32*)RTA_DATA(tb[TCA_FW_CLASSID-1]);
                        cl = tp->q->ops->cl_ops->bind_tcf(tp->q, base, f->res.classid);
                        cl = cls_set_class(tp, &f->res.class, cl);
                        if (cl)
                                tp->q->ops->cl_ops->unbind_tcf(tp->q, cl);
                }
#ifdef CONFIG_NET_CLS_POLICE
                if (tb[TCA_FW_POLICE-1]) {
                        struct tcf_police *police = tcf_police_locate(tb[TCA_FW_POLICE-1],
                              tca[TCA_RATE-1]);
```

```
                        tcf_tree_lock(tp);
                        police = xchg(&f->police, police);
                        tcf_tree_unlock(tp);

                        tcf_police_release(police);
                }
#endif
                return 0;
        }
```

Figure 9.75 Firewall classifier API—change classifier iii: `linux/net/sched/cls_fw.c`.

```
        if (!handle)
                return -EINVAL;

        if (head == NULL) {
                head = kmalloc(sizeof(struct fw_head), GFP_KERNEL);
                if (head == NULL)
                        return -ENOBUFS;
                memset(head, 0, sizeof(*head));

                tcf_tree_lock(tp);
                tp->root = head;
                tcf_tree_unlock(tp);
        }

        f = kmalloc(sizeof(struct fw_filter), GFP_KERNEL);
        if (f == NULL)
                return -ENOBUFS;
        memset(f, 0, sizeof(*f));

        f->id = handle;
```

Figure 9.76 Firewall classifier API—change classifier iv: `linux/net/sched/cls_fw.c`.

```
        if (tb[TCA_FW_CLASSID-1]) {
                err = -EINVAL;
                if (RTA_PAYLOAD(tb[TCA_FW_CLASSID-1]) != 4)
                        goto errout;
                f->res.classid = *(u32*)RTA_DATA(tb[TCA_FW_CLASSID-1]);
                cls_set_class(tp, &f->res.class, tp->q->ops->cl_ops->bind_tcf(tp->q, base,
                     f->res.classid));
        }

#ifdef CONFIG_NET_CLS_POLICE
        if (tb[TCA_FW_POLICE-1])
                f->police = tcf_police_locate(tb[TCA_FW_POLICE-1], tca[TCA_RATE-1]);
#endif

```

```
        f->next = head->ht[fw_hash(handle)];
        tcf_tree_lock(tp);
        head->ht[fw_hash(handle)] = f;
        tcf_tree_unlock(tp);

        *arg = (unsigned long)f;
        return 0;

errout:
        if (f)
                kfree(f);
        return err;
}
```

TC Classifiers

These classifiers follow the traffic control rules.

Figure 9.77 TC classifier API—defines: `linux/net/sched/cls_tcindex.c.`

```
/*
 * Not quite sure if we need all the xchgs Alexey uses when accessing things.
 * Can always add them later ... :)
 */

/*
 * Passing parameters to the root seems to be done more awkwardly than really
 * necessary. At least, u32 doesn't seem to use such dirty hacks. To be
 * verified. FIXME.
 */

#define PERFECT_HASH_THRESHOLD 64   /* use perfect hash if not bigger */
#define DEFAULT_HASH_SIZE     64    /* optimized for diffserv */


#if 1 /* control */
#define DPRINTK(format,args...) printk(KERN_DEBUG format,##args)
#else
#define DPRINTK(format,args...)
#endif

#if 0 /* data */
#define D2PRINTK(format,args...) printk(KERN_DEBUG format,##args)
#else
#define D2PRINTK(format,args...)
#endif


#define PRIV(tp)      ((struct tcindex_data *) (tp)->root)


```

```
struct tcindex_filter_result {
	struct tcf_police *police;
	struct tcf_result res;
};

struct tcindex_filter {
	__u16 key;
	struct tcindex_filter_result result;
	struct tcindex_filter *next;
};


struct tcindex_data {
	struct tcindex_filter_result *perfect; /* perfect hash; NULL if none */
	struct tcindex_filter **h; /* imperfect hash; only used if !perfect;
				      NULL if unused */
	__u16 mask;		/* AND key with mask */
	int shift;		/* shift ANDed key to the right */
	int hash;		/* hash table size; 0 if undefined */
	int alloc_hash;		/* allocated size */
	int fall_through;	/* 0: only classify if explicit match */
};
```

Figure 9.78 TC classifier API—lookup: `linux/net/sched/cls_tcindex.c`.

```
static struct tcindex_filter_result *lookup(struct tcindex_data *p,__u16 key)
{
	struct tcindex_filter *f;

	if (p->perfect)
		return p->perfect[key].res.classid ? p->perfect+key : NULL;
	if (!p->h)
		return NULL;
	for (f = p->h[key % p->hash]; f; f = f->next) {
		if (f->key == key)
			return &f->result;
	}
	return NULL;
}
```

Figure 9.79 TC classifier API—classifier: `linux/net/sched/cls_tcindex.c`.

```
static int tcindex_classify(struct sk_buff *skb, struct tcf_proto *tp,
			    struct tcf_result *res)
{
	struct tcindex_data *p = PRIV(tp);
	struct tcindex_filter_result *f;

	D2PRINTK("tcindex_classify(skb %p,tp %p,res %p),p %p\n",skb,tp,res,p);

```

```
98              f = lookup(p,(skb->tc_index & p->mask) >> p->shift);
99              if (!f) {
100                     if (!p->fall_through)
101                             return -1;
102                     res->classid = TC_H_MAKE(TC_H_MAJ(tp->q->handle),
103                         (skb->tc_index& p->mask) >> p->shift);
104                     res->class = 0;
105                     D2PRINTK("alg 0x%x\n",res->classid);
106                     return 0;
107             }
108             *res = f->res;
109             D2PRINTK("map 0x%x\n",res->classid);
110     #ifdef CONFIG_NET_CLS_POLICE
111             if (f->police) {
112                     int result;
113
114                     result = tcf_police(skb,f->police);
115                     D2PRINTK("police %d\n",res);
116                     return result;
117             }
118     #endif
119             return 0;
120     }
```

Figure 9.80 TC classifier API—miscellaneous: `linux/net/sched/cls_tcindex.c`.

```
122
123     static unsigned long tcindex_get(struct tcf_proto *tp, u32 handle)
124     {
125             DPRINTK("tcindex_get(tp %p,handle 0x%08x)\n",tp,handle);
126             return (unsigned long) lookup(PRIV(tp),handle);
127     }
128
129
130     static void tcindex_put(struct tcf_proto *tp, unsigned long f)
131     {
132             DPRINTK("tcindex_put(tp %p,f 0x%lx)\n",tp,f);
133     }
134
135
136     static int tcindex_init(struct tcf_proto *tp)
137     {
138             struct tcindex_data *p;
139
140             DPRINTK("tcindex_init(tp %p)\n",tp);
141             MOD_INC_USE_COUNT;
142             p = kmalloc(sizeof(struct tcindex_data),GFP_KERNEL);
143             if (!p) {
144                     MOD_DEC_USE_COUNT;
145                     return -ENOMEM;
146             }
147             tp->root = p;
```

```
148            p->perfect = NULL;
149            p->h = NULL;
150            p->hash = 0;
151            p->mask = 0xffff;
152            p->shift = 0;
153            p->fall_through = 1;
154            return 0;
155    }
```

Figure 9.81 TC classifier API—delete classifier: `linux/net/sched/cls_tcindex.c`.

```
158    static int tcindex_delete(struct tcf_proto *tp, unsigned long arg)
159    {
160            struct tcindex_data *p = PRIV(tp);
161            struct tcindex_filter_result *r = (struct tcindex_filter_result *) arg;
162            struct tcindex_filter *f = NULL;
163            unsigned long cl;
164
165            DPRINTK("tcindex_delete(tp %p,arg 0x%lx),p %p,f %p\n",tp,arg,p,f);
166            if (p->perfect) {
167                    if (!r->res.classid)
168                            return -ENOENT;
169            } else {
170                    int i;
171                    struct tcindex_filter **walk = NULL;
172
173                    for (i = 0; i < p->hash; i++)
174                            for (walk = p->h+i; *walk; walk = &(*walk)->next)
175                                    if (&(*walk)->result == r)
176                                            goto found;
177                    return -ENOENT;
178
179    found:
180                    f = *walk;
181                    tcf_tree_lock(tp);
182                    *walk = f->next;
183                    tcf_tree_unlock(tp);
184            }
185            cl = __cls_set_class(&r->res.class,0);
186            if (cl)
187                    tp->q->ops->cl_ops->unbind_tcf(tp->q,cl);
188    #ifdef CONFIG_NET_CLS_POLICE
189            tcf_police_release(r->police);
190    #endif
191            if (f)
192                    kfree(f);
193            return 0;
194    }
```

Figure 9.82 TC classifier API—destroy classifier: `linux/net/sched/cls_tcindex.c`.

```
377
378   static int tcindex_destroy_element(struct tcf_proto *tp,
379       unsigned long arg, struct tcf_walker *walker)
380   {
381           return tcindex_delete(tp,arg);
382   }
383
384
385   static void tcindex_destroy(struct tcf_proto *tp)
386   {
387           struct tcindex_data *p = PRIV(tp);
388           struct tcf_walker walker;
389
390           DPRINTK("tcindex_destroy(tp %p),p %p\n",tp,p);
391           walker.count = 0;
392           walker.skip = 0;
393           walker.fn = &tcindex_destroy_element;
394           tcindex_walk(tp,&walker);
395           if (p->perfect)
396                   kfree(p->perfect);
397           if (p->h)
398                   kfree(p->h);
399           kfree(p);
400           tp->root = NULL;
401           MOD_DEC_USE_COUNT;
402   }
```

Figure 9.83 TC classifier API—change classifier i: `linux/net/sched/cls_tcindex.c`.

```
202   static int tcindex_change(struct tcf_proto *tp,unsigned long base,u32 handle,
203       struct rtattr **tca,unsigned long *arg)
204   {
205           struct tcindex_filter_result new_filter_result = {
206                   NULL,          /* no policing */
207                   { 0,0 },       /* no classification */
208           };
209           struct rtattr *opt = tca[TCA_OPTIONS-1];
210           struct rtattr *tb[TCA_TCINDEX_MAX];
211           struct tcindex_data *p = PRIV(tp);
212           struct tcindex_filter *f;
213           struct tcindex_filter_result *r = (struct tcindex_filter_result *) *arg;
214           struct tcindex_filter **walk;
215           int hash;
216           __u16 mask;
217
218           DPRINTK("tcindex_change(tp %p,handle 0x%08x,tca %p,arg %p),opt %p,"
219               "p %p,r %p\n",tp,handle,tca,arg,opt,p,r);
220           if (arg)
221                   DPRINTK("*arg = 0x%lx\n",*arg);
222           if (!opt)
```

```
        return 0;
    if (rtattr_parse(tb,TCA_TCINDEX_MAX,RTA_DATA(opt),RTA_PAYLOAD(opt)) < 0)
        return -EINVAL;
    if (!tb[TCA_TCINDEX_HASH-1]) {
        hash = p->hash;
    } else {
        if (RTA_PAYLOAD(tb[TCA_TCINDEX_HASH-1]) < sizeof(int))
            return -EINVAL;
        hash = *(int *) RTA_DATA(tb[TCA_TCINDEX_HASH-1]);
    }
    if (!tb[TCA_TCINDEX_MASK-1]) {
        mask = p->mask;
    } else {
        if (RTA_PAYLOAD(tb[TCA_TCINDEX_MASK-1]) < sizeof(__u16))
            return -EINVAL;
        mask = *(__u16 *) RTA_DATA(tb[TCA_TCINDEX_MASK-1]);
    }
    if (p->perfect && hash <= mask)
        return -EBUSY;
    if ((p->perfect || p->h) && hash > p->alloc_hash)
        return -EBUSY;
```

Figure 9.84 TC classifier API—change classifier ii: `linux/net/sched/cls_tcindex.c`.

```
    p->hash = hash;
    p->mask = mask;
    if (tb[TCA_TCINDEX_SHIFT-1]) {
        if (RTA_PAYLOAD(tb[TCA_TCINDEX_SHIFT-1]) < sizeof(__u16))
            return -EINVAL;
        p->shift = *(int *) RTA_DATA(tb[TCA_TCINDEX_SHIFT-1]);
    }
    if (tb[TCA_TCINDEX_FALL_THROUGH-1]) {
        if (RTA_PAYLOAD(tb[TCA_TCINDEX_FALL_THROUGH-1]) < sizeof(int))
            return -EINVAL;
        p->fall_through =
           *(int *) RTA_DATA(tb[TCA_TCINDEX_FALL_THROUGH-1]);
    }
    DPRINTK("classid/police %p/%p\n",tb[TCA_TCINDEX_CLASSID-1],
       tb[TCA_TCINDEX_POLICE-1]);
    if (!tb[TCA_TCINDEX_CLASSID-1] && !tb[TCA_TCINDEX_POLICE-1])
        return 0;
    if (!p->hash) {
        if (p->mask < PERFECT_HASH_THRESHOLD) {
            p->hash = p->mask+1;
        } else {
            p->hash = DEFAULT_HASH_SIZE;
        }
    }
```

Figure 9.85 TC classifier API—change classifier iii: `linux/net/sched/cls_tcindex.c`.

```
268          if (!p->perfect && !p->h) {
269                  p->alloc_hash = p->hash;
270                  DPRINTK("hash %d mask %d\n",p->hash,p->mask);
271                  if (p->hash > p->mask) {
272                          p->perfect = kmalloc(p->hash*
273                              sizeof(struct tcindex_filter_result),GFP_KERNEL);
274                          if (!p->perfect)
275                                  return -ENOMEM;
276                          memset(p->perfect, 0,
277                                  p->hash * sizeof(struct tcindex_filter_result));
278                  } else {
279                          p->h = kmalloc(p->hash*sizeof(struct tcindex_filter *),
280                              GFP_KERNEL);
281                          if (!p->h)
282                                  return -ENOMEM;
283                          memset(p->h, 0, p->hash*sizeof(struct tcindex_filter *));
284                  }
285          }
286          if (handle > p->mask)
287                  return -EINVAL;
288          if (p->perfect) {
289                  r = p->perfect+handle;
290          } else {
291                  r = lookup(p,handle);
292                  DPRINTK("r=%p\n",r);
293                  if (!r)
294                          r = &new_filter_result;
295          }
296          DPRINTK("r=%p\n",r);
```

Figure 9.86 TC classifier API—change classifier iv: `linux/net/sched/cls_tcindex.c`.

```
297          if (tb[TCA_TCINDEX_CLASSID-1]) {
298              unsigned long cl = cls_set_class(tp,&r->res.class,0);
299
300              if (cl)
301                      tp->q->ops->cl_ops->unbind_tcf(tp->q,cl);
302              r->res.classid = *(__u32 *) RTA_DATA(tb[TCA_TCINDEX_CLASSID-1]);
303              r->res.class = tp->q->ops->cl_ops->bind_tcf(tp->q,base,
304                                                      r->res.classid);
305              if (!r->res.class) {
306                      r->res.classid = 0;
307                      return -ENOENT;
308              }
309          }
310 #ifdef CONFIG_NET_CLS_POLICE
311      if (!tb[TCA_TCINDEX_POLICE-1]) {
312              r->police = NULL;
313      } else {
314              struct tcf_police *police =
315                  tcf_police_locate(tb[TCA_TCINDEX_POLICE-1],NULL);
```

```

                tcf_tree_lock(tp);
                police = xchg(&r->police,police);
                tcf_tree_unlock(tp);
                tcf_police_release(police);
        }
#endif
        if (r != &new_filter_result)
                return 0;
        f = kmalloc(sizeof(struct tcindex_filter),GFP_KERNEL);
        if (!f)
                return -ENOMEM;
        f->key = handle;
        f->result = new_filter_result;
        f->next = NULL;
        for (walk = p->h+(handle % p->hash); *walk; walk = &(*walk)->next)
                /* nothing */;
        wmb();
        *walk = f;
        return 0;
}
```

9.10 Queuing Discipline

Linux 2.4 supports a wide variety of queuing disciplines, ranging from simple elementary schedulers, through to the complex, multi-tiered compound systems. The current list is:

FIFO. This represents the default, best-effort Internet service.

Priority. This is the simplest way to achieve some level of traffic differentiation.

RED. This is the well-known queue management technique for distributing fairness amongst rate-adaptive (*TCP-friendly*) flows.

Generalized RED. A special Linux version of RED.

Differentiated service marker. The queuing discipline needs to do marking rather than dropping.

Stochastic fairness queue. SFQ is an approximate technique for fairness.

Token bucket flow. A token bucket policing queue.

Traffic equalizer. Traffic equalization is an EPFL special.

CBQ. CBQ and CSZ are techniques for combining other queuing disciplines into a structure. This is not necessarily, but usually hierarchical).

CSZ. David Clark, Scott Shenker, and Lixia Zhang carried out some of the earliest integrated services research.

ATM VC manager. In the closing years of the second millenium, Internet core networks were often built around a level 2, ATM-switched infrastructure. This is a way to manage the IP QoS overlay on top of the ATM layer—other techniques (e.g., MPLS) are evolving.

9.11 Scheduler Framework

The API to the entire scheduling system looks like the code segments given in the next subsection.

9.11.1 Scheduling API

Figure 9.87 Scheduler API i: `linux/net/sched/sch_api.c.`

```
/*

   Short review.
   -------------

   This file consists of two interrelated parts:

   1. queueing disciplines manager frontend.
   2. traffic classes manager frontend.

   Generally, queueing discipline ("qdisc") is a black box,
   which is able to enqueue packets and to dequeue them (when
   device is ready to send something) in order and at times
   determined by algorithm hidden in it.

   qdisc's are divided to two categories:
   - "queues", which have no internal structure visible from outside.
   - "schedulers", which split all the packets to "traffic classes",
     using "packet classifiers" (look at cls_api.c)

   In turn, classes may have child qdiscs (as rule, queues)
   attached to them etc. etc. etc.

   The goal of the routines in this file is to translate
   information supplied by user in the form of handles
   to more intelligible for kernel form, to make some sanity
   checks and part of work, which is common to all qdiscs
   and to provide rtnetlink notifications.

   All real intelligent work is done inside qdisc modules.



   Every discipline has two major routines: enqueue and dequeue.

   ---dequeue

```

```
  dequeue usually returns a skb to send. It is allowed to return NULL,
  but it does not mean that queue is empty, it just means that
  discipline does not want to send anything this time.
  Queue is really empty if q->q.qlen == 0.
  For complicated disciplines with multiple queues q->q is not
  real packet queue, but however q->q.qlen must be valid.

  ---enqueue

  enqueue returns 0, if packet was enqueued successfully.
  If packet (this one or another one) was dropped, it returns
  not zero error code.
  NET_XMIT_DROP      - this packet dropped
    Expected action: do not backoff, but wait until queue will clear.
  NET_XMIT_CN        - probably this packet enqueued, but another one dropped.
    Expected action: backoff or ignore
  NET_XMIT_POLICED   - dropped by police.
    Expected action: backoff or error to real-time apps.
```

Figure 9.88 Scheduler API—auxiliary routines: `linux/net/sched/sch_api.c`.

```

  Auxiliary routines:

  ---requeue

  requeues once dequeued packet. It is used for non-standard or
  just buggy devices, which can defer output even if dev->tbusy=0.

  ---reset

  returns qdisc to initial state: purge all buffers, clear all
  timers, counters (except for statistics) etc.

  ---init

  initializes newly created qdisc.

  ---destroy

  destroys resources allocated by init and during lifetime of qdisc.

  ---change

  changes qdisc parameters.
 */

/* Protects list of registered TC modules. It is pure SMP lock. */
static rwlock_t qdisc_mod_lock = RW_LOCK_UNLOCKED;
```

Figure 9.89 Scheduler API—all the disciplines: `linux/net/sched/sch_api.c`.

```
/************************************************
 *      Queueing disciplines manipulation.  *
 ************************************************/


/* The list of all installed queueing disciplines. */

static struct Qdisc_ops *qdisc_base = NULL;
```

Figure 9.90 Scheduler API—register/unregister a discipline: `linux/net/sched/sch_api.c`.

```
int register_qdisc(struct Qdisc_ops *qops)
{
        struct Qdisc_ops *q, **qp;

        write_lock(&qdisc_mod_lock);
        for (qp = &qdisc_base; (q=*qp)!=NULL; qp = &q->next) {
                if (strcmp(qops->id, q->id) == 0) {
                        write_unlock(&qdisc_mod_lock);
                        return -EEXIST;
                }
        }

        if (qops->enqueue == NULL)
                qops->enqueue = noop_qdisc_ops.enqueue;
        if (qops->requeue == NULL)
                qops->requeue = noop_qdisc_ops.requeue;
        if (qops->dequeue == NULL)
                qops->dequeue = noop_qdisc_ops.dequeue;

        qops->next = NULL;
        *qp = qops;
        write_unlock(&qdisc_mod_lock);
        return 0;
}

int unregister_qdisc(struct Qdisc_ops *qops)
{
        struct Qdisc_ops *q, **qp;
        int err = -ENOENT;

        write_lock(&qdisc_mod_lock);
        for (qp = &qdisc_base; (q=*qp)!=NULL; qp = &q->next)
                if (q == qops)
                        break;
        if (q) {
                *qp = q->next;
                q->next = NULL;
                err = 0;
```

```
185             }
186             write_unlock(&qdisc_mod_lock);
187             return err;
188    }
```

Figure 9.91 Scheduler API—find a discipline by handle: `linux/net/sched/sch_api.c`.

```
190    /* We know handle. Find qdisc among all qdisc's attached to device
191       (root qdisc, all its children, children of children etc.)
192     */
193
194    struct Qdisc *qdisc_lookup(struct net_device *dev, u32 handle)
195    {
196            struct Qdisc *q;
197
198            for (q = dev->qdisc_list; q; q = q->next) {
199                    if (q->handle == handle)
200                            return q;
201            }
202            return NULL;
203    }
204
205    struct Qdisc *qdisc_leaf(struct Qdisc *p, u32 classid)
206    {
207            unsigned long cl;
208            struct Qdisc *leaf;
209            struct Qdisc_class_ops *cops = p->ops->cl_ops;
210
211            if (cops == NULL)
212                    return NULL;
213            cl = cops->get(p, classid);
214
215            if (cl == 0)
216                    return NULL;
217            leaf = cops->leaf(p, cl);
218            cops->put(p, cl);
219            return leaf;
220    }
```

Figure 9.92 Scheduler API—find a discipline by name: `linux/net/sched/sch_api.c`.

```
224    struct Qdisc_ops *qdisc_lookup_ops(struct rtattr *kind)
225    {
226            struct Qdisc_ops *q = NULL;
227
228            if (kind) {
229                    read_lock(&qdisc_mod_lock);
230                    for (q = qdisc_base; q; q = q->next) {
231                            if (rtattr_strcmp(kind, q->id) == 0)
232                                    break;
```

```
			}
			read_unlock(&qdisc_mod_lock);
		}
		return q;
}
```

Figure 9.93 Scheduler API—find a discipline by rate: `linux/net/sched/sch_api.c`.

```
struct qdisc_rate_table *qdisc_get_rtab(struct tc_ratespec *r, struct rtattr *tab)
{
		struct qdisc_rate_table *rtab;

		for (rtab = qdisc_rtab_list; rtab; rtab = rtab->next) {
			if (memcmp(&rtab->rate, r, sizeof(struct tc_ratespec)) == 0) {
				rtab->refcnt++;
				return rtab;
			}
		}

		if (tab == NULL || r->rate == 0 || r->cell_log == 0 || RTA_PAYLOAD(tab) != 1024)
			return NULL;

		rtab = kmalloc(sizeof(*rtab), GFP_KERNEL);
		if (rtab) {
			rtab->rate = *r;
			rtab->refcnt = 1;
			memcpy(rtab->data, RTA_DATA(tab), 1024);
			rtab->next = qdisc_rtab_list;
			qdisc_rtab_list = rtab;
		}
		return rtab;
}
```

Figure 9.94 Scheduler API—free rate table entry: `linux/net/sched/sch_api.c`.

```
void qdisc_put_rtab(struct qdisc_rate_table *tab)
{
		struct qdisc_rate_table *rtab, **rtabp;

		if (!tab || --tab->refcnt)
			return;

		for (rtabp = &qdisc_rtab_list; (rtab=*rtabp) != NULL; rtabp = &rtab->next) {
			if (rtab == tab) {
				*rtabp = rtab->next;
				kfree(rtab);
				return;
			}
		}
}
```

Figure 9.95 Scheduler API—allocate discipline to a unique handle: `linux/net/sched/sch_api.c.`

```
u32 qdisc_alloc_handle(struct net_device *dev)
{
        int i = 0x10000;
        static u32 autohandle = TC_H_MAKE(0x80000000U, 0);

        do {
                autohandle += TC_H_MAKE(0x10000U, 0);
                if (autohandle == TC_H_MAKE(TC_H_ROOT, 0))
                        autohandle = TC_H_MAKE(0x80000000U, 0);
        } while (qdisc_lookup(dev, autohandle) && --i > 0);

        return i>0 ? autohandle : 0;
}
```

Figure 9.96 Scheduler API—graft-queue discipline to a device: `linux/net/sched/sch_api.c.`

```
/* Attach toplevel qdisc to device dev */

static struct Qdisc *
dev_graft_qdisc(struct net_device *dev, struct Qdisc *qdisc)
{
        struct Qdisc *oqdisc;

        if (dev->flags & IFF_UP)
                dev_deactivate(dev);

        write_lock(&qdisc_tree_lock);
        spin_lock_bh(&dev->queue_lock);
        if (qdisc && qdisc->flags&TCQ_F_INGRES) {
                oqdisc = dev->qdisc_ingress;
                /* Prune old scheduler */
                if (oqdisc && atomic_read(&oqdisc->refcnt) <= 1) {
                        /* delete */
                        qdisc_reset(oqdisc);
                        dev->qdisc_ingress = NULL;
                } else { /* new */
                        dev->qdisc_ingress = qdisc;
                }

        } else {

                oqdisc = dev->qdisc_sleeping;

                /* Prune old scheduler */
                if (oqdisc && atomic_read(&oqdisc->refcnt) <= 1)
                        qdisc_reset(oqdisc);

                /* ... and graft new one */
                if (qdisc == NULL)
```

```
332                        qdisc = &noop_qdisc;
333                dev->qdisc_sleeping = qdisc;
334                dev->qdisc = &noop_qdisc;
335        }
336
337        spin_unlock_bh(&dev->queue_lock);
338        write_unlock(&qdisc_tree_lock);
339
340        if (dev->flags & IFF_UP)
341                dev_activate(dev);
342
343        return oqdisc;
344 }
```

Figure 9.97 Scheduler API—graft-queue discipline child to parent class: `linux/net/sched/sch_api.c`.

```
347 /* Graft qdisc "new" to class "classid" of qdisc "parent" or
348    to device "dev".
349
350    Old qdisc is not destroyed but returned in *old.
351  */
352
353 int qdisc_graft(struct net_device *dev, struct Qdisc *parent, u32 classid,
354                 struct Qdisc *new, struct Qdisc **old)
355 {
356        int err = 0;
357        struct Qdisc *q = *old;
358
359
360        if (parent == NULL) {
361                if (q && q->flags&TCQ_F_INGRES) {
362                        *old = dev_graft_qdisc(dev, q);
363                } else {
364                        *old = dev_graft_qdisc(dev, new);
365                }
366        } else {
367                struct Qdisc_class_ops *cops = parent->ops->cl_ops;
368
369                err = -EINVAL;
370
371                if (cops) {
372                        unsigned long cl = cops->get(parent, classid);
373                        if (cl) {
374                                err = cops->graft(parent, cl, new, old);
375                                cops->put(parent, cl);
376                        }
377                }
378        }
379        return err;
380 }
```

Figure 9.98 Scheduler API—allocate and initialize new queue discipline: `linux/net/sched/sch_api.c`.

```
/*
   Allocate and initialize new qdisc.

   Parameters are passed via opt.
 */

static struct Qdisc *
qdisc_create(struct net_device *dev, u32 handle, struct rtattr **tca, int *errp)
{
        int err;
        struct rtattr *kind = tca[TCA_KIND-1];
        struct Qdisc *sch = NULL;
        struct Qdisc_ops *ops;
        int size;

        ops = qdisc_lookup_ops(kind);
#ifdef CONFIG_KMOD
        if (ops==NULL && tca[TCA_KIND-1] != NULL) {
                char module_name[4 + IFNAMSIZ + 1];

                if (RTA_PAYLOAD(kind) <= IFNAMSIZ) {
                        sprintf(module_name, "sch_%s", (char*)RTA_DATA(kind));
                        request_module (module_name);
                        ops = qdisc_lookup_ops(kind);
                }
        }
#endif
```

Figure 9.99 Scheduler API—allocate and initialize new queue discipline: `linux/net/sched/sch_api.c`.

```
        err = -EINVAL;
        if (ops == NULL)
                goto err_out;

        size = sizeof(*sch) + ops->priv_size;

        sch = kmalloc(size, GFP_KERNEL);
        err = -ENOBUFS;
        if (!sch)
                goto err_out;

        /* Grrr... Resolve race condition with module unload */

        err = -EINVAL;
        if (ops != qdisc_lookup_ops(kind))
                goto err_out;

        memset(sch, 0, size);
```

Figure 9.100 Scheduler API—allocate and initialize new queue discipline: `linux/net/sched/sch_api.c`.

```
        skb_queue_head_init(&sch->q);

        if (handle == TC_H_INGRESS)
                sch->flags |= TCQ_F_INGRES;

        sch->ops = ops;
        sch->enqueue = ops->enqueue;
        sch->dequeue = ops->dequeue;
        sch->dev = dev;
        atomic_set(&sch->refcnt, 1);
        sch->stats.lock = &dev->queue_lock;
        if (handle == 0) {
                handle = qdisc_alloc_handle(dev);
                err = -ENOMEM;
                if (handle == 0)
                        goto err_out;
        }

        if (handle == TC_H_INGRESS)
                sch->handle =TC_H_MAKE(TC_H_INGRESS, 0);
        else
                sch->handle = handle;

        if (!ops->init || (err = ops->init(sch, tca[TCA_OPTIONS-1])) == 0) {
                write_lock(&qdisc_tree_lock);
                sch->next = dev->qdisc_list;
                dev->qdisc_list = sch;
                write_unlock(&qdisc_tree_lock);
#ifdef CONFIG_NET_ESTIMATOR
                if (tca[TCA_RATE-1])
                        qdisc_new_estimator(&sch->stats, tca[TCA_RATE-1]);
#endif
                return sch;
        }

err_out:
        *errp = err;
        if (sch)
                kfree(sch);
        return NULL;
}
```

Figure 9.101 Scheduler API—modify new queue discipline: `linux/net/sched/sch_api.c`.

```
static int qdisc_change(struct Qdisc *sch, struct rtattr **tca)
{
        if (tca[TCA_OPTIONS-1]) {
                int err;

                if (sch->ops->change == NULL)
```

```
479                            return -EINVAL;
480                    err = sch->ops->change(sch, tca[TCA_OPTIONS-1]);
481                    if (err)
482                            return err;
483            }
484    #ifdef CONFIG_NET_ESTIMATOR
485            if (tca[TCA_RATE-1]) {
486                    qdisc_kill_estimator(&sch->stats);
487                    qdisc_new_estimator(&sch->stats, tca[TCA_RATE-1]);
488            }
489    #endif
490            return 0;
491    }
```

Figure 9.102 Scheduler API—detect loops in queue operations graph: `linux/net/sched/sch_api.c`.

```
493    struct check_loop_arg
494    {
495            struct qdisc_walker   w;
496            struct Qdisc          *p;
497            int                   depth;
498    };
499
500    static int check_loop_fn(struct Qdisc *q, unsigned long cl, struct qdisc_walker *w);
501
502    static int check_loop(struct Qdisc *q, struct Qdisc *p, int depth)
503    {
504            struct check_loop_arg arg;
505
506            if (q->ops->cl_ops == NULL)
507                    return 0;
508
509            arg.w.stop = arg.w.skip = arg.w.count = 0;
510            arg.w.fn = check_loop_fn;
511            arg.depth = depth;
512            arg.p = p;
513            q->ops->cl_ops->walk(q, &arg.w);
514            return arg.w.stop ? -ELOOP : 0;
515    }
516
517    static int
518    check_loop_fn(struct Qdisc *q, unsigned long cl, struct qdisc_walker *w)
519    {
520            struct Qdisc *leaf;
521            struct Qdisc_class_ops *cops = q->ops->cl_ops;
522            struct check_loop_arg *arg = (struct check_loop_arg *)w;
523
524            leaf = cops->leaf(q, cl);
525            if (leaf) {
526                    if (leaf == arg->p || arg->depth > 7)
527                            return -ELOOP;
528                    return check_loop(leaf, arg->p, arg->depth + 1);
```

```
529            }
530            return 0;
531    }
```

Figure 9.103 Scheduler API—destroy queue discipline entry: linux/net/sched/sch_
api.c.

```
537    static int tc_get_qdisc(struct sk_buff *skb, struct nlmsghdr *n, void *arg)
538    {
539            struct tcmsg *tcm = NLMSG_DATA(n);
540            struct rtattr **tca = arg;
541            struct net_device *dev;
542            u32 clid = tcm->tcm_parent;
543            struct Qdisc *q = NULL;
544            struct Qdisc *p = NULL;
545            int err;
546
547            if ((dev = __dev_get_by_index(tcm->tcm_ifindex)) == NULL)
548                    return -ENODEV;
549
550            if (clid) {
551                    if (clid != TC_H_ROOT) {
552                            if (TC_H_MAJ(clid) != TC_H_MAJ(TC_H_INGRESS)) {
553                                    if ((p = qdisc_lookup(dev, TC_H_MAJ(clid))) == NULL)
554                                            return -ENOENT;
555                                    q = qdisc_leaf(p, clid);
556                            } else { /* ingress */
557                                    q = dev->qdisc_ingress;
558                            }
559                    } else {
560                            q = dev->qdisc_sleeping;
561                    }
562                    if (!q)
563                            return -ENOENT;
564
565                    if (tcm->tcm_handle && q->handle != tcm->tcm_handle)
566                            return -EINVAL;
567            } else {
568                    if ((q = qdisc_lookup(dev, tcm->tcm_handle)) == NULL)
569                            return -ENOENT;
570            }
```

Figure 9.104 Scheduler API—destroy queue discipline entry: linux/net/sched/sch_
api.c.

```
572            if (tca[TCA_KIND-1] && rtattr_strcmp(tca[TCA_KIND-1], q->ops->id))
573                    return -EINVAL;
574
575            if (n->nlmsg_type == RTM_DELQDISC) {
576                    if (!clid)
```

```
577                      return -EINVAL;
578              if (q->handle == 0)
579                      return -ENOENT;
580              if ((err = qdisc_graft(dev, p, clid, NULL, &q)) != 0)
581                      return err;
582              if (q) {
583                      qdisc_notify(skb, n, clid, q, NULL);
584                      spin_lock_bh(&dev->queue_lock);
585                      qdisc_destroy(q);
586                      spin_unlock_bh(&dev->queue_lock);
587              }
588      } else {
589              qdisc_notify(skb, n, clid, NULL, q);
590      }
591      return 0;
592 }
```

Changing Scheduler Discipline Parameters

Figure 9.105 Scheduler API—change queue discipline entry: `linux/net/sched/sch_api.c`.

```
598 static int tc_modify_qdisc(struct sk_buff *skb, struct nlmsghdr *n, void *arg)
599 {
600      struct tcmsg *tcm = NLMSG_DATA(n);
601      struct rtattr **tca = arg;
602      struct net_device *dev;
603      u32 clid = tcm->tcm_parent;
604      struct Qdisc *q = NULL;
605      struct Qdisc *p = NULL;
606      int err;
607
608      if ((dev = __dev_get_by_index(tcm->tcm_ifindex)) == NULL)
609              return -ENODEV;
610
611      if (clid) {
612              if (clid != TC_H_ROOT) {
613                      if (clid != TC_H_INGRESS) {
614                              if ((p = qdisc_lookup(dev, TC_H_MAJ(clid))) == NULL)
615                                      return -ENOENT;
616                              q = qdisc_leaf(p, clid);
617                      } else { /*ingress */
618                              q = dev->qdisc_ingress;
619                      }
620              } else {
621                      q = dev->qdisc_sleeping;
622              }
623
624              /* It may be default qdisc, ignore it */
625              if (q && q->handle == 0)
626                      q = NULL;
627
```

```
        if (!q || !tcm->tcm_handle || q->handle != tcm->tcm_handle) {
            if (tcm->tcm_handle) {
                if (q && !(n->nlmsg_flags&NLM_F_REPLACE))
                    return -EEXIST;
                if (TC_H_MIN(tcm->tcm_handle))
                    return -EINVAL;
                if ((q = qdisc_lookup(dev, tcm->tcm_handle)) == NULL)
                    goto create_n_graft;
                if (n->nlmsg_flags&NLM_F_EXCL)
                    return -EEXIST;
                if (tca[TCA_KIND-1] && rtattr_strcmp(tca[TCA_KIND-1], q->ops->id))
                    return -EINVAL;
                if (q == p ||
                    (p && check_loop(q, p, 0)))
                    return -ELOOP;
                atomic_inc(&q->refcnt);
                goto graft;
            } else {
```

Figure 9.106 Scheduler API—change queue discipline entry: `linux/net/sched/sch_api.c`.

```
                if (q == NULL)
                    goto create_n_graft;

                /* This magic test requires explanation.
                 *
                 *  We know, that some child q is already
                 *  attached to this parent and have choice:
                 *  either to change it or to create/graft new one.
                 *
                 *  1. We are allowed to create/graft only
                 *  if CREATE and REPLACE flags are set.
                 *
                 *  2. If EXCL is set, requestor wanted to say,
                 *  that qdisc tcm_handle is not expected
                 *  to exist, so that we choose create/graft too.
                 *
                 *  3. The last case is when no flags are set.
                 *  Alas, it is sort of hole in API, we
                 *  cannot decide what to do unambiguously.
                 *  For now we select create/graft, if
                 *  user gave KIND, which does not match existing.
                 */
                if ((n->nlmsg_flags&NLM_F_CREATE) &&
                    (n->nlmsg_flags&NLM_F_REPLACE) &&
                    ((n->nlmsg_flags&NLM_F_EXCL) ||
                     (tca[TCA_KIND-1] &&
                      rtattr_strcmp(tca[TCA_KIND-1], q->ops->id))))
                    goto create_n_graft;
            }
        }
    } else {
```

```
        if (!tcm->tcm_handle)
                return -EINVAL;
        q = qdisc_lookup(dev, tcm->tcm_handle);
    }
```

Figure 9.107 Scheduler API—change queue discipline entry: `linux/net/sched/sch_api.c`.

```
    /* Change qdisc parameters */
    if (q == NULL)
            return -ENOENT;
    if (n->nlmsg_flags&NLM_F_EXCL)
            return -EEXIST;
    if (tca[TCA_KIND-1] && rtattr_strcmp(tca[TCA_KIND-1], q->ops->id))
            return -EINVAL;
    err = qdisc_change(q, tca);
    if (err == 0)
            qdisc_notify(skb, n, clid, NULL, q);
    return err;

create_n_graft:
    if (!(n->nlmsg_flags&NLM_F_CREATE))
            return -ENOENT;
    if (clid == TC_H_INGRESS)
            q = qdisc_create(dev, tcm->tcm_parent, tca, &err);
    else
            q = qdisc_create(dev, tcm->tcm_handle, tca, &err);
    if (q == NULL)
            return err;

graft:
    if (1) {
            struct Qdisc *old_q = NULL;
            err = qdisc_graft(dev, p, clid, q, &old_q);
            if (err) {
                    if (q) {
                            spin_lock_bh(&dev->queue_lock);
                            qdisc_destroy(q);
                            spin_unlock_bh(&dev->queue_lock);
                    }
                    return err;
            }
            qdisc_notify(skb, n, clid, old_q, q);
            if (old_q) {
                    spin_lock_bh(&dev->queue_lock);
                    qdisc_destroy(old_q);
                    spin_unlock_bh(&dev->queue_lock);
            }
    }
    return 0;
}
```

RTNetlink to Scheduler Interface

Figure 9.108 Scheduler API—report stats via RT: `linux/net/sched/sch_api.c`.

```
int qdisc_copy_stats(struct sk_buff *skb, struct tc_stats *st)
{
        spin_lock_bh(st->lock);
        RTA_PUT(skb, TCA_STATS, (char*)&st->lock - (char*)st, st);
        spin_unlock_bh(st->lock);
        return 0;

rtattr_failure:
        spin_unlock_bh(st->lock);
        return -1;
}
```

Figure 9.109 Scheduler API—NLM message: `linux/net/sched/sch_api.c`.

```

static int tc_fill_qdisc(struct sk_buff *skb, struct Qdisc *q, u32 clid,
                         u32 pid, u32 seq, unsigned flags, int event)
{
        struct tcmsg *tcm;
        struct nlmsghdr *nlh;
        unsigned char  *b = skb->tail;

        nlh = NLMSG_PUT(skb, pid, seq, event, sizeof(*tcm));
        nlh->nlmsg_flags = flags;
        tcm = NLMSG_DATA(nlh);
        tcm->tcm_family = AF_UNSPEC;
        tcm->tcm_ifindex = q->dev ? q->dev->ifindex : 0;
        tcm->tcm_parent = clid;
        tcm->tcm_handle = q->handle;
        tcm->tcm_info = atomic_read(&q->refcnt);
        RTA_PUT(skb, TCA_KIND, IFNAMSIZ, q->ops->id);
        if (q->ops->dump && q->ops->dump(q, skb) < 0)
                goto rtattr_failure;
        q->stats.qlen = q->q.qlen;
        if (qdisc_copy_stats(skb, &q->stats))
                goto rtattr_failure;
        nlh->nlmsg_len = skb->tail - b;
        return skb->len;

nlmsg_failure:
rtattr_failure:
        skb_trim(skb, b - skb->data);
        return -1;
}
```

Figure 9.110 Scheduler API—notify RTNetlink: `linux/net/sched/sch_api.c`.

```
static int qdisc_notify(struct sk_buff *oskb, struct nlmsghdr *n,
                        u32 clid, struct Qdisc *old, struct Qdisc *new)
{
        struct sk_buff *skb;
        u32 pid = oskb ? NETLINK_CB(oskb).pid : 0;

        skb = alloc_skb(NLMSG_GOODSIZE, GFP_KERNEL);
        if (!skb)
                return -ENOBUFS;

        if (old && old->handle) {
                if (tc_fill_qdisc(skb, old, clid, pid, n->nlmsg_seq, 0, RTM_DELQDISC) < 0)
                        goto err_out;
        }
        if (new) {
                if (tc_fill_qdisc(skb, new, clid, pid, n->nlmsg_seq, old ? NLM_F_REPLACE : 0,
                   RTM_NEWQDISC) < 0)
                        goto err_out;
        }

        if (skb->len)
                return rtnetlink_send(skb, pid, RTMGRP_TC, n->nlmsg_flags&NLM_F_ECHO);

err_out:
        kfree_skb(skb);
        return -EINVAL;
}
```

Figure 9.111 Scheduler API—dump statistics to RT: `linux/net/sched/sch_api.c`.

```
static int tc_dump_qdisc(struct sk_buff *skb, struct netlink_callback *cb)
{
        int idx, q_idx;
        int s_idx, s_q_idx;
        struct net_device *dev;
        struct Qdisc *q;

        s_idx = cb->args[0];
        s_q_idx = q_idx = cb->args[1];
        read_lock(&dev_base_lock);
        for (dev=dev_base, idx=0; dev; dev = dev->next, idx++) {
                if (idx < s_idx)
                        continue;
                if (idx > s_idx)
                        s_q_idx = 0;
                read_lock(&qdisc_tree_lock);
                for (q = dev->qdisc_list, q_idx = 0; q;
                     q = q->next, q_idx++) {
                        if (q_idx < s_q_idx)
                                continue;
                        if (tc_fill_qdisc(skb, q, 0, NETLINK_CB(cb->skb).pid,
```

```
                        cb->nlh->nlmsg_seq, NLM_F_MULTI, RTM_NEWQDISC) <= 0) {
                    read_unlock(&qdisc_tree_lock);
                    goto done;
                }
            }
            read_unlock(&qdisc_tree_lock);
        }

done:
        read_unlock(&dev_base_lock);

        cb->args[0] = idx;
        cb->args[1] = q_idx;

        return skb->len;
}
```

Figure 9.112 Scheduler API—traffic class control: `linux/net/sched/sch_api.c`.

```
static int tc_ctl_tclass(struct sk_buff *skb, struct nlmsghdr *n, void *arg)
{
        struct tcmsg *tcm = NLMSG_DATA(n);
        struct rtattr **tca = arg;
        struct net_device *dev;
        struct Qdisc *q = NULL;
        struct Qdisc_class_ops *cops;
        unsigned long cl = 0;
        unsigned long new_cl;
        u32 pid = tcm->tcm_parent;
        u32 clid = tcm->tcm_handle;
        u32 qid = TC_H_MAJ(clid);
        int err;

        if ((dev = __dev_get_by_index(tcm->tcm_ifindex)) == NULL)
              return -ENODEV;

        /*
           parent == TC_H_UNSPEC - unspecified parent.
           parent == TC_H_ROOT - class is root, which has no parent.
           parent == X:0       - parent is root class.
           parent == X:Y       - parent is a node in hierarchy.
           parent == 0:Y       - parent is X:Y, where X:0 is qdisc.

           handle == 0:0       - generate handle from kernel pool.
           handle == 0:Y       - class is X:Y, where X:0 is qdisc.
           handle == X:Y       - clear.
           handle == X:0       - root class.
         */
```

Figure 9.113 Scheduler API—traffic class control: `linux/net/sched/sch_api.c`.

```
872                /* Step 1. Determine qdisc handle X:0 */
873
874        if (pid != TC_H_ROOT) {
875                u32 qid1 = TC_H_MAJ(pid);
876
877            if (qid && qid1) {
878                    /* If both majors are known, they must be identical. */
879                    if (qid != qid1)
880                            return -EINVAL;
881            } else if (qid1) {
882                    qid = qid1;
883            } else if (qid == 0)
884                    qid = dev->qdisc_sleeping->handle;
885
886            /* Now qid is genuine qdisc handle consistent
887               both with parent and child.
888
889               TC_H_MAJ(pid) still may be unspecified, complete it now.
890             */
891            if (pid)
892                    pid = TC_H_MAKE(qid, pid);
893        } else {
894            if (qid == 0)
895                    qid = dev->qdisc_sleeping->handle;
896        }
897
898        /* OK. Locate qdisc */
899        if ((q = qdisc_lookup(dev, qid)) == NULL)
900                return -ENOENT;
901
902        /* An check that it supports classes */
903        cops = q->ops->cl_ops;
904        if (cops == NULL)
905                return -EINVAL;
```

Figure 9.114 Scheduler API—traffic class control: `linux/net/sched/sch_api.c`.

```
907        /* Now try to get class */
908        if (clid == 0) {
909                if (pid == TC_H_ROOT)
910                        clid = qid;
911        } else
912                clid = TC_H_MAKE(qid, clid);
913
914        if (clid)
915                cl = cops->get(q, clid);
916
917        if (cl == 0) {
918                err = -ENOENT;
919                if (n->nlmsg_type != RTM_NEWTCLASS || !(n->nlmsg_flags&NLM_F_CREATE))
920                        goto out;
921        } else {
922                switch (n->nlmsg_type) {
```

```
923                 case RTM_NEWTCLASS:
924                         err = -EEXIST;
925                         if (n->nlmsg_flags&NLM_F_EXCL)
926                                 goto out;
927                         break;
928                 case RTM_DELTCLASS:
929                         err = cops->delete(q, cl);
930                         if (err == 0)
931                                 tclass_notify(skb, n, q, cl, RTM_DELTCLASS);
932                         goto out;
933                 case RTM_GETTCLASS:
934                         err = tclass_notify(skb, n, q, cl, RTM_NEWTCLASS);
935                         goto out;
936                 default:
937                         err = -EINVAL;
938                         goto out;
939                 }
940         }
```

Figure 9.115 Scheduler API—traffic class control: `linux/net/sched/sch_api.c`.

```
942         new_cl = cl;
943         err = cops->change(q, clid, pid, tca, &new_cl);
944         if (err == 0)
945                 tclass_notify(skb, n, q, new_cl, RTM_NEWTCLASS);
946
947  out:
948         if (cl)
949                 cops->put(q, cl);
950
951         return err;
952  }
```

Figure 9.116 Scheduler API—traffic class report to RTNetlink: `linux/net/sched/sch_api.c`.

```
1016  static int tc_dump_tclass(struct sk_buff *skb, struct netlink_callback *cb)
1017  {
1018         int t;
1019         int s_t;
1020         struct net_device *dev;
1021         struct Qdisc *q;
1022         struct tcmsg *tcm = (struct tcmsg*)NLMSG_DATA(cb->nlh);
1023         struct qdisc_dump_args arg;
1024
1025         if (cb->nlh->nlmsg_len < NLMSG_LENGTH(sizeof(*tcm)))
1026                 return 0;
1027         if ((dev = dev_get_by_index(tcm->tcm_ifindex)) == NULL)
1028                 return 0;
1029
1030         s_t = cb->args[0];
1031
```

```
        read_lock(&qdisc_tree_lock);
        for (q=dev->qdisc_list, t=0; q; q = q->next, t++) {
              if (t < s_t) continue;
              if (!q->ops->cl_ops) continue;
              if (tcm->tcm_parent && TC_H_MAJ(tcm->tcm_parent) != q->handle)
                    continue;
              if (t > s_t)
                    memset(&cb->args[1], 0, sizeof(cb->args)-sizeof(cb->args[0]));
              arg.w.fn = qdisc_class_dump;
              arg.skb = skb;
              arg.cb = cb;
              arg.w.stop = 0;
              arg.w.skip = cb->args[1];
              arg.w.count = 0;
              q->ops->cl_ops->walk(q, &arg.w);
              cb->args[1] = arg.w.count;
              if (arg.w.stop)
                    break;
        }
        read_unlock(&qdisc_tree_lock);

        cb->args[0] = t;

        dev_put(dev);
        return skb->len;
}
```

This code is now actually scheduling packets.

Figure 9.117 Scheduler API—packet scheduling: `linux/net/sched/sch_api.c`.

```
int psched_us_per_tick = 1;
int psched_tick_per_us = 1;

#ifdef CONFIG_PROC_FS
static int psched_read_proc(char *buffer, char **start, off_t offset,
                            int length, int *eof, void *data)
{
        int len;

        len = sprintf(buffer, "%08x %08x %08x %08x\n",
                      psched_tick_per_us, psched_us_per_tick,
                      1000000, HZ);

        len -= offset;

        if (len > length)
              len = length;
        if(len < 0)
              len = 0;

        *start = buffer + offset;
```

```
1081            *eof = 1;
1082
1083            return len;
1084    }
1085    #endif
1086
1087    #if PSCHED_CLOCK_SOURCE == PSCHED_GETTIMEOFDAY
1088    int psched_tod_diff(int delta_sec, int bound)
1089    {
1090            int delta;
1091
1092            if (bound <= 1000000 || delta_sec > (0x7FFFFFFF/1000000)-1)
1093                    return bound;
1094            delta = delta_sec * 1000000;
1095            if (delta > bound)
1096                    delta = bound;
1097            return delta;
1098    }
1099    #endif
1100
1101    psched_time_t psched_time_base;
1102
1103    #if PSCHED_CLOCK_SOURCE == PSCHED_CPU
1104    psched_tdiff_t psched_clock_per_hz;
1105    int psched_clock_scale;
1106    #endif
1107
1108    #ifdef PSCHED_WATCHER
1109    PSCHED_WATCHER psched_time_mark;
1110
1111    static void psched_tick(unsigned long);
1112
1113    static struct timer_list psched_timer =
1114            { function: psched_tick };
```

Figure 9.118 Scheduler API—packet scheduling tick: `linux/net/sched/sch_api.c`.

```
1116    static void psched_tick(unsigned long dummy)
1117    {
1118    #if PSCHED_CLOCK_SOURCE == PSCHED_CPU
1119            psched_time_t dummy_stamp;
1120            PSCHED_GET_TIME(dummy_stamp);
1121            /* It is OK up to 4GHz cpu */
1122            psched_timer.expires = jiffies + 1*HZ;
1123    #else
1124            unsigned long now = jiffies;
1125            psched_time_base = ((u64)now)<<PSCHED_JSCALE;
1126            psched_time_mark = now;
1127            psched_timer.expires = now + 60*60*HZ;
1128    #endif
1129            add_timer(&psched_timer);
1130    }
```

Figure 9.119 Scheduler API—packet scheduling tick: `linux/net/sched/sch_api.c`.

```
#if PSCHED_CLOCK_SOURCE == PSCHED_CPU
int __init psched_calibrate_clock(void)
{
        psched_time_t stamp, stamp1;
        struct timeval tv, tv1;
        psched_tdiff_t delay;
        long rdelay;
        unsigned long stop;

#ifdef PSCHED_WATCHER
        psched_tick(0);
#endif
        stop = jiffies + HZ/10;
        PSCHED_GET_TIME(stamp);
        do_gettimeofday(&tv);
        while (time_before(jiffies, stop))
                barrier();
        PSCHED_GET_TIME(stamp1);
        do_gettimeofday(&tv1);

        delay = PSCHED_TDIFF(stamp1, stamp);
        rdelay = tv1.tv_usec - tv.tv_usec;
        rdelay += (tv1.tv_sec - tv.tv_sec)*1000000;
        if (rdelay > delay)
                return -1;
        delay /= rdelay;
        psched_tick_per_us = delay;
        while ((delay>>=1) != 0)
                 psched_clock_scale++;
        psched_us_per_tick = 1<<psched_clock_scale;
        psched_clock_per_hz = (psched_tick_per_us*(1000000/HZ))>>psched_clock_scale;
        return 0;
}
#endif
```

Starting Up Packet Scheduling

Figure 9.120 Scheduler API—packet scheduling initialization: `linux/net/sched/sch_api.c`.

```
int __init pktsched_init(void)
{
#ifdef CONFIG_RTNETLINK
        struct rtnetlink_link *link_p;
#endif

#if PSCHED_CLOCK_SOURCE == PSCHED_CPU
        if (psched_calibrate_clock() < 0)
                return -1;
#elif PSCHED_CLOCK_SOURCE == PSCHED_JIFFIES
        psched_tick_per_us = HZ<<PSCHED_JSCALE;
```

```
1179            psched_us_per_tick = 1000000;
1180    #ifdef PSCHED_WATCHER
1181            psched_tick(0);
1182    #endif
1183    #endif
1184
1185    #ifdef CONFIG_RTNETLINK
1186            link_p = rtnetlink_links[PF_UNSPEC];
1187
1188            /* Setup rtnetlink links. It is made here to avoid
1189              exporting large number of public symbols.
1190             */
1191
1192            if (link_p) {
1193                    link_p[RTM_NEWQDISC-RTM_BASE].doit = tc_modify_qdisc;
1194                    link_p[RTM_DELQDISC-RTM_BASE].doit = tc_get_qdisc;
1195                    link_p[RTM_GETQDISC-RTM_BASE].doit = tc_get_qdisc;
1196                    link_p[RTM_GETQDISC-RTM_BASE].dumpit = tc_dump_qdisc;
1197                    link_p[RTM_NEWTCLASS-RTM_BASE].doit = tc_ctl_tclass;
1198                    link_p[RTM_DELTCLASS-RTM_BASE].doit = tc_ctl_tclass;
1199                    link_p[RTM_GETTCLASS-RTM_BASE].doit = tc_ctl_tclass;
1200                    link_p[RTM_GETTCLASS-RTM_BASE].dumpit = tc_dump_tclass;
1201            }
```

Figure 9.121 Scheduler API—packet scheduling initialization: `linux/net/sched/sch_api.c.`

```
1203
1204    #define INIT_QDISC(name) { \
1205            extern struct Qdisc_ops name##_qdisc_ops; \
1206            register_qdisc(& name##_qdisc_ops);   \
1207            }
1208
1209            INIT_QDISC(pfifo);
1210            INIT_QDISC(bfifo);
```

Figure 9.122 Scheduler API—packet scheduling initialization: `linux/net/sched/sch_api.c.`

```
1212    #ifdef CONFIG_NET_SCH_CBQ
1213            INIT_QDISC(cbq);
1214    #endif
1215    #ifdef CONFIG_NET_SCH_CSZ
1216            INIT_QDISC(csz);
1217    #endif
1218    #ifdef CONFIG_NET_SCH_HPFQ
1219            INIT_QDISC(hpfq);
1220    #endif
1221    #ifdef CONFIG_NET_SCH_HFSC
1222            INIT_QDISC(hfsc);
```

```
#endif
#ifdef CONFIG_NET_SCH_RED
        INIT_QDISC(red);
#endif
#ifdef CONFIG_NET_SCH_GRED
        INIT_QDISC(gred);
#endif
#ifdef CONFIG_NET_SCH_INGRESS
        INIT_QDISC(ingress);
#endif
#ifdef CONFIG_NET_SCH_DSMARK
        INIT_QDISC(dsmark);
#endif
#ifdef CONFIG_NET_SCH_SFQ
        INIT_QDISC(sfq);
#endif
#ifdef CONFIG_NET_SCH_TBF
        INIT_QDISC(tbf);
#endif
#ifdef CONFIG_NET_SCH_TEQL
        teql_init();
#endif
#ifdef CONFIG_NET_SCH_PRIO
        INIT_QDISC(prio);
#endif
#ifdef CONFIG_NET_SCH_ATM
        INIT_QDISC(atm);
#endif
#ifdef CONFIG_NET_CLS
        tc_filter_init();
#endif

#ifdef CONFIG_PROC_FS
        create_proc_read_entry("net/psched", 0, 0, psched_read_proc, NULL);
#endif
```

9.11.2 Scheduler Framework

Figure 9.123 Packet scheduler interface—QDisc walker definition: `linux/include/net/pkt_sched.h`.

```

struct qdisc_walker
{
        int     stop;
        int     skip;
        int     count;
        int     (*fn)(struct Qdisc *, unsigned long cl, struct qdisc_walker *);
};
```

Figure 9.124 Packet scheduler interface—QDisc class operations: `linux/include/net/pkt_sched.h`.

```
struct Qdisc_class_ops
{
        /* Child qdisc manipulation */
        int                 (*graft)(struct Qdisc *, unsigned long cl, struct Qdisc *, struct Qdisc **);
        struct Qdisc *      (*leaf)(struct Qdisc *, unsigned long cl);

        /* Class manipulation routines */
        unsigned long       (*get)(struct Qdisc *, u32 classid);
        void                (*put)(struct Qdisc *, unsigned long);
        int                 (*change)(struct Qdisc *, u32, u32, struct rtattr **, unsigned long *);
        int                 (*delete)(struct Qdisc *, unsigned long);
        void                (*walk)(struct Qdisc *, struct qdisc_walker * arg);

        /* Filter manipulation */
        struct tcf_proto ** (*tcf_chain)(struct Qdisc *, unsigned long);
        unsigned long       (*bind_tcf)(struct Qdisc *, unsigned long, u32 classid);
        void                (*unbind_tcf)(struct Qdisc *, unsigned long);

        /* rtnetlink specific */
        int                 (*dump)(struct Qdisc *, unsigned long, struct sk_buff *skb, struct tcmsg*);
};
```

Figure 9.125 Packet scheduler interface—QDisc operations: `linux/include/net/pkt_sched.h`.

```
struct Qdisc_ops
{
        struct Qdisc_ops        *next;
        struct Qdisc_class_ops *cl_ops;
        char                    id[IFNAMSIZ];
        int                     priv_size;

        int                     (*enqueue)(struct sk_buff *, struct Qdisc *);
        struct sk_buff *        (*dequeue)(struct Qdisc *);
        int                     (*requeue)(struct sk_buff *, struct Qdisc *);
        int                     (*drop)(struct Qdisc *);

        int                     (*init)(struct Qdisc *, struct rtattr *arg);
        void                    (*reset)(struct Qdisc *);
        void                    (*destroy)(struct Qdisc *);
        int                     (*change)(struct Qdisc *, struct rtattr *arg);

        int                     (*dump)(struct Qdisc *, struct sk_buff *);
};
```

Figure 9.126 Packet scheduler interface–QDisc structure: `linux/include/net/pkt_sched.h`.

```
struct Qdisc
{
        int                    (*enqueue)(struct sk_buff *skb, struct Qdisc *dev);
        struct sk_buff *       (*dequeue)(struct Qdisc *dev);
        unsigned               flags;
#define TCQ_F_BUILTIN 1
#define TCQ_F_THROTTLED 2
#define TCQ_F_INGRES  4
        struct Qdisc_ops       *ops;
        struct Qdisc           *next;
        u32                    handle;
        atomic_t               refcnt;
        struct sk_buff_head    q;
        struct net_device      *dev;

        struct tc_stats        stats;
        int                    (*reshape_fail)(struct sk_buff *skb, struct Qdisc *q);

        /* This field is deprecated, but it is still used by CBQ
         * and it will live until better solution will be invented.
         */
        struct Qdisc           *__parent;

        char                   data[0];
};
```

Figure 9.127 Packet scheduler interface–QDisc operations: `linux/include/net/pkt_sched.h`.

```
struct qdisc_rate_table
{
        struct tc_ratespec rate;
        u32             data[256];
        struct qdisc_rate_table *next;
        int             refcnt;
};

static inline void sch_tree_lock(struct Qdisc *q)
{
        write_lock(&qdisc_tree_lock);
        spin_lock_bh(&q->dev->queue_lock);
}

static inline void sch_tree_unlock(struct Qdisc *q)
{
        spin_unlock_bh(&q->dev->queue_lock);
        write_unlock(&qdisc_tree_lock);
}

static inline void tcf_tree_lock(struct tcf_proto *tp)
```

```
{
        write_lock(&qdisc_tree_lock);
        spin_lock_bh(&tp->q->dev->queue_lock);
}

static inline void tcf_tree_unlock(struct tcf_proto *tp)
{
        spin_unlock_bh(&tp->q->dev->queue_lock);
        write_unlock(&qdisc_tree_lock);
}


static inline unsigned long
cls_set_class(struct tcf_proto *tp, unsigned long *clp, unsigned long cl)
{
        unsigned long old_cl;

        tcf_tree_lock(tp);
        old_cl = *clp;
        *clp = cl;
        tcf_tree_unlock(tp);
        return old_cl;
}

static inline unsigned long
__cls_set_class(unsigned long *clp, unsigned long cl)
{
        unsigned long old_cl;

        old_cl = *clp;
        *clp = cl;
        return old_cl;
}
```

Figure 9.128 Packet scheduler interface—clock comment: `linux/include/net/pkt_sched.h`.

```
/*
   Timer resolution MUST BE < 10% of min_schedulable_packet_size/bandwidth

   Normal IP packet size ~ 512byte, hence:

   0.5Kbyte/1Mbyte/sec = 0.5msec, so that we need 50usec timer for
   10Mbit ethernet.

   10msec resolution -> <50Kbit/sec.

   The result: [34]86 is not good choice for QoS router :-(

   The things are not so bad, because we may use artifical
   clock evaluated by integration of network data flow
   in the most critical places.

```

```
   Note: we do not use fastgettimeofday.
   The reason is that, when it is not the same thing as
   gettimeofday, it returns invalid timestamp, which is
   not updated, when net_bh is active.

   So, use PSCHED_CLOCK_SOURCE = PSCHED_CPU on alpha and pentiums
   with rtdsc. And PSCHED_JIFFIES on all other architectures, including [34]86
   and pentiums without rtdsc.
   You can use PSCHED_GETTIMEOFDAY on another architectures,
   which have fast and precise clock source, but it is too expensive.
 */

/* General note about internal clock.

   Any clock source returns time intervals, measured in units
   close to 1usec. With source PSCHED_GETTIMEOFDAY it is precisely
   microseconds, otherwise something close but different chosen to minimize
   arithmetic cost. Ratio usec/internal untis in form nominator/denominator
   may be read from /proc/net/psched.
 */
```

Figure 9.129 Scheduler API ii: `linux/net/sched/sch_api.c`.

```
#ifdef CONFIG_RTNETLINK
static int qdisc_notify(struct sk_buff *oskb, struct nlmsghdr *n, u32 clid,
                        struct Qdisc *old, struct Qdisc *new);
static int tclass_notify(struct sk_buff *oskb, struct nlmsghdr *n,
                         struct Qdisc *q, unsigned long cl, int event);
#endif
```

Figure 9.130 Scheduler API—discussion: `linux/net/sched/sch_api.c`.

```
/*

   Short review.
   -------------

   This file consists of two interrelated parts:

   1. queueing disciplines manager frontend.
   2. traffic classes manager frontend.

   Generally, queueing discipline ("qdisc") is a black box,
   which is able to enqueue packets and to dequeue them (when
   device is ready to send something) in order and at times
   determined by algorithm hidden in it.

   qdisc's are divided to two categories:
   - "queues", which have no internal structure visible from outside.
   - "schedulers", which split all the packets to "traffic classes",
```

```
  using "packet classifiers" (look at cls_api.c)

In turn, classes may have child qdiscs (as rule, queues)
attached to them etc. etc. etc.
```

Figure 9.131 Scheduler API—more discussion: `linux/net/sched/sch_api.c`.

```
The goal of the routines in this file is to translate
information supplied by user in the form of handles
to more intelligible for kernel form, to make some sanity
checks and part of work, which is common to all qdiscs
and to provide rtnetlink notifications.

All real intelligent work is done inside qdisc modules.
```

Figure 9.132 Scheduler API—more discussion: `linux/net/sched/sch_api.c`.

```
Every discipline has two major routines: enqueue and dequeue.

---dequeue

dequeue usually returns a skb to send. It is allowed to return NULL,
but it does not mean that queue is empty, it just means that
discipline does not want to send anything this time.
Queue is really empty if q->q.qlen == 0.
For complicated disciplines with multiple queues q->q is not
real packet queue, but however q->q.qlen must be valid.

---enqueue

enqueue returns 0, if packet was enqueued successfully.
If packet (this one or another one) was dropped, it returns
not zero error code.
NET_XMIT_DROP      - this packet dropped
  Expected action: do not backoff, but wait until queue will clear.
NET_XMIT_CN        - probably this packet enqueued, but another one dropped.
  Expected action: backoff or ignore
NET_XMIT_POLICED   - dropped by police.
  Expected action: backoff or error to real-time apps.
```

Figure 9.133 Scheduler API—more discussion: `linux/net/sched/sch_api.c`.

```
Auxiliary routines:

---requeue

requeues once dequeued packet. It is used for non-standard or
just buggy devices, which can defer output even if dev->tbusy=0.
```

```

    ---reset

    returns qdisc to initial state: purge all buffers, clear all
    timers, counters (except for statistics) etc.

    ---init

    initializes newly created qdisc.

    ---destroy

    destroys resources allocated by init and during lifetime of qdisc.

    ---change

    changes qdisc parameters.
  */
```

Generic Scheduler

Here is a generic example of a scheduler that acts to try to help clarify the API.

Figure 9.134 A generic scheduler—queue discipline lock comment: `linux/net/sched/sch_generic.c`.

```
 *             2 of the License, or (at your option) any later version.
 *
 * Authors:    Alexey Kuznetsov, <kuznet@ms2.inr.ac.ru>
 *             Jamal Hadi Salim, <hadi@nortelnetworks.com> 990601
 *             - Ingress support
 */

#include <asm/uaccess.h>
#include <asm/system.h>
#include <asm/bitops.h>
#include <linux/config.h>
#include <linux/types.h>
#include <linux/kernel.h>
#include <linux/sched.h>
#include <linux/string.h>
#include <linux/mm.h>
#include <linux/socket.h>
#include <linux/sockios.h>
#include <linux/in.h>
#include <linux/errno.h>
#include <linux/interrupt.h>
#include <linux/netdevice.h>
#include <linux/skbuff.h>
#include <linux/rtnetlink.h>
#include <linux/init.h>
```

```
#include <net/sock.h>
#include <net/pkt_sched.h>

/* Main transmission queue. */

/* Main qdisc structure lock.

   However, modifications
   to data, participating in scheduling must be additionally
   protected with dev->queue_lock spinlock.

   The idea is the following:
   - enqueue, dequeue are serialized via top level device
     spinlock dev->queue_lock.
   - tree walking is protected by read_lock(qdisc_tree_lock)
     and this lock is used only in process context.
   - updates to tree are made only under rtnl semaphore,
     hence this lock may be made without local bh disabling.

   qdisc_tree_lock must be grabbed BEFORE dev->queue_lock!
 */
rwlock_t qdisc_tree_lock = RW_LOCK_UNLOCKED;

/*
   dev->queue_lock serializes queue accesses for this device
   AND dev->qdisc pointer itself.

   dev->xmit_lock serializes accesses to device driver.

   dev->queue_lock and dev->xmit_lock are mutually exclusive,
   if one is grabbed, another must be free.
 */
```

Figure 9.135 A generic scheduler i: `linux/net/sched/sch_generic.c`.

```
/* Kick device.
   Note, that this procedure can be called by a watchdog timer, so that
   we do not check dev->tbusy flag here.

   Returns: 0  - queue is empty.
           >0  - queue is not empty, but throttled.
           <0  - queue is not empty. Device is throttled, if dev->tbusy != 0.

   NOTE: Called under dev->queue_lock with locally disabled BH.
*/
```

Figure 9.136 A generic scheduler i: `linux/net/sched/sch_generic.c`.

```
int qdisc_restart(struct net_device *dev)
{
        struct Qdisc *q = dev->qdisc;
        struct sk_buff *skb;

        /* Dequeue packet */
        if ((skb = q->dequeue(q)) != NULL) {
                if (spin_trylock(&dev->xmit_lock)) {
                        /* Remember that the driver is grabbed by us. */
                        dev->xmit_lock_owner = smp_processor_id();

                        /* And release queue */
                        spin_unlock(&dev->queue_lock);

                        if (!netif_queue_stopped(dev)) {
                                if (netdev_nit)
                                        dev_queue_xmit_nit(skb, dev);

                                if (dev->hard_start_xmit(skb, dev) == 0) {
                                        dev->xmit_lock_owner = -1;
                                        spin_unlock(&dev->xmit_lock);

                                        spin_lock(&dev->queue_lock);
                                        return -1;
                                }
                        }

                        /* Release the driver */
                        dev->xmit_lock_owner = -1;
                        spin_unlock(&dev->xmit_lock);
                        spin_lock(&dev->queue_lock);
                        q = dev->qdisc;
```

Figure 9.137 A generic scheduler ii: `linux/net/sched/sch_generic.c`.

```
                } else {
                        /* So, someone grabbed the driver. */

                        /* It may be transient configuration error,
                           when hard_start_xmit() recurses. We detect
                           it by checking xmit owner and drop the
                           packet when deadloop is detected.
                         */
                        if (dev->xmit_lock_owner == smp_processor_id()) {
                                kfree_skb(skb);
                                if (net_ratelimit())
                                        printk(KERN_DEBUG "Dead loop on netdevice %s, fix it
                                              urgently!\n", dev->name);
                                return -1;
                        }
                        netdev_rx_stat[smp_processor_id()].cpu_collision++;
```

```
                }

                /* Device kicked us out :(
                   This is possible in three cases:

                   0. driver is locked
                   1. fastroute is enabled
                   2. device cannot determine busy state
                      before start of transmission (f.e. dialout)
                   3. device is buggy (ppp)
                 */

                q->ops->requeue(skb, q);
                netif_schedule(dev);
                return 1;
        }
        return q->q.qlen;
}
```

Figure 9.138 A generic scheduler—watchdog timers: `linux/net/sched/sch_generic.c`.

```
static void dev_watchdog(unsigned long arg)
{
        struct net_device *dev = (struct net_device *)arg;

        spin_lock(&dev->xmit_lock);
        if (dev->qdisc != &noop_qdisc) {
                if (netif_device_present(dev) &&
                    netif_running(dev) &&
                    netif_carrier_ok(dev)) {
                        if (netif_queue_stopped(dev) &&
                            (jiffies - dev->trans_start) > dev->watchdog_timeo) {
                                printk(KERN_INFO "NETDEV WATCHDOG: %s: transmit timed out\n", dev->
                                      name);
                                dev->tx_timeout(dev);
                        }
                        if (!mod_timer(&dev->watchdog_timer, jiffies + dev->watchdog_timeo))
                                dev_hold(dev);
                }
        }
        spin_unlock(&dev->xmit_lock);

        dev_put(dev);
}

static void dev_watchdog_init(struct net_device *dev)
{
        init_timer(&dev->watchdog_timer);
        dev->watchdog_timer.data = (unsigned long)dev;
        dev->watchdog_timer.function = dev_watchdog;
}

void __netdev_watchdog_up(struct net_device *dev)
```

```
174    {
175            if (dev->tx_timeout) {
176                    if (dev->watchdog_timeo <= 0)
177                            dev->watchdog_timeo = 5*HZ;
178                    if (!mod_timer(&dev->watchdog_timer, jiffies + dev->watchdog_timeo))
179                            dev_hold(dev);
180            }
181    }
182
183    static void dev_watchdog_up(struct net_device *dev)
184    {
185            spin_lock_bh(&dev->xmit_lock);
186            __netdev_watchdog_up(dev);
187            spin_unlock_bh(&dev->xmit_lock);
188    }
189
190    static void dev_watchdog_down(struct net_device *dev)
191    {
192            spin_lock_bh(&dev->xmit_lock);
193            if (del_timer(&dev->watchdog_timer))
194                    __dev_put(dev);
195            spin_unlock_bh(&dev->xmit_lock);
196    }
```

Figure 9.139 A generic scheduler—noop scheduler: `linux/net/sched/sch_generic.c`.

```
198    /* "NOOP" scheduler: the best scheduler, recommended for all interfaces
199       under all circumstances. It is difficult to invent anything faster or
200       cheaper.
201     */
202
203    static int
204    noop_enqueue(struct sk_buff *skb, struct Qdisc * qdisc)
205    {
206            kfree_skb(skb);
207            return NET_XMIT_CN;
208    }
209
210    static struct sk_buff *
211    noop_dequeue(struct Qdisc * qdisc)
212    {
213            return NULL;
214    }
215
216    static int
217    noop_requeue(struct sk_buff *skb, struct Qdisc* qdisc)
218    {
219            if (net_ratelimit())
220                    printk(KERN_DEBUG "%s deferred output. It is buggy.\n", skb->dev->name);
221            kfree_skb(skb);
222            return NET_XMIT_CN;
223    }
```

Figure 9.140 A generic scheduler—operations: `linux/net/sched/sch_generic.c`.

```
struct Qdisc_ops noop_qdisc_ops =
{
        NULL,
        NULL,
        "noop",
        0,

        noop_enqueue,
        noop_dequeue,
        noop_requeue,
};

struct Qdisc noop_qdisc =
{
        noop_enqueue,
        noop_dequeue,
        TCQ_F_BUILTIN,
        &noop_qdisc_ops,
};


struct Qdisc_ops noqueue_qdisc_ops =
{
        NULL,
        NULL,
        "noqueue",
        0,

        noop_enqueue,
        noop_dequeue,
        noop_requeue,

};

struct Qdisc noqueue_qdisc =
{
        NULL,
        noop_dequeue,
        TCQ_F_BUILTIN,
        &noqueue_qdisc_ops,
};
```

Figure 9.141 A generic scheduler—PFIFO operations: `linux/net/sched/sch_generic.c`.

```
268   static const u8 prio2band[TC_PRIO_MAX+1] =
269   { 1, 2, 2, 2, 1, 2, 0, 0 , 1, 1, 1, 1, 1, 1, 1, 1 };
270
271   /* 3-band FIFO queue: old style, but should be a bit faster than
272      generic prio+fifo combination.
273    */
274
275   static int
276   pfifo_fast_enqueue(struct sk_buff *skb, struct Qdisc* qdisc)
277   {
278          struct sk_buff_head *list;
279
280          list = ((struct sk_buff_head*)qdisc->data) +
281                    prio2band[skb->priority&TC_PRIO_MAX];
282
283          if (list->qlen <= skb->dev->tx_queue_len) {
284                 __skb_queue_tail(list, skb);
285                 qdisc->q.qlen++;
286                 return 0;
287          }
288          qdisc->stats.drops++;
289          kfree_skb(skb);
290          return NET_XMIT_DROP;
291   }
```

Figure 9.142 A generic scheduler—PFIFO operations: `linux/net/sched/sch_generic.c`.

```
293   static struct sk_buff *
294   pfifo_fast_dequeue(struct Qdisc* qdisc)
295   {
296          int prio;
297          struct sk_buff_head *list = ((struct sk_buff_head*)qdisc->data);
298          struct sk_buff *skb;
299
300          for (prio = 0; prio < 3; prio++, list++) {
301                 skb = __skb_dequeue(list);
302                 if (skb) {
303                        qdisc->q.qlen--;
304                        return skb;
305                 }
306          }
307          return NULL;
308   }
309
310   static int
311   pfifo_fast_requeue(struct sk_buff *skb, struct Qdisc* qdisc)
312   {
313          struct sk_buff_head *list;
314
315          list = ((struct sk_buff_head*)qdisc->data) +
316                    prio2band[skb->priority&TC_PRIO_MAX];
```

```
317
318            __skb_queue_head(list, skb);
319            qdisc->q.qlen++;
320            return 0;
321    }
322
323    static void
324    pfifo_fast_reset(struct Qdisc* qdisc)
325    {
326            int prio;
327            struct sk_buff_head *list = ((struct sk_buff_head*)qdisc->data);
328
329            for (prio=0; prio < 3; prio++)
330                    skb_queue_purge(list+prio);
331            qdisc->q.qlen = 0;
332    }
333
334    static int pfifo_fast_init(struct Qdisc *qdisc, struct rtattr *opt)
335    {
336            int i;
337            struct sk_buff_head *list;
338
339            list = ((struct sk_buff_head*)qdisc->data);
340
341            for (i=0; i<3; i++)
342                    skb_queue_head_init(list+i);
343
344            return 0;
345    }
```

Figure 9.143 A generic scheduler—PFIFO declare: `linux/net/sched/sch_generic.c`.

```
347    static struct Qdisc_ops pfifo_fast_ops =
348    {
349            NULL,
350            NULL,
351            "pfifo_fast",
352            3 * sizeof(struct sk_buff_head),
353
354            pfifo_fast_enqueue,
355            pfifo_fast_dequeue,
356            pfifo_fast_requeue,
357            NULL,
358
359            pfifo_fast_init,
360            pfifo_fast_reset,
361    };
```

Figure 9.144 A generic scheduler—create default entry: `linux/net/sched/sch_generic.c`.

```
struct Qdisc * qdisc_create_dflt(struct net_device *dev, struct Qdisc_ops *ops)
{
        struct Qdisc *sch;
        int size = sizeof(*sch) + ops->priv_size;

        sch = kmalloc(size, GFP_KERNEL);
        if (!sch)
                return NULL;
        memset(sch, 0, size);

        skb_queue_head_init(&sch->q);
        sch->ops = ops;
        sch->enqueue = ops->enqueue;
        sch->dequeue = ops->dequeue;
        sch->dev = dev;
        sch->stats.lock = &dev->queue_lock;
        atomic_set(&sch->refcnt, 1);
        if (!ops->init || ops->init(sch, NULL) == 0)
                return sch;

        kfree(sch);
        return NULL;
}
```

9.12 Class-Based Queuing

CBQ is a framework, or if you prefer, a metadiscipline, within which subdisciplines are placed. Initially, a filter will run to classify a packet, which will then be handed to the CBQ discipline—within this discipline, the same filter/classify/queue steps are recursively rerun to decide which subclass the packet belongs to. This can go on as long as you like. The CSZ framework discussed later is similar.

Figure 9.145 CBQ—initial comment i: `linux/net/sched/sch_cbq.c`.

```
/*      Class-Based Queueing (CBQ) algorithm.
        =======================================

        Sources: [1] Sally Floyd and Van Jacobson, "Link-sharing and Resource
                 Management Models for Packet Networks",
                 IEEE/ACM Transactions on Networking, Vol.3, No.4, 1995

                 [2] Sally Floyd, "Notes on CBQ and Guaranted Service", 1995

                 [3] Sally Floyd, "Notes on Class-Based Queueing: Setting
                 Parameters", 1996

```

```
        [4] Sally Floyd and Michael Speer, "Experimental Results
        for Class-Based Queueing", 1998, not published.

-----------------------------------------------------------------------

Algorithm skeleton was taken from NS simulator cbq.cc.
If someone wants to check this code against the LBL version,
he should take into account that ONLY the skeleton was borrowed,
the implementation is different. Particularly:

--- The WRR algorithm is different. Our version looks more
reasonable (I hope) and works when quanta are allowed to be
less than MTU, which is always the case when real time classes
have small rates. Note, that the statement of [3] is
incomplete, delay may actually be estimated even if class
per-round allotment is less than MTU. Namely, if per-round
allotment is W*r_i, and r_1+...+r_k = r < 1

delay_i <= ([MTU/(W*r_i)]*W*r + W*r + k*MTU)/B

In the worst case we have IntServ estimate with D = W*r+k*MTU
and C = MTU*r. The proof (if correct at all) is trivial.
```

Figure 9.146 CBQ—initial comment ii: `linux/net/sched/sch_cbq.c`.

```
--- It seems that cbq-2.0 is not very accurate. At least, I cannot
interpret some places, which look like wrong translations
from NS. Anyone is advised to find these differences
and explain to me, why I am wrong 8).

--- Linux has no EOI event, so that we cannot estimate true class
idle time. Workaround is to consider the next dequeue event
as sign that previous packet is finished. This is wrong because of
internal device queueing, but on a permanently loaded link it is true.
Moreover, combined with clock integrator, this scheme looks
very close to an ideal solution. */
```

Figure 9.147 CBQ—class structure definition i: `linux/net/sched/sch_cbq.c`.

```
struct cbq_sched_data;


struct cbq_class
{
        struct cbq_class        *next;          /* hash table link */
        struct cbq_class        *next_alive;    /* next class with backlog in this priority band */

/* Parameters */
        u32                     classid;
        unsigned char           priority;       /* class priority */
```

Figure 9.148 CBQ—class structure definition i: `linux/net/sched/sch_cbq.c`.

```
        unsigned char           priority2;      /* priority to be used after overlimit */
        unsigned char           ewma_log;       /* time constant for idle time calculation */
        unsigned char           ovl_strategy;
#ifdef CONFIG_NET_CLS_POLICE
        unsigned char           police;
#endif

        u32                     defmap;
```

Figure 9.149 CBQ—class structure definition ii: `linux/net/sched/sch_cbq.c`.

```
        /* Link-sharing scheduler parameters */
        long                    maxidle;        /* Class paramters: see below. */
        long                    offtime;
        long                    minidle;
        u32                     avpkt;
        struct qdisc_rate_table *R_tab;

        /* Overlimit strategy parameters */
        void                    (*overlimit)(struct cbq_class *cl);
        long                    penalty;

        /* General scheduler (WRR) parameters */
        long                    allot;
        long                    quantum;        /* Allotment per WRR round */
        long                    weight;         /* Relative allotment: see below */

        struct Qdisc            *qdisc;         /* Ptr to CBQ discipline */
        struct cbq_class        *split;         /* Ptr to split node */
        struct cbq_class        *share;         /* Ptr to LS parent in the class tree */
        struct cbq_class        *tparent;       /* Ptr to tree parent in the class tree */
        struct cbq_class        *borrow;        /* NULL if class is bandwidth limited;
                                                   parent otherwise */
        struct cbq_class        *sibling;       /* Sibling chain */
        struct cbq_class        *children;      /* Pointer to children chain */

        struct Qdisc            *q;             /* Elementary queueing discipline */
```

Figure 9.150 CBQ—class structure definition iii: `linux/net/sched/sch_cbq.c`.

```
/* Variables */
        unsigned char           cpriority;      /* Effective priority */
        unsigned char           delayed;
        unsigned char           level;          /* level of the class in hierarchy:
                                                   0 for leaf classes, and maximal
                                                   level of children + 1 for nodes.
                                                 */

        psched_time_t           last;           /* Last end of service */
```

Figure 9.151 CBQ—class structure definition iv: `linux/net/sched/sch_cbq.c`.

```
        psched_time_t       undertime;
        long                avgidle;
        long                deficit;        /* Saved deficit for WRR */
        unsigned long       penalized;
        struct tc_stats     stats;
        struct tc_cbq_xstats xstats;

        struct tcf_proto    *filter_list;

        int                 refcnt;
        int                 filters;

        struct cbq_class    *defaults[TC_PRIO_MAX+1];
};
```

Figure 9.152 CBQ—scheduling data forwarding: `linux/net/sched/sch_cbq.c`.

```
struct cbq_sched_data
{
        struct cbq_class    *classes[16];        /* Hash table of all classes */
        int                 nclasses[TC_CBQ_MAXPRIO+1];
        unsigned            quanta[TC_CBQ_MAXPRIO+1];

        struct cbq_class    link;

        unsigned            activemask;
        struct cbq_class    *active[TC_CBQ_MAXPRIO+1];   /* List of all classes
                                                            with backlog */

#ifdef CONFIG_NET_CLS_POLICE
        struct cbq_class    *rx_class;
#endif
        struct cbq_class    *tx_class;
        struct cbq_class    *tx_borrowed;
        int                 tx_len;
        psched_time_t       now;            /* Cached timestamp */
        psched_time_t       now_rt;         /* Cached real time */
        unsigned            pmask;

        struct timer_list   delay_timer;
        struct timer_list   wd_timer;       /* Watchdog timer,
                                               started when CBQ has
                                               backlog, but cannot
                                               transmit just now */
        long                wd_expires;
        int                 toplevel;
        u32                 hgenerator;
};
```

The Actual Classifier

Figure 9.153 CBQ—classifier i: `linux/net/sched/sch_cbq.c`.

```
/* Classify packet. The procedure is pretty complicated, but
   it allows us to combine link sharing and priority scheduling
   transparently.

   Namely, you can put link sharing rules (f.e. route based) at root of CBQ,
   so that it resolves to split nodes. Then packets are classified
   by logical priority, or a more specific classifier may be attached
   to the split node.
 */

static struct cbq_class *
cbq_classify(struct sk_buff *skb, struct Qdisc *sch)
{
        struct cbq_sched_data *q = (struct cbq_sched_data*)sch->data;
        struct cbq_class *head = &q->link;
        struct cbq_class **defmap;
        struct cbq_class *cl = NULL;
        u32 prio = skb->priority;
        struct tcf_result res;

        /*
         * Step 1. If skb->priority points to one of our classes, use it.
         */
        if (TC_H_MAJ(prio^sch->handle) == 0 &&
            (cl = cbq_class_lookup(q, prio)) != NULL)
                return cl;

        for (;;) {
                int result = 0;

                defmap = head->defaults;

                /*
                 * Step 2+n. Apply classifier.
                 */
                if (!head->filter_list || (result = tc_classify(skb, head->filter_list, &res))
                        < 0)
                        goto fallback;

                if ((cl = (void*)res.class) == NULL) {
                        if (TC_H_MAJ(res.classid))
                                cl = cbq_class_lookup(q, res.classid);
                        else if ((cl = defmap[res.classid&TC_PRIO_MAX]) == NULL)
                                cl = defmap[TC_PRIO_BESTEFFORT];

                        if (cl == NULL || cl->level >= head->level)
                                goto fallback;
                }
```

Figure 9.154 CBQ—classifier ii: `linux/net/sched/sch_cbq.c`.

```
278    #ifdef CONFIG_NET_CLS_POLICE
279                    switch (result) {
280                    case TC_POLICE_RECLASSIFY:
281                            return cbq_reclassify(skb, cl);
282                    case TC_POLICE_SHOT:
283                            return NULL;
284                    default:
285                    }
286    #endif
287                    if (cl->level == 0)
288                            return cl;
289
290                    /*
291                     * Step 3+n. If classifier selected a link sharing class,
292                     *       apply agency specific classifier.
293                     *       Repeat this procdure until we hit a leaf node.
294                     */
295                    head = cl;
296            }
297
298    fallback:
299            cl = head;
300
301            /*
302             * Step 4. No success...
303             */
304            if (TC_H_MAJ(prio) == 0 &&
305                !(cl = head->defaults[prio&TC_PRIO_MAX]) &&
306                !(cl = head->defaults[TC_PRIO_BESTEFFORT]))
307                    return head;
308
309            return cl;
310    }
```

Figure 9.155 CBQ—reclassifier: `linux/net/sched/sch_cbq.c`.

```
216    static struct cbq_class *
217    cbq_reclassify(struct sk_buff *skb, struct cbq_class *this)
218    {
219            struct cbq_class *cl, *new;
220
221            for (cl = this->tparent; cl; cl = cl->tparent)
222                    if ((new = cl->defaults[TC_PRIO_BESTEFFORT]) != NULL && new != this)
223                            return new;
224
225            return NULL;
226    }
```

Using a Class

Figure 9.156 CBQ—activate or deactivate a class: `linux/net/sched/sch_cbq.c`.

```
/*
   A packet has just been enqueued on the empty class.
   cbq_activate_class adds it to the tail of active class list
   of its priority band.
 */

static __inline__ void cbq_activate_class(struct cbq_class *cl)
{
        struct cbq_sched_data *q = (struct cbq_sched_data*)cl->qdisc->data;
        int prio = cl->cpriority;
        struct cbq_class *cl_tail;

        cl_tail = q->active[prio];
        q->active[prio] = cl;

        if (cl_tail != NULL) {
                cl->next_alive = cl_tail->next_alive;
                cl_tail->next_alive = cl;
        } else {
                cl->next_alive = cl;
                q->activemask |= (1<<prio);
        }
}
```

Figure 9.157 CBQ—activate or deactivate a class: `linux/net/sched/sch_cbq.c`.

```
/*
   Unlink class from active chain.
   Note that this same procedure is done directly in cbq_dequeue*
   during round-robin procedure.
 */

static void cbq_deactivate_class(struct cbq_class *this)
{
        struct cbq_sched_data *q = (struct cbq_sched_data*)this->qdisc->data;
        int prio = this->cpriority;
        struct cbq_class *cl;
        struct cbq_class *cl_prev = q->active[prio];

        do {
                cl = cl_prev->next_alive;
                if (cl == this) {
                        cl_prev->next_alive = cl->next_alive;
                        cl->next_alive = NULL;

                        if (cl == q->active[prio]) {
                                q->active[prio] = cl_prev;
                                if (cl == q->active[prio]) {
                                        q->active[prio] = NULL;
```

```
                                        q->activemask &= ~(1<<prio);
                                        return;
                                }
                        }

                        cl = cl_prev->next_alive;
                        return;
                }
        } while ((cl_prev = cl) != q->active[prio]);
}
```

Marking a Class

Figure 9.158 CBQ—mark top level: `linux/net/sched/sch_cbq.c`.

```
static void
cbq_mark_toplevel(struct cbq_sched_data *q, struct cbq_class *cl)
{
        int toplevel = q->toplevel;

        if (toplevel > cl->level && !(cl->q->flags&TCQ_F_THROTTLED)) {
                psched_time_t now;
                psched_tdiff_t incr;

                PSCHED_GET_TIME(now);
                incr = PSCHED_TDIFF(now, q->now_rt);
                PSCHED_TADD2(q->now, incr, now);

                do {
                        if (PSCHED_TLESS(cl->undertime, now)) {
                                q->toplevel = cl->level;
                                return;
                        }
                } while ((cl=cl->borrow) != NULL && toplevel > cl->level);
        }
}
```

CBQ Queuing Actions

Figure 9.159 CBQ—enqueue: `linux/net/sched/sch_cbq.c`.

```
static int
cbq_enqueue(struct sk_buff *skb, struct Qdisc *sch)
{
        struct cbq_sched_data *q = (struct cbq_sched_data *)sch->data;
        struct cbq_class *cl = cbq_classify(skb, sch);
        int len = skb->len;
        int ret = NET_XMIT_POLICED;

#ifdef CONFIG_NET_CLS_POLICE
```

```
        q->rx_class = cl;
#endif
        if (cl) {
#ifdef CONFIG_NET_CLS_POLICE
                cl->q->__parent = sch;
#endif
                if ((ret = cl->q->enqueue(skb, cl->q)) == 0) {
                        sch->q.qlen++;
                        sch->stats.packets++;
                        sch->stats.bytes+=len;
                        cbq_mark_toplevel(q, cl);
                        if (!cl->next_alive)
                                cbq_activate_class(cl);
                        return 0;
                }
        }

        sch->stats.drops++;
        if (cl == NULL)
                kfree_skb(skb);
        else {
                cbq_mark_toplevel(q, cl);
                cl->stats.drops++;
        }
        return ret;
}
```

Figure 9.160 CBQ—requeue: `linux/net/sched/sch_cbq.c`.

```
static int
cbq_requeue(struct sk_buff *skb, struct Qdisc *sch)
{
        struct cbq_sched_data *q = (struct cbq_sched_data *)sch->data;
        struct cbq_class *cl;
        int ret;

        if ((cl = q->tx_class) == NULL) {
                kfree_skb(skb);
                sch->stats.drops++;
                return NET_XMIT_CN;
        }
        q->tx_class = NULL;

        cbq_mark_toplevel(q, cl);

#ifdef CONFIG_NET_CLS_POLICE
        q->rx_class = cl;
        cl->q->__parent = sch;
#endif
        if ((ret = cl->q->ops->requeue(skb, cl->q)) == 0) {
                sch->q.qlen++;
                if (!cl->next_alive)
                        cbq_activate_class(cl);
```

```
452                  return 0;
453         }
454         sch->stats.drops++;
455         cl->stats.drops++;
456         return ret;
457 }
```

Here are the overlimit functions.

Figure 9.161 CBQ—overlimit: `linux/net/sched/sch_cbq.c`.

```
459 /* Overlimit actions */
460
461 /* TC_CBQ_OVL_CLASSIC: (default) penalize leaf class by adding offtime */
462
463 static void cbq_ovl_classic(struct cbq_class *cl)
464 {
465         struct cbq_sched_data *q = (struct cbq_sched_data *)cl->qdisc->data;
466         psched_tdiff_t delay = PSCHED_TDIFF(cl->undertime, q->now);
467
468         if (!cl->delayed) {
469                 delay += cl->offtime;
470
471                 /*
472                    Class goes to sleep, so that it will have no
473                    chance to work avgidle. Let's forgive it 8)
474
475                    BTW cbq-2.0 has a crap in this
476                    place, apparently they forgot to shift it by cl->ewma_log.
477                  */
478                 if (cl->avgidle < 0)
479                         delay -= (-cl->avgidle) - ((-cl->avgidle) >> cl->ewma_log);
480                 if (cl->avgidle < cl->minidle)
481                         cl->avgidle = cl->minidle;
482                 if (delay <= 0)
483                         delay = 1;
484                 PSCHED_TADD2(q->now, delay, cl->undertime);
485
486                 cl->xstats.overactions++;
487                 cl->delayed = 1;
488         }
489         if (q->wd_expires == 0 || q->wd_expires > delay)
490                 q->wd_expires = delay;
491
492         /* Dirty work! We must schedule wakeups based on
493            real available rate, rather than leaf rate,
494            which may be tiny (even zero).
495          */
496         if (q->toplevel == TC_CBQ_MAXLEVEL) {
497                 struct cbq_class *b;
498                 psched_tdiff_t base_delay = q->wd_expires;
```

```

                for (b = cl->borrow; b; b = b->borrow) {
                        delay = PSCHED_TDIFF(b->undertime, q->now);
                        if (delay < base_delay) {
                                if (delay <= 0)
                                        delay = 1;
                                base_delay = delay;
                        }
                }

                q->wd_expires = delay;
        }
}
```

Figure 9.162 CBQ—overlimit: reclassify: `linux/net/sched/sch_cbq.c.`

```
/* TC_CBQ_OVL_RCLASSIC: penalize by offtime classes in hierarchy, when
   they go overlimit
 */

static void cbq_ovl_rclassic(struct cbq_class *cl)
{
        struct cbq_sched_data *q = (struct cbq_sched_data *)cl->qdisc->data;
        struct cbq_class *this = cl;

        do {
                if (cl->level > q->toplevel) {
                        cl = NULL;
                        break;
                }
        } while ((cl = cl->borrow) != NULL);

        if (cl == NULL)
                cl = this;
        cbq_ovl_classic(cl);
}
```

Figure 9.163 CBQ—overlimit: delay: `linux/net/sched/sch_cbq.c.`

```
/* TC_CBQ_OVL_DELAY: delay until it will go to underlimit */

static void cbq_ovl_delay(struct cbq_class *cl)
{
        struct cbq_sched_data *q = (struct cbq_sched_data *)cl->qdisc->data;
        psched_tdiff_t delay = PSCHED_TDIFF(cl->undertime, q->now);

        if (!cl->delayed) {
                unsigned long sched = jiffies;

                delay += cl->offtime;
                if (cl->avgidle < 0)
```

```
                        delay -= (-cl->avgidle) - ((-cl->avgidle) >> cl->ewma_log);
                if (cl->avgidle < cl->minidle)
                        cl->avgidle = cl->minidle;
                PSCHED_TADD2(q->now, delay, cl->undertime);

                if (delay > 0) {
                        sched += PSCHED_US2JIFFIE(delay) + cl->penalty;
                        cl->penalized = sched;
                        cl->cpriority = TC_CBQ_MAXPRIO;
                        q->pmask |= (1<<TC_CBQ_MAXPRIO);
                        if (del_timer(&q->delay_timer) &&
                            (long)(q->delay_timer.expires - sched) > 0)
                                q->delay_timer.expires = sched;
                        add_timer(&q->delay_timer);
                        cl->delayed = 1;
                        cl->xstats.overactions++;
                        return;
                }
                delay = 1;
        }
        if (q->wd_expires == 0 || q->wd_expires > delay)
                q->wd_expires = delay;
}
```

Figure 9.164 CBQ—overlimit: lower priority or even drop: `linux/net/sched/sch_cbq.c`.

```
/* TC_CBQ_OVL_LOWPRIO: penalize class by lowering its priority band */

static void cbq_ovl_lowprio(struct cbq_class *cl)
{
        struct cbq_sched_data *q = (struct cbq_sched_data*)cl->qdisc->data;

        cl->penalized = jiffies + cl->penalty;

        if (cl->cpriority != cl->priority2) {
                cl->cpriority = cl->priority2;
                q->pmask |= (1<<cl->cpriority);
                cl->xstats.overactions++;
        }
        cbq_ovl_classic(cl);
}

/* TC_CBQ_OVL_DROP: penalize class by dropping */

static void cbq_ovl_drop(struct cbq_class *cl)
{
        if (cl->q->ops->drop)
                if (cl->q->ops->drop(cl->q))
                        cl->qdisc->q.qlen--;
        cl->xstats.overactions++;
        cbq_ovl_classic(cl);
}
```

Figure 9.165 CBQ—watchdog timer: `linux/net/sched/sch_cbq.c`.

```
static void cbq_watchdog(unsigned long arg)
{
	struct Qdisc *sch = (struct Qdisc*)arg;

	sch->flags &= ~TCQ_F_THROTTLED;
	netif_schedule(sch->dev);
}
```

Figure 9.166 CBQ—remove delay priority penalty: `linux/net/sched/sch_cbq.c`.

```
static unsigned long cbq_undelay_prio(struct cbq_sched_data *q, int prio)
{
	struct cbq_class *cl;
	struct cbq_class *cl_prev = q->active[prio];
	unsigned long now = jiffies;
	unsigned long sched = now;

	if (cl_prev == NULL)
		return now;

	do {
		cl = cl_prev->next_alive;
		if ((long)(now - cl->penalized) > 0) {
			cl_prev->next_alive = cl->next_alive;
			cl->next_alive = NULL;
			cl->cpriority = cl->priority;
			cl->delayed = 0;
			cbq_activate_class(cl);

			if (cl == q->active[prio]) {
				q->active[prio] = cl_prev;
				if (cl == q->active[prio]) {
					q->active[prio] = NULL;
					return 0;
				}
			}

			cl = cl_prev->next_alive;
		} else if ((long)(sched - cl->penalized) > 0)
			sched = cl->penalized;
	} while ((cl_prev = cl) != q->active[prio]);

	return (long)(sched - now);
}
```

Figure 9.167 CBQ—remove delay penalty: `linux/net/sched/sch_cbq.c`.

```
static void cbq_undelay(unsigned long arg)
{
        struct Qdisc *sch = (struct Qdisc*)arg;
        struct cbq_sched_data *q = (struct cbq_sched_data*)sch->data;
        long delay = 0;
        unsigned pmask;

        pmask = q->pmask;
        q->pmask = 0;

        while (pmask) {
                int prio = ffz(~pmask);
                long tmp;

                pmask &= ~(1<<prio);

                tmp = cbq_undelay_prio(q, prio);
                if (tmp > 0) {
                        q->pmask |= 1<<prio;
                        if (tmp < delay || delay == 0)
                                delay = tmp;
                }
        }

        if (delay) {
                q->delay_timer.expires = jiffies + delay;
                add_timer(&q->delay_timer);
        }

        sch->flags &= ~TCQ_F_THROTTLED;
        netif_schedule(sch->dev);
}
```

Figure 9.168 CBQ—reshape: `linux/net/sched/sch_cbq.c`.

```

static int cbq_reshape_fail(struct sk_buff *skb, struct Qdisc *child)
{
        int len = skb->len;
        struct Qdisc *sch = child->__parent;
        struct cbq_sched_data *q = (struct cbq_sched_data *)sch->data;
        struct cbq_class *cl = q->rx_class;

        q->rx_class = NULL;

        if (cl && (cl = cbq_reclassify(skb, cl)) != NULL) {

                cbq_mark_toplevel(q, cl);

                q->rx_class = cl;
                cl->q->__parent = sch;

```

```
            if (cl->q->enqueue(skb, cl->q) == 0) {
                sch->q.qlen++;
                sch->stats.packets++;
                sch->stats.bytes+=len;
                if (!cl->next_alive)
                    cbq_activate_class(cl);
                return 0;
            }
            sch->stats.drops++;
            return 0;
        }

        sch->stats.drops++;
        return -1;
}
```

We need to propagate the occupancy of each child up to the top of the CBQ tree to make sure we get the underlimit/overlimit and borrow actions correct.

Figure 9.169 CBQ—update top-level occupancy: `linux/net/sched/sch_cbq.c`.

```
/*
   It is mission critical procedure.

   We "regenerate" toplevel cutoff, if transmitting class
   has backlog and it is not regulated. It is not part of
   original CBQ description, but looks more reasonable.
   Probably, it is wrong. This question needs further investigation.
*/

static __inline__ void
cbq_update_toplevel(struct cbq_sched_data *q, struct cbq_class *cl,
                    struct cbq_class *borrowed)
{
        if (cl && q->toplevel >= borrowed->level) {
                if (cl->q->q.qlen > 1) {
                        do {
                                if (PSCHED_IS_PASTPERFECT(borrowed->undertime)) {
                                        q->toplevel = borrowed->level;
                                        return;
                                }
                        } while ((borrowed=borrowed->borrow) != NULL);
                }
#if 0
        /* It is not necessary now. Uncommenting it
           will save CPU cycles, but decrease fairness.
         */
                q->toplevel = TC_CBQ_MAXLEVEL;
#endif
        }
}
```

Then we propagate this to each level.

Figure 9.170 CBQ—update each level's occupancy i: `linux/net/sched/sch_cbq.c`.

```
static void
cbq_update(struct cbq_sched_data *q)
{
        struct cbq_class *this = q->tx_class;
        struct cbq_class *cl = this;
        int len = q->tx_len;

        q->tx_class = NULL;

        for ( ; cl; cl = cl->share) {
                long avgidle = cl->avgidle;
                long idle;

                cl->stats.packets++;
                cl->stats.bytes += len;

                /*
                   (now - last) is total time between packet right edges.
                   (last_pktlen/rate) is "virtual" busy time, so that

                         idle = (now - last) - last_pktlen/rate
                 */

                idle = PSCHED_TDIFF(q->now, cl->last);
                if ((unsigned long)idle > 128*1024*1024) {
                        avgidle = cl->maxidle;
                } else {
                        idle -= L2T(cl, len);

                /* true_avgidle := (1-W)*true_avgidle + W*idle,
                   where W=2^{-ewma_log}. But cl->avgidle is scaled:
                   cl->avgidle == true_avgidle/W,
                   hence:
                 */
                        avgidle += idle - (avgidle>>cl->ewma_log);
                }
```

Figure 9.171 CBQ—update each level's occupancy ii: `linux/net/sched/sch_cbq.c`.

```

                        if (avgidle < cl->minidle)
                                avgidle = cl->minidle;

                        cl->avgidle = avgidle;

                        /* Calculate expected time, when this class
                           will be allowed to send.
                           It will occur, when:
                           (1-W)*true_avgidle + W*delay = 0, i.e.
```

```
                        idle = (1/W - 1)*(-true_avgidle)
                        or
                        idle = (1 - W)*(-cl->avgidle);
                      */
                     idle = (-avgidle) - ((-avgidle) >> cl->ewma_log);

                     /*
                        That is not all.
                        To maintain the rate allocated to the class,
                        we add to undertime virtual clock,
                        necesary to complete transmitted packet.
                        (len/phys_bandwidth has been already passed
                        to the moment of cbq_update)
                      */

                     idle -= L2T(&q->link, len);
                     idle += L2T(cl, len);

                     PSCHED_AUDIT_TDIFF(idle);

                     PSCHED_TADD2(q->now, idle, cl->undertime);
```

Figure 9.172 CBQ—update each level's occupancy iii: `linux/net/sched/sch_cbq.c`.

```
              } else {
                     /* Underlimit */

                     PSCHED_SET_PASTPERFECT(cl->undertime);
                     if (avgidle > cl->maxidle)
                            cl->avgidle = cl->maxidle;
                     else
                            cl->avgidle = avgidle;
              }
              cl->last = q->now;
       }

       cbq_update_toplevel(q, this, q->tx_borrowed);
}
```

If a level is underlimit, we may need to lend capacity.

Figure 9.173 CBQ—underlimit actions: `linux/net/sched/sch_cbq.c`.

```
static __inline__ struct cbq_class *
cbq_under_limit(struct cbq_class *cl)
{
       struct cbq_sched_data *q = (struct cbq_sched_data*)cl->qdisc->data;
       struct cbq_class *this_cl = cl;
```

```

        if (cl->tparent == NULL)
              return cl;

        if (PSCHED_IS_PASTPERFECT(cl->undertime) ||
            !PSCHED_TLESS(q->now, cl->undertime)) {
              cl->delayed = 0;
              return cl;
        }

        do {
              /* It is very suspicious place. Now overlimit
                 action is generated for not bounded classes
                 only if link is completely congested.
                 Though it is in agree with ancestor-only paradigm,
                 it looks very stupid. Particularly,
                 it means that this chunk of code will either
                 never be called or result in strong amplification
                 of burstiness. Dangerous, silly, and, however,
                 no another solution exists.
               */
              if ((cl = cl->borrow) == NULL) {
                    this_cl->stats.overlimits++;
                    this_cl->overlimit(this_cl);
                    return NULL;
              }
              if (cl->level > q->toplevel)
                    return NULL;
        } while (!PSCHED_IS_PASTPERFECT(cl->undertime) &&
                 PSCHED_TLESS(q->now, cl->undertime));

        cl->delayed = 0;
        return cl;
}
```

If we are dequeuing a packet, which is first?

Figure 9.174 CBQ—dequeue by priorities i: `linux/net/sched/sch_cbq.c`.

```
static __inline__ struct sk_buff *
cbq_dequeue_prio(struct Qdisc *sch, int prio)
{
        struct cbq_sched_data *q = (struct cbq_sched_data *)sch->data;
        struct cbq_class *cl_tail, *cl_prev, *cl;
        struct sk_buff *skb;
        int deficit;

        cl_tail = cl_prev = q->active[prio];
        cl = cl_prev->next_alive;

        do {
```

```
877                     deficit = 0;
878
879                     /* Start round */
880                     do {
881                             struct cbq_class *borrow = cl;
882
883                             if (cl->q->q.qlen &&
884                                 (borrow = cbq_under_limit(cl)) == NULL)
885                                     goto skip_class;
886
887                             if (cl->deficit <= 0) {
888                                     /* Class exhausted its allotment per
889                                        this round. Switch to the next one.
890                                      */
891                                     deficit = 1;
892                                     cl->deficit += cl->quantum;
893                                     goto next_class;
894                             }
895
896                             skb = cl->q->dequeue(cl->q);
```

Figure 9.175 CBQ—dequeue by priorities ii: `linux/net/sched/sch_cbq.c`.

```
898                             /* Class did not give us any skb :-(
899                                It could occur even if cl->q->q.qlen != 0
900                                f.e. if cl->q == "tbf"
901                              */
902                             if (skb == NULL)
903                                     goto skip_class;
904
905                             cl->deficit -= skb->len;
906                             q->tx_class = cl;
907                             q->tx_borrowed = borrow;
908                             if (borrow != cl) {
909     #ifndef CBQ_XSTATS_BORROWS_BYTES
910                                     borrow->xstats.borrows++;
911                                     cl->xstats.borrows++;
912     #else
913                                     borrow->xstats.borrows += skb->len;
914                                     cl->xstats.borrows += skb->len;
915     #endif
916                             }
917                             q->tx_len = skb->len;
918
919                             if (cl->deficit <= 0) {
920                                     q->active[prio] = cl;
921                                     cl = cl->next_alive;
922                                     cl->deficit += cl->quantum;
923                             }
924                             return skb;
```

Figure 9.176 CBQ—dequeue by priorities iii: `linux/net/sched/sch_cbq.c`.

```
skip_class:
                        if (cl->q->q.qlen == 0 || prio != cl->cpriority) {
                                /* Class is empty or penalized.
                                   Unlink it from active chain.
                                 */
                                cl_prev->next_alive = cl->next_alive;
                                cl->next_alive = NULL;

                                /* Did cl_tail point to it? */
                                if (cl == cl_tail) {
                                        /* Repair it! */
                                        cl_tail = cl_prev;

                                        /* Was it the last class in this band? */
                                        if (cl == cl_tail) {
                                                /* Kill the band! */
                                                q->active[prio] = NULL;
                                                q->activemask &= ~(1<<prio);
                                                if (cl->q->q.qlen)
                                                        cbq_activate_class(cl);
                                                return NULL;
                                        }
```

Figure 9.177 CBQ—dequeue by priorities iv: `linux/net/sched/sch_cbq.c`.

```
                                        q->active[prio] = cl_tail;
                                }
                                if (cl->q->q.qlen)
                                        cbq_activate_class(cl);

                                cl = cl_prev;
                        }

next_class:
                        cl_prev = cl;
                        cl = cl->next_alive;
                } while (cl_prev != cl_tail);
        } while (deficit);

        q->active[prio] = cl_prev;

        return NULL;
}
```

Figure 9.178 CBQ—dequeue 1: `linux/net/sched/sch_cbq.c`.

```
static __inline__ struct sk_buff *
cbq_dequeue_1(struct Qdisc *sch)
{
        struct cbq_sched_data *q = (struct cbq_sched_data *)sch->data;
        struct sk_buff *skb;
        unsigned activemask;

        activemask = q->activemask&0xFF;
        while (activemask) {
                int prio = ffz(~activemask);
                activemask &= ~(1<<prio);
                skb = cbq_dequeue_prio(sch, prio);
                if (skb)
                        return skb;
        }
        return NULL;
}
```

Figure 9.179 CBQ—main dequeue functon i: `linux/net/sched/sch_cbq.c`.

```
static struct sk_buff *
cbq_dequeue(struct Qdisc *sch)
{
        struct sk_buff *skb;
        struct cbq_sched_data *q = (struct cbq_sched_data *)sch->data;
        psched_time_t now;
        psched_tdiff_t incr;

        PSCHED_GET_TIME(now);
        incr = PSCHED_TDIFF(now, q->now_rt);

        if (q->tx_class) {
                psched_tdiff_t incr2;
                /* Time integrator. We calculate EOS time
                   by adding expected packet transmittion time.
                   If real time is greater, we warp artificial clock,
                   so that:

                   cbq_time = max(real_time, work);
                 */
                incr2 = L2T(&q->link, q->tx_len);
                PSCHED_TADD(q->now, incr2);
                cbq_update(q);
                if ((incr -= incr2) < 0)
                        incr = 0;
        }
        PSCHED_TADD(q->now, incr);
        q->now_rt = now;
```

Figure 9.180 CBQ—main dequeue functon: linux/net/sched/sch_cbq.c.

```
1015            for (;;) {
1016                    q->wd_expires = 0;
1017
1018                    skb = cbq_dequeue_1(sch);
1019                    if (skb) {
1020                            sch->q.qlen--;
1021                            sch->flags &= ~TCQ_F_THROTTLED;
1022                            return skb;
1023                    }
1024
1025                    /* All the classes are overlimit.
1026
1027                       It is possible, if:
1028
1029                       1. Scheduler is empty.
1030                       2. Toplevel cutoff inhibited borrowing.
1031                       3. Root class is overlimit.
1032
1033                       Reset 2d and 3d conditions and retry.
1034
1035                       Note, that NS and cbq-2.0 are buggy, peeking
1036                       an arbitrary class is appropriate for ancestor-only
1037                       sharing, but not for toplevel algorithm.
1038
1039                       Our version is better, but slower, because it requires
1040                       two passes, but it is unavoidable with top-level sharing.
1041                     */
1042
1043                    if (q->toplevel == TC_CBQ_MAXLEVEL &&
1044                        PSCHED_IS_PASTPERFECT(q->link.undertime))
1045                            break;
1046
1047                    q->toplevel = TC_CBQ_MAXLEVEL;
1048                    PSCHED_SET_PASTPERFECT(q->link.undertime);
1049            }
```

Figure 9.181 CBQ—main dequeue functon: linux/net/sched/sch_cbq.c.

```
1051            /* No packets in scheduler or nobody wants to give them to us :-(
1052               Sigh... start watchdog timer in the last case. */
1053
1054            if (sch->q.qlen) {
1055                    sch->stats.overlimits++;
1056                    if (q->wd_expires && !netif_queue_stopped(sch->dev)) {
1057                            long delay = PSCHED_US2JIFFIE(q->wd_expires);
1058                            del_timer(&q->wd_timer);
1059                            if (delay <= 0)
1060                                    delay = 1;
1061                            q->wd_timer.expires = jiffies + delay;
1062                            add_timer(&q->wd_timer);
1063                            sch->flags |= TCQ_F_THROTTLED;
```

```
            }
        }
        return NULL;
}
```

Figure 9.182 CBQ—maintenance functions: `linux/net/sched/sch_cbq.c.`

```
/* CBQ class maintanance routines */

static void cbq_adjust_levels(struct cbq_class *this)
{
        if (this == NULL)
                return;

        do {
                int level = 0;
                struct cbq_class *cl;

                if ((cl = this->children) != NULL) {
                        do {
                                if (cl->level > level)
                                        level = cl->level;
                        } while ((cl = cl->sibling) != this->children);
                }
                this->level = level+1;
        } while ((this = this->tparent) != NULL);
```

Then we initialize the CBQ machinery.

Figure 9.183 CBQ—initialize CBQ i: `linux/net/sched/sch_cbq.c.`

```
static int cbq_init(struct Qdisc *sch, struct rtattr *opt)
{
        struct cbq_sched_data *q = (struct cbq_sched_data*)sch->data;
        struct rtattr *tb[TCA_CBQ_MAX];
        struct tc_ratespec *r;

        if (rtattr_parse(tb, TCA_CBQ_MAX, RTA_DATA(opt), RTA_PAYLOAD(opt)) < 0 ||
            tb[TCA_CBQ_RTAB-1] == NULL || tb[TCA_CBQ_RATE-1] == NULL ||
            RTA_PAYLOAD(tb[TCA_CBQ_RATE-1]) < sizeof(struct tc_ratespec))
                return -EINVAL;

        if (tb[TCA_CBQ_LSSOPT-1] &&
            RTA_PAYLOAD(tb[TCA_CBQ_LSSOPT-1]) < sizeof(struct tc_cbq_lssopt))
                return -EINVAL;

        r = RTA_DATA(tb[TCA_CBQ_RATE-1]);

```

```
        MOD_INC_USE_COUNT;
        if ((q->link.R_tab = qdisc_get_rtab(r, tb[TCA_CBQ_RTAB-1])) == NULL) {
                MOD_DEC_USE_COUNT;
                return -EINVAL;
        }
```

Figure 9.184 CBQ—initialize CBQ ii: `linux/net/sched/sch_cbq.c`.

```
        q->link.refcnt = 1;
        q->link.sibling = &q->link;
        q->link.classid = sch->handle;
        q->link.qdisc = sch;
        if (!(q->link.q = qdisc_create_dflt(sch->dev, &pfifo_qdisc_ops)))
                q->link.q = &noop_qdisc;

        q->link.priority = TC_CBQ_MAXPRIO-1;
        q->link.priority2 = TC_CBQ_MAXPRIO-1;
        q->link.cpriority = TC_CBQ_MAXPRIO-1;
        q->link.ovl_strategy = TC_CBQ_OVL_CLASSIC;
        q->link.overlimit = cbq_ovl_classic;
        q->link.allot = psched_mtu(sch->dev);
        q->link.quantum = q->link.allot;
        q->link.weight = q->link.R_tab->rate.rate;

        q->link.ewma_log = TC_CBQ_DEF_EWMA;
        q->link.avpkt = q->link.allot/2;
        q->link.minidle = -0x7FFFFFFF;
        q->link.stats.lock = &sch->dev->queue_lock;
```

Figure 9.185 CBQ—initialize CBQ iii: `linux/net/sched/sch_cbq.c`.

```
        init_timer(&q->wd_timer);
        q->wd_timer.data = (unsigned long)sch;
        q->wd_timer.function = cbq_watchdog;
        init_timer(&q->delay_timer);
        q->delay_timer.data = (unsigned long)sch;
        q->delay_timer.function = cbq_undelay;
        q->toplevel = TC_CBQ_MAXLEVEL;
        PSCHED_GET_TIME(q->now);
        q->now_rt = q->now;

        cbq_link_class(&q->link);

        if (tb[TCA_CBQ_LSSOPT-1])
                cbq_set_lss(&q->link, RTA_DATA(tb[TCA_CBQ_LSSOPT-1]));

        cbq_addprio(q, &q->link);
        return 0;
}
```

Now we manage the whole system.

Figure 9.186 CBQ—grafting and pruning classes i: `linux/net/sched/sch_cbq.c`.

```
1660    static int cbq_graft(struct Qdisc *sch, unsigned long arg, struct Qdisc *new,
1661                        struct Qdisc **old)
1662    {
1663            struct cbq_class *cl = (struct cbq_class*)arg;
1664
1665            if (cl) {
1666                    if (new == NULL) {
1667                            if ((new = qdisc_create_dflt(sch->dev, &pfifo_qdisc_ops)) == NULL)
1668                                    return -ENOBUFS;
1669                    } else {
1670    #ifdef CONFIG_NET_CLS_POLICE
1671                            if (cl->police == TC_POLICE_RECLASSIFY)
1672                                    new->reshape_fail = cbq_reshape_fail;
1673    #endif
1674                    }
1675                    sch_tree_lock(sch);
1676                    *old = cl->q;
1677                    cl->q = new;
1678                    qdisc_reset(*old);
1679                    sch_tree_unlock(sch);
1680
1681                    return 0;
1682            }
1683            return -ENOENT;
1684    }
```

Figure 9.187 CBQ—grafting and pruning classes ii: `linux/net/sched/sch_cbq.c`.

```
1686    static struct Qdisc *
1687    cbq_leaf(struct Qdisc *sch, unsigned long arg)
1688    {
1689            struct cbq_class *cl = (struct cbq_class*)arg;
1690
1691            return cl ? cl->q : NULL;
1692    }
1693
1694    static unsigned long cbq_get(struct Qdisc *sch, u32 classid)
1695    {
1696            struct cbq_sched_data *q = (struct cbq_sched_data *)sch->data;
1697            struct cbq_class *cl = cbq_class_lookup(q, classid);
1698
1699            if (cl) {
1700                    cl->refcnt++;
1701                    return (unsigned long)cl;
1702            }
1703            return 0;
1704    }
```

Figure 9.188 CBQ—grafting and pruning classes iii: `linux/net/sched/sch_cbq.c`.

```
static void cbq_destroy_filters(struct cbq_class *cl)
{
        struct tcf_proto *tp;

        while ((tp = cl->filter_list) != NULL) {
                cl->filter_list = tp->next;
                tp->ops->destroy(tp);
        }
}

static void cbq_destroy_class(struct cbq_class *cl)
{
        cbq_destroy_filters(cl);
        qdisc_destroy(cl->q);
        qdisc_put_rtab(cl->R_tab);
#ifdef CONFIG_NET_ESTIMATOR
        qdisc_kill_estimator(&cl->stats);
#endif
        kfree(cl);
}
```

Here's the core part of CBQ.

Figure 9.189 CBQ: `linux/net/sched/sch_cbq.c`.

```
static int
cbq_change_class(struct Qdisc *sch, u32 classid, u32 parentid, struct rtattr **tca,
                 unsigned long *arg)
{
        int err;
        struct cbq_sched_data *q = (struct cbq_sched_data *)sch->data;
        struct cbq_class *cl = (struct cbq_class*)*arg;
        struct rtattr *opt = tca[TCA_OPTIONS-1];
        struct rtattr *tb[TCA_CBQ_MAX];
        struct cbq_class *parent;
        struct qdisc_rate_table *rtab = NULL;

        if (opt==NULL ||
            rtattr_parse(tb, TCA_CBQ_MAX, RTA_DATA(opt), RTA_PAYLOAD(opt)))
                return -EINVAL;

        if (tb[TCA_CBQ_OVL_STRATEGY-1] &&
            RTA_PAYLOAD(tb[TCA_CBQ_OVL_STRATEGY-1]) < sizeof(struct tc_cbq_ovl))
                return -EINVAL;

        if (tb[TCA_CBQ_FOPT-1] &&
            RTA_PAYLOAD(tb[TCA_CBQ_FOPT-1]) < sizeof(struct tc_cbq_fopt))
                return -EINVAL;

```

```
        if (tb[TCA_CBQ_RATE-1] &&
            RTA_PAYLOAD(tb[TCA_CBQ_RATE-1]) < sizeof(struct tc_ratespec))
                        return -EINVAL;

        if (tb[TCA_CBQ_LSSOPT-1] &&
            RTA_PAYLOAD(tb[TCA_CBQ_LSSOPT-1]) < sizeof(struct tc_cbq_lssopt))
                        return -EINVAL;

        if (tb[TCA_CBQ_WRROPT-1] &&
            RTA_PAYLOAD(tb[TCA_CBQ_WRROPT-1]) < sizeof(struct tc_cbq_wrropt))
                        return -EINVAL;

#ifdef CONFIG_NET_CLS_POLICE
        if (tb[TCA_CBQ_POLICE-1] &&
            RTA_PAYLOAD(tb[TCA_CBQ_POLICE-1]) < sizeof(struct tc_cbq_police))
                        return -EINVAL;
#endif

        if (cl) {
                /* Check parent */
                if (parentid) {
                        if (cl->tparent && cl->tparent->classid != parentid)
                                return -EINVAL;
                        if (!cl->tparent && parentid != TC_H_ROOT)
                                return -EINVAL;
                }

                if (tb[TCA_CBQ_RATE-1]) {
                        rtab = qdisc_get_rtab(RTA_DATA(tb[TCA_CBQ_RATE-1]), tb[TCA_CBQ_RTAB-1]);
                        if (rtab == NULL)
                                return -EINVAL;
                }
```

Figure 9.190 CBQ: linux/net/sched/sch_cbq.c.

```
                /* Change class parameters */
                sch_tree_lock(sch);

                if (cl->next_alive != NULL)
                        cbq_deactivate_class(cl);

                if (rtab) {
                        rtab = xchg(&cl->R_tab, rtab);
                        qdisc_put_rtab(rtab);
                }

                if (tb[TCA_CBQ_LSSOPT-1])
                        cbq_set_lss(cl, RTA_DATA(tb[TCA_CBQ_LSSOPT-1]));

                if (tb[TCA_CBQ_WRROPT-1]) {
                        cbq_rmprio(q, cl);
                        cbq_set_wrr(cl, RTA_DATA(tb[TCA_CBQ_WRROPT-1]));
                }
```

```
	if (tb[TCA_CBQ_OVL_STRATEGY-1])
		cbq_set_overlimit(cl, RTA_DATA(tb[TCA_CBQ_OVL_STRATEGY-1]));

#ifdef CONFIG_NET_CLS_POLICE
	if (tb[TCA_CBQ_POLICE-1])
		cbq_set_police(cl, RTA_DATA(tb[TCA_CBQ_POLICE-1]));
#endif

	if (tb[TCA_CBQ_FOPT-1])
		cbq_set_fopt(cl, RTA_DATA(tb[TCA_CBQ_FOPT-1]));

	if (cl->q->q.qlen)
		cbq_activate_class(cl);

	sch_tree_unlock(sch);
```

Figure 9.191 CBQ: `linux/net/sched/sch_cbq.c.`

```
#ifdef CONFIG_NET_ESTIMATOR
		if (tca[TCA_RATE-1]) {
			qdisc_kill_estimator(&cl->stats);
			qdisc_new_estimator(&cl->stats, tca[TCA_RATE-1]);
		}
#endif
		return 0;
	}

	if (parentid == TC_H_ROOT)
		return -EINVAL;

	if (tb[TCA_CBQ_WRROPT-1] == NULL || tb[TCA_CBQ_RATE-1] == NULL ||
	    tb[TCA_CBQ_LSSOPT-1] == NULL)
		return -EINVAL;

	rtab = qdisc_get_rtab(RTA_DATA(tb[TCA_CBQ_RATE-1]), tb[TCA_CBQ_RTAB-1]);
	if (rtab == NULL)
		return -EINVAL;

	if (classid) {
		err = -EINVAL;
		if (TC_H_MAJ(classid^sch->handle) || cbq_class_lookup(q, classid))
			goto failure;
	} else {
		int i;
		classid = TC_H_MAKE(sch->handle,0x8000);

		for (i=0; i<0x8000; i++) {
			if (++q->hgenerator >= 0x8000)
				q->hgenerator = 1;
			if (cbq_class_lookup(q, classid|q->hgenerator) == NULL)
				break;
		}
```

```
                err = -ENOSR;
                if (i >= 0x8000)
                        goto failure;
                classid = classid|q->hgenerator;
        }
```

Figure 9.192 CBQ: linux/net/sched/sch_cbq.c.

```
        parent = &q->link;
        if (parentid) {
                parent = cbq_class_lookup(q, parentid);
                err = -EINVAL;
                if (parent == NULL)
                        goto failure;
        }

        err = -ENOBUFS;
        cl = kmalloc(sizeof(*cl), GFP_KERNEL);
        if (cl == NULL)
                goto failure;
        memset(cl, 0, sizeof(*cl));
        cl->R_tab = rtab;
        rtab = NULL;
        cl->refcnt = 1;
        if (!(cl->q = qdisc_create_dflt(sch->dev, &pfifo_qdisc_ops)))
                cl->q = &noop_qdisc;
        cl->classid = classid;
        cl->tparent = parent;
        cl->qdisc = sch;
        cl->allot = parent->allot;
        cl->quantum = cl->allot;
        cl->weight = cl->R_tab->rate.rate;
        cl->stats.lock = &sch->dev->queue_lock;

        sch_tree_lock(sch);
        cbq_link_class(cl);
        cl->borrow = cl->tparent;
        if (cl->tparent != &q->link)
                cl->share = cl->tparent;
        cbq_adjust_levels(parent);
        cl->minidle = -0x7FFFFFFF;
        cbq_set_lss(cl, RTA_DATA(tb[TCA_CBQ_LSSOPT-1]));
        cbq_set_wrr(cl, RTA_DATA(tb[TCA_CBQ_WRROPT-1]));
        if (cl->ewma_log==0)
                cl->ewma_log = q->link.ewma_log;
        if (cl->maxidle==0)
                cl->maxidle = q->link.maxidle;
        if (cl->avpkt==0)
                cl->avpkt = q->link.avpkt;
        cl->overlimit = cbq_ovl_classic;
        if (tb[TCA_CBQ_OVL_STRATEGY-1])
                cbq_set_overlimit(cl, RTA_DATA(tb[TCA_CBQ_OVL_STRATEGY-1]));
```

Figure 9.193 CBQ: `linux/net/sched/sch_cbq.c`.

```
1946    #ifdef CONFIG_NET_CLS_POLICE
1947            if (tb[TCA_CBQ_POLICE-1])
1948                    cbq_set_police(cl, RTA_DATA(tb[TCA_CBQ_POLICE-1]));
1949    #endif
1950            if (tb[TCA_CBQ_FOPT-1])
1951                    cbq_set_fopt(cl, RTA_DATA(tb[TCA_CBQ_FOPT-1]));
1952            sch_tree_unlock(sch);
1953
1954    #ifdef CONFIG_NET_ESTIMATOR
1955            if (tca[TCA_RATE-1])
1956                    qdisc_new_estimator(&cl->stats, tca[TCA_RATE-1]);
1957    #endif
1958
1959            *arg = (unsigned long)cl;
1960            return 0;
1961
1962    failure:
1963            qdisc_put_rtab(rtab);
1964            return err;
1965    }
```

Figure 9.194 CBQ—delete CBQ from Qdisc : `linux/net/sched/sch_cbq.c`.

```
1967    static int cbq_delete(struct Qdisc *sch, unsigned long arg)
1968    {
1969            struct cbq_sched_data *q = (struct cbq_sched_data *)sch->data;
1970            struct cbq_class *cl = (struct cbq_class*)arg;
1971
1972            if (cl->filters || cl->children || cl == &q->link)
1973                    return -EBUSY;
1974
1975            sch_tree_lock(sch);
1976
1977            if (cl->next_alive)
1978                    cbq_deactivate_class(cl);
1979
1980            if (q->tx_borrowed == cl)
1981                    q->tx_borrowed = q->tx_class;
1982            if (q->tx_class == cl) {
1983                    q->tx_class = NULL;
1984                    q->tx_borrowed = NULL;
1985            }
1986    #ifdef CONFIG_NET_CLS_POLICE
1987            if (q->rx_class == cl)
1988                    q->rx_class = NULL;
1989    #endif
1990
1991            cbq_unlink_class(cl);
1992            cbq_adjust_levels(cl->tparent);
1993            cl->defmap = 0;
1994            cbq_sync_defmap(cl);
```

```

        cbq_rmprio(q, cl);
        sch_tree_unlock(sch);

        if (--cl->refcnt == 0)
             cbq_destroy_class(cl);

        return 0;
}
```

Clark/Shenker/Zhang Scheduling

Clark, Shenker, and Zhang [19] suggested a different structure for a hierarchical classification architecture.

Figure 9.195 Clark/Shenker/Zhang scheduling—initial comment: `linux/net/sched/sch_csz.c`.

```
/*      Clark-Shenker-Zhang algorithm.
        =======================================

        SOURCE.

        David D. Clark, Scott Shenker and Lixia Zhang
        "Supporting Real-Time Applications in an Integrated Services Packet
        Network: Architecture and Mechanism".

        CBQ presents a flexible universal algorithm for packet scheduling,
        but it has pretty poor delay characteristics.
        Round-robin scheduling and link-sharing goals
        apparently contradict minimization of network delay and jitter.
        Moreover, correct handling of predictive flows seems to be
        impossible in CBQ.

        CSZ presents a more precise but less flexible and less efficient
        approach. As I understand it, the main idea is to create
        WFQ flows for each guaranteed service and to allocate
        the rest of bandwith to dummy flow-0. Flow-0 comprises
        the predictive services and the best effort traffic;
        it is handled by a priority scheduler with the highest
        priority band allocated for predictive services, and the rest ---
        to the best effort packets.

        Note that in CSZ flows are NOT limited to their bandwidth. It
        is supposed that the flow passed admission control at the edge
        of the QoS network and it doesn't need further shaping. Any
        attempt to improve the flow or to shape it to a token bucket
        at intermediate hops will introduce undesired delays and raise
        jitter.
```

```
	At the moment CSZ is the only scheduler that provides
	true guaranteed service. Another schemes (including CBQ)
	do not provide guaranteed delay and randomize jitter.
	There is a proof (Sally Floyd), that delay
	can be estimated by a IntServ compliant formula.
	This result is true formally, but it is wrong in principle.
	It takes into account only round-robin delays,
	ignoring delays introduced by link sharing i.e. overlimiting.
	Note that temporary overlimits are inevitable because
	real links are not ideal, and the real algorithm must take this
	into account.
```

Figure 9.196 CSZ notation: `linux/net/sched/sch_csz.c`.

```
	--- Notations.

	$B$ is link bandwidth (bits/sec).

	$I$ is set of all flows, including flow $0$.
	Every flow $a \in I$ has associated bandwidth slice $r_a < 1$ and
	$\sum_{a \in I} r_a = 1$.

	--- Flow model.

	Let $m_a$ is the number of backlogged bits in flow $a$.
	The flow is {\em active}, if $m_a > 0$.
	This number is a discontinuous function of time;
	when a packet $i$ arrives:
	\[
	m_a(t_i+0) - m_a(t_i-0) = L^i,
	\]
	where $L^i$ is the length of the arrived packet.
	The flow queue is drained continuously until $m_a == 0$:
	\[
	{d m_a \over dt} = - { B r_a \over \sum_{b \in A} r_b}.
	\]
	I.e. flow rates are their allocated rates proportionally
	scaled to take all available link bandwidth. Apparently,
	it is not the only possible policy. F.e. CBQ classes
	without borrowing would be modelled by:
	\[
	{d m_a \over dt} = - B r_a .
	\]
	More complicated hierarchical bandwidth allocation
	policies are possible, but unfortunately, the basic
	flow equations have a simple solution only for proportional
	scaling.
```

Figure 9.197 CSZ departure times: linux/net/sched/sch_csz.c.

```
120        --- Departure times.
121
122        We calculate the time until the last bit of packet is sent:
123        \[
124        E_a^i(t) = { m_a(t_i) - \delta_a(t) \over r_a },
125        \]
126        where $\delta_a(t)$ is number of bits drained since $t_i$.
127        We have to evaluate $E_a^i$ for all queued packets,
128        then find the packet with minimal $E_a^i$ and send it.
129
130        This sounds good, but direct implementation of the algorithm
131        is absolutely infeasible. Luckily, if flow rates
132        are scaled proportionally, the equations have a simple solution.
133
134        The differential equation for $E_a^i$ is
135        \[
136        {d E_a^i (t) \over dt } = - { d \delta_a(t) \over dt} { 1 \over r_a} =
137        { B \over \sum_{b \in A} r_b}
138        \]
139        with initial condition
140        \[
141        E_a^i (t_i) = { m_a(t_i) \over r_a } .
142        \]
143
144        Let's introduce an auxiliary function $R(t)$:
```

Figure 9.198 CSZ—the round: linux/net/sched/sch_csz.c.

```
146        --- Round number.
147
148        Consider the following model: we rotate over active flows,
149        sending $r_a B$ bits from every flow, so that we send
150        $B \sum_{a \in A} r_a$ bits per round, that takes
151        $\sum_{a \in A} r_a$ seconds.
152
153        Hence, $R(t)$ (round number) is a monotonically increasing
154        linear function of time when $A$ is not changed
155        \[
156        { d R(t) \over dt } = { 1 \over \sum_{a \in A} r_a }
157        \]
158        and it is continuous when $A$ changes.
159
160        The central observation is that the quantity
161        $F_a^i = R(t) + E_a^i(t)/B$ does not depend on time at all!
162        $R(t)$ does not depend on flow, so that $F_a^i$ can be
163        calculated only once on packet arrival, and we need not
164        recalculate $E$ numbers and resorting queues.
165        The number $F_a^i$ is called finish number of the packet.
166        It is just the value of $R(t)$ when the last bit of packet
167        is sent out.
168
```

```
Maximal finish number on flow is called finish number of flow
and minimal one is "start number of flow".
Apparently, flow is active if and only if $F_a \leq R$.
```

Figure 9.199 CSZ—the round: `linux/net/sched/sch_csz.c`.

```
When a packet of length $L_i$ bit arrives to flow $a$ at time $t_i$,
we calculate $F_a^i$ as:

If flow was inactive ($F_a < R$):
$F_a^i = R(t) + {L_i \over B r_a}$
otherwise
$F_a^i = F_a + {L_i \over B r_a}$

These equations complete the algorithm specification.
```

Figure 9.200 CSZ discussion: `linux/net/sched/sch_csz.c`.

```
It looks pretty hairy, but there is a simple
procedure for solving these equations.
See procedure csz_update(), that is a generalization of
the algorithm from S. Keshav's thesis Chapter 3
"Efficient Implementation of Fair Queeing".

NOTES.

* We implement only the simplest variant of CSZ,
when flow-0 is a explicit 4band priority fifo.
This is bad, but we need a "peek" operation in addition
to "dequeue" to implement complete CSZ.
I do not want to do that, unless it is absolutely
necessary.
```

Figure 9.201 CSZ discussion: `linux/net/sched/sch_csz.c`.

```
* A primitive support for token bucket filtering
presents itself too. It directly contradicts CSZ, but
even though the Internet is on the globe ... :-)
"the edges of the network" really exist.

BUGS.

* Fixed point arithmetic is overcomplicated, suboptimal and even
wrong. Check it later. */
```

The code and data structures are similar to CBQ, so we don't cover those here.

9.13 Queue Management

As discussed previously, queue management is really about what to do when the queue occupancy is becoming a source of problems.

9.13.1 Best-Effort (Also Known as FIFO) Scheduler

Here we see the classic set of standard queue management functions for the simplest (default) case, that of FIFO queuing.

Figure 9.202 FIFO queuing scheduler—data: `linux/net/sched/sch_fifo.c`.

```
/* 1 band FIFO pseudo-"scheduler" */

struct fifo_sched_data
{
        unsigned limit;
};
```

Figure 9.203 FIFO queuing scheduler—enqueue: `linux/net/sched/sch_fifo.c`.

```
static int
bfifo_enqueue(struct sk_buff *skb, struct Qdisc* sch)
{
        struct fifo_sched_data *q = (struct fifo_sched_data *)sch->data;

        if (sch->stats.backlog <= q->limit) {
                __skb_queue_tail(&sch->q, skb);
                sch->stats.backlog += skb->len;
                sch->stats.bytes += skb->len;
                sch->stats.packets++;
                return 0;
        }
        sch->stats.drops++;
#ifdef CONFIG_NET_CLS_POLICE
        if (sch->reshape_fail==NULL || sch->reshape_fail(skb, sch))
#endif
                kfree_skb(skb);
        return NET_XMIT_DROP;
}
```

Figure 9.204 FIFO queuing scheduler—requeue: `linux/net/sched/sch_fifo.c`.

```
static int
bfifo_requeue(struct sk_buff *skb, struct Qdisc* sch)
{
        __skb_queue_head(&sch->q, skb);
        sch->stats.backlog += skb->len;
        return 0;
}
```

Figure 9.205 FIFO queuing scheduler—dequeue: `linux/net/sched/sch_fifo.c`.

```
static struct sk_buff *
bfifo_dequeue(struct Qdisc* sch)
{
        struct sk_buff *skb;

        skb = __skb_dequeue(&sch->q);
        if (skb)
                sch->stats.backlog -= skb->len;
        return skb;
}
```

Figure 9.206 FIFO queuing scheduler—drop: `linux/net/sched/sch_fifo.c`.

```
static int
fifo_drop(struct Qdisc* sch)
{
        struct sk_buff *skb;

        skb = __skb_dequeue_tail(&sch->q);
        if (skb) {
                sch->stats.backlog -= skb->len;
                kfree_skb(skb);
                return 1;
        }
        return 0;
}
```

Figure 9.207 FIFO queuing scheduler—reset: `linux/net/sched/sch_fifo.c`.

```
static void
fifo_reset(struct Qdisc* sch)
{
        skb_queue_purge(&sch->q);
        sch->stats.backlog = 0;
}
```

Then we also have to have reshaping versions of all of those functions.

Figure 9.208 FIFO queuing scheduler—enqueue: `linux/net/sched/sch_fifo.c`.

```
pfifo_enqueue(struct sk_buff *skb, struct Qdisc* sch)
{
        struct fifo_sched_data *q = (struct fifo_sched_data *)sch->data;

        if (sch->q.qlen <= q->limit) {
                __skb_queue_tail(&sch->q, skb);
                sch->stats.bytes += skb->len;
                sch->stats.packets++;
                return 0;
        }
        sch->stats.drops++;
#ifdef CONFIG_NET_CLS_POLICE
        if (sch->reshape_fail==NULL || sch->reshape_fail(skb, sch))
#endif
                kfree_skb(skb);
        return NET_XMIT_DROP;
}
```

Figure 9.209 FIFO queuing scheduler—requeue: `linux/net/sched/sch_fifo.c`.

```
static int
pfifo_requeue(struct sk_buff *skb, struct Qdisc* sch)
{
        __skb_queue_head(&sch->q, skb);
        return 0;
}
```

Figure 9.210 FIFO queuing scheduler—dequeue: `linux/net/sched/sch_fifo.c`.

```
static struct sk_buff *
pfifo_dequeue(struct Qdisc* sch)
{
        return __skb_dequeue(&sch->q);
}
```

Figure 9.211 FIFO queuing scheduler—init: `linux/net/sched/sch_fifo.c`.

```
{
        struct fifo_sched_data *q = (void*)sch->data;

        if (opt == NULL) {
                if (sch->ops == &bfifo_qdisc_ops)
```

```
                q->limit = sch->dev->tx_queue_len*sch->dev->mtu;
            else
                q->limit = sch->dev->tx_queue_len;
        } else {
            struct tc_fifo_qopt *ctl = RTA_DATA(opt);
            if (opt->rta_len < RTA_LENGTH(sizeof(*ctl)))
                return -EINVAL;
            q->limit = ctl->limit;
        }
        return 0;
}
```

This is how the system estimates rates.

Figure 9.212 Rate estimator—general purpose block comment: `linux/net/sched/estimator.c`.

```
/*
   This code is NOT intended to be used for statistics collection,
   its purpose is to provide a base for statistical multiplexing
   for controlled load service.
   If you need only statistics, run a user level daemon which
   periodically reads byte counters.

   Unfortunately, rate estimation is not a very easy task.
   F.e. I did not find a simple way to estimate the current peak rate
   and even failed to formulate the problem 8)8)

   So I preferred not to built an estimator into the scheduler,
   but run this task separately.
   Ideally, it should be kernel thread(s), but for now it runs
   from timers, which puts apparent top bounds on the number of rated
   flows, has minimal overhead on small, but is enough
   to handle controlled load service, sets of aggregates.

   We measure rate over A=(1<<interval) seconds and evaluate EWMA:

   avrate = avrate*(1-W) + rate*W

   where W is chosen as negative power of 2: W = 2^(-ewma_log)

   The resulting time constant is:

   T = A/(-ln(1-W))


   NOTES.

   * The stored value for avbps is scaled by 2^5, so that maximal
     rate is ~1Gbit, avpps is scaled by 2^10.

   * Minimal interval is HZ/4=250msec (it is the greatest common divisor
```

```
68        for HZ=100 and HZ=1024 8)), maximal interval
69        is (HZ/4)*2^EST_MAX_INTERVAL = 8sec. Shorter intervals
70        are too expensive, longer ones can be implemented
71        at user level painlessly.
72   */
```

Figure 9.213 Rate estimator—data: `linux/net/sched/estimator.c`.

```
74   #if (HZ%4) != 0
75   #error Bad HZ value.
76   #endif
77
78   #define EST_MAX_INTERVAL      5
79
80   struct qdisc_estimator
81   {
82           struct qdisc_estimator *next;
83           struct tc_stats        *stats;
84           unsigned               interval;
85           int                    ewma_log;
86           u64                    last_bytes;
87           u32                    last_packets;
88           u32                    avpps;
89           u32                    avbps;
90   };
91
92   struct qdisc_estimator_head
93   {
94           struct timer_list    timer;
95           struct qdisc_estimator *list;
96   };
97
98   static struct qdisc_estimator_head elist[EST_MAX_INTERVAL+1];
99
100  /* Estimator array lock */
101  static rwlock_t est_lock = RW_LOCK_UNLOCKED;
```

Figure 9.214 Rate estimator—timer routine for estimation: `linux/net/sched/estimator.c`.

```
103  static void est_timer(unsigned long arg)
104  {
105          int idx = (int)arg;
106          struct qdisc_estimator *e;
107
108          read_lock(&est_lock);
109          for (e = elist[idx].list; e; e = e->next) {
110                  struct tc_stats *st = e->stats;
111                  u64 nbytes;
112                  u32 npackets;
113                  u32 rate;
```

```

                spin_lock(st->lock);
                nbytes = st->bytes;
                npackets = st->packets;
                rate = (nbytes - e->last_bytes)<<(7 - idx);
                e->last_bytes = nbytes;
                e->avbps += ((long)rate - (long)e->avbps) >> e->ewma_log;
                st->bps = (e->avbps+0xF)>>5;

                rate = (npackets - e->last_packets)<<(12 - idx);
                e->last_packets = npackets;
                e->avpps += ((long)rate - (long)e->avpps) >> e->ewma_log;
                e->stats->pps = (e->avpps+0x1FF)>>10;
                spin_unlock(st->lock);
        }

        mod_timer(&elist[idx].timer, jiffies + ((HZ/4)<<idx));
        read_unlock(&est_lock);
}
```

Figure 9.215 Rate estimator–add a timer routine for estimation: `linux/net/sched/estimator.c`.

```
int qdisc_new_estimator(struct tc_stats *stats, struct rtattr *opt)
{
        struct qdisc_estimator *est;
        struct tc_estimator *parm = RTA_DATA(opt);

        if (RTA_PAYLOAD(opt) < sizeof(*parm))
                return -EINVAL;

        if (parm->interval < -2 || parm->interval > 3)
                return -EINVAL;

        est = kmalloc(sizeof(*est), GFP_KERNEL);
        if (est == NULL)
                return -ENOBUFS;

        memset(est, 0, sizeof(*est));
        est->interval = parm->interval + 2;
        est->stats = stats;
        est->ewma_log = parm->ewma_log;
        est->last_bytes = stats->bytes;
        est->avbps = stats->bps<<5;
        est->last_packets = stats->packets;
        est->avpps = stats->pps<<10;

        est->next = elist[est->interval].list;
        if (est->next == NULL) {
                init_timer(&elist[est->interval].timer);
                elist[est->interval].timer.data = est->interval;
                elist[est->interval].timer.expires = jiffies + ((HZ/4)<<est->interval);
                elist[est->interval].timer.function = est_timer;
```

```
                add_timer(&elist[est->interval].timer);
        }
        write_lock_bh(&est_lock);
        elist[est->interval].list = est;
        write_unlock_bh(&est_lock);
        return 0;
}
```

Figure 9.216 Rate estimator–stop estimation timer routine for estimation: `linux/net/sched/estimator.c`.

```
void qdisc_kill_estimator(struct tc_stats *stats)
{
        int idx;
        struct qdisc_estimator *est, **pest;

        for (idx=0; idx <= EST_MAX_INTERVAL; idx++) {
                int killed = 0;
                pest = &elist[idx].list;
                while ((est=*pest) != NULL) {
                        if (est->stats != stats) {
                                pest = &est->next;
                                continue;
                        }

                        write_lock_bh(&est_lock);
                        *pest = est->next;
                        write_unlock_bh(&est_lock);

                        kfree(est);
                        killed++;
                }
                if (killed && elist[idx].list == NULL)
                        del_timer(&elist[idx].timer);
        }
}
```

Here we see what the *policer* functions look like.

Figure 9.217 Policer i: `linux/net/sched/police.c`.

```
#define L2T(p,L) ((p)->R_tab->data[(L)>>(p)->R_tab->rate.cell_log])
#define L2T_P(p,L) ((p)->P_tab->data[(L)>>(p)->P_tab->rate.cell_log])

static u32 idx_gen;
static struct tcf_police *tcf_police_ht[16];
/* Policer hash table lock */
static rwlock_t police_lock = RW_LOCK_UNLOCKED;

/* Each policer is serialized by its individual spinlock */

```

```
static __inline__ unsigned tcf_police_hash(u32 index)
{
        return index&0xF;
}

static __inline__ struct tcf_police * tcf_police_lookup(u32 index)
{
        struct tcf_police *p;

        read_lock(&police_lock);
        for (p = tcf_police_ht[tcf_police_hash(index)]; p; p = p->next) {
                if (p->index == index)
                        break;
        }
        read_unlock(&police_lock);
        return p;
}

static __inline__ u32 tcf_police_new_index(void)
{
        do {
                if (++idx_gen == 0)
                        idx_gen = 1;
        } while (tcf_police_lookup(idx_gen));

        return idx_gen;
}
```

Figure 9.218 Policer ii—destroy policer: `linux/net/sched/police.c.`

```
void tcf_police_destroy(struct tcf_police *p)
{
        unsigned h = tcf_police_hash(p->index);
        struct tcf_police **p1p;

        for (p1p = &tcf_police_ht[h]; *p1p; p1p = &(*p1p)->next) {
                if (*p1p == p) {
                        write_lock_bh(&police_lock);
                        *p1p = p->next;
                        write_unlock_bh(&police_lock);
#ifdef CONFIG_NET_ESTIMATOR
                        qdisc_kill_estimator(&p->stats);
#endif
                        if (p->R_tab)
                                qdisc_put_rtab(p->R_tab);
                        if (p->P_tab)
                                qdisc_put_rtab(p->P_tab);
                        kfree(p);
                        return;
                }
        }
        BUG_TRAP(0);
}
```

Figure 9.219 Policer iii—locate: `linux/net/sched/police.c`.

```
struct tcf_police * tcf_police_locate(struct rtattr *rta, struct rtattr *est)
{
        unsigned h;
        struct tcf_police *p;
        struct rtattr *tb[TCA_POLICE_MAX];
        struct tc_police *parm;

        if (rtattr_parse(tb, TCA_POLICE_MAX, RTA_DATA(rta), RTA_PAYLOAD(rta)) < 0)
              return NULL;

        if (tb[TCA_POLICE_TBF-1] == NULL)
              return NULL;

        parm = RTA_DATA(tb[TCA_POLICE_TBF-1]);

        if (parm->index && (p = tcf_police_lookup(parm->index)) != NULL) {
              p->refcnt++;
              return p;
        }

        p = kmalloc(sizeof(*p), GFP_KERNEL);
        if (p == NULL)
              return NULL;
```

Figure 9.220 Policer iv—locate: `linux/net/sched/police.c`.

```

        memset(p, 0, sizeof(*p));
        p->refcnt = 1;
        spin_lock_init(&p->lock);
        p->stats.lock = &p->lock;
        if (parm->rate.rate) {
              if ((p->R_tab = qdisc_get_rtab(&parm->rate, tb[TCA_POLICE_RATE-1])) == NULL)
                    goto failure;
              if (parm->peakrate.rate &&
                  (p->P_tab = qdisc_get_rtab(&parm->peakrate, tb[TCA_POLICE_PEAKRATE-1])) ==
                     NULL)
                    goto failure;
        }
        if (tb[TCA_POLICE_RESULT-1])
              p->result = *(int*)RTA_DATA(tb[TCA_POLICE_RESULT-1]);
#ifdef CONFIG_NET_ESTIMATOR
        if (tb[TCA_POLICE_AVRATE-1])
              p->ewma_rate = *(u32*)RTA_DATA(tb[TCA_POLICE_AVRATE-1]);
#endif
        p->toks = p->burst = parm->burst;
        p->mtu = parm->mtu;
        if (p->mtu == 0) {
              p->mtu = ~0;
              if (p->R_tab)
                    p->mtu = 255<<p->R_tab->rate.cell_log;
```

```
144             }
145             if (p->P_tab)
146                     p->ptoks = L2T_P(p, p->mtu);
147             PSCHED_GET_TIME(p->t_c);
148             p->index = parm->index ? : tcf_police_new_index();
149             p->action = parm->action;
```

Figure 9.221 Policer v—the police: `linux/net/sched/police.c`.

```
149             p->action = parm->action;
150     #ifdef CONFIG_NET_ESTIMATOR
151             if (est)
152                     qdisc_new_estimator(&p->stats, est);
153     #endif
154             h = tcf_police_hash(p->index);
155             write_lock_bh(&police_lock);
156             p->next = tcf_police_ht[h];
157             tcf_police_ht[h] = p;
158             write_unlock_bh(&police_lock);
159             return p;
160
161     failure:
162             if (p->R_tab)
163                     qdisc_put_rtab(p->R_tab);
164             kfree(p);
165             return NULL;
166     }
```

Figure 9.222 Policer vi—the police: `linux/net/sched/police.c`.

```
168     int tcf_police(struct sk_buff *skb, struct tcf_police *p)
169     {
170             psched_time_t now;
171             long toks;
172             long ptoks = 0;
173
174             spin_lock(&p->lock);
175
176             p->stats.bytes += skb->len;
177             p->stats.packets++;
178
179     #ifdef CONFIG_NET_ESTIMATOR
180             if (p->ewma_rate && p->stats.bps >= p->ewma_rate) {
181                     p->stats.overlimits++;
182                     spin_unlock(&p->lock);
183                     return p->action;
184             }
185     #endif
186
187             if (skb->len <= p->mtu) {
188                     if (p->R_tab == NULL) {
```

```
189                      spin_unlock(&p->lock);
190                      return p->result;
191              }
192
193              PSCHED_GET_TIME(now);
194
195              toks = PSCHED_TDIFF_SAFE(now, p->t_c, p->burst, 0);
```

Figure 9.223 Policer vii—the police: `linux/net/sched/police.c`.

```
197              if (p->P_tab) {
198                      ptoks = toks + p->ptoks;
199                      if (ptoks > (long)L2T_P(p, p->mtu))
200                              ptoks = (long)L2T_P(p, p->mtu);
201                      ptoks -= L2T_P(p, skb->len);
202              }
203              toks += p->toks;
204              if (toks > (long)p->burst)
205                      toks = p->burst;
206              toks -= L2T(p, skb->len);
207
208              if ((toks|ptoks) >= 0) {
209                      p->t_c = now;
210                      p->toks = toks;
211                      p->ptoks = ptoks;
212                      spin_unlock(&p->lock);
213                      return p->result;
214              }
215      }
216
217      p->stats.overlimits++;
218      spin_unlock(&p->lock);
219      return p->action;
220 }
```

9.13.2 Ingress Queuing

Ingress queuing is useful when we want to give a specific forwarding behavior based on what the input process looks like for packet processing.

Figure 9.224 Ingress queuing scheduler—data: `linux/net/sched/sch_ingress.c`.

```
47 struct ingress_qdisc_data {
48       struct Qdisc        *q;
49       struct tcf_proto    *filter_list;
50 };
```

Figure 9.225 Ingress queuing—tree handling: `linux/net/sched/sch_ingress.c`.

```
static int ingress_graft(struct Qdisc *sch,unsigned long arg,
                    struct Qdisc *new,struct Qdisc **old)
{
#ifdef DEBUG_INGRESS
        struct ingress_qdisc_data *p = PRIV(sch);
#endif

        DPRINTK("ingress_graft(sch %p,[qdisc %p],new %p,old %p)\n",
                sch, p, new, old);
        DPRINTK("\n ingress_graft: You cannot add qdiscs to classes");
        return 1;
}


static struct Qdisc *ingress_leaf(struct Qdisc *sch, unsigned long arg)
{
        return NULL;
}


static unsigned long ingress_get(struct Qdisc *sch,u32 classid)
{
#ifdef DEBUG_INGRESS
        struct ingress_qdisc_data *p = PRIV(sch);
#endif
        DPRINTK("ingress_get(sch %p,[qdisc %p],classid %x)\n", sch, p, classid);
        return TC_H_MIN(classid) + 1;
}


static unsigned long ingress_bind_filter(struct Qdisc *sch,
    unsigned long parent, u32 classid)
{
        return ingress_get(sch, classid);
}


static void ingress_put(struct Qdisc *sch, unsigned long cl)
{
}
```

Figure 9.226 Ingress queuing—change parameters: `linux/net/sched/sch_ingress.c`.

```
static int ingress_change(struct Qdisc *sch, u32 classid, u32 parent,
                          struct rtattr **tca, unsigned long *arg)
{
#ifdef DEBUG_INGRESS
        struct ingress_qdisc_data *p = PRIV(sch);
#endif
        DPRINTK("ingress_change(sch %p,[qdisc %p],classid %x,parent %x),"
                "arg 0x%lx\n", sch, p, classid, parent, *arg);
        DPRINTK("No effect. sch_ingress doesnt maintain classes at the moment");
        return 0;
}
```

Figure 9.227 Ingress queuing—walk tree: `linux/net/sched/sch_ingress.c`.

```
static void ingress_walk(struct Qdisc *sch,struct qdisc_walker *walker)
{
#ifdef DEBUG_INGRESS
        struct ingress_qdisc_data *p = PRIV(sch);
#endif
        DPRINTK("ingress_walk(sch %p,[qdisc %p],walker %p)\n", sch, p, walker);
        DPRINTK("No effect. sch_ingress doesnt maintain classes at the moment");
}


static struct tcf_proto **ingress_find_tcf(struct Qdisc *sch,unsigned long cl)
{
        struct ingress_qdisc_data *p = PRIV(sch);

        return &p->filter_list;
}
```

Figure 9.228 Ingress queuing—enqueue: `linux/net/sched/sch_ingress.c`.

```
static int ingress_enqueue(struct sk_buff *skb,struct Qdisc *sch)
{
        struct ingress_qdisc_data *p = PRIV(sch);
        struct tcf_result res;
        int result;

        D2PRINTK("ingress_enqueue(skb %p,sch %p,[qdisc %p])\n", skb, sch, p);
        result = tc_classify(skb, p->filter_list, &res);
        D2PRINTK("result %d class 0x%04x\n", result, res.classid);
        /*
         * Unlike normal "enqueue" functions, ingress_enqueue returns a
         * firewall FW_* code.
         */
        switch (result) {
#ifdef CONFIG_NET_CLS_POLICE
                case TC_POLICE_SHOT:
```

```
                        result = NF_DROP;
                        break;
                case TC_POLICE_RECLASSIFY: /* DSCP remarking here ? */
                case TC_POLICE_OK:
                case TC_POLICE_UNSPEC:
                default:
                        result = NF_ACCEPT;
                        break;
#endif
        };

        skb->tc_index = TC_H_MIN(res.classid);
        return result;
}
```

Figure 9.229 Ingress queuing—dequeue: `linux/net/sched/sch_ingress.c`.

```
static struct sk_buff *ingress_dequeue(struct Qdisc *sch)
{
/*
        struct ingress_qdisc_data *p = PRIV(sch);
        D2PRINTK("ingress_dequeue(sch %p,[qdisc %p])\n",sch,PRIV(p));
*/
        return NULL;
}
```

Figure 9.230 Ingress queuing—requeue: `linux/net/sched/sch_ingress.c`.

```
static int ingress_requeue(struct sk_buff *skb,struct Qdisc *sch)
{
/*
        struct ingress_qdisc_data *p = PRIV(sch);
        D2PRINTK("ingress_requeue(skb %p,sch %p,[qdisc %p])\n",skb,sch,PRIV(p));
*/
        return 0;
}
```

Figure 9.231 Ingress queuing—drop: `linux/net/sched/sch_ingress.c`.

```
static int ingress_drop(struct Qdisc *sch)
{
#ifdef DEBUG_INGRESS
        struct ingress_qdisc_data *p = PRIV(sch);
#endif
        DPRINTK("ingress_drop(sch %p,[qdisc %p])\n", sch, p);
        return 0;
}
```

9.13.3 Differentiated Services Marker

Differentiated services are based on packet marking. The DSCode points have to be configured according to various filters or classifiers, then acted upon, based on the source behavior.

Figure 9.232 Differentiated services field marker—data types: linux/net/sched/sch_dsmark.c.

```
#define PRIV(sch) ((struct dsmark_qdisc_data *) (sch)->data)


/*
 * classid     class          marking
 * -------     -----          -------
 *   n/a         0            n/a
 *   x:0         1            use entry [0]
 *   ...        ...           ...
 *   x:y y>0    y+1           use entry [y]
 *   ...        ...           ...
 * x:indices-1 indices        use entry [indices-1]
 */


struct dsmark_qdisc_data {
        struct Qdisc            *q;
        struct tcf_proto        *filter_list;
        __u8                    *mask;  /* "owns" the array */
        __u8                    *value;
        __u16                   indices;
        __u16                   default_index;
        int                     set_tc_index;
};
```

Figure 9.233 Differentiated services field marker—tree functions: linux/net/sched/sch_dsmark.c.

```
/* ------------------------- Class/flow operations ------------------------- */


static int dsmark_graft(struct Qdisc *sch,unsigned long arg,
                          struct Qdisc *new,struct Qdisc **old)
{
        struct dsmark_qdisc_data *p = PRIV(sch);

        DPRINTK("dsmark_graft(sch %p,[qdisc %p],new %p,old %p)\n",sch,p,new,
            old);
        if (!new)
                new = &noop_qdisc;
        sch_tree_lock(sch);
```

```
        *old = xchg(&p->q,new);
        if (*old)
              qdisc_reset(*old);
        sch_tree_unlock(sch); /* @@@ move up ? */
        return 0;
}


static struct Qdisc *dsmark_leaf(struct Qdisc *sch, unsigned long arg)
{
        return NULL;
}


static unsigned long dsmark_get(struct Qdisc *sch,u32 classid)
{
        struct dsmark_qdisc_data *p __attribute__((unused)) = PRIV(sch);

        DPRINTK("dsmark_get(sch %p,[qdisc %p],classid %x)\n",sch,p,classid);
        return TC_H_MIN(classid)+1;
}


static unsigned long dsmark_bind_filter(struct Qdisc *sch,
    unsigned long parent, u32 classid)
{
        return dsmark_get(sch,classid);
}


static void dsmark_put(struct Qdisc *sch, unsigned long cl)
{
}
```

Figure 9.234 Differentiated services field marker—change parameters: `linux/net/sched/sch_dsmark.c`.

```

static int dsmark_change(struct Qdisc *sch, u32 classid, u32 parent,
                              struct rtattr **tca, unsigned long *arg)
{
        struct dsmark_qdisc_data *p = PRIV(sch);
        struct rtattr *opt = tca[TCA_OPTIONS-1];
        struct rtattr *tb[TCA_DSMARK_MAX];

        DPRINTK("dsmark_change(sch %p,[qdisc %p],classid %x,parent %x),"
                "arg 0x%lx\n",sch,p,classid,parent,*arg);
        if (*arg > p->indices)
              return -ENOENT;
        if (!opt || rtattr_parse(tb, TCA_DSMARK_MAX, RTA_DATA(opt),
                                RTA_PAYLOAD(opt)))
              return -EINVAL;
        if (tb[TCA_DSMARK_MASK-1]) {
```

```
		if (!RTA_PAYLOAD(tb[TCA_DSMARK_MASK-1]))
			return -EINVAL;
		p->mask[*arg-1] = *(__u8 *) RTA_DATA(tb[TCA_DSMARK_MASK-1]);
	}
	if (tb[TCA_DSMARK_VALUE-1]) {
		if (!RTA_PAYLOAD(tb[TCA_DSMARK_VALUE-1]))
			return -EINVAL;
		p->value[*arg-1] = *(__u8 *) RTA_DATA(tb[TCA_DSMARK_VALUE-1]);
	}
	return 0;
}
```

Figure 9.235 Marker—delete: `linux/net/sched/sch_dsmark.c`.

```
static int dsmark_delete(struct Qdisc *sch,unsigned long arg)
{
	struct dsmark_qdisc_data *p = PRIV(sch);

	if (!arg || arg > p->indices)
		return -EINVAL;
	p->mask[arg-1] = 0xff;
	p->value[arg-1] = 0;
	return 0;
}
```

Figure 9.236 Marker—walk: `linux/net/sched/sch_dsmark.c`.

```
static void dsmark_walk(struct Qdisc *sch,struct qdisc_walker *walker)
{
	struct dsmark_qdisc_data *p = PRIV(sch);
	int i;

	DPRINTK("dsmark_walk(sch %p,[qdisc %p],walker %p)\n",sch,p,walker);
	if (walker->stop)
		return;
	for (i = 0; i < p->indices; i++) {
		if (p->mask[i] == 0xff && !p->value[i])
			continue;
		if (walker->count >= walker->skip) {
			if (walker->fn(sch, i+1, walker) < 0) {
				walker->stop = 1;
				break;
			}
		}
		walker->count++;
	}
}
```

Figure 9.237 Marker—find: `linux/net/sched/sch_dsmark.c`.

```
static struct tcf_proto **dsmark_find_tcf(struct Qdisc *sch,unsigned long cl)
{
        struct dsmark_qdisc_data *p = PRIV(sch);

        return &p->filter_list;
}
```

Figure 9.238 Marker—enqueue i: `linux/net/sched/sch_dsmark.c`.

```
static int dsmark_enqueue(struct sk_buff *skb,struct Qdisc *sch)
{
        struct dsmark_qdisc_data *p = PRIV(sch);
        struct tcf_result res;
        int result;
        int ret;

        D2PRINTK("dsmark_enqueue(skb %p,sch %p,[qdisc %p])\n",skb,sch,p);
        if (p->set_tc_index) {
                switch (skb->protocol) {
                        case __constant_htons(ETH_P_IP):
                                skb->tc_index = ipv4_get_dsfield(skb->nh.iph);
                                break;
                        case __constant_htons(ETH_P_IPV6):
                                skb->tc_index = ipv6_get_dsfield(skb->nh.ipv6h);
                                break;
                        default:
                                skb->tc_index = 0;
                                break;
                };
        }
```

Figure 9.239 Marker—enqueue ii: `linux/net/sched/sch_dsmark.c`.

```
        result = TC_POLICE_OK; /* be nice to gcc */
        if (TC_H_MAJ(skb->priority) == sch->handle) {
                skb->tc_index = TC_H_MIN(skb->priority);
        } else {
                result = tc_classify(skb,p->filter_list,&res);
                D2PRINTK("result %d class 0x%04x\n",result,res.classid);
                switch (result) {
#ifdef CONFIG_NET_CLS_POLICE
                        case TC_POLICE_SHOT:
                                kfree_skb(skb);
                                break;
#if 0
                        case TC_POLICE_RECLASSIFY:
                                /* FIXME: what to do here ??? */
#endif
#endif
                        case TC_POLICE_OK:
```

```
215                                 skb->tc_index = TC_H_MIN(res.classid);
216                                 break;
217                         case TC_POLICE_UNSPEC:
218                                 /* fall through */
219                         default:
220                                 if (p->default_index)
221                                         skb->tc_index = p->default_index;
222                                 break;
223                 };
224         }
225         if (
226 #ifdef CONFIG_NET_CLS_POLICE
227             result == TC_POLICE_SHOT ||
228 #endif
229
230             ((ret = p->q->enqueue(skb,p->q)) != 0)) {
231                 sch->stats.drops++;
232                 return 0;
233         }
234         sch->stats.bytes += skb->len;
235         sch->stats.packets++;
236         sch->q.qlen++;
237         return ret;
238 }
```

Figure 9.240 Marker—dequeue: `linux/net/sched/sch_dsmark.c`.

```
240
241 static struct sk_buff *dsmark_dequeue(struct Qdisc *sch)
242 {
243         struct dsmark_qdisc_data *p = PRIV(sch);
244         struct sk_buff *skb;
245         int index;
246
247         D2PRINTK("dsmark_dequeue(sch %p,[qdisc %p])\n",sch,p);
248         skb = p->q->ops->dequeue(p->q);
249         if (!skb)
250                 return NULL;
251         sch->q.qlen--;
252         index = skb->tc_index & (p->indices-1);
253         D2PRINTK("index %d->%d\n",skb->tc_index,index);
254         switch (skb->protocol) {
255                 case __constant_htons(ETH_P_IP):
256                         ipv4_change_dsfield(skb->nh.iph,
257                             p->mask[index],p->value[index]);
258                         break;
259                 case __constant_htons(ETH_P_IPV6):
260                         ipv6_change_dsfield(skb->nh.ipv6h,
261                             p->mask[index],p->value[index]);
262                         break;
263                 default:
264                         /*
265                          * Only complain if a change was actually attempted.
```

```
266                          * This way, we can send non-IP traffic through dsmark
267                          * and don't need yet another qdisc as a bypass.
268                          */
269                         if (p->mask[index] != 0xff || p->value[index])
270                                 printk(KERN_WARNING "dsmark_dequeue: "
271                                         "unsupported protocol %d\n",
272                                         htons(skb->protocol));
273                         break;
274             };
275         return skb;
276  }
```

Figure 9.241 Marker—requeue: `linux/net/sched/sch_dsmark.c`.

```
279  static int dsmark_requeue(struct sk_buff *skb,struct Qdisc *sch)
280  {
281         int ret;
282         struct dsmark_qdisc_data *p = PRIV(sch);
283
284         D2PRINTK("dsmark_requeue(skb %p,sch %p,[qdisc %p])\n",skb,sch,p);
285         if ((ret = p->q->ops->requeue(skb, p->q)) == 0) {
286                 sch->q.qlen++;
287                 return 0;
288         }
289         sch->stats.drops++;
290         return ret;
291  }
```

Figure 9.242 Marker—drop: `linux/net/sched/sch_dsmark.c`.

```
294  static int dsmark_drop(struct Qdisc *sch)
295  {
296         struct dsmark_qdisc_data *p = PRIV(sch);
297
298         DPRINTK("dsmark_reset(sch %p,[qdisc %p])\n",sch,p);
299         if (!p->q->ops->drop)
300                 return 0;
301         if (!p->q->ops->drop(p->q))
302                 return 0;
303         sch->q.qlen--;
304         return 1;
305  }
```

Figure 9.243 Marker—init: `linux/net/sched/sch_dsmark.c`.

```
int dsmark_init(struct Qdisc *sch,struct rtattr *opt)
{
        struct dsmark_qdisc_data *p = PRIV(sch);
        struct rtattr *tb[TCA_DSMARK_MAX];
        __u16 tmp;

        DPRINTK("dsmark_init(sch %p,[qdisc %p],opt %p)\n",sch,p,opt);
        if (rtattr_parse(tb,TCA_DSMARK_MAX,RTA_DATA(opt),RTA_PAYLOAD(opt)) < 0 ||
            !tb[TCA_DSMARK_INDICES-1] ||
            RTA_PAYLOAD(tb[TCA_DSMARK_INDICES-1]) < sizeof(__u16))
                return -EINVAL;
        memset(p,0,sizeof(*p));
        p->filter_list = NULL;
        p->indices = *(__u16 *) RTA_DATA(tb[TCA_DSMARK_INDICES-1]);
        if (!p->indices)
                return -EINVAL;
        for (tmp = p->indices; tmp != 1; tmp >>= 1) {
                if (tmp & 1)
                        return -EINVAL;
        }
        p->default_index = 0;
        if (tb[TCA_DSMARK_DEFAULT_INDEX-1]) {
                if (RTA_PAYLOAD(tb[TCA_DSMARK_DEFAULT_INDEX-1]) < sizeof(__u16))
                        return -EINVAL;
                p->default_index =
                    *(__u16 *) RTA_DATA(tb[TCA_DSMARK_DEFAULT_INDEX-1]);
                if (!p->default_index || p->default_index >= p->indices)
                        return -EINVAL;
        }
        p->set_tc_index = !!tb[TCA_DSMARK_SET_TC_INDEX-1];
        p->mask = kmalloc(p->indices*2,GFP_KERNEL);
        if (!p->mask)
                return -ENOMEM;
        p->value = p->mask+p->indices;
        memset(p->mask,0xff,p->indices);
        memset(p->value,0,p->indices);
        if (!(p->q = qdisc_create_dflt(sch->dev, &pfifo_qdisc_ops)))
                p->q = &noop_qdisc;
        DPRINTK("dsmark_init: qdisc %p\n",&p->q);
        MOD_INC_USE_COUNT;
        return 0;
}
```

Figure 9.244 Marker—reset: `linux/net/sched/sch_dsmark.c`.

```
static void dsmark_reset(struct Qdisc *sch)
{
        struct dsmark_qdisc_data *p = PRIV(sch);

        DPRINTK("dsmark_reset(sch %p,[qdisc %p])\n",sch,p);
        qdisc_reset(p->q);
        sch->q.qlen = 0;
}
```

Figure 9.245 Marker—destroy: `linux/net/sched/sch_dsmark.c`.

```
static void dsmark_destroy(struct Qdisc *sch)
{
        struct dsmark_qdisc_data *p = PRIV(sch);
        struct tcf_proto *tp;

        DPRINTK("dsmark_destroy(sch %p,[qdisc %p])\n",sch,p);
        while (p->filter_list) {
                tp = p->filter_list;
                p->filter_list = tp->next;
                tp->ops->destroy(tp);
        }
        qdisc_destroy(p->q);
        p->q = &noop_qdisc;
        kfree(p->mask);
        MOD_DEC_USE_COUNT;
}
```

Figure 9.246 Marker—dump class: `linux/net/sched/sch_dsmark.c`.

```
static int dsmark_dump_class(struct Qdisc *sch, unsigned long cl,
    struct sk_buff *skb, struct tcmsg *tcm)
{
        struct dsmark_qdisc_data *p = PRIV(sch);
        unsigned char *b = skb->tail;
        struct rtattr *rta;

        DPRINTK("dsmark_dump_class(sch %p,[qdisc %p],class %ld\n",sch,p,cl);
        if (!cl || cl > p->indices)
                return -EINVAL;
        tcm->tcm_handle = TC_H_MAKE(TC_H_MAJ(sch->handle),cl-1);
        rta = (struct rtattr *) b;
        RTA_PUT(skb,TCA_OPTIONS,0,NULL);
        RTA_PUT(skb,TCA_DSMARK_MASK,1,&p->mask[cl-1]);
        RTA_PUT(skb,TCA_DSMARK_VALUE,1,&p->value[cl-1]);
        rta->rta_len = skb->tail-b;
        return skb->len;

rtattr_failure:
        skb_trim(skb,b-skb->data);
        return -1;
}
```

Figure 9.247 Marker—dump: `linux/net/sched/sch_dsmark.c`.

```
static int dsmark_dump(struct Qdisc *sch, struct sk_buff *skb)
{
        struct dsmark_qdisc_data *p = PRIV(sch);
        unsigned char *b = skb->tail;
        struct rtattr *rta;

```

```
        rta = (struct rtattr *) b;
        RTA_PUT(skb,TCA_OPTIONS,0,NULL);
        RTA_PUT(skb,TCA_DSMARK_INDICES,sizeof(__u16),&p->indices);
        if (p->default_index)
                RTA_PUT(skb,TCA_DSMARK_DEFAULT_INDEX, sizeof(__u16),
                        &p->default_index);
        if (p->set_tc_index)
                RTA_PUT(skb, TCA_DSMARK_SET_TC_INDEX, 0, NULL);
        rta->rta_len = skb->tail-b;
        return skb->len;

rtattr_failure:
        skb_trim(skb,b-skb->data);
        return -1;
}
```

Figure 9.248 Marker—operations registration: `linux/net/sched/sch_dsmark.c`.

```
static struct Qdisc_class_ops dsmark_class_ops =
{
        dsmark_graft,                   /* graft */
        dsmark_leaf,                    /* leaf */
        dsmark_get,                     /* get */
        dsmark_put,                     /* put */
        dsmark_change,                  /* change */
        dsmark_delete,                  /* delete */
        dsmark_walk,                    /* walk */

        dsmark_find_tcf,                /* tcf_chain */
        dsmark_bind_filter,             /* bind_tcf */
        dsmark_put,                     /* unbind_tcf */

#ifdef CONFIG_RTNETLINK
        dsmark_dump_class,              /* dump */
#endif
};

struct Qdisc_ops dsmark_qdisc_ops =
{
        NULL,                           /* next */
        &dsmark_class_ops,              /* cl_ops */
        "dsmark",
        sizeof(struct dsmark_qdisc_data),

        dsmark_enqueue,                 /* enqueue */
        dsmark_dequeue,                 /* dequeue */
        dsmark_requeue,                 /* requeue */
        dsmark_drop,                    /* drop */

        dsmark_init,                    /* init */
        dsmark_reset,                   /* reset */
        dsmark_destroy,                 /* destroy */
        NULL,                           /* change */
```

```
#ifdef CONFIG_RTNETLINK
        dsmark_dump                     /* dump */
#endif
};

#ifdef MODULE
int init_module(void)
{
        return register_qdisc(&dsmark_qdisc_ops);
}


void cleanup_module(void)
{
        unregister_qdisc(&dsmark_qdisc_ops);
}
```

9.13.4 RED and Friends

Random early detection is one of several scalable queue management techniques.

Figure 9.249 Random Early Detection (RED) queue—introductory remarks: `linux/net/sched/sch_red.c`.

```
#define RED_ECN_ECT 0x02
#define RED_ECN_CE 0x01


/*      Random Early Detection (RED) algorithm.
        =======================================

        Source: Sally Floyd and Van Jacobson, "Random Early Detection Gateways
        for Congestion Avoidance", 1993, IEEE/ACM Transactions on Networking.

        This file codes a "divisionless" version of RED algorithm
        as written down in Fig.17 of the paper.

Short description.
------------------

        When a new packet arrives we calculate the average queue length:

        avg = (1-W)*avg + W*current_queue_len,

        W is the filter time constant (choosen as 2^(-Wlog)), it controls
        the inertia of the algorithm. To allow larger bursts, W should be
        decreased.
```

Figure 9.250 RED queue—behavior: `linux/net/sched/sch_red.c`.

```
        if (avg > th_max) -> packet marked (dropped).
        if (avg < th_min) -> packet passes.
        if (th_min < avg < th_max) we calculate probability:

        Pb = max_P * (avg - th_min)/(th_max-th_min)

        and mark (drop) packet with this probability.
        Pb changes from 0 (at avg==th_min) to max_P (avg==th_max).
        max_P should be small (not 1), usually 0.01..0.02 is good value.

        max_P is chosen as a number, so that max_P/(th_max-th_min)
        is a negative power of two in order arithmetics to contain
        only shifts.


        Parameters, settable by user:
        -----------------------------

        limit          - bytes (must be > qth_max + burst)

        Hard limit on queue length, should be chosen >qth_max
        to allow packet bursts. This parameter does not
        affect the algorithms behaviour and can be chosen
        arbitrarily high (well, less than ram size)
        Really, this limit will never be reached
        if RED works correctly.
```

Figure 9.251 RED queue—parameters: `linux/net/sched/sch_red.c`.

```
        qth_min        - bytes (should be < qth_max/2)
        qth_max        - bytes (should be at least 2*qth_min and less limit)
        Wlog           - bits (<32) log(1/W).
        Plog           - bits (<32)

        Plog is related to max_P by formula:

        max_P = (qth_max-qth_min)/2^Plog;

        F.e. if qth_max=128K and qth_min=32K, then Plog=22
        corresponds to max_P=0.02

        Scell_log
        Stab

        Lookup table for log((1-W)^(t/t_ave).
```

Figure 9.252 RED queue—notes: `linux/net/sched/sch_red.c`.

```
113   NOTES:
114
115   Upper bound on W.
116   -----------------
117
118         If you want to allow bursts of L packets of size S,
119         you should choose W:
120
121         L + 1 - th_min/S < (1-(1-W)^L)/W
122
123         th_min/S = 32       th_min/S = 4
124
125         log(W)  L
126         -1      33
127         -2      35
128         -3      39
129         -4      46
130         -5      57
131         -6      75
132         -7      101
133         -8      135
134         -9      190
135         etc.
136   */
```

Figure 9.253 RED—scheduler data: `linux/net/sched/sch_red.c`.

```
138   struct red_sched_data
139   {
140   /* Parameters */
141         u32           limit;        /* HARD maximal queue length */
142         u32           qth_min;      /* Min average length threshold: A scaled */
143         u32           qth_max;      /* Max average length threshold: A scaled */
144         u32           Rmask;
145         u32           Scell_max;
146         unsigned char flags;
147         char          Wlog;         /* log(W)              */
148         char          Plog;         /* random number bits */
149         char          Scell_log;
150         u8            Stab[256];
151
152   /* Variables */
153         unsigned long qave;         /* Average queue length: A scaled */
154         int           qcount;       /* Packets since last random number generation */
155         u32           qR;           /* Cached random number */
156
157         psched_time_t qidlestart;   /* Start of idle period      */
158         struct tc_red_xstats st;
159   };
```

9.13.5 Explicit Congestion Notification

Explicit congestion notification (ECN) is an alternative to packet dropping that TCP can act on (as discussed in Chapter 6).

Figure 9.254 RED—ECN bit handling: `linux/net/sched/sch_red.c`.

```
static int red_ecn_mark(struct sk_buff *skb)
{
	if (skb->nh.raw + 20 > skb->tail)
		return 0;

	switch (skb->protocol) {
	case __constant_htons(ETH_P_IP):
	{
		u8 tos = skb->nh.iph->tos;

		if (!(tos & RED_ECN_ECT))
			return 0;

		if (!(tos & RED_ECN_CE))
			IP_ECN_set_ce(skb->nh.iph);

		return 1;
	}

	case __constant_htons(ETH_P_IPV6):
	{
		u32 label = *(u32*)skb->nh.raw;

		if (!(label & __constant_htonl(RED_ECN_ECT<<20)))
			return 0;
		label |= __constant_htonl(RED_ECN_CE<<20);
		return 1;
	}

	default:
		return 0;
	}
}
```

RED Enqueue and Dequeue Functions

Here's an interesting comment, too.

Figure 9.255 RED—enqueue i: `linux/net/sched/sch_red.c`.

```
static int
red_enqueue(struct sk_buff *skb, struct Qdisc* sch)
{
```

```
        struct red_sched_data *q = (struct red_sched_data *)sch->data;

        psched_time_t now;

        if (!PSCHED_IS_PASTPERFECT(q->qidlestart)) {
                long us_idle;
                int  shift;

                PSCHED_GET_TIME(now);
                us_idle = PSCHED_TDIFF_SAFE(now, q->qidlestart, q->Scell_max, 0);
                PSCHED_SET_PASTPERFECT(q->qidlestart);

/*
   The problem: ideally, average length queue recalcultion should
   be done over constant clock intervals. This is too expensive, so that
   the calculation is driven by outgoing packets.
   When the queue is idle we have to model this clock by hand.

   SF+VJ proposed to "generate" m = idletime/(average_pkt_size/bandwidth)
   dummy packets as a burst after idle time, i.e.

          q->qave *= (1-W)^m

   This is an apparently overcomplicated solution (f.e. we have to precompute
   a table to make this calculation in reasonable time)
   I believe that a simpler model may be used here,
   but it is field for experiments.
*/
```

Figure 9.256 RED—enqueue ii: `linux/net/sched/sch_red.c`.

```
                shift = q->Stab[us_idle>>q->Scell_log];

                if (shift) {
                        q->qave >>= shift;
                } else {
                        /* Approximate initial part of exponent
                           with linear function:
                           (1-W)^m ~= 1-mW + ...

                           Seems, it is the best solution to
                           problem of too coarce exponent tabulation.
                         */

                        us_idle = (q->qave * us_idle)>>q->Scell_log;
                        if (us_idle < q->qave/2)
                                q->qave -= us_idle;
                        else
                                q->qave >>= 1;
                }
        } else {
                q->qave += sch->stats.backlog - (q->qave >> q->Wlog);
                /* NOTE:
```

```
248                            q->qave is fixed point number with point at Wlog.
249                            The formulae above is equvalent to floating point
250                            version:
251
252                            qave = qave*(1-W) + sch->stats.backlog*W;
253                                                         --ANK (980924)
254                    */
255            }
```

Figure 9.257 RED—enqueue iii: `linux/net/sched/sch_red.c`.

```
257            if (q->qave < q->qth_min) {
258                    q->qcount = -1;
259     enqueue:
260                    if (sch->stats.backlog <= q->limit) {
261                            __skb_queue_tail(&sch->q, skb);
262                            sch->stats.backlog += skb->len;
263                            sch->stats.bytes += skb->len;
264                            sch->stats.packets++;
265                            return NET_XMIT_SUCCESS;
266                    } else {
267                            q->st.pdrop++;
268                    }
269                    kfree_skb(skb);
270                    sch->stats.drops++;
271                    return NET_XMIT_DROP;
272            }
273            if (q->qave >= q->qth_max) {
274                    q->qcount = -1;
275                    sch->stats.overlimits++;
276     mark:
277                    if  (!(q->flags&TC_RED_ECN) || !red_ecn_mark(skb)) {
278                            q->st.early++;
279                            goto drop;
280                    }
281                    q->st.marked++;
282                    goto enqueue;
283            }
```

Here is how we map the randomness into the queue position.

Figure 9.258 RED—enqueue i: `linux/net/sched/sch_red.c`.

```
285            if (++q->qcount) {
286                    /* The formula used below causes questions.
287
288                       OK. qR is random number in the interval 0..Rmask
289                       i.e. 0..(2^Plog). If we used floating point
290                       arithmetics, it would be: (2^Plog)*rnd_num,
291                       where rnd_num is less 1.
292
```

```
                   Taking into account, that qave have fixed
                   point at Wlog, and Plog is related to max_P by
                   max_P = (qth_max-qth_min)/2^Plog; two lines
                   below have the following floating point equivalent:

                   max_P*(qave - qth_min)/(qth_max-qth_min) < rnd/qcount

                   Any questions? --ANK (980924)
                 */
                if (((q->qave - q->qth_min)>>q->Wlog)*q->qcount < q->qR)
                        goto enqueue;
                q->qcount = 0;
                q->qR = net_random()&q->Rmask;
                sch->stats.overlimits++;
                goto mark;
        }
        q->qR = net_random()&q->Rmask;
        goto enqueue;

drop:
        kfree_skb(skb);
        sch->stats.drops++;
        return NET_XMIT_CN;
}
```

Figure 9.259 RED—requeue and dequeue: `linux/net/sched/sch_red.c`.

```
static int
red_requeue(struct sk_buff *skb, struct Qdisc* sch)
{
        struct red_sched_data *q = (struct red_sched_data *)sch->data;

        PSCHED_SET_PASTPERFECT(q->qidlestart);

        __skb_queue_head(&sch->q, skb);
        sch->stats.backlog += skb->len;
        return 0;
}

static struct sk_buff *
red_dequeue(struct Qdisc* sch)
{
        struct sk_buff *skb;
        struct red_sched_data *q = (struct red_sched_data *)sch->data;

        skb = __skb_dequeue(&sch->q);
        if (skb) {
                sch->stats.backlog -= skb->len;
                return skb;
        }
        PSCHED_GET_TIME(q->qidlestart);
        return NULL;
}
```

Figure 9.260 RED—drop: `linux/net/sched/sch_red.c`.

```
static int
red_drop(struct Qdisc* sch)
{
        struct sk_buff *skb;
        struct red_sched_data *q = (struct red_sched_data *)sch->data;

        skb = __skb_dequeue_tail(&sch->q);
        if (skb) {
                sch->stats.backlog -= skb->len;
                sch->stats.drops++;
                q->st.other++;
                kfree_skb(skb);
                return 1;
        }
        PSCHED_GET_TIME(q->qidlestart);
        return 0;
}
```

Figure 9.261 RED—reset: `linux/net/sched/sch_red.c`.

```
static void red_reset(struct Qdisc* sch)
{
        struct red_sched_data *q = (struct red_sched_data *)sch->data;
        struct sk_buff *skb;

        while((skb=__skb_dequeue(&sch->q))!=NULL)
                kfree_skb(skb);
        sch->stats.backlog = 0;
        PSCHED_SET_PASTPERFECT(q->qidlestart);
        q->qave = 0;
        q->qcount = -1;
}
```

Figure 9.262 RED—change: `linux/net/sched/sch_red.c`.

```
static int red_change(struct Qdisc *sch, struct rtattr *opt)
{
        struct red_sched_data *q = (struct red_sched_data *)sch->data;
        struct rtattr *tb[TCA_RED_STAB];
        struct tc_red_qopt *ctl;

        if (opt == NULL ||
            rtattr_parse(tb, TCA_RED_STAB, RTA_DATA(opt), RTA_PAYLOAD(opt)) ||
            tb[TCA_RED_PARMS-1] == 0 || tb[TCA_RED_STAB-1] == 0 ||
            RTA_PAYLOAD(tb[TCA_RED_PARMS-1]) < sizeof(*ctl) ||
            RTA_PAYLOAD(tb[TCA_RED_STAB-1]) < 256)
                return -EINVAL;

        ctl = RTA_DATA(tb[TCA_RED_PARMS-1]);

        sch_tree_lock(sch);
```

```
        q->flags = ctl->flags;
        q->Wlog = ctl->Wlog;
        q->Plog = ctl->Plog;
        q->Rmask = ctl->Plog < 32 ? ((1<<ctl->Plog) - 1) : ~0UL;
        q->Scell_log = ctl->Scell_log;
        q->Scell_max = (255<<q->Scell_log);
        q->qth_min = ctl->qth_min<<ctl->Wlog;
        q->qth_max = ctl->qth_max<<ctl->Wlog;
        q->limit = ctl->limit;
        memcpy(q->Stab, RTA_DATA(tb[TCA_RED_STAB-1]), 256);

        q->qcount = -1;
        if (skb_queue_len(&sch->q) == 0)
                PSCHED_SET_PASTPERFECT(q->qidlestart);
        sch_tree_unlock(sch);
        return 0;
}
```

Figure 9.263 RED—init: `linux/net/sched/sch_red.c`.

```
static int red_init(struct Qdisc* sch, struct rtattr *opt)
{
        int err;

        MOD_INC_USE_COUNT;

        if ((err = red_change(sch, opt)) != 0) {
                MOD_DEC_USE_COUNT;
        }
        return err;
}
```

9.13.6 GRED

GRED is a generalized version of RED that includes the idea of a 1-bit penalty box (RED in/out) for TCPs that do not conform to their contract. It is structurally very similar to RED, so we don't include a detailed discussion of the code here.

9.13.7 Token Bucket Queue

The token bucket was described earlier in the chapter.

Figure 9.264 Token bucket filter queue—initial remarks: `linux/net/sched/sch_tbf.c`.

```
/*      Simple Token Bucket Filter.
        =======================================

        SOURCE.
        -------
```

```

        None.

        Description.
        ------------

        A data flow obeys TBF with rate R and depth B, if for any
        time interval t_i...t_f the number of transmitted bits
        does not exceed B + R*(t_f-t_i).

        Packetized version of this definition:
        The sequence of packets of sizes s_i served at moments t_i
        obeys TBF, if for any i<=k:

        s_i+....+s_k <= B + R*(t_k - t_i)

        Algorithm.
        ----------

        Let N(t_i) be B/R initially and N(t) grow continuously with time as:

        N(t+delta) = min{B/R, N(t) + delta}

        If the first packet in queue has length S, it may be
        transmited only at the time t_* when S/R <= N(t_*),
        and in this case N(t) jumps:

        N(t_* + 0) = N(t_* - 0) - S/R.
```

Figure 9.265 Token bucket filter queue—algorithm/notes: `linux/net/sched/sch_tbf.c`.

```

        Actually, QoS requires two TBF to be applied to a data stream.
        One of them controls steady state burst size, another
        one with rate P (peak rate) and depth M (equal to link MTU)
        limits bursts at a smaller time scale.

        It is easy to see that P>R, and B>M. If P is infinity, this double
        TBF is equivalent to a single one.

        When TBF works in reshaping mode, latency is estimated as:

        lat = max ((L-B)/R, (L-M)/P)


        NOTES.
        ------

        If TBF throttles, it starts a watchdog timer, which will wake it up
        when it is ready to transmit.
        Note that the minimal timer resolution is 1/HZ.
        If no new packets arrive during this period,
        or if the device is not awaken by EOI for some previous packet,
        TBF can stop its activity for 1/HZ.
```

```


	This means, that with depth B, the maximal rate is

	R_crit = B*HZ

	F.e. for 10Mbit ethernet and HZ=100 the minimal allowed B is ~10Kbytes.

	Note that the peak rate TBF is much more tough: with MTU 1500
	P_crit = 150Kbytes/sec. So, if you need greater peak
	rates, use alpha with HZ=1000 :-)
*/
```

Figure 9.266 Token bucket filter queue—data: `linux/net/sched/sch_tbf.c`.

```
struct tbf_sched_data
{
/* Parameters */
	u32		limit;		/* Maximal length of backlog: bytes */
	u32		buffer;		/* Token bucket depth/rate: MUST BE >= MTU/B */
	u32		mtu;
	u32		max_size;
	struct qdisc_rate_table *R_tab;
	struct qdisc_rate_table *P_tab;

/* Variables */
	long	tokens;			/* Current number of B tokens */
	long	ptokens;		/* Current number of P tokens */
	psched_time_t t_c;		/* Time check-point */
	struct timer_list wd_timer;	/* Watchdog timer */
};

#define L2T(q,L) ((q)->R_tab->data[(L)>>(q)->R_tab->rate.cell_log])
#define L2T_P(q,L) ((q)->P_tab->data[(L)>>(q)->P_tab->rate.cell_log])
```

Figure 9.267 TBF—enqueue: `linux/net/sched/sch_tbf.c`.

```
static int
tbf_enqueue(struct sk_buff *skb, struct Qdisc* sch)
{
	struct tbf_sched_data *q = (struct tbf_sched_data *)sch->data;

	if (skb->len > q->max_size)
		goto drop;
	__skb_queue_tail(&sch->q, skb);
	if ((sch->stats.backlog += skb->len) <= q->limit) {
		sch->stats.bytes += skb->len;
		sch->stats.packets++;
		return 0;
	}

```

```
145              /* Drop action: undo the things that we just did,
146               * i.e. make tail drop
147               */
148
149              __skb_unlink(skb, &sch->q);
150              sch->stats.backlog -= skb->len;
151
152      drop:
153              sch->stats.drops++;
154      #ifdef CONFIG_NET_CLS_POLICE
155              if (sch->reshape_fail==NULL || sch->reshape_fail(skb, sch))
156      #endif
157                      kfree_skb(skb);
158              return NET_XMIT_DROP;
159      }
```

Figure 9.268 TBF—requeue and drop: `linux/net/sched/sch_tbf.c`.

```
161      static int
162      tbf_requeue(struct sk_buff *skb, struct Qdisc* sch)
163      {
164              __skb_queue_head(&sch->q, skb);
165              sch->stats.backlog += skb->len;
166              return 0;
167      }
168
169      static int
170      tbf_drop(struct Qdisc* sch)
171      {
172              struct sk_buff *skb;
173
174              skb = __skb_dequeue_tail(&sch->q);
175              if (skb) {
176                      sch->stats.backlog -= skb->len;
177                      sch->stats.drops++;
178                      kfree_skb(skb);
179                      return 1;
180              }
181              return 0;
182      }
```

Figure 9.269 TBF—watchdog: `linux/net/sched/sch_tbf.c`.

```
184      static void tbf_watchdog(unsigned long arg)
185      {
186              struct Qdisc *sch = (struct Qdisc*)arg;
187
188              sch->flags &= ~TCQ_F_THROTTLED;
189              netif_schedule(sch->dev);
190      }
```

Figure 9.270 TBF—dequeue: linux/net/sched/sch_tbf.c.

```
192   static struct sk_buff *
193   tbf_dequeue(struct Qdisc* sch)
194   {
195         struct tbf_sched_data *q = (struct tbf_sched_data *)sch->data;
196         struct sk_buff *skb;
197
198         skb = __skb_dequeue(&sch->q);
199
200         if (skb) {
201               psched_time_t now;
202               long toks;
203               long ptoks = 0;
204
205               PSCHED_GET_TIME(now);
206
207               toks = PSCHED_TDIFF_SAFE(now, q->t_c, q->buffer, 0);
208
209               if (q->P_tab) {
210                     ptoks = toks + q->ptokens;
211                     if (ptoks > (long)q->mtu)
212                           ptoks = q->mtu;
213                     ptoks -= L2T_P(q, skb->len);
214               }
215               toks += q->tokens;
216               if (toks > (long)q->buffer)
217                     toks = q->buffer;
218               toks -= L2T(q, skb->len);
```

Figure 9.271 TBF—dequeue: linux/net/sched/sch_tbf.c.

```
220               if ((toks|ptoks) >= 0) {
221                     q->t_c = now;
222                     q->tokens = toks;
223                     q->ptokens = ptoks;
224                     sch->stats.backlog -= skb->len;
225                     sch->flags &= ~TCQ_F_THROTTLED;
226                     return skb;
227               }
228
229               if (!netif_queue_stopped(sch->dev)) {
230                     long delay = PSCHED_US2JIFFIE(max(-toks, -ptoks));
231
232                     if (delay == 0)
233                           delay = 1;
234
235                     mod_timer(&q->wd_timer, jiffies+delay);
236               }
237
238               /* Maybe we have a shorter packet in the queue,
239                  which can be sent now. It sounds cool,
240                  but, however, this is wrong in principle.
241                  We MUST NOT reorder packets under these circumstances.
```

```

              Really, if we split the flow into independent
              subflows, it would be a very good solution.
              This is the main idea of all FQ algorithms
              (cf. CSZ, HPFQ, HFSC)
             */
            __skb_queue_head(&sch->q, skb);

            sch->flags |= TCQ_F_THROTTLED;
            sch->stats.overlimits++;
        }
        return NULL;
}
```

Figure 9.272 TBF—reset: `linux/net/sched/sch_tbf.c`.

```
static void
tbf_reset(struct Qdisc* sch)
{
        struct tbf_sched_data *q = (struct tbf_sched_data *)sch->data;

        skb_queue_purge(&sch->q);
        sch->stats.backlog = 0;
        PSCHED_GET_TIME(q->t_c);
        q->tokens = q->buffer;
        q->ptokens = q->mtu;
        sch->flags &= ~TCQ_F_THROTTLED;
        del_timer(&q->wd_timer);
}
```

Figure 9.273 TBF—change: `linux/net/sched/sch_tbf.c`.

```
static int tbf_change(struct Qdisc* sch, struct rtattr *opt)
{
        int err = -EINVAL;
        struct tbf_sched_data *q = (struct tbf_sched_data *)sch->data;
        struct rtattr *tb[TCA_TBF_PTAB];
        struct tc_tbf_qopt *qopt;
        struct qdisc_rate_table *rtab = NULL;
        struct qdisc_rate_table *ptab = NULL;
        int max_size;

        if (rtattr_parse(tb, TCA_TBF_PTAB, RTA_DATA(opt), RTA_PAYLOAD(opt)) ||
            tb[TCA_TBF_PARMS-1] == NULL ||
            RTA_PAYLOAD(tb[TCA_TBF_PARMS-1]) < sizeof(*qopt))
                goto done;

        qopt = RTA_DATA(tb[TCA_TBF_PARMS-1]);
        rtab = qdisc_get_rtab(&qopt->rate, tb[TCA_TBF_RTAB-1]);
        if (rtab == NULL)
                goto done;

```

```
        if (qopt->peakrate.rate) {
              if (qopt->peakrate.rate > qopt->rate.rate)
                    ptab = qdisc_get_rtab(&qopt->peakrate, tb[TCA_TBF_PTAB-1]);
              if (ptab == NULL)
                    goto done;
        }

        max_size = psched_mtu(sch->dev);
        if (ptab) {
              int n = max_size>>qopt->peakrate.cell_log;
              while (n>0 && ptab->data[n-1] > qopt->mtu) {
                    max_size -= (1<<qopt->peakrate.cell_log);
                    n--;
              }
        }
        if (rtab->data[max_size>>qopt->rate.cell_log] > qopt->buffer)
              goto done;

        sch_tree_lock(sch);
        q->limit = qopt->limit;
        q->mtu = qopt->mtu;
        q->max_size = max_size;
        q->buffer = qopt->buffer;
        q->tokens = q->buffer;
        q->ptokens = q->mtu;
        rtab = xchg(&q->R_tab, rtab);
        ptab = xchg(&q->P_tab, ptab);
        sch_tree_unlock(sch);
        err = 0;
done:
        if (rtab)
              qdisc_put_rtab(rtab);
        if (ptab)
              qdisc_put_rtab(ptab);
        return err;
}
```

Figure 9.274 TBF—init: `linux/net/sched/sch_tbf.c`.

```
static int tbf_init(struct Qdisc* sch, struct rtattr *opt)
{
        int err;
        struct tbf_sched_data *q = (struct tbf_sched_data *)sch->data;

        if (opt == NULL)
              return -EINVAL;

        MOD_INC_USE_COUNT;

        PSCHED_GET_TIME(q->t_c);
        init_timer(&q->wd_timer);
        q->wd_timer.function = tbf_watchdog;
        q->wd_timer.data = (unsigned long)sch;
```

```
        if ((err = tbf_change(sch, opt)) != 0) {
                MOD_DEC_USE_COUNT;
        }
        return err;
}
```

Figure 9.275 TBF—destroy: `linux/net/sched/sch_tbf.c.`

```
static void tbf_destroy(struct Qdisc *sch)
{
        struct tbf_sched_data *q = (struct tbf_sched_data *)sch->data;

        del_timer(&q->wd_timer);

        if (q->P_tab)
                qdisc_put_rtab(q->P_tab);
        if (q->R_tab)
                qdisc_put_rtab(q->R_tab);

        MOD_DEC_USE_COUNT;
}
```

9.13.8 Ingress Queuing

Figure 9.276 Ingress queuing—ingress hook: `linux/net/sched/sch_ingress.c.`

```
static unsigned int
ing_hook(unsigned int hook, struct sk_buff **pskb,
                             const struct net_device *indev,
                             const struct net_device *outdev,
                             int (*okfn)(struct sk_buff *))
{

        struct Qdisc *q;
        struct sk_buff *skb = *pskb;
        struct net_device *dev = skb->dev;
        int fwres=NF_ACCEPT;

        DPRINTK("ing_hook: skb %s dev=%s len=%u\n",
                skb->sk ? "(owned)" : "(unowned)",
                skb->dev ? (*pskb)->dev->name : "(no dev)",
                skb->len);

/*
revisit later: Use a private since lock dev->queue_lock is also
used on the egress (might slow things for an iota)
*/

        if (dev->qdisc_ingress) {
                spin_lock(&dev->queue_lock);
                if ((q = dev->qdisc_ingress) != NULL)
```

```
218                         fwres = q->enqueue(skb, q);
219                 spin_unlock(&dev->queue_lock);
220         }
221
222         return fwres;
223 }
```

Figure 9.277 Ingress queuing—operations and initialization: `linux/net/sched/sch_ingress.c`.

```
225  /* after ipt_filter */
226  static struct nf_hook_ops ing_ops =
227  {
228          { NULL, NULL},
229          ing_hook,
230          PF_INET,
231          NF_IP_PRE_ROUTING,
232          NF_IP_PRI_FILTER + 1
233  };
234
235  int ingress_init(struct Qdisc *sch,struct rtattr *opt)
236  {
237          struct ingress_qdisc_data *p = PRIV(sch);
238
239          DPRINTK("ingress_init(sch %p,[qdisc %p],opt %p)\n",sch,p,opt);
240          memset(p, 0, sizeof(*p));
241          p->filter_list = NULL;
242          p->q = &noop_qdisc;
243  #ifndef MODULE
244          if (nf_register_hook(&ing_ops) < 0) {
245                  printk("Unable to register ingress \n");
246                  goto error;
247          }
248  #endif
249          DPRINTK("ingress_init: qdisc %p\n", sch);
250          MOD_INC_USE_COUNT;
251          return 0;
252  #ifndef MODULE
253  error:
254  #endif
255          return -EINVAL;
256  }
257
258
259  static void ingress_reset(struct Qdisc *sch)
260  {
261          struct ingress_qdisc_data *p = PRIV(sch);
262
263          DPRINTK("ingress_reset(sch %p,[qdisc %p])\n", sch, p);
264
265  /*
266  #if 0
267  */
268  /* for future use */
```

```
        qdisc_reset(p->q);
/*
#endif
*/
}
```

Figure 9.278 Ingress queuing—destroy: `linux/net/sched/sch_ingress.c`.

```
static void ingress_destroy(struct Qdisc *sch)
{
        struct ingress_qdisc_data *p = PRIV(sch);
        struct tcf_proto *tp;

        DPRINTK("ingress_destroy(sch %p,[qdisc %p])\n", sch, p);
        while (p->filter_list) {
                tp = p->filter_list;
                p->filter_list = tp->next;
                tp->ops->destroy(tp);
        }
        memset(p, 0, sizeof(*p));
        p->filter_list = NULL;

#if 0
/* for future use */
        qdisc_destroy(p->q);
#endif

#ifndef MODULE
        nf_unregister_hook(&ing_ops);
#endif

        MOD_DEC_USE_COUNT;
}
```

9.13.9 Priority Queuing

Priority queuing is just about the simplest way to implement traffic differentiation.

Figure 9.279 Priority queue: `linux/net/sched/sch_prio.c`.

```
struct prio_sched_data
{
        int bands;
        struct tcf_proto *filter_list;
        u8  prio2band[TC_PRIO_MAX+1];
        struct Qdisc *queues[TCQ_PRIO_BANDS];
};
```

Figure 9.280 Priority classifier: `linux/net/sched/sch_prio.c`.

```
static __inline__ unsigned prio_classify(struct sk_buff *skb, struct Qdisc *sch)
{
	struct prio_sched_data *q = (struct prio_sched_data *)sch->data;
	struct tcf_result res;
	u32 band;

	band = skb->priority;
	if (TC_H_MAJ(skb->priority) != sch->handle) {
		if (!q->filter_list || tc_classify(skb, q->filter_list, &res)) {
			if (TC_H_MAJ(band))
				band = 0;
			return q->prio2band[band&TC_PRIO_MAX];
		}
		band = res.classid;
	}
	band = TC_H_MIN(band) - 1;
	return band < q->bands ? band : q->prio2band[0];
}
```

Figure 9.281 Priority enqueue: `linux/net/sched/sch_prio.c`.

```
static int
prio_enqueue(struct sk_buff *skb, struct Qdisc* sch)
{
	struct prio_sched_data *q = (struct prio_sched_data *)sch->data;
	struct Qdisc *qdisc;
	int ret;

	qdisc = q->queues[prio_classify(skb, sch)];

	if ((ret = qdisc->enqueue(skb, qdisc)) == 0) {
		sch->stats.bytes += skb->len;
		sch->stats.packets++;
		sch->q.qlen++;
		return 0;
	}
	sch->stats.drops++;
	return ret;
}
```

Figure 9.282 Priority requeue and dequeue: `linux/net/sched/sch_prio.c`.

```

static int
prio_requeue(struct sk_buff *skb, struct Qdisc* sch)
{
	struct prio_sched_data *q = (struct prio_sched_data *)sch->data;
	struct Qdisc *qdisc;
```

```
94              int ret;
95
96              qdisc = q->queues[prio_classify(skb, sch)];
97
98              if ((ret = qdisc->ops->requeue(skb, qdisc)) == 0) {
99                      sch->q.qlen++;
100                     return 0;
101             }
102             sch->stats.drops++;
103             return ret;
104     }
105
106
107     static struct sk_buff *
108     prio_dequeue(struct Qdisc* sch)
109     {
110             struct sk_buff *skb;
111             struct prio_sched_data *q = (struct prio_sched_data *)sch->data;
112             int prio;
113             struct Qdisc *qdisc;
114
115             for (prio = 0; prio < q->bands; prio++) {
116                     qdisc = q->queues[prio];
117                     skb = qdisc->dequeue(qdisc);
118                     if (skb) {
119                             sch->q.qlen--;
120                             return skb;
121                     }
122             }
123             return NULL;
124
125     }
```

Figure 9.283 Priority drop: `linux/net/sched/sch_prio.c`.

```
127     static int
128     prio_drop(struct Qdisc* sch)
129     {
130             struct prio_sched_data *q = (struct prio_sched_data *)sch->data;
131             int prio;
132             struct Qdisc *qdisc;
133
134             for (prio = q->bands-1; prio >= 0; prio--) {
135                     qdisc = q->queues[prio];
136                     if (qdisc->ops->drop(qdisc)) {
137                             sch->q.qlen--;
138                             return 1;
139                     }
140             }
141             return 0;
142     }
```

This is to show how to change priority parameters.

Figure 9.284 Priority—tune: `linux/net/sched/sch_prio.c`.

```
static int prio_tune(struct Qdisc *sch, struct rtattr *opt)
{
        struct prio_sched_data *q = (struct prio_sched_data *)sch->data;
        struct tc_prio_qopt *qopt = RTA_DATA(opt);
        int i;

        if (opt->rta_len < RTA_LENGTH(sizeof(*qopt)))
                return -EINVAL;
        if (qopt->bands > TCQ_PRIO_BANDS || qopt->bands < 2)
                return -EINVAL;

        for (i=0; i<=TC_PRIO_MAX; i++) {
                if (qopt->priomap[i] >= qopt->bands)
                        return -EINVAL;
        }

        sch_tree_lock(sch);
        q->bands = qopt->bands;
        memcpy(q->prio2band, qopt->priomap, TC_PRIO_MAX+1);

        for (i=q->bands; i<TCQ_PRIO_BANDS; i++) {
                struct Qdisc *child = xchg(&q->queues[i], &noop_qdisc);
                if (child != &noop_qdisc)
                        qdisc_destroy(child);
        }
        sch_tree_unlock(sch);

        for (i=0; i<=TC_PRIO_MAX; i++) {
                int band = q->prio2band[i];
                if (q->queues[band] == &noop_qdisc) {
                        struct Qdisc *child;
                        child = qdisc_create_dflt(sch->dev, &pfifo_qdisc_ops);
                        if (child) {
                                sch_tree_lock(sch);
                                child = xchg(&q->queues[band], child);

                                if (child != &noop_qdisc)
                                        qdisc_destroy(child);
                                sch_tree_unlock(sch);
                        }
                }
        }
        return 0;
}
```

9.13.10 Stochastic Fairness Queuing

Figure 9.285 Stochastic fairness queuing scheduler—introductory remarks: `linux/net/sched/sch_sfq.c`.

```
/*      Stochastic Fairness Queuing algorithm.
        =======================================

        Source:
        Paul E. McKenney "Stochastic Fairness Queuing",
        IEEE INFOCOMM'90 Proceedings, San Francisco, 1990.

        Paul E. McKenney "Stochastic Fairness Queuing",
        "Interworking: Research and Experience", v.2, 1991, p.113-131.


        See also:
        M. Shreedhar and George Varghese "Efficient Fair
        Queuing using Deficit Round Robin", Proc. SIGCOMM 95.


        This is not the thing that is usually called (W)FQ nowadays.
        It does not use any timestamp mechanism, but instead
        processes queues in round-robin order.

        ADVANTAGE:

        - It is very cheap. Both CPU and memory requirements are minimal.

        DRAWBACKS:

        - "Stochastic" -> It is not 100% fair.
        When hash collisions occur, several flows are considered as one.

        - "Round-robin" -> It introduces larger delays than virtual clock
        based schemes, and should not be used for isolating interactive
        traffic from non-interactive. It means, that this scheduler
        should be used as leaf of CBQ or P3, which put interactive traffic
        to higher priority band.

        We still need true WFQ for top level CSZ, but using WFQ
        for the best effort traffic is absolutely pointless:
        SFQ is superior for this purpose.
```

Figure 9.286 Stochastic fairness queuing scheduler—introductory remarks: `linux/net/sched/sch_sfq.c` continued.

```

        IMPLEMENTATION:
        This implementation limits maximal queue length to 128;
        maximal mtu to 2^15-1; number of hash buckets to 1024.
        The only goal of this restrictions was that all data
        fit into one 4K page :-). Struct sfq_sched_data is
        organized in anti-cache manner: all the data for a bucket
        are scattered over different locations. This is not good,
        but it allowed me to put it into 4K.

        It is easy to increase these values, but not in flight. */
```

9.13.11 Priority Queuing

Figure 9.287 Priority queue: `linux/net/sched/sch_prio.c`.

```
/*
 * net/sched/sch_prio.c Simple 3-band priority "scheduler".
 *
 *           This program is free software; you can redistribute it and/or
 *           modify it under the terms of the GNU General Public License
 *           as published by the Free Software Foundation; either version
 *           2 of the License, or (at your option) any later version.
 *
 * Authors:  Alexey Kuznetsov, <kuznet@ms2.inr.ac.ru>
 * Fixes:    19990609: J Hadi Salim <hadi@nortelnetworks.com>:
 *           Init -- EINVAL when opt undefined
 */

#include <linux/config.h>
#include <linux/module.h>
#include <asm/uaccess.h>
#include <asm/system.h>
#include <asm/bitops.h>
#include <linux/types.h>
#include <linux/kernel.h>
#include <linux/sched.h>
#include <linux/string.h>
#include <linux/mm.h>
#include <linux/socket.h>
#include <linux/sockios.h>
#include <linux/in.h>
#include <linux/errno.h>
#include <linux/interrupt.h>
#include <linux/if_ether.h>
#include <linux/inet.h>
```

9.13.12 Stochastic Fairness Queuing

Figure 9.288 Stochastic fairness queuing scheduler–introductory remarks: `linux/net/sched/sch_sfq.c`.

```
/*      Stochastic Fairness Queuing algorithm.
        =======================================

        Source:
        Paul E. McKenney "Stochastic Fairness Queuing",
        IEEE INFOCOMM'90 Proceedings, San Francisco, 1990.

        Paul E. McKenney "Stochastic Fairness Queuing",
        "Interworking: Research and Experience", v.2, 1991, p.113-131.


        See also:
        M. Shreedhar and George Varghese "Efficient Fair
        Queuing using Deficit Round Robin", Proc. SIGCOMM 95.


        This is not the thing that is usually called (W)FQ nowadays.
        It does not use any timestamp mechanism, but instead
        processes queues in round-robin order.

        ADVANTAGE:

        - It is very cheap. Both CPU and memory requirements are minimal.

        DRAWBACKS:

        - "Stochastic" -> It is not 100% fair.
        When hash collisions occur, several flows are considered as one.

        - "Round-robin" -> It introduces larger delays than virtual clock
        based schemes, and should not be used for isolating interactive
        traffic from non-interactive. It means, that this scheduler
        should be used as leaf of CBQ or P3, which put interactive traffic
        to higher priority band.

        We still need true WFQ for top level CSZ, but using WFQ
        for the best effort traffic is absolutely pointless:
        SFQ is superior for this purpose.

        IMPLEMENTATION:
        This implementation limits maximal queue length to 128;
        maximal mtu to 2^15-1; number of hash buckets to 1024.
        The only goal of this restrictions was that all data
        fit into one 4K page :-). Struct sfq_sched_data is
        organized in anti-cache manner: all the data for a bucket
        are scattered over different locations. This is not good,
        but it allowed me to put it into 4K.

        It is easy to increase these values, but not in flight. */
```

Figure 9.289 SFQ—data structures: `linux/net/sched/sch_sfq.c`.

```
#define SFQ_DEPTH          128
#define SFQ_HASH_DIVISOR     1024

/* This type should contain at least SFQ_DEPTH*2 values */
typedef unsigned char sfq_index;

struct sfq_head
{
        sfq_index      next;
        sfq_index      prev;
};

struct sfq_sched_data
{
/* Parameters */
        int            perturb_period;
        unsigned       quantum;       /* Allotment per round: MUST BE >= MTU */

/* Variables */
        struct timer_list perturb_timer;
        int            perturbation;
        sfq_index      tail;          /* Index of current slot in round */
        sfq_index      max_depth;     /* Maximal depth */

        sfq_index      ht[SFQ_HASH_DIVISOR]; /* Hash table */
        sfq_index      next[SFQ_DEPTH];     /* Active slots link */
        short          allot[SFQ_DEPTH];    /* Current allotment per slot */
        unsigned short hash[SFQ_DEPTH];     /* Hash value indexed by slots */
        struct sk_buff_head  qs[SFQ_DEPTH];        /* Slot queue */
        struct sfq_head dep[SFQ_DEPTH*2];   /* Linked list of slots, indexed by depth */
};
```

Figure 9.290 SFQ—queue hash functions: `linux/net/sched/sch_sfq.c`.

```
static __inline__ unsigned sfq_fold_hash(struct sfq_sched_data *q, u32 h, u32 h1)
{
        int pert = q->perturbation;

        /* Have we any rotation primitives? If not, WHY? */
        h ^= (h1<<pert) ^ (h1>>(0x1F - pert));
        h ^= h>>10;
        return h & 0x3FF;
}

#ifndef IPPROTO_ESP
#define IPPROTO_ESP 50
#endif

static unsigned sfq_hash(struct sfq_sched_data *q, struct sk_buff *skb)
{
        u32 h, h2;

        switch (skb->protocol) {
        case __constant_htons(ETH_P_IP):
        {
                struct iphdr *iph = skb->nh.iph;
                h = iph->daddr;
                h2 = iph->saddr^iph->protocol;
                if (!(iph->frag_off&htons(IP_MF|IP_OFFSET)) &&
                    (iph->protocol == IPPROTO_TCP ||
                     iph->protocol == IPPROTO_UDP ||
                     iph->protocol == IPPROTO_ESP))
                        h2 ^= *(((u32*)iph) + iph->ihl);
                break;
        }
        case __constant_htons(ETH_P_IPV6):
        {
                struct ipv6hdr *iph = skb->nh.ipv6h;
                h = iph->daddr.s6_addr32[3];
                h2 = iph->saddr.s6_addr32[3]^iph->nexthdr;
                if (iph->nexthdr == IPPROTO_TCP ||
                    iph->nexthdr == IPPROTO_UDP ||
                    iph->nexthdr == IPPROTO_ESP)
                        h2 ^= *(u32*)&iph[1];
                break;
        }
        default:
                h = (u32)(unsigned long)skb->dst^skb->protocol;
                h2 = (u32)(unsigned long)skb->sk;
        }
        return sfq_fold_hash(q, h, h2);
}
```

Figure 9.291 SFQ–queue decrement/increment functions: `linux/net/sched/sch_sfq.c`.

```
extern __inline__ void sfq_link(struct sfq_sched_data *q, sfq_index x)
{
        sfq_index p, n;
        int d = q->qs[x].qlen + SFQ_DEPTH;

        p = d;
        n = q->dep[d].next;
        q->dep[x].next = n;
        q->dep[x].prev = p;
        q->dep[p].next = q->dep[n].prev = x;
}

extern __inline__ void sfq_dec(struct sfq_sched_data *q, sfq_index x)
{
        sfq_index p, n;

        n = q->dep[x].next;
        p = q->dep[x].prev;
        q->dep[p].next = n;
        q->dep[n].prev = p;

        if (n == p && q->max_depth == q->qs[x].qlen + 1)
                q->max_depth--;

        sfq_link(q, x);
}

extern __inline__ void sfq_inc(struct sfq_sched_data *q, sfq_index x)
{
        sfq_index p, n;
        int d;

        n = q->dep[x].next;
        p = q->dep[x].prev;
        q->dep[p].next = n;
        q->dep[n].prev = p;
        d = q->qs[x].qlen;
        if (q->max_depth < d)
                q->max_depth = d;

        sfq_link(q, x);
}
```

Figure 9.292 SFQ—queue drop function: `linux/net/sched/sch_sfq.c`.

```
215  static int sfq_drop(struct Qdisc *sch)
216  {
217          struct sfq_sched_data *q = (struct sfq_sched_data *)sch->data;
218          sfq_index d = q->max_depth;
219          struct sk_buff *skb;
220
221          /* Queue is full! Find the longest slot and
222             drop a packet from it */
223
224          if (d > 1) {
225                  sfq_index x = q->dep[d+SFQ_DEPTH].next;
226                  skb = q->qs[x].prev;
227                  __skb_unlink(skb, &q->qs[x]);
228                  kfree_skb(skb);
229                  sfq_dec(q, x);
230                  sch->q.qlen--;
231                  sch->stats.drops++;
232                  return 1;
233          }
234
235          if (d == 1) {
236                  /* It is difficult to believe, but ALL THE SLOTS HAVE LENGTH 1. */
237                  d = q->next[q->tail];
238                  q->next[q->tail] = q->next[d];
239                  q->allot[q->next[d]] += q->quantum;
240                  skb = q->qs[d].prev;
241                  __skb_unlink(skb, &q->qs[d]);
242                  kfree_skb(skb);
243                  sfq_dec(q, d);
244                  sch->q.qlen--;
245                  q->ht[q->hash[d]] = SFQ_DEPTH;
246                  sch->stats.drops++;
247                  return 1;
248          }
249
250          return 0;
251  }
```

Figure 9.293 SFQ—enqueue function: `linux/net/sched/sch_sfq.c`.

```
253  static int
254  sfq_enqueue(struct sk_buff *skb, struct Qdisc* sch)
255  {
256          struct sfq_sched_data *q = (struct sfq_sched_data *)sch->data;
257          unsigned hash = sfq_hash(q, skb);
258          sfq_index x;
259
260          x = q->ht[hash];
261          if (x == SFQ_DEPTH) {
262                  q->ht[hash] = x = q->dep[SFQ_DEPTH].next;
263                  q->hash[x] = hash;
```

```
264         }
265         __skb_queue_tail(&q->qs[x], skb);
266         sfq_inc(q, x);
267         if (q->qs[x].qlen == 1) {            /* The flow is new */
268                 if (q->tail == SFQ_DEPTH) { /* It is the first flow */
269                         q->tail = x;
270                         q->next[x] = x;
271                         q->allot[x] = q->quantum;
272                 } else {
273                         q->next[x] = q->next[q->tail];
274                         q->next[q->tail] = x;
275                         q->tail = x;
276                 }
277         }
278         if (++sch->q.qlen < SFQ_DEPTH-1) {
279                 sch->stats.bytes += skb->len;
280                 sch->stats.packets++;
281                 return 0;
282         }
283
284         sfq_drop(sch);
285         return NET_XMIT_CN;
286 }
```

Figure 9.294 SFQ—requeue function: `linux/net/sched/sch_sfq.c`.

```
255 {
256         struct sfq_sched_data *q = (struct sfq_sched_data *)sch->data;
257         unsigned hash = sfq_hash(q, skb);
258         sfq_index x;
259
260         x = q->ht[hash];
261         if (x == SFQ_DEPTH) {
262                 q->ht[hash] = x = q->dep[SFQ_DEPTH].next;
263                 q->hash[x] = hash;
264         }
265         __skb_queue_tail(&q->qs[x], skb);
266         sfq_inc(q, x);
267         if (q->qs[x].qlen == 1) {            /* The flow is new */
268                 if (q->tail == SFQ_DEPTH) { /* It is the first flow */
269                         q->tail = x;
270                         q->next[x] = x;
271                         q->allot[x] = q->quantum;
272                 } else {
273                         q->next[x] = q->next[q->tail];
274                         q->next[q->tail] = x;
275                         q->tail = x;
276                 }
277         }
278         if (++sch->q.qlen < SFQ_DEPTH-1) {
279                 sch->stats.bytes += skb->len;
280                 sch->stats.packets++;
281                 return 0;
```

```
282              }
283
284          sfq_drop(sch);
285          return NET_XMIT_CN;
286      }
287
288      static int
289      sfq_requeue(struct sk_buff *skb, struct Qdisc* sch)
290      {
291          struct sfq_sched_data *q = (struct sfq_sched_data *)sch->data;
292          unsigned hash = sfq_hash(q, skb);
293          sfq_index x;
294
295          x = q->ht[hash];
296          if (x == SFQ_DEPTH) {
297                  q->ht[hash] = x = q->dep[SFQ_DEPTH].next;
298                  q->hash[x] = hash;
299          }
300          __skb_queue_head(&q->qs[x], skb);
301          sfq_inc(q, x);
302          if (q->qs[x].qlen == 1) {            /* The flow is new */
303                  if (q->tail == SFQ_DEPTH) {  /* It is the first flow */
304                          q->tail = x;
305                          q->next[x] = x;
306                          q->allot[x] = q->quantum;
307                  } else {
308                          q->next[x] = q->next[q->tail];
309                          q->next[q->tail] = x;
310                          q->tail = x;
311                  }
312          }
313          if (++sch->q.qlen < SFQ_DEPTH-1)
314                  return 0;
315
316          sch->stats.drops++;
317          sfq_drop(sch);
318          return NET_XMIT_CN;
319      }
```

Figure 9.295 SFQ—dequeue function: `linux/net/sched/sch_sfq.c`.

```
324      static struct sk_buff *
325      sfq_dequeue(struct Qdisc* sch)
326      {
327          struct sfq_sched_data *q = (struct sfq_sched_data *)sch->data;
328          struct sk_buff *skb;
329          sfq_index a, old_a;
330
331          /* No active slots */
332          if (q->tail == SFQ_DEPTH)
333                  return NULL;
334
335          a = old_a = q->next[q->tail];
```

```
336
337            /* Grab packet */
338            skb = __skb_dequeue(&q->qs[a]);
339            sfq_dec(q, a);
340            sch->q.qlen--;
341
342            /* Is the slot empty? */
343            if (q->qs[a].qlen == 0) {
344                    a = q->next[a];
345                    if (a == old_a) {
346                            q->tail = SFQ_DEPTH;
347                            return skb;
348                    }
349                    q->next[q->tail] = a;
350                    q->allot[a] += q->quantum;
351            } else if ((q->allot[a] -= skb->len) <= 0) {
352                    q->tail = a;
353                    a = q->next[a];
354                    q->allot[a] += q->quantum;
355            }
356            return skb;
357    }
```

Figure 9.296 SFQ—reset: `linux/net/sched/sch_sfq.c`.

```
359    static void
360    sfq_reset(struct Qdisc* sch)
361    {
362            struct sk_buff *skb;
363
364            while ((skb = sfq_dequeue(sch)) != NULL)
365                    kfree_skb(skb);
366    }
```

Figure 9.297 SFQ—perturb queue: `linux/net/sched/sch_sfq.c`.

```
368    static void sfq_perturbation(unsigned long arg)
369    {
370            struct Qdisc *sch = (struct Qdisc*)arg;
371            struct sfq_sched_data *q = (struct sfq_sched_data *)sch->data;
372
373            q->perturbation = net_random()&0x1F;
374            q->perturb_timer.expires = jiffies + q->perturb_period;
375
376            if (q->perturb_period) {
377                    q->perturb_timer.expires = jiffies + q->perturb_period;
378                    add_timer(&q->perturb_timer);
379            }
380    }
```

9.13.13 Link Equalization

Figure 9.298 Traffic equalization/load balance queue—initial remarks: `linux/net/sched/sch_teql.c`.

```
/*
   How to setup it.
   ----------------

   After loading this module you will find a new device teqlN
   and new qdisc with the same name. To join a slave to the equalizer
   you should just set this qdisc on a device f.e.

   # tc qdisc add dev eth0 root teql0
   # tc qdisc add dev eth1 root teql0

   That's all. Full PnP 8)

   Applicability.
   --------------

   1. Slave devices MUST be active devices, i.e., they must raise the tbusy
      signal and generate EOI events. If you want to equalize virtual devices
      like tunnels, use a normal eql device.
   2. This device puts no limitations on physical slave characteristics
      f.e. it will equalize 9600baud line and 100Mb ethernet perfectly :-)
      Certainly, large difference in link speeds will make the resulting
      eqalized link unusable, because of huge packet reordering.
      I estimate an upper useful difference as ~10 times.
   3. If the slave requires address resolution, only protocols using
      neighbour cache (IPv4/IPv6) will work over the equalized link.
      Other protocols are still allowed to use the slave device directly,
      which will not break load balancing, though native slave
      traffic will have the highest priority. */
```

Figure 9.299 TE data: `linux/net/sched/sch_teql.c`.

```
struct teql_master
{
        struct Qdisc_ops qops;
        struct net_device dev;
        struct Qdisc *slaves;
        struct net_device_stats stats;
};

struct teql_sched_data
{
        struct Qdisc *next;
        struct teql_master *m;
        struct neighbour *ncache;
        struct sk_buff_head q;
};

```

```
#define NEXT_SLAVE(q) (((struct teql_sched_data*)((q)->data))->next)

#define FMASK (IFF_BROADCAST|IFF_POINTOPOINT|IFF_BROADCAST)
```

Figure 9.300 TE enqueue, requeue, dequeue: `linux/net/sched/sch_teql.c`.

```
/* "teql*" qdisc routines */

static int
teql_enqueue(struct sk_buff *skb, struct Qdisc* sch)
{
        struct net_device *dev = sch->dev;
        struct teql_sched_data *q = (struct teql_sched_data *)sch->data;

        __skb_queue_tail(&q->q, skb);
        if (q->q.qlen <= dev->tx_queue_len) {
                sch->stats.bytes += skb->len;
                sch->stats.packets++;
                return 0;
        }

        __skb_unlink(skb, &q->q);
        kfree_skb(skb);
        sch->stats.drops++;
        return NET_XMIT_DROP;
}

static int
teql_requeue(struct sk_buff *skb, struct Qdisc* sch)
{
        struct teql_sched_data *q = (struct teql_sched_data *)sch->data;

        __skb_queue_head(&q->q, skb);
        return 0;
}

static struct sk_buff *
teql_dequeue(struct Qdisc* sch)
{
        struct teql_sched_data *dat = (struct teql_sched_data *)sch->data;
        struct sk_buff *skb;

        skb = __skb_dequeue(&dat->q);
        if (skb == NULL) {
                struct net_device *m = dat->m->dev.qdisc->dev;
                if (m) {
                        dat->m->slaves = sch;
                        netif_wake_queue(m);
                }
        }
        sch->q.qlen = dat->q.qlen + dat->m->dev.qdisc->q.qlen;
        return skb;
}
```

Figure 9.301 TE release, reset, destroy: linux/net/sched/sch_teql.c.

```
static __inline__ void
teql_neigh_release(struct neighbour *n)
{
        if (n)
                neigh_release(n);
}

static void
teql_reset(struct Qdisc* sch)
{
        struct teql_sched_data *dat = (struct teql_sched_data *)sch->data;

        skb_queue_purge(&dat->q);
        sch->q.qlen = 0;
        teql_neigh_release(xchg(&dat->ncache, NULL));
}

static void
teql_destroy(struct Qdisc* sch)
{
        struct Qdisc *q, *prev;
        struct teql_sched_data *dat = (struct teql_sched_data *)sch->data;
        struct teql_master *master = dat->m;

        if ((prev = master->slaves) != NULL) {
                do {
                        q = NEXT_SLAVE(prev);
                        if (q == sch) {
                                NEXT_SLAVE(prev) = NEXT_SLAVE(q);
                                if (q == master->slaves) {
                                        master->slaves = NEXT_SLAVE(q);
                                        if (q == master->slaves) {
                                                master->slaves = NULL;
                                                spin_lock_bh(&master->dev.queue_lock);
                                                qdisc_reset(master->dev.qdisc);
                                                spin_unlock_bh(&master->dev.queue_lock);
                                        }
                                }
                                skb_queue_purge(&dat->q);
                                teql_neigh_release(xchg(&dat->ncache, NULL));
                                break;
                        }

                } while ((prev = q) != master->slaves);
        }

        MOD_DEC_USE_COUNT;
}
```

Figure 9.302 TE initialization: `linux/net/sched/sch_teql.c`.

```
184   static int teql_qdisc_init(struct Qdisc *sch, struct rtattr *opt)
185   {
186           struct net_device *dev = sch->dev;
187           struct teql_master *m = (struct teql_master*)sch->ops;
188           struct teql_sched_data *q = (struct teql_sched_data *)sch->data;
189
190           if (dev->hard_header_len > m->dev.hard_header_len)
191                   return -EINVAL;
192
193           if (&m->dev == dev)
194                   return -ELOOP;
195
196           q->m = m;
197
198           skb_queue_head_init(&q->q);
199
200           if (m->slaves) {
201                   if (m->dev.flags & IFF_UP) {
202                           if ((m->dev.flags&IFF_POINTOPOINT && !(dev->flags&IFF_POINTOPOINT))
203                                   || (m->dev.flags&IFF_BROADCAST && !(dev->flags&IFF_BROADCAST))
204                                   || (m->dev.flags&IFF_MULTICAST && !(dev->flags&IFF_MULTICAST))
205                                   || dev->mtu < m->dev.mtu)
206                                           return -EINVAL;
207                   } else {
208                           if (!(dev->flags&IFF_POINTOPOINT))
209                                   m->dev.flags &= ~IFF_POINTOPOINT;
210                           if (!(dev->flags&IFF_BROADCAST))
211                                   m->dev.flags &= ~IFF_BROADCAST;
212                           if (!(dev->flags&IFF_MULTICAST))
213                                   m->dev.flags &= ~IFF_MULTICAST;
214                           if (dev->mtu < m->dev.mtu)
215                                   m->dev.mtu = dev->mtu;
216                   }
217                   q->next = NEXT_SLAVE(m->slaves);
218                   NEXT_SLAVE(m->slaves) = sch;
219           } else {
220                   q->next = sch;
221                   m->slaves = sch;
222                   m->dev.mtu = dev->mtu;
223                   m->dev.flags = (m->dev.flags&~FMASK)|(dev->flags&FMASK);
224           }
225
226           MOD_INC_USE_COUNT;
227           return 0;
228   }
```

Figure 9.303 TE net device resolve: `linux/net/sched/sch_teql.c`.

```
230   /* "teql*" netdevice routines */
231
232   static int
233   __teql_resolve(struct sk_buff *skb, struct sk_buff *skb_res, struct net_device *dev)
```

```
234   {
235           struct teql_sched_data *q = (void*)dev->qdisc->data;
236           struct neighbour *mn = skb->dst->neighbour;
237           struct neighbour *n = q->ncache;
238
239           if (mn->tbl == NULL)
240                   return -EINVAL;
241           if (n && n->tbl == mn->tbl &&
242               memcmp(n->primary_key, mn->primary_key, mn->tbl->key_len) == 0) {
243                   atomic_inc(&n->refcnt);
244           } else {
245                   n = __neigh_lookup_errno(mn->tbl, mn->primary_key, dev);
246                   if (IS_ERR(n))
247                           return PTR_ERR(n);
248           }
249           if (neigh_event_send(n, skb_res) == 0) {
250                   int err;
251                   read_lock(&n->lock);
252                   err = dev->hard_header(skb, dev, ntohs(skb->protocol), n->ha, NULL, skb->len);
253                   read_unlock(&n->lock);
254                   if (err < 0) {
255                           neigh_release(n);
256                           return -EINVAL;
257                   }
258                   teql_neigh_release(xchg(&q->ncache, n));
259                   return 0;
260           }
261           neigh_release(n);
262           return (skb_res == NULL) ? -EAGAIN : 1;
263   }
264
265   static __inline__ int
266   teql_resolve(struct sk_buff *skb, struct sk_buff *skb_res, struct net_device *dev)
267   {
268           if (dev->hard_header == NULL ||
269               skb->dst == NULL ||
270               skb->dst->neighbour == NULL)
271                   return 0;
272           return __teql_resolve(skb, skb_res, dev);
273   }
```

Figure 9.304 TE net device transmit: `linux/net/sched/sch_teql.c`.

```
275   static int teql_master_xmit(struct sk_buff *skb, struct net_device *dev)
276   {
277           struct teql_master *master = (void*)dev->priv;
278           struct Qdisc *start, *q;
279           int busy;
280           int nores;
281           int len = skb->len;
282           struct sk_buff *skb_res = NULL;
283
284           start = master->slaves;
```

```
285
286   restart:
287          nores = 0;
288          busy = 0;
289
290          if ((q = start) == NULL)
291                  goto drop;
```

Figure 9.305 TE net device transmit ii: `linux/net/sched/sch_teql.c`.

```
293          do {
294                  struct net_device *slave = q->dev;
295
296                  if (slave->qdisc_sleeping != q)
297                          continue;
298                  if (netif_queue_stopped(slave) || ! netif_running(slave)) {
299                          busy = 1;
300                          continue;
301                  }
302
303                  switch (teql_resolve(skb, skb_res, slave)) {
304                  case 0:
305                          if (spin_trylock(&slave->xmit_lock)) {
306                                  slave->xmit_lock_owner = smp_processor_id();
307                                  if (!netif_queue_stopped(slave) &&
308                                      slave->hard_start_xmit(skb, slave) == 0) {
309                                          slave->xmit_lock_owner = -1;
310                                          spin_unlock(&slave->xmit_lock);
311                                          master->slaves = NEXT_SLAVE(q);
312                                          netif_wake_queue(dev);
313                                          master->stats.tx_packets++;
314                                          master->stats.tx_bytes += len;
315                                          return 0;
316                                  }
317                                  slave->xmit_lock_owner = -1;
318                                  spin_unlock(&slave->xmit_lock);
319                          }
320                          if (netif_queue_stopped(dev))
321                                  busy = 1;
322                          break;
323                  case 1:
324                          master->slaves = NEXT_SLAVE(q);
325                          return 0;
326                  default:
327                          nores = 1;
328                          break;
329                  }
330                  __skb_pull(skb, skb->nh.raw - skb->data);
331          } while ((q = NEXT_SLAVE(q)) != start);
```

Figure 9.306 TE net device transmit iii: `linux/net/sched/sch_teql.c`.

```
333            if (nores && skb_res == NULL) {
334                    skb_res = skb;
335                    goto restart;
336            }
337
338            if (busy) {
339                    netif_stop_queue(dev);
340                    return 1;
341            }
342            master->stats.tx_errors++;
343
344    drop:
345            master->stats.tx_dropped++;
346            dev_kfree_skb(skb);
347            return 0;
348    }
```

Figure 9.307 TE net device open: `linux/net/sched/sch_teql.c`.

```
350    static int teql_master_open(struct net_device *dev)
351    {
352            struct Qdisc * q;
353            struct teql_master *m = (void*)dev->priv;
354            int mtu = 0xFFFE;
355            unsigned flags = IFF_NOARP|IFF_MULTICAST;
356
357            if (m->slaves == NULL)
358                    return -EUNATCH;
359
360            flags = FMASK;
361
362            q = m->slaves;
363            do {
364                    struct net_device *slave = q->dev;
365
366                    if (slave == NULL)
367                            return -EUNATCH;
368
369                    if (slave->mtu < mtu)
370                            mtu = slave->mtu;
371                    if (slave->hard_header_len > LL_MAX_HEADER)
372                            return -EINVAL;
373
374                    /* If all the slaves are BROADCAST, master is BROADCAST
375                       If all the slaves are PtP, master is PtP
376                       Otherwise, master is NBMA.
377                     */
378                    if (!(slave->flags&IFF_POINTOPOINT))
379                            flags &= ~IFF_POINTOPOINT;
380                    if (!(slave->flags&IFF_BROADCAST))
381                            flags &= ~IFF_BROADCAST;
```

```
		if (!(slave->flags&IFF_MULTICAST))
			flags &= ~IFF_MULTICAST;
	} while ((q = NEXT_SLAVE(q)) != m->slaves);

	m->dev.mtu = mtu;
	m->dev.flags = (m->dev.flags&~FMASK) | flags;
	netif_start_queue(&m->dev);
	MOD_INC_USE_COUNT;
	return 0;
}
```

Figure 9.308 TE net device close and stats: `linux/net/sched/sch_teql.c`.

```
static int teql_master_close(struct net_device *dev)
{
	netif_stop_queue(dev);
	MOD_DEC_USE_COUNT;
	return 0;
}

static struct net_device_stats *teql_master_stats(struct net_device *dev)
{
	struct teql_master *m = (void*)dev->priv;
	return &m->stats;
}
```

Figure 9.309 TE net device mtu: `linux/net/sched/sch_teql.c`.

```
static int teql_master_mtu(struct net_device *dev, int new_mtu)
{
	struct teql_master *m = (void*)dev->priv;
	struct Qdisc *q;

	if (new_mtu < 68)
		return -EINVAL;

	q = m->slaves;
	if (q) {
		do {
			if (new_mtu > q->dev->mtu)
				return -EINVAL;
		} while ((q=NEXT_SLAVE(q)) != m->slaves);
	}

	dev->mtu = new_mtu;
	return 0;
}
```

Figure 9.310 TE net device master initialization: `linux/net/sched/sch_teql.c`.

```
426   static int teql_master_init(struct net_device *dev)
427   {
428           dev->open           = teql_master_open;
429           dev->hard_start_xmit = teql_master_xmit;
430           dev->stop           = teql_master_close;
431           dev->get_stats      = teql_master_stats;
432           dev->change_mtu     = teql_master_mtu;
433           dev->type           = ARPHRD_VOID;
434           dev->mtu            = 1500;
435           dev->tx_queue_len   = 100;
436           dev->flags          = IFF_NOARP;
437           dev->hard_header_len = LL_MAX_HEADER;
438           return 0;
439   }
440
441   static struct teql_master the_master = {
442   {
443           NULL,
444           NULL,
445           "",
446           sizeof(struct teql_sched_data),
447
448           teql_enqueue,
449           teql_dequeue,
450           teql_requeue,
451           NULL,
452
453           teql_qdisc_init,
454           teql_reset,
455           teql_destroy,
456           NULL,
457   },};
```

Figure 9.311 TE net device register: `linux/net/sched/sch_teql.c`.

```
459
460   #ifdef MODULE
461   int init_module(void)
462   #else
463   int __init teql_init(void)
464   #endif
465   {
466           int err;
467
468           rtnl_lock();
469
470           the_master.dev.priv = (void*)&the_master;
471           err = dev_alloc_name(&the_master.dev, "teql%d");
472           if (err < 0)
473                   return err;
474           memcpy(the_master.qops.id, the_master.dev.name, IFNAMSIZ);
```

```
        the_master.dev.init = teql_master_init;

        err = register_netdevice(&the_master.dev);
        if (err == 0) {
                err = register_qdisc(&the_master.qops);
                if (err)
                        unregister_netdevice(&the_master.dev);
        }
        rtnl_unlock();
        return err;
}

#ifdef MODULE
void cleanup_module(void)
{
        rtnl_lock();
        unregister_qdisc(&the_master.qops);
        unregister_netdevice(&the_master.dev);
        rtnl_unlock();
}
#endif
```

9.13.14 Profiling

Figure 9.312 Profiling—timer: `linux/net/core/profile.c`.

```
atomic_t net_profile_active;
struct timeval net_profile_adjust;

NET_PROFILE_DEFINE(total);

struct net_profile_slot *net_profile_chain = &net_prof_total;

#ifdef __alpha__
__u32 alpha_lo;
long alpha_hi;

static void alpha_tick(unsigned long);

static struct timer_list alpha_timer =
        { NULL, NULL, 0, 0L, alpha_tick };

void alpha_tick(unsigned long dummy)
{
        struct timeval dummy_stamp;
        net_profile_stamp(&dummy_stamp);
        alpha_timer.expires = jiffies + 4*HZ;
        add_timer(&alpha_timer);
}

#endif
```

Figure 9.313 Profiling—white hole interface: `linux/net/core/profile.c`.

```
struct iphdr whitehole_iph;
int whitehole_count;

static int whitehole_xmit(struct sk_buff *skb, struct net_device *dev)
{
        struct net_device_stats *stats;

        stats = (struct net_device_stats *)dev->priv;
        stats->tx_packets++;
        stats->tx_bytes+=skb->len;

        dev_kfree_skb(skb);
        return 0;
}

static void whitehole_inject(unsigned long);
int whitehole_init(struct net_device *dev);

static struct timer_list whitehole_timer =
        { NULL, NULL, 0, 0L, whitehole_inject };

static struct net_device whitehole_dev = {
        "whitehole", 0x0, 0x0, 0x0, 0x0, 0, 0, 0, 0, 0, NULL, whitehole_init, };
```

Figure 9.314 Profiling—white hole interface: `linux/net/core/profile.c`.

```
static int whitehole_open(struct net_device *dev)
{
        whitehole_count = 100000;
        whitehole_timer.expires = jiffies + 5*HZ;
        add_timer(&whitehole_timer);
        return 0;
}

static int whitehole_close(struct net_device *dev)
{
        del_timer(&whitehole_timer);
        return 0;
}

static void whitehole_inject(unsigned long dummy)
{
        struct net_device_stats *stats = (struct net_device_stats *)whitehole_dev.priv;
        extern int netdev_dropping;

        do {
                struct iphdr *iph;
                struct sk_buff *skb = alloc_skb(128, GFP_ATOMIC);
                if (!skb)
                        break;
                skb_reserve(skb, 32);
```

```
                iph = (struct iphdr*)skb_put(skb, sizeof(*iph));
                skb->mac.raw = ((u8*)iph) - 14;
                memcpy(iph, &whitehole_iph, sizeof(*iph));
                skb->protocol = __constant_htons(ETH_P_IP);
                skb->dev = &whitehole_dev;
                skb->pkt_type = PACKET_HOST;
                stats->rx_packets++;
                stats->rx_bytes += skb->len;
                netif_rx(skb);
                whitehole_count--;
        } while (netdev_dropping == 0 && whitehole_count>0);
        if (whitehole_count > 0) {
                whitehole_timer.expires = jiffies + 1;
                add_timer(&whitehole_timer);
        }
}
```

Figure 9.315 Profiling—white hole—stats and init: `linux/net/core/profile.c`.

```
static struct net_device_stats *whitehole_get_stats(struct net_device *dev)
{
        struct net_device_stats *stats = (struct net_device_stats *) dev->priv;
        return stats;
}

int __init whitehole_init(struct net_device *dev)
{
        dev->priv = kmalloc(sizeof(struct net_device_stats), GFP_KERNEL);
        if (dev->priv == NULL)
                return -ENOBUFS;
        memset(dev->priv, 0, sizeof(struct net_device_stats));
        dev->get_stats = whitehole_get_stats;
        dev->hard_start_xmit = whitehole_xmit;
        dev->open = whitehole_open;
        dev->stop = whitehole_close;
        ether_setup(dev);
        dev->tx_queue_len = 0;
        dev->flags |= IFF_NOARP;
        dev->flags &= ~(IFF_BROADCAST|IFF_MULTICAST);
        dev->iflink = 0;
        whitehole_iph.ihl = 5;
        whitehole_iph.version = 4;
        whitehole_iph.ttl = 2;
        whitehole_iph.saddr = in_aton("193.233.7.21");
        whitehole_iph.daddr = in_aton("193.233.7.10");
        whitehole_iph.tot_len = htons(20);
        whitehole_iph.check = ip_compute_csum((void *)&whitehole_iph, 20);
        return 0;
}
```

Figure 9.316 Profiling—white hole—register/unregister: `linux/net/core/profile.c`.

```
239   int net_profile_register(struct net_profile_slot *slot)
240   {
241           cli();
242           slot->next = net_profile_chain;
243           net_profile_chain = slot;
244           sti();
245           return 0;
246   }
247
248   int net_profile_unregister(struct net_profile_slot *slot)
249   {
250           struct net_profile_slot **sp, *s;
251
252           for (sp = &net_profile_chain; (s = *sp) != NULL; sp = &s->next) {
253                   if (s == slot) {
254                           cli();
255                           *sp = s->next;
256                           sti();
257                           return 0;
258                   }
259           }
260           return -ESRCH;
261   }
262
263
264   int __init net_profile_init(void)
265   {
266           int i;
267
268   #ifdef CONFIG_PROC_FS
269           create_proc_read_entry("net/profile", 0, 0, profile_read_proc, NULL);
270   #endif
271
272           register_netdevice(&whitehole_dev);
273
274           printk("Evaluating net profiler cost ...");
275   #ifdef __alpha__
276           alpha_tick(0);
277   #endif
278           for (i=0; i<1024; i++) {
279                   NET_PROFILE_ENTER(total);
280                   NET_PROFILE_LEAVE(total);
281           }
282           if (net_prof_total.accumulator.tv_sec) {
283                   printk(" too high!\n");
284           } else {
285                   net_profile_adjust.tv_usec = net_prof_total.accumulator.tv_usec>>10;
286                   printk("%ld units\n", net_profile_adjust.tv_usec);
287           }
288           net_prof_total.hits = 0;
289           net_profile_stamp(&net_prof_total.entered);
290           return 0;
291   }
292
293   #endif
```

Almesberger/EPFL ATM VC Scheduling

ATM is a pretty special case, where a level 2 network does the real work, but we can interface to this—Almesberger [1] did some nice work here providing a clean integrated interface.

Figure 9.317 ATM scheduling–author: `linux/net/sched/sch_atm.c`.

```
/* net/sched/sch_atm.c - ATM VC selection "queueing discipline" */

/* Written 1998-2000 by Werner Almesberger, EPFL ICA */
```

Figure 9.318 ATM scheduling–introductory remarks: `linux/net/sched/sch_atm.c`.

```
/*
 * The ATM queuing discipline provides a framework for invoking classifiers
 * (aka "filters"), which in turn select classes of this queuing discipline.
 * Each class maps the flow(s) it is handling to a given VC. Multiple classes
 * may share the same VC.
 *
 * When creating a class, VCs are specified by passing the number of the open
 * socket descriptor by which the calling process references the VC. The kernel
 * keeps the VC open at least until all classes using it are removed.
 *
 * In this file, most functions are named atm_tc_* to avoid confusion with all
 * the atm_* in net/atm. This naming convention differs from what's used in the
 * rest of net/sched.
 *
 * Known bugs:
 *  - sometimes messes up the IP stack
 *  - any manipulations besides the few operations described in the README, are
 *    untested and likely to crash the system
 *  - should lock the flow while there is data in the queue (?)
 */
```

Figure 9.319 ATM scheduling–data structures: `linux/net/sched/sch_atm.c`.

```
#define PRIV(sch) ((struct atm_qdisc_data *) (sch)->data)
#define VCC2FLOW(vcc) ((struct atm_flow_data *) ((vcc)->user_back))


struct atm_flow_data {
        struct Qdisc            *q;             /* FIFO, TBF, etc. */
        struct tcf_proto        *filter_list;
        struct atm_vcc          *vcc;           /* VCC; NULL if VCC is closed */
        void (*old_pop)(struct atm_vcc *vcc,struct sk_buff *skb); /* chaining */
        struct atm_qdisc_data *parent;          /* parent qdisc */
        struct socket           *sock;          /* for closing */
        u32                     classid;        /* x:y type ID */
        int                     ref;            /* reference count */
```

```
        struct tc_stats       stats;
        struct atm_flow_data  *next;
        struct atm_flow_data  *excess;       /* flow for excess traffic;
                                                NULL to set CLP instead */
        int                   hdr_len;
        unsigned char         hdr[0];        /* header data; MUST BE LAST */
};

struct atm_qdisc_data {
        struct atm_flow_data  link;          /* unclassified skbs go here */
        struct atm_flow_data  *flows;        /* NB: "link" is also on this
                                                list */
        struct tasklet_struct task;          /* requeue tasklet */
};
```

Figure 9.320 ATM scheduling—finding flows i: `linux/net/sched/sch_atm.c`.

```
/* ------------------------- Class/flow operations ------------------------- */


static int find_flow(struct atm_qdisc_data *qdisc,struct atm_flow_data *flow)
{
        struct atm_flow_data *walk;

        DPRINTK("find_flow(qdisc %p,flow %p)\n",qdisc,flow);
        for (walk = qdisc->flows; walk; walk = walk->next)
                if (walk == flow) return 1;
        DPRINTK("find_flow: not found\n");
        return 0;
}


static __inline__ struct atm_flow_data *lookup_flow(struct Qdisc *sch,
    u32 classid)
{
        struct atm_flow_data *flow;

        for (flow = PRIV(sch)->flows; flow; flow = flow->next)
                if (flow->classid == classid) break;
        return flow;
}
```

Figure 9.321 ATM scheduling—trees of flows: `linux/net/sched/sch_atm.c`.

```
static int atm_tc_graft(struct Qdisc *sch,unsigned long arg,
    struct Qdisc *new,struct Qdisc **old)
{
        struct atm_qdisc_data *p = PRIV(sch);
        struct atm_flow_data *flow = (struct atm_flow_data *) arg;

        DPRINTK("atm_tc_graft(sch %p,[qdisc %p],flow %p,new %p,old %p)\n",sch,
```

```
            p,flow,new,old);
        if (!find_flow(p,flow)) return -EINVAL;
        if (!new) new = &noop_qdisc;
        *old = xchg(&flow->q,new);
        if (*old) qdisc_reset(*old);
        return 0;
}


static struct Qdisc *atm_tc_leaf(struct Qdisc *sch,unsigned long cl)
{
        struct atm_flow_data *flow = (struct atm_flow_data *) cl;

        DPRINTK("atm_tc_leaf(sch %p,flow %p)\n",sch,flow);
        return flow ? flow->q : NULL;
}
```

Figure 9.322 ATM scheduling–more finding flows: `linux/net/sched/sch_atm.c`.

```
static unsigned long atm_tc_get(struct Qdisc *sch,u32 classid)
{
        struct atm_qdisc_data *p __attribute__((unused)) = PRIV(sch);
        struct atm_flow_data *flow;

        DPRINTK("atm_tc_get(sch %p,[qdisc %p],classid %x)\n",sch,p,classid);
        flow = lookup_flow(sch,classid);
        if (flow) flow->ref++;
        DPRINTK("atm_tc_get: flow %p\n",flow);
        return (unsigned long) flow;
}


static unsigned long atm_tc_bind_filter(struct Qdisc *sch,
    unsigned long parent, u32 classid)
{
        return atm_tc_get(sch,classid);
}
```

Figure 9.323 ATM scheduling–destroy filters: `linux/net/sched/sch_atm.c`.

```
static void destroy_filters(struct atm_flow_data *flow)
{
        struct tcf_proto *filter;

        while ((filter = flow->filter_list)) {
                DPRINTK("destroy_filters: destroying filter %p\n",filter);
                flow->filter_list = filter->next;
                filter->ops->destroy(filter);
        }
}
```

Figure 9.324 ATM scheduling—destroy all filters: `linux/net/sched/sch_atm.c`.

```
/*
 * atm_tc_put handles all destructions, including the ones that are explicitly
 * requested (atm_tc_destroy, etc.). The assumption here is that we never drop
 * anything that still seems to be in use.
 */

static void atm_tc_put(struct Qdisc *sch, unsigned long cl)
{
        struct atm_qdisc_data *p = PRIV(sch);
        struct atm_flow_data *flow = (struct atm_flow_data *) cl;
        struct atm_flow_data **prev;

        DPRINTK("atm_tc_put(sch %p,[qdisc %p],flow %p)\n",sch,p,flow);
        if (--flow->ref) return;
        DPRINTK("atm_tc_put: destroying\n");
        for (prev = &p->flows; *prev; prev = &(*prev)->next)
                if (*prev == flow) break;
        if (!*prev) {
                printk(KERN_CRIT "atm_tc_put: class %p not found\n",flow);
                return;
        }
        *prev = flow->next;
        DPRINTK("atm_tc_put: qdisc %p\n",flow->q);
        qdisc_destroy(flow->q);
        destroy_filters(flow);
        if (flow->sock) {
                DPRINTK("atm_tc_put: f_count %d\n",
                    file_count(flow->sock->file));
                flow->vcc->pop = flow->old_pop;
                sockfd_put(flow->sock);
        }
        if (flow->excess) atm_tc_put(sch,(unsigned long) flow->excess);
        if (flow != &p->link) kfree(flow);
        /*
         * If flow == &p->link, the qdisc no longer works at this point and
         * needs to be removed. (By the caller of atm_tc_put.)
         */
}
```

Now we have to worry about virtual circuit management too.

Figure 9.325 ATM scheduling—pop a VC: `linux/net/sched/sch_atm.c`.

```
static void sch_atm_pop(struct atm_vcc *vcc,struct sk_buff *skb)
{
        struct atm_qdisc_data *p = VCC2FLOW(vcc)->parent;

        D2PRINTK("sch_atm_pop(vcc %p,skb %p,[qdisc %p])\n",vcc,skb,p);
        VCC2FLOW(vcc)->old_pop(vcc,skb);
        tasklet_schedule(&p->task);
}
```

In a way, the level 2 network inherits changes from the level 3 network. If we were really clever, we might think of ATM (and any MPLS-type QoS-aware network) as being a leaf level below the IP leaf level.

Figure 9.326 ATM scheduling–change ATM TC parameters i: `linux/net/sched/sch_atm.c`.

```
static int atm_tc_change(struct Qdisc *sch, u32 classid, u32 parent,
    struct rtattr **tca, unsigned long *arg)
{
        struct atm_qdisc_data *p = PRIV(sch);
        struct atm_flow_data *flow = (struct atm_flow_data *) *arg;
        struct atm_flow_data *excess = NULL;
        struct rtattr *opt = tca[TCA_OPTIONS-1];
        struct rtattr *tb[TCA_ATM_MAX];
        struct socket *sock;
        int fd,error,hdr_len;
        void *hdr;

        DPRINTK("atm_tc_change(sch %p,[qdisc %p],classid %x,parent %x,"
            "flow %p,opt %p)\n",sch,p,classid,parent,flow,opt);
        /*
         * The concept of parents doesn't apply for this qdisc.
         */
        if (parent && parent != TC_H_ROOT && parent != sch->handle)
                return -EINVAL;
        /*
         * ATM classes cannot be changed. In order to change properties of the
         * ATM connection, that socket needs to be modified directly (via the
         * native ATM API. In order to send a flow to a different VC, the old
         * class needs to be removed and a new one added. (This may be changed
         * later.)
         */
        if (flow) return -EBUSY;
        if (opt == NULL || rtattr_parse(tb,TCA_ATM_MAX,RTA_DATA(opt),
            RTA_PAYLOAD(opt))) return -EINVAL;
        if (!tb[TCA_ATM_FD-1] || RTA_PAYLOAD(tb[TCA_ATM_FD-1]) < sizeof(fd))
                return -EINVAL;
        fd = *(int *) RTA_DATA(tb[TCA_ATM_FD-1]);
        DPRINTK("atm_tc_change: fd %d\n",fd);
```

Figure 9.327 ATM scheduling–change ATM TC parameters ii: `linux/net/sched/sch_atm.c`.

```
                hdr_len = RTA_PAYLOAD(tb[TCA_ATM_HDR-1]);
                hdr = RTA_DATA(tb[TCA_ATM_HDR-1]);
        }
        else {
                hdr_len = RFC1483LLC_LEN;
                hdr = NULL; /* default LLC/SNAP for IP */
        }
        if (!tb[TCA_ATM_EXCESS-1]) excess = NULL;
```

```
	else {
		if (RTA_PAYLOAD(tb[TCA_ATM_EXCESS-1]) != sizeof(u32))
			return -EINVAL;
		excess = (struct atm_flow_data *) atm_tc_get(sch,
		    *(u32 *) RTA_DATA(tb[TCA_ATM_EXCESS-1]));
		if (!excess) return -ENOENT;
	}
	DPRINTK("atm_tc_change: type %d, payload %d, hdr_len %d\n",
	    opt->rta_type,RTA_PAYLOAD(opt),hdr_len);
	if (!(sock = sockfd_lookup(fd,&error))) return error; /* f_count++ */
	DPRINTK("atm_tc_change: f_count %d\n",file_count(sock->file));
	if (sock->ops->family != PF_ATMSVC && sock->ops->family != PF_ATMPVC) {
		error = -EPROTOTYPE;
		goto err_out;
	}
	/* @@@ should check if the socket is really operational or we'll crash
	   on vcc->send */
	if (classid) {
		if (TC_H_MAJ(classid ^ sch->handle)) {
			DPRINTK("atm_tc_change: classid mismatch\n");
			error = -EINVAL;
			goto err_out;
		}
		if (find_flow(p,flow)) {
			error = -EEXIST;
			goto err_out;
		}
	}
```

Figure 9.328 ATM scheduling—change ATM TC parameters iii: `linux/net/sched/sch_atm.c`.

```
	else {
		int i;
		unsigned long cl;

		for (i = 1; i < 0x8000; i++) {
			classid = TC_H_MAKE(sch->handle,0x8000 | i);
			if (!(cl = atm_tc_get(sch,classid))) break;
			atm_tc_put(sch,cl);
		}
	}
	DPRINTK("atm_tc_change: new id %x\n",classid);
	flow = kmalloc(sizeof(struct atm_flow_data)+hdr_len,GFP_KERNEL);
	DPRINTK("atm_tc_change: flow %p\n",flow);
	if (!flow) {
		error = -ENOBUFS;
		goto err_out;
	}
	memset(flow,0,sizeof(*flow));
	flow->filter_list = NULL;
	if (!(flow->q = qdisc_create_dflt(sch->dev,&pfifo_qdisc_ops)))
		flow->q = &noop_qdisc;
```

```
        DPRINTK("atm_tc_change: qdisc %p\n",flow->q);
        flow->sock = sock;
        flow->vcc = ATM_SD(sock); /* speedup */
        flow->vcc->user_back = flow;
        DPRINTK("atm_tc_change: vcc %p\n",flow->vcc);
        flow->old_pop = flow->vcc->pop;
        flow->parent = p;
        flow->vcc->pop = sch_atm_pop;
        flow->classid = classid;
        flow->ref = 1;
        flow->excess = excess;
        flow->next = p->link.next;
        p->link.next = flow;
        flow->hdr_len = hdr_len;
        if (hdr) memcpy(flow->hdr,hdr,hdr_len);
        else {
                memcpy(flow->hdr,llc_oui,sizeof(llc_oui));
                ((u16 *) flow->hdr)[3] = htons(ETH_P_IP);
        }
        *arg = (unsigned long) flow;
        return 0;
err_out:
        if (excess) atm_tc_put(sch,(unsigned long) excess);
        sockfd_put(sock);
        return error;
}
```

Figure 9.329 ATM scheduling—delete TC: `linux/net/sched/sch_atm.c`.

```
static int atm_tc_delete(struct Qdisc *sch,unsigned long arg)
{
        struct atm_qdisc_data *p = PRIV(sch);
        struct atm_flow_data *flow = (struct atm_flow_data *) arg;

        DPRINTK("atm_tc_delete(sch %p,[qdisc %p],flow %p)\n",sch,p,flow);
        if (!find_flow(PRIV(sch),flow)) return -EINVAL;
        if (flow->filter_list || flow == &p->link) return -EBUSY;
        /*
         * Reference count must be 2: one for "keepalive" (set at class
         * creation), and one for the reference held when calling delete.
         */
        if (flow->ref < 2) {
                printk(KERN_ERR "atm_tc_delete: flow->ref == %d\n",flow->ref);
                return -EINVAL;
        }
        if (flow->ref > 2) return -EBUSY; /* catch references via excess, etc.*/
        atm_tc_put(sch,arg);
        return 0;
}
```

Here we have a more general level of management.

Figure 9.330 ATM scheduling—walk TC: `linux/net/sched/sch_atm.c`.

```
static void atm_tc_walk(struct Qdisc *sch,struct qdisc_walker *walker)
{
        struct atm_qdisc_data *p = PRIV(sch);
        struct atm_flow_data *flow;

        DPRINTK("atm_tc_walk(sch %p,[qdisc %p],walker %p)\n",sch,p,walker);
        if (walker->stop) return;
        for (flow = p->flows; flow; flow = flow->next) {
                if (walker->count >= walker->skip)
                        if (walker->fn(sch,(unsigned long) flow,walker) < 0) {
                                walker->stop = 1;
                                break;
                        }
                walker->count++;
        }
}
```

Figure 9.331 ATM scheduling—find TCF: `linux/net/sched/sch_atm.c`.

```
static struct tcf_proto **atm_tc_find_tcf(struct Qdisc *sch,unsigned long cl)
{
        struct atm_qdisc_data *p = PRIV(sch);
        struct atm_flow_data *flow = (struct atm_flow_data *) cl;

        DPRINTK("atm_tc_find_tcf(sch %p,[qdisc %p],flow %p)\n",sch,p,flow);
        return flow ? &flow->filter_list : &p->link.filter_list;
}
```

Figure 9.332 ATM scheduling—enqueue i: `linux/net/sched/sch_atm.c`.

```
static int atm_tc_enqueue(struct sk_buff *skb,struct Qdisc *sch)
{
        struct atm_qdisc_data *p = PRIV(sch);
        struct atm_flow_data *flow = NULL ; /* @@@ */
        struct tcf_result res;
        int result;
        int ret = NET_XMIT_POLICED;

        D2PRINTK("atm_tc_enqueue(skb %p,sch %p,[qdisc %p])\n",skb,sch,p);
        result = TC_POLICE_OK; /* be nice to gcc */
        if (TC_H_MAJ(skb->priority) != sch->handle ||
            !(flow = (struct atm_flow_data *) atm_tc_get(sch,skb->priority)))
                for (flow = p->flows; flow; flow = flow->next)
                        if (flow->filter_list) {
                                result = tc_classify(skb,flow->filter_list,
```

```
408                          &res);
409                     if (result < 0) continue;
410                     flow = (struct atm_flow_data *) res.class;
411                     if (!flow) flow = lookup_flow(sch,res.classid);
412                     break;
413                 }
414         if (!flow) flow = &p->link;
```

Figure 9.333 ATM scheduling—enqueue ii: `linux/net/sched/sch_atm.c`.

```
415        else {
416             if (flow->vcc)
417                 ATM_SKB(skb)->atm_options = flow->vcc->atm_options;
418                 /*@@@ looks good ... but it's not supposed to work :-)*/
419  #ifdef CONFIG_NET_CLS_POLICE
420             switch (result) {
421                 case TC_POLICE_SHOT:
422                     kfree_skb(skb);
423                     break;
424                 case TC_POLICE_RECLASSIFY:
425                     if (flow->excess) flow = flow->excess;
426                     else {
427                         ATM_SKB(skb)->atm_options |=
428                             ATM_ATMOPT_CLP;
429                         break;
430                     }
431                     /* fall through */
432                 case TC_POLICE_OK:
433                     /* fall through */
434                 default:
435                     break;
436             }
437  #endif
438        }
```

Figure 9.334 ATM scheduling—enqueue iii: `linux/net/sched/sch_atm.c`.

```
439        if (
440  #ifdef CONFIG_NET_CLS_POLICE
441            result == TC_POLICE_SHOT ||
442  #endif
443            (ret = flow->q->enqueue(skb,flow->q)) != 0) {
444             sch->stats.drops++;
445             if (flow) flow->stats.drops++;
446             return ret;
447        }
448        sch->stats.bytes += skb->len;
449        sch->stats.packets++;
450        flow->stats.bytes += skb->len;
451        flow->stats.packets++;
```

```
	/*
	 * Okay, this may seem weird. We pretend we've dropped the packet if
	 * it goes via ATM. The reason for this is that the outer qdisc
	 * expects to be able to q->dequeue the packet later on if we return
	 * success at this place. Also, sch->q.qdisc needs to reflect whether
	 * there is a packet egligible for dequeuing or not. Note that the
	 * statistics of the outer qdisc are necessarily wrong because of all
	 * this. There's currently no correct solution for this.
	 */
	if (flow == &p->link) {
		sch->q.qlen++;
		return 0;
	}
	tasklet_schedule(&p->task);
	return NET_XMIT_BYPASS;
}
```

Figure 9.335 ATM scheduling—dequeue: `linux/net/sched/sch_atm.c`.

```
/*
 * Dequeue packets and send them over ATM. Note that we quite deliberately
 * avoid checking net_device's flow control here, simply because sch_atm
 * uses its own channels, which have nothing to do with any CLIP/LANE/or
 * non-ATM interfaces.
 */


static void sch_atm_dequeue(unsigned long data)
{
	struct Qdisc *sch = (struct Qdisc *) data;
	struct atm_qdisc_data *p = PRIV(sch);
	struct atm_flow_data *flow;
	struct sk_buff *skb;

	D2PRINTK("sch_atm_dequeue(sch %p,[qdisc %p])\n",sch,p);
	for (flow = p->link.next; flow; flow = flow->next)
		/*
		 * If traffic is properly shaped, this won't generate nasty
		 * little bursts. Otherwise, it may ... (but that's okay)
		 */
		while ((skb = flow->q->dequeue(flow->q))) {
			if (!atm_may_send(flow->vcc,skb->truesize)) {
				(void) flow->q->ops->requeue(skb,flow->q);
				break;
			}
			D2PRINTK("atm_tc_deqeueue: sending on class %p\n",flow);
			/* remove any LL header somebody else has attached */
			skb_pull(skb,(char *) skb->nh.iph-(char *) skb->data);
			if (skb_headroom(skb) < flow->hdr_len) {
				struct sk_buff *new;

				new = skb_realloc_headroom(skb,flow->hdr_len);
				dev_kfree_skb(skb);
```

```
                        if (!new) continue;
                        skb = new;
                }
                D2PRINTK("sch_atm_dequeue: ip %p, data %p\n",
                    skb->nh.iph,skb->data);
                ATM_SKB(skb)->vcc = flow->vcc;
                memcpy(skb_push(skb,flow->hdr_len),flow->hdr,
                    flow->hdr_len);
                atomic_add(skb->truesize,&flow->vcc->tx_inuse);
                ATM_SKB(skb)->iovcnt = 0;
                /* atm.atm_options are already set by atm_tc_enqueue */
                (void) flow->vcc->send(flow->vcc,skb);
        }
}
```

Figure 9.336 ATM scheduling—TC dequeue: `linux/net/sched/sch_atm.c`.

```
static struct sk_buff *atm_tc_dequeue(struct Qdisc *sch)
{
        struct atm_qdisc_data *p = PRIV(sch);
        struct sk_buff *skb;

        D2PRINTK("atm_tc_dequeue(sch %p,[qdisc %p])\n",sch,p);
        tasklet_schedule(&p->task);
        skb = p->link.q->dequeue(p->link.q);
        if (skb) sch->q.qlen--;
        return skb;
}
```

Figure 9.337 ATM scheduling—TC requeue: `linux/net/sched/sch_atm.c`.

```

static int atm_tc_requeue(struct sk_buff *skb,struct Qdisc *sch)
{
        struct atm_qdisc_data *p = PRIV(sch);
        int ret;

        D2PRINTK("atm_tc_requeue(skb %p,sch %p,[qdisc %p])\n",skb,sch,p);
        ret = p->link.q->ops->requeue(skb,p->link.q);
        if (!ret) sch->q.qlen++;
        else {
                sch->stats.drops++;
                p->link.stats.drops++;
        }
        return ret;
}
```

Figure 9.338 ATM scheduling—TC drop: `linux/net/sched/sch_atm.c.`

```
static int atm_tc_drop(struct Qdisc *sch)
{
        struct atm_qdisc_data *p = PRIV(sch);
        struct atm_flow_data *flow;

        DPRINTK("atm_tc_drop(sch %p,[qdisc %p])\n",sch,p);
        for (flow = p->flows; flow; flow = flow->next)
                if (flow->q->ops->drop && flow->q->ops->drop(flow->q))
                        return 1;
        return 0;
}
```

Figure 9.339 ATM scheduling—initialize: `linux/net/sched/sch_atm.c.`

```
#ifdef MODULE
int init_module(void)
{
        return register_qdisc(&atm_qdisc_ops);
}


void cleanup_module(void)
{
        unregister_qdisc(&atm_qdisc_ops);
}
#endif
```

9.14 Managing Forwarding Treatment Information—the TC Command

Linux now has sophisticated (and complex) traffic control facilities—these could be managed through some distributed resource reservation or traffic engineering algorithm, or manually set up at each site. The TC command is an application that lets you configure the facilities on a specific Linux system.

9.14.1 Traffic Control—Using the Tool

```
******************************
#!/bin/sh
TC=/src/iproute2/tc/tc
DEV="dev eth0"
efrate="2Mbit"
MTU="1.5kB"
```

```
#$TC qdisc add $DEV handle 1:0 root dsmark indices 64 set_tc_index
#$TC filter add $DEV parent 1:0 protocol ip prio 1 tcindex mask 0xfc shift 2

$TC qdisc add $DEV handle 1:0 root dsmark indices 64
$TC qdisc add $DEV parent 1:0 handle 2:0 prio

#
# EF class: Maximum about one MTU sized packet allowed on the queue
#
$TC filter add $DEV parent 1:0 protocol ip prio 1 handle 0x22 tcindex \
         classid 2:1
$TC qdisc add $DEV parent 2:1 tbf rate $efrate burst $MTU limit 2.5kB

$TC filter add $DEV parent 1:0 protocol ip prio 2 handle 0x2f tcindex mask
0xff\
         classid 2:2
$TC qdisc add $DEV parent 2:2 handle 3:0 gred setup DPs 2 default 2 grio

#
# AF class
#
$TC filter add $DEV parent 1:0 protocol ip prio 3 handle 0x24 tcindex \
         classid 3:1
$TC qdisc add $DEV handle 3: gred limit 90KB min 55KB max 65KB \
        burst 90 avpkt 1000 bandwidth 10Mbit DP 1 probability 0.05 prio 2
#
# BE class
#
$TC filter add $DEV parent 1:0 protocol ip prio 3 handle 0x26 tcindex \
        classid 3:2
$TC qdisc add $DEV handle 3: gred limit 90KB min 35KB max 50KB burst 90 \
         avpkt 1000 bandwidth 10Mbit DP 2 probability 0.1 prio 3
```

9.14.2 Traffic Control—How the Tool Is Implemented

Figure 9.340 TC—main: `tc/tc.c`.

```
void *BODY;
static struct qdisc_util * qdisc_list;
static struct filter_util * filter_list;

static int print_noqopt(struct qdisc_util *qu, FILE *f, struct rtattr *opt)
{
```

9.14.3 TC Command Usage

The TC command usage is fairly complex, since there are three intertwined types of object one can set up. As described earlier, we have a filter type, a class, and then the actual queuing discipline with its parameters. Normally, one uses `tc` to select a queuing discipline for a device, then attaches a filter to the device to direct packets to the appropriate queue. In more complex cases, this recurses via CBQ or CSZ and the use of class identifiers, as well as filters.

```
tc [ OPTIONS ] OBJECT { COMMAND | help }
where  OBJECT := \{ qdisc | class | filter \}
       OPTIONS := \ { -s[tatistics] | -d[etails] | -r[aw] \} }
```

TC Qdisc Command

As discussed in the rest of this chapter, the queuing discipline is currently one of `{ atm | [p|b]fifo | tbf | prio | hfsc | hpfq | sfq | cbq | csz | red | gred | dsmark | ingress | etc. }`.

```
tc qdisc [ add | del | replace | change | get ] dev STRING
        [ handle QHANDLE ] [ root | ingress | parent CLASSID ]
        [ estimator INTERVAL TIME_CONSTANT ]
        [ [ QDISC_KIND ] [ help | OPTIONS ] ] }
```

We can be adding a base queue discipline optionally with a handle, or as a child in a class hierarchy (usually previously defined by CBQ or CSZ), or we can be adding an estimator. One exceptional case is ingress queuing.

The *estimator* takes an interval and a time constant over which the estimate decays. This is used to monitor queue occupancy, without running too many cycles up doing so.

When we add or modify a given queuing discipline, there are configuration parameters we also must set up. The options each queuing discipline can be configured with are (roughly) as follows:

atm. IP over ATM can set up ATM parameters as part of a class hierarchy. These include the type of ATM VC in use, and the VC class (in the ATM sense, in other words, UBR, VBR, and so on). The ATM AAL-level parameters such as SDU (packet size, usually 9,280 bytes), and any ATM-level addressing information (e.g., whether E164 or ISO addresses are used to indentify the link layer next hop address, or in other words the ATM VC end point).

```
atm ( pvc <addr> | svc <addr> [ sap <sap> ] ) | qos <qos> [
sndbuf <bytes> ] | hdr <hex> | excess ( <class id> | clp )
clip
```

fifo. FIFO takes one parameter, which is the maximum queue length.

```
[p|b]fifo [limit <n>]
```

tbf. The token bucket filter takes a queue length, `limit`, and a latency (in microseconds), or a burst specification in terms of a buffer and a burst length, as well as mean and peak rate parameters. Also, it can take an MTU parameter and a maximum path unit packet size parameter.

```
tbf limit <bytes> burst <bytes>[/<bytes>] rate <kbps> [ mtu
<bytes>[/<bytes>] ]
```

prio. Priority queues are configured with a number of bands, then a map of the identifiers (so that they can be used later in a filter).

```
prio bands <n> priomap <P1> <P2> ...
```

hfsc. The hierarchical fair service curve is not part of the current release.

hpfq. Hierarchical packet fair queuing is not in the current release at the time of writing.

sfq. Stochastic fairness queuing can be set up with a perturbation and a quantum, which represent the input to the statistical nature of this approximate fair-queuing technique.

```
sfq [ perturb <seconds> ] [ quantum <bytes> ]
```

cbq.

```
cbq bandwidth <bps> rate <bps> maxburst <npkts> [ avpkt <bytes> ]
        [ minburst <npkts> ] [ bounded ] [ isolated ]
        [ allot <bytes> ] [ mpu <bytes> ] [ weight <rate> ]
        [ prio <n> ] [ cell <bytes> ] [ ewma <log> ]
        [ estimator <interval> <time constant> ]
        [ split <class id> ] [ defmap <mask>/<change> ]
```

or

```
cbq bandwidth <bps> avpkt <bytes> [ mpu <bytes> ]
        [ cell <bytes> ] [ ewma <log> ]
```

csz. Is not currently implemented.

red. RED sets up the parameters for random early detection, basically in line with the research that describes RED—for example, the minimum and maximum threshold and average number of packets in the queue that trigger and set the drop (or marking) probability (marking if ECN is set).

```
red limit <bytes> min <bytes> max <bytes> avpkt <bytes>
burst <n packets> red probability <probability> bandwidth
<kbps> [ ecn ]
```

gred. GRED includes a range of drop probabilities suitable, for example, for the differentiated services AF class.

```
gred DP drop-probability limit <bytes> min <bytes> max
<bytes> gred avpkt <bytes> burst <n pkts> probability <prob>
bandwidth <kbps> gred [prio value] gred setup DPs <no. of
DPs> default <default DP> [grio]
```

dsmark. Differentiated services marking involves setting up a set of indices to a set of mask/value pairs.

```
dsmark indices <indices> [ default index <default index> ]
 [ set_tc_index ]
```

ingress. Takes an IP address as a parameter. `tc qdisc list` will show the current set of queuing disciplines instantiated.

TC Class Command

```
tc class [ add | del | change | get ] dev <string>
       [ classid <class id> ] [ root | parent <class id> ]
       [ [ <qdisc kind> ] [ help | <options> ] ]}
```

Essentially, class identifiers are attached to queuing disciplines, and are either a root, or are attached to parent classes. A class can also have an estimator attached.

TC Filter Command

```
tc filter [ add | del | change | get ] dev <string>
       [ pref <priority> ] [ protocol <protocol> ]
       [ estimator <interval> <time constant> ]
       [ root | classid <class id> ] [ handle <filter id> ]
       [ [ <filter type> ] [ help | <options> ] ]

       tc filter show [ dev <string> ] [ root | parent <class id> ]
```

Where:

```
FILTER_TYPE := { rsvp | u32 | fw | route | etc. }
FILTERID := ... format depends on classifier, see there
OPTIONS := ... try tc filter add <desired FILTER_KIND> help
```

Filters are set up as per RSVP flow specifications, on specific unsigned 32-bit identifiers, according to a route classifier, or as a firewall filter. Filters have a handle, and can have a parent, a priority, a preference, and possibly a protocol, as well as possibly also adding an estimator.

9.15 BSD

Recent releases of BSD UNIX have added a class-based queuing that was developed by Kenjiro Cho in the Wide Project in Japan. This system predates the Linux system, and is quite similar, although less general in its current form. As in the Linux code, it has a classifier, a queuing discipline, and a policing system (called a *regulator*). The pipeline for these components is the same as in the Linux CBQ structure, but less general in that the order is not reprogrammable.

Readers familiar with the BSD network device output interface will see immediately how it fits in:

```
ip_output()
calls
if_output()
which
classifies
enqueues

if_start()
dequeues a packet and
regulates it
```

Other functions manage the queue parameters such as maximum length. There are a variety of possible regulators, but the default one is a token bucket one, which has a rate and bucket size as in the Linux case.

9.16 Summary

In this chapter we have looked at the various forwarding treatments that Linux offers as a routing platform, and the tools to manage the packet forwarding scheduler, queue manager, and associated drop behaviors.

In the next chapter, we look at Interprocess communication.

CHAPTER 10 Security

10.1 Roadmap

In this chapter we will consider some of the security facilities offered by the Linux kernel. The main security features are implemented as part of the netfilter work. This enables firewalls and masquerading routers to be built. Towards the end of the chapter there will be a discussion of IPSec and SSL.

10.2 Security Scenarios

10.2.1 Firewalls

A firewall is a mechanism placed between the Internet and the operating system and applications of the host you wish to protect. Traditional firewalls were placed on or near the main gateway router, but there is now a trend of personal firewalls that run on the system being protected. The purpose of a firewall is to block traffic that may be malicious in nature. Such traffic could be attacks that exploit holes in the operating system or attempt denial-of-service attacks on a host. Using a firewall is akin to locking the front door of your home, rather than fitting individual locks on each of the insecure doors inside. One main door can protect a large number of smaller doors. In this way a site system administrator can protect their users without necessarily involving the users in the protection.

10.2.2 NAT—Network Address Translation

NAT is a scheme to translate parts of an IP datagram—notably the source and destination addresses and ports. The purpose of NAT is to provide other services such as port forwarding, transparent proxying, and masquerading. NAT works by monitoring certain parts of packets, and if they match a particular pattern, then modifying the packet accordingly before forwarding it.

Masquerading. This is a scheme where a LAN containing many hosts can be connected to the Internet even if the ISP has provided only a single IP address for a single host. One machine is configured as a masquerading router, and this translates packets in and out of the network acting on behalf of (masquerading as) individual hosts on the LAN. Consider the network in Figure 10.1. Here a masquerading router M is routing packets from three hosts on a private network, A, B, and C. Consider the case when host A wishes to download a Web page from some site on the Internet, called W, with an address of 3.4.5.6. A's packets will be initially sent towards M, with the IP source address of A and an ephemeral port a, and with a destination address of D, port 80. M will rewrite the packet, inserting its own IP address as the source and its own ephemeral source port (m). The packet will travel across the Internet, and eventually a response packet will be found. This will be addressed towards $M : m$, but the NAT code in M will match this packet and rewrite it, addressing it toward $A : a$. See Figure 10.2, and note that A's address and port never make it outside of the masqueraded LAN.

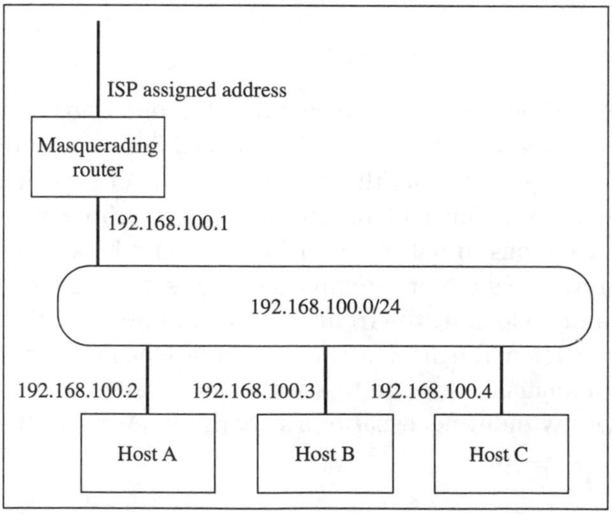

Figure 10.1 Masquerading router.

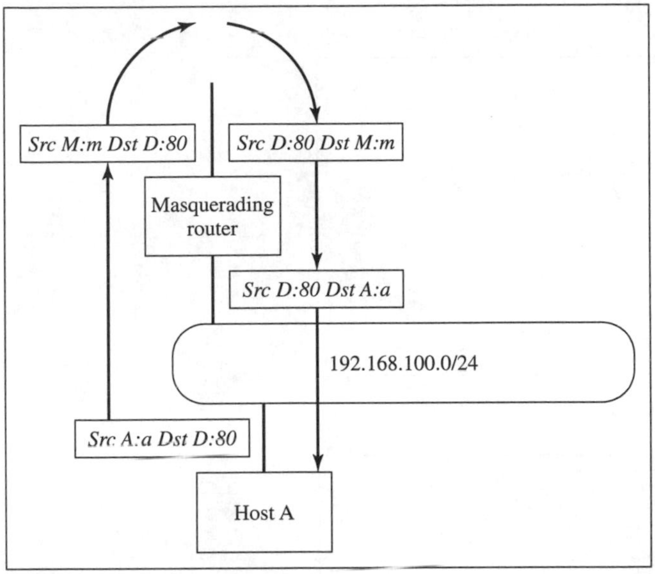

Figure 10.2 Masquerading example.

Port forwarding. Consider the situation where a corporate Web server is behind a masquerading, firewalling router. Any request from outside the organization needs to be directed towards this machine's Web server port. However, as this machine is within a masqueraded network, then its IP address is not globally valid. The solution is to publish the firewall's address, *F*, as the Web service, and forward requests arriving at the firewall to the actual machine, using NAT (see Figure 10.3). Here, an incoming Web request from a machine out on the Internet, *R*, is forwarded to the Web server, *W*. *W* generates its reply and sends the result back to *M*, which translates it for its return path to *R*.

Transparent proxying. A transparent proxying server allows for a service to be proxied on an intermediate host, with the knowledge, and therefore reconfiguration, of the client machine. By proxying we mean an additional service being performed on behalf of the client. The usual example of proxying is a caching web server. Here a server monitors requests and stores (caches) the responses. If a second or further request for the same Web page arrives, this can be responded to with the saved data immediately without waiting for a response from the origin host. Another benefit of proxy caches is that they can run on a firewalling machine forwarding requests from a protected domain within an organization (see Figure 10.5). Here host *A* is using *M* is a proxying Web cache. Therefore, any Web page requests are sent to *M* using port 3128 in this example. *M* then makes a check of its stored objects, and if the requested object is not

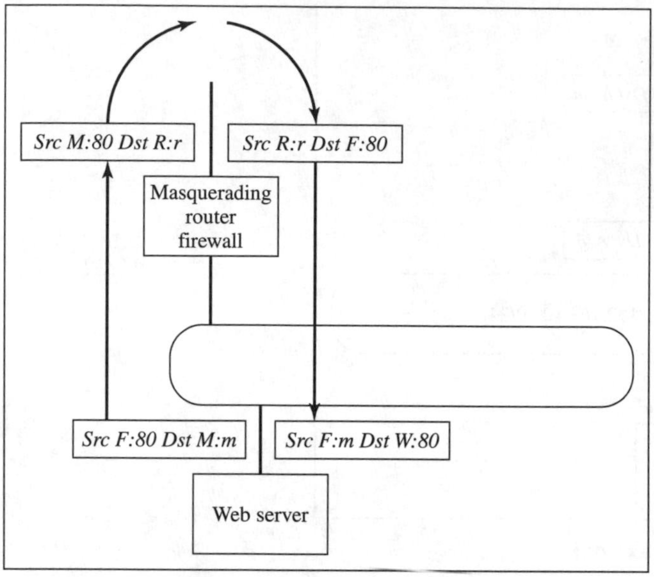

Figure 10.3 Port forwarding with a firewall.

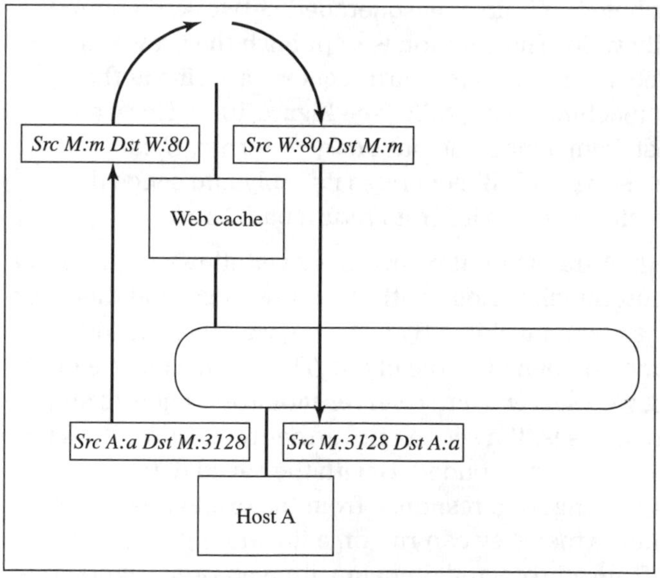

Figure 10.4 A proxy cache.

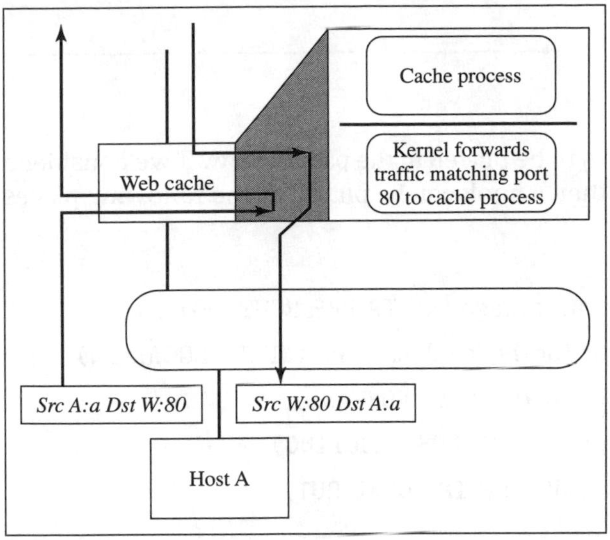

Figure 10.5 A transparent proxy cache.

available, then it itself requests the page from the actual site $W : 80$ (this information will be in the HTTP GET message). The site responds and M relays the response to A. Host A must be configured to allow this mode of operation by informing the browser to request pages from the Web cache rather than the origin Web site. A transparent Web cache employs port forwarding to prevent this need for reconfiguration, and thus save system administrators time and improve ISP profits (or reduce losses) (see Figure 10.5). The Web cache machine takes all packets with 80 as a destination port (i.e., most Web traffic) and forwards it to some application level caching software. If there is a match in the cache, then a response can be formulated and the corresponding IP header information placed in the response packet (i.e., place the destination address/port of the request in the response source address/port). If the page is not cached, then the cache can request it using the address of the original requesting machine. To both the Web server and the browsing host, the operation of the cache goes unnoticed except for possibly the improvement or reduction in performance.

It is possible for masquerading, firewalling, and transparent proxying functionality to be combined on a single machine. This is left as an exercise for the reader.

Each of the above functionalities is available through the netfilter system in Linux, which is described now.

10.3 Netfilter

10.3.1 Introduction

The netfilter code allows hooks to be placed in the packet flow. If we consider a Linux box acting as a router, then a hook can be placed at the following places (see Figure 10.6):

1. After input, before the routing stage (`NF_IP_PRE_ROUTING`)
2. After input if the packet is for the local machine (`NF_IP_LOCAL_IN`)
3. If the packet is to be forwarded (`NF_IP_FORWARD`)
4. Before the packet is output (`NF_IP_POST_ROUTING`)
5. If the packet is created locally (`NF_IP_LOCAL_OUT`)

Netfilter allows the following actions to be performed at a filtering hook:

- ACCEPT—Indicates that the packet should be allowed to continue; that is, the next hook should be called.
- DROP—The packet should be dropped by the kernel.
- STEEL—The packet will be handled by another process.
- QUEUE—The packets should be queued for processing; usually this is to pass a packet to user space.
- REPEAT—Repeat the call to this hook.

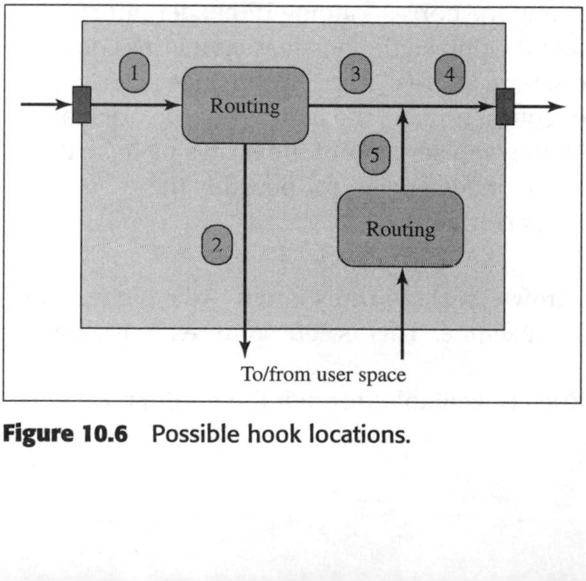

Figure 10.6 Possible hook locations.

10.3.2 IP Tables

IP tables is a mechanism where a list of rules can be applied to selected packets. Included within the Linux kernel are a set of default tables that support:

- Filtering
- Mangling
- Connection tracking
- NAT

Taking filtering as an example, see `net/ipv4/netfilter/iptable_filter.c`. Here a structure is built that is hooked into just the `NF_IP_LOCAL_IN`, `NF_IP_FORWARD`, and `NF_IP_LOCAL_OUT` hooks. Rules are then added to the table under control of user space programs that indicate which packets match and should be dropped.

10.3.3 Summary

IP tables is a complex and extendable security system involving both user and kernel space code. This section has concentrated on the deep kernel code. For more information on the user space code and setting up IP tables secured systems, refer to the Bibliography.

10.4 IPSec

IPSec is an IP datagram layer security system that introduces extra headers for authentication (authentication header—AH) and encryption (encapsulation security protocol—ESP) of individual packets. IPSec is described in RFCs 2401–2412. An implementation of IPSec is not currently part of the Linux kernel.

10.5 SSL

The Secure Sockets Layer uses a combination of public key and symmetric key cryptography to provide a secure transport layer between hosts. Its most common implementations are within Web browsers for access to secure Web sites, and the SSH program to allow secure communication and logins between hosts. Currently SSH is entirely implemented by user space programs.

10.6 Summary

This chapter has taken a look at netfilter code in the Linux kernel, and how it can be used to provide security for sites and users. A brief mention has been made of IPSec and SSL, but these are not part of the Linux kernel at the time of writing, although the FreeSWAN project does provide an IPSec implementation.

Afterword

When I started writing this, I compared it to the task faced by the translators who prepared the famous first King James Bible—they were not the first to attempt a translation from Latin, nor the last. Nor was a large part of the book originally written in Latin (but rather in Aramaic and Greek in the Old and New Testaments respectively). Similarly, this book is in English, but is about the Linux communications stack, which is written in C, and implements a system designed by the Internet pioneers in RFCs, written in the semiformal language used by protocol specifiers. Furthermore, there already is a "King James' translation" of one C implementation, so I guess I have to think of this as a new English version.

As is often the case, much has been lost in the translation, and while I (like Spike Milligan and mathematics) speak C like a native, and have written RFCs, that only means that I must take the blame even more readily for any such errors.

That's all for now, folks!

Glossary

AAL (ATM Adaptation Layer) (see ATM). AALs are framing and protocol layers between the cell transmission layer and layer three (IP).

ACK. Common abbreviation for acknowledgment.

Admission Control. Call admission, CAC, and decision traffic (packets) are allowed to flow because of some decision based on past, current, and expected conditions.

1. The decision can be based on parameters in the packet (simplest is the destination address—so-called destination-based routing), ToS, precedence, current traffic load (e.g., buffer overload calls for *call blocking*), or packet dropping. Which packet gets dropped from an overloaded queue is an interesting question (see RED). Keeping queues short (underload) is a good thing.
2. The decision can also be based on out-of-band signaled parameters about the traffic flow (see QoS and RSVP), and on downstream conditions (is QoS available all the way(s) to the destination?). Such information on downstream conditions is typically disseminated by QoS routing protocols.

Adspec. An Adspec is an object in a path message that carries a package of OPWA advertising information (see OPWA).

ADU (Application Data Unit). The unit of transmission or reception from an application protocol such as FTP or HTTP.

AF (Assured Forwarding). One of the differentiated services, classes, or behaviors. Defined in terms of loss preference.

Aggregation (see scale). Traffic can be aggregated—the Internet does stat muxing currently; it also aggregates state about traffic flows for destination-based routing by aggregating addresses hierarchically (see CIDR). Other forms of aggregation are possible:

1. Routing considerations (link state advertisements) can be constrained to areas, and then inter-area routing can be considered separately.
2. Traffic flow conditions downstream can be aggregated by routing area.

AIMD (additive increase, multiplicative decrease). The control law for a TCP-like protocol when seeing no or some congestion indication.

Alternate path routing A routing technique in which multiple paths, rather than just the shortest (typically most opportunistic) path between a source and a destination are utilized to route traffic. One of the objectives of alternate path routing might be to distribute load among multiple paths in the network (or conversely to reduce dependence on single mode/path failure).

API (application programming interface). The set of functions and parameters needed by a higher-level protocol to use a lower-level protocol.

AppleTalk. A proprietary family of protocols defined by Apple Computer systems.

ARP (Address Resolution Protocol). Used to map dynamically between layer three (IP) addresses and layer two (MAC) addresses.

ARPA, DARPA (Advanced Research Projects Agency, Defense Advanced Research Projects Agency). U.S. DoD research funding agency that underwrote a lot of the invention and development of the Internet.

ARPANET. The research network funded by the Advanced Research Projects Agency (ARPA) on which the Internet protocols were first developed.

AS (autonomous system). An AS runs a single routing protocol (e.g., RIP or OSPF) and interfaces to other ASs via an interdomain routing protocol—today, BGP.

ASM (assembly). Mnemonic version (human readable) of machine program language.

Assured Forwarding. PHB for differentiated service that allows multiple forwarding classes with (orthogonally) multiple drop priorities. Aimed at supported mixes of RTP/UDP and TCP traffic. Might use RED.

ATM (Asynchronous Transfer Mode) (see B-ISDN). A link layer technology that may be used to optimize packet transfer times by cut-through packet forwarding (also known as IP switching). ATM has its own entire architecture for traffic management.

1. VCI/VPI—Virtual Circuit Identifier/Path Identifier; used as a two-level tag for a flow.
2. UBR, VBR(rt—nrt), ABR, CBR—Unspecified bit rate, variable bit rate, available bit rate and constant bit rate service classes.
3. MCR, PCR, SCR—Mean cell rate, peak cell rate, sustainable cell rate.
4. CDV, BT—Cell delay variation, burst tolerance.
5. RM cells—Resource management cells.
6. PNNI, IPNNI—Private Network Network Interface; signaling and QoS routing from the ATM Forum.

ATM PVC (ATM Permanent Virtual Circuit). A configured resource on an ATM level two network.

Autonomous system (AS). A routing domain which has a common intradomain routing protocol and administrative authority

AX.25. The amateur packet radio network's version of the old X.25 protocol, used to mask errors on the packet radio network so that it can carry IP packets more effectively.

BGP (Border Gateway Protocol). The interdomain routing protocol in use worldwide today.

Blockade state. Blockade state helps to solve a *killer reservation* problem.

BPF (Berkeley Packet Filter). Programmable mechanism for general packet classification.

BSD (Berkeley Standard Definition). One of the main family trees of UNIX alongside System V, Linux, and others.

CAM (Content Addressable Memory). CAMs are useful for various associative-type lookup operations where we want to find the index position of something via its value rather than the other way around.

CBQ (Class Based Queuing). This is an architecture for integrating a number of service levels implemented by a variety of queuing disciplines, and associating them with collections or aggregates of users (e.g., by agency or address prefix).

CIDR (Classless InterDomain Routing). Address aggregation—currently used to compact destination-based forwarding tables; could be used for sources or even for logical (e.g., multicast class D or mobile) addresses, but isn't yet.

Class (also known as profile, template) (see generalized port specification). A traffic class is a contract *type*; a contract is a contract type plus a set of values for the parameters for that type. The contract type specifies the parameters of the admission control; for example:

1. Best Effort—has no parameters (beyond source plus destination address, ToS, and precedence).
2. Controlled Load—Specifies a contract that looks to the source (sink) like a lightly loaded network with the specified mean rate. The borrowing of capacity between a flow that has a burst at a higher rate and ones that are currently at a lower rate is possible. The control of this over the short time frame is a factor in selecting a packet scheduling algorithm (see schedule).
3. Guaranteed Service—This is very much like the ATM CBR contract, but it is also like the VBR rt service—it specifies delay bounds as well as throughput parameters. These are actually implemented end-to-end and hop-by-hop, so are somewhat different from the CDV parameter that is a traffic behavior specification rather than a contract request.
4. Slack—A term in RSVP for how to divvy up variation along the hops of a path.
5. Controlled Delay—This and the next two parameters are proposed service contracts.
6. Committed Rate.
7. Predictive.

Classifier. An implementation of a rule to decide the provenance of a packet and assign it to a class.

Congestion. A state of the network and its offered load where traffic is partially or largely not being carried usefully—for example, traffic flows across a link to a bottleneck, only to be dropped. Also, in multiservice networks with reservations, can refer to high call blocking probability—actually, this is simply scarcity of resource.

Crankback. A technique where a flow setup is recursively backtracked along the partial flow path up to the first node that can determine an alternative path to the destination.

CSMA (Carrier Sense Multiple Access). Building block for shared media network mediation.

CSZ (Clark, Shenker, and Zhang). Alternative model to CBQ.

cwnd (congestion window). This is an important parameter in the TCP congestion avoidance algorithm discussed in Chapter 7.

Daemon. Always on UNIX user-space process that handles various service requests and enhances kernel level functionality.

Datagram. An IP packet.

DECnet. The Digital Equipment Corporation's old network architecture.

Destination routing. Current standard way that a route is chosen for each and every packet in the Internet—the destination address is used to look up the shortest (by some metric, whether hop count, highest throughput, lowest delay, or whatever) path out of the graph that is the network mesh map, which may have multiple potential different paths. To select more than one path, one could use external state (e.g., random number, traffic load from other sources), but this might lead to high degrees of packets arriving out of order at a destination. To use more than a single path, one needs to distinguish flows based on other information—for example, source, or source plus ToS (plus Precedence(plus signaled QoS)) or generalized port information. Alternatively, a fast lookup key associated with this information, whatever it is, could be installed—for example, by the signaling protocol, or by implicit recognition of the existence of a *flow*, by a *tag* or *flow label* installation protocol. Such tags might be hop-specific.

DHCP (Dynamic Host Configuration Protocol). Used to autoconfigure a computer when it's connected or booted on a new network.

Differentiated Services. Class of service rather than quality of service. Uses edge devices and per hop behaviors instead of hop-by-hop and end-to-end services. Typically, subscription-based rather than signaled. Allows aggregation by class.

DMA (direct memory access). Means for an I/O device to send and receive data from memory without involving the CPU.

DNS (Domain Name System). The service that maps human-useful names for computers and services to IP addresses.

DRR (Deficit Round Robin). A common and efficient approximation to Weighted Fair Queuing.

DVMRP (Distance Vector Multicast Routing Protocol). A deprecated routing protocol for IP multicast.

E.164. The addressing used in ATM networks.

ECN (Explicit Congestion Notification). A means to feed back information to end systems about incipient congestion at a router in the Internet by explicit (binary) marking of IP packets.

ECONET. Low-performance, low-price local network technology.

EGP (Exterior Gateway Protocol). Old term and protocol for interdomain routing.

Entry policing. Traffic policing done at the first RSVP- (and policing)capable router on a data path. Also known as ingress policing.

Ethernet. A family of local area network technologies in very widespread use.

Expedited Forwarding. A PHB for diff serve designed to achieve virtual leased line. Typically, uses a priority queue.

Explicit sender selection. A (reservation-)style attribute; all reserved senders are to be listed explicitly in the reservation message (see also wildcard sender selection).

FCFS (first come first served). Effectively the same as FIFO.

FF style. Fixed filter reservation style in RSVP, which has explicit sender selection and distinct attributes.

FIFO (first in first out). A simple queuing discipline.

Filterspec. Together with the session information, in RSVP defines the set of data packets to receive the QoS specified in a flowspec. The filterspec is used to set parameters in the packet classifier function.

Flow. A sequence of packets from a source to a destination (possibly a group) constituting a single activity (e.g., transfer of a file, a Web page, an audio/video stream, and so on) that is usefully temporally as well as spatially correlated.

Flow Admission Control (FAC). A process by which it is determined whether a link or a node has sufficient resources to satisfy the QoS required for a flow. FAC is typically applied by each node in the path of a flow during flow set-up to check local resource availability.

Flow descriptor. The combination of a flowspec and a filterspec.

Flow label. A shortcut key for looking up a flow rather than the set of typical IP (TCP and UDP) protocol fields that routers seem poor at looking at (though hosts seem to manage somehow.)

Flow identifier. An IPv6 field that might serve as a globally allocated flow ID, or might not.

Flow set-up. The act of determining the path for a flow, and attempting to establish state in routers along the flow path to satisfy its QoS requirement.

Flowspec. Defines the QoS to be provided for a flow. The flowspec is used to set parameters in the packet scheduling function to provide the requested quality of service. A flowspec is carried in a FLOWSPEC object. The flowspec format is opaque to RSVP, and is defined by the Integrated Services Working Group.

Gateway. Older term for router.

Generalized port specification. RSVP uses this to identify an IPv4 flow. The component of a session definition that provides further transport or application protocol layer demultiplexing beyond DestAddress. (see session).

GPL (GNU Public License). A license often used to protocol open source software.

GPS (Global Positioning System). Satellite based location system.

GRE (Generic Routing Encapsulation). Generalized recursive tunnelling.

GUI (graphical user interface). X Windows, and so on.

Higher-level admission control. A process by which it is determined whether or not a flow setup should proceed, based on estimates of the overall resource usage by the flow. Higher-level admission control may result in the failure of a flow setup even when FAC at each node along the flow path indicates resource availability.

HTML. Hypertext Markup Language.

HTTP. Hypertext Transfer Protocol.

IANA (Internet Assigned Numbers Authority). Assigns codepoints in Internet protocols.

ICMP (Internet Control Message Protocol). IP layer diagnostic and error reporting protocol.

IETF (Internet Engineering Task Force). Internet standards working groups body.

IGMP (Internet Group Management Protocol). IP multicast management protocol.

IGP (Interior Gateway Protocol). Generic term for protocols used within a single AS (see AS)—for example, OSPF, ISIS, and so on.

Integrated Services Internet. An enhanced Internet which offers controlled load and guaranteed services as well as the normal best effort service.

Integrated Service over Specific Link Layers.

ATM
RSVP/Q.2931 or PNNI mapping
QoS parameter mapping
802.1q
FR
SMDS
Native

IP flow (or simply flow). An IP packet stream from a source to a destination (unicast or multicast) with an associated quality of service (see QoS) and higher-level demultiplexing information. The associated QoS could be best-effort.

IPC (interprocess communication). Mechanism such as sockets.

IPSec (Internet protocol security). Term for both architecture and mechanisms.

IPX. Novell network layer 3 protocol.

IPv4, IPv6. Main two versions of IP extant.

IRQ (interrupt request). Logical channel for interrupt from a device on PC hardware.

ISP (Internet service provider). Generic term for organizations and companies that provide carriage for IP.

ISR (interrupt service routing). Software handler for dealing with interrupts.

ITU (International Telecommunication Union). Standards body for telecommunications.

Killer reservation problem. The killer reservation problem describes a case where a receiver attempting and failing to make a large QoS reservation prevents smaller QoS reservations from being established.

LAN. Local area network.

LIH (Logical Interface Handle). The LIH is used to help deal with non-RSVP clouds.

LILO (Linux Loader). The first stage disk bootstrap program for Linux.

Linux. Linux is not UNIX, really.

Local repair. Allows RSVP to rapidly adapt its reservations to changes in routing.

LRU (least-recently used). Cache replacement strategy.

Police. When traffic specifies a service contract, it should keep to it (especially if there are tariff (whether per-use- or per-subscription-based) considerations. To check this, traffic is typically monitored as it is placed into appropriate queues for appropriate schedules—if a contract is exceeded, packets can be treated in a number of ways:

1. Move to a lower class—This can be tricky given the lower class may have a policy associated with it. For example, maybe it gets an overall minimum share.
2. Drop—This is easy, especially with RED.
3. Mark as in breach of contract—No field currently in IP to do this, unless the packet was in a class because of priority or precedence, in

which case the field could be overwritten, but this would invalidate the IP (v4 header) checksum unless restored after the current piece of network.

Merge policing. Traffic policing that takes place at a data merge point of a shared reservation.

Merging. The process of taking the maximum (or more generally, the least-upper bound) of the reservations arriving on outgoing interfaces, and forwarding this maximum on the incoming interface.

MFC (multicast forwarding cache). Fast lookup structure for commonly used IP multicast routing entries.

MMU. Memory management unit.

MPLS (Multi-Protocol Label Switching). Generalized version of ATM.

MPOA. Multi-protocol Over ATM.

MSDP (Multicast Source Distribution Protocol). Part of IP multicast interdomain routing framework.

MSS (maximum segment size). Largest packet TCP will try to send whatever the size of the user request. Generally set or discovered to try to avoid or minimize IP fragmentation (see MTU). Allows for TCP header.

MTU (Maximum Transfer Unit). Largest packet IP can send without fragmentation (see MSS).

Multicast path (or multicast tree). A subtree of the network topology in which all the leaves and zero or more interior nodes are members of the same multicast group. A multicast path may be per-source, in which case the subtree is rooted at the source.

Nagle. Researcher, known in the TCP community for an algorithm used to reduce IP/TCP packet count for slow intermittent applications.

NAT (network address translator). Mechanism to map between locally significant IP addresses and globally allocated ones so that a site can move without renumbering its hosts, or can share a small pool of addresses amongst a small set of active hosts drawn from a larger internal pool.

Netfilter. Mechanism for packet filtering in Linux (see Chapter 10).

Netlink. Mechanism for user-to-kernel communication to manage network layer systems.

Netstat. Commonly used application to get IP and lower-level statistics.

NFS (Network File System). Popular UNIX file-sharing protocol.

NHOP. An RSVP object that carries the next hop information in RSVP control messages.

NIC. Network interface card (e.g., 3Com 3c509 Ethernet board).

NIS (Network Information Service). Local-only service like DNS, only more extensible.

NNTP (Network News Transfer Protocol). For Bboards.

NSF (National Science Foundation). Popular U.S. research funding agency.

NTFS (NT file system). A filesystem type supported by Linux.

OpenSSL. Implementation of Secure Sockets Layer system.

OPWA (One Pass With Advertising). Describes a reservation setup model in which (path) messages sent downstream gather information that the receiver(s) can use to predict the end-to-end service. The information that is gathered is called an advertisement (see also Adspec).

OSPF (Open Shortest Path First). Commonly used intradomain IP routing protocol.

Path state. Information kept in routers and hosts about all RSVP senders.

PathErr. Path Error RSVP control message.

PathTear. Path Teardown RSVP control message.

PHB (per-hop behavior). A service description based around behavior rather than mechanism, and local, rather than path gobal (see expedited and assured forwarding groups).

PHOP. An object that carries the previous hop information in RSVP control messages.

PIM (Protocol Independant Multicast). Prevalent routing protocol now for IP multicast packets.

PPP (Point-to-Point Protocol). Widely used link layer for carrying IP on serial lines.

PVC, PVP (permanent virtual circuit, permanent virtual path). Configured VC or VP on an ATM network.

Quality of service (QoS). A set of service requirements to be met by the network while transporting a flow. Quality of service or route:

RSVP defines some fields that carry QoS descriptions—the actual meanings of these are as per the int-serv classes/templates. Given a service class, a flow also is covered by:

1. Tspec—the traffic spec, what the flow actually looks like.
2. A leaky bucket spec, Rspec—the QoS desired.
3. A leaky bucket spec, ADSpec—advertised flow spec used by OPWA.
4. OPWA—One Path With Advertising.

Qdisc. Queuing discipline.

QoS-based routing. A routing mechanism under which paths for flows are determined based on some knowledge of resource availability in the network as well as the QoS requirement of flows.

Queue management. Queues exist to smooth traffic in a statistically multiplexed network. In a TDM multiplexed network, queues rarely happen.

RED (Random Early Detection). A technique for controlling best-effort queue lengths—might also be used on out-of-contract packets within a class better than best effort.

Reservation style. Describes a set of attributes for a reservation, including the sharing attributes and sender selection attributes.

Resv message. Reservation request RSVP control message.

ResvConf. Reservation confirmation RSVP control message confirms successful installation of a reservation at some upstream node.

ResvErr. Reservation error control message indicates that a reservation request has failed or an active reservation has been preempted.

ResvTear. Reservation teardown RSVP control message deletes reservation state.

RIP (Routing Information Protocol). Simple but effective intradomain routing protocol commonly used on modest-sized site networks.

Route (ToS, QoS, QoR). Type of service is a well-understood field in the IPv4 header—some systems even implement setting it. Some forwarding software (e.g., slip drivers) use this, but routers. QoS, refers to a route derived from consideration of network topology, edge costs and traffic conditions. QoR refers to routes derived solely from edge fixed parameters.

Route pinning. A mechanism to keep a flow path fixed for a duration of time.

Rspec. The component of a flowspec that defines a desired QoS. The Rspec format is opaque to RSVP, and is defined by the Integrated Services Working Group of the IETF.

RSVP (Resource Reservation Protocol). The proposed Internet signaling protocol.

RTNetlink. Controlling and managing the routing systems between the kernel and user space.

RTP, RTCP. Real-Time Transport Protocol, Real-Time Transport Control Protocol.

RTT (Round-Trip Time). One of the critical performance parameters for a TCP flow.

Scale (see aggregation). QoS requires state. State incurs costs in memory and in messages to establish it. The state may simply be a constant increase over the state needed for destination routing—however, usually destinations are heavily aggregated (e.g., at least by network number, but also by CIDR, and so on). Flows are per-user, and may be present in much larger numbers than host IDs, although if the phone net is anything to go by, this is not true.

SCFQ. Self-Clocked Fair Queuing.

Schedule. A neat way to think about scheduling is to take a picture of a resource shared over time and picture how it is *decreased* by someone else asking for special circumstances.

1. FIFO/FCFS (first in, first out; first come, first served)—A strange but widespread service discipline in IP (and multiprotocol) routers.
2. Drop policy—Drop tail, drop head, random (see RED). When the queue is full, which packet gets lost?
3. Priority queue—When there is more than one packet in a queue, which gets fowarded? Note priority queuing can starve lower-priority packets of ever seeing service.
4. Precedence queuing—Priority queue based on the precedence bits in the IP header.
5. Custom queuing—A (proprietary, but commonly used if by other names) scheme to give certain flows a minimum performance through hardwired classifications and minimum queue service rates.
6. Fair queuing (FQ)—Round robin.
7. Weighted Fair Queuing (WFQ)—Rounder robin (rounding error is to allow for variable length packets—weight in WFQ sometimes used to refer to unfair share; actually, its the P in PGPS—see GPS and PGPS).
8. Virtual Clock—A service scheme for TDM that still stat muxes.
9. Generalized Processor Sharing (GPS)—The theory of WFQ—fluid flow.
10. Packet Generalized Processor Sharing (PGPS)—The practice of WFQ—packet flow.
11. Earliest Due Date (EDD)—A neat alternative scheduler for delay bounding.

SE style. Shared explicit reservation style, which has explicit sender selection and shared attributes.

Service. A single packet cannot be said to see a service contract. A flow of packets can see statistical properties with distributions such as interarrival and departure times, drop probabilities, reordering probabilities, erroring probabilities, and so on. The difference between distributions before and after service are the result of the scheduling discipline, combined possibly with the other traffic (especially true for best-effort and priority queuing). The state mathematics theory is such that we typically cannot derive anything beyond mean and bounds (if they exist) for typical service classes and worst-case traffic. The Internet largely survives because of FIFO and drop tail's amazing ability to survive many traffic arrival patterns, and under engineering. RED appears to improve this.

Session. An RSVP session defines one simplex unicast or multicast data flow for which reservations are required. A session is identified by the destination address, transport layer protocol, and an optional (generalized) destination port.

Shape. Traffic may be within contract, but incur extra jitter due to bursts of other traffic when going through a switch. The jury is still out on whether one should then reshape the traffic to its mean rate—typically, if a path has 2* bandwidth* delay of buffering, then it can sustain any burstiness; however, there may be stat-muxing synergy to having a minimum (and maximum) amount of burstiness—there is probably some statistical thermodynamic theory that could show this (e.g., diffusion model, or lattice gas occupancy analogy), but it's beyond me right now.

Shared style. A (reservation) style attribute; all reserved senders share the same reserved resources (see also distinct style).

Signal (see RSVP).

Soft state. Control state in hosts and routers that will expire if not refreshed within a specified amount of time.

Source. A host or router that can be identified by a unique unicast IP address.

Source routing. A technique for selecting a path out of many at the source—requires network to deliver choice to the source, and the source to be able to indicate choice in packet, or in signaling. Useful for policies, not for scaling.

SSH. Secure Shell.

State. Incurred from route, QoS, QoR, and signaled information.

SYN (synchronize). A bit set in the TCP header to indicate part of the three-way handshake to start a connection (by setting initial sequence numbers and other initial state).

Tag switching. A technique for optimizing the lookup for forwarding packets—reduces router memory limits by a constant factor (see flow labeling). Can be used on per-flow by detection (autocorrelation of destination and time), by route (output port), or by application.

Tariff. A tariff structure has a per-parameter, per-service class price structure that may include time of day, or even other traffic related factors. The more complex the service model and the tariff structure, the more expensive it is to collect usage-based revenue.

Tasklet. Ultra-lightweight way to schedule families of low-level kernel events including software and other deferred interrupts.

TBF. Token bucket/leaky bucket.

Token Rate	Bucket Depth
The Tspec/Rspec parameters—Version	Maximum Transmission Unit
Token Bucket Rate	Token Bucket Size
Maximum Transmission Rate	Minimum Delay Noticed
Maximum Delay Variation	Loss Sensitivity
Burst Loss Sensitivity	Loss Interval
Quality of Guarantee	

TSpec. A traffic parameter set that describes a flow. The format of a Tspec is opaque to RSVP and is defined by the Integrated Service.

UDP. User Datagram Protocol.

UDP encapsulation. A way for hosts that cannot use raw sockets to participate in RSVP by encapsulating the RSVP protocol (raw) packets in ordinary UDP packets.

Unicast destination. A host or router that can be identified by a unique unicast IP address.

VFS. Virtual File System.

Virtual Circuit/Channel Call. Not an IP concept yet, or ever, if we can help it.

VJ-CC (Van Jacobson Congestion Control). End-to-end arguments—a control theoretical model-based scheme for limiting traffic going in to the network based on history. Given a delayed feedback loop of what has arrived, what can we say about what can be sent? Hard (but not impossible) to apply to multicast flows.

Van has perpetrated this algorithm no less than three times:

1. Congestion Control.
2. Adaptive Playout (in Vat).
3. Class-Based Queuing and RED.

VoIP (Voice over IP). Killer application for QoS.

WF style. Wildcard filter reservation style, which has wildcard sender selection and shared attributes.

WFQ. Weighted Fair Queuing.

Wildcard sender selection. A (reservation) style attribute; traffic from any sender to a specific session receives the same QoS (see also explicit sender selection).

WRR. Weighted Round Robin.

Bibliography

[1] "Linux Traffic Control—Implementation Overview," Werner Almesberger, Tech Report, EPFL, Switzerland.

[2] "Linux—Advanced Networking Overview," Sravanan Rhadakkrishnan, Tech Report, University of Kansas, Lawrence, KS, USA.

[3] "Network Buffers and Memory Management," Alan Cox, *Kernel Korner, Linux Journal*, Vol. 1, No. 30, Oct. 1996. `http://www.ssc.com/lj/issue30/kk30.html`

[4] "Linux IP Networking," Glenn Herrin, from Masters Project Report, Computer Science, University of New Hampshire. `http://pubpages.unh.edu/gherrin/project/linux-net.html`

[5] "Linux Kernel Internals," Michael Beck et al., Addison Wesley, Harlow, England, 1997.

[6] *Linux IP Stacks Commentary*, In-Depth Code Annotation, Coriolis Open Press, Stephen T. Satchell, H.B.J. Clifford, 2000.

[7] *Understanding the Linux Kernel*, Daniel Bovet and Marco Cesati, O'Reilly, Jan. 2001.

[8] *TCP/IP Illustrated*, Vol. 1, 2, and 3, W. Richard Stevens, Addison Wesley Professional Computing Series, 1992, 1994, 1996.

[9] "End-to-End Arguments in System Design," J. H. Saltzer, D. P. Reed, D. D. Clark, *ACM Transactions on Computer Systems*, Vol. 2, No. 4, pp. 277–288, Nov. 1984.

[10] "UNIX Systems for Modern Architectures," In *Symmetric Multiprocessing and Caching for Kernel Programmers*, Curt Schimmel, 1994 Addison Wesley Professional Computing Series.

[11] "The GNU Coding Standards," Richard Stallman et al., `http://www.gnu.org/prep/standards_toc.html`

[12] "Scalable High Speed IP Routing Lookups," Marcel Waldvogel (ETH), George Varghese, Jon Turner, and Bernhard Plattner, *Computer Communication Review*, a publication of ACM SIGCOMM, Vol. 27, No. 4, Oct. 1997.

[13] "Small Forwarding Tables for Fast Routing Lookups," M. Degermark, A. Brodnik, S. Carlsson, and S. Pink, ACM SIGCOMM, Cannes, France, Vol. 27, No. 4, pp. 3–15, Oct. 1997.

[14] "Trends in Wide Area IP Traffic Patterns," Sean McCreary and Kimberly C. Claffy, in *Proc. of ITC Specialist Seminar on IP Traffic Measurement, Modeling and Management* (Monterey, California), Sept. 2000.

[15] *OSPF: Anatomy of an Internet Routing Protocol*, John T. Moy, Addison-Wesley, 1998.

[16] "Generalized Processor Sharing," Abhey Parekh, PhD Thesis, MIT Laboratory for Decision Systems, MIT, 1993.

[17] "Modelling TCP Throughput: A Simple Model and its Empirical Validation," J. Padhye, V. Firoiu, D. Towsley, J. Kurose, *Proceedings of Sigcomm'98*, Vancouver, WA, Sept. 1998.

[18] "Strawman Specification for TCP Friendly (Reliable) Multicast Congestion Control (TFMCC)," M. Handley, S. Floyd, B. Whetten, IRTF, Reliable Multicast Working Group, work in progress, 1999.

[19] "Supporting Real-Time Applications in an Integrated Services Packet Network: Architecture and Mechanism," David D. Clark, Scott Shenker, and Lixia Zhang, in *Sigcomm* (Baltimore, Maryland), pp. 14–26, Aug. 1992.

[20] "Link-Sharing and Resource Management Models for Packet Networks," S. Floyd and V. Jacobson, *IEEE/ACM Transactions on Networking*, Vol. 3, No. 4, pp. 365–386, Aug. 1995.

[21] "Managing Traffic with ALTQ," Kenjiro Cho, in 1999 USENIX Annual Technical Conference (Monterey, California, USA), Jun. 1999.

[22] "Implementing Real-Time Packet Forwarding Policies Using Streams," Ian Wakeman, Atanu Ghosh, Jon Crowcroft, Van Jacobson, and Sally Floyd, in USENIX 1995 Technical Conference (New Orleans, Louisiana), Jan. 1995.

[23] *Operating System Concepts*, A. Silberschatz, J. Peterson, Addison Wesley, 1988.

[24] "Computer Organisation and Design," In *The Hardware Software Interface*, D. A. Patterson, J. L. Hennessy, Morgan Kauffman, 1998.

[25] *Computer Networking: A Top Down Approach Featuring the Internet*, J. Kurose, K. Ross, Addison Wesley, 2001.

[26] "The Click Modular Router," Eddie Kohler, Robert Morris, Benjie Chen, John Jannotti, and M. Frans Kaashoek, *ACM Transactions on Computer Systems* Vol. 18, No. 3, pp. 263–297, Aug. 2000.

[27] *Linux Routers: A Primer for Network Administrators*, Tony Mancill, Prentice Hall, 2001.

[28] *Firewalls and Internet Security: Repelling the Wily Hacker*, William R. Cheswick, Steven M. Bellovin (Contributor), 2nd edition, Addison-Wesley, Oct. 2001.

RFCs Cited in Code

RFCs are the famous *Request for Comments* series of documents about the Internet protocol suite. Some are standards and some are purely informational (and some are historical or just mere entertainment). There are many points in the Linux kernel code (and elsewhere) that implementors refer to the relevant RFC. Here we give the list. See `http://www.ietf.org` for availability and status information about these documents and the protocols and services they describe.

0791 Internet Protocol. J. Postel. Sep-01-1981.

0793 Transmission Control Protocol. J. Postel. Sep-01-1981.

0815 IP Datagram Reassembly Algorithms. D. D. Clark. Jul-01-1982.

0826 Ethernet Address Resolution Protocol. D. C. Plummer. Nov-01-1982.

0950 Internet Standard Subnetting Procedure. J. C. Mogul, J. Postel. Aug-01-1985.

0961 Official ARPA-Internet protocols. J. K. Reynolds, J. Postel. Dec-01-1985.

1042 Standard for the transmission of IP datagrams over IEEE 802 networks. J. Postel, J. K. Reynolds. Feb-01-1988.

1048 BOOTP vendor information extensions. P. A. Prindeville. Feb-01-1988.

1051 Standard for the transmission of IP datagrams and ARP packets over ARCNET networks. P. A. Prindeville. Mar-01-1988.

1063 IP MTU discovery options. J. C. Mogul, C. A. Kent, C. Partridge, K. McCloghrie. Jul-01-1988.

1112 Host extensions for IP multicasting. S. E. Deering. Aug-01-1989.

1122 Requirements for Internet Hosts—Communication Layers. R. T. Braden. Oct-01-1989.

1191 Path MTU Discovery. J. C. Mogul, S. E. Deering. Nov-01-1990.

1201 Transmitting IP traffic over ARCNET networks. D. Provan. Feb-01-1991.

1323 TCP Extensions for High Performance. V. Jacobson, R. Braden, D. Borman. May 1992.

1337 TIME-WAIT Assassination Hazards in TCP. R. Braden. May 1992.

1390 Transmission of IP and ARP over FDDI Networks. D. Katz. January 1993.

1414 Identification MIB. M. St. Johns, M. Rose. January 1993.

1469 IP Multicast over Token-Ring Local Area Networks. T. Pusateri. June 1993.

1483 Multiprotocol Encapsulation over ATM Adaptation Layer 5. Juha Heinanen. July 1993.

1490 Multiprotocol Interconnect over Frame Relay. T. Bradley, C. Brown, A. Malis. July 1993.

1512 FDDI Management Information Base. J. Case, A. Rijsinghani. September 1993.

1577 Classical IP and ARP over ATM. M. Laubach. January 1994.

1584 Multicast Extensions to OSPF. J. Moy. March 1994.

1589 A Kernel Model for Precision Timekeeping. D. Mills. March 1994.

1626 Default IP MTU for use over ATM AAL5. R. Atkinson. May 1994.

1701 Generic Routing Encapsulation (GRE). S. Hanks, T. Li, D. Farinacci, P. Traina. October 1994.

1702 Generic Routing Encapsulation over IPv4 networks. S. Hanks, T. Li, D. Farinacci, P. Traina. October 1994.

1762 The PPP DECnet Phase IV Control Protocol (DNCP). S. Senum. March 1995.

1812 Requirements for IP Version 4 Routers. F. Baker. June 1995.

1826 IP Authentication Header. R. Atkinson. August 1995.

1883 Internet Protocol, Version 6 (IPv6) Specification. S. Deering, R. Hinden. December 1995.

1885 Internet Control Message Protocol (ICMPv6) for the Internet Protocol Version 6 (IPv6). A. Conta, S. Deering. December 1995.

1945 Hypertext Transfer Protocol—HTTP/1.0. T. Berners-Lee, R. Fielding, H. Frystyk. May 1996.

2003 IP Encapsulation within IP. C. Perkins. October 1996.

2067 IP over HIPPI. J. Renwick. January 1997.

2131 Dynamic Host Configuration Protocol. R. Droms. March 1997.

2133 Basic Socket Interface Extensions for IPv6. R. Gilligan, S. Thomson, J. Bound, W. Stevens. April 1997.

2207 RSVP Extensions for IPSEC Data Flows. L. Berger, T. O'Malley. September 1997.

2402 IP Authentication Header. S. Kent, R. Atkinson. November 1998.

2460 Internet Protocol, Version 6 (IPv6) Specification. S. Deering, R. Hinden. December 1998.

2481 A Proposal to add Explicit Congestion Notification (ECN) to IP. K. Ramakrishnan, S. Floyd. January 1999.

2516 Method for Transmitting PPP Over Ethernet (PPPoE). L. Mamakos, K. Lidl, J. Evarts, D. Carrel, D. Simone, R. Wheeler. February 1999.

2553 Basic Socket Interface Extensions for IPv6. R. Gilligan, S. Thomson, J. Bound, W. Stevens. March 1999.

2581 TCP Congestion Control. M. Allman, V. Paxson, W. Stevens. April 1999.

2582 The New Reno Modification to TCP's Fast Recovery Algorithm. S. Floyd, T. Henderson. April 1999.

2861 TCP Congestion Window Validation. M. Handley, J. Padhye, S. Floyd. June 2000.

2988 Computing TCP's Retransmission Timer. V. Paxson, M. Allman. November 2000.

Code Authors

```
<chexum@bankinf.banki.hu>
<Tim_Alpaerts@toyota-motor-europe.com>
Aage Kvalnes <aage@cs.uit.no>
Adam Sulmicki <adam@cfar.umd.edu>
Al Longyear <longyear@netcom.com>
Alan Cox <alan.cox@linux.org>
Alexey Kuznetsov <kuznet@ms2.inr.ac.ru>
Andrey V. Savochkin <saw@msu.ru>
Arnaldo Carvalho de Melo <acme@conectiva.com.br>
Arnt Gulbrandsen <agulbra@nvg.unit.no>
```

Charles Hedrick <hedrick@klinzhai.rutgers.edu>
<chihjenc@scf.usc.edu> and <tsusheng@scf.usc.edu>
<chris@cybernet.co.nz>
Martin Mares <mj@atrey.karlin.mff.cuni.cz>
Corey Minyard <wf-rch!minyard@relay.EU.net>
Dag Brattli <dag@brattli.net>
Dave Airlie, University of Limerick, Ireland <airlied@linux.ie>
David Hinds <dhinds@allegro.stanford.edu>
David S. Miller <davem@caip.rutgers.edu>
Donald Becker <becker@super.org>
E.M. Serrat <emserrat@geocities.com>
Eduardo Marcelo Serrat <emserrat@geocities.com>
Emmanuel Roger <winfield@freegates.be>
<emserrat@geocities.com>
Erik Schoenfelder <schoenfr@ibr.cs.tu-bs.de>
Florian La Roche <rzsfl@rz.uni-sb.de>
Fred Baumgarten <dc6iq@insu1.etec.uni-karlsruhe.de>
Fred N. van Kempen <waltje@uwalt.nl.mugnet.org>
Gerald J. Heim <heim@peanuts.informatik.uni-tuebingen.de>
Herv? Eychenne <eychenne@info.enserb.u-bordeaux.fr>
Horst von Brand <vonbrand@sleipnir.valparaiso.cl>
Ian P. Morris <I.P.Morris@soton.ac.uk>
Issam Chehab <ichehab@madge1.demon.co.uk>
J Hadi Salim <hadi@nortelnetworks.com>
Jacques Gelinas <jacques@solucorp.qc.ca>
Jamal Hadi Salim <hadi@nortelnetworks.com>
Jay Schulist <jschlst@turbolinux.com>
Jay Schulist <jschlst@turbolinux.com>
Jean II - <jt@hpl.hp.com>
Jean Tourrilhes <jt@hpl.hp.com>
Jrme de Vivie <devivie@info.enserb.u-bordeaux.fr>
Jes Sorensen <Jes.Sorensen@cern.ch>
Jim Freeman <jfree@caldera.com>
Joerg Reuter DL1BKE <jreuter@yaina.de>
John McDonald <jm@dataprotect.com>
Jonathan Naylor <g4klx@g4klx.demon.co.uk>
Jorge Cwik <jorge@laser.satlink.net>
Jos Vos <jos@xos.nl>
<jreuter@yaina.de>
Kleen <ak@muc.de>
Laurence Culhane <loz@holmes.demon.co.uk>
Lawrence V. Stefani <stefani@lkg.dec.com>
Lennert Buytenhek <buytenh@gnu.org>

Linus Torvalds <Linus.Torvalds@helsinki.fi>
<majordomo@oss.sgi.com>
Marc Santoro <ultima@snicker.emoti.com>
Marc Zyngier <mzyngier@freesurf.fr>
Mark Evans <evansmp@uhura.aston.ac.uk>
<Mark.Bush@prg.ox.ac.uk>
Marko Kiiskila <carnil@cs.tut.fi>
Martijn van Oosterhout <kleptogimp@geocities.com>
Matthew Dillon <dillon@apollo.west.oic.com>
Michael Callahan <callahan@maths.ox.ac.uk>
Michael Neuling <Michael.Neuling@rustcorp.com.au>
Mike <pall@rz.uni-karlsruhe.de>
Mike Shaver <shaver@ingenia.com>
MvS <miquels@drinkel.ow.org>
Olaf Kirch <okir@monad.swb.de>
<p.norton@computer.org>
Patrick Caulfield <patrick@pandh.demon.co.uk>
Paul Norton <pnorton@cts.com>
Paul Russell <Paul.Russell@rustcorp.com.au>
Pedro Roque <roque@di.fc.ul.pt>
Pekka Riikonen <priikone@poesidon.pspt.fi>
Philip Blundell <philb@gnu.org>
<greg@caldera.com>
<rco@di.uminho.pt>
Report socket allocation statistics <mea@utu.fi>
Richard Underwood <richard@wuzz.demon.co.uk>
Rick Sladkey <jrs@world.std.com>
Ross Biro <bir7@leland.Stanford.Edu>
Rusty Russell <rusty@rustcorp.com.au>
Sam Lantinga <slouken@cs.ucdavis.edu>
Stefan Becker <stefanb@yello.ping.de>
Steve Whitehouse <SteveW@ACM.org>
Thomas Davis <ratbert@radiks.net>,
Thomas Lopatic <tl@dataprotect.com>
Tim Kordas <tjk@nostromo.eeap.cwru.edu>
Tim MacKenzie <tym@dibbler.cs.monash.edu.au>
Trond Myklebust <trond.myklebust@fys.uio.no>
Vineet Abraham <vma@iol.unh.edu>
Wesley Craig <netatalk@umich.edu>
Willy Konynenberg <willy@xos.nl>

Index

Numbers

A

D

E

F

G

P

Q

S

U

V

W

X